Eleventh Dialog System Technology Challenge

Prague, Czech Republic
11 September 2023

ISBN: 978-1-7138-9030-0

Printed from e-media with permission by:

Curran Associates, Inc.
57 Morehouse Lane
Red Hook, NY 12571

Some format issues inherent in the e-media version may also appear in this print version.

Printed with permission by Curran Associates, Inc. (2025)

Association for Computational Linguistics
209 N. Eighth Street
Stroudsburg, Pennsylvania 18360

Phone: 1-570-476-8006
Fax: 1-570-476-0860

acl@aclweb.org

Additional copies of this publication are available from:

Curran Associates, Inc.
57 Morehouse Lane
Red Hook, NY 12571 USA
Phone: 845-758-0400
Fax: 845-758-2633
Email: curran@proceedings.com
Web: www.proceedings.com

TABLE OF CONTENTS

Exploring Prompt-Based Multi-Task Learning for Multimodal Dialog State Tracking and Immersive Multimodal Conversation 1
Yirong Chen, Ya Li, Tao Wang, Xiaofen Xing, Xiangmin Xu, Quan Liu, Cong Liu, Guoping Hu

Multi-Task Learning for Ambiguous Candidate Identification with Pre-Trained Model 9
Daesik Jang, Hyewon Choi

Improving Situated Conversational Agents with Step-By-Step Multi-Modal Logic Reasoning 15
Yuxing Long, Huibin Zhang, Binyuan Hui, Zhenglu Yang, Caixia Yuan, Xiaojie Wang, Fei Huang, Yongbin Li

Contrastively Pretrained Vision-Language Transformers and Domain Adaptation Methods for Multimodal TOD Systems 25
Youngjae Chang, Doo Young Kim, Jinyoung Kim, Keunha Kim, Hyunmook Cha, Suyoung Min, Youngjoong Ko, Kye-Hwan Lee, Joonwoo Park

Multi-Stage Coarse-To-Fine Contrastive Learning for Conversation Intent Induction 31
Caiyuan Chu, Ya Li, Yifan Liu, Jia-Chen Gu, Quan Liu, Yongxin Ge, Guoping Hu

DORIC : Domain Robust Fine-Tuning for Open Intent Clustering Through Dependency Parsing 40
Jihyun Lee, Seungyeon Seo, Yunsu Kim, Gary Geunbae Lee

A Two-Stage Progressive Intent Clustering for Task-Oriented Dialogue 48
Bingzhu Du, Nan Su, Yuchi Zhang, Yongliang Wang

Analysis of Utterance Embeddings and Clustering Methods Related to Intent Induction for Task-Oriented Dialogue 57
Jeiyoon Park, Yoonna Jang, Chanhee Lee, Heuiseok Lim

Multi-View Zero-Shot Open Intent Induction from Dialogues: Multi Domain Batch and Proxy Gradient Transfer 67
Hyukhun Koh, Haesung Pyun, Nakyeong Yang, Kyomin Jung

Adapting Text-Based Dialogue State Tracker for Spoken Dialogues 81
Jaeseok Yoon, Seunghyun Hwang, Han Ran, Jeong-Uk Bang, Kee-Eung Kim

CopyT5: Copy Mechanism and Post-Trained T5 for Speech-Aware Dialogue State Tracking System 89
Cheonyoung Park, Eunji Ha, Yewon Jeong, Chi-young Kim, Haeun Yu, Joo-won Sung

OLISIA: A Cascade System for Spoken Dialogue State Tracking 95
Léo Jacqmin, Lucas Druart, Yannick Estève, Benoît Favre, Lina M Rojas, Valentin Vielzeuf

Speech-Aware Multi-Domain Dialogue State Generation with ASR Error Correction Modules 105
Ridong Jiang, Wei Shi, Bin Wang, Chen Zhang, Yan Zhang, Chunlei Pan, Jung Jae Kim, Haizhou Li

Three Ways of Using Large Language Models to Evaluate Chat 113
Ondřej Plátek, Vojtech Hudecek, Patricia Schmidtova, Mateusz Lango, Ondrej Dusek

Parallel Corpora Alignment Framework for Multilingual and Robust Automatic Dialogue Evaluation 123
Xinglin Wang, Jiayi Shi, Peiwen Yuan, Kan Li

Simple LLM Prompting is State-Of-The-Art for Robust and Multilingual Dialogue Evaluation 133
John Mendonça, Patrícia Pereira, Helena Moniz, Joao Paulo Carvalho, Alon Lavie, Isabel Trancoso

Towards Optimizing Pre-Trained Language Model Ensemble Learning for Task-Oriented Dialogue System 144
Zhiyuan Zhu, Yusheng Liao, Zhe Chen, Yu Wang, Yunfeng Guan

Enhancing Task-Oriented Dialog System with Subjective Knowledge: A Large Language Model-Based Data Augmentation Framework 150
Haein Jung, Heuiyeen Yeen, Jeehyun Lee, Minju Kim, Namo Bang, Myoung-Wan Koo

Semantic Data Augmentation for Meaning Maintenance on Task-Oriented Conversation with Large-Size Language Model 166
Jaehwan Lee, Kwanyoung Son, Eugene Kim

Ensemble Method Via Ranking Model for Conversational Modeling with Subjective Knowledge 177
Xin Huang, Kye Min Tan, Richeng Duan, Bowei Zou

Exploring Back Translation with Typo Noise for Enhanced Inquiry Understanding in Task-Oriented Dialogue 185
Jihyun Lee, Junseok Kim, Gary Geunbae Lee

Leveraging Few-Shot Data Augmentation and Waterfall Prompting for Response Generation....................... 193
Lea Krause, Selene Báez Santamaría, Michiel van der Meer, Urja Khurana

Leveraging Ensemble Techniques and Metadata for Subjective Knowledge-Grounded Conversational Systems.......... 206
Seongho Joo, Kang-il Lee, Kyungmin Min, Joongbo Shin, Janghoon Han, Seungpil Won, Kyomin Jung

A Difference-Aware Ensemble Method for Task-Oriented Dialogue with Subjective Knowledge................. 216
Changxin Ke, Churui Sun, Longxuan Ma, Wei-Nan Zhang, Ting Liu

DSTC-11: Speech Aware Task-Oriented Dialog Modeling Track 226
Hagen Soltau, Izhak Shafran, Mingqiu Wang, Abhinav Rastogi, Wei Han, Yuan Cao

Overview of Situated and Interactive Multimodal Conversations (SIMMC) 2.1 Track at DSTC 11 235
Satwik Kottur, Seungwhan Moon

Intent Induction from Conversations for Task-Oriented Dialogue Track at DSTC 11 242
James Gung, Raphael Shu, Emily Moeng, Wesley Rose, Salvatore Romeo, Arshit Gupta, Yassine Benajiba, Saab Mansour, Yi Zhang

Overview of Robust and Multilingual Automatic Evaluation Metricsfor Open-Domain Dialogue Systems at DSTC 11 Track 4 260
Mario Rodríguez-Cantelar, Chen Zhang, Chengguang Tang, Ke Shi, Sarik Ghazarian, João Sedoc, Luis Fernando D'Haro, Alexander I. Rudnicky

Task-Oriented Conversational Modeling with Subjective Knowledge Track in DSTC11.......... 274
Seokhwan Kim, Spandana Gella, Chao Zhao, Di Jin, Alexandros Papangelis, Behnam Hedayatnia, Yang Liu, Dilek Z Hakkani-Tur

Author Index

Exploring Prompt-based Multi-task Learning for Multimodal Dialog State Tracking and Immersive Multimodal Conversation

Yirong Chen[1]*, Ya Li[2]†, Tao Wang[2], Xiaofen Xing[1], Xiangmin Xu[3,4], Quan Liu[2,5], Cong Liu[2,6], Guoping Hu[2,5]

[1]Guangdong Provincial Key Laboratory of Human Digital Twin, School of EE., South China University of Technology, Guangzhou, China

[2]iFLYTEK Research, Hefei, China [3]Pazhou Lab, Guangzhou, China

[4]School of Future Technology, South China University of Technology, Guangzhou, China

[5]State Key Laboratory of Cognitive Intelligence, Hefei, China [6]National Engineering Research Center of Speech and Language Information Processing, Hefei, China

eeyirongchen@mail.scut.edu.cn, {yali8, taowang49}@iflytek.com
{xfxing, xmxu}@scut.edu.cn, {quanliu, congliu2, gphu}@iflytek.com

Abstract

With the rise of the metaverse, immersive multimodal conversation has attracted more and more researchers' attention. Multimodal contexts will become more important for human-computer interaction in the metaverse, especially in shopping domain. Unlike traditional conversation tasks, immersive multimodal conversation has challenges such as multimodal ambiguous candidate identification and multimodal coreference resolution, which makes it more difficult to dialog state tracking and response generation, as described in SIMMC 2.1 challenge, a part of DSTC11. In particular, as the number of objects in the scene increases, the difficulty will increase dramatically. We proposed PMTLED (**P**rompt-based **M**ulti-**T**ask **L**earning **E**ncoder-**D**ecoder), in which different subtasks use different prompts to make the model tend to focus on the current subtask. We achieve the winner in ambiguous candidates indentification and runner-up in multimodal coreference resolution (MM-Coref), multimodal dialog state tracking (MM-DST) and assistant response generation. Our code and model are made publicly available at `https://github.com/scutcyr/dstc11-simmc2.1-scut-bds-lab`.

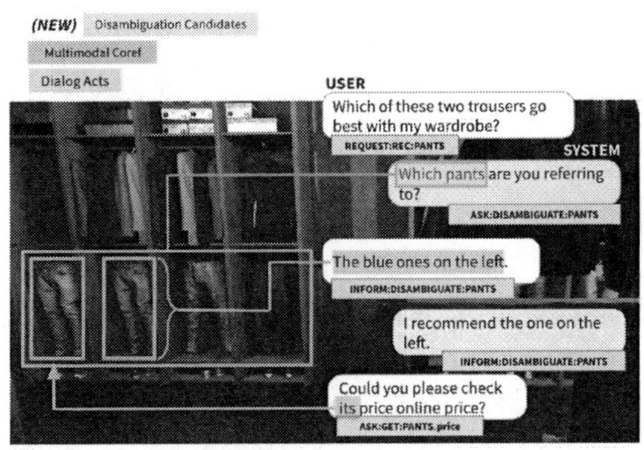

Figure 1: Overview of SIMMC2.1 challenge. The user ambiguously uses 'these two trousers', so that the system needs to identify all the ambiguous objects on the scene to help further disambiguation and coreference resolution.

1 Introduction

With the rise of the metaverse(Mystakidis, 2022) and virtual reality (VR), immersive multimodal conversation has attracted more and more researchers' attention. Unlike traditional conversation tasks, immersive multimodal conversation has challenges such as multimodal ambiguous candidate identification and multimodal coreference resolution, which makes it difficult to dialog state tracking and response generation. To this end, Facebook released multimodal conversational dataset (SIMMC 2.1) and proposed the SIMMC 2.1 challenge (Kottur et al., 2021), in which the virtual assistant shares the same scene with the user.

In the past, the SIMMC 1.0 (Moon et al., 2020) challenge provided the controllable and sanitized multimodal contexts, while the SIMMC2.0 (Kottur et al., 2021) challenge provied the cluttered and closer-to-real-world multimodal contexts, in which there is no clear correspondence between textual context and objects in the scene. On the basis of the SIMMC 1.0 and SIMMC 2.0, SIMMC 2.1 proposed a new subtask (ambiguous candidate identification) in order to attract more attention on the key challenge of fine-grained visual disambiguation, as shown in Figure 1. Different from the SIMMC 2.0, SIMMC 2.1 has been annotated with additional labels (i.e. identification of all possible

*Work done during an internship at iFLYTEK Research.
†Corresponding author. Email: yali8@iflytek.com

Proceedings of The Eleventh Dialog System Technology Challenge, pages 1–8
September 11, 2023 ©2023 Association for Computational Linguistics

referent candidates given ambiguous mentions). In particular, the number of objects in a scene ranges from 6 to 141. Each object is different due to its visual or non-visual attributes. There are multiple objects with one same attribute in the scene, but the number of user-mentioned objects is less than the count in the scene, which makes the virtual assistant unable to identify the specific object that the user refers to, thus causing ambiguity.

The SIMMC2.1 challenge has four different subtasks, which are ambiguous candidates indentification (ACI), multimodal coreference resolution (MM-Coref), multimodal dialog state tracking (MM-DST) and assistant response generation. Due to the introduction of ACI, the other three subtasks are affected accordingly. In addition, ambiguous candidates and multimodal coreferential objects do not appear at the same time based on statistical analysis of the dataset.

The state-of-the-art method in the previous SIMMC challenge (Lee et al., 2022a,b) adopt BART and joint-learning approach on all subtasks. However, the performance of the original framework will be limited after adding the ambiguous candidates indentification task. In addition, The model also ignores the ground truth APIs in terms of response generation performance. Modeling MM-DST tasks as sequential prediction tasks is also easy to cause instability in prediction. For example, the model may forget to generate "<EOB>" tokens or ")" in some test samples. In order to consider both the performance and robustness of the model, we propose a prompt-based multi-task learning Transformer framework to address the above problems. In particular, ACI, MM-Coref and MM-DST share the same prompt, while the assistant response generation task uses another set of prompts alone, which will make full use of ground-truth APIs when generating responses.

Our model was declared as the **winner** of the subtask 1 (ambiguous candidates indentification) with 70.50% ambiguous object identification F1. Moreover, our model was declared as the **runner-up** in the official evaluation on all other subtasks, in which we achieved 80.28% coreference F1, 92.66% slot F1, 97.75% intent F1 (rank #1) and 0.3650 BLEU-4.

2 Related Work

2.1 Multi-task Learning for Task-oriented Dialog System

Task-oriented dialog systems have explicit goals (e.g. request to compare, request to get, etc.), making dialog understanding important before generating response. When using multi-task learning, the subtasks related to dialogue understanding and dialogue generation in task-oriented dialog system can be modeled into one model. In the Encoder-Decoder (e.g. Transformer (Vaswani et al., 2017)) or UniLM (Dong et al., 2019) framework, the classification tasks can be further modeled based on the output of Encoder, and the generation tasks can be further modeled based on Decoder. In recent years, there has been an increasing amount of literature on multi-task learning for task-oriented dialog system (Zhao et al., 2022; Su et al., 2022). Recently, a unified dialog model named SPACE-3 (He et al., 2022) has verified that the performance of various tasks can be significantly improved by conducting multi-task joint pretraining on large-scale task-oriented dialog corpus, in which the authors proposed 5 tasks, including span masked language modeling, understanding semantic modeling, semantic region modeling, policy semantic modeling and response generation modeling. In the SIMMC 2.1 challenge of DSTC-10, multi-task learning has been verified to be effective for task-oriented dialog system (Lee et al., 2022a; Nguyen et al., 2022).

2.2 Prompt Learning

With the rise of large-scale pre-trained language models (Devlin et al., 2019; Han et al., 2021), prompt learning has recently been widely studied by the NLP community, e.g. AutoPrompt (Shin et al., 2020), Prefix-Tuning (Li and Liang, 2021) and etc. Both discrete and continuous prompts are widely used to solve downstream tasks with pre-trained models. Some prompt-based works are proposed for task-oriented dialog system, such as UniTranSeR (Ma et al., 2022), Cins (Mi et al., 2022), SPACE-3 (He et al., 2022) and etc. SPACE-3 employed two kinds of prompts to extract semantics with three subtasks for helping pass the task-flow in a task-oriented dialog system. We use prompts to model MM-DST task as several different prompt-based classification tasks and used the ground-truth APIs to design the prompts for response generation.

Total # dialogs	11,244
Total # utterances	117,236
Total # scenes	3,133
Avg # words per user turns	12
Avg # words per assistant turns	13.7
Avg # utterances per dialog	10.4
Avg # objects mentioned per dialog	4.7
Avg # objects in scene per dialog	19.7
Avg # candidates per ambiguous turn	5.6

Table 1: Summary of SIMMC 2.1 dataset statistics.

Figure 2: An example of the scene.

3 SIMMC2.1 Dataset

SIMMC 2.1[1] is a dataset for studying immersive multimodal conversations in the form of a co-observed image or virtual reality (VR) environment(Kottur et al., 2021) in two shopping domain: furniture (4k dialogs) and fashion (7.2k dialogs). Different from other task-oriented dialog datasets. SIMMC 2.1 is highly structured with abundant annotation information, including dialog act, slot values, coreference objects, ambiguous candidate objects, scene images, metadata of all objects, bounding boxes and etc. The statistics of SIMMC 2.1 is shown in Table 1. For the SIMMC 2.1 challenge, the dataset is split into 4 sets: train, dev, devtest and teststd according to the ratio of 6.4:0.5:1.5:1.5. Each turn of dialog has a corresponding scene image (e.g., Figure 2), the objects in which have corresponding canonical ID(s) for subtasks ACI or MM-Coref. In particular, all the subtasks are prohibited from using visual metadata of the objects, but non-visual metadata is allowed to use. Both subtask ACI and MM-Coref formally look for subsets from a set of objects and return them as prediction results. The number of ambiguous candidates ranges from 2 to count of all objects in a scene image, while the number of coreference objects is commonly less than 4.

[1] `https://github.com/facebookresearch/simmc2`

4 Method

In this section, we demonstrate the implementation of the proposed PMTLED for solving each subtask. The architecture for subtasks 1, 2 and 3 is shown in Figure 3 (a), and the architecture for subtask 4 is shown in Figure 3 (b). We first introduce the input of the model and the model architecture. Then we elaborate on objectives of each subtask and auxiliary tasks.

4.1 Model Architecture

Similar to (Lee et al., 2022a), We choose BART (Lewis et al., 2020) as our backbone model for both dialog understanding tasks and dialog generation task. BART contains a Transformer Encoder and a Transformer Decoder, which is particularly effective when fine tuned for both dialog understanding and response generation. Let $\mathcal{D}$ denotes a dialog with L_{turn} turns in SIMMC2.1 dataset. $\mathcal{D}$ can be defined as:

$$\mathcal{D} := \{(U_i, A_i, M_i, B_i^u, B_i^a, S_i)\}_{i=1}^{L_{turn}} \quad (1)$$

where U_i and A_i are the user and system utterances at turn i, M_i is the multimodal context that consists of a set of object indices mentioned by the system, B_i^u and B_i^a are the user and system belief states, S_i is the scene context including both the scene image and all objects in it.

4.2 Input Representation

As shown in Figure 3, the input is concatenated as in Equation 2. We adopt the same separator tokens and other special tokens described in (Lee et al., 2022a), including "<DISAM>", "<NOCOREF>", "<SOM>", "<EOM>", "<SOO>", "<EOO>", "<OBJ>", "<PREVIOBJ>" and etc. The objects in the scene is represented by their canonical object ID tokens with the form of "<obj_scene_index>" (e.g. "<1>") and their unique meta ID with the form of "<obj_meta_id>" (e.g. "<@1001>"). In addition, in order to obtain the better representation of scene context S_i, the embedding of the objects is added with the representation of the bounding box information and all the embedding of non-visual attributes (*customerReview*, *brand*, *price*, *size*, *materials*). We follow the object box embedding method used in (Lee et al., 2022a) to obtain representation of the bounding box through the encoding process $(x_1/w - 0.5, y_1/h - 0.5, x_2/w - 0.5, y_2/h - 0.5, (x_2 - x_1)(y_2 - y_1)/(h \cdot w))$ and then pass it

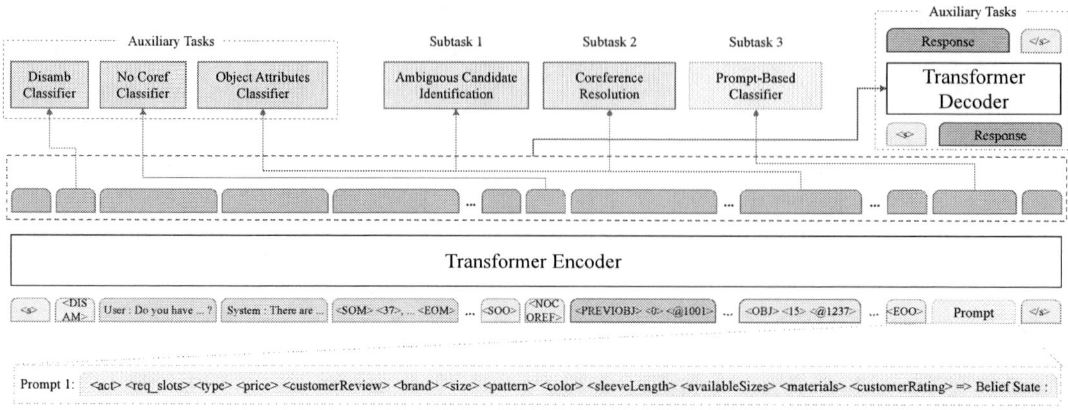

(a) PMTLED$_{\mathcal{P}_f}$: The architecture for subtask 1, 2 and 3, of which the inputs successively includes textual context, multimodal context and a fixed prompt $\mathcal{P}_f$. Prompt-Based Classifier is used for predicting intent and slot values. Each prompt token corresponds to a classifier, e.g. the last hidden state of <act> is for intent recognition. Three task objectives and several auxiliary objectives are carried out to optimize the model jointly in a multi-task paradigm.

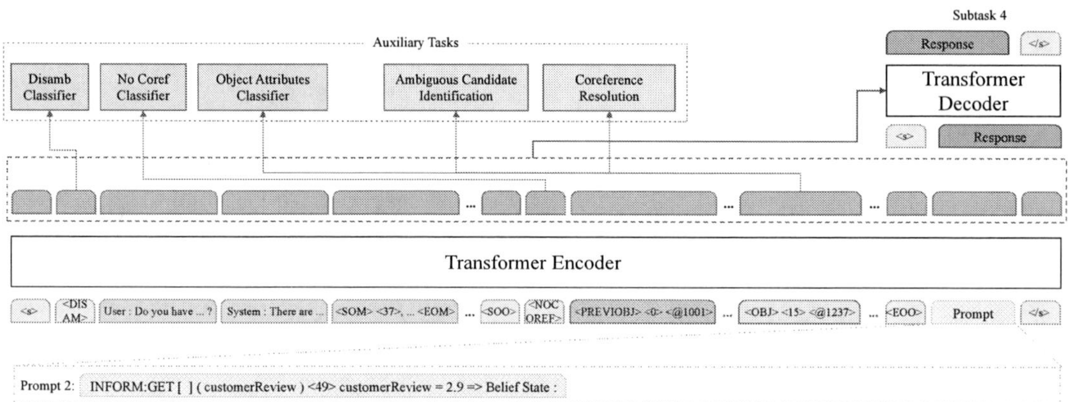

(b) PMTLED$_{\mathcal{P}_d}$: the architecture for subtask 4, of which the inputs successively includes textual context, multimodal context and a dynamic prompt $\mathcal{P}_d$. For the system response generation task, the system's belief state is designed as prompt. Three task objectives and several auxiliary objectives are carried out to optimize the model jointly in a multi-task paradigm.

Figure 3: Overview of multi-task jointly fine-tuning and prompt-tuning for each subtask.

to a fully-connected layer followed by LayerNorm by its upper-left vertex (x_1, y_1), lower-right vertex (x_2, y_2), height h and width w.

$$input_i = [(U, A, M)_{i-\ell:i}, U_i, S_i, P_i] \quad (2)$$

where $(U, A, M)_{i-\ell:i}$ are the previous user utterances, system utterances and multimodal context with dialog history up to ℓ turns to limit the length of input. P_i is the prompt designed at turn i.

In this work, we designed the fixed prompt $\mathcal{P}_f$ for MM-DST and the dynamic prompt $\mathcal{P}_d$ for response generation.

4.3 Fixed Prompt for MM-DST

In SIMMC 2.0, the MM-DST is universally considered as an auto-regressive language modeling task (Lee et al., 2022a; Nguyen et al., 2022), which makes the model unstable in the inference process. Therefore, we adopt a fixed prompt $\mathcal{P}_f$= "<act> <req_slots> <type> <price> <customerReview> <brand> <size> <pattern> <color> <sleeveLength> <availableSizes> <materials> <customerRating>", the output of which are used for classification for MM-DST. For example, the last hidden state of the prompt token "<act>" is passed into a classifier for intent recognition. All the prompt-based classification tasks can be expressed as:

$$\boldsymbol{C}_{\boldsymbol{p_t}} = \boldsymbol{W}_{\boldsymbol{p_t}} \boldsymbol{h}^{\boldsymbol{\ell}}_{\boldsymbol{p_t}} + \boldsymbol{b}_{\boldsymbol{p_t}}, p_t \in \mathcal{P}_f \quad (3)$$

where $h^{\ell}_{p_t}$ denotes the last hidden state of the prompt token p_t, $\boldsymbol{W}_{\boldsymbol{p_t}} \in \mathbb{R}^{n \times d}$ and $\boldsymbol{b}_{\boldsymbol{p_t}} \in \mathbb{R}^n$ are the trainable parameters. n is the number of categories for the classification task on the prompt token p_t. d is the dimension of the hidden states.

We denote the prompt-based MM-DST classification loss $\mathcal{L}_{dst}$ for all prompt token in $\mathcal{P}_f$ by

$$\mathcal{L}_{dst} = -\sum_{p_t \in \mathcal{P}_f} \sum_{c \in \mathcal{C}_{p_t}} \mathbb{L}\{c = y_{p_t}\} \log P(c) \quad (4)$$

where $\mathcal{C}_{p_t}$ is the set of all classes on the classification task of prompt token p_t, y_{p_t} the label, and $\mathbb{L}$ is an indicator function.

4.4 Dynamic Prompt for Response Generation

Since the annotation information *system_transcript_annotated* of current turn is allow to use in subtask response generation, we use *act*, *slot_values* and *request_slots* to design the dynamic prompt $\mathcal{P}_d$ in both the training and testing phases. Key-value pairs similar to *"Object ID: 36": {"customerReview": 4.3}* will be characterized as "*<36> customerReview = 4.3*", which makes the representation of the objects consistent with that of scene context S_i. In the end, the process of response generation is split into two phases: (i) dynamic prompt generation driven by *system_transcript_annotated* and (ii) response generation driven by both the multimodal context and dynamic prompt. Then the cross-entropy loss is employed to calculate the subtask loss:

$$\mathcal{L}_{lm} = -\sum_{i=1}^{L} \log P(t_i | t_1, t_2, \cdots, t_{i-1}) \quad (5)$$

where t_i is the i-th target token and L the total length of the response.

4.5 Classification for ACI and MM-Coref

Both subtsk 1 and subtask 2 can be formulateed as a binary classification on all objects in the scene image. For the obj_i in the scene, the last hidden states of the canonical object ID token and its unique meta ID token is concatenated to obtain the joint representation h_{obj_i} as follows:

$$\boldsymbol{h_{obj_i}} = concat(\boldsymbol{h^{\ell}_{pos_i}}, \boldsymbol{h^{\ell}_{pos_i+1}}) \quad (6)$$

where pos_i is the position of the canonical object ID token in the input sequence, $h^{\ell}_{pos_i}$ the last hidden state of the canonical object ID token, $h^{\ell}_{pos_i+1}$ the last hidden state of the unique meta ID.

Then, the joint representation h_{obj_i} is passed to a ACI classifier (see Equation 7) and MM-Coref classifier (see Equation 8) to predict true or false. Both the ACI classifier and MM-Coref classifier are fully-connected layers. Then, the ACI loss $\mathcal{L}_{aci}$ and MM-Coref loss $\mathcal{L}_{coref}$ can be calculated by using cross-entropy loss.

$$\boldsymbol{C_{ACI}} = \boldsymbol{W_{ACI} h_{obj_i}} + \boldsymbol{b_{ACI}} \quad (7)$$

$$\boldsymbol{C_{coref}} = \boldsymbol{W_{coref} h_{obj_i}} + \boldsymbol{b_{coref}} \quad (8)$$

where $\boldsymbol{W_{ACI}} \in \mathbb{R}^{2\times 2d}$, $\boldsymbol{b_{ACI}} \in \mathbb{R}^2$, $\boldsymbol{W_{coref}} \in \mathbb{R}^{2\times 2d}$ and $\boldsymbol{b_{coref}} \in \mathbb{R}^2$ are the trainable parameters.

4.6 Auxiliary tasks

Similar to (Lee et al., 2022a), we adopt three same auxiliary tasks for both the model of subtask 1 to 3 and the model of subtask 4: (i) Binary prediction for disambiguation with task objective $\mathcal{L}_{disamb}$, (ii) Binary prediction for empty coreference set with task objective $\mathcal{L}_{nocoref}$ and (iii) Prediction for object attributes with task objective $\mathcal{L}_{attr}$ as shown in Equation 9.

$$\mathcal{L}_{attr} = -\sum_{j \in \mathcal{O}_s} \sum_{n=1}^{N} \sum_{c \in \mathcal{C}_n} \mathbb{L}\{c = y_{jn}\} \log P(c) \quad (9)$$

where $\mathcal{O}_s$ is the set of objects in the scene history, N the number of attributes, $\mathcal{C}_n$ the set of all classes of the n-th attribute, y_{jn} the label of the n-th attribute of the j-th object, and $\mathbb{L}$ is an indicator function.

The auxiliary objective can be calculated by

$$\begin{aligned}\mathcal{L}_{aux} = &\lambda_{attr}\mathcal{L}_{attr} + \lambda_{disamb}\mathcal{L}_{disamb} \\ &+ \lambda_{nocoref}\mathcal{L}_{nocoref}\end{aligned} \quad (10)$$

where λ_{attr}, λ_{disamb} and $\lambda_{nocoref}$ are the hyperparameters.

4.7 Training Objective

As shown in Figure 3, the model for subtask 1 to 3 and the model for subtask 4 has different multi-task join objective. To sum up, the overall training objective of the model for subtask 1 to 3 $\mathcal{L}_{subtask123}$ can be defined as follows:

$$\begin{aligned}\mathcal{L}_{subtask123} = &\lambda_{aci}\mathcal{L}_{aci} + \lambda_{coref}\mathcal{L}_{coref} \\ &+ \lambda_{dst}\mathcal{L}_{dst} + \lambda_{lm}\mathcal{L}_{lm} + \mathcal{L}_{aux}\end{aligned} \quad (11)$$

where λ_{aci}, λ_{coref}, λ_{dst} and λ_{lm} are the hyperparameters.

Toward the model for subtask 4, the overall training objective is defined as:

$$\begin{aligned}\mathcal{L}_{subtask4} = &\lambda_{aci}\mathcal{L}_{aci} + \lambda_{coref}\mathcal{L}_{coref} \\ &+ \lambda_{lm}\mathcal{L}_{lm} + \mathcal{L}_{aux}\end{aligned} \quad (12)$$

Team ID	Models	Subtask #1	Subtask #2	Subtask #3		Subtask #4
		Object F1	Object f1	Slot F1	Act. F1	BLEU-4
0(baseline)	GPT2	18.00%	26.50%	73.50%	93.00%	0.192
	GPT-2(MM)	43.20%	-	-	-	-
	BERT(MM)	43.90%	-	-	-	-
	MTN	-	-	75.00%	94.30%	0.210
1	Longformer	67.26%†	-	-	-	-
	Longformer	-	**94.29%**	-	-	-
	Longformer	-	-	**94.24%**	95.98%	-
	OFA	-	-	-	-	**0.4093**
2	CoCondenser	65.17%	-	-	-	-
3	ALBEF	63.84%	75.85%	-	-	-
	BART	-	-	90.48%	96.77%	0.3029
4	COMBINER	-	-	-	-	0.2519
5(ours)	PMTLED$_{\mathcal{P}_f}$	**70.50%**	80.28%†	92.66%†	**97.30%**	-
	PMTLED$_{\mathcal{P}_d}$	-	-	-	-	0.3650†

Table 2: The official leaderboard of DSTC11 SIMMC 2.1 Challenge on the teststd set. The subtask winners are bold-faced and runner-ups are marked with †. "-" means that the model did not participate in that subtask.

5 Experiments

5.1 Settings and Hyperparameters

The BART-large[2] (Lewis et al., 2020) model is used as the backbone. The whole implementation was based on the *Huggingface Transformers* (Wolf et al., 2020)[3]. The maximum length of dialog turns L_{turn} is set to 6 and the max sequence length is 1,024. The model is finetuned for 30 epochs with an initial learning rate 5e-5 and a batch size of 16 per GPU with AdamW optimizer (Loshchilov and Hutter, 2018). Besides, the linear warmup schedule with warmup ratio of 0.1 and clip gradient norms of 1.0 are equipped. The weight decay and dropout rate are set to 0.1. The value of λ_{aci}, λ_{coref}, λ_{dst} and λ_{lm} are set to 1.0, while the value of λ_{attr}, λ_{disamb} and $\lambda_{nocoref}$ are set to 0.1 based on the performance in validation set. We finetuned all models on a Linux server with Centos and 4 GPU of NVIDIA Tesla A100.

5.2 Results and Analysis

The results on the teststd set is shown in Table 2. The proposed model mt-bart-dstcla was declared as the winner of the subtask 1 with 70.50% ambiguous object identification F1, and was declared as the runner-up of the subtask 2 and 3 with 80.28% coreference F1 in MM-Coref, 92.66% slot F1 and 97.30% Act. F1 in MM-DST. The proposed dynamic prompt-based multi-task model mt-bart-sys-ensemble was declared as the runner-up with 0.3650 BLEU-4 in response generation. For comparison, the Entry #1 used separate models Longformer (Beltagy et al., 2020) for subtask 1, 2 and 3 and adopted the mode of jointly multi-task training of current task and auxiliary tasks. In particular, for Task 3, Entry #1 adopted a fixed prompt for MM-DST task, similar to our approach. Different from us, Entry #1 has designed two different fixed prompts and adopted different classifiers for two different domain: furniture and fashion. This has resulted in higher Act. F1 (1.32%↑) for our proposed model and higher Slot F1 (1.58%↑) for the model of Entry #1. Torward subtask 4, both Entry #1 and us bsed the *system_transcript_annotated* to design the dynamic prompt for response generation. However, we do not use the mentioned objects of the current turn, while Entry #1 use the mentioned objects and their non-visual attributes, which is one of the core factors that they get a higher BLEU-4 (0.0443↑). As for subtask 1, Entry #1 only use the samples with *disambiguation_label*=1 to finetuned the ACI classifier, in which other subtasks do not participate in joint fine-tuning process. Therefore, we finally achieved the higher ambiguous object identification F1 (3.24%↑).

[2] https://huggingface.co/facebook/bart-large

[3] https://github.com/huggingface/transformers

Models	Subtask #1	Subtask #2	Subtask #3		Subtask #4
	Object F1	Object f1	Slot F1	Act. F1	BLEU-4
baseline (Lee et al., 2022a)	-	75.9%	90.%	97.4%	0.3193
PMTLED$_{\mathcal{P}_f}$	68.5%	78.4%	92.0%	97.5%	-
w/o $\mathcal{P}_f$	65.7%	77.3%	88.4%	96.6%	-
PMTLED$_{\mathcal{P}_d}$	-	-	-	-	0.3874
w/o $\mathcal{P}_d$	-	-	-	-	0.3433

Table 3: Results on the devtest set. $\mathcal{P}_f$: fixed prompt. $\mathcal{P}_d$: dynamic prompt.

5.3 Ablation Study

We conduct ablation experiments to answer the questions: (i) Wherther the fixed prompt and dynamic prompt are useful? Table 3 provides detailed results on the devtest for our ablation study. The second row of results is obtained according to the hyperparameters setting of (Lee et al., 2022a). As shown in the row 3 and 4, the performance of the model without $\mathcal{P}_f$ degrades largely on subtask 1, 2 and 3, demonstrating the effectiveness of using the fixed prompt. According to the row 5 and 6, BLEU-4 significantly deteriorates if we discard the dynamic prompt $\mathcal{P}_d$, suggesting that dynamic prompt generated by *system_transcript_annotated* is crucial component for the response generation task.

6 Conclusion and Future Work

In this paper, we proposed a prompt-based multitask learning method for multimodal dialog state tracking and immersive multimodal conversation. The proposed model used fixed prompt for multimodal dialog state tracking and dynamic prompt for immersive multimodal conversation based on Transformer framework. Experiments demonstrated that the proposed fixed prompt and dynamic prompt are effective on jointly fine-tuning the model for the SIMMC 2.1 Challenge. In the future, we will continue exploring the design of the prompt, promoting the model to apply more knowledge as much as possible, e.g. the mentioned objects of current turn of the assistant, the scene image and etc. In addition, the current version of the model depends on domain information, which makes it difficult to apply to other scenarios. Further research needs to solve the domain dependency.

7 Acknowledgement

This work was supported by the Science and Technology Project of Guangzhou (202103010002), the Natural Science Foundation of Guangdong Province (2022A1515011588), the National Key R&D Program of China (2022YFB4500600), the Science and Technology Project of Guangdong (2022B0101010003), the National Natural Science Foundation of China under Grant U1801262 and Guangdong Provincial Key Laboratory of Human Digital Twin (2022B1212010004).

References

Iz Beltagy, Matthew E. Peters, and Arman Cohan. 2020. Longformer: The long-document transformer. *CoRR*, abs/2004.05150.

Jacob Devlin, Ming-Wei Chang, Kenton Lee, and Kristina Toutanova. 2019. BERT: Pre-training of deep bidirectional transformers for language understanding. In *Proceedings of the 2019 Conference of the North American Chapter of the Association for Computational Linguistics: Human Language Technologies, Volume 1 (Long and Short Papers)*, pages 4171–4186, Minneapolis, Minnesota. Association for Computational Linguistics.

Li Dong, Nan Yang, Wenhui Wang, Furu Wei, Xiaodong Liu, Yu Wang, Jianfeng Gao, Ming Zhou, and Hsiao-Wuen Hon. 2019. Unified language model pre-training for natural language understanding and generation. In *Advances in Neural Information Processing Systems*, volume 32. Curran Associates, Inc.

Xu Han, Zhengyan Zhang, Ning Ding, Yuxian Gu, Xiao Liu, Yuqi Huo, Jiezhong Qiu, Yuan Yao, Ao Zhang, Liang Zhang, Wentao Han, Minlie Huang, Qin Jin, Yanyan Lan, Yang Liu, Zhiyuan Liu, Zhiwu Lu, Xipeng Qiu, Ruihua Song, Jie Tang, Ji-Rong Wen, Jinhui Yuan, Wayne Xin Zhao, and Jun Zhu. 2021. Pre-trained models: Past, present and future. *AI Open*, 2:225–250.

Wanwei He, Yinpei Dai, Min Yang, Jian Sun, Fei Huang, Luo Si, and Yongbin Li. 2022. Unified dialog model pre-training for task-oriented dialog understanding and generation. In *Proceedings of the 45th International ACM SIGIR Conference on Research and Development in Information Retrieval*, SIGIR '22, page 187–200, New York, NY, USA. Association for Computing Machinery.

Satwik Kottur, Seungwhan Moon, Alborz Geramifard, and Babak Damavandi. 2021. SIMMC 2.0: A task-oriented dialog dataset for immersive multimodal conversations. In *Proceedings of the 2021 Conference on Empirical Methods in Natural Language Processing*, pages 4903–4912, Online and Punta Cana, Dominican Republic. Association for Computational Linguistics.

Haeju Lee, Oh Joon Kwon, Yunseon Choi, Jinhyeon Kim, Youngjune Lee, Ran Han, Yoonhyung Kim, Minho Park, Kangwook Lee, Haebin Shin, et al. 2022a. Tackling situated multi-modal task-oriented dialogs with a single transformer model. In *DSTC 10 Workshop @ AAAI 2022*.

Haeju Lee, Oh Joon Kwon, Yunseon Choi, Minho Park, Ran Han, Yoonhyung Kim, Jinhyeon Kim, Youngjune Lee, Haebin Shin, Kangwook Lee, and Kee-Eung Kim. 2022b. Learning to embed multi-modal contexts for situated conversational agents. In *Findings of the Association for Computational Linguistics: NAACL 2022*, pages 813–830, Seattle, United States. Association for Computational Linguistics.

Mike Lewis, Yinhan Liu, Naman Goyal, Marjan Ghazvininejad, Abdelrahman Mohamed, Omer Levy, Veselin Stoyanov, and Luke Zettlemoyer. 2020. BART: Denoising sequence-to-sequence pre-training for natural language generation, translation, and comprehension. In *Proceedings of the 58th Annual Meeting of the Association for Computational Linguistics*, pages 7871–7880, Online. Association for Computational Linguistics.

Xiang Lisa Li and Percy Liang. 2021. Prefix-tuning: Optimizing continuous prompts for generation. In *Proceedings of the 59th Annual Meeting of the Association for Computational Linguistics and the 11th International Joint Conference on Natural Language Processing (Volume 1: Long Papers)*, pages 4582–4597, Online. Association for Computational Linguistics.

I Loshchilov and F Hutter. 2018. Fixing weight decay regularization in adam, iclr 2018 conference. In *Vancouver, BC, Canada: Vancouver Convention Center.[Google Scholar]*.

Zhiyuan Ma, Jianjun Li, Guohui Li, and Yongjing Cheng. 2022. UniTranSeR: A unified transformer semantic representation framework for multimodal task-oriented dialog system. In *Proceedings of the 60th Annual Meeting of the Association for Computational Linguistics (Volume 1: Long Papers)*, pages 103–114, Dublin, Ireland. Association for Computational Linguistics.

Fei Mi, Yasheng Wang, and Yitong Li. 2022. Cins: Comprehensive instruction for few-shot learning in task-oriented dialog systems. In *Proceedings of the AAAI Conference on Artificial Intelligence*, volume 36, pages 11076–11084.

Seungwhan Moon, Satwik Kottur, Paul Crook, Ankita De, Shivani Poddar, Theodore Levin, David Whitney, Daniel Difranco, Ahmad Beirami, Eunjoon Cho, Rajen Subba, and Alborz Geramifard. 2020. Situated and interactive multimodal conversations. In *Proceedings of the 28th International Conference on Computational Linguistics*, pages 1103–1121, Barcelona, Spain (Online). International Committee on Computational Linguistics.

Stylianos Mystakidis. 2022. Metaverse. *Encyclopedia*, 2(1):486–497.

Thanh-Tung Nguyen, Wei Shi, Ridong Jiang, and Jung jae Kim. 2022. Multimodal and joint learning generation models for simmc 2.0. In *DSTC 10 Workshop @ AAAI 2022*.

Taylor Shin, Yasaman Razeghi, Robert L. Logan IV, Eric Wallace, and Sameer Singh. 2020. AutoPrompt: Eliciting Knowledge from Language Models with Automatically Generated Prompts. In *Proceedings of the 2020 Conference on Empirical Methods in Natural Language Processing (EMNLP)*, pages 4222–4235, Online. Association for Computational Linguistics.

Yixuan Su, Lei Shu, Elman Mansimov, Arshit Gupta, Deng Cai, Yi-An Lai, and Yi Zhang. 2022. Multi-task pre-training for plug-and-play task-oriented dialogue system. In *Proceedings of the 60th Annual Meeting of the Association for Computational Linguistics (Volume 1: Long Papers)*, pages 4661–4676, Dublin, Ireland. Association for Computational Linguistics.

Ashish Vaswani, Noam Shazeer, Niki Parmar, Jakob Uszkoreit, Llion Jones, Aidan N Gomez, Ł ukasz Kaiser, and Illia Polosukhin. 2017. Attention is all you need. In *Advances in Neural Information Processing Systems*, volume 30. Curran Associates, Inc.

Thomas Wolf, Lysandre Debut, Victor Sanh, Julien Chaumond, Clement Delangue, Anthony Moi, Pierric Cistac, Tim Rault, Remi Louf, Morgan Funtowicz, Joe Davison, Sam Shleifer, Patrick von Platen, Clara Ma, Yacine Jernite, Julien Plu, Canwen Xu, Teven Le Scao, Sylvain Gugger, Mariama Drame, Quentin Lhoest, and Alexander Rush. 2020. Transformers: State-of-the-art natural language processing. In *Proceedings of the 2020 Conference on Empirical Methods in Natural Language Processing: System Demonstrations*, pages 38–45, Online. Association for Computational Linguistics.

Meng Zhao, Lifang Wang, Zejun Jiang, Ronghan Li, Xinyu Lu, and Zhongtian Hu. 2022. Multi-task learning with graph attention networks for multi-domain task-oriented dialogue systems. *Knowledge-Based Systems*, page 110069.

Multi-Task Learning for Ambiguous Candidate Identification with Pre-trained Model

Daesik Jang* **and Hyewon Choi***
daesik0320@gmail.com, hyewon4999@gmail.com

Abstract

Recently, research using multimodal datasets containing image and text information has been conducted actively. One of them is the SIMMC2.1 dataset. It is a more complicated dataset than answering a conversation using only text because it should predict an answer after understanding the relationship between images and text. Therefore, there are limitations to answering a conversation only using text-based models such as BERT or GPT-2, so models with both image and language understanding abilities should be considered. We propose a new model that is effective for the ambiguous candidate identification task in DSTC11 SIMMC2.1 Tark. It consists of a simple pipeline model structure, which has two steps. The first step is to check whether there is ambiguity in the current user utterance, and the second step is to extract objects mentioned in the ambiguous utterance of the user. We suggest a new learning framework with a pre-trained image model and text model that is effective for the ambiguous candidate identification task. Experiments show that the proposed method can improve the model performance, and our model achieved 3rd place in sub-task 1 of the SIMMC2.1 track.

1 Introduction

Conversations with multiple contexts, and multi-modal components, have been actively explored (Das et al., 2017; De Vries et al., 2017; Antol et al., 2015). When developing the conversational agent in the real world, visual information is essential for effective conversation agents so that they can easily adapt to user situations. In this paper, we present our ambiguous candidate identification model, which was submitted to the SIMMC2.1 challenge (Kottur et al., 2021). We focus on the ambiguous candidate identification task of SIMMC2.1, among other tasks. It is the task of detecting ambiguity in conversations and extracting objects mentioned in the user utterance predicted as ambiguous. For example, ambiguities may occur for several reasons, such as when the user does not give enough details to single out a unique referent (e.g., "What is the price of that t-shirt?" instead of "What is the price of the t-shirt on the left?") (Kottur et al., 2021). If a conversational agent needs to answer an ambiguous utterance of the user like the example, the agent may not be able to predict a correct answer effectively. Therefore, for an agent to generate a correct answer to the ambiguous utterance of the user, it is critical to find out the information about objects mentioned in the utterance and help the agent to generate the answer.

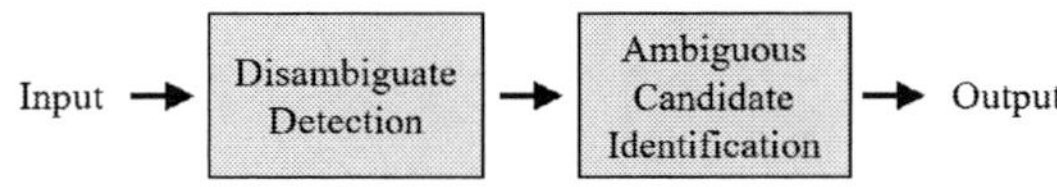

Figure 1: An illusion of the two-step pipeline model framework.

To solve this problem, we use the SIMMC2.1 dataset. For each scene in the data, there is a JSON file with every object's information including its name, ID, bounding box (bbox), location, and relationship. We use the objects' metadata(e.g., color, pattern, type) to determine whether the current user utterance is ambiguous and extract all objects mentioned in the user utterance predicted as ambiguous. Figure 1 is the structure of our proposed model. We construct a two-step pipeline model to solve the task. First, we detect whether the current user utterance is ambiguous using a binary classification model. Then, we use the dialogue history and object information to extract all objects in the ambiguous utterance of the user. This paper has two main contributions as follows:

1. Contrastive loss (Chen et al., 2020; Kim et al., 2021) and binary cross-entropy loss are re-

*These authors contributed equally to this work

Proceedings of The Eleventh Dialog System Technology Challenge, pages 9–14
September 11, 2023 ©2023 Association for Computational Linguistics

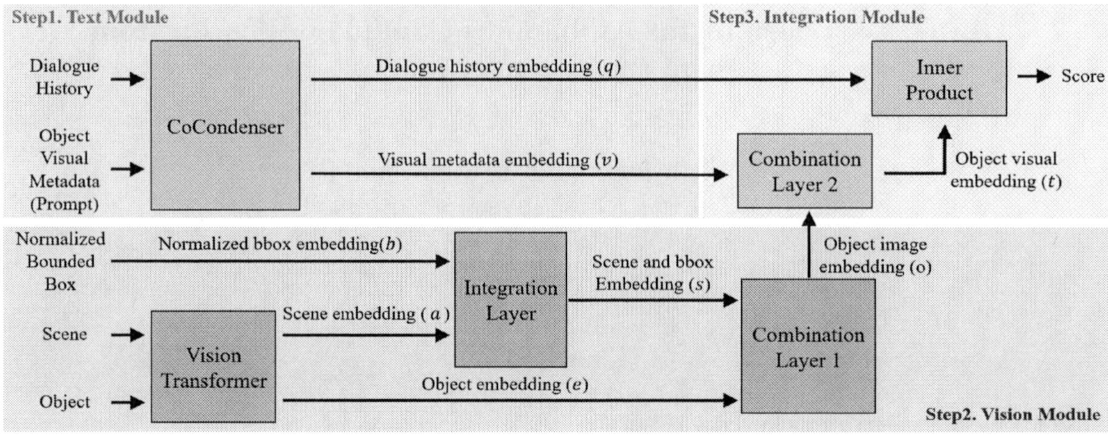

Figure 2: An illustration of the ambiguous candidate identification model using pre-trained model.

garded as different tasks to train a model using the MT-DNN (Liu et al., 2019) method.

2. An effective embedding generation for ambiguous candidate identification task is done by additionally inputting abundant linguistic information of metadata into the model using the prompt we created. Then, we efficiently adjust the encoding ratio according to data characteristics with a linear combination (Choi and Ko, 2022) to create object visual embedding.

Experiments show that our method can improve the model performance. As a result, we gained 3rd place in sub-task 1 of the SIMMC2.1 track.

2 Task and Data Description

DSTC11 Track 1 SIMMC2.1 consists of four subtasks. SIMMC 2.1 provides different datasets for each sub-task, such as the object metadata and the scene image corresponding to dialogue. Among them, we solve sub-task 1, which is the ambiguous candidate identification task. The ambiguous candidate identification task focuses on identifying the ambiguity in the current user utterance given dialogue context and scene information and finding object candidates corresponding to the ambiguity. This task is very effective for multi-modal interactive AI assistants to generate clear utterances from the next utterance.

3 Method

We solve the ambiguous candidate identification task with a two-step pipeline model. Figure 1 is the structure of our proposed model. We describe the disambiguate detection in 3.1 and the ambiguous candidate identification in 3.2.

3.1 Disambiguate Detection

First, disambiguate detection determines whether the current user utterance is ambiguous through binary classification using CoCondenser proposed in Gao and Callan (2022). The CoCondenser is a pre-trained language model based on an encoder suitable for contrastive learning. These Transformer (Vaswani et al., 2017) blocks are divided into three groups, early backbone encoder layers, late backbone encoder layers, and head layers. The head takes the `[CLS]` representation from the late representations, and the token representations from the early layers using a skip connection. The skip connection from the early layers to the head layers lets the model's `[CLS]` token have the global meaning of the input text. We use a pre-trained CoCondenser to generate `[CLS]` token embedding containing the global meaning of dialogue history. The input sequence is as follows:

`[CLS]` Current user utterance `[SEP]` Dialogue context `[SEP]`

Let $C \in \mathbb{R}^h$ be the final hidden vector of `[CLS]` token using CoCondenser, $W_{DD} \in \mathbb{R}^{2\times h}$ be a classification layer for disambiguate detection layer, and we minimize a binary cross-entropy loss.

$$f(x) = softmax\left(CW_{DD}^T\right) = [\hat{y_0}, \hat{y_1}] \quad (1)$$

$$\mathcal{L} = -\sum_{x\in D} y\ log\,\hat{y_1} + (1-y)\ log\,\hat{y_0} \quad (2)$$

where $f(x)$ is the final output of the model and $y \in \{0, 1\}$ is a label.

3.2 Ambiguous Candidate Identification

Figure 2 shows the entire structure of ambiguous candidate identification. The ambiguous candidate identification consists of three major parts. The first is the Text Module, the second is the Vision Module, and the last is the Integration Module which fuses the text and image information.

3.2.1 Text Module

We use the pre-trained language model CoCodenser in the Text Module. The Text Module is used for encoding both the dialogue history and object visual metadata. The input of dialogue history is the same as the input format of Disambiguate Detection. Object visual metadata is composed of prompts to contain rich metadata information. We have structured the prompts for two domains: Fashion and Furniture. The examples of prompts are as below.

Fashion metadata

- Absence of "Sleeve Length"
  - This <Type> with <Pattern> pattern and colored <Color>.
  - Ex) This is jean with denim pattern and colored dark blue.
- Presence of "Sleeve Length"
  - This <Sleeve Length> sleeve <Type> with <Pattern> pattern and colored <Color>.
  - Ex) This is long sleeve blouse with plaid pattern and colored red, white, yellow.

Furniture metadata

- This is <Color> <Type>.
- Ex) This is red area rug.

For the fashion data, the configured prompt varies depending on the presence or absence of "Sleeve Length" in metadata. We create the dialogue history embedding and visual metadata embedding using `[CLS]` token embedding in the last layer.

3.2.2 Vision Module

The Vision Module uses a scene of the current user utterance and an object included in it to encode visual information corresponding to that utterance. We use Vision Transformer (ViT) (Dosovitskiy et al., 2020) to encode a scene and an object effectively. Scene embedding and object embedding are created using the class token embedding of the last layer with a pre-trained ViT without further fine-tuning. Then, we add the normalized bbox information to supplement the object's relative position information to the scene embedding. It is necessary to normalize the bbox as shown in Equations (3-6) with the method proposed in YOLO (Redmon et al., 2016). The normalized bbox information provides relative positioning information for the object in the scene.

$$x_{center} = \frac{\left(x + \frac{width}{2}\right)}{width\ of\ whole\ image} \tag{3}$$

$$y_{center} = \frac{\left(y + \frac{height}{2}\right)}{height\ of\ whole\ image} \tag{4}$$

$$w_{ratio} = \frac{width}{width\ of\ whole\ image} \tag{5}$$

$$h_{ratio} = \frac{height}{height\ of\ whole\ image} \tag{6}$$

$$b = [x_{center}; y_{center}; w_{ratio}; h_{ratio}] \tag{7}$$

As shown in Equation (7), the normalized bbox embedding b is generated through concatenation. Then, the bbox embedding b is concatenated with the scene embedding $a \in \mathbb{R}^h$ to produce the embedding $s \in \mathbb{R}^h$ using the learnable parameter $W_{Integration} \in \mathbb{R}^{h \times (h+4)}$.

$$s = W_{Integration} \cdot [a; b] \tag{8}$$

The embedding s and the object embedding $e \in \mathbb{R}^h$ are concatenated as in Equation (9) to obtain the weight $m_1 \in \mathbb{R}^h$ through a learnable parameter, $W_\gamma \in \mathbb{R}^{h \times 2h}$. The object image embedding $o \in \mathbb{R}^h$ is produced through a linear combination using the weight m_1.

$$m_1 = \sigma\left(W_\gamma \cdot [e; s]\right) \tag{9}$$

$$o = m_1 \circ e + (1 - m_1) \circ s \tag{10}$$

where $\circ$ is the element-wise product.

3.2.3 Integration Module

The Visual metadata embedding, $v \in \mathbb{R}^h$, and the object image embedding, o, are linearly combined.

$$m_2 = \sigma\left(W_\alpha \cdot [v; o]\right) \tag{11}$$

$$t = m_2 \circ v + (1 - m_2) \circ o \tag{12}$$

When extracting the ambiguous candidate, the importance of visual metadata and object image information may vary depending on the situation. Thus, we use a linear combination to dynamically adjust the amount of the visual metadata and object image information to generate an embedding $t \in \mathbb{R}^h$ that is effective for extracting ambiguous candidates. The final score is calculated dialogue history embedding $q \in \mathbb{R}^h$ and inner product with the embedding t containing the object visual information created in Equations (11) and (12) as in Equation (13) and (14).

$$\hat{y} = q \cdot t \tag{13}$$

$$score = sigmoid\left(\hat{y}\right) \tag{14}$$

At inference time, if the $score$ value exceeds the threshold value δ, it is determined as an ambiguous candidate.

3.2.4 Training Method

We train a model using the binary cross-entropy loss and contrastive loss. In binary cross-entropy loss, we train positive samples to have scores close to 1 and negative ones to 0.

$$\mathcal{L}_{BCE} = -y\, log\, \sigma\left(\hat{y}\right) + (1-y)\ log\ \left(1-\sigma\left(\hat{y}\right)\right) \tag{15}$$

After obtaining scores using positive and negative pairs of dialogue history and objects, a contrastive loss is calculated.

$$\mathcal{L}_{Contrastive} = -log\, \frac{exp\left(q \cdot t_{+}/\tau\right)}{\sum_k exp\left(q \cdot t_k/\tau\right)} \tag{16}$$

We adopt the multi-task learning framework, MT-DNN, and train the model with both binary cross-entropy loss and contrastive loss.

4 Experiments

4.1 Training Setup

We utilized CoCondenser pre-trained with Wikipedia data and pre-trained ViT. We obtained the class token embedding of the last layer from the pre-trained ViT, which was released in Dosovitskiy et al. (2020). The optimizer used for training is Adam (Kingma and Ba, 2014) and we use the linear scheduler with a learning rate of 5e-5. We trained our model for 10 epochs on one RTX 3090.

4.2 Comparison with other models

Table 1 shows the performance results of our proposed model and other models on devtest dataset and teststd dataset. The proposed model was evaluated using the two steps pipeline model. Our model achieved 3rd place in both devtest dataset and teststd dataset. The results prove that our learning method is effective for the ambiguous candidate identification task.

TeamID	Devtest F1-score	Teststd F1-score
1	70.31%	67.26%
2 (Our model)	66.22%	65.17%
3	62.45%	63.84%
4	68.47%	70.50%

Table 1: The performance comparison on devtest and teststd dataset.

Type	Loss function	Precision	Recall	F1-score
1	Contrastive Loss	29.28%	93.73%	44.62%
2	Binary Cross-entropy Loss	62.23%	69.46%	66.20%
3	Contrastive Loss + Binary Cross-entropy Loss	**63.64%**	**76.10%**	**69.28%**

Table 2: Experimental results according to loss type on devtest dataset.

Type	Loss function	Positive	Negative
1	Contrastive Loss	12.76	2.93
2	Binary Cross-entropy Loss	2.81	-3.88
3	Contrastive Loss + Binary Cross-entropy Loss	6.06	-8.30

Table 3: Experimental results of averaging the positive and negative samples $\hat{y}$ value on devtest dataset.

4.3 Effect of loss type

Table 2 is the model performance according to the loss type, and Table 3 presents the score values derived at inference time from the model trained with each loss type. If a score value obtained from Equation (14) is 0.5 or higher, we regard the value as an ambiguous candidate. Positive and negative scores in Table 3 are the results of averaging $\hat{y}$ values obtained from Equation (13) of the positive and negative samples of all evaluation data during inference.

First, Type 1 contrastive loss shows relatively low performance with an F1-score of 44.62%. Then, recall is a very high value of 93.73%. In Type 1, most positive and negative $\hat{y}$ values were higher than 0. We can see that the contrastive loss simply distances a positive $\hat{y}$ value from a negative one without any directional information about an object.

Second, Type 2 binary cross-entropy loss is an F1-score of 66.20%, achieving relatively higher performance than Type 1. The recall of Type 2 is 69.46%, which is lower than that of Type 1. Unlike the contrastive loss, the binary cross-entropy learns positive scores as close to 1 and negative scores as close to 0. In this way, it helps the model absorb the directional information about an object. Therefore, we can see the Type 2 scores in Table 3 evenly distributed as positive sample $\hat{y}$ values as positive numbers and negative sample $\hat{y}$ values as negative numbers based on 0.

Finally, Type 3 is a model with binary cross-entropy loss and contrastive loss using the method proposed in MT-DNN. The result was an F1-score of 69.28%, which is about 3%p higher than that of Type 2. In MT-DNN multi-task learning framework, models can have benefits of both contrastive loss and binary cross-entropy loss. That is, while learning directional information about an object, positive $\hat{y}$ values are evenly distributed as positive numbers and negative $\hat{y}$ values as negative numbers. Also, we can see that the contrastive loss distances a positive score from a negative one with directional information about an object, unlike Type 1. This can extract ambiguous candidates more effectively than Type 1 and Type 2 when identifying them.

4.4 Ablation study

In Table 4, the Text Module of Figure 2 uses the same method to encode dialogue history and object visual metadata. We tested by setting the Vision Module encoding method differently.

Method	Model	Precision	Recall	F1-score
1	CoCondenser + Scene embedding + Normalized bbox	43.44%	51.15%	46.98%
2	CoCondenser + Scene embedding + Normalized bbox **+ Object embedding**	57.74%	58.02%	57.88% (+10.9%p)
3	CoCondenser + Scene embedding + Normalized bbox + Object embedding **+ Visual metadata** **(Our model)**	**63.64%**	**76.01%**	**69.28%** **(+22.3%p)**

Table 4: The experiments to examine the vision module encoding method on devtest dataset.

First, we encode image information using scene embedding and normalized bbox information. The result is an F1-score of 46.98%. Second, using object embedding together improved performance by about 11%p. These evaluation results demonstrate that we can create richer object image embedding by using the image information of an object itself with the scene information. Finally, when we use our own prompt, there is as much as 11%p performance improvement with an F1-score of 69.28%. This shows that information on each object's prompt plays a significant role in resolving the ambiguous candidate identification tasks.

4.5 Effect of encoding method

When combining two embeddings, we used a linear combination instead of concatenating and projecting them through weights. The structure helps the model dynamically adjust the encoding ratio depending on the situation. A simple weighted method concatenates two embeddings and then projects them through the weights W to create one embedding.

Combination layer 1	Combination layer 2	F1-score
simple weight	simple weight	66.74%
linear combination	simple weight	67.37%
linear combination	linear combination	**69.28%**

Table 5: The effect of the linear combination on devtest dataset.

We evaluated three forms to prove the contribution of our proposed linear combination. First, when using the simple weights for the combination layers 1 and 2, an F1-score of 66.74% shows relatively low performance. Second, when using a linear combination for combination layer 1 and simple weights for combination layer 2, an F1-score of 69.28% achieves higher performance than when applying simple weights to both layers. Finally, using a linear combination for both layers gives the highest performing an F1-score of 69.28%. These results prove our hypothesis that our proposed linear combination method effectively solves ambiguous candidate identification tasks by dynamically adjusting the encoding ratio according to the data characteristics.

5 Conclusion

Our proposed model places 3rd in the ambiguous candidate identification task of the SIMMC2.1 track. There are two main contributions. First, we consider both the contrastive loss and the binary cross-entropy loss and use a multi-task learning framework, MT-DNN. By learning a model in this way, it can have both benefits of contrastive loss and binary cross-entropy loss. We have demonstrated through testing that our proposed learning method is effective for ambiguous candidate identification. Second, by using our prompt to further input metadata information into a model, we create richer embeddings for successful ambiguous candidate identification. Then, we use a linear combination to adjust the encoding ratio according to the data characteristics to create embeddings suitable for object extraction. Through ablation studies, evaluation results show that visual metadata information using prompts improve performance. In particular, model performance increased by about 11%p through visual metadata information (prompt), proving the effectiveness of our prompts.

We suggest a novel two-step pipeline system for the ambiguous candidate identification task. In the future, we are planning to work on an End2End system instead of a two-step pipeline system.

References

Stanislaw Antol, Aishwarya Agrawal, Jiasen Lu, Margaret Mitchell, Dhruv Batra, C Lawrence Zitnick, and Devi Parikh. 2015. Vqa: Visual question answering. In *Proceedings of the IEEE international conference on computer vision*, pages 2425–2433.

Ting Chen, Simon Kornblith, Mohammad Norouzi, and Geoffrey Hinton. 2020. A simple framework for contrastive learning of visual representations. In *International conference on machine learning*, pages 1597–1607. PMLR.

Hyewon Choi and Youngjoong Ko. 2022. Effective fake news video detection using domain knowledge and multimodal data fusion on youtube. *Pattern Recognition Letters*, 154:44–52.

Abhishek Das, Satwik Kottur, Khushi Gupta, Avi Singh, Deshraj Yadav, José MF Moura, Devi Parikh, and Dhruv Batra. 2017. Visual dialog. In *Proceedings of the IEEE conference on computer vision and pattern recognition*, pages 326–335.

Harm De Vries, Florian Strub, Sarath Chandar, Olivier Pietquin, Hugo Larochelle, and Aaron Courville. 2017. Guesswhat?! visual object discovery through multi-modal dialogue. In *Proceedings of the IEEE Conference on Computer Vision and Pattern Recognition*, pages 5503–5512.

Alexey Dosovitskiy, Lucas Beyer, Alexander Kolesnikov, Dirk Weissenborn, Xiaohua Zhai, Thomas Unterthiner, Mostafa Dehghani, Matthias Minderer, Georg Heigold, Sylvain Gelly, et al. 2020. An image is worth 16x16 words: Transformers for image recognition at scale. *arXiv preprint arXiv:2010.11929*.

Luyu Gao and Jamie Callan. 2022. Unsupervised corpus aware language model pre-training for dense passage retrieval. In *Proceedings of the 60th Annual Meeting of the Association for Computational Linguistics (Volume 1: Long Papers)*, pages 2843–2853.

Bosung Kim, Hyewon Choi, Haeun Yu, and Youngjoong Ko. 2021. Query reformulation for descriptive queries of jargon words using a knowledge graph based on a dictionary. In *Proceedings of the 30th ACM International Conference on Information & Knowledge Management*, pages 854–862.

Diederik P Kingma and Jimmy Ba. 2014. Adam: A method for stochastic optimization. *arXiv preprint arXiv:1412.6980*.

Satwik Kottur, Seungwhan Moon, Alborz Geramifard, and Babak Damavandi. 2021. Simmc 2.0: A task-oriented dialog dataset for immersive multimodal conversations. In *Proceedings of the 2021 Conference on Empirical Methods in Natural Language Processing*, pages 4903–4912.

Xiaodong Liu, Pengcheng He, Weizhu Chen, and Jianfeng Gao. 2019. Multi-task deep neural networks for natural language understanding. In *Proceedings of the 57th Annual Meeting of the Association for Computational Linguistics*, pages 4487–4496.

Joseph Redmon, Santosh Divvala, Ross Girshick, and Ali Farhadi. 2016. You only look once: Unified, real-time object detection. In *Proceedings of the IEEE conference on computer vision and pattern recognition*, pages 779–788.

Ashish Vaswani, Noam Shazeer, Niki Parmar, Jakob Uszkoreit, Llion Jones, Aidan N Gomez, Łukasz Kaiser, and Illia Polosukhin. 2017. Attention is all you need. *Advances in neural information processing systems*, 30.

Improving Situated Conversational Agents with Step-by-Step Multi-modal Logic Reasoning

Yuxing Long[1*], **Huibin Zhang**[1*], **Binyuan Hui**[1*], **Zhenglu Yang**[2], **Caixia Yuan**[2], **Xiaojie Wang**[2], **Fei Huang**[1], **Yongbin Li**[1†]

[1] DAMO Academy, Alibaba Group, [2] Independent Researcher

{longyuxing.lyx,zhanghuibin.zhb,binyuan.hby,f.huang,shuide.lyb}@alibaba-inc.com

Abstract

To fulfill complex user requirements in a situated conversational scenario, the agent needs to conduct step-by-step multi-modal logic reasoning, which includes locating objects, querying information and searching objects. However, existing methods omit this multi-step procedure and therefore constitute the risk of shortcuts when making predictions. For example, they may directly copy the information from the dialogue history or simply use the textual description without visual reasoning. To address this issue and further boost the system performance, we apply the dual process theory to plug a reasoner into the original transformer-based model for step-by-step reasoning. When system 2 completes multi-step reasoning, its output is regarded as the final prediction. Our proposed method achieved the 1st rank on the summing scores across all four DSTC-11 SIMMC 2.1 sub-tasks.

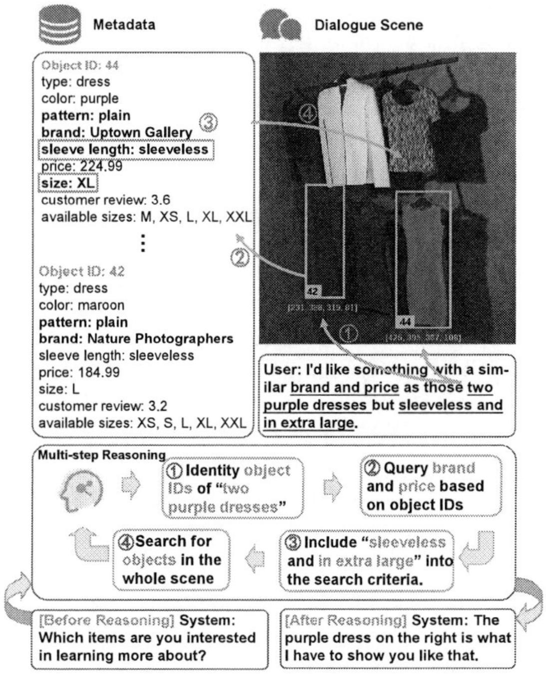

Figure 1: The multi-modal multi-step reasoning process for complex user requirements in the real world. Numbers ❶❷❸❹ represent the sequence of reasoning steps. To make the response to user, the situated conversational agent needs to identify objects on the scene image, query information from metadata, add extra user requirements and search for the target object in the whole scene. Without such a reasoning process, the agent fails to give an effective answer.

1 Introduction

A situated conversational agent (Moon et al., 2020) engages in a conversation in an embedded multi-modal context, which may involve a virtual environment, a real physical world, etc. This task features language understanding, visual perception, decision feedback, and abundant interactions and reasoning among various modalities. Recently, (Kottur et al., 2021) proposed virtual shopping scenarios based on fashion and furniture, i.e. SIMMC, and it becomes a popular benchmark for the situated conversational task.

Current efforts (Lee et al., 2022; Lee and Han, 2021; Nguyen et al., 2021) on SIMMC target this task by designing unique model structures, auxiliary losses, and pre-training strategies. Although their approaches could improve the model's performance in predicting metadata related answer, such improvements partially come from shortcuts that have been revealed in recent studies (Ye and Kovashka, 2021; Dancette et al., 2021; Si et al., 2022; Ye et al., 2023). These shortcuts include directly copying keywords from dialogue history or making predictions simply based on textual mappings without performing visual reasoning. Apparently, shortcuts could harm the model performance especially for complex user requests. Instead, explicitly modeling the multi-step reasoning chain can provide a clear clue to help the model yield more reliable predictions. For instance, as shown

*Equal Contribution
†Corresponding Author

Proceedings of The Eleventh Dialog System Technology Challenge, pages 15–24
September 11, 2023

in Fig. 1, when the agent responds to a user query, *I'd like something with a similar brand and price as those two purple dresses but sleeveless and in extra large*, it needs to go through the subsequent step-by-step deliberation process. Step ❶, clarify the user's reference, i.e., identify the object id of the `two purple dresses`, based on the dialogue history and the current visual scene. Step ❷, check the corresponding brands and prices for the `two purple dresses` based on their object ids. Step ❸, include the newly stated requirements of the user in the search criteria: `sleeveless` and `extra large`. Step ❹, the eligible objects in the current visual scene are identified by incorporating the information from our query and the new requirements stated by the speaker.

Additionally, according to the *Dual process theory* (Evans, 2003), human cognition is produced by the interaction of ***System 1***, which is in charge of quick, unconscious, implicit judgments, and ***System 2***, which is in charge of complex, explicit, step-by-step reasoning. The cognitive ability of humans is mediated by the interaction of *System 1* and *System 2*. However, current situated conversational agents solely rely on intuition to derive answers from straightforward processing of input data (analogous to *System 1*). These responses are frequently inaccurate when the questions are complex because of the lack of interlocking logical reasoning (analogous to *System 2*). Therefore, we argue that the acquisition of the reasoning capabilities performed by humans in *System 2*, especially step-by-step multi-modal reasoning, is a crucial component of situated conversational agents.

To this end, inspired by cognitive theory, we propose a step-by-step multi-modal reasoning framework. Concretely, in our framework, **System 1**'s implicit understanding is handled by the conventional encoder-decoder, while the explicit step-by-step reasoning of **System 2** is handled by the newborn reasoner. Besides, we propose a simple, unsupervised step-by-step reasoning process generation approach based on rewriting the original user utterance as a learning signal for the reasoner.

We evaluate our model on the 11th Dialog System Technology Challenge (DSTC-11) SIMMC 2.1 (Kottur et al., 2021) track. SIMMC 2.1 includes four sub-tasks of situated conversational task, i.e., ambiguous candidate identification (Task 1 Ambigu.), multi-modal coreference resolution (Task 2 MM-Coref), multi-modal dialog state tracking (Task 3 MM-DST) and multi-modal dialog response generation (Task 4 Res. Gen.). Notably, after the official evaluation of the DSTC-11 committee, **our proposed model achieved the 1st rank on the summing scores across all four sub-tasks**.

2 Related Work

2.1 Situated Conversational Agents

Situated conversational agents aim at holding a meaningful conversation with humans based on natural images or real visual scene (Chen et al., 2020c). Recently, the flourishing of visual and language representation learning poses great demand for multi-modal dialog systems. Several datasets have been proposed to evaluate multi-modal dialog system, e.g., VisDial (Das et al., 2017), MMD (Saha et al., 2018), SIMMC (Moon et al., 2020), JDDC (Chen et al., 2020b) and JDDC 2.0 (Zhao et al., 2021). These datasets, however, are image-oriented dialogue systems without a comprehension of real-world visual scenes. To address the aforementioned issue, SIMMC 2.0 and 2.1 (Kottur et al., 2021) have been proposed, which are datasets for situated interactive multi-modal dialogue system and serve as official datasets for DSTC-10 and DSTC-11 challenge respectively. To solve this challenge, (Kottur et al., 2021) proposes a multi-modal GPT-2 (Radford et al., 2019) model as task baseline to generate current belief states and system response auto-regressively. (Huang et al., 2021) suggested using the rich multi-modal input and the pre-trained UNITER (Chen et al., 2020d) model to predict user mentioned objects. (Lee et al., 2022) encodes multi-modal context by special tokens and designs auxiliary tasks to predict object metadata so that the single-stream model can better utilize this information to respond to user requirements. All existing methods make efforts to improve representations of scene objects and fluency of agent response, but they ignore modeling logic in the multi-modal multi-step reasoning. Therefore, these methods often make mistakes when dealing with complex user requirements. Unlike them and (Long et al., 2023; He et al., 2022c,a,b), we first notice the step-by-step multi-modal reasoning based on cognitive theory in situated conversational agents.

2.2 Multi-modal Reasoning

Widely used multi-modal datasets, such as VQA (Goyal et al., 2017), VisDial (Das et al., 2017), FVQA (Wang et al., 2018) and

KVQA (Shah et al., 2019), all contains complex multi-modal questions or user utterances which require multi-modal agent to conduct multi-step reasoning on the image, text or structural data to predict answers. For VQA task and VisDial task, existing models, like ReDAN (Gan et al., 2019), DMRM (Chen et al., 2020a) MUREL (Cadène et al., 2019), GoG (Chen et al., 2021), design special modules or graphs to increase multi-modal agent's attention on the target image objects step-by-step under user guidance. In fact, these methods just complete visual grounding of objects by understanding the multi-hop keywords in textual instruction. when dealing with multiple actions in context, they are not equipped with abilities of multi-step logic reasoning. For FVQA task, (Zhu et al., 2020) builds convolutional graph network for retrieved facts and performs graph multi-step reasoning through message passing scheme utilizing graph convolution. For KVQA task, (Heo et al., 2022) constructs hypergraphs with multi-modal multi-hop information and creates Hypergraph Transformer to predict answers. Although their methods conduct multi-step logic reasoning, their reasoning actions are limited to querying information. Besides, the reasoning chain of all these methods is invisible to users, which makes their prediction result lack of interpretation. Compared with their method, our approach can generate a detailed multi-step logic reasoning process dealing with multiple actions according to user requirements, which is more interpretable and can be easily plugged into existing model architecture.

3 Task Descriptions

Ambiguous Candidate Identification (Ambigu.) During the conversation, the user's expressions tend to be more colloquial and accompanied by ambiguous object references. The ambiguous candidate identification task focuses on identifying all possible candidates that match the user's description. (*e.g.* U:"Can you tell me how much the brown piece costs? I'd like the rating too." ⇒ All of the brown objects in the current scene need to be predicted by the model.).

Multi-modal Coreference Resolution (MM-Coref) Similar to the ambiguous candidate identification task, the user will refer to specific items in the current scene when they are expressing their meaning accurately. Based on the current dialogue context and visual scene, the task requires the model to anticipate which object the user is referring to.

Multi-modal Dialog State Tracking (MM-DST) Dialogue state tracking task requires the model to track the speaker's belief state cumulative across multiple turns. In addition to comprehending the dialogue history, the MM-DST task requires the model to reason about the objects and their attributes in the current scene. (*e.g.* U: "Do you have something in a similar brand as that grey coat" ⇒ It is necessary to predict the object id and brand attribute of that grey coat.)

Multi-modal Dialog Response Generation (Res. Gen.) Similar to text-driven dialog response generation, this task requires the model to generate assistant responses based on the dialog history and the current scene.

4 Method

Our model contains a dual system, similar to the human cognitive system, consisting of System 1 and System 2. System 1 consists of a conventional Encoder-Decoder, which is dedicated to a specific task. System 2 consists of a generative Reasoner capable of producing step-by-step multi-modal reasoning path generation.

4.1 System 1: Encoder-Decoder

The design of System 1 is followed by (Lee et al., 2022) and it can perform SIMMC 2.1 sub-tasks end-to-end by unique task loss. Here we describe the architecture of System 1 in detail.

Encoder As Figure 2 shows, the encoder takes multi-modal information as input. The textual input includes dialogue history, current user utterance and special tokens, e.g., `"[act]"`, `"[obj]"` and `"[type]"`. The visual input of the encoder is all scene object region features encoded by pretrained models, e.g., ResNet-50 (He et al., 2016), which are projected to visual embedding with the same size as textual embedding. The projected bounding box coordinates are added to object visual embedding to represent spatial relations. Besides, similar to (Lee et al., 2022), we add auxiliary tasks for encoder to enhance the understanding of visual and non-visual attributes.

For predicting user act, user mentioned object IDs and slot values, the additional heads on special tokens as classification layer, which are optimized by cross-entropy losses.

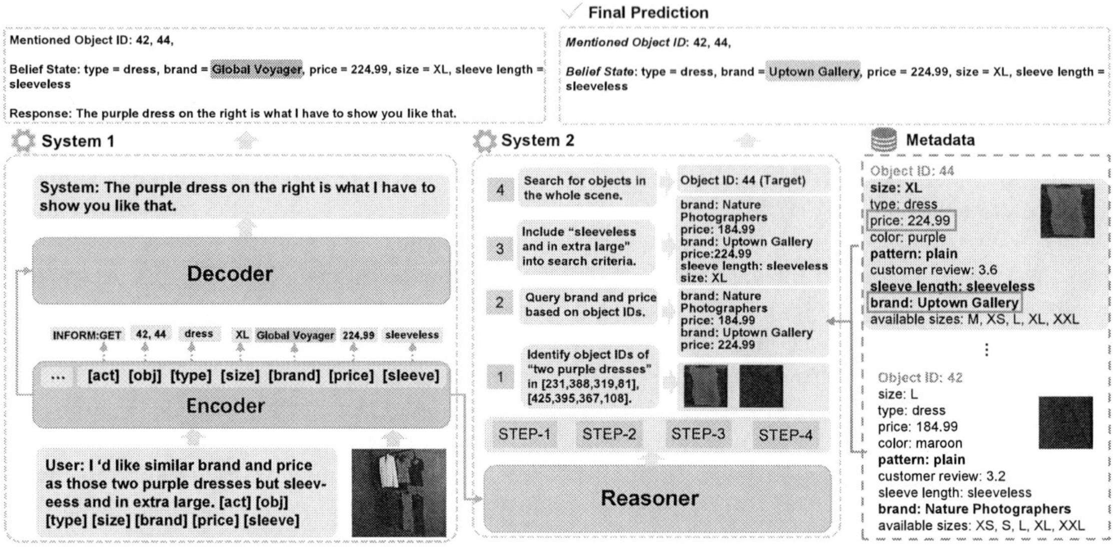

Figure 2: Overview of our proposed framework. We reuse the example in Figure 1. According to the user utterance, the encoder predicts the belief state and intent action of user, and the reasoner generates the detailed reasoning steps of situated conversational agents. The Decoder is in charge of generating system response based on the current multi-modal context. In the inference stage, the output of the reasoner is regarded as the final prediction if it completes multi-step reasoning.

Decoder The decoder takes hidden representation H from the encoder as input and generates output auto-regressively. For response generation, the response decoder is optimized by the standard left-to-right language modeling loss $\mathcal{L}_{\text{dec}}$ as the following.

$$\mathcal{L}_{\text{dec}} = \sum_{i=1}^{L} - \log P_{\theta_{dec}} \left(\omega_{dec}^{i} \mid \omega_{dec}^{1}, \ldots, \omega_{dec}^{i-1}, H \right) \tag{1}$$

where H denotes the last hidden states of encoder, ω_{dec}^{i} represents i-th target response token, L_{dec} is the total length of target response and θ_{dec} means decoder learnable parameters.

4.2 System 2: Reasoner

The aim of system 2 is to generate a concrete inferring process step-by-step and implement corresponding actions on the scene image and metadata to get information about object IDs, bounding boxes and attributes. The core module of system 2 is a reasoner whose architecture is also a Transformer-based auto-regressive decoder. As Figure 2 shows, the reasoner takes encoded multi-modal representation from the encoder as module input and auto-regressively generates reasoning steps.

According to reasoning intention, the generated reasoning steps can be categorized into: **Locate Object**, **Query Information**, **Add Requirement**, **Search Object**, **Compare** and **Disambiguate**. **1)** In the step of locating objects, the reasoner extracts object detailed description from the input text and then predicts corresponding bounding box coordinates on the scene image, which can be used to crop object region visual features. The cropped region feature is compared with object screenshots in the metadata to identify IDs of objects mentioned in the current user utterance. **2)** In the step of querying information, the reasoner extracts user required attribute types, such as *"brand"* and *"price"*, about mentioned objects from inputted text and queries metadata values based on identified object IDs and attribute types. These queried values are regarded as search requirements. **3)** In the step of adding requirement, the reasoner extracts user extra requirements attribute values, like *"sleeveless"* and *"in extra large"*, from inputted text and adds them into search requirements. **4)** In the step of searching objects, the reasoner takes all search requirements as criteria and searches for objects satisfying all requirements among metadata. **5)** In the step of comparing, the reasoner retrieves all metadata attribute of object 1 and object 2 and compare their similarity and difference. **6)** In the step of disambiguation, the reasoner extracts object detailed description from the input text and transverses all metadata of scene objects to find out

REASONING TYPE	REASONING TEMPLATE
`Locate Object`	Identify object IDs of "**[Referring Expression]**" in **[x1, y1, x2, y2]**.
`Query Information`	Query **[Metadata Type]** of object **[Object ID]**.
`Add Requirement`	Include "**[Attribute Value]**" into search criteria.
`Search Object`	Search for objects in the whole scene.
`Compare`	Compare metadata of object **[Object 1 ID]** and **[Object 2 ID]**.
`Disambiguate`	Find all possible "**[Referring Expressions]**" in the whole scene.

Table 1: Six types of reasoning step templates designed for SIMMC 2.1. "[*]" is the template slots to be filled. By extracting information from user utterances and filling the templates, multi-step reasoning data can be generated as reasoner training data.

matched objects.

Reasoning Process Generation By analyzing complex user utterances in the multimodal conversation datasets (Kottur et al., 2021; Moon et al., 2020; Saha et al., 2018), we find that there are signal words, like *"similar"*, *"but"* and *"as"*, exist in the user utterance, which indicates the start of essential information. In this case, original user utterance can be divided into different reasoning semantics by these signal words. For example, user utterance *"I'd like similar brand and price as those two purple dresses but sleeveless and in extra large"* can be splitted into referring expression *"as those two purple dresses"*, information inquiry *"similar brand and price"* and new requirements *"but sleeveless and in extra large"*. Based on common reasoning semantics in the SIMMC 2.1, we design six types of reasoning step templates as Table 1 shows. After determining the template by signal words, regular expressions are utilized to extract attribute types and values from splitted reasoning semantics to fill template slots. In this way, a multi-step reasoning process can be generated from the original user utterance. If there are no signal words in the utterance, the generation target is set to *"No multi-step reasoning"*.

Reasoning Task The reasoner is optimized by the standard left-to-right language modeling loss $\mathcal{L}_{\text{rea}}$ as the following.

$$\mathcal{L}_{\text{rea}} = \sum_{i=1}^{L} -\log P_{\theta_{rea}}\left(\omega_{rea}^{i} \mid \omega_{rea}^{1}, \ldots, \omega_{rea}^{i-1}, H\right) \tag{2}$$

where ω_{rea}^{i} represents i-th target reasoning process token, L_{rea} is the total length of target reasoning process and θ_{rea} is reasoner learnable parameters.

After the reasoner executes all steps, it can obtain object IDs mentioned by current user utterance, user utterance slot values and object information to be responded by agent, which is collected as the output of system 2. Compared with system 1, system 2 is more reliable because system 2 completes the whole reasoning process explicitly instead of utilizing shortcuts to respond to complex user requirements. Therefore, in the inference stage, system 2 output is chosen as the final prediction result if its output exists.

5 Experiments

5.1 Dataset

The SIMMC 2.1 dataset follows the setting of SIMMC 2.0 (Kottur et al., 2021), which is geared towards building virtual assistant that generates conversations with users in the form of co-observation and immersive virtual reality (VR) environments. The conversation's content may take several turns, and the context is dynamically modified based on the user's activities at each turn. There are a total of 11244 dialogues and 1566 scenes gathered in the SIMMC 2.1 dataset, which uses a two-stage pipeline to collect dialogues (multi-modal dialogue simulation and manual interpretation). The dialogue of SIMMC 2.1 involves two domains: fashion (7.2k dialogs) and furniture (4k dialogs), which are randomly divided into four splits: train (64%), dev (5%), dev-test (15%), and test-std (15%). The test-std split is used as the evaluation dataset for the DSTC-11 Challenge[2] and its data annotation is not publicly available.

5.2 Evaluation Metric

In order to evaluate the performance of the multimodal dialogue system, SIMMC 2.1 employs different evaluation metrics for each subtask. For Ambiguous Candidate Identification task and Multimodal Coreference Resolution task, the performance is mainly evaluated by the F1 score of object

[2]https://dstc11.dstc.community

	Model	Task 1 Ambigu. Object F1 (↑)	Task 2 MM-Coref Object F1 (↑)	Task 3 MM-DST Slot F1 (↑)	Task 3 MM-DST Act F1 (↑)	Task 4 Res. Gen. BLEU-4 (↑)
Baseline	GPT-2	18.00%	26.50%	73.50%	93.00%	19.20
	MTN	43.20%	–	75.00%	94.30%	21.00
	BERT	43.90%	–	–	–	–
DSTC-10	I2R Singapore	–	40.50%	86.40%	96.30%	34.62
	Sogang University	–	46.97%	88.25%	96.13%	28.38
	Kakao Enterprise	–	60.80%	–	–	28.50
	KAIST	–	73.50%	88.30%	96.30%	33.10
DSTC-11	#2	62.45%	73.78%	92.48%	97.30%	30.00
	#3	69.28%	–	–	–	–
	#5	68.46%	78.64%	92.05%	97.82%	39.09
	(Ours) #1	**70.30%**	**94.40%**	**93.32%**	**99.19%**	**42.55**
	- Reasoner	65.10%	79.65%	89.42%	96.53%	41.24

Table 2: Results on the SIMMC 2.1 devtest set. The first block shows the baselines, which are separately trained on each subtask. The second block and third block provide the complete results and ablation study on DSTC-10 & DSTC-11 model: "- Reasoner" means taking system 1 prediction as the final prediction under all cases without system 2 participation. Task 1 is the new task of DSTC-11, hence it isn't included in the result of DSTC-10.

prediction (Object F1). For the Multi-modal Dialog State Tracking task, the performance is mainly evaluated by the F1 score of dialog action and slot-values prediction (Slot F1 & Act F1). For the Multi-modal Dialog Response Generation task, the performance is mainly evaluated by the BLEU-4 for generated system response (BELU-4).

5.3 Baselines

The official SIMMC 2.1 proposer provided three baseline models, the finetuned **GPT-2** baseline generates the results of tasks 1 to 4 in a way similar to the language model. The **MTN** and **BERT** baselines combine visual scene information and dialogue history to generate user belief state and system response (these two models are not involved in all tasks). The visual features for the corresponding bounding boxes in each scene have been extracted by using pretrained ResNet-50 (He et al., 2016). Additionally, we have included the result from other DSTC-10 and DSTC-11 participating teams. In table 2, We display the teams with publicly available results due to certain teams still not publishing their performance on devtest set. In table 3 we display the official leaderboard of DSTC-11 & DSTC-10 on the teststd set of SIMMC 2.1.

5.4 Implementation Detail

For the encoder module in System 1, we employ the pre-trained longformer-base (Beltagy et al., 2020) model provided by HuggingFace's transformers library (Wolf et al., 2020). The decoder in System 1 and the reasoner in System 2 are designed as 6 hidden layers with a size of 512 and 8 attention heads. In our training stage, the batch size is set to 64 and the number of training epochs is set to 100. We introduce a cosine warm-up mechanism and set the warm-up rate and learning rate to 0.1 and 5e-5. The AdamW optimizer is used to optimize all models and all experiments are conducted with PyTorch. Our source code will be released online.

5.5 Experimental Results

5.5.1 Comparison Analysis

From the evaluation results in Table 2, it can be observed that our model achieves state-of-the-art performance on each task. In particular, the performance on multi-modal coreference resolution (Task 2) and response generation (Task 4) exceed the runner-up for a large margin (15.76 (78.64 $\rightarrow$ 94.40) in object f1-score and 6.30 (39.09 $\rightarrow$ 45.39) in Bleu-4 score), which demonstrates the effectiveness of introducing the step-by-step multi-modal reasoning strategy. By introducing the reasoning generation process of system 2, our model can better comprehend the coreference relationship and implicit reasoning logic in the dialogue. For the ambiguous candidate identification (Task 1) and multi-modal dialog state tracking task (Task 3), we apply a similar framework and achieve favorable performance. Additionally, in contrast to other teams which employ an autoregressive language approach to deal with the MM-DST, We first utilize the encoder module for processing. We also conducted an ablation analysis on the primary modules in the framework.

	Model Entry	Task 1 Ambigu. Object F1 (↑)	Task 2 MM-Coref Object F1 (↑)	Task 3 MM-DST Slot F1 (↑)	Task 3 MM-DST Act F1 (↑)	Task 4 Res. Gen. BLEU-4 (↑)
DSTC-10	I2R Singapore	–	42.20%	87.80%	96.20%	25.60
	Sogang University	–	52.10%	88.30%	96.30%	28.50
	QS goal Diggers	–	56.40%	89.30%	96.40%	32.20
	Kakao Enterprise	–	68.20%	4.000%	41.40%	29.70
	Hariot-Watt University	–	68.20%	87.70%	95.80%	32.70
	New York University	–	73.30%	–	–	–
	KAIST	–	75.80%	90.30%	95.90%	29.50
	UCLA	–	78.30%	–	–	–
DSTC-11	**#2**	65.17%	–	–	–	–
	#3	63.84%	75.85%	90.48%	96.77%	30.29
	#4	–	–	–	–	25.19
	#5	**70.50%**	80.28%	92.66%	**97.75%**	36.50
	(Ours) #1	67.26%	**94.29%**	**94.24%**	95.98%	**40.93**

Table 3: The official leaderboard of DSTC-11 & DSTC-10 on the teststd set of SIMMC 2.1. The first block shows the results of DSTC-10 and the second block shows the results of DSTC-11. The task winners are bold-faced and runner-ups are marked with underline.'-' means that the entry did not participate in that task. Task 1 is the new task of DSTC-11, hence it isn't included in the result of DSTC-10. Our entry is officially announced as the Winner of Subtask 2,3,4 (MM-Coref, MM-DST, Res. Gen.) and Runner-up of Subtask 1 (Ambigu.)[1].

As indicated by the last row of Table 2, the removal of the reasoner weakens our model's performance on all sub-tasks. Especially, reasoner has a huge influence on the Task 1 and Task 2. The reason may lay on the fact that these two tasks require the model to ground all mentioned objects or possible referred objects in the scene image, which leads to the failure of shortcuts. The ablation study reflects the significance of the step-by-step multi-modal reasoning for the multi-modal dialog system.

For the official evaluation, we generate the evaluation file in accordance with the competition settings[3]. As shown in table 3 our model achieved the 1st rank when summing the metrics across all four sub-tasks. We withheld the names of the DSTC-11 participating teams in order to comply with the anonymity requirement.

5.5.2 Human Evaluation

The human evaluation for response generation mainly focuses on 4 aspects: **fluency**, **relevance**, **correctness**, and **informativeness**, which are important for task-oriented dialogue systems. First, We randomly select 500 dialogues from SIMMC 2.1 dev-test dataset as candidates. According to SIMMC rule, only the last response of each dialogue in devtest is evaluated. Therefore, we choose the last responses of these selected 500 dialogues generated by KAIST, I2R Singapore, and

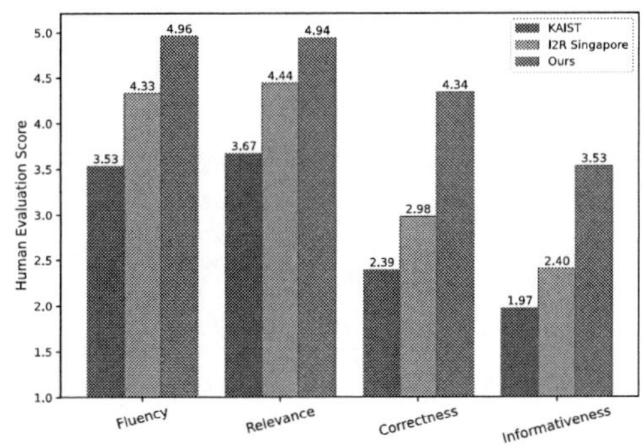

Figure 3: The human evaluation results on SIMMC 2.1 from four aspects. Our model displays significant improvement on **correctness** and **informativeness**.

our model. We release human evaluation task on Amazon Mechanical Turk (AMT) platform and hire 10 evaluators with different AMT ID. Every evaluator is assigned with these 1500 randomly shuffled evaluation data samples. Each data sample contains complete GT dialogue, scene images and last generated response without the model name. Evaluators need to score from four aspects on a scale of 1-5. The final score of each aspect of each model is the average score of 10 evaluators on 500 responses generated by corresponding model on this aspect. To guarantee the effectiveness of our human evaluation result, we respectively calculate Fleiss Kappa scores for fluency, relevance, correctness, and informativeness, which are 0.9077, 0.9189, 0.8813, 0.8698. As shown in 3, it can be observed that our model consistently outperforms

[3]https://github.com/facebookresearch/simmc2

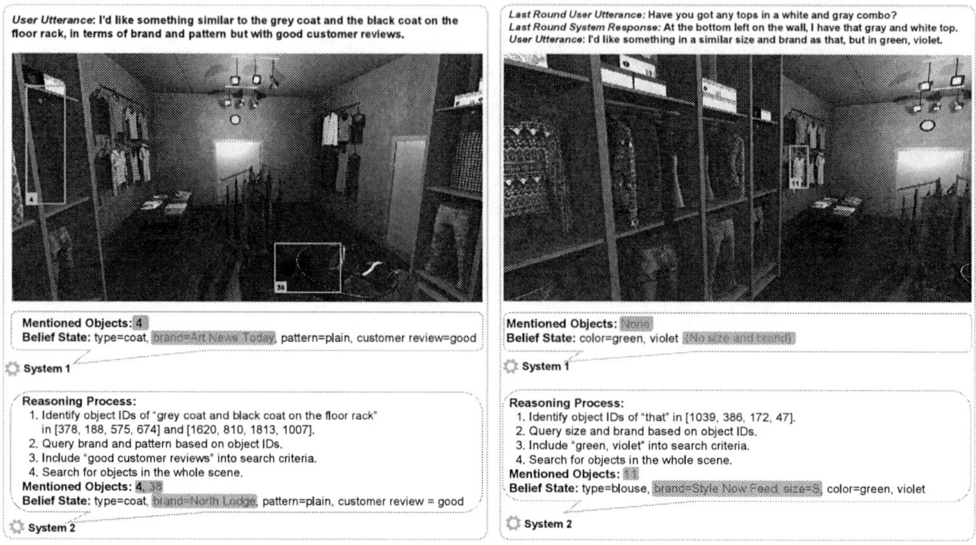

Figure 4: The left case: in which system 1 fails to predict user mentioned "*black coat*" and slot value of the brand while system 2 conducts a complete reasoning process and predicts the correct mentioned object ID "38" and brand slot value "*North Lodge*". The right case: in which system 1 fails to resolve user coreference "*that*" and misses slot values of size and brand while system 2 identifies "*grey and white top*" referred by "*that*" in the last round system response and predicts correct mentioned object ID "11", brand "*StyleNow Feed*" and size "*S*".

the other two models on all metrics, which is in line with automatic evaluation results.

5.5.3 Case Study

To better illustrate the advantage of our method on multi-step reasoning, we visualize several system responses to complex user utterances generated by our model and existing SOTA models.

As shown in the left part of Figure 4, system 1 fails to predict the corresponding object ID of "*black coat*" and therefore directly uses the brand of "*grey coat*" and copies pattern "*plain*" and customer review "*good*" in the user utterance to answer. Compared with system 1, system 2 successfully identifies object IDs of "*grey coat*" and "*black coat*" and conducts multi-step reasoning to obtain the correct brand of target object. As shown in the right part of Figure 4, system 1 is confused about coreference word "*that*" and unable to link it to "*grey and white top*" in the dialogue history. In this case, system 1 simply judges there is no mentioned object in the current the user utterance and ignores brand and size slots. It only predicts color slot by copying user requirement about color "*green, violet*". Compared with system 1, system 2 successfully links "*that*" to "*grey and white top*" and predicts its IDs, brand and size by multi-step reasoning.

From the above cases, it can be observed that: (1) our model is able to locate user mentioned objects more accurately on the scene image when more than one object exists in the user utterance. (2) our model has the ability to resolve corefence like "*that*", "*those*" and "*these*" in the dialogue history and link them to corresponding object IDs. (3) our model predicts slot values about complex user utterances through implementing reasoning actions step-by-step instead of directly copying information from the current user utterance or simply using the textual description without visual reasoning.

6 Conclusion

In this paper, we propose to enhance the ability of situated conversational agents by emphasizing step-by-step multi-modal reasoning. Specifically, the original user utterance is rewritten into a step-by-step reasoning process by introducing a knowledge- and semantic-based extraction approach. In light of dual process theory, we propose a step-by-step multi-modal reasoning framework, and transmit complicated multi-step reasoning and implicit multi-modal comprehension to different modules. Extensive experiments on benchmarks SIMMC validate the superiority of our framework. After the official evaluation of the 11th Dialog System Technology Challenge (DSTC-11) SIMMC 2.1 track, our model is ranked at the 1st of the summing score of all sub-tasks.

References

Iz Beltagy, Matthew E. Peters, and Arman Cohan. 2020. Longformer: The long-document transformer. *CoRR*, abs/2004.05150.

Rémi Cadène, Hédi Ben-Younes, Matthieu Cord, and Nicolas Thome. 2019. MUREL: multimodal relational reasoning for visual question answering. In *IEEE Conference on Computer Vision and Pattern Recognition, CVPR 2019, Long Beach, CA, USA, June 16-20, 2019*, pages 1989–1998. Computer Vision Foundation / IEEE.

Feilong Chen, Xiuyi Chen, Fandong Meng, Peng Li, and Jie Zhou. 2021. Gog: Relation-aware graph-over-graph network for visual dialog. In *Findings of the Association for Computational Linguistics: ACL/IJCNLP 2021, Online Event, August 1-6, 2021*, volume ACL/IJCNLP 2021 of *Findings of ACL*, pages 230–243. Association for Computational Linguistics.

Feilong Chen, Fandong Meng, Jiaming Xu, Peng Li, Bo Xu, and Jie Zhou. 2020a. DMRM: A dual-channel multi-hop reasoning model for visual dialog. In *The Thirty-Fourth AAAI Conference on Artificial Intelligence, AAAI 2020, The Thirty-Second Innovative Applications of Artificial Intelligence Conference, IAAI 2020, The Tenth AAAI Symposium on Educational Advances in Artificial Intelligence, EAAI 2020, New York, NY, USA, February 7-12, 2020*, pages 7504–7511. AAAI Press.

Meng Chen, Ruixue Liu, Lei Shen, Shaozu Yuan, Jingyan Zhou, Youzheng Wu, Xiaodong He, and Bowen Zhou. 2020b. The JDDC corpus: A large-scale multi-turn chinese dialogue dataset for e-commerce customer service. In *Proceedings of The 12th Language Resources and Evaluation Conference, LREC 2020, Marseille, France, May 11-16, 2020*, pages 459–466. European Language Resources Association.

Xiaofan Chen, Songyang Lao, and Ting Duan. 2020c. Multimodal fusion of visual dialog: A survey. In *RICAI 2020: 2nd International Conference on Robotics, Intelligent Control and Artificial Intelligence, Shanghai, China, October, 2020*, pages 302–308. ACM.

Yen-Chun Chen, Linjie Li, Licheng Yu, Ahmed El Kholy, Faisal Ahmed, Zhe Gan, Yu Cheng, and Jingjing Liu. 2020d. UNITER: universal image-text representation learning. In *Computer Vision - ECCV 2020 - 16th European Conference, Glasgow, UK, August 23-28, 2020, Proceedings, Part XXX*, volume 12375 of *Lecture Notes in Computer Science*, pages 104–120. Springer.

Corentin Dancette, Rémi Cadène, Damien Teney, and Matthieu Cord. 2021. Beyond question-based biases: Assessing multimodal shortcut learning in visual question answering. In *2021 IEEE/CVF International Conference on Computer Vision, ICCV 2021, Montreal, QC, Canada, October 10-17, 2021*, pages 1554–1563. IEEE.

Abhishek Das, Satwik Kottur, Khushi Gupta, Avi Singh, Deshraj Yadav, José M. F. Moura, Devi Parikh, and Dhruv Batra. 2017. Visual dialog. In *2017 IEEE Conference on Computer Vision and Pattern Recognition, CVPR 2017, Honolulu, HI, USA, July 21-26, 2017*, pages 1080–1089. IEEE Computer Society.

Jonathan St BT Evans. 2003. In two minds: dual-process accounts of reasoning. *Trends in cognitive sciences*, 7(10):454–459.

Zhe Gan, Yu Cheng, Ahmed Kholy, Linjie Li, Jingjing Liu, and Jianfeng Gao. 2019. Multi-step reasoning via recurrent dual attention for visual dialog. In *Proceedings of the 57th Annual Meeting of the Association for Computational Linguistics*, pages 6463–6474, Florence, Italy. Association for Computational Linguistics.

Yash Goyal, Tejas Khot, Douglas Summers-Stay, Dhruv Batra, and Devi Parikh. 2017. Making the V in VQA matter: Elevating the role of image understanding in Visual Question Answering. In *Conference on Computer Vision and Pattern Recognition (CVPR)*.

Kaiming He, Xiangyu Zhang, Shaoqing Ren, and Jian Sun. 2016. Deep residual learning for image recognition. In *Proceedings of the IEEE Conference on Computer Vision and Pattern Recognition*, pages 770–778.

Wanwei He, Yinpei Dai, Binyuan Hui, Min Yang, Zheng Cao, Jianbo Dong, Fei Huang, Luo Si, and Yongbin Li. 2022a. Space-2: Tree-structured semi-supervised contrastive pre-training for task-oriented dialog understanding. In *Proceedings of the 29th International Conference on Computational Linguistics*.

Wanwei He, Yinpei Dai, Min Yang, Jian Sun, Fei Huang, Luo Si, and Yongbin Li. 2022b. Space-3: Unified dialog model pre-training for task-oriented dialog understanding and generation. In *Proceedings of the 45th International ACM SIGIR Conference on Research and Development in Information Retrieval*, pages 187–200.

Wanwei He, Yinpei Dai, Yinhe Zheng, Yuchuan Wu, Zheng Cao, Dermot Liu, Peng Jiang, Min Yang, Fei Huang, Luo Si, et al. 2022c. Space: A generative pre-trained model for task-oriented dialog with semi-supervised learning and explicit policy injection. *Proceedings of the AAAI Conference on Artificial Intelligence*.

Yu-Jung Heo, Eun-Sol Kim, Woo Suk Choi, and Byoung-Tak Zhang. 2022. Hypergraph Transformer: Weakly-supervised multi-hop reasoning for knowledge-based visual question answering. In *Proceedings of the 60th Annual Meeting of the Association for Computational Linguistics (Volume 1: Long Papers)*, pages 373–390, Dublin, Ireland. Association for Computational Linguistics.

Yichen Huang, Yuchen Wang, and Yik-Cheung Tam. 2021. Uniter-based situated coreference resolution with rich multimodal input. *CoRR*, abs/2112.03521.

Satwik Kottur, Seungwhan Moon, Alborz Geramifard, and Babak Damavandi. 2021. SIMMC 2.0: A task-oriented dialog dataset for immersive multimodal conversations. In *Proceedings of the 2021 Conference on Empirical Methods in Natural Language Processing, EMNLP 2021, Virtual Event / Punta Cana, Dominican Republic, 7-11 November, 2021*, pages 4903–4912. Association for Computational Linguistics.

Haeju Lee, Oh Joon Kwon, Yunseon Choi, Minho Park, Ran Han, Yoonhyung Kim, Jinhyeon Kim, Youngjune Lee, Haebin Shin, Kangwook Lee, and Kee-Eung Kim. 2022. Learning to embed multimodal contexts for situated conversational agents. In *Findings of the Association for Computational Linguistics: NAACL 2022, Seattle, WA, United States, July 10-15, 2022*, pages 813–830. Association for Computational Linguistics.

Joosung Lee and Kijong Han. 2021. Multimodal interactions using pretrained unimodal models for SIMMC 2.0. In *DSTC10 challenge wokrshop at AAAI*.

Yuxing Long, Binyuan Hui, Fulong Ye, Yanyang Li, Zhuoxin Han, Caixia Yuan, Yongbin Li, and Xiaojie Wang. 2023. SPRING: situated conversation agent pretrained with multimodal questions from incremental layout graph. *Proceedings of the AAAI Conference on Artificial Intelligence*.

Seungwhan Moon, Satwik Kottur, Paul A. Crook, Ankita De, Shivani Poddar, Theodore Levin, David Whitney, Daniel Difranco, Ahmad Beirami, Eunjoon Cho, Rajen Subba, and Alborz Geramifard. 2020. Situated and interactive multimodal conversations. In *Proceedings of the 28th International Conference on Computational Linguistics, COLING 2020, Barcelona, Spain (Online), December 8-13, 2020*, pages 1103–1121. International Committee on Computational Linguistics.

Thanh-Tung Nguyen, Wei Shi, Ridong Jiang, and Jung jae Kim. 2021. Multimodal and joint learning generation models for simmc 2.0. In *DSTC10 challenge wokrshop at AAAI*.

Alec Radford, Jeffrey Wu, Rewon Child, David Luan, Dario Amodei, Ilya Sutskever, et al. 2019. Language models are unsupervised multitask learners. *OpenAI blog*, 1(8):9.

Amrita Saha, Mitesh M. Khapra, and Karthik Sankaranarayanan. 2018. Towards building large scale multimodal domain-aware conversation systems. In *Proceedings of the Thirty-Second AAAI Conference on Artificial Intelligence, (AAAI-18), the 30th innovative Applications of Artificial Intelligence (IAAI-18), and the 8th AAAI Symposium on Educational Advances in Artificial Intelligence (EAAI-18), New Orleans, Louisiana, USA, February 2-7, 2018*, pages 696–704. AAAI Press.

Sanket Shah, Anand Mishra, Naganand Yadati, and Partha Pratim Talukdar. 2019. KVQA: knowledge-aware visual question answering. In *The Thirty-Third AAAI Conference on Artificial Intelligence, AAAI 2019, The Thirty-First Innovative Applications of Artificial Intelligence Conference, IAAI 2019, The Ninth AAAI Symposium on Educational Advances in Artificial Intelligence, EAAI 2019, Honolulu, Hawaii, USA, January 27 - February 1, 2019*, pages 8876–8884. AAAI Press.

Qingyi Si, Fandong Meng, Mingyu Zheng, Zheng Lin, Yuanxin Liu, Peng Fu, Yanan Cao, Weiping Wang, and Jie Zhou. 2022. Language prior is not the only shortcut: A benchmark for shortcut learning in VQA. *CoRR*, abs/2210.04692.

Peng Wang, Qi Wu, Chunhua Shen, Anthony R. Dick, and Anton van den Hengel. 2018. FVQA: fact-based visual question answering. *IEEE Trans. Pattern Anal. Mach. Intell.*, 40(10):2413–2427.

Thomas Wolf, Lysandre Debut, Victor Sanh, Julien Chaumond, Clement Delangue, Anthony Moi, Pierric Cistac, Tim Rault, Rémi Louf, Morgan Funtowicz, Joe Davison, Sam Shleifer, Patrick von Platen, Clara Ma, Yacine Jernite, Julien Plu, Canwen Xu, Teven Le Scao, Sylvain Gugger, Mariama Drame, Quentin Lhoest, and Alexander M. Rush. 2020. Transformers: State-of-the-art natural language processing. In *Proceedings of the 2020 Conference on Empirical Methods in Natural Language Processing: System Demonstrations*, pages 38–45, Online. Association for Computational Linguistics.

Keren Ye and Adriana Kovashka. 2021. A case study of the shortcut effects in visual commonsense reasoning. In *Thirty-Fifth AAAI Conference on Artificial Intelligence, AAAI 2021, Thirty-Third Conference on Innovative Applications of Artificial Intelligence, IAAI 2021, The Eleventh Symposium on Educational Advances in Artificial Intelligence, EAAI 2021, Virtual Event, February 2-9, 2021*, pages 3181–3189. AAAI Press.

Yunhu Ye, Binyuan Hui, Min Yang, Binhua Li, Fei Huang, and Yongbin Li. 2023. Large language models are versatile decomposers: Decompose evidence and questions for table-based reasoning. *CoRR*, abs/2301.13808.

Nan Zhao, Haoran Li, Youzheng Wu, Xiaodong He, and Bowen Zhou. 2021. The JDDC 2.0 corpus: A large-scale multimodal multi-turn chinese dialogue dataset for e-commerce customer service. *CoRR*, abs/2109.12913.

Zihao Zhu, Jing Yu, Yujing Wang, Yajing Sun, Yue Hu, and Qi Wu. 2020. Mucko: Multi-layer cross-modal knowledge reasoning for fact-based visual question answering. In *Proceedings of the Twenty-Ninth International Joint Conference on Artificial Intelligence, IJCAI-20*, pages 1097–1103. International Joint Conferences on Artificial Intelligence Organization. Main track.

Contrastively Pretrained Vision-Language Transformers and Domain Adaptation Methods for Multimodal TOD Systems

Youngjae Chang[1], Dooyoung Kim[1], Jinyoung Kim[1], Hyunmook Cha[1], Keunha Kim[1], Sooyoung Min[1], Youngjoong Ko[1]*, Kye-Hwan Lee[2], Joonwoo Park[2]
Sungkyunkwan University[1], LG Electronics[2]
{youngjaechang0, kdysunleo98, jeankim941, chahyunmook, keunhakim98, sujae9704}@gmail.com, yjko@skku.edu, {kyehwan.lee, joonwoo.park}@lge.com

Abstract

The Situated Interactive MultiModal Conversations (SIMMC2.1) Challenge 2022 is hosted by the Eleventh Dialog System Technology Challenge (DSTC11). The task of SIMMC is to create a shopping assistant agent that can communicate with customers in a virtual store. It requires processing store scenes and product catalogs along with the customer's request which could be decomposed into four steps and each becomes a subtask. In this work, we investigate monolithic transformers, fusion transformers, and language transformers as three distinct multimodal modeling approaches, and evaluate the potential of each. We also devise a retrieval-based method to acquire meta-data of each object which enhances the accuracy of predicted object characteristics significantly. Furthermore, we identify a discrepancy in using pretrained language models for dialog tasks and propose a simple domain-adaptation method. Our model came in third place for object coreferencing, dialog state tracking, and response generation tasks.

1 Introduction

Task-oriented dialog system refers to a system that communicates with users with a specific purpose, such as restaurant recommendation or accommodation reservation. The system should be able to analyze the user's utterance to track the dialog state and generate a response accordingly to fulfill the user's purpose. Recent advances in pretrained language models and new dialog datasets such as MultiWOZ have accelerated the research on task-oriented dialogs (Budzianowski et al., 2018).

To this end, Situated Interactive MultiModal Conversations (SIMMC) Challenge was proposed to introduce multimodality to the task-oriented dialog tasks (Crook et al., 2019). The challenge consists of a virtual shopping scenario in the fashion and furniture domain. Each dialog is based on up to two virtual scenes, and the user interacts with the system to purchase items in the corresponding domain. The system is required to process user utterances, previous dialogues, images of the scenes, and metadata files for the objects appearing in the scenes to find the adequate belief state and generate a response. An example of dialog is given in Figure 1, where the user seeks two pairs of trousers to purchase. As the dialogues are grounded on virtual scenes, the system should not only have a powerful language understanding but also should be able to process images and fuse the two modalities. In the Eleventh Dialog System Technology Challenge (DSTC11), SIMMC2.1 was held as the first track for competition. The SIMMC2.1 challenge decomposes the requirements of multimodal task-oriented systems into the following four subtasks: 1) Ambiguous Candidate Identification, 2) Multimodal Coreference Resolution, 3) Multimodal Dialog State Tracking, 4) Multimodal Dialog Response Generation. The only change from SIMMC2.0 (Kottur et al., 2021) is the first subtask, where the

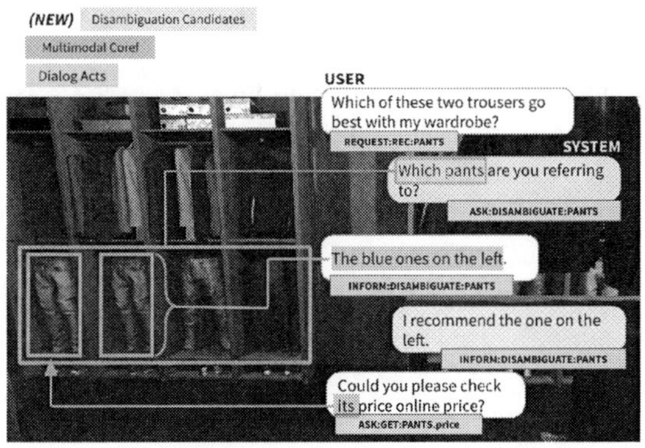

Figure 1: The SIMMC2.1 dataset consists of the dialogues between a user and a clerk, with an image of the virtual store's scene and the metadata for every object that appears in the scene. To achieve high performance on the given four subtasks, it is important to utilize all possible modalities with the most adequate method.

* Corresponding author

Proceedings of The Eleventh Dialog System Technology Challenge, pages 25–30
September 11, 2023

binary classification task developed to be a more challenging candidate identification task.

Past studies have proposed various designs for solving the SIMMC task. For instance, Huang (Huang et al., 2021) proposed a model based on a vision-language transformer model and condensed various metadata and visual data of objects into a single token. Lee (Lee and Han, 2021) utilized contrastive learning to pretrain a dual encoder model to project image data and language data into the same semantic space. Son (Son et al., 2022) converted image data to a natural language form with multiple attribute classifiers and leveraged the power of a large pretrained language model for better language generation results. Likewise, approaches vary widely on how to process data from different modalities.

In this study, we identify three methods that are commonly used to model multimodality which is; monolithic vision language transformers, dual encoding vision language transformers, and language-centric multimodal transformers. We select a representative model from each category and conduct experiments on SIMMC2.1 to compare the performance of each method. We also develop a retrieval-oriented approach for obtaining the meta-data of individual objects, which substantially improves the precision of the predicted attributes for each object.

We find it unsuitable to fine-tune pretrained language models for the SIMMC task. Most pretrained language models pretrain on large text datasets that are crawled from the internet, which are predominantly web pages and documents. However, dialogues have different characteristics compared to typical text data because the vocabulary for colloquial style differs from written text (Zhang et al., 2020; Kulhánek et al., 2021). To be specific, spoken language tends to have frequent coreferencing and ellipsis, which require earlier contexts to understand. To this end, we experiment with several domain-adaptation methods based on pretraining to alleviate the problem.

2 Task Description

- **#1. Ambiguous Candidate Identification** The user utterance may be ambiguous depending on the given scene in the background. More than one item in the scene could match the user's description of an object, in which case there is the need to disambiguate the user's utterance. The goal of this subtask is to find all the ambiguous candidate objects in the scene that matches the user's description. As the objects are distinguished by canonical ID(s), the model should output all the canonical ID(s) of the ambiguous candidates.

- **#2. Multimodal Coreference Resolution** The system should know the object the user is referring to before preparing a response. To minimize error propagation, this step comes in high priority in the multimodal task-oriented dialog task. Similar to the first subtask, the model should output all the canonical ID(s) for the object the user is referring to.

- **#3. Multimodal Dialog State Tracking (MM-DST)** Task-oriented dialogues have a structured form of dialog states, also known as belief states. They are abstracts of the dialog and contain essential information for the system to fulfill the user's goals. This subtask involves predicting the correct user intent, and pairs of slot values the user provides.

- **#4. Multimodal Dialog Response Generation** The ultimate goal of the system is to generate an adequate answer to the user utterance. Utilizing the results from previous subtasks would give accurate guidance for generating a response. This task is evaluated by the similarity of the model output compared to the human response.

3 Methods

We present three representative methods for solving multimodal tasks and a pretraining method to enhance performance by adapting large pretrained language models to the dialog domain.

3.1 Monolithic Vision-Language Transformer

Previous studies have defined this category of vision-language transformers as monolithic because it tends to drastically simplify the processing of the visual inputs to be the same as the convolution-free manner in processing textual inputs (Kim et al., 2021). As depicted in <A> of Figure 2, we build object embeddings for every object in the scene by leveraging visual embeddings extracted from each object image, bounding box information, and textual embeddings extracted from the metadata. The information of different

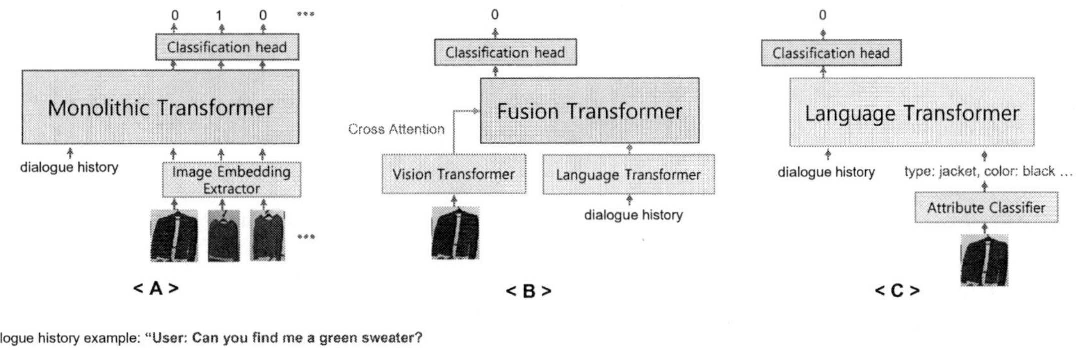

Figure 2: Recent studies have commonly used the three methods above for modeling multimodality. <A> model represents the Monolithic Vision-Language Transformer while <B> and <C> represent the Dual Vision-Language Transformer and the Language-Centric Multimodal Transformer, respectively.

modalities concatenated and projected by an MLP layer to match the hidden size of the monolithic vision-language transformer. All of the object embeddings are concatenated consecutively to the embeddings of dialog history and are processed by the monolithic vision-language transformer. Given a dialog, the dialog history will have consecutive turns, $(DH_i = t_1, t_2, ..., t_{i-1})$ where each turn as a user and system utterance $(t_i = u_i, s_i)$, and background scene with objects, $(S = o_1, o_2, ..., o_n)$, is created. Then, the input x for the model could be described as follows:

$$x_i = [DH_i \oplus u_i \oplus OA] \quad (1)$$

Where object attributes *OA* can be obtained by the following equation:

$$OA = MLP(VM(S) \oplus PLM(S) \oplus bbox) \quad (2)$$

The visual embedding extractor is a pretrained vision model *VM* and the textual embedding is a pretrained language model *PLM*.

3.2 Dual Vision-Language Transformer

We define vision-language models that use a separate encoder for modeling visual inputs and textual inputs as dual vision-language models. They are pretrained by a contrastive learning loss which induces the embeddings of visual inputs and image inputs to become similar if they contain the same semantics information (Lee and Han, 2021; Li et al., 2021). In <B> of Figure 2, a single object image and the dialog history are each processed by the vision transformer and the language transformer. The two output embeddings are fused by the cross-attention mechanism in the fusion transformer to be classified for final output. We use non-visual metadata as additional textual inputs for more coherence between vision and language encoders.

3.3 Language-Centric Multimodal Transformer

This method takes a pipeline approach to handle multimodal inputs, by converting data that are not language to a textual form. Recent studies have tested this method with various multimodal tasks such as visual question answering and yielded robust performance on those that generate natural language (Gao et al., 2022). We build an efficient input template for reflecting all the textual data for the language transformer to process. Each part is explained in detail as follows:

- **Object Metadata Prediction** We train the object data on a CNN model to extract attributes from the object images which can be obtained by utilizing the bounding box information and the scenes of the dialog data. We devise a retrieval-based method to reduce the search space of all possible attributes by training the image classifier to find the object itself among all the candidates in the catalog, instead of classifying each of the attributes. This way we drastically reduce the prediction space of each attribute and limit the model from outputting non-existent sets of attributes such as "pink check-patterned jeans". We convert the attributes extracted to a language form using a simple template for each attribute in the form of "[attribute type] is [predicted value].".

- **Language Transformer** As shown in <C> of Figure 2, we leverage the preprocessed objects and dialog history and perform classification on each of the objects with the output hidden representation of the language transformer. Instead of using the [CLS] token for classification, we utilized the soft-prompting technique by building an input template with extra learnable prompts. Prompt tuning (Lester et al., 2021) is simple to implement, yet efficient and explicitly changes the model behavior with additional input. Given that object description OD_j is the natural language form of attributes object o_j has, the following equation describes the template of input x.

$$x_i = [DH_i \oplus u_i \oplus [P1], [P2], [MASK] \oplus OD_j] \quad (3)$$

[P1], [P2] correspond to the two soft prompts we have used for this method, and the output of the [MASK] token is used for classification.

3.4 Domain-Adaptation Method

To mitigate the discrepancy between pretrained language models and dialog tasks, various methods of domain-adaptation have been proposed, and by far pretraining on a target domain has been most successful (He et al., 2022; Zhang et al., 2019). We conducted two different types of pretraining on the task dataset, which are random masked language modeling and noun prioritized masked language modeling. As we are pretraining an encoder-decoder model for generation, random masked language modeling works identically to the Token Masking of the BART reconstruction task. In the Token Masking task is masking a sequence randomly, and regenerate the masked sequence to its original form. This differs from fine-tuning because the objective is to learn general language representations by self-restoration. For the noun prioritized masked language modeling, we utilize the nltk POS tagger (Bird et al., 2009) to give additional weights to the nouns of the input for masking before applying the reconstruction loss. We presumed that this method would nudge the model to focus on the noun components of the input. This adjustment will mitigate the discrepancy problem because coreferencing and ellipsis usually occur on nouns in an utterance if they were mentioned earlier on in the dialogue. Given a sequence of tokens, $(T = t_1, t_2, ..., t_n)$, the corrupted version of the sequence, $(C = c_1, c_2, ..., c_m)$, the reconstruction loss can be described as follows:

$$\mathcal{L}_{RL} = -\sum_{i=1}^{|T|} \log p(t_i | C, t_1, t_2, ..., t_{i-1}; \theta) \quad (4)$$

Model	Disambiguation F1(%)	Coreferencing F1(%)
UNITER	57.0	67.5
ALBEF	**62.4**	**73.7**
RoBERTa-large	-	65.6

Table 1: Devtest evaluation of the three Representative methods of modeling multimodality. The disambiguation performance of RoBERTa-large is not evaluated due to its lack of performance on the easier task, coreferencing.

Name	DST		Response
	Intent F1(%)	Slot F1(%)	BLEU-4
BART	97.15	89.81	0.291
w/ pretrain	**97.35**	91.8	0.288
w/ noun priority	97.31	**92.1**	**0.297**

Table 2: Devtest evaluation of domain-adaptation methods.

4 Experiments

4.1 Experiment Settings

All three methods for modeling multimodality used a binary cross entropy loss for training and were evaluated on subtasks 1 and 2, where visual information plays a crucial role along with the input texts. For the monolithic vision-language transformer, we used the UNITER-based model (Huang et al., 2021) with visual embeddings extracted from our image preprocessor. In the case of the dual vision-language transformer, we leveraged ALBEF (Li et al., 2021) with a custom input template for the textual encoder. For the language-centric multimodal transformer, we set RoBERTa-large (Liu et al., 2019) as the backbone and utilized the ResNext101 model (Xie et al., 2017) as the attribute extractor.

For subtasks 3 and 4, we speculated that dialog state tracking and response generation rely heavily on the language understanding and generation power of the model. To address our speculation, we fine-tuned the BART model, a large pretrained language model that met our requirements. We experimented with the domain-adaptation methods by guiding BART with additional pretraining on our target dataset.

Team ID	Subtask 1	Subtask 2	Subtask 3		Subtask4
	F1	F1	Slot F1	Intent F1	BLEU-4
Team 1	0.6726	**0.9429**	**0.9424**	0.9598	**0.4093**
Team 2	0.6517	-	-	-	-
Team 3(Ours)	0.6384	0.7585	0.9048	0.9677	0.3029
Team 4	-	-	-	-	0.2519
Team 5	**0.705**	0.8028	0.9266	**0.9775**	0.365

Table 3: Final Results on the teststd split for SIMMC2.1 competition

4.2 Results

The results for the multimodal modeling methods are presented in Table 1, where ALBEF, the dual vision-language transformer yielded the highest performance followed by the monolithic vision-language transformer, UNITER. The language-centric multimodal model based on RoBERTa, had the worst performance. Given that the gap between the ALBEF and UNITER is significant, it is presumable that processing multiple objects at once may harm the performance of the system.

Performances on the domain-adaption method can be found in Table 2. The slot F1 score had a higher priority than the intent F1 score according to the rules of the competition. Under such criteria, the noun priority masking method for pre-training became the most preferable way for both dialog state tracking and response generation as it had higher performances in slot F1 and BLEU-4. In our analysis of specific cases of the model outputs, it was observed that the domain-adapted version demonstrates greater expressiveness, referencing past dialogues to employ a more comprehensive selection of adjectives for object elaboration. For instance, the baseline model provides a response with "I'll add that top to your cart", while the domain-adapted model produces a more expressive response, such as "I'll put that light grey tank top in your cart", which would in turn assist the user with a clearer understanding of the whole situation.

Table 3 presents the official results of SIMMC2.1 evaluated on the teststd data split. Before comparing our model with others, it should be acknowledged that we had different circumstances with teams 1 and 5. The two high-ranking teams have reused certain codes from a submission in SIMMC2.0 that might be problematic due to the changes in the allowed inputs during inference. The problem was about the same objects appearing in the train and test, which made it possible for the model to memorize all the attributes of the object by using the unique id and simple attribute classification heads. Disregarding this issue, we achieved 3rd place in subtasks 2, 3, and 4 with a marginal gap in performance for subtask 3.

5 Conclusion

In this work, we have identified 3 common ways to model multimodality and conducted experiments to find the best fit for multimodal task-oriented dialog systems. Despite that we found the dual vision-language transformer to have higher performance over other methods we did not set specific criteria for each method to be fairly evaluated such as the size of parameters and number of training steps. We also investigated domain-adaptation methods to enhance language understanding and generation in the dialog domain, where we found the noun-prioritized masking effective. It should be interesting to leverage part-of-speech tags for domain-adaptation to other domains, which could be material for future work.

6 Acknowledgements

This work was supported in part by LG Electronics (CTO/AI lab) and in part by the National Research Foundation of Korea (NRF) grant funded by the Korea government (MSIT) (No. NRF-2020R1A2C2100362).

References

Steven Bird, Ewan Klein, and Edward Loper. 2009. *Natural language processing with Python: analyzing text with the natural language toolkit.* " O'Reilly Media, Inc.".

Paweł Budzianowski, Tsung-Hsien Wen, Bo-Hsiang Tseng, Inigo Casanueva, Stefan Ultes, Osman Ramadan, and Milica Gašić. 2018. Multiwoz–a large-scale multi-domain wizard-of-oz dataset for task-oriented dialogue modelling. *arXiv preprint arXiv:1810.00278.*

Paul A Crook, Shivani Poddar, Ankita De, Semir Shafi, David Whitney, Alborz Geramifard, and Rajen Subba. 2019. Simmc: Situated interactive multi-modal conversational data collection and evaluation platform. *arXiv preprint arXiv:1911.02690*.

Feng Gao, Qing Ping, Govind Thattai, Aishwarya Reganti, Ying Nian Wu, and Prem Natarajan. 2022. Transform-retrieve-generate: Natural language-centric outside-knowledge visual question answering. In *Proceedings of the IEEE/CVF Conference on Computer Vision and Pattern Recognition*, pages 5067–5077.

Wanwei He, Yinpei Dai, Yinhe Zheng, Yuchuan Wu, Zheng Cao, Dermot Liu, Peng Jiang, Min Yang, Fei Huang, Luo Si, et al. 2022. Galaxy: A generative pre-trained model for task-oriented dialog with semi-supervised learning and explicit policy injection. In *Proceedings of the AAAI Conference on Artificial Intelligence*, volume 36, pages 10749–10757.

Yichen Huang, Yuchen Wang, and Yik-Cheung Tam. 2021. Uniter-based situated coreference resolution with rich multimodal input. *arXiv preprint arXiv:2112.03521*.

Wonjae Kim, Bokyung Son, and Ildoo Kim. 2021. Vilt: Vision-and-language transformer without convolution or region supervision. In *International Conference on Machine Learning*, pages 5583–5594. PMLR.

Satwik Kottur, Seungwhan Moon, Alborz Geramifard, and Babak Damavandi. 2021. Simmc 2.0: A task-oriented dialog dataset for immersive multimodal conversations. *arXiv preprint arXiv:2104.08667*.

Jonáš Kulhánek, Vojtech Hudecek, Tomáš Nekvinda, and Ondrej Dušek. 2021. Augpt: Dialogue with pre-trained language models and data augmentation. *arXiv preprint arXiv:2102.05126*.

Joosung Lee and Kijong Han. 2021. Multimodal interactions using pretrained unimodal models for simmc 2.0. *arXiv preprint arXiv:2112.05328*.

Brian Lester, Rami Al-Rfou, and Noah Constant. 2021. The power of scale for parameter-efficient prompt tuning. *arXiv preprint arXiv:2104.08691*.

Junnan Li, Ramprasaath Selvaraju, Akhilesh Gotmare, Shafiq Joty, Caiming Xiong, and Steven Chu Hong Hoi. 2021. Align before fuse: Vision and language representation learning with momentum distillation. *Advances in neural information processing systems*, 34:9694–9705.

Yinhan Liu, Myle Ott, Naman Goyal, Jingfei Du, Mandar Joshi, Danqi Chen, Omer Levy, Mike Lewis, Luke Zettlemoyer, and Veselin Stoyanov. 2019. Roberta: A robustly optimized bert pretraining approach. *arXiv preprint arXiv:1907.11692*.

Dongcheol Son, Youngjae Chang, Youngjoong Ko, and Jaehwan Lee. 2022. Domain Adaptive Task-Oriented Dialog System for Deep Understanding of Multimodal Conversation.

Saining Xie, Ross Girshick, Piotr Dollár, Zhuowen Tu, and Kaiming He. 2017. Aggregated residual transformations for deep neural networks. In *Proceedings of the IEEE conference on computer vision and pattern recognition*, pages 1492–1500.

Yichi Zhang, Zhijian Ou, Huixin Wang, and Junlan Feng. 2020. A probabilistic end-to-end task-oriented dialog model with latent belief states towards semi-supervised learning. *arXiv preprint arXiv:2009.08115*.

Yizhe Zhang, Siqi Sun, Michel Galley, Yen-Chun Chen, Chris Brockett, Xiang Gao, Jianfeng Gao, Jingjing Liu, and Bill Dolan. 2019. Dialogpt: Large-scale generative pre-training for conversational response generation. *arXiv preprint arXiv:1911.00536*.

Multi-Stage Coarse-to-Fine Contrastive Learning for Conversation Intent Induction

Caiyuan Chu[1*†], **Ya Li**[2†‡], **Yifan Liu**[2], **Jia-Chen Gu**[4],
Quan Liu[2,3], **Yongxin Ge**[1], **Guoping Hu**[2,3]
[1]Chongqing University, Chongqing, China
[2]iFLYTEK Research, Hefei, China [3]State Key Laboratory of Cognitive Intelligence
[4]University of Science and Technology of China, Hefei, China
{Chucy,yongxinge}@cqu.edu.cn, gujc@ustc.edu.cn,
{yali8,yfliu7,quanliu,gphu}@iflytek.com

Abstract

Intent recognition is critical for task-oriented dialogue systems. However, for emerging domains and new services, it is difficult to accurately identify the key intent of a conversation due to time-consuming data annotation and comparatively poor model transferability. Therefore, the automatic induction of dialogue intention is very important for intelligent dialogue systems. This paper presents our solution to Track 2 of Intent Induction from Conversations for Task-Oriented Dialogue at the Eleventh Dialogue System Technology Challenge (DSTC11). The essence of intention clustering lies in distinguishing the representation of different dialogue utterances. The key to automatic intention induction is that, for any given set of new data, the sentence representation obtained by the model can be well distinguished from different labels. Therefore, we propose a multi-stage coarse-to-fine contrastive learning model training scheme including unsupervised contrastive learning pre-training, supervised contrastive learning pre-training, and fine-tuning with joint contrastive learning and clustering to obtain a better dialogue utterance representation model for the clustering task. In the released DSTC11 Track 2 evaluation results, our proposed system ranked first on both of the two subtasks of this Track.

1 Introduction

The design of dialogue mode is very important for the development of task-oriented dialogue system. It typically consists of a set of intents with corresponding slots for capturing and handling domain-specific dialogue box states. Previous work on schema-guided dialogue (Rastogi et al., 2020a,b; Ruan et al., 2020; Lee et al., 2022) focused on data-efficient joint dialogue state modeling across domains and zero-shot generalization to new APIs. However, for new emerging domains and novel services, the identification of key intents of such schema typically requires domain expertise and/or laborious analysis of a large volume of conversation transcripts. As the demand for and adoption of virtual assistants continues to increase, recent work has investigated ways to accelerate pattern design through the automatic induction of intentions (Hakkani-Tür et al., 2015; Haponchyk et al., 2018; Perkins and Yang, 2019; Chatterjee and Sengupta, 2020) or the induction of slots and dialogue states (Min et al., 2020; Hudeček et al., 2021). However, the lack of realistic shared benchmarks with public datasets, metrics, and task definitions has made it difficult to track progress in this area. For this reason, the Eleventh Dialogue System Technology Challenge (DSTC11) proposed a track of Intent Induction from Conversations for Task-Oriented Dialogue. This Track is composed of two subtasks, which are organized as shown in Fig. 1. 1) Intent Clustering, which needs to cluster the given dialogue statements and evaluate them using standard clustering metrics. 2) Open Intent Induction, in which participants are required to generate a set of intents, each represented by a list of sample utterances. The induced intents and utterances will be evaluated using their performance on a downstream classification task over reference intents. Both subtasks aim to discover intents from conversations. This Track is very challenging due to the lack of labeled data and the unknown number of conversation intents.

This paper presents a system that is evaluated in this Track. For these tasks, in order to obtain a better dialogue utterance representation model under the condition that the data is unlabeled, we propose a multi-stage coarse-to-fine contrast learning model training scheme. The backbone of our multi-stage training scheme is the RoBERTa-large (Liu et al., 2019). Firstly, pre-training is performed

[*]Work done during the internship at iFLYTEK Research.
[†]Equal contribution.
[‡]Corresponding author.

Proceedings of The Eleventh Dialog System Technology Challenge, pages 31–39
September 11, 2023

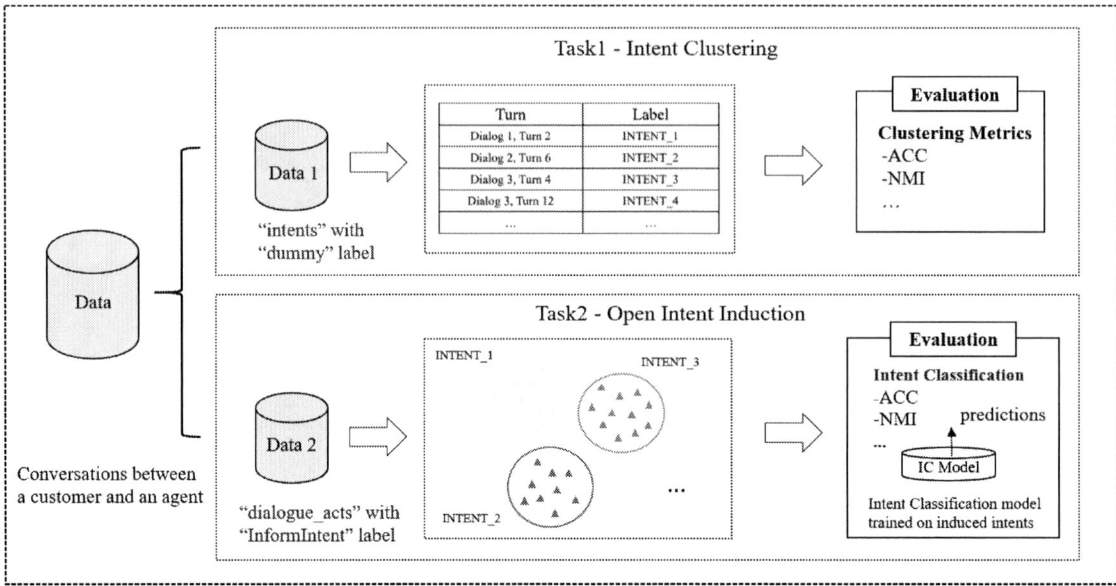

Figure 1: An overview of the tasks in this Track, including the tasks of Intent Clustering and Open Intent Induction.

by unsupervised contrastive learning in a large number of consecutive conversations. Secondly, the model is fine-tuned using a dataset with labels from the same domain as that of the target data for supervised comparative learning. Finally, the model obtained after the above two training steps is further fine-tuned on the target data by joint clustering and contrastive learning to obtain the final model. In addition, for the selection of the number of clustering categories k, we adopted the automatic parameter optimization method based on silhouette coefficients (Rousseeuw, 1987) provided in the baseline code. As shown in the released evaluation results, our proposed model ranked first on both subtasks. Furthermore, experimental results are analyzed by ablation tests. Finally, we draw conclusions and give an overview of our future work.

2 Related Work

Labeled data for task-oriented dialogue systems is often scarce because of the high cost of data annotation. Consequently, learning generic dialogue representations that effectively capture dialogue semantics at various granularities (Hou et al., 2020; Krone et al., 2020; Gu et al., 2019; Yu et al., 2021) lays a good foundation for handling a variety of downstream tasks (Vinyals et al., 2016; Snell et al., 2017). Contrastive learning has recently demonstrated promising results in the processing of natural language. Among which SimCSE (Gao et al., 2021) and TOD-BERT (Wu et al., 2020) get a very good performance on general texts and dialogues, respectively. DSE (Zhou et al., 2022) set new state-of-the-art results on general dialogues.

SimCSE (Gao et al., 2021) uses Dropout (Srivastava et al., 2014) to construct positive pairs by passing a sentence through the encoder twice to generate two different embeddings. Despite the fact that SimCSE performs better than ordinary data augmentation that directly manipulates discrete text, it has proven to be a poor performer in the field of dialogue, which is confirmed in the DSE (Zhou et al., 2022). Moreover, TOD-BERT takes an utterance and the concatenation of all the previous utterances in the dialogue as a positive pair. Although showing promise on the same tasks, TOD-BERT's semantic granularity and data statistics in many other dialogue tasks differ from those evaluated in their paper. DSE learns from dialogues by taking consecutive utterances of the same dialogue as positive pairs for contrastive learning, and state-of-the-art results are obtained in several tasks, including intention classification. Recently, MTP-CLNN (Zhang et al., 2022) set new state-of-the-art results in the New Intent Discovery field. However, the supervised pre-training part of it requires the data to have a small number of labels to get better results. According to our experimental verification, the generalization ability of the pre-trained model in the first stage is poor for data with no labels at all. In addition, recent research results

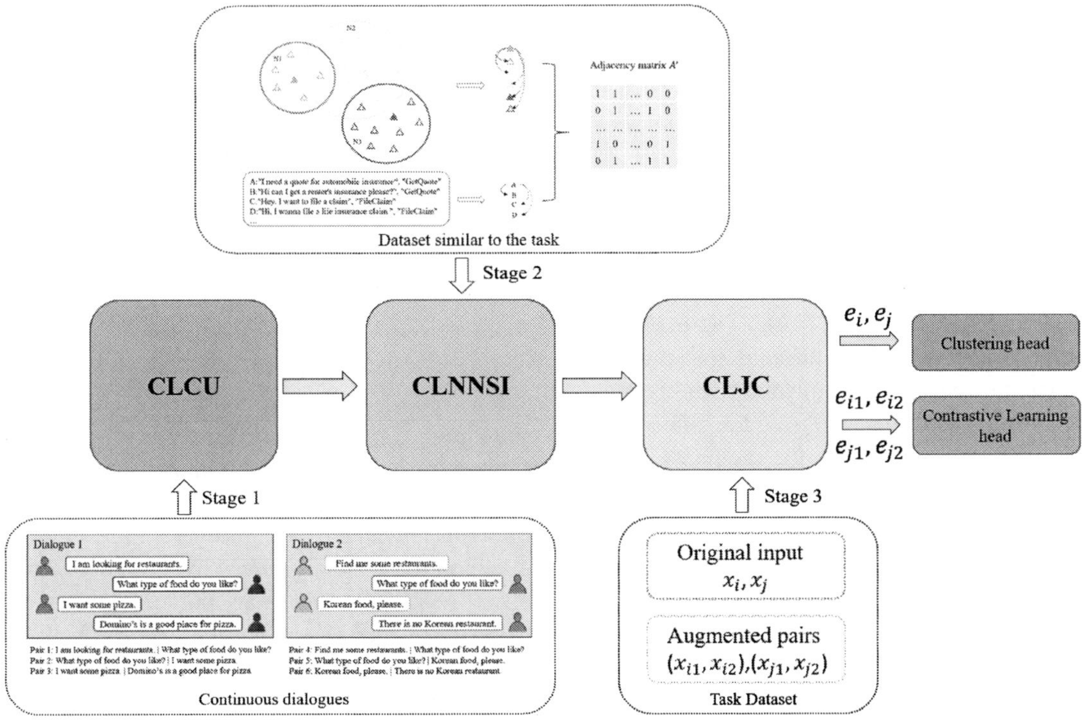

Figure 2: The framework of our proposed multi-stage coarse-to-fine contrastive learning model training scheme.

on short text clustering show that the combined training method based on clustering and contrastive learning, SCCL (Zhang et al., 2021) achieves very good results. However, a better pre-trained model for the clustering task as encoded by SCCL can further improve the results of clustering. To this end, the goal of our work in the first two stages is to continue pre-training language models to derive better representations for downstream tasks.

3 Methodology

Our proposed multi-stage coarse-to-fine model training scheme consists of three stages: Contrastive Learning with Consecutive Utterances (CLCU), Contrastive Learning with the Nearest Neighbors and the Same Intent (CLNNSI) and Contrastive Learning with Joint Clustering (CLJC). This is shown in Fig. 2. In the first stage, a pre-trained model is obtained by performing unsupervised contrastive learning on a large amount of dialogue data using consecutive discourses of the same dialogue as positive pairs. In the second stage, for labeled data in the same domain, we treat that sample with its neighboring samples or samples with the same intention as a positive pairs, and then fine-tune the model by contrastive learning. The third stage further fine-tunes the model by joint contrastive learning and clustering jointly on the target data. The negative pairs for contrastive learning are collected by small batches of negative sampling in the above three stages of model training. After training, we employ a simple non-parametric clustering algorithm named k-means to obtain clustering results. In this section, we describe our multi-stage coarse-to-fine contrastive learning model training scheme in detail below.

3.1 Stage 1: CLCU

CLCU encourages the model to treat an utterance as similar to its neighboring utterances and dissimilar to utterances that are not subsequent to it or that belong to other dialogues when doing contrastive learning on consecutive utterances. Consecutive utterances contain implicit categorical information, which benefits dialogue classification tasks (e.g., intent classification). Consider pairs 1 and 4 in Fig. 2 stage 1: We implicitly learn similar representations of *I am looking for restaurants* and *Find me some restaurants*, since they are both consecutive with *What type of food do you like?*. In contrast, SimCSE does not enjoy these benefits by simply using Dropout as data augmentation. Although

TOD-BERT also leverages the intrinsic semantics of dialogue by combining an utterance with its dialogue context as a positive pair, the context is often a concatenation of 5 to 15 utterances. Due to the large discrepancy in both semantics and data statistics between each utterance and its context, simply optimizing the similarity between them leads to less satisfying representations on many dialogue tasks. Just like the experimental results in DSE (Zhou et al., 2022). TOD-BERT can even lead to degenerated representations on some downstream tasks when compared to the original BERT (Devlin et al., 2019) model. Therefore, in the first stage, we adopt the method of DSE, which learns from dialogues by taking consecutive utterances of the same dialogue as positive pairs for contrastive learning, and directly use the model they trained on a large number of datasets as our first stage model.

3.2 Stage 2: CLNNSI

In the second stage, a small number of labeled datasets in the same domain as the target data are used, which makes our model have stronger generalization ability. And adopt an objective that pulls neighboring instances together and pushes distant ones away in the embedding space to learn compact representations for clustering. To be specific, we first encode the utterances with the pre-trained model from stage 1. The inner product is then used as a distance metric to find the top-K nearest neighbors of each utterance x_i in the embedding space, forming a neighborhood N_i. During training, for each minibatch of utterances B $= \{x_i\}_{i=1}^{M}$ and each utterance $x_i \in$ B, we uniformly sample one neighbor x_i' from its neighborhood N_i. Then use data augmentation to generate $\tilde{x}_i$ and $\tilde{x}_i'$ for x_i and x_i' respectively. Here, $\tilde{x}_i$ and $\tilde{x}_i'$ are treated as a positive pair. We then obtain an augmented batch $B' = \{\tilde{x}_i, \tilde{x}_i'\}_{i=1}^{M}$ with all the generated samples. To compute contrastive loss, we construct an adjacency matrix A' for B', which is a 2M $\times$ 2M binary matrix where 1 indicates positive relations (either being neighbors or having the same intent label) and 0 indicates negative relations. Hence, the contrastive loss can writed as:

$$l_i = -\frac{1}{|\mathcal{C}_i|} \sum_{j \in C_i} \log \frac{\exp\left(\operatorname{sim}\left(\tilde{e}_i, \tilde{e}_j\right)/\tau\right)}{\sum_{k \neq i}^{2M} \exp\left(\operatorname{sim}\left(\tilde{e}_i, \tilde{e}_k\right)/\tau\right)}, \quad (1)$$

$$L_{stg2} = \frac{1}{2M} \sum_{i=1}^{2M} l_i, \quad (2)$$

where $C_i = \left\{A_{ij}' = 1 \mid j \in \{1, \ldots, 2M\}\right\}$ denotes the set of instances having positive relation with $\tilde{x}_i$ and $|C_i|$ is the cardinality. $\tilde{e}_i$ is the embedding for utterance $\tilde{x}_i$, τ is the temperature parameter. $sim(.,.)$ is a similarity function on a pair of normalized feature vectors. Has the following advantages by introducing the notion of neighborhood relationships in contrastive learning: 1) Similar instances are pulled together and dissimilar instances are pushed away to achieve more compact clusters; and 2) known intents are naturally incorporated with the adjacency matrix.

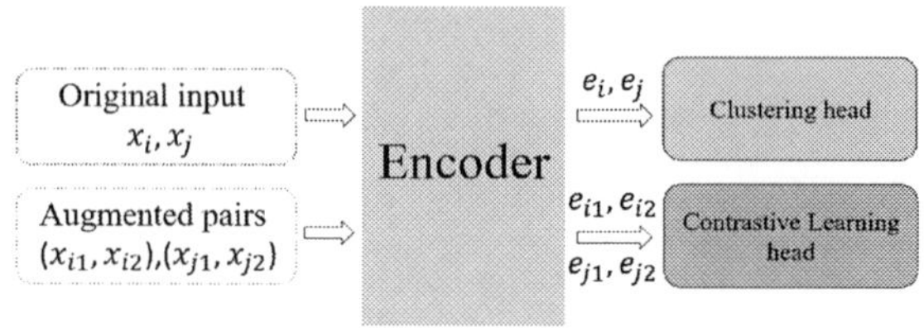

Figure 3: The training framework for stage 3.

3.3 Stage 3: CLJC

Previous research efforts focused on integrating clustering with deep representation learning by optimizing a clustering objective defined in the representation space (Zhang et al., 2017; Shaham et al., 2018). Despite promising improvements, the clustering performance is still inadequate, especially in the presence of complex data with a large number of clusters. One possible reason is that, even with a deep neural network, data still has significant overlap across categories before clustering starts. Consequently, the clusters learned by optimizing various distance or similarity-based clustering objectives suffer from poor purity. Moreover, contrastive learning has recently achieved remarkable success in self-monitoring (Wu et al., 2018; Chen et al., 2020), as the name suggests, a contrastive loss is adopted to pull together samples augmented from the same instance in the original dataset while pushing apart those from different ones. This beneficial property can be leveraged to support clustering by scattering apart the overlapped categories. Hence, in the third stage, for target data, we adopt the method of joint clustering and contrastive learning to further fine-tune the model. The training framework stage3 is shown in Fig. 3. Among them, x_{i_1},x_{i_2} and x_{j_1},x_{j_2} are obtained by means of data augmentation. In this paper, we adopt the contextual augmenter data

dataset	dial.	test-utt.	task1-utt.	task2-utt.
dev	948	913	1205	4332
banking	1000	407	1503	3696
finance	2000	1130	1597	6676

Table 1: Statistics of the DSTC11-Track 2 datasets. utt.: utterance, dial.: dialogue.

augment in the form of a pre-trained transformers to find the top-n suitable words of the input text for insertion or substitution. We used word substitution to augment the data and chose Bertbase and Robertabase to generate augmented pairs. And the overall objective is:

$$L_{stg3} = L_{CL} + \eta L_{Clu}, \quad (3)$$

where L_{CL} and L_{Clu} are the loss functions of comparative learning and clustering, respectively. η balances between the contrastive loss and the clustering loss of stage3, for simplicity, it is set to 10 in our experiment.

4 Experiments

4.1 Dataset

For this Track, one development dataset and two test datasets are provided. Each dataset consists of 1) some human-to-human conversations between a customer and an agent, and 2) a set of testing samples with corresponding intent annotations. The task1-utterances and task2-utterances are utterances in which "intents" are non-empty and "dialogue_acts" are "InformIntent" in dialogues in each dataset, respectively. Detailed statistics of the dataset are summarized in Table 1.

4.2 Metrics

Task 1 and task 2 are both evaluated by the following six metrics,: accuracy (ACC) (Huang et al., 2014), normalized mutual information (NMI), F1-score, Recall, Precision, and adjusted rand index (ARI). But the ACC is the primary metric used for ranking system submissions. Metrics dependent on reference intents will be computed using an automatic alignment of cluster labels to reference intent labels. For task 1, alignments will be computed based on turn-level reference intent labels. For task 2, to avoid the need to assign labels to turns in the input transcripts, alignments will be computed using classifier predictions on the set of utterances held out for evaluation. In both cases, 1:1 alignments between induced intents and reference intents will be computed using the Hungarian algorithm (Kuhn, 1955).

Team	ACC	P	R	F1	NMI	ARI
T23	**69.79**	76.09	76.12	76.00	75.05	59.23
T07	69.59	72.01	81.64	**76.50**	73.48	60.13
T35	69.31	**78.41**	73.35	75.78	74.30	58.67
T05	69.06	73.26	78.32	75.70	**75.54**	**61.38**
T02	68.83	73.04	78.06	75.46	75.13	60.88
T17	67.15	70.49	78.48	74.10	73.20	60.86
T36	66.32	71.86	74.46	73.13	73.64	58.05
T24	66.19	71.17	77.36	74.13	74.72	58.15
T00	64.92	71.42	74.80	73.05	71.08	50.37
T34	63.73	71.01	74.84	72.59	72.98	52.77
...	...	...	...	...	...	...
baseline	55.80	64.97	62.98	63.26	62.98	39.85

Table 2: The summary of the task 1 evaluation results on the two datasets, with the best score in bold.

Team	ACC	P	R	F1	NMI	ARI
T23	**76.30**	78.68	**89.86**	83.55	87.42	**71.82**
T02	75.34	78.18	88.18	82.86	87.32	68.87
T36	74.85	78.81	87.59	82.85	87.00	71.36
T24	74.70	79.76	87.62	83.42	87.45	70.71
T05	74.52	79.50	87.49	83.17	87.88	70.26
T17	73.79	**83.25**	84.87	**83.99**	**88.11**	71.42
T14	69.55	70.68	87.97	78.27	83.67	65.11
T13	69.43	82.66	74.47	78.26	82.29	62.13
T27	68.70	80.29	77.51	78.76	83.69	63.83
T19	67.50	69.09	89.4	77.92	83.73	63.67
...	...	...	...	...	...	...
baseline	63.61	68.93	79.59	73.86	80.09	57.24

Table 3: The summary of the task 2 evaluation results on the two datasets, with the best score in bold.

4.3 Experiment Results

The final summary results of the test-banking dataset and the test-finance dataset for the two subtasks are shown in Tables 2 and 3. Our model ranks first in the test sets for both subtasks. Compared with the baseline, where the baseline model in the above tables is the official provided baseline model mpnet by Track 2 of DSTC11. It is trained on a large and diverse dataset of over 1 billion training pairs. And the test ACC of our model is improved by 13.99% and 12.69% on tasks 1 and 2, respectively. It shows the effectiveness of

	task1	task2
GloVe (Pennington et al., 2014)	20.58	29.12
MPNet (Song et al., 2020)	46.14	60.23
SimCSE (Gao et al., 2021)	47.39	57.74
DSE (Zhou et al., 2022)	58.67	64.18
SCCL (Zhang et al., 2021)	65.32	78.34
Our model	**75.68**	**85.76**

Table 4: Comparison of the accuracy of different models on the development dataset for the two tasks.

our method.

In addition, we give the results of our method on the development dataset compared with some representative baseline models. We compared with the following baseline models: **(1) GloVe** (Pennington et al., 2014). One of the official baseline models provided by the Track 2 of DSTC11, which is a sentence-transformers model. It maps sentences or paragraphs to a 300 dimensional dense vector space and can be used for tasks like clustering or semantic search. **(2) MPNet** (Song et al., 2020). Another official baseline model provided by Track 2 of DSTC11, which is trained on a large and diverse dataset of over 1 billion training pairs. The base model is MPNet-base. **(3) SimCSE** (Gao et al., 2021). The model we chose is trained on 10^6 randomly sampled sentences from English Wikipedia by unsupervised contrastive learning, and its base model is RoBERTa-large. **(4) DSE** (Zhou et al., 2022). It is trained on a large number of training pairs constructed in the style of consecutive conversational sentences as positive pair using multiple conversational datasets. And the base model is RoBERTa-large. **(5) SCCL** (Zhang et al., 2021). Fine-tuning of the baseline model using the development dataset by joint training with clustering and contrastive learning, where the baseline model is the DSE-trained model described above.

As can be seen from the experimental results in Table 4, our model obtained the best results in both subtasks compared to several other representative baseline models, with accuracy rates of 75.68% and 85.76%, respectively. On task 1, the accuracy of our model outperformed GloVe by 55.1%, outperformed MPNet by 29.54%, outperformed SimCSE by 28.29%, outperformed DSE by 17.01%, and outperformed SCCL by 10.36%. On task 2, the accuracy of our model outperformed GloVe by 56.64%, outperformed MPNet by 25.53%, outperformed SimCSE by 28.02%, outperformed DSE by 21.56%, and outperformed SCCL by 7.42%. This illustrates the soundness of our approach.

	task1	task2
model	75.68	85.76
w/o. stage1,stage2 and stage3	46.14	60.24
w/o. stage2 and stage3	58.59	60.90
w/o. stage3	70.71	80.28

Table 5: Accuracy of ablation experiment on the development set.

4.4 Ablation Study

Through ablation experiments with a random seed set to 42 in the clustering algorithm on the development dataset, the experimental results are shown in Table 5. When there is no stage1, stage2 and stag3 (this is the case is the baseline), the ACC of the test on task1 and task2 are 46.14%, 60.24% respectively. when stage1, stage2 and stage3 are performed, the results on task1 are improved by 12.45%, 12.12% and the results on task2 improved by 0.68%, 19.38%, and 5.48%, respectively. In addition, the TSNE visualization of the utterances representation of the model obtained at each stage on the development set is shown in Fig. 4. It can be observed from the figure that each cluster becomes more and more compact after each stage compared to the baseline model. That verifies the rationality of each stage.

5 Conclusion

In this paper, we present our solution to the challenge of Intent Induction from Conversations for task-Oriented Dialogue of DSTC11. Firstly, we chose RoBERTa-large, which was pre-trained on a large number of continuous dialogues. Since continuous utterances also contain implicit classification information, they are beneficial for the task of dialogue intention classification. Secondly, the use of some labeled datasets in the same domain as the target data makes our model have stronger transfer ability. And we adopt KNN to select the positive pair for contrastive learning in order to pull neighboring instances together and push distant ones away in the embedding space to learn compact representations for clustering. Lastly, the joint training method of clustering

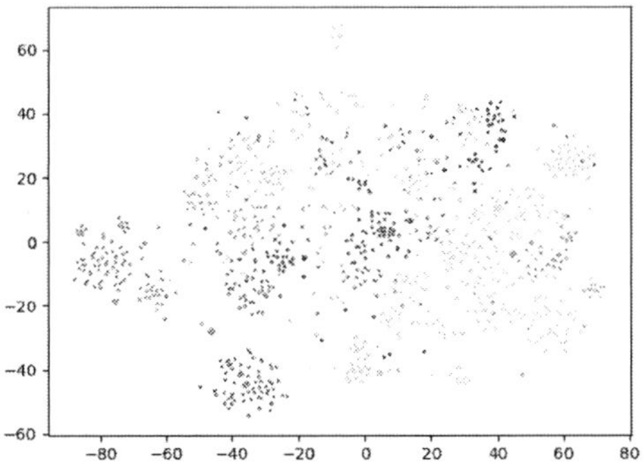

(a) Baseline

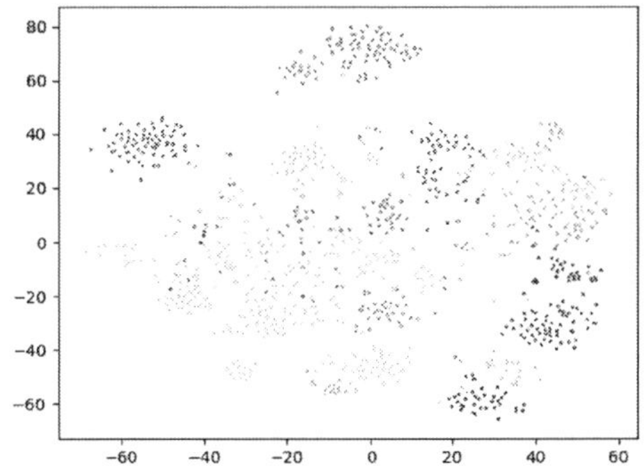

(b) Stage 1

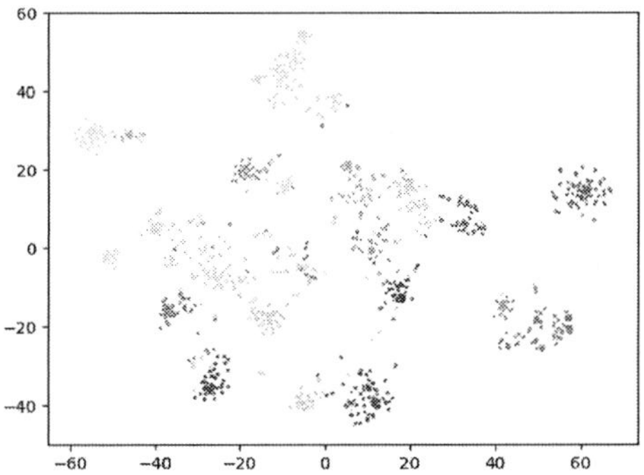

(c) Stage 2

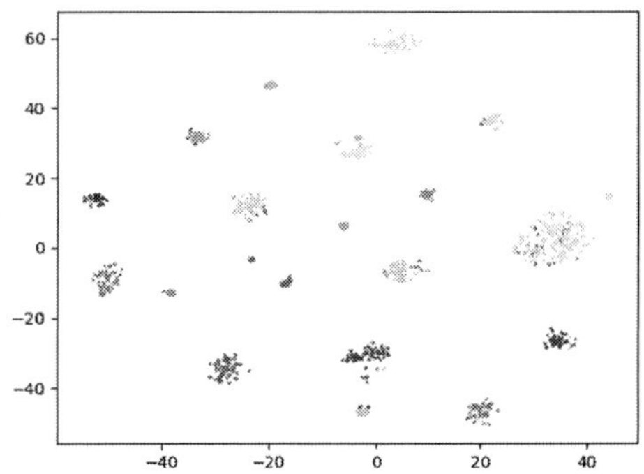

(d) Stage 3

Figure 4: TSNE visualization (Van der Maaten and Hinton, 2008) of the dialogue representations provides by baseline and three stages on the development set, each color indicates a ground truth semantic category.

and contrastive learning makes the advantages of clustering and contrastive learning complementary. Experimental results demonstrate that our methods can effectively cluster the utterances with intention in the dialogue. Our method of competitive performance achieved first place in two subtasks. In the future, we will explore better ways to obtain a better dialogue utterance representation model for the clustering task.

Acknowledgements

We thank anonymous reviewers for their valuable comments.

References

Ajay Chatterjee and Shubhashis Sengupta. 2020. Intent mining from past conversations for conversational agent. *CoRR*, abs/2005.11014.

Ting Chen, Simon Kornblith, Mohammad Norouzi, and Geoffrey Hinton. 2020. A simple framework for contrastive learning of visual representations. In *International conference on machine learning*, pages 1597–1607. PMLR.

Jacob Devlin, Ming-Wei Chang, Kenton Lee, and Kristina Toutanova. 2019. BERT: Pre-training of deep bidirectional transformers for language understanding. In *Proceedings of the 2019 Conference of the North American Chapter of the Association for Computational Linguistics: Human Language Technologies, Volume 1 (Long and Short Papers)*, pages 4171–4186, Minneapolis, Minnesota. Association for Computational Linguistics.

Tianyu Gao, Xingcheng Yao, and Danqi Chen. 2021. Simcse: Simple contrastive learning of sentence embeddings. In *Proceedings of the 2021 Conference on Empirical Methods in Natural Language Processing, EMNLP 2021, Virtual Event / Punta Cana, Dominican Republic, 7-11 November, 2021*, pages 6894–6910. Association for Computational Linguistics.

Jia-Chen Gu, Zhen-Hua Ling, and Quan Liu. 2019. Interactive matching network for multi-turn response selection in retrieval-based chatbots. In *Proceedings of the 28th ACM International Conference on Information and Knowledge Management, CIKM 2019*, pages 2321–2324. ACM.

Dilek Hakkani-Tür, Yun-Cheng Ju, Geoffrey Zweig, and Gokhan Tur. 2015. Clustering novel intents in a conversational interaction system with semantic parsing. In *Sixteenth Annual Conference of the International Speech Communication Association*.

Iryna Haponchyk, Antonio Uva, Seunghak Yu, Olga Uryupina, and Alessandro Moschitti. 2018. Supervised clustering of questions into intents for dialog system applications. In *Proceedings of the 2018 Conference on Empirical Methods in Natural Language Processing*, pages 2310–2321.

Yutai Hou, Wanxiang Che, Yongkui Lai, Zhihan Zhou, Yijia Liu, Han Liu, and Ting Liu. 2020. Few-shot slot tagging with collapsed dependency transfer and label-enhanced task-adaptive projection network. In *Proceedings of the 58th Annual Meeting of the Association for Computational Linguistics*, pages 1381–1393.

Peihao Huang, Yan Huang, Wei Wang, and Liang Wang. 2014. Deep embedding network for clustering. In *2014 22nd International conference on pattern recognition*, pages 1532–1537. IEEE.

Vojtěch Hudeček, Ondřej Dušek, and Zhou Yu. 2021. Discovering dialogue slots with weak supervision. In *Proceedings of the 59th Annual Meeting of the Association for Computational Linguistics and the 11th International Joint Conference on Natural Language Processing (Volume 1: Long Papers)*, pages 2430–2442.

Jason Krone, Yi Zhang, and Mona T. Diab. 2020. Learning to classify intents and slot labels given a handful of examples. *CoRR*, abs/2004.10793.

Harold W Kuhn. 1955. The hungarian method for the assignment problem. *Naval research logistics quarterly*, 2(1-2):83–97.

Harrison Lee, Raghav Gupta, Abhinav Rastogi, Yuan Cao, Bin Zhang, and Yonghui Wu. 2022. Sgd-x: A benchmark for robust generalization in schema-guided dialogue systems. In *Proceedings of the AAAI Conference on Artificial Intelligence*, volume 36, pages 10938–10946.

Yinhan Liu, Myle Ott, Naman Goyal, Jingfei Du, Mandar Joshi, Danqi Chen, Omer Levy, Mike Lewis, Luke Zettlemoyer, and Veselin Stoyanov. 2019. Roberta: A robustly optimized BERT pretraining approach. *CoRR*, abs/1907.11692.

Qingkai Min, Libo Qin, Zhiyang Teng, Xiao Liu, and Yue Zhang. 2020. Dialogue state induction using neural latent variable models. In *Proceedings of the Twenty-Ninth International Joint Conference on Artificial Intelligence, IJCAI 2020*, pages 3845–3852. ijcai.org.

Jeffrey Pennington, Richard Socher, and Christopher D. Manning. 2014. Glove: Global vectors for word representation. In *Proceedings of the 2014 Conference on Empirical Methods in Natural Language Processing, EMNLP 2014, October 25-29, 2014, Doha, Qatar, A meeting of SIGDAT, a Special Interest Group of the ACL*, pages 1532–1543. ACL.

Hugh Perkins and Yi Yang. 2019. Dialog intent induction with deep multi-view clustering. In *Proceedings of the 2019 Conference on Empirical Methods in Natural Language Processing and the 9th International Joint Conference on Natural Language Processing, EMNLP-IJCNLP 2019, Hong Kong, China, November 3-7, 2019*, pages 4014–4023. Association for Computational Linguistics.

Abhinav Rastogi, Xiaoxue Zang, Srinivas Sunkara, Raghav Gupta, and Pranav Khaitan. 2020a. Schema-guided dialogue state tracking task at DSTC8. *CoRR*, abs/2002.01359.

Abhinav Rastogi, Xiaoxue Zang, Srinivas Sunkara, Raghav Gupta, and Pranav Khaitan. 2020b. Towards scalable multi-domain conversational agents: The schema-guided dialogue dataset. In *Proceedings of the AAAI Conference on Artificial Intelligence*, volume 34, pages 8689–8696.

Peter J Rousseeuw. 1987. Silhouettes: a graphical aid to the interpretation and validation of cluster analysis. *Journal of computational and applied mathematics*, 20:53–65.

Yu-Ping Ruan, Zhen-Hua Ling, Jia-Chen Gu, and Quan Liu. 2020. Fine-tuning BERT for schema-guided zero-shot dialogue state tracking. In *Proceedings of the Thirty-Fourth AAAI Conference on Artificial Intelligence, AAAI 2020, Workshop on the Eighth Dialog System Technology Challenge, DSTC8*.

Uri Shaham, Kelly P. Stanton, Henry Li, Ronen Basri, Boaz Nadler, and Yuval Kluger. 2018. Spectralnet: Spectral clustering using deep neural networks. In *6th International Conference on Learning Representations, ICLR 2018, Vancouver, BC, Canada, April 30 - May 3, 2018, Conference Track Proceedings*. OpenReview.net.

Jake Snell, Kevin Swersky, and Richard Zemel. 2017. Prototypical networks for few-shot learning. *Advances in neural information processing systems*, 30.

Kaitao Song, Xu Tan, Tao Qin, Jianfeng Lu, and Tie-Yan Liu. 2020. Mpnet: Masked and permuted pre-training for language understanding. In *Advances in Neural Information Processing Systems 33: Annual Conference on Neural Information Processing Systems 2020, NeurIPS 2020, December 6-12, 2020, virtual*.

Nitish Srivastava, Geoffrey Hinton, Alex Krizhevsky, Ilya Sutskever, and Ruslan Salakhutdinov. 2014. Dropout: a simple way to prevent neural networks from overfitting. *The journal of machine learning research*, 15(1):1929–1958.

Laurens Van der Maaten and Geoffrey Hinton. 2008. Visualizing data using t-sne. *Journal of machine learning research*, 9(11).

Oriol Vinyals, Charles Blundell, Timothy Lillicrap, Daan Wierstra, et al. 2016. Matching networks for one shot learning. *Advances in neural information processing systems*, 29.

Chien-Sheng Wu, Steven C. H. Hoi, Richard Socher, and Caiming Xiong. 2020. TOD-BERT: pre-trained natural language understanding for task-oriented dialogue. In *Proceedings of the 2020 Conference on Empirical Methods in Natural Language Processing, EMNLP 2020, Online, November 16-20, 2020*, pages 917–929. Association for Computational Linguistics.

Zhirong Wu, Yuanjun Xiong, Stella X Yu, and Dahua Lin. 2018. Unsupervised feature learning via non-parametric instance discrimination. In *Proceedings of the IEEE conference on computer vision and pattern recognition*, pages 3733–3742.

Dian Yu, Luheng He, Yuan Zhang, Xinya Du, Panupong Pasupat, and Qi Li. 2021. Few-shot intent classification and slot filling with retrieved examples. In *Proceedings of the 2021 Conference of the North American Chapter of the Association for Computational Linguistics: Human Language Technologies, NAACL-HLT 2021, Online, June 6-11, 2021*, pages 734–749. Association for Computational Linguistics.

Dejiao Zhang, Feng Nan, Xiaokai Wei, Shang-Wen Li, Henghui Zhu, Kathleen R. McKeown, Ramesh Nallapati, Andrew O. Arnold, and Bing Xiang. 2021. Supporting clustering with contrastive learning. In *Proceedings of the 2021 Conference of the North American Chapter of the Association for Computational Linguistics: Human Language Technologies, NAACL-HLT 2021, Online, June 6-11, 2021*, pages 5419–5430. Association for Computational Linguistics.

Dejiao Zhang, Yifan Sun, Brian Eriksson, and Laura Balzano. 2017. Deep unsupervised clustering using mixture of autoencoders. *arXiv preprint arXiv:1712.07788*.

Yuwei Zhang, Haode Zhang, Li-Ming Zhan, Xiao-Ming Wu, and Albert Y. S. Lam. 2022. New intent discovery with pre-training and contrastive learning. In *Proceedings of the 60th Annual Meeting of the Association for Computational Linguistics (Volume 1: Long Papers), ACL 2022, Dublin, Ireland, May 22-27, 2022*, pages 256–269. Association for Computational Linguistics.

Zhihan Zhou, Dejiao Zhang, Wei Xiao, Nicholas Dingwall, Xiaofei Ma, Andrew O. Arnold, and Bing Xiang. 2022. Learning dialogue representations from consecutive utterances. In *Proceedings of the 2022 Conference of the North American Chapter of the Association for Computational Linguistics: Human Language Technologies, NAACL 2022, Seattle, WA, United States, July 10-15, 2022*, pages 754–768. Association for Computational Linguistics.

DORIC : Domain Robust Fine-Tuning for Open Intent Clustering through Dependency Parsing

Jihyun Lee[1], **Seungyeon Seo**[1], **Yunsu Kim**[1,2], **Gary Geunbae Lee**[1,2]
[1]Graduate School of Artificial Intelligence, POSTECH, Republic of Korea
[2]Department of Computer Science and Engineering, POSTECH, Republic of Korea
{jihyunlee, ssy319, yunsu.kim, gblee}@postech.ac.kr

Abstract

We present our work on Track 2 in the Dialog System Technology Challenges 11 (DSTC11). DSTC11-Track2 aims to provide a benchmark for zero-shot, cross-domain, intent-set induction. In the absence of in-domain training dataset, robust utterance representation that can be used across domains is necessary to induce users' intentions. To achieve this, we leveraged a multi-domain dialogue dataset to fine-tune the language model and proposed extracting Verb-Object pairs to remove the artifacts of unnecessary information. Furthermore, we devised the method that generates each cluster's name for the explainability of clustered results. Our approach achieved 3rd place in the precision score and showed superior accuracy and normalized mutual information (NMI) score than the baseline model on various domain datasets.

1 Introduction

Understanding the user's intent plays an important role in task-oriented dialogue (TOD) systems. Traditionally, understanding the user's intent requires supervised training using intent-annotated dialogue datasets (Xu et al., 2013; Wang et al., 2015; Kim et al., 2017; Goo et al., 2018). However, for new emerging domains and services, defining the intent set is challenging and also requires an expert's knowledge. Therefore, finding an automatic method that identifies intents from raw conversational data is desirable to reduce costs.

The intent clustering task of the 11th Dialog System Technology Challenge (DSTC11) aims to provide a realistic benchmark for the intent induction problem. This track evaluates automatic customer intent induction methods from dialogues between human agents and customers, and the DSTC11 challenge participants are required to create a set of intent labels based on the conversations. To provide a realistic setting, the number of intents and domain of the test set are not provided until the development phase ends.

In this paper, we introduce an automatic intent induction framework that effectively utilizes a public TOD dataset. First, we fine-tuned the language model with multi-domain TOD datasets so that it has a domain-robust semantic representation. Here, we extract verbs and object from utterance to remove the artifacts of unnecessary information. For the training, we applied supervised contrastive learning (SCL), which is known to be stable in language model fine-tuning (Gunel et al., 2020). Second, to infer a new intent set from the unseen domain dataset, we applied a clustering technique that groups the utterances based on the fine-tuned embedding model's representation. Furthermore, we generate a label name for each cluster to obtain an interpretable result. The cluster label generation method could reduce the effort of examining each set manually to understand the clustering results.

In the experiment with the test dataset (finance and banking domain), we achieved 3rd place in terms of precision and demonstrated superior accuracy (ACC) and a higher normalized mutual information (NMI) score than the baseline. Furthermore, the generated clustering labels reasonably explain each cluster. Finally, we analyzed our model with comparable options and demonstrated the result on development, test, and TOD datasets. We named our framework DORIC, which means **DO**main **R**obust fine-tuning for open **I**ntent **C**lustering through dependency parsing.

2 Related Work

2.1 Intent Classification

Traditionally, benchmark datasets (Price, 1990; Coucke et al., 2018; Eric et al., 2019) for intent identification have sufficient labeled datasets for training, and the task has been solved through the classification method. For example, Goo et al. (2018) classified the intent and slot information using the attention mechanism, and Kim et al. (2017)

Proceedings of The Eleventh Dialog System Technology Challenge, pages 40–47
September 11, 2023 ©2023 Association for Computational Linguistics

enriched word embeddings by using semantic lexicons and adapted this strategy to the intent classification. In addition, Wang et al. (2015) grouped the intent of tweets into six categories, used a graph embedding consisting of tweet nodes, and classified their intents. However, labeling the intent for the raw dialogue dataset requires extensive human labor, so building a new labeled intent dataset in the real world is challenging. Therefore, a robust intent induction model that can be applied to a new domain as an unsupervised method is required.

2.2 Intent induction with unsupervised method

The representative method of unsupervised intent induction utilizes the clustering method. Liu et al. (2021) is one example of research that enhanced the clustering algorithm. They proposed a balanced score metric to obtain similar-sized clusters in K-means clustering and found proper K-values that were more stable than naive K-means. Chatterjee and Sengupta (2020) also enhanced the clustering algorithm by utilizing the outlier information of the density-based clustering model, which is called ITER-DBSCAN. Their work shows greater accuracy on imbalanced intent data. On the other hand, there has been research that improved the dialogue representations for better clustering results. For example, Perkins and Yang (2019) iteratively enhanced the dialogue embedding by reflecting the clustering score, and Lin and Xu (2019) proposed a BiLSTM (Mesnil et al., 2014) embedding model with margin loss that is effective in detecting unknown intents. However, robust intent induction in diverse domains was not examined in previous research. Therefore, as a strategy for enhancing the embedding dialogue model, we propose the DORIC method, which robustly embeds diverse dialogue domains.

3 DSTC11 Intent Clustering Task

In this task, participants are required to assign an intent label to each dialogue turn. A set of dialogues are provided as input, and each turn is pre-labeled with both its speaker role (i.e., Agent or Customer) and dialogue acts (i.e., InformIntent or not). One development dataset and two test datasets are provided, and each dataset consists of approximately 1K customer support spoken conversations with manual transcriptions and annotations. The development dataset derives from an insurance-related customer support service, and each conversation has an average of 70 turns. In addition, the development dataset contains ground truth intent annotations that allow participants to test and evaluate the model. The number of intent types and the domains of the test dataset are not revealed until the development phase ends. Note that no training dataset is given, as this challenge aims to zero-shot intent induction.

4 Method

4.1 Semantic representation

With the advance of the pre-trained langue model, leveraging these models for embedding dialogue has exhibited promising results (Ham et al., 2020; Lin et al., 2020; Yang et al., 2021; Lee and Lee, 2022). Following their success, we utilize the pre-trained SBERT (Reimers and Gurevych, 2019) as a backbone model; SBERT has a siamese network structure and performs well in classification (Reimers and Gurevych, 2019), summarization (Zhong et al., 2020), and intent clustering (Liu et al., 2021).

The SBERT model is pre-trained on a written form text dataset that has a different linguistic pattern with the dialogue utterances. This difference could hurt the accuracy on dialogue related tasks (Wu et al., 2020). Therefore, we fine-tuned the model with the multi-domain public task-oriented dialogue dataset MultiWOZ 2.2 (Eric et al., 2019). This dataset has nine intents types, and we fine-tuned the model to learn the embedding of utterances according to intent type. In this data, intents are spanned multiple turns, and some utterances contain multiple intents in one utterance. To clarify the match between the utterance and the intent label, we used only the first utterance of the spanned intent dialogue and excluded utterances that contained multiple intents. We analyze the processed fine-tuning dataset in Table 1.

As we aim for unsupervised intent induction, domain robust fine-tuning is crucial to identify the intents across the domain. To do so, we extract Verb-Object structure from the utterance using the dependency parser[1]. This additional pre-process removes the effect of non-relevant words or utterance styles when fine-tuning the SBERT model. However, at inference time, we used whole utterances for clustering as preliminary experiments demon-

[1]https://spacy.io/

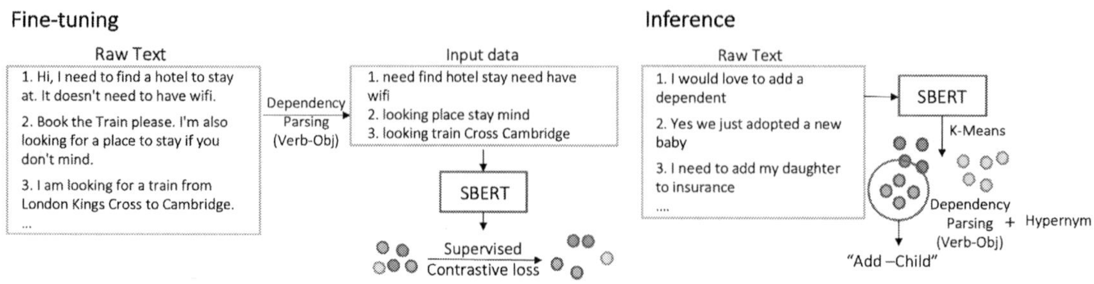

Figure 1: Fine-tuning and inference method of our proposed methods.

Intent	Count
FindRestaurants	3561
SearchHotel	3375
FindTrains	3262
FindAttractions	2795
ReserveHotel	1951
GetTrainTickets	1926
ReserveRestaurant	1600
GetRide	1262
FindPolice	229
Total	19961

Table 1: Type and number of intents of the fine-tuning dataset.

Inference data	NMI	ACC
Verb-Object	41.89	30.79
Sentence	**65.16**	**56.68**

Table 2: The comparison of using whole sentence and Verb-Object format in inference. NMI and accuracy result on DSTC11 development are reported.

strated better results (Table 2). We demonstrate our overall method in Figure 1.

4.2 Supervised contrastive learning

Recently, there have been several successful studies using contrastive learning (CL) in the computer vision and language domain (Chen et al., 2020; Liu and Abbeel, 2020; Wu et al., 2018; Gunel et al., 2020) and CL shows more generalize and robustness to language model training than cross-entropy loss (Gunel et al., 2020). Following their success, we utilize supervised contrastive learning (SCL) (Khosla et al., 2020) in fine-tuning.

SCL is a modified version of the CL approach, which utilize the label information. In CL, only the anchor and its augmented object are regarded as positive objects, and others are used as negative object in training. However, SCL set the same label objects as positive and others as negative, so more accurate embedding representation learning is possible.

For the N randomly sampled object $\{x_k, y_k\}_{k=1...N}$, mini batch used for training is consists of $2N$ pair, $\{\tilde{x}_k, \tilde{y}_k\}_{k=1...2N}$. In $\{\tilde{x}_k, \tilde{y}_k\}_{k=1...2N}$, $\{\tilde{x}_k, \tilde{y}_k\}_{k=1...N}$ is same as original sampled $\{x_k, y_k\}_{k=1...N}$ and $\{\tilde{x}_k, \tilde{y}_k\}_{k=N...2N}$ is augmented pair of original sampled data. Wordnet (Miller, 1995) based synonym augmentation[2] is used for augmentation. Φ denotes the SBERT encoder and τ is scalar temperature parameter to adjust the separation strength. The overall loss is given by the following equations, and visualization of the training results are shown in Figure 2:

$$\mathcal{L}^{sup} = \sum_{i=1}^{2N} \mathcal{L}_i^{sup} \tag{1}$$

$$L_i^{sup} = -\frac{1}{2N_{\tilde{y}} - 1} \sum_{j=1}^{2N} \mathbf{1}_{i \neq j} \cdot \mathbf{1}_{\tilde{y} = \tilde{y}} \cdot \log \frac{\exp(\Phi_i \cdot \Phi_j / \tau)}{\sum_{k=1}^{2N} \mathbf{1}_{i \neq k} \exp(\Phi_i \cdot \Phi_j / \tau)} \tag{2}$$

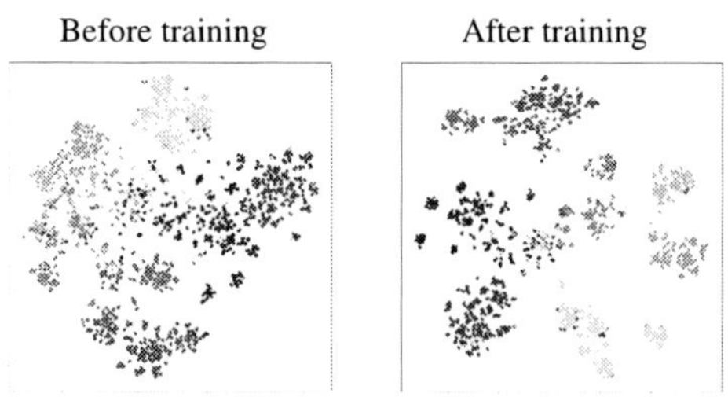

Figure 2: Visualization of Multiwoz 2.2 test dataset. The left is utterance representation before training, and the right is after training.

4.3 Intent label generation

To improve the explainability of the clustering results, we automatically generated the semantic labels from the clustering results. Following the intent datasets, which usually represent the intent

[2] https://github.com/makcedward/nlpaug

name as a verb and object pair (Zang et al., 2020; Coucke et al., 2018; Rastogi et al., 2020), we also named our induced clusters as Verb-Object forms using a dependency parser. In the previous method, Liu et al. (2021) counted the common Verb-Object pairs in the cluster and used the most common pair as the cluster name. However, this method did not create a proper label when detailed words appeared in the object. For example, a pair of `call-son` and `call-daughter` cannot be grouped as `call-child` using the previous method.

To overcome this limitation, we propose a method that uses the object word's hypernyms. By adopting hypernyms, we could obtain a proper word containing detailed information. More precisely, we generate *verb-hyper(object)* and *verb-hyper(hyper(object))* pairs from existing Verb-Object pairs and calculate the most common pair from this generated result. We employ this rule when the number of the most common pair and second place does not differ by more than α times, and we set α to 2.0 in the experiment. Word-net (Miller, 1995) is used to get the hypernyms.

5 Experiment

5.1 Experimental setup

Dataset To demonstrate the performance of our model, we used the development (dev) (insurance), test1 (banking), and test2 (finance) datasets. These datasets have domains that are different from the fine-tuning dataset (tourism), so we were able to examine our method's effectiveness in diverse domains. Additionally, we used the Schema-Guided Dialogue Dataset (SGD) dataset; we extracted tourism-related domains from the SGD dataset to make the same domain environment with fine-tuning dataset. The number of intents for each dataset is shown in Table 3.

Dataset	Domain	# of intents
Dev	Insurance	22
Test1	Banking	29
Test2	Fianace	39
SGD	Tourism	6

Table 3: Domain and number of intents type for each dataset.

Evaluation NMI and accuracy were the primary metrics used for the evaluation, and to provide additional metrics, precision was also used. The higher NMI value denotes that clustering has reduced more entropy. 1:1 alignments between the induced intents and the gold intents were computed by the Hungarian algorithm (Kuhn, 1955).

Setup We employ the pre-trained SBERT (Reimers and Gurevych, 2019) for the baseline embedding model. The pre-trained parameters were from the huggingface (Wolf et al., 2019) *all-mpnet-base-v2* version. In the SCL function, we set the τ as 0.07 and trained a maximum of five epochs with early stopping. In the K-means clustering, we set the minimum cluster number as five and the max cluster number as 50 and use silhouette score for comparing the clustered result, which is based on tightness and separation (Rousseeuw, 1987).

5.2 Intent clustering result

Model	Data	NMI	ACC	Precision
Different Domain with Fine-tuning Dataset				
Baseline	Dev(Insurance)	59.31	46.14	65.98
DORIC	Dev(Insurance)	**65.16**	**56.68**	**67.63**
Baseline	Test1(Banking)	65.71	51.85	60.68
DORIC	Test1(Banking)	**71.02**	**52.35**	**73.92**
Baseline	Test2(Finance)	60.26	59.75	69.25
DORIC	Test2(Finance)	**69.64**	**65.14**	**75.14**
Same Domain with Fine-tuning Dataset				
Baseline	SGD(Tourism)	60.54	63.67	49.90
DORIC	SGD(Tourism)	**65.32**	**68.36**	**51.00**

Table 4: Comparison of baseline and DORIC in different dataset. NMI, ACC and Precision are reported.

The results of DORIC after evaluation on the dev (insurance), test1 (finance), test2 (banking), and SGD (tourism) datasets are shown in Table 4. These results show that our model outperforms the baseline model in terms of the NMI, ACC, and precision on all datasets. Except for the SGD dataset, the dataset's domains are all different from the fine-tuning dataset MultiWOZ2.2 (tourism), which demonstrates that our intent induction framework is robust to diverse domain datasets. The visualization of experimental results in Figure 3 also exhibits the aligned result with Table 4; compared to the baseline, DORIC embeds utterances with the same label at a closer distance.

5.3 Intent label generation with hypernym

Table 5 shows examples of the generated intent labels, and cluster with †denotes the clusters with the hypernyms following section 4.3. As shown in the table, our proposed method successfully explains the cluster results compared to the ground truth label. Furthermore, using hypernyms enables the grouping of detailed information in the cluster. For

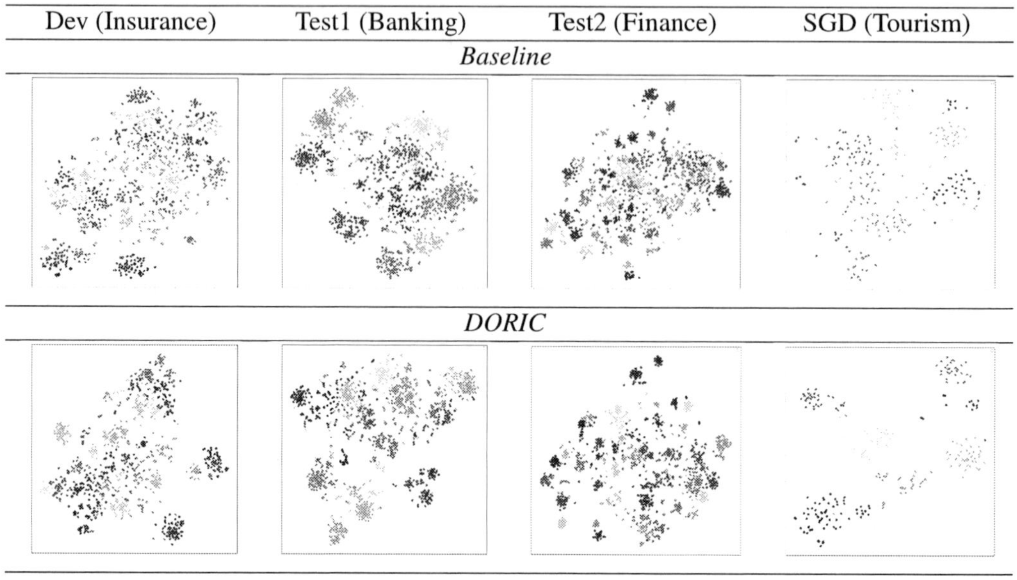

Figure 3: Visulization on dev (insurance), test1 (banking), test2 (finance) and SGD (tourism) dataset.

Idx	Generated name	Ground-truth
0	create-account	CreateAccount
1	cancel-billing	CancelAutomaticBilling
2†	**add-child**	AddDependent
3	report-accident	ReportAutomobileAccident
4	change-address	ChangeAddress
5†	get-quote	GetQuote
6	change-plan	ChangePlan
7	file-claim	FileClaim
8	pay-bill	PayBill
9	check-balance	CheckAccountBalance
10	change-question	ChangeSecurityQuestion
11	cancel-plan	CancelPlan
	Without hypernym	
2	**add-son**	AddDependent
5	get-quote	GetQuote

Table 5: Example of generated intent labels and ground truth. Cluster name with †means using hypernym.

Method	Dataset (domain)	NMI	ACC
Different Domain with Fine-tuning Dataset			
Sentence	Dev (Insurance)	62.13	55.35
Verb-Obj	Dev (Insurance)	**65.16**	**56.68**
Sentence	Test1 (Banking)	68.91	**53.22**
Verb-Obj	Test1 (Banking)	**71.02**	52.35
Sentence	Test2 (Finance)	64.94	**67.07**
Verb-Obj	Test2 (Finance)	**69.64**	65.14
Same Domain with Fine-tuning Dataset			
Sentence	SGD (Tourism)	65.24	68.35
Verb-Obj	SGD (Tourism)	**65.32**	**68.36**

Table 6: The NMI and accuracy result on DSTC11 development, test, and SGD dataset according to fine-tuning utterance format.

instance, Cluster 2 obtains a more comprehensive label, `add-child` than `add-son` by using the hypernyms. We also present the more detailed results for the dev and test data in Appendix A.1.

6 Analysis

6.1 Verb-Object structure in fine-tuning

To examine the effect of extracting Verb-Object structures from the sentence, we compare our proposed method with methods that use the whole sentence during the fine-tuning stage (Table 6). Using the Verb-Object structure demonstrates superior NMI results in both different-domain and same-domain environments; this result indicates that fine-tuning with Verb-Object information has helped reduce the clustering uncertainty. However, the accuracy doesn't significantly differ between the Verb-Object form and the whole sentence form in the tourism domain, which is identical to the fine-tuning dataset domain.

6.2 Analysis of loss

To investigate the effect of SCL during fine-tuning, we compare the result with the cross-entropy loss in Table 7. In most cases, the SCL loss demonstrates better results by a large margin; however, on the SGD dataset, the NMI and ACC results were slightly or no different than the cross-entropy loss. Considering that the SGD dataset is the only dataset with the same domain with the fine-tuning dataset (tourism), this result indicates that SCL is more useful when it is used in a domain-across environment.

Loss function	Dataset (domain)	NMI	ACC
Different Domain with Fine-tuning Dataset			
Cross Entropy	Dev (Insurance)	61.98	53.69
SCL	Dev (Insurance)	**65.16**	**56.68**
Cross Entropy	Test1 (Banking)	67.67	52.16
SCL	Test1 (Banking)	**71.02**	**52.35**
Cross Entropy	Test2 (Finance)	64.09	63.07
SCL	Test2 (Finance)	**69.64**	**65.14**
Same Domain with Fine-tuning Dataset			
Cross Entropy	SGD (Tourism)	64.11	**70.31**
SCL	SGD (Tourism)	**65.32**	68.36

Table 7: The NMI and accuracy result on DSTC11 development, test, and SGD dataset according to the loss function.

7 Conclusion

In this paper, we describe our solution for the DSTC11 intent induction competition. We leveraged the SBERT model to embed sentences and fine-tuned the model using dependency parsing results. Additionally, we used supervised contrastive loss during fine-tuning to make the model robust in multiple domains. During the analysis, both dependency parsing and SCL helped to make the intent induction model more domain robust. Furthermore, our intent label generation with hypernym methods allows us to explain the clustering results. According to the results, our approach achieved 3rd place in terms of the precision score and demonstrated better NMI and accuracy compared to the baseline model.

Limitations

Our contribution has two limitations. First, although DORIC shows superior performance in the domain across the environment, the increase was insignificant in the same domain environment. Second, we thoroughly examine the embedding methods, but we adapt this method only to the K-means clustering. In the future, we plan to devise a progressed clustering method that fits our embedding method.

Acknowledgements

This work was partly supported by Institute of Information & communications Technology Planning & Evaluation (IITP) grant funded by the Korea government(MSIT) (No.2019-0-01906, Artificial Intelligence Graduate School Program(POSTECH)) and ITRC(Information Technology Research Center) support program(IITP-2023-2020-0-01789).

References

Ajay Chatterjee and Shubhashis Sengupta. 2020. Intent mining from past conversations for conversational agent. *arXiv preprint arXiv:2005.11014*.

Ting Chen, Simon Kornblith, Mohammad Norouzi, and Geoffrey Hinton. 2020. A simple framework for contrastive learning of visual representations. In *International conference on machine learning*, pages 1597–1607. PMLR.

Alice Coucke, Alaa Saade, Adrien Ball, Théodore Bluche, Alexandre Caulier, David Leroy, Clément Doumouro, Thibault Gisselbrecht, Francesco Caltagirone, Thibaut Lavril, et al. 2018. Snips voice platform: an embedded spoken language understanding system for private-by-design voice interfaces. *arXiv preprint arXiv:1805.10190*.

Mihail Eric, Rahul Goel, Shachi Paul, Adarsh Kumar, Abhishek Sethi, Peter Ku, Anuj Kumar Goyal, Sanchit Agarwal, Shuyang Gao, and Dilek Hakkani-Tur. 2019. Multiwoz 2.1: A consolidated multi-domain dialogue dataset with state corrections and state tracking baselines. *arXiv preprint arXiv:1907.01669*.

Chih-Wen Goo, Guang Gao, Yun-Kai Hsu, Chih-Li Huo, Tsung-Chieh Chen, Keng-Wei Hsu, and Yun-Nung Chen. 2018. Slot-gated modeling for joint slot filling and intent prediction. In *Proceedings of the 2018 Conference of the North American Chapter of the Association for Computational Linguistics: Human Language Technologies, Volume 2 (Short Papers)*, pages 753–757.

Beliz Gunel, Jingfei Du, Alexis Conneau, and Ves Stoyanov. 2020. Supervised contrastive learning for pre-trained language model fine-tuning. *arXiv preprint arXiv:2011.01403*.

Donghoon Ham, Jeong-Gwan Lee, Youngsoo Jang, and Kee-Eung Kim. 2020. End-to-end neural pipeline for goal-oriented dialogue systems using gpt-2. In *Proceedings of the 58th Annual Meeting of the Association for Computational Linguistics*, pages 583–592.

Prannay Khosla, Piotr Teterwak, Chen Wang, Aaron Sarna, Yonglong Tian, Phillip Isola, Aaron Maschinot, Ce Liu, and Dilip Krishnan. 2020. Supervised contrastive learning. *Advances in Neural Information Processing Systems*, 33:18661–18673.

Young-Bum Kim, Sungjin Lee, and Karl Stratos. 2017. Onenet: Joint domain, intent, slot prediction for spoken language understanding. In *2017 IEEE Automatic Speech Recognition and Understanding Workshop (ASRU)*, pages 547–553. IEEE.

Harold W Kuhn. 1955. The hungarian method for the assignment problem. *Naval research logistics quarterly*, 2(1-2):83–97.

Jihyun Lee and Gary Geunbae Lee. 2022. Sf-dst: Few-shot self-feeding reading comprehension dialogue state tracking with auxiliary task. *arXiv preprint arXiv:2209.07742*.

Ting-En Lin and Hua Xu. 2019. Deep unknown intent detection with margin loss. *arXiv preprint arXiv:1906.00434*.

Zhaojiang Lin, Andrea Madotto, Genta Indra Winata, and Pascale Fung. 2020. Mintl: Minimalist transfer learning for task-oriented dialogue systems. *arXiv preprint arXiv:2009.12005*.

Hao Liu and Pieter Abbeel. 2020. Hybrid discriminative-generative training via contrastive learning. *arXiv preprint arXiv:2007.09070*.

Pengfei Liu, Youzhang Ning, King Keung Wu, Kun Li, and Helen Meng. 2021. Open intent discovery through unsupervised semantic clustering and dependency parsing. *arXiv preprint arXiv:2104.12114*.

Grégoire Mesnil, Yann Dauphin, Kaisheng Yao, Yoshua Bengio, Li Deng, Dilek Hakkani-Tur, Xiaodong He, Larry Heck, Gokhan Tur, Dong Yu, et al. 2014. Using recurrent neural networks for slot filling in spoken language understanding. *IEEE/ACM Transactions on Audio, Speech, and Language Processing*, 23(3):530–539.

George A Miller. 1995. Wordnet: a lexical database for english. *Communications of the ACM*, 38(11):39–41.

Hugh Perkins and Yi Yang. 2019. Dialog intent induction with deep multi-view clustering. *arXiv preprint arXiv:1908.11487*.

Patti Price. 1990. Evaluation of spoken language systems: The atis domain. In *Speech and Natural Language: Proceedings of a Workshop Held at Hidden Valley, Pennsylvania, June 24-27, 1990*.

Abhinav Rastogi, Xiaoxue Zang, Srinivas Sunkara, Raghav Gupta, and Pranav Khaitan. 2020. Schema-guided dialogue state tracking task at dstc8. *arXiv preprint arXiv:2002.01359*.

Nils Reimers and Iryna Gurevych. 2019. Sentence-bert: Sentence embeddings using siamese bert-networks. *arXiv preprint arXiv:1908.10084*.

Peter J Rousseeuw. 1987. Silhouettes: a graphical aid to the interpretation and validation of cluster analysis. *Journal of computational and applied mathematics*, 20:53–65.

Jinpeng Wang, Gao Cong, Xin Wayne Zhao, and Xiaoming Li. 2015. Mining user intents in twitter: A semi-supervised approach to inferring intent categories for tweets. In *Twenty-Ninth AAAI Conference on Artificial Intelligence*.

Thomas Wolf, Lysandre Debut, Victor Sanh, Julien Chaumond, Clement Delangue, Anthony Moi, Pierric Cistac, Tim Rault, Rémi Louf, Morgan Funtowicz, et al. 2019. Huggingface's transformers: State-of-the-art natural language processing. *arXiv preprint arXiv:1910.03771*.

Chien-Sheng Wu, Steven Hoi, Richard Socher, and Caiming Xiong. 2020. Tod-bert: Pre-trained natural language understanding for task-oriented dialogue. *arXiv preprint arXiv:2004.06871*.

Zhirong Wu, Yuanjun Xiong, Stella X Yu, and Dahua Lin. 2018. Unsupervised feature learning via non-parametric instance discrimination. In *Proceedings of the IEEE conference on computer vision and pattern recognition*, pages 3733–3742.

Juan Xu, Qi Zhang, and Xuanjing Huang. 2013. Understanding the semantic intent of domain-specific natural language query. In *Proceeding of International Joint Conference on Natural Language Processing*, pages 552–560.

Yunyi Yang, Yunhao Li, and Xiaojun Quan. 2021. Ubar: Towards fully end-to-end task-oriented dialog system with gpt-2. In *Proceedings of the AAAI Conference on Artificial Intelligence*, volume 35, pages 14230–14238.

Xiaoxue Zang, Abhinav Rastogi, Srinivas Sunkara, Raghav Gupta, Jianguo Zhang, and Jindong Chen. 2020. Multiwoz 2.2: A dialogue dataset with additional annotation corrections and state tracking baselines. *arXiv preprint arXiv:2007.12720*.

Ming Zhong, Pengfei Liu, Yiran Chen, Danqing Wang, Xipeng Qiu, and Xuanjing Huang. 2020. Extractive summarization as text matching. *arXiv preprint arXiv:2004.08795*.

A Appendix

A.1 Generated cluster label name in detail.

Cluster	TOP 3 Verb-Object Pairs	Example	Ground-truth
0	('create-account', 13), ('make-account', 5), ('open-account', 3)	~create an account for my new renter policy.	CreateAccount
1	('cancel-billing', 6), ('stop-payment', 3), ('cancel-payment', 2)	~to cancel the automatic billing of my account ~	CancelAutomaticBilling
2†	('add-child', 10), ('add-son', 5), ('add-male_offspring', 5)	Oh good, help me add my son.	AddDependent
3	('report-accident', 10), ('file-claim', 1), ('start-process', 1)	Hey yeah, I have to call and report an accident.	ReportAutomobileAccident
4	('change-address', 31), ('update-address', 9), ('update-information', 2)	Hi, I'd like to change my address to a new one ~	ChangeAddress
5†	('get-quote', 10), ('get-punctuation', 10), ('get-interruption', 10)	~to get a quote from you guys.	GetQuote
6	('change-plan', 9), ('upgrade-plan', 1), ('get-quote', 1)	Eee yeah I think I want to change my plan	ChangePlan
7	('file-claim', 20), ('report-claim', 3), ('make-claim', 2)	I'd like to file a property claim.	FileClaim
8	('pay-bill', 17), ('get-bill', 2), ('take-care', 2)	Well, I'm calling to pay my bill.	PayBill
9	('check-balance', 4), ('pay-bill', 2), ('confirm-balance', 2)	Yes I need to check the balance ~	CheckAccountBalance
10	('change-question', 10), ('remember-question', 2), ('keep-stuff', 1)	~to change my security question and answer.	ChangeSecurityQuestion
11	('cancel-plan', 24), ('cancel-policy', 8), ('cancel-insurance', 6)	~I need to cancel my plan.	CancelPlan

Table 8: Generated intent cluster label, example, and ground truth on dev (insurance) dataset. Cluster name with †means using hypernym.

Cluster	TOP 3 Verb-Object Pairs	Example	Ground-truth
0	('dispute-transaction', 17), ('have-transaction', 3), ('dispute-charge', 2)	almost. I need to dispute this transaction I found for Piggly Wiggly.	DisputeCharge
1	('open-account', 56), ('set-banking', 2), ('set-account', 2)	~ so I would need to open a checking account then, right?	OpenBankingAccount
2	('update-address', 19), ('change-address', 7), ('do-address', 1)	I'd like to update my address I believe when ~	UpdateStreetAddress
3†	('transfer-money', 23), ('transfer-medium_of_exchange', 23), ('transfer-standard', 18)	And transfer the money from that to my checking.	InternalFundsTransfer
4	('check-balance', 68), ('get-balance', 8), ('give-balance', 7)	yes I need to check the my account balance ~	CheckAccountBalance
5†	('make-transfer', 23), ('make-movement', 23), ('make-change', 23)	Yeah, I needed to make a wire transfer ~	ExternalWireTransfer
6	('find-branch', 19), ('locate-branch', 5), ('help-branch', 4)	Yes. I need help with the with finding the nearest branch to my location.	FindBranch

Table 9: Generated intent cluster label, example, and ground truth on test1 (banking) dataset. Cluster name with †means using hypernym.

Cluster	TOP 3 Verb-Object Pairs	Example	Ground-truth
0	('check-balance', 18), ('check-account', 4), ('check-checking', 2)	~ I am calling to check my account balance.	CheckAccountBalance
1†	('update-number', 13), ('update-amount', 13), ('update-assets', 13)	~ and next update my phone number for my business~	UpdatePhoneNumber
2	('check-balance', 16), ('get-balance', 6), ('know-balance', 3)	I need to check the balance on my credit card please	CheckAccountBalance
3	('update-address', 17), ('change-address', 6), ('change-piece', 1)	yeah I need to update my street address on ~	UpdateStreetAddress
4†	('open-account', 11), ('open-record', 11), ('open-evidence', 11)	~ I was thinking about opening another account for ~	OpenAccount
5	('add-user', 10), ('have-access', 2), ('bring-people', 1)	Yeah I need to add some additional users to my account	AddUserToAccount
6†	('make-transfer', 13), ('make-movement', 13), ('make-change', 13)	Hi Jerry. I need to make a wire transfer man.	MakeTransfer

Table 10: Generated intent cluster label, example, and ground truth on test2 (finance) dataset. Cluster name with †means using hypernym.

A Two-Stage Progressive Intent Clustering for Task-Oriented Dialogue

Bingzhu Du and **Nan Su** and **Yuchi Zhang** and **Yongliang Wang**
Ant Group, Beijing, China

Abstract

Natural Language Understanding (NLU) is one of the most critical components of task-oriented dialogue, and it is often considered as an intent classification task. To achieve outstanding intent identification performance, system designers often need to hire a large number of domain experts to label the data, which is inefficient and costly. To address this problem, researchers' attention has gradually shifted to automatic intent clustering methods, which employ low-resource unsupervised approaches to solve classification problems. The classical framework for clustering is deep clustering, which uses deep neural networks (DNNs) to jointly optimize non-clustering loss and clustering loss. However, for new conversational domains or services, utterances required to assign intents are scarce and the performance of DNNs is often dependent on large amounts of data. In addition, although re-clustering with k-means algorithm after training the network usually leads to better results, k-means methods often suffer from poor stability. To address these problems, we propose an effective two-stage progressive approach to refine the clustering. Firstly, we pre-train the network with contrastive loss using all conversations data and then optimize the clustering loss and contrastive loss simultaneously. Secondly, we propose adaptive progressive k-means to alleviate the randomness of vanilla k-means, achieving better performance and smaller deviation. Our method ranks second in DSTC11 Track2 Task 1, a benchmark for intent clustering of task-oriented dialogue, demonstrating the superiority and effectiveness of our method.

1 Introduction

Task-oriented dialogue technique is of great popularity and is widely adopted in various applications, such as Microsoft's XiaoIce (Zhou et al., 2020), Google Assistant etc. Natural Language Understanding (NLU) is one of the most crucial components of task-oriented dialogue, and it is often considered as an intent classification task. Supervised deep networks are the most widely used methods for intent classification due to their high performance, such as classification head based on pre-trained language models. However, such kind of methods require a large amount of labeled data that is collected through painstaking analysis of conversation transcripts by domain experts. This is not feasible for many commercial operations, especially in emerging domains or services.

Therefore, researchers have proposed low-resource unsupervised intent clustering methods to address this problem, as described in Table 1. An intent clustering procedure assigns an intent label to each dialogue turn labeled with "informIntent" dialogue act based on the conversation between the customer and the agent. Such kind of unsupervised approach has tackled the above mentioned low resource dilemma for task-oriented dialogue systems. The most commonly used clustering method is k-means (Macqueen, 1967; Lloyd, 1982) due to its simplicity and efficiency. However, its clustering performance depends on data representation, which is often ineffective for high-dimensional data. To alleviate this problem, Principal Component Analysis (PCA) and Non-negative Matrix Factorization (NMF) were proposed. They are non-parametric linear transformations and followed by clustering algorithms sequentially. Now there is more work focusing on nonlinear dimensionality reduction and co-optimization of clustering objectives using DNNs, called deep clustering. Two surveys provide detailed descriptions of this approach. Min et al. (2018) gives a review from the perspective of network structure. Aljalbout et al. (2018) presents a systematic taxonomy of clustering methods using DNNs.

Xie et al. (2016) proposed Deep Embedded Clustering (DEC), a method for the first time combining DNN with clustering, which uses deep neural networks to iteratively optimize sentence represen-

Proceedings of The Eleventh Dialog System Technology Challenge, pages 48–56
September 11, 2023 ©2023 Association for Computational Linguistics

Speaker Role	Utterances	Dialog Acts	Gold Intent
Agent	How can I help you today?		
Customer	**I want to pay my auto insurance bill.**	InformIntent	Intent1
Agent	I will need your account number.		
Customer	It's two three one five six four eight seven nine.		
Agent	Okay. Thank you.		
Customer	**So what is my payment?**	InformIntent	Intent2
Agent	Okay. I'm showing that no payment is due until April.		

Table 1: Intent Clustering. The utterance written in bold is target utterance required to assign intents and its proportion is relatively small from the conversations.

tation and cluster assignment. Hadifar et al. (2019) applied DEC approach with sentence embedded by Smooth Inverse Frequency (SIF) to perform short text clustering following a multi-stage approach. To facilitate better data separation, Supporting Clustering with Contrastive Learning (SCCL) (Zhang et al., 2021) is the first method to introduce contrastive learning into clustering by jointly optimizing contrastive loss and clustering loss.

However, DNNs usually rely on large amounts of data to update model parameters or proper initialization to speed up convergence. In addition, the acquisition of intent utterances is limited and difficult, especially in emerging dialogue domains or services, so we improve the clustering performance from the perspective of model initialization. Meanwhile, in order to get better cluster assignments, re-run clustering using k-means is generally performed after training the network. It is known that K-means suffer from poor stability due to the way of obtaining initial centroids. To solve these problems, we propose an effective two-stage progressive intent clustering from conversations. Our main contributions are as follows:

- Pre-training with contrastive learning. To obtain a proper parameter initialization, we pretrain the network before jointly learning utterance representations and clustering. Due to the lack of target utterances, contrastive learning is introduced and trained with all conversations. The introduction of pre-training increases the robustness of the model and also outputs better initial parameters for subsequent joint training.

- Progressive k-means. To alleviate the stability of vanilla k-means, we propose progressive k-means, an improved cluster algorithm that is adaptive to deep clustering. As the deep representation is learned, the distance loss is gradually minimized until convergence. The cluster centroids are no longer chosen randomly but are replaced by high-confidence cluster centers.

- Our approach ranks second in ACC metrics and first in F1 metrics on the DSTC11 Track2 task1, a benchmark for intent clustering from conversations for task-oriented dialogue, demonsrating the effectiveness and superiority on two different domain datasets.

2 Proposed Approach

To refine the performance of automatic intent clustering for task-oriented dialogues, we propose a two-stage progressive approach. Our specific method pipeline is shown in Figure 1.

- Estimating number of intent. According to the task description, the number of clusters is unknown, so we need to automatically estimate the number of clusters. We consider it as a parameter and explore the search space based on a predefined objective function to decide the optimal value. The utterance representation is extracted by all-mpnet-base-v2, which is the best model for learning sentence representations. The specific parameter estimation methods are described in 3.2.

- Stage one. Due to the shortage of target utterances, we used the entire conversations to pretrain the network with the help of contrastive learning (see 2.1). During training, we use progressive K-means (see 2.4) to assign intent labels to the target utterance. Besides, the progressive k-means outputs a high-confidence cluster centers named as High-Score-Center,

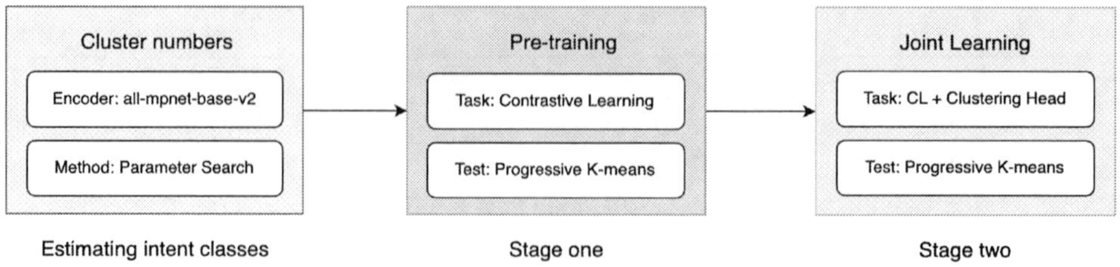

Figure 1: Task Pipeline

which is used as the initial center of clustering head in the second stage. Pre-training can provides better initial parameters for subsequent joint learning and thus converge to a better position.

- Stage two. During the second stage of the approach, we jointly optimize contrastive loss and clustering loss on target utterances, which can iteratively refine the cluster assignments alongside improving utterance representations (see 2.2; 2.3). The parameters of linear layer of clustering head are initialized by High-Score-Center which is obtained in the first stage. In order to get better cluster assignments, progressive k-means is performed on target utterances during the training process.

2.1 Contrastive Learning

Learning universal sentence embedding is a significant problem in natural language processing (Kiros et al., 2015; Hill et al., 2016; Conneau et al., 2017; Logeswaran and Lee, 2018). Much recent research has shown that contrastive learning can be extremely effective to advance the sentence embeddings (Henderson et al., 2020; Zhang et al., 2020). Contrastive learning aims to learn effective representation by pulling semantically close neighbors together and pushing apart non-neighbors (Hadsell et al., 2006). It refines representation learning by using a contrastive prediction task. The training data consists of positive pairs and negative pairs constructed from unlabeled or labeled datasets.

We follow the contrastive learning framework proposed in SimCLR by Chen et al. (2020), using the normalized temperature-scaled cross-entropy loss as the training loss which is also called InfoNCE in the previous literature (Hjelm et al., 2019). The specific contrastive learning method we adopt is SimCSE (Gao et al., 2021), which uses dropout coupled with pre-trained language models as the minimal data augmentation strategy compared with previous explicit data augmentation strategies. This simple strategy proved to be superior to many traditional data augmentation techniques in natural language processing such as word deletion, reordering and substitution and back translation, etc. Given a minibatch of N examples $D = \{x_i\}_{i=1}^N$. Let h_i and h_i^+ denote the representation of example x_i, which is the output obtained by feeding x_i into the encoder twice by applying different dropout masks z_i and z_i^+, constituting a positive pair. The negative pair is derived from two different examples within the minibatch D. The contrastive learning objective x_i is as follows,

$$l_i^{CL} = -log(\frac{e^{sim(h_i,h_i^+)/\tau}}{\sum_{j=1}^{N} e^{sim(h_i,h_j^+)/\tau}}) \quad (1)$$

$$h_i = f_\theta(x_i, z_i), h_i^+ = f_\theta(x_i, z_i^+) \quad (2)$$

$f_\theta(.)$ denotes the encoder, τ denotes the temperature parameter which we set as 0.5, $sim(h_1, h_2)$ is the cosine similarity $\frac{h_1^T h_2}{||h_1||.||h_2||}$.

The contrastive learning approach can also be replaced by EsimCSE (Wu et al., 2021), which refines the positive and negative construction method called Enhanced SimCSE. Since positive pairs are of the same length, EsimCSE breaks this length pattern by using word repetitions that do not destroy the meaning of the sentence. In addition, by introducing momentum contrast (He et al., 2020), more negative pairs can be leveraged to guide the model to achieve a better representation.

2.2 Clustering with KL divergence

DEC was proposed by Xie et al. (2016), which trains the auto-encoder by minimizing reconstruction loss and then fine-tunes the encoder network by optimizing KL-divergence with an auxiliary target distribution. Let e_i denote the representation of instance x_i, u_k, $k \in 1, ..., K$ denote the cluster centroid. Following Laurens and Hinton (2008), we use the Student's t-distribution to measure the similarity between embedded point e_i and centroid

k,

$$q_{ik} = \frac{(1 + ||e_i - u_k||^2/\alpha)^{-\frac{\alpha+1}{2}}}{\sum_{k'=1}^{K}(1 + ||e_i - u'_k||^2/\alpha)^{-\frac{\alpha+1}{2}}} \quad (3)$$

q_{ik} can be regarded as the probability of assigning x_i to the k cluster and then be used as a soft assignment of embeddings to cluster centers, α denotes the degree of freedom of the Student's t-distribution which we set as 1.

We use a linear layer to approximate the centroids of each cluster and optimize it iteratively by leveraging an auxiliary distribution. let p_{ik} denote the auxiliary probability which has stricter probabilities compared to the similarity score q_{ik},

$$p_{ik} = \frac{q_{ik}^2/f_k}{\sum_{k'=1}^{K} q_{ik}^2/f'_k} \quad (4)$$

Here $f_k = \sum_{i=1}^{N} q_{ik}, k = 1, ..., K$ can be interpreted as the soft cluster frequencies. By quadratic sharpening of the soft assignments q_{ik}, this target distribution can assign more weight to high-confidence instances and less weights to low-confidence instances. In addition, by using soft cluster frequencies for normalization, the bias caused by large clusters can be avoided.

Finally, we use KL divergence, which can measure the similarity between two probability distributions P and Q, as the training objective to achieve pushing the soft assignments to the target distribution. The specific loss is as follows,

$$l_i^C = KL[p_i||q_i] = \sum_{k=1}^{K} p_{ik} log \frac{p_{ik}}{q_{ik}} \quad (5)$$

Unlike SCCL, in which the parameters of the linear layer that fits the clustering centroids are initialized by the cluster centers generated by standard K-means in the hidden space h. We instead use the clustering centers computed from the high-scoring instances generated by the progressive k-means (detailed as 2.4) we iterated during pre-training.

2.3 Joint Learning

We adopt joint learning where simultaneous optimization of representation learning and clustering is performed. In the second stage of our method, we adopt joint learning. Its specific structure is shown in Figure 2. First, the encoder maps the input data to the representation space, followed by the clustering head and contrastive head modules described in detail above. Inspired by SimCSE, we pass the input data into the encoder twice with different dropout masks. The overall training objective is the weighted sum of the contrast loss and clustering loss as follows.

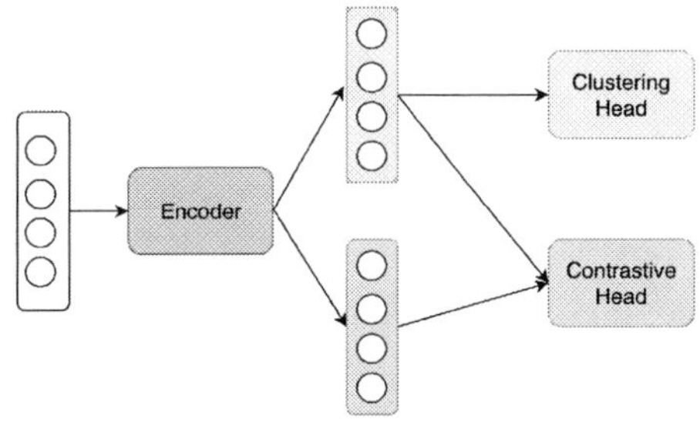

Figure 2: Joint Modeling Framework

$$L = L_{Instance-CL} + \eta L_{Cluster} \quad (6)$$

$$L_{Instance-CL} = \sum_{i=1}^{N} l_i^{CL}/N \quad (7)$$

$$L_{Cluster} = \sum_{i=1}^{N} l_i^{C}/N \quad (8)$$

$L_{Instance-CL}$ denotes the contrastive loss, the average loss over the minibatch. $L_{Cluster}$ denotes the average clustering loss on minibatch.

2.4 Progressive K-means

Deep clustering is a method that uses deep neural networks to jointly optimize representation learning and clustering. We propose progressive K-means, which is adaptive to this method, introducing an updated representation of instances for iteration in the outer layer of the original K-means iteration.

Except for the first starting centers, we use the improved cluster centroids generated by the last optimization. K-means is a well-known clustering algorithm that is widely used due to its simplicity and efficiency. However, the arbitrary nature of its initial centers leads to relatively large differences between cluster assignments, which ultimately does not guarantee the accuracy of the results. K-means++ (Arthur and Vassilvitskii, 2007) improves the method of selecting the starting center. The centroids are selected based on the weight of the data points, which are calculated based on their squared distance from the nearest center. Despite the significant improvements, the clustering

Dataset	Conversation		Cluster			
	Nums	Turns	Turns	Len	Labels	L/S
Insurance	948	66875	1205	17	22	10
Finance	2000	130274	1597	27	39	45
Banking	1000	59180	1503	23	29	63

Table 2: Dataset statistics. Nums: number of conversations; Len: average number of words in each cluster query; Labels: number of clusters; L/S: the ratio of the size of the largest cluster to that of the smallest cluster.

Method	ACC	Precision	Recall	F1	NMI	ARI	#cluster
Baseline	55.80	64.97	62.98	63.26	62.98	39.85	29
T23(best)	**69.79**	76.09	76.12	76.00	75.05	59.23	30.5
T07(ours)	69.59	72.01	81.64	**76.50**	73.48	60.13	27.5

Table 3: Overall performance. Average experimental results of different methods on two test datasets; ACC-ARI is metric introduced as 3.3; Cluster is the predicted number of clusters and the true cluster numbers is 34; The highest value for each metric is written in bold

performance is still inadequate. To solve this problem, we propose an improved K-means which is adaptive to successive iterative representations.

Algorithm 1 Progressive K-means

for $epoch = 1, Ts//Interval$ **do**
  Obtain the representation from the network
  if $epoch = 1$ **then**
    Kmeans++
    Save High-Score-Centers
  else
    Kmeans++ initialized with High-Score-Centers
    Update High-Score-Centers
  end if
end for

Algorithm 1 summarizes the progressive K-means, where Ts denotes the total training steps, $Interval$ denotes the frequency of cluster updates, K-means++ denotes the original complete iterative process, and High-Score-Centers are the average embedding of the first 20 high silhouette coefficient score instances in each cluster, which will be used as the initial centroids of subsequent iterations. This approach can be used in combination with deep clustering methods. Except for the first iteration, K-means++ uses the latest representation of the instance with better separation in each new iteration and uses High-Score-Centers as the initial centroid. Thus, it results in an asymptotic and stable cluster assignment that greatly mitigates the randomness and deviation of K-means.

3 Experiments and Results

3.1 Datasets

We evaluated the proposed method on one development dataset and two test datasets provided by the organizers of DSTC11 Track2. The performance on the test dataset validates the effectiveness of our method. The ablation studies performed on the development dataset demonstrate the properties of different parts of our method.

The three datasets mentioned above are from different domains, namely insurance, finance and banking. The dataset contains about 1K customer-supported spoken conversations with manual transcription and annotation. Both customers and agents are real people. Each conversation has an average of 70 turns. Detailed statistics are presented in Table 2.

3.2 Experimental Setup

We adopt all-mpnet-base-v2 (Song et al., 2020) in the Sentence Transformers Library (Reimers and Gurevych, 2019) as an encoder, which is a pre-trained language model that can learn state-of-the-art universal sentence representations. Same with Zhang et al. (2021), the clustering head is implemented by a linear layer with size $768 \times K$, where K denotes the number of clusters, and the contrastive head is implemented using MLP with an input hidden size of 768 and an output hidden size of 128. We use the Adam optimizer with batch size

Method	ACC	Precision	Recall	F1	NMI	ARI	#cluster
Baseline	51.85	69.25	53.98	60.67	65.71	33.61	46
(T23)Best	**68.13**	70.95	76.52	73.63	72.85	55.52	32
(T07)Ours	67.06	71.82	78.71	**75.11**	74.48	**55.77**	41

Table 4: Performance of Finance dataset; the gold cluster numbers is 39; The highest value for each metric is written in bold

Method	ACC	Precision	Recall	F1	NMI	ARI	#cluster
Baseline	59.75	60.68	71.99	65.85	60.26	46.10	12
(T05)Best	**75.25**	78.78	82.50	**80.60**	**78.45**	**70.69**	26
(T07)Ours	72.12	72.19	84.56	77.89	72.47	64.50	14

Table 5: Performance of Banking dataset; the gold cluster numbers is 29; The highest value for each metric is written in bold

of 400 and set the maximum sentence length to 64, 100, and 100 for insurance, finance, and banking, respectively. We use a constant learning rate of 1e-6 to optimize the encoder while setting a learning rate of 1e-4 to optimize the rest of our model.

Hyperparameter Optimization (Hyperopt) (Bergstra et al., 2013) is used to search for the optimal number of clusters between 5 and 50. In this paper, we use Tree of Parzen Estimators (TPE) to search for the best parameters in a specified search space based on a predefined objective function. Specifically, we perform k-means with different numbers of clusters and then output the number with the highest silhouette coefficient score. Considering that the choice of initial centroids has a considerable impact on the clustering performance when applying the k-means algorithm, we conducted multiple search experiments. First we performed 30 Hypteropt search experiments with different seeds to obtain 30 optimal clustering numbers, and then we chose the mode of data points greater than the 60th percentile as the final clustering number. Outliers are considered here, and not all data points are used.

In the ablation study, K-means++ is executed after training the network to obtain clustering results. Similar to Xie et al. (2016), we run K-means++ with 20 restarts and select the best centroids. The experimental results are the average of 7 trials, and the standard deviation is also shown as Hadifar et al. (2019).

We measure the performance of our method on test datasets using fusion results of 7 trials. We fuse the results by voting. If the number of votes is greater than half, the result is used, otherwise the result of the model with the largest sample size is used. In this way, the more authoritative the model, the more likely it is to be chosen.

3.3 Experiment results

We evaluate the clustering performance from two perspectives and six standard metrics. Clustering accuracy (ACC), Adjusted Rand Index (ARI) and Normalized Mutual Information (NMI) focus more on model performance itself (Huang et al., 2014; Wang et al., 2017) while Precision, Recall and F1 forcus more on performance of practical application (Hadifar et al., 2019). They are used together to provide a comprehensive measure of overall system performance. ACC is used as the primary metric for evaluating system submission rankings and is calculated using the following logic:

$$ACC = \frac{\sum_{i=1}^{N} \delta(map(c_i) = y_i)}{N} \quad (9)$$

$\delta(.)$ is an indicator function, c_i is the clustering label for x_i, $map(.)$ is a mapping between the predicted labels and ground-truth labels using the Hungarian algorithm (Kuhn, 1955) for 1:1 assignment. It is a mapping between predicted labels and ground truth labels using the Hungarian algorithm for 1:1 assignment. For Precision, Recall and F1, the predicted categories will be assigned to the most frequent target categories, allowing a many-to-one assignment to ensure maximum sample matching.

The organizers ranked the submitted systems using the average ACC metric calculated on the

Datase	ACC	Precision	Recall	F1	NMI	ARI
SCCL	56.57±2.38	65.37±1.68	61.67±1.97	63.46±1.66	64.33±1.33	41.71±1.76
+Pretraining	62.16±1.68	67.94±1.58	75.46±0.92	71.49±0.78	69.65±0.65	46.90±2.01
+Refined centers	65.15±1.78	71.22±1.82	74.70±0.19	72.90±0.87	70.86±0.59	51.12±1.26
Our Method	**66.72±0.59**	**72.96±0.41**	**74.20±0.51**	**73.57±0.42**	**71.30±0.23**	**51.89±0.70**

Table 6: Ablation results on Insurance dataset. Performance was assessed by the mean results and standard deviation of 7 trials

financial and banking datasets. We first compare our approach with the baseline and the best model, and the results are presented in Table 3. Obviously, our model outperforms the baseline model by a large margin.

- **Baseline**. It adopts a traditional sequential modeling approach where feature representations are first extracted before using K-means. Clustering is performed directly in the feature space generated by the pre-trained language model all-mpnet-base-v2 in the sentence transformation library. Hyperopt is used to estimate the number of clusters.

- **Submission System**. T23 is the model ranking first and our method is denoted as T07.

As shown in Table 3, our system ranks second with the ACC (0.2% lower than the first place) and first with the F1 (0.5% higher than T23), indicating that our model is more competitive in the actual dialogue system development. In terms of other metrics, it has good and bad. In addition, our predicted number of clusters is 27.5, which differs from the ground truth figure by 6.5 (ground truth is 34).

To further analyze the performance of our system, we report the performance on the Finance and Banking datasets, respectively, as shown in Table 4 and Table 5. On the Finance dataset, our system ranks second in terms of ACC (1.07% lower than first) and outperforms T23 on the other five metrics. Notably, our model ranks first in the F1 and ARI metrics, outperforming T23 by 1.48% and 0.25%, respectively. The target cluster count is 39, while our prediction is 41. On the banking dataset, our system is 3.13% lower than the best model on the acc metric, ranking sixth. The performance is not satisfactory compared to the financial dataset, which may be caused by the bias brought by the estimated clusters counts. The ground truth label is 29 and our predicted value is 14, resulting in a difference of 15 data points.

Furthermore, T23 has the best result in the financial dataset but ranks 8th in the banking dataset, while T05 has the best result in the banking dataset but ranks 6th in the financial dataset. It demonstrates that none of these models guarantee accuracy and that there is much room for improvement, particularly in terms of stability. In addition, it also reflects that this task is difficult and the performance of clustering can be affected by a variety of factors. The two approaches we propose: improving the clustering algorithm and improving the initialization, are stable and effective in various domains. In the future, we will concentrate on doing more work on the estimation of the number of clusters.

3.4 Ablation Study

In order to improve the effectiveness of the automatic intent clustering method in dialogues, we refined the SCCL method from different perspectives. To investigate the effectiveness of each part of our proposed method, we performed an ablation study on the insurance dataset, by adding each module to SCCL in turn. Details are shown in Table 6. **+Pretraining:** A pre-training module with contrastive loss is added to the SCCL approach, which is trained using the entire conversations. It shows an improvement of almost 6% in the Acc metric and significant improvements in other metrics. In addition, the bias of the model is reduced due to better learned representations. **+Refined centers:** The parameters in the clustering head are initialized with the High-Score-Centers generated by the progressive k-means in pre-training. The results show an improvement of nearly 3%, demonstrating the great impact of initialization and the effectiveness of our proposed progressive k-means. **Our Method:** In addition to the above modifications, we performed progressive k-means after training the network to replace the previous k-means method. The performance is also slightly improved by 1.6% and the bias is reduced to within 1%.

4 Conclusion

In this paper, to refine the performance of automatic intent clustering for task-oriented dialogue, we propose a two-stage progressive approach. To alleviate the lack of target utterance, we introduce pre-training before joint learning to increase the robustness of the model. In addition, we propose progressive K-means, an enhanced K-means method, which is compatible with deep clustering. Also, we use the High-Score-Center obtained by performing progressive K-means in the first stage to initialize the parameters of the clustering head in the second stage. Ultimately, our model results in better performance and lower deviation. Our proposed system proved its effectiveness by ranking second in ACC metrics and first in F1 metrics in DSTC11 Track2 Task 1. In addition, we conducted an ablation study to verify the performance of each component.

References

E. Aljalbout, V. Golkov, Y. Siddiqui, M. Strobel, and D. Cremers. 2018. Clustering with deep learning: Taxonomy and new methods.

D. Arthur and S. Vassilvitskii. 2007. K-means++: The advantages of careful seeding. In *Proceedings of the Eighteenth Annual ACM-SIAM Symposium on Discrete Algorithms, SODA 2007, New Orleans, Louisiana, USA, January 7-9, 2007.*

James Bergstra, Daniel Yamins, and David D. Cox. 2013. Making a science of model search: Hyperparameter optimization in hundreds of dimensions for vision architectures. In *Proceedings of the 30th International Conference on Machine Learning, ICML 2013, Atlanta, GA, USA, 16-21 June 2013*, volume 28 of *JMLR Workshop and Conference Proceedings*, pages 115–123. JMLR.org.

Ting Chen, Simon Kornblith, Mohammad Norouzi, and Geoffrey E. Hinton. 2020. A simple framework for contrastive learning of visual representations. In *Proceedings of the 37th International Conference on Machine Learning, ICML 2020, 13-18 July 2020, Virtual Event*, volume 119 of *Proceedings of Machine Learning Research*, pages 1597–1607. PMLR.

Alexis Conneau, Douwe Kiela, Holger Schwenk, Loïc Barrault, and Antoine Bordes. 2017. Supervised learning of universal sentence representations from natural language inference data. In *Proceedings of the 2017 Conference on Empirical Methods in Natural Language Processing*, pages 670–680, Copenhagen, Denmark. Association for Computational Linguistics.

Tianyu Gao, Xingcheng Yao, and Danqi Chen. 2021. SimCSE: Simple contrastive learning of sentence embeddings. In *Empirical Methods in Natural Language Processing (EMNLP)*.

Amir Hadifar, Lucas Sterckx, Thomas Demeester, and Chris Develder. 2019. A self-training approach for short text clustering. In *Proceedings of the 4th Workshop on Representation Learning for NLP (RepL4NLP-2019)*, pages 194–199, Florence, Italy. Association for Computational Linguistics.

R. Hadsell, S. Chopra, and Y. LeCun. 2006. Dimensionality reduction by learning an invariant mapping. In *2006 IEEE Computer Society Conference on Computer Vision and Pattern Recognition (CVPR'06)*, volume 2, pages 1735–1742.

Kaiming He, Haoqi Fan, Yuxin Wu, Saining Xie, and Ross B. Girshick. 2020. Momentum contrast for unsupervised visual representation learning. In *2020 IEEE/CVF Conference on Computer Vision and Pattern Recognition, CVPR 2020, Seattle, WA, USA, June 13-19, 2020*, pages 9726–9735. IEEE.

Matthew Henderson, Iñigo Casanueva, Nikola Mrkšić, Pei-Hao Su, Tsung-Hsien Wen, and Ivan Vulić. 2020. ConveRT: Efficient and accurate conversational representations from transformers. In *Findings of the Association for Computational Linguistics: EMNLP 2020*, pages 2161–2174, Online. Association for Computational Linguistics.

Felix Hill, Kyunghyun Cho, and Anna Korhonen. 2016. Learning distributed representations of sentences from unlabelled data. In *Proceedings of the 2016 Conference of the North American Chapter of the Association for Computational Linguistics: Human Language Technologies*, pages 1367–1377, San Diego, California. Association for Computational Linguistics.

R. Devon Hjelm, Alex Fedorov, Samuel Lavoie-Marchildon, Karan Grewal, Philip Bachman, Adam Trischler, and Yoshua Bengio. 2019. Learning deep representations by mutual information estimation and maximization. In *7th International Conference on Learning Representations, ICLR 2019, New Orleans, LA, USA, May 6-9, 2019*. OpenReview.net.

Peihao Huang, Yan Huang, Wei Wang, and Liang Wang. 2014. Deep embedding network for clustering. In *2014 22nd International Conference on Pattern Recognition*, pages 1532–1537.

Ryan Kiros, Yukun Zhu, Ruslan Salakhutdinov, Richard S. Zemel, Raquel Urtasun, Antonio Torralba, and Sanja Fidler. 2015. Skip-thought vectors. In *Advances in Neural Information Processing Systems 28:*

Annual Conference on Neural Information Processing Systems 2015, December 7-12, 2015, Montreal, Quebec, Canada, pages 3294–3302.

H. W. Kuhn. 1955. The hungarian method for the assignment problem. *Naval Research Logistics*, 2(1):83–98.

Van Der Maaten Laurens and Geoffrey Hinton. 2008. Visualizing data using t-sne. *Journal of Machine Learning Research*, 9(2605):2579–2605.

S. P. Lloyd. 1982. Least square quantization in pcm. *IEEE Transactions on Information Theory*, 28.

Lajanugen Logeswaran and Honglak Lee. 2018. An efficient framework for learning sentence representations. In *6th International Conference on Learning Representations, ICLR 2018, Vancouver, BC, Canada, April 30 - May 3, 2018, Conference Track Proceedings*. OpenReview.net.

J. Macqueen. 1967. Some methods for classification and analysis of multivariate observations. *Proc. Symp. Math. Statist. and Probability, 5th*, 1.

Erxue Min, Xifeng Guo, Qiang Liu, Gen Zhang, Jianjing Cui, and Jun Long. 2018. A survey of clustering with deep learning: From the perspective of network architecture. *IEEE Access*, 6:39501–39514.

Nils Reimers and Iryna Gurevych. 2019. Sentence-BERT: Sentence embeddings using Siamese BERT-networks. In *Proceedings of the 2019 Conference on Empirical Methods in Natural Language Processing and the 9th International Joint Conference on Natural Language Processing (EMNLP-IJCNLP)*, pages 3982–3992, Hong Kong, China. Association for Computational Linguistics.

K. Song, X. Tan, T. Qin, J. Lu, and T. Y. Liu. 2020. Mpnet: Masked and permuted pre-training for language understanding.

Wang, Peng, Xu, Bo, Zheng, Suncong, Zhao, Jun, Jiaming, and Tian. 2017. Self-taught convolutional neural networks for short text clustering. *Neural Networks the Official Journal of the International Neural Network Society*.

Xing Wu, Chaochen Gao, Liangjun Zang, Jizhong Han, Zhongyuan Wang, and Songlin Hu. 2021. ESimCSE: Enhanced Sample Building Method for Contrastive Learning of Unsupervised Sentence Embedding. *arXiv e-prints*, page arXiv:2109.04380.

Junyuan Xie, Ross B. Girshick, and Ali Farhadi. 2016. Unsupervised deep embedding for clustering analysis. In *Proceedings of the 33nd International Conference on Machine Learning, ICML 2016, New York City, NY, USA, June 19-24, 2016*, volume 48 of *JMLR Workshop and Conference Proceedings*, pages 478–487. JMLR.org.

Dejiao Zhang, Feng Nan, Xiaokai Wei, Shang-Wen Li, Henghui Zhu, Kathleen McKeown, Ramesh Nallapati, Andrew O. Arnold, and Bing Xiang. 2021. Supporting clustering with contrastive learning. In *Proceedings of the 2021 Conference of the North American Chapter of the Association for Computational Linguistics: Human Language Technologies*, pages 5419–5430, Online. Association for Computational Linguistics.

Yan Zhang, Ruidan He, Zuozhu Liu, Kwan Hui Lim, and Lidong Bing. 2020. An unsupervised sentence embedding method by mutual information maximization. In *Proceedings of the 2020 Conference on Empirical Methods in Natural Language Processing (EMNLP)*, pages 1601–1610, Online. Association for Computational Linguistics.

Li Zhou, Jianfeng Gao, Di Li, and Heung-Yeung Shum. 2020. The design and implementation of XiaoIce, an empathetic social chatbot. *Computational Linguistics*, 46(1):53–93.

Analysis of Utterance Embeddings and Clustering Methods Related to Intent Induction for Task-Oriented Dialogue

Jeiyoon Park[1,3], Yoonna Jang[1], Chanhee Lee[2], Heuiseok Lim[1]
[1]Department of Computer Science and Engineering, Korea University
[2]Naver Corporation
[3]LLSOLLU
{k4ke, morelychee, limhseok}@korea.ac.kr, chanhee.lee@navercorp.com

Abstract

The focus of this work is to investigate unsupervised approaches to overcome quintessential challenges in designing task-oriented dialog schema: assigning intent labels to each dialog turn (*intent clustering*) and generating a set of intents based on the intent clustering methods (*intent induction*). We postulate there are two salient factors for automatic induction of intents: (1) clustering algorithm for intent labeling and (2) user utterance embedding space. We compare existing off-the-shelf clustering models and embeddings based on DSTC11 evaluation. Our extensive experiments demonstrate that the combined selection of utterance embedding and clustering method in the intent induction task should be carefully considered. We also present that pretrained MiniLM with Agglomerative clustering shows significant improvement in NMI, ARI, F1, accuracy and example coverage in intent induction tasks. The source codes are available at `https://github.com/Jeiyoon/dstc11-track2`.

1 Introduction

Why Intent Induction? We humans are generalists. During a conversation, we listen to the other person's utterance and naturally grasp which intent of the utterance is. With the skyrocketing demand for conversational AI, however, the more user utterances a dialogue system encounters, the more unknown intents it does. Predefining user intent is expensive and it is impossible to annotate all the user intents.

Since provided user utterances are unlabeled, intent induction (Haponchyk et al., 2018; Perkins and Yang, 2019; Chatterjee and Sengupta, 2020; Zeng et al., 2021; Zhang et al., 2022) focuses on discovering user intents from user utterances. However, previous studies did not conduct an in-depth analysis of the application of existing models to intent induction that might cause performance degradation problems (Zeng et al., 2021).

Agent: Hello, you are currently speaking with Rivetown Insurance customer service. My name is Julian, How may I be of service to you?

Customer: The services I have being receiving from your company has been encouraging and my intent is to increase or enroll for more plans with you.

Agent: Whoa, that is such an encouraging word coming from you. So, which of the plans do you wish to register for?

Customer: I would like to enroll for the life insurance policy.

dialog act: ['*InformIntent*'], intent: ['*EnrollInPlan*']

Agent: That won't be an issue, I can help you get registered right away.

Customer: Ok then, but first can I get my current policy number.

dialog act: ['*InformIntent*'], intent: ['*GetPolicyNumber*']

Agent: Of course, I can help you get that.

Figure 1: A sample segment of conversation transcript.

Dataset	Domain	#Intents	#Utterances
DSTC11_{dev}	*insurance*	22	66,875
DSTC11_{test}	*insurance*	22	913

Table 1: Statistics of development dataset.

Our Approach. Intuitively, for good intent induction, user utterances must be well represented in the embedding space, and good clustering algorithms must be employed to capture latent barycenters of user intent clusters to handle both predefined and unseen intents well.

In this paper, We postulate there are two salient factors for automatic induction of intents: (1) clustering algorithm for intent labeling (Cheung and Li, 2012; Hakkani-Tür et al., 2015; Padmasundari, 2018) and (2) user utterance embedding space (Wang et al., 2020; Song et al., 2020; Gao et al., 2021; Chuang et al., 2022; Nishikawa et al., 2022).

We analyze how the two key factors affect to user intent clustering and intent induction. Our extensive experiments with existing models demonstrate

Proceedings of The Eleventh Dialog System Technology Challenge, pages 57–66
September 11, 2023

that pretrained MiniLM with Agglomerative clustering shows significant improvement in NMI, ARI, F1, accuracy and example coverage.

2 Task 1: Intent Clustering

2.1 Task Description.

A set of conversation transcripts are given as Figure 1, intent clustering model aims to (i) generate intent labels and (ii) align each utterance annotated with dialog act (i.e., *"InformIntent"*).

Dataset. We conduct experiments on DSTC11 development dataset. It consists of 948 human-to-human conversation transcript with speaker role, utterance, dialog act, and intent. Testset is composed of 913 customer utterances and corresponding user intents. The dataset statistics are summarized in Table 1.

Metrics. We follow the same experimental metrics employed in the DSTC11 task proposal: Normalized mutual information (NMI), Adjusted rand index (ARI), Accuracy (ACC), Precision, Recall, F1 score, Intent example coverage, and the number of clusters (#K).

NMI is used for measuring dependency between two different distributions:

$$NMI(X,Y) = \frac{\mathbb{I}(X;Y)}{\min(\mathbb{H}(X), \mathbb{H}(Y))} \quad (1)$$

, where $X = [X_1, ..., X_r]$ denote clustered labels, $Y = [Y_1, ..., Y_s]$ are reference labels, $\mathbb{I}$ stands for mutual information, and $\mathbb{H}$ is entropy.

ARI is a measure for computing similarities between clustered results and reference labels:

$$ARI(X,Y) = \frac{\sum_{ij}\binom{n_{ij}}{2} - [AB]/\binom{n}{2}}{\frac{1}{2}[A+B] - [AB]/\binom{n}{2}} \quad (2)$$

, where $A = \sum_i \binom{a_i}{2}$, $B = \sum_j \binom{b_j}{2}$, $n_{ij} = |X_i \cap Y_j|$, a_i is the number of clustered label X_i and b_j is the number of reference label Y_j.

Both Precision and Recall measure many-to-one alignments from clustered labels to reference labels. F1 score is a harmonic mean between precision and recall. After performing a many-to-one alignment, Intent example coverage is determined as percent of examples whose reference has a corresponding predicted result.

2.2 Methods

Clustering Algorithm. Intent clustering focuses on assigning dialog intents to each dialog. K-means clustering (Lloyd, 1982), for example, regards a set of conversation transcript $\mathcal{T}_1, ..., \mathcal{T}_m$. Each transcript $\mathcal{T}$ consists of turn-level dialog acts, speaker's role, whether it is Agent or Customer, and dialog utterances $X_1, ..., X_n \in \mathbb{R}^p$. K-means minimizes the following equation in the Euclidean embedding space:

$$\min_{\beta_1,...\beta_K \in \mathbb{R}^d} \sum_{i=1}^{n} \min_{k\in[K]} \mu_{ik} ||X_i - \beta_k||_2^2 \quad (3)$$

, where $\{\beta_k\}_{k=1}^K$ denotes centroid of each intent cluster, $[K] = 1, 2, ..., K$, μ_{ik} is alignment factor. Equation 1 can be expressed as:

$$\min_{V_1,...V_K} \left\{ \sum_{k=1}^{K} \sum_{i\in V_k} \mu_{ik} ||X_i - \beta_k||_2^2 : \bigsqcup_{k=1}^{K} V_k = [n] \right\} \quad (4)$$

, where $\sqcup$ stands for disjoint union, and $\{V_k\}_{k=1}^K$ is intent cluster, determined by Voronoi diagram in utterance embedding space.

Given initial intent centroids $\{\beta_k^1\}_{k=1}^K$, we assign each utterance embedding to its nearest centroid (a.k.a., Expectation step):

$$V_k^t = \{ i \in [n] : ||X_i - \beta_k||_2^2 \leq ||X_i - \beta_j||_2^2, \} \quad (5)$$

, where $\forall j \in [K]$. Then, we update the location of centroids (a.k.a., Maximization step):

$$\beta_k^{t+1} = \frac{1}{|V_k^t|} \sum_{i\in V_k^t} X_i \quad (6)$$

We iterate equation 5 and equation 6 alternatively until equation 4 converges.

In this paper, we conduct experiments with K-means (Lloyd, 1982), BIRCH (Zhang et al., 1996), Agglomerative clustering (Steinbach et al., 2000), Spectral clustering (Yu and Shi, 2003), Bisecting K-means (Di and Gou, 2018), and Variational optimal transportation (VOT) (Mi et al., 2018).

Embeddings. User utterance should be represented in the embedding space which is able to capture universal and rich semantic information. MiniLM (Wang et al., 2020) is an effective task-agnostic distillation to compress transformer-based language models. MPNet (Song et al., 2020) proposes permuted language model for dependency among predicted tokens and makes the model to see a full sentence and auxiliary position information. SimCSE (Gao et al., 2021) leverages a simple contrastive learning framework. DiffCSE (Chuang

Clustering Method	K-means Clustering							
Metric	NMI	ARI	ACC	Precision	Recall	F1	Example Coverage	#K
$\text{EASE}^{m}_{ROBERTA}$	33.4	14.2	28.0	28.0	**69.0**	39.9	43.9	5
EASE_{BERT}	36.1	18.1	35.3	36.8	58.9	45.3	53.5	8
EASE^{m}_{BERT}	38.4	10.9	23.6	42.7	24.2	30.9	87.6	44
$\text{EASE}_{ROBERTA}$	45.8	25.4	40.0	43.7	60.7	50.9	65.6	12
$\text{DiffCSE}^{trans}_{BERT}$	43.8	15.5	29.4	49.5	30.6	37.8	90.1	40
$\text{DiffCSE}^{sts}_{BERT}$	46.6	16.9	29.9	50.4	30.8	38.2	89.9	43
$\text{DiffCSE}^{sts}_{ROBERTA}$	53.9	29.0	45.1	57.2	46.8	51.5	91.1	30
$\text{DiffCSE}^{trans}_{ROBERTA}$	55.0	23.1	35.7	60.6	35.7	44.9	96.7	50
SimCSE^{u}_{BERT}	31.7	13.3	27.9	27.9	<u>65.0</u>	39.0	43.9	5
$\text{SimCSE}^{u}_{BERT+}$	47.0	25.7	38.4	46.9	46.9	46.9	76.8	19
$\text{SimCSE}^{u}_{ROBERTA}$	51.2	29.0	44.4	49.7	61.6	55.0	70.5	14
SimCSE_{BERT+}	53.0	27.8	39.8	55.0	42.2	47.8	91.0	31
SimCSE_{BERT}	53.1	24.4	39.0	60.5	39.5	47.8	96.3	44
$\text{SimCSE}^{u}_{ROBERTA+}$	53.2	25.9	42.2	56.8	43.8	49.5	91.7	32
$\text{SimCSE}_{ROBERTA}$	56.6	28.8	42.7	60.8	43.3	50.6	91.3	36
$\text{SimCSE}_{ROBERTA+}$	56.8	28.9	41.3	62.5	41.6	49.9	98.4	42
Glove^{avg}	30.5	7.0	20.6	34.6	22.2	27.0	92.2	50
MPNet	59.3	32.3	46.1	66.0	47.1	54.9	96.5	42
MiniLM_{L6}	59.3	35.7	52.6	62.2	54.9	58.4	92.4	28
$\text{MiniLM}_{MULTIQA}$	<u>61.7</u>	<u>38.2</u>	**55.1**	<u>66.6</u>	55.4	<u>60.5</u>	<u>98.8</u>	30
MiniLM_{L12}	**63.1**	**38.9**	<u>54.9</u>	**68.0**	54.9	**60.8**	**100.0**	31

Table 2: Clustering results on DSTC11 dataset. We employ K-means clustering algorithm to all utterance embeddings. m denotes multilingual model, u stands for unsupervised model, and $+$ means large model.

Method	DiffCSE	SimCSE	MPNet	MiniLM
# Param	250M	125M	110M	21.3M

Table 3: The number of parameters. Both DiffCSE and SimCSE denote $\text{RoBERTa}_{\text{base}}$ model.

et al., 2022) learns the difference between the original sentence and a stochastically masked sentence. EASE (Nishikawa et al., 2022) exploits sentence embedding via contrastive learning between the original sentence and its related entities.

2.3 Result Analysis

To analyze the effects of both embedding and clustering algorithm, We first heuristically fix the clustering algorithm and find the most meaningful embedding. Then, we opt for the most suitable clustering method based on the embedding.

Analysis of Embeddings. We show the experimental results for analyzing the effect of embedding space in Table 2. We observe that EASE records poor performance in all metrics, followed by averaged Glove embedding which shows the worst result, though EASE is a large-scale model. Note that both entity-aware contrastive learning and multilingual setting cause performance degradation in dialog intent clustering task.

The results for DiffCSE also show that unsupervised contrastive learning between original utterance and edited utterance exacerbates model performance in both STS and Trans tasks. Despite the model size being twice smaller than DiffCSE as shown in Table 3, SimCSE gets comparable scores to MPNet, with a similar model size. Note that MiniLM achieves remarkable performances in both $L12$ setting[1] and $MULTIQA$ setting[2] in all metrics. These results demonstrate that (i) performance increases as the number of parameter decreases, which means excessively large embedding model leads to performance degradation, and (ii) the use of a student network which is trained by the teacher's self-attention distributions and guiding layer improves intent clustering performance.

Visualization. Figure 2 gives UMAP (McInnes et al., 2018) visualization of clustering results. Note that we employ UMAP, instead of t-SNE (van der Maaten and Hinton, 2008), because

[1] https://huggingface.co/sentence-transformers/all-MiniLM-L12-v2

[2] https://huggingface.co/sentence-transformers/multi-qa-MiniLM-L6-cos-v1

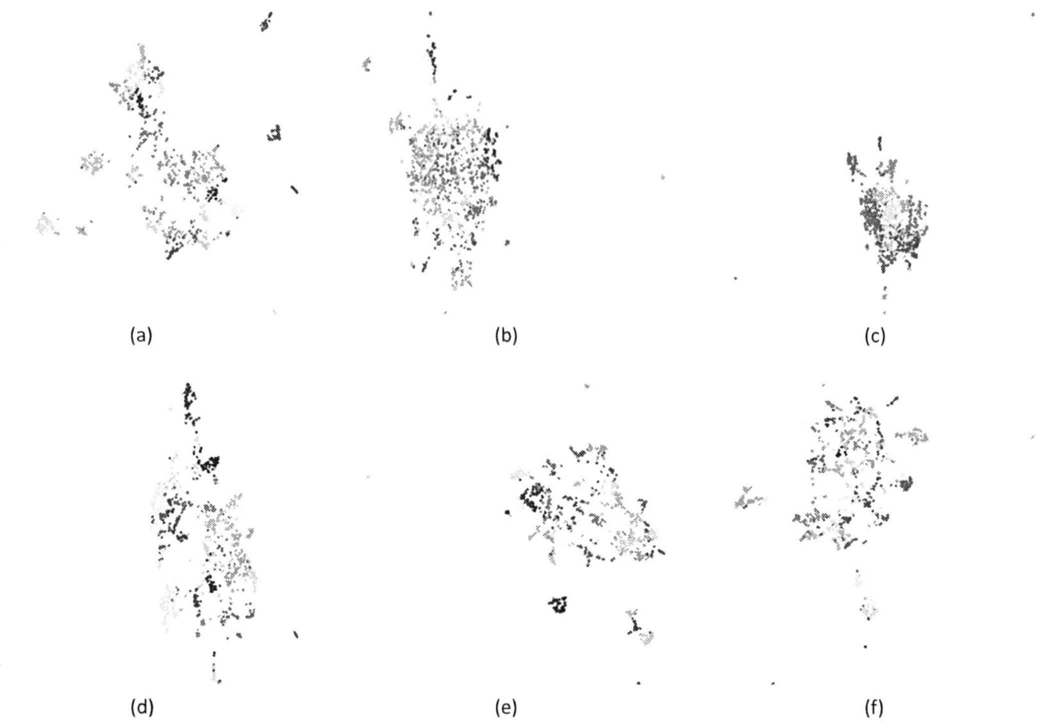

Figure 2: UMAP visualization of intent clustering results with different embeddings based on DSTC11 development dataset: (a) MiniLM, (b) Glove, (c) Ease-roberta, (d) DiffCSE-roberta, (e) SimCSE-roberta, and (f) MPNet. We apply K-means clustering algorithm to (a)-(e) experiments.

Utterance Embedding				**MiniLM$_{L12}$**				
Metric	**NMI**	**ARI**	**ACC**	**Precision**	**Recall**	**F1**	**Example Coverage**	**#K**
Bisect K-means	32.2	13.9	23.8	26.0	**67.4**	37.5	37.0	5
VOT	53.8	31.8	48.5	54.1	53.5	53.8	84.8	20
Spectral	57.6	34.9	51.3	58.8	56.1	57.4	82.9	24
Agglomerative	57.9	34.2	51.8	58.0	55.4	56.7	88.6	23
BIRCH	59.9	32.9	46.3	64.6	47.0	54.4	**100.0**	47
K-means	**63.1**	**38.9**	**54.9**	**68.0**	54.9	**60.8**	**100.0**	31

Table 4: Clustering results on DSTC11 dataset. We apply MiniLM$_{L12}$ utterance embedding to all clustering methods.

UMAP preserves more global structure than t-SNE. We observe that (b) - (d) vertically degenerated into each embedding space. We also find that (a) presents the most well-clustered result and covers all intents (i.e., Example Coverage is 100.0) while (e) and (f) embeddings suffer from relatively ill-clustered result and outliers.

Analysis of Clustering Methods. In Table 4, we observe that K-means method outperforms the other models, followed by BIRCH. Note that VOT records poor performance which means optimal transportation with the variational principle deteriorates the result in intent clustering task. Bisect K-means clustering algorithm calculates the point density and average density of all points to initialize cluster barycenters. However, K-means with K-means++ (Arthur and Vassilvitskii, 2007) initializer shows much better performance, contributing to the overall cluster inertia.

Voronoi Diagram. Figure 3 gives UMAP visualization of clustering results with Voronoi diagram. The number of barycenters of Bisect K-means is five which means this ill-clustering model is not able to cover all latent user intents. Though BIRCH records compatible results to K-means, the number of predicted barycenters is excessively large compared to the number of reference K. It causes outlier barycenter problem that barycenter contains a few utterances and disrupts universal clustering representation. It also demonstrates that hierarchi-

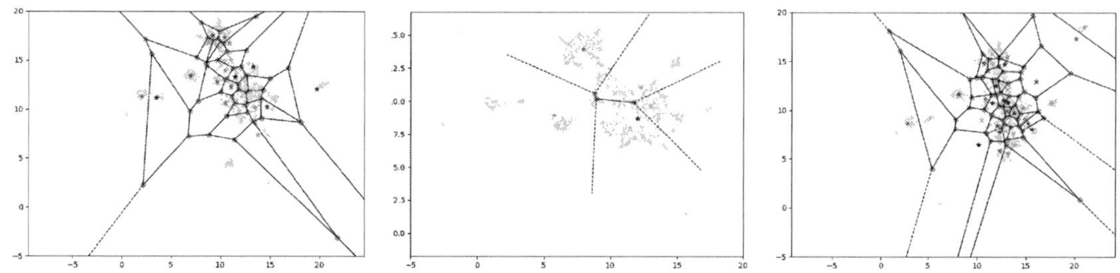

(a) (b) (c)

Figure 3: Voronoi diagram visualization of intent clustering results with different clustering algorithms based on DSTC11 development dataset: (a) K-means, (b) Bisect K-means, and (c) BIRCH. We apply MiniLM$_{L12}$ user utterance embedding to (a)-(c) experiments. * stands for barycenter of each cluster and x represents outlier barycenter with fewer than five utterances.

Clustering Method	K**-means Clustering**							
Metric	**NMI**	**ARI**	**ACC**	**Precision**	**Recall**	**F1**	**Example Coverage**	**#K**
EASE$^{m}_{BERT}$	27.0	12.3	23.9	24.1	72.9	36.2	26.4	5
EASE$_{BERT}$	53.1	25.6	42.8	50.2	57.4	53.5	80.0	26
EASE$^{m}_{ROBERTA}$	59.6	41.8	53.7	57.8	68.8	62.8	86.0	34
EASE$_{ROBERTA}$	60.5	50.7	52.7	55.8	70.0	62.1	83.1	28
DiffCSE$^{trans}_{BERT}$	21.0	11.5	23.3	23.7	77.5	36.3	32.5	6
DiffCSE$^{sts}_{BERT}$	49.6	22.3	40.2	46.1	58.4	51.5	93.2	31
DiffCSE$^{sts}_{ROBERTA}$	65.4	42.3	53.7	59.4	65.9	62.5	89.8	31
DiffCSE$^{trans}_{ROBERTA}$	65.4	53.3	57.6	63.1	71.1	66.8	90.0	28
SimCSE$^{u}_{BERT+}$	33.1	19.1	28.0	28.0	77.5	41.2	33.4	5
SimCSE$^{u}_{BERT}$	58.3	29.6	46.4	58.5	59.1	58.8	83.1	32
SimCSE$_{BERT+}$	59.4	29.1	47.0	54.2	60.5	57.2	86.2	30
SimCSE$_{ROBERTA}$	61.4	34.3	47.1	54.3	62.0	57.9	80.3	29
SimCSE$_{BERT}$	62.7	37.3	52.6	63.4	59.8	61.6	89.6	34
SimCSE$^{u}_{ROBERTA+}$	67.8	51.1	57.7	64.2	70.2	67.1	86.4	32
SimCSE$^{u}_{ROBERTA}$	68.6	48.0	54.7	65.6	71.2	68.3	86.1	31
SimCSE$_{ROBERTA+}$	69.2	38.7	52.1	62.4	70.0	66.0	**93.8**	32
Glove^{avg}	35.0	18.8	29.1	36.3	51.2	42.4	77.0	29
MPNet	72.8	41.6	60.2	65.6	76.3	70.6	86.5	26
MiniLM$_{L12}$	73.2	47.1	57.1	66.0	72.2	69.0	83.1	25
MiniLM$_{L6}$	74.7	52.8	61.2	**70.5**	74.9	72.7	83.4	25
MiniLM$_{MULTIQA}$	**77.4**	**54.5**	**63.2**	**70.5**	**79.1**	**74.6**	80.0	24

Table 5: Intent induction results on DSTC11 dataset. We employ K-means clustering algorithm to all utterance embeddings. m denotes multilingual model, u stands for unsupervised model, and $+$ means large model.

cal process of BIRCH including removing outliers and cluster refining does not have a substantial impact.

3 Task 2: Intent Induction

3.1 Task Description

Unlike Task 1, intent induction takes different transcripts which annotate only the speaker's role and intent label. The goal of intent induction is to create a set of intents and match them to each utterance without access to the ground-truth dialog acts. In this paper, we use DSTC11 dataset as shown in Table 1, exploit the same clustering algorithms and utterance embeddings, and evaluate methods using NMI, ARI, Accuracy, F1, and Example coverage. We employ the provided automatic dialog act predictions.

3.2 Result Analysis

Analysis of Embeddings. Table 5 demonstrates that MiniLM-based utterance embedding can im-

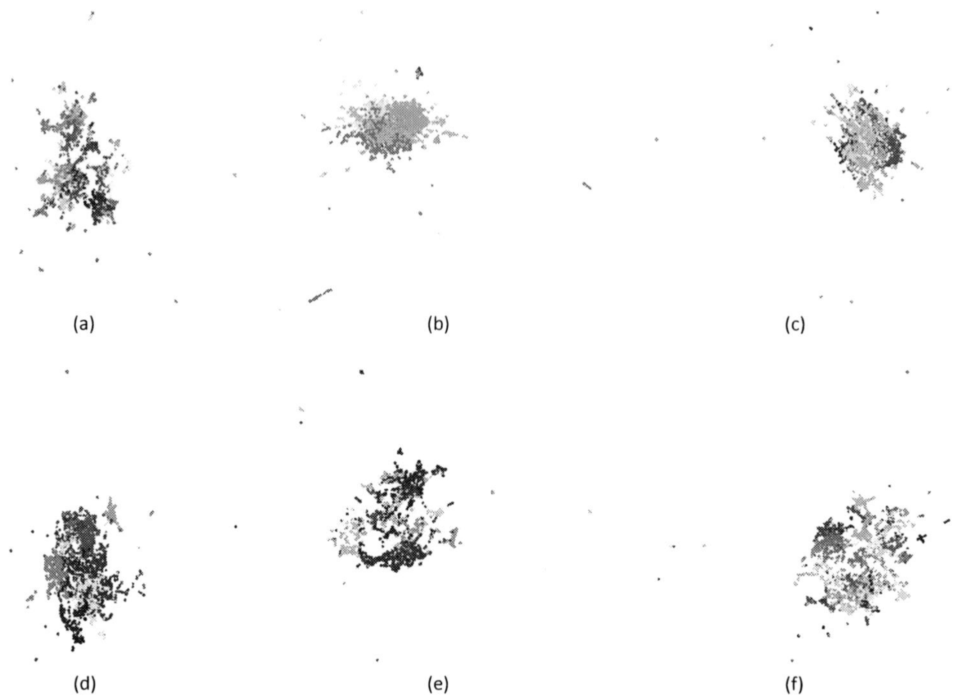

Figure 4: UMAP visualization of intent induction results with different embeddings based on DSTC11 development dataset: (a) MiniLM, (b) Glove, (c) Ease-roberta, (d) DiffCSE-roberta, (e) SimCSE-roberta, and (f) MPNet. We apply Agglomerative clustering algorithm to (a)-(e) experiments.

Utterance Embedding			**MiniLM$_{\text{MULTIQA}}$**					
Metric	**NMI**	**ARI**	**ACC**	**Precision**	**Recall**	**F1**	**Example Coverage**	**#K**
Bisect K-means	72.3	55.7	57.4	63.0	81.2	70.9	76.8	27
VOT	75.3	50.6	60.0	71.9	72.3	72.1	**93.4**	33
Spectral	75.0	51.7	59.0	67.7	75.9	71.6	86.3	23
K-means	77.4	54.5	63.2	70.5	79.1	74.6	80.0	24
BIRCH	79.5	62.8	**68.1**	71.9	**84.6**	77.7	89.9	24
Agglomerative	**81.0**	**64.2**	66.5	**75.5**	80.6	**78.0**	86.2	25

Table 6: Intent induction results on DSTC11 dataset. We apply MiniLM$_{\text{MULTIQA}}$ utterance embedding to all clustering methods.

prove induction performance for user intents. Unlike Task 1, MiniLM$_{\text{MULTIQA}}$ outperforms the other methods, followed by MiniLM$_{\text{L6}}$[3]. It represents that MiniLM with 6 layers and 384 hidden size can learn universal utterance representation and capture meaningful information. Though the performance tends to increase as the size of each embedding model increases, we observe that larger models do not always perform better. Note that DiffCSE$^{trans}_{BERT}$ and EASE$^{m}_{BERT}$ record high recall because the number of clusters K is disastrously low. We observe that it dampens overall model performance. As shown in both Task 1 and Task 2 results, (i) entity-aware contrastive learning, (ii) multilingual setting, (iii) contrastive learning between the original utterance and edited utterance are ultimately not the optimal choice to improve intent induction performance.

[3]https://huggingface.co/sentence-transformers/all-MiniLM-L6-v2

Visualization. We present UMAP visualization of intent induction results with different utterance embeddings (Figure 4). It corroborates that MiniLM-based intent induction can provide wider and well-separated results preserving its meaningful embedding space.

Analysis of Clustering Methods. In Table 6, we show the results of intent induction comparing models that clustering algorithms. Unlike the results in Task 1, Agglomerative clustering and BIRCH out-

Method	Voronoi Diagram	Examples	Label
Agglomerative + MiniLM	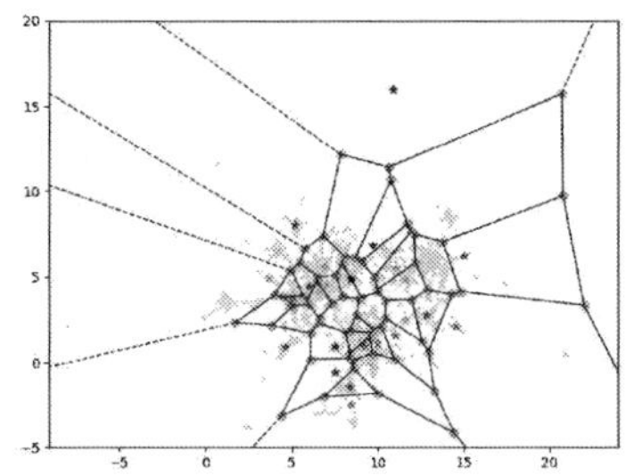	*Would it be on like any of my other bills?* *Oh okay. Where at on the bill. I'm looking now.* *Okay. When will I see that in my bill?* *Hi I am calling because I received a wrong bill.* *Thank you. How much will this make my bill go up?* *Yeah, so exactly how does this work? Do I just send a bill or what?* *crap! Well what can I do now? Can I make the payment and have the same policy that I had before?*	34
Agglomerative + DiffCSE	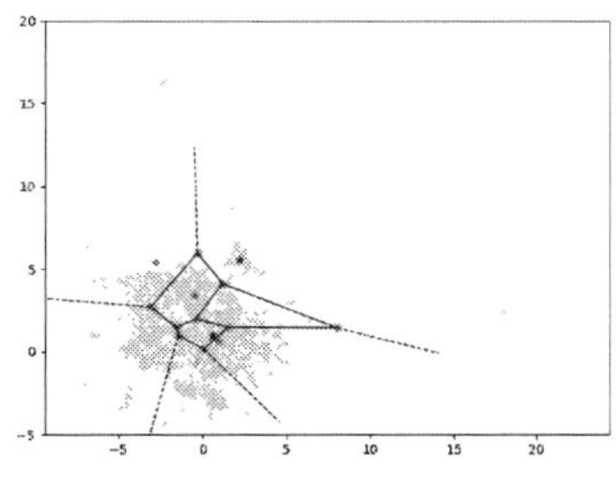	*Would it be on like any of my other bills?*	5
		Oh okay. Where at on the bill. I'm looking now.	2
		Okay. When will I see that in my bill?	7
		Hi I am calling because I received a wrong bill.	6
		Thank you. How much will this make my bill go up?	0
		Yeah, so exactly how does this work? Do I just send a bill or what?	1
		crap! Well what can I do now? Can I make the payment and have the same policy that I had before?	4

Figure 5: Qualitative result on DSTC11 dataset comparing MiniLM-based and DiffCSE-based models. We fix the clustering model as Agglomerative clustering in this experiment.

perform the other baselines. Agglomerative clustering starts with the utterances as individual clusters and merges them if they have similar intents. The experiment shows that the approach exploiting $\text{MiniLM}_{\text{MULTIQA}}$ and Agglomerative clustering achieves state-of-the-art results among the other methods in the intent induction task.

3.3 Qualitative Results

Figure 5 shows the qualitative result for intent induction on DSTC11 dataset. We generate user intent labels using two different models. We observe that Agglomerative clustering on MiniLM utterance embedding can classify bill-related utterances well. However, Agglomerative clustering on DiffCSE utterance embedding is not able to discern user intent well and amalgamate completely different user utterances into a single intent cluster. Note that all clusters have bill-related user utterances which means it is an ill-clustered result.

We conclude that user utterance embedding is one of the most important factors affecting performance, and we should add a huge caveat that selection of utterance embedding in intent induction task should be very careful. Further analyzing how to leverage an embedding model is an interesting direction for future work.

Our extensive experiments demonstrate that the combined selection of utterance embedding and clustering method in the intent induction task should be carefully considered.

3.4 Quantitative Results

We conduct quantitative experiments to analyze (i) the correlation between the number of inducted clusters and performance, and (ii) the correlation between the number of utterances per intent and performance (Figure 6). Note that the maximum number of sample utterances aligned to intent is limited to 50. First, We find that NMI and ARI increase as the number of inducted clusters approaches the reference K. We also observe that Example coverage decreases as the number of inducted clusters go toward the reference K. We demonstrate that there is a trade-off relationship between NMI, ARI and Example coverage. Second, the correlation between the number of utterances per intent and performance shows the same pattern as the correlation between the number of inducted clusters and performance.

4 Conclusion

The conclusion of this paper is threefold:

- We empirically demonstrate that the combined selection of utterance embedding and clustering method in the intent induction task should

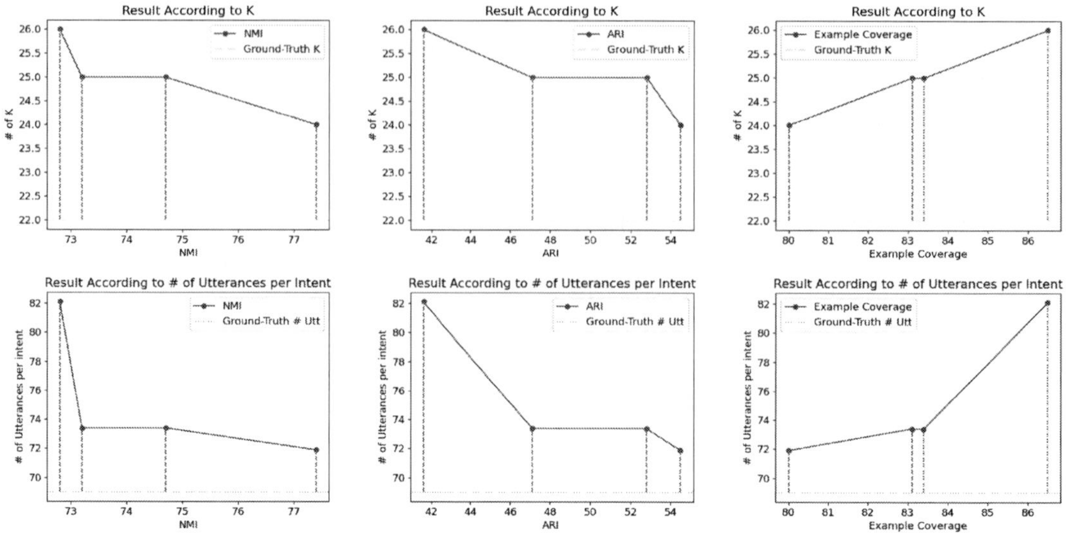

Figure 6: Quantitative results on DSTC11 dataset related to NMI, ARI, F1 score, and Example coverage. We analyze using four results with the best performance introduced in Table 5.

be carefully considered.

- We also present that pretrained MiniLM with Agglomerative clustering shows significant improvement in NMI, ARI, F1, accuracy and example coverage in intent induction tasks.
- We find that there is a trade-off relationship between NMI, ARI and Example coverage.

5 Discussion and Future Work

In clustering, broadly, there are three categories of methods: (i) Barycenter-based formulation, (ii) Density-based formulation, and (iii) Distance-based formulation. In this paper, we mainly dealt with barycenter-based methods. Indeed, K-means clustering method, for instance, theoretically produce the same result as barycenter-based formulation and distacne-based formulation in Euclidean embedding space:

$$\sum_{i,j=1}^{n} ||X_i - X_j||_2^2 = 2n \sum_{i=1}^{n} ||X_i - \beta||_2^2 \quad (7)$$

, where $\beta = \frac{1}{n}\sum_{i=1}^{n} X_i$. Besides, barycenter-based K-means in Euclidean space can circumvent the problem frequently caused by the location of barycenter in different measure space (e.g., Wasserstein space (Zhuang et al., 2022)):

$$\sum_{i=1}^{n} ||X - X_i||_2^2 = n||X - \beta||_2^2 + \sum_{i=1}^{n} ||X - X_i||_2^2 \geqslant n||X - \beta||_2^2 \quad (8)$$

However, K-means clustering in Euclidean space often loses salient geometric information of dataset, due to its formulation. In the same vein, though we didn't add the experimental result of Density-based formulation to the table, the performance was disastrous. DBSCAN (Ester et al., 1996), for example, recorded 7.7 NMI, 0.0 ARI, 16.1 Accuracy, 27.6 F1 score, and 41.0 Example coverage in intent clustering task. Therefore, both clustering in different measure spaces and clustering using embedding density should be investigated. Further analyzing how to leverage an embedding model is also an interesting direction for future work.

Acknowledgements

This work was supported by Institute of Information & communications Technology Planning & Evaluation(IITP) grant funded by the Korea government(MSIT) (No. 2020-0-00368, A Neural-Symbolic Model for Knowledge Acquisition and Inference Techniques). This research was supported by the MSIT(Ministry of Science and ICT), Korea, under the ITRC(Information Technology Research Center) support program(IITP-2022-2018-0-01405) supervised by the IITP(Institute for Information & Communications Technology Planning & Evaluation).

References

David Arthur and Sergei Vassilvitskii. 2007. K-means++: The advantages of careful seeding. In

Proceedings of the Eighteenth Annual ACM-SIAM Symposium on Discrete Algorithms, SODA '07, page 1027–1035, USA. Society for Industrial and Applied Mathematics.

Ajay Chatterjee and Shubhashis Sengupta. 2020. Intent mining from past conversations for conversational agent. In *Proceedings of the 28th International Conference on Computational Linguistics*, pages 4140–4152, Barcelona, Spain (Online). International Committee on Computational Linguistics.

Jackie Chi Kit Cheung and Xiao Li. 2012. Sequence clustering and labeling for unsupervised query intent discovery. In *Proceedings of the Fifth International Conference on Web Search and Web Data Mining, WSDM 2012, Seattle, WA, USA, February 8-12, 2012*, pages 383–392. ACM.

Yung-Sung Chuang, Rumen Dangovski, Hongyin Luo, Yang Zhang, Shiyu Chang, Marin Soljacic, Shang-Wen Li, Scott Yih, Yoon Kim, and James Glass. 2022. DiffCSE: Difference-based contrastive learning for sentence embeddings. In *Proceedings of the 2022 Conference of the North American Chapter of the Association for Computational Linguistics: Human Language Technologies*, pages 4207–4218, Seattle, United States. Association for Computational Linguistics.

Jian Di and Xinyue Gou. 2018. Bisecting k-means algorithm based on k-valued selfdetermining and clustering center optimization. *J. Comput.*, 13(6):588–595.

Martin Ester, Hans-Peter Kriegel, Jörg Sander, and Xiaowei Xu. 1996. A density-based algorithm for discovering clusters in large spatial databases with noise. In *Proceedings of the Second International Conference on Knowledge Discovery and Data Mining*, KDD'96, page 226–231. AAAI Press.

Tianyu Gao, Xingcheng Yao, and Danqi Chen. 2021. SimCSE: Simple contrastive learning of sentence embeddings. In *Proceedings of the 2021 Conference on Empirical Methods in Natural Language Processing*, pages 6894–6910, Online and Punta Cana, Dominican Republic. Association for Computational Linguistics.

Dilek Hakkani-Tür, Yun-Cheng Ju, Geoffrey Zweig, and Gokhan Tur. 2015. Clustering novel intents in a conversational interaction system with semantic parsing. In *Sixteenth Annual Conference of the International Speech Communication Association*.

Iryna Haponchyk, Antonio Uva, Seunghak Yu, Olga Uryupina, and Alessandro Moschitti. 2018. Supervised clustering of questions into intents for dialog system applications. In *Proceedings of the 2018 Conference on Empirical Methods in Natural Language Processing*, pages 2310–2321.

Stuart P. Lloyd. 1982. Least squares quantization in pcm. *IEEE Trans. Inf. Theory*, 28(2):129–136.

L. McInnes, J. Healy, and J. Melville. 2018. UMAP: Uniform Manifold Approximation and Projection for Dimension Reduction. *ArXiv e-prints*.

Liang Mi, Wen Zhang, Xianfeng Gu, and Yalin Wang. 2018. Variational Wasserstein clustering. In *Proceedings of the European Conference on Computer Vision (ECCV)*, pages 322–337.

Sosuke Nishikawa, Ryokan Ri, Ikuya Yamada, Yoshimasa Tsuruoka, and Isao Echizen. 2022. EASE: Entity-aware contrastive learning of sentence embedding. In *Proceedings of the 2022 Conference of the North American Chapter of the Association for Computational Linguistics: Human Language Technologies*, pages 3870–3885, Seattle, United States. Association for Computational Linguistics.

Srinivas Bangalore Padmasundari. 2018. Intent discovery through unsupervised semantic text clustering. In *Proc. Interspeech*, volume 2018, pages 606–610.

Hugh Perkins and Yi Yang. 2019. Dialog intent induction with deep multi-view clustering. In *EMNLP*.

Kaitao Song, Xu Tan, Tao Qin, Jianfeng Lu, and Tie-Yan Liu. 2020. Mpnet: Masked and permuted pre-training for language understanding. In *Advances in Neural Information Processing Systems*, volume 33, pages 16857–16867. Curran Associates, Inc.

M. Steinbach, G. Karypis, and V. Kumar. 2000. A comparison of document clustering techniques. In *KDD Workshop on Text Mining*.

Laurens van der Maaten and Geoffrey E. Hinton. 2008. Visualizing data using t-sne. *Journal of Machine Learning Research*, 9:2579–2605.

Wenhui Wang, Furu Wei, Li Dong, Hangbo Bao, Nan Yang, and Ming Zhou. 2020. Minilm: Deep self-attention distillation for task-agnostic compression of pre-trained transformers. In *Advances in Neural Information Processing Systems*, volume 33, pages 5776–5788. Curran Associates, Inc.

Stella X. Yu and Jianbo Shi. 2003. Multiclass spectral clustering. In *ICCV*, pages 313–319. IEEE Computer Society.

Zengfeng Zeng, Dan Ma, Haiqin Yang, Zhen Gou, and Jianping Shen. 2021. Automatic intent-slot induction for dialogue systems. In *Proceedings of the Web Conference 2021*, WWW '21, page 2578–2589, New York, NY, USA. Association for Computing Machinery.

Tian Zhang, Raghu Ramakrishnan, and Miron Livny. 1996. Birch: an efficient data clustering method for very large databases. In *SIGMOD '96: Proceedings of the 1996 ACM SIGMOD international conference on Management of data*, pages 103–114, New York, NY, USA. ACM.

Yuwei Zhang, Haode Zhang, Li-Ming Zhan, Xiao-Ming Wu, and Albert Lam. 2022. New intent discovery with pre-training and contrastive learning. In *Proceedings of the 60th Annual Meeting of the Association for Computational Linguistics (Volume 1: Long Papers)*, pages 256–269, Dublin, Ireland. Association for Computational Linguistics.

Yubo Zhuang, Xiaohui Chen, and Yun Yang. 2022. Wasserstein k-means for clustering probability distributions. *Thirty-sixth Conference on Neural Information Processing Systems*.

Multi-View Zero-Shot Open Intent Induction from Dialogues: Multi Domain Batch and Proxy Gradient Transfer

Hyukhun Koh[1], **Haesung Pyun**[2], **Nakyeong Yang**[1], **Kyomin Jung**[1]
Seoul National University[1], Hanyang University[2]
{hyukhunkoh-ai, yny0506, kjung}@snu.ac.kr
haesung.pyun@gmail.com

Abstract

In Task Oriented Dialogue (TOD) system, detecting and inducing new intents are two main challenges to apply the system in the real world. In this paper, we suggest the semantic multi-view model to resolve these two challenges: (1) SBERT for General Embedding (GE), (2) Multi Domain Batch (MDB) for dialogue domain knowledge, and (3) Proxy Gradient Transfer (PGT) for cluster-specialized semantic. MDB feeds diverse dialogue datasets to the model at once to tackle the multi-domain problem by learning the multiple domain knowledge. We introduce a novel method PGT, which employs the Siamese network to fine-tune the model with a clustering method directly. Our model can learn how to cluster dialogue utterances by using PGT. Experimental results demonstrate that our multi-view model with MDB and PGT significantly improves the Open Intent Induction performance compared to baseline systems.

1 Introduction

In developing Task Oriented Dialogue (TOD) systems, it is important to understand the user's intent, such as opening a new account in banking and reporting accidents in finance. In this circumstance, TOD system is used to capture the intents automatically within some dialogue turns, generating appropriate responses to users. Since Pretrained Language Models (PLMs) have become mainstream among the recent NLP tasks, various kinds of research to apply the PLMs to a dialogue system have appeared. (Henderson et al. (2019), Bao et al. (2020), Majumder et al. (2020), Zhao et al. (2020))

In TOD systems, one of the core tasks is intent detection, which seeks to discern user intentions from their utterances. However, most of the typical intent detection modules depend heavily on the domain to be applied. Due to the domain-lopsided characteristic, it is necessary for typical models to collect the data of the domain to be serviced and go through a cumbersome process to train a model for each domain from scratch. Besides, no standard conventions exist for defining and labeling the intents within the same domain. For example, Banking77, an intent classification dataset, has 77 intents. In contrast, Banking from DSTC 11 has 29 intents and some of the intents, "AskAboutATM-Fees" and "GetBranchInfo," are not included in Banking77. Hence, it is tricky to apply a model trained with Banking77 directly to Banking dataset. For example, Banking77, an intent classification dataset, has 77 intents. In contrast, Banking from DSTC 11 has 29 intents and some of the intents, "AskAboutATMFees" and "GetBranchInfo," are not included in Banking77. Hence, it is impossible to directly apply a model trained with Banking77 to Banking dataset. In addition, customers may not communicate within only predefined intent sets. Summing up, intent detection modules should induce intents from utterances beyond each domain dataset.

Previous researches utilized BERT to produce hidden representations and passed them to clustering algorithms in order to discern intents of utterances (Lin et al., 2019, Aharoni and Goldberg, 2020). However, utterances in dialogue data are usually shorter and colloquial compared to generic text where the ellipsis and omission are less likely to occur. Furthermore, BERT representations are insufficient to capture the intent information for dialogue since it is only trained to focus on learning the context of the generic text. Additional methods are required to contain the domain-specific information since the meaning of a sentence can also be interpreted in various ways depending on its domain. Therefore, some researchers have trained PLMs with dialogue data (Shen et al., 2021, Zhang et al., 2021a, Zhang et al., 2021b, Zhang et al., 2021c). However, they mostly have conducted experiments within a few-shot setting where some portion of a target dataset is available, rather than

Proceedings of The Eleventh Dialog System Technology Challenge, pages 67–80
September 11, 2023

a zero-shot setting where target domain data is not accessible. In accordance with the study by Zhang et al. (2022), they handled such problems in semi-supervised learning schemes. Zhang et al. (2022) showed that it is beneficial to train PLM with external intent detection datasets. They also proposed a contrastive learning method based on K-nearest neighbor algorithm. Nevertheless, the performance gap between few-shot and zero-shot settings has been still large.

Our whole pipeline is the same as the baseline used in DSTC 11 task2[1]. Details are presented in Section 4 Task Description. Following the baseline pipeline, we only feed some utterances with labeled as InformIntent without any modification. Similar utterances should be clustered in the hidden representation space.

In this paper, we aim to improve Open Intent Induction which requires inducing intent sets in various domains without additional training on target domain datasets (zero-shot setting). We suggest the semantic multi-view model to resolve aforementioned problem using three methods : (1) SBERT for general embedding (GE), (2) Multi Domain Batch (MDB) for dialogue domain knowledge, and (3) Proxy Gradient Transfer (PGT) for cluster-specialized semantics. By MDB and PGT methods, constructed domain-agnostic model is not necessary to update parameters further when applying to a different target domain. MDB makes a model to learn various domain knowledge by composing a batch with six groups of samples, sampling from each of the six different dataset. PGT is a way of fine-tuning with K-means to improve on the clustering capability, especially in inducing intents properly. Although K-means is an integer assignment problem that is impossible to differentiate, PGT allows a differentiable comparison of K-means labels and ground truth labels by adopting Siamese network learning process.

From our experiment, combining the General Embedding (GE) module and the MDB module showed an excellent performance. In addition, when applying the PGT method to these two modules for the clustering, the performance was improved as well. Finally, we found that Spectral clustering with all three modules (GE, MDB, PGT) works better, compared to K-means clustering. The codes are available in the github repository[2]

[1]DSTC11 Track Proposal: Intent Induction from Conversations for Task-Oriented Dialogue

[2]Multi_View_Zero_Shot_Open_Intent_Induction

This paper has three contributions:

1. We suggest the multi-view model composed with GE, MDB, PGT modules.

2. We suggest a novel method PGT to directly fine-tune a model onto a clustering. PGT contributes to better performance and deals with a non-differentiable problem.

3. Our model demonstrates excellent performance in Banking and Finance, outperforming the baseline in Open Intent Induction task.

2 Background

In this section, we will briefly cover PLMs (2.1) and explore how PLMs are applied to TOD systems (2.2). Finally, we will introduce existing clustering methods (2.3).

2.1 Pretrained Language Models

There are two streams of PLM which is trained on massive corpus, Auto-Regressive (AR) and Auto-Encoding (AE) model. GPT-3 (Brown et al., 2020) and FLAN (Wei et al., 2022) are well known for AR model using Transformer decoder which are optimized to maximize the likelihood of the next word generation given preceding tokens. In comparison, BERT (Devlin et al., 2019), a representative of AE model, is a pretrained Transformer encoder with Masked Language Modeling (MLM). BERT variant models have been introduced since BERT has shown an outstanding performance in Natural Language Understanding (NLU) tasks. RoBERTa (Liu et al., 2020) enhanced BERT with Dynamic Masking method and larger dataset. Sentence Transformer SBERT (Reimers and Gurevych, 2019) derives more semantically meaningful sentence embeddings by training a model with NLI task in the scheme of Siamese network.

Some studies tried to overcome the disadvantage of AR and AE model by combining MLM with permutation methods: XLNet (Yang et al., 2019), MPNet (Song et al., 2020). XLNet (Yang et al., 2019) proposed an autoregressive pretraining by permutating tokens to capture long dependencies. MPNet unifies MLM and permutation pretraining methods, employing a two-stream attention to capture position information.

2.2 Dialogue Systems with PLMs

Despite its universal applications of PLMs, there is a discrepancy between a general corpus and a dialogue corpus. Therefore, there are some studies which trained the PLMs on a dialogue corpus further, rather than directly applying PLMs to the TOD task. TOD-BERT (Wu et al., 2020) pretrained BERT on TOD corpus. IntentBERT (Zhang et al., 2021b) proposed regularized supervised learning and showed that it is promising in a few-shot intent detection task. Vulic et al. (2021) proposed two-stage procedures. They used a universal conversational encoder with small conversational data samples, subsequently fine-tuned an encoder for a sentence similarity task. These studies focus on pretraining with the dialogue corpus and applying it to a specific dataset.

2.3 Clustering Methods

There are several candidates when cluster task is necessary. K-means (MacQueen, 1967) clusters the inputs based on Euclidean distance. It has problems when the real clusters do not have spherical shape or have a huge imbalance in size. Furthermore, Clustering performance heavily relies on the predefined K. Agglomerative (Chidananda Gowda and Krishna, 1978), one of hierarchical clusterings which build clusters based on the proximity matrix, starts with N clusters. However, it is often deficient in robustness, sensitive to noise, and computationally expensive. DBSCAN (Ester et al., 1996) is a density-based approach, which finds every point's neighbors and identifies the core points. DBSCAN is robust to noise and outliers. Nevertheless, it is slower than K-means clustering. It is also difficult to choose distance threshold epsilon and minimum points. ITER-DBSCAN (Chatterjee and Sengupta, 2020) extends DBSCAN with label propagation technique and dialog act classification. Gaussian Mixture Model (GMM) clusters based on the probability of a mixture of multiple unknown Gaussian distributions. This method does not assume the real cluster to be a specific shape but requires high computational costs. Spectral clustering (Ng et al., 2001) is based on Ratio Cut algorithm using the Laplacian matrix. This algorithm calculates the Laplacian matrix upon the similarity matrix and obtains eigenvectors from the matrix. This method can cluster the data type of non-global shape. Nonetheless, the number of clusters is essential in advance.

3 Related Works

Studies related to OOD detection and intent discovery are very relevant to Open Intent Induction task in terms of the fact that they need to handle unseen intents. The researchers of those studies are interested in how to make a good representation and how to connect it well by using a grouping algorithm. Perkins and Yang (2019) proposed the method which utilized content view and utterance view to yield the cluster assignments. Lin and Xu (2019) introduced margin loss on Bi-Directional Long Short Term Memory (BiLSTM) (Mesnil et al., 2015) for inter-class discrimination and intra-class compactness. They applied local outlier factor (LOF) (Breunig et al., 2000) to detect unknown intents based on the nearest-neighbor's density. Chatterjee and Sengupta (2020) introduced ITER-DBSCAN which extended DBSCAN with a label propagation technique. However, the methods mentioned above require domain specific knowledge and laborious feature engineering. Also, those methods often cannot fully leverage the prior knowledge and cannot accurately capture fine-grained intents. Lin et al. (2020) leveraged PLM and limited labeled data for supervised intent classification. They used the sentence similarity and filtered out low confidence assignment which is for refining clusters. Deep Aligned Clustering (Zhang et al., 2021a) pretrained BERT model with known intent samples to inject prior knowledge. As a next step, they produced pseudo-labels by the cluster assignment for self-supervised learning. CPFT (Zhang et al., 2021c) performed a contrastive learning with MLM to learn discriminative ability on utterance semantics. Shen et al. (2021) suggested the supervised contrastive scheme with dialogue domain labeled dataset on the basis of MPNet. After that, they applied K-means clustering with estimated K based on Bayesian Optimization. Zhou et al. (2022) focused on training fine-grained discriminative semantic features to deal with OOD intents among in-domain (IND) distribution. They utilize K-nearest neighbors of IND intents sample. The limitation of those studies is that they mainly focused on a few-shot performance where the premise is that few target-related labels are available.

Chen et al. (2022) pretrained Transformer with dialogue data and introduced a domain adaptive pretraining method which shows good performance in Open Intent Discovery task. Since their domain adaptive pretraining method shows promising results, we adopt it with some variations. Zhang et al. (2022) embedded rich information for the clustering by exploiting external and internal data. They show comparable results in the setting where target-related labels are unprovided. However, there is a still big gap between a few-shot setting and a zero-shot setting.

In this paper, we suggest two learning methods to induce intents from dialogues efficiently: 1. For MDB, how to appropriately inject prior external knowledge in PLM model to be robust whenever the domain changes and 2. For PGT, how the capability of model can be boosted in terms of clustering performance. Using two methods, the performance of Banking and Finance significantly increased compared to the model exposed in a few-shot setting.

4 Task Description

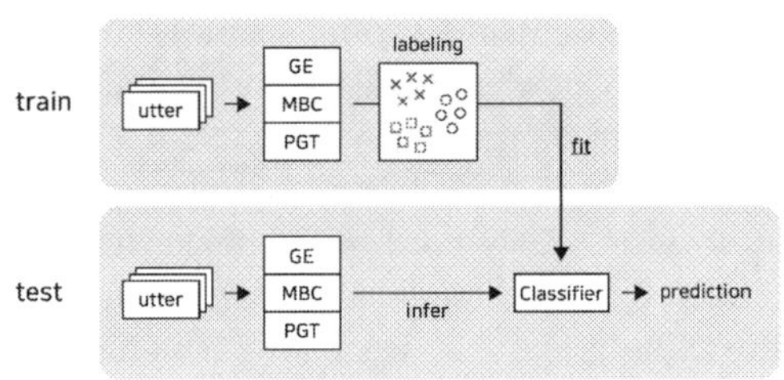

Figure 1: This is the outline of DSTC 11 task 2 Open Intent Induction. By concatenating representations of GE, MDB, and PGT modules, a clustering algorithm clusters those multi-view representations of train-utterances to construct an intent schema which consists of utterances and predicted labels. Next, we train the linear classifier with the intent schema. At test phase, multi-view representations of test-utterances go into the trained classifier to induce labels.

The second track of DSTC11 challenge is Intent Induction task based on TOD, such as Banking and Finance. This challenge aims to automatically induce intent sets for a task-oriented chatbot without training on target datasets which is a customer service interaction between the chatbot and clients.

There are three given datasets(Insurance, Banking, Finance) from 1K customer support spoken conversations, Insurance for development and others for evaluation. Each dataset has two divided data, one for training an evaluation classifier and the other for testing the performance of Open Intent Induction. The challenge assumes that utterances have only speaker roles without labels such as dialog act and intents, the number of which ranges from 5 to 50.

The task consists of three subtasks: Label Construction, Classifier Construction, and Inducing Intent. Label Construction subtask clusters the train-utterances in order to make a set of intents while predicting what the number of intents is. Classifier Construction subtask is for training a classifier with train-utterances and predicted labels which are from Label Construction subtask. Inducing Intent subtask predicts the labels for test-utterances based on a trained classifier.

4.1 Problem Formulation

$$\begin{gathered}\{\ d_1 \cdots d_n\ \} \rightarrow \{\ u_1 \cdots u_m\ \}, \\ d_i \subset D\ and\ u_i \subset U\end{gathered} \tag{1}$$

According to equation (1), we denote a dialogue set as $\mathbf{D} = \{\mathbf{d_1} \cdots \mathbf{d_n}\}$, where $\mathbf{d_i}$ represents the i-th utterance in a given dialogue, n is the total number of the dialogue sets. Extracted utterances denote as $\mathbf{U} = \{\mathbf{u_1} \cdots \mathbf{u_m}\}$, where $\mathbf{u_i}$ represents the i-th candidate utterance which seems to have intent, labeled as InformIntent, and m is the number of utterances selected from $\mathbf{D}$. Each single turn utterance becomes an input to the model and $\mathbf{U}$ may have some noises containing utterances without intents.

For Label Construction subtask, K-means attaches labels to train-utterances on hidden representation spaces that our model(GE-MDB-PGT) generates. For Classifier Construction subtask, train-utterances and their labels are used to train Linear Regression classifier. For Inducing Intent subtask, test-utterances sequentially go into our model and trained classifier to induce intents. The whole pipeline of DSTC 11 task 2 is in Figure 1.

5 Methods

In this section, we cover our methodology in detail. We adopt the baseline model structure of the DSTC 11 challenge as it is, but we investigate how the performance can be boosted by further learning. Our goal is for the model to automatically induce and generate meaningful intents from a collection of unlabeled utterances. SBERT, the baseline model proposed by DSTC 11, is used as the backbone.

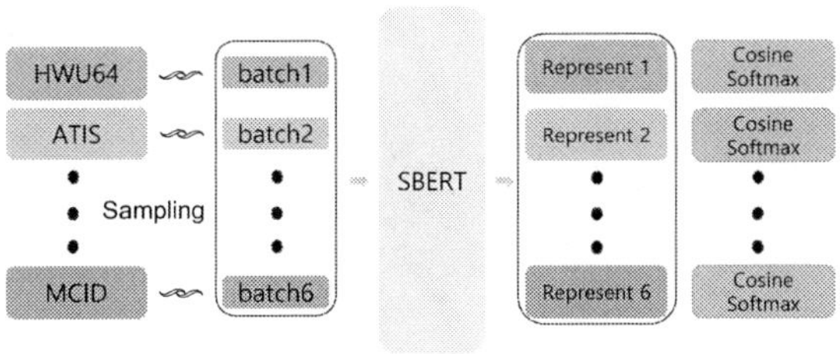

Figure 2: It shows the procedure of MDB to learn how to make appropriate domain-agnostic hidden representations. Multi-domain samples from each dataset construct the total batch (HWU64, ATIS, ..., MCID). Next, SBERT converts the total batch to hidden representations. Finally, the loss is calculated by applying cosine softmax for samples of each dataset.

5.1 Multi-View Model

Utterances from U enter into our three modules for taking the different perspectives into account, which is a multi-view approach. By passing U through them, we get each of three hidden representations of utterance.

$$\begin{aligned} Z_1 &= GE(U) \\ Z_2 &= MDB(U) \\ Z_3 &= PGT(U) \\ H &= Concat\{Z_1, Z_2, Z_3\} \end{aligned} \quad (2)$$

Hidden representation Z_1 is drawn using the General Embedding(GE) module, which interprets utterances in terms of a general linguistic perspective. Z_2 is created through a module learned by MDB to extract the dialogue-viewed representation. Hidden representation Z_3 is induced by the PGT module for tuning an encoder and a clustering module in order to boost the performance. H is constructed by concatenating all those hidden representations.

In the last step, K-means or Spectral clustering groups the concatenated representations to make intent schema by Bayesian Optimization (BO). BO method samples the number of clusters from a uniform distribution between 5 to 50 and estimates the optimal K based on the silhouette score. In the test process, Hungarian algorithm maps predicted labels to reference labels in order to evaluate the performance.

5.2 Multi Domain Batch Cosine Softmax (MDB)

As mentioned earlier, SBERT (the baseline of DSTC 11) is not enough to make a proper representation of the dialogue domain due to the discrepancy between the generic corpus and the dialogue corpus. Therefore, training PLM with a dialogue corpus is indispensable. In that sense, Multi Domain Batch (MDB) proved to be efficient in Chen et al. (2022). Unlike Chen et al. (2022), we directly apply MDB to PLM with some variations. The Figure 2 explains the process step by step. MDB uses six external datasets which are publicly available. In the process of MDB training, six different dialogue datasets configure the batch. For example, if the batch size is 36, the model would convert six samples for one dataloader to hidden representations where samples for one dataset are independent of the other datasets. The last layer of MDB is cosine softmax which is already proven to be more advantageous than naive softmax in Chen et al. (2022). We add a term τ for a numerical and denominator part.

$$j^{th}\ Cosine\ Softmax = \frac{exp(\bar{h_j}^T \bar{w^k}/\tau)}{\sum_i^{L^k} exp(\bar{h_i}^T \bar{w^k}/\tau)}, \quad (3)$$

where k is the kth dataset, $\bar{h_i}$ for h_i divided by norm(h_i), $\bar{w^k}$ for k^{th} dataset's linear normalized weight, τ for the temperature, and L^k for the kth dataset's number of intent categories.

The benefit of this methodology is that we do not have to preprocess collected datasets to unify the intent category sets. It saves lots of time to merge the datasets because different domains have different intent label categories, and even the same domain has different ways of defining intent labels. Next, the model can acquire multiple dialogue domain knowledge at once, which is not dependent on a specific dataset. It indicates that we no longer train the model further when applying the model to other TOD industrial fields. Besides, as well known fact that catastrophic forgetting could occur when sequentially training the model, MDB prevents this problem by parallelly training which is much more efficient in terms of learning time.

5.3 Proxy Gradient Transfer(PGT)

In Open Intent Induction task, the model induces a set of intents by clustering methods. Therefore, the model needs to know how to cluster well from the perspective of clustering methods. In that sense, Proxy Gradient Transfer(PGT) is a way of learning how to interpret utterances in terms of clustering methods, grounded on the MDB module. Since K-means self-supervised learning is proven to be

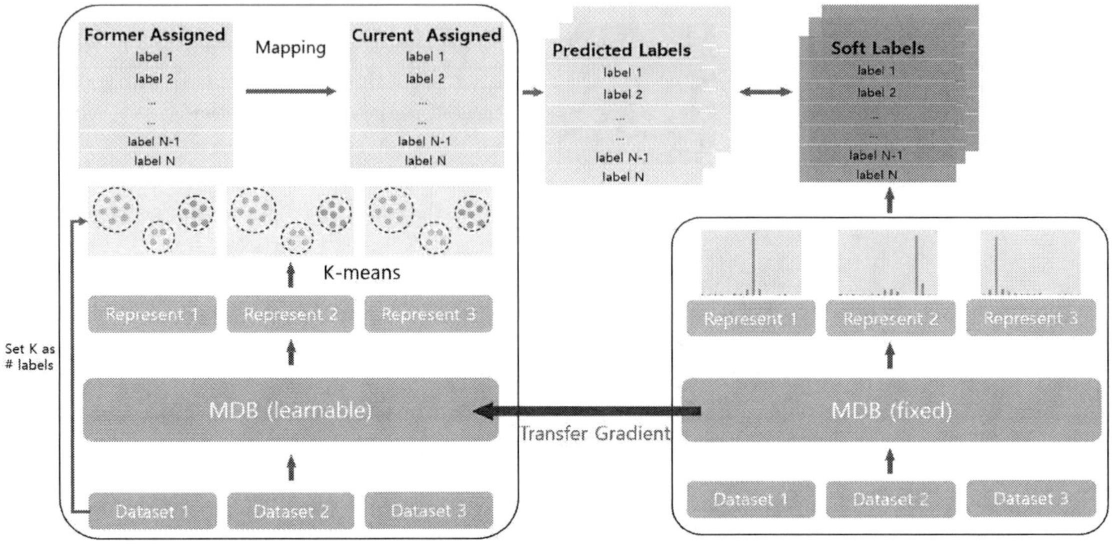

Figure 3: MDB signifies the SBERT trained by MDB method. First, two same MDB are initialized. Second, MDB (learnable) predicts the labels for train utterances using K-means. Third, MDB (fixed) calculates gradients based on cross entropy loss between predicted labels and soft labels. Fourth, MDB (fixed) transfers the gradients to MDB (learnable), considering a weight difference. Finally, MDB (learnable) is optimized with transferred gradients.

efficient in Zhang et al. (2021a), we choose K-means as a clustering module. Details are in Figure 3. However, there are three obstacles to overcome. It is not straightforward to select the K for K-means and it is impossible to differentiate. Furthermore, K-means is non-convex, whose result highly depends on fortunate initialized centroids. At last, the labels of clusters can vary each step even though their contents do not change.

First, we use the number of intent labels for each dataset to determine K. The premise is that K does not change during PGT training. Second, Siamese network learning process makes the model differentiate. In the process of PGT training, one of two identical encoders in Siamese network (MDB-learnable) predicts labels from K-means clustering. The other (MDB-fixed) generates representations to use them as soft labels and vicariously calculates gradients based on the cross entropy loss between predicted labels and soft labels. Afterward, the gradients are assigned from MDB(fixed) to MDB(learnable), reflecting equation (4).

$$Grad_{learned} = Grad_{fixed} + W_{learned} - W_{fixed} \quad (4)$$

where $Grad_{learned}$ is the gradient of MDB (learnable), $Grad_{fixed}$ for the gradient of MDB (fixed), $W_{learned}$ for the weight of MDB (learnable), and W_{fixed} for the weight of MDB (fixed). In the next step, MDB(learnable) is optimized with allotted gradients. Third, when the performance of MDB is reasonably good, the effect of initialized centroids diminishes. Though few initial randomnesses can still remain, we consider it as an augmentation. Lastly, the cluster label is adjusted through Hungarian mapping according to the similarity among the clusters' centroids.

6 Experiment

6.1 Dataset

We separate our datasets into two groups, a train dataset and a test dataset. For MDB and PGT training, we introduce six datasets.

Train Banking77 (Casanueva et al., 2020) is banking dialogue divided into Out-Of-Domain (OOD) intent and In-Domain (IND) intent. We use fine-grained 77 intents as train data. ATIS (Hemphill et al., 1990) is made of airplane travel transcripts. We preprocess them to extract the 17 intent categories. Clinc150 (Larson et al., 2019) is for evaluating the intent detection system. HWU64 (Liu et al., 2019) is for developing a home robot with various scenarios to serve as personal assistance, comprised of multi-domain(21 domains). MCID (Levy and Wang, 2020) is involved in Covid-19, a chatbot dataset consisting of user and agent. Restaurants-8k (Coope et al., 2020) is a set of 8,198 utterances gathered from the actual restaurant booking system. The details of the training dataset with specific data statistics are in table 1.

Test We test our model on two different domain datasets without further training. Finance and Banking are the released test datasets of DSTC 11.

6.2 Baseline

In DSTC 11 task2 Open Intent Induction, "glove-840b-300d" and "sentence-transformer/all-mpnet-base-v2" are base encoders. Afterward, K-means clusters the hidden representations from encoders to induce an intent schema. Utterances with "InformIntent" are used as input, which implies that some noises might be included as well.

- KGlove + K-means clustering
- SBERT + K-means clustering

6.3 Metrics

There are five evaluation metrics: accuracy (ACC), normalized mutual information (NMI), Adjusted rand index (ARI), Precision, Recall, and F1 score. ACC is the main evaluation. NMI is defined as

$$\mathbf{NMI}(\mathbf{Y},\mathbf{C}) = \frac{2 * I(Y;C)}{[H(Y) + H(C)]}, \quad (5)$$

where Y is class labels, C for cluster labels, H for entropy, and I for mutual information. Following the baseline code, we used hyperopt packages to identify the optimal alignment.

6.4 Implementation

The "sentence-transforemr/all-mpnet-base-v2" model is our backbone. In MDB training process, we split each dataset into three sets (Train 70 : valid 20 : test 10). Since each dataset has its own various sizes, we set the number of iterations per epoch according to the largest dataset's length (i.e., 22,500 of CLINC150 dataset) divided by the batch size 64.

We train MDB and PGT modules 40 epochs in total. The optimizer is AdamW with cosine annealing and warm-up scheduler, whose learning rate is 5e-6, weight decay for 1e-2, and warm-up steps for 10% of total iterations. To calculate the loss in the MDB training, we set temperature τ as 0.05 for each dataset, whereas PGT uses cross entropy loss.

In our experiments with the grouping algorithms, K-Means and Spectral clustering use n init 10. As mentioned in Section 5 Methods, we sample from the uniform distribution between 5 and 50 until finding optimal K. The type of affinity is 'nearest neighbors' for Spectral clustering.

7 Results

We show the results on the Banking and Finance DSTC 11 datasets in Table 2. We ablate each module to find the best combination. We notate T(True) and F(False) to signify each module's existence (GE-MDB-PGT). For example, TTF-kmeans means that we concatenate representations of GE and MDB, subsequently clustering those with K-means algorithm.

First, an encoder with Spectral clustering outperforms one with K-Means clustering in most cases by at least around 5% in ACC and at most 16% in ACC. Spectral clustering additionally constructs an affinity matrix using the similarity based on the nearest neighbors and clusters utterances based on K-means in a Laplacian embedding space. Therefore, the result implies that Spectral clustering is advantageous for Finance and Banking as it clusters data by considering the connectivity between data points rather than compactness around the cluster center. More details are in Appendix A and Appendix B

Next, the MDB module significantly plays a significant role in Open Intent Induction task beyond the domain. For instance, on Banking dataset, FTF-spectral outperforms Baseline by around 13% in ACC, 5% in NMI, and 7% in F1 score. On Finance Dataset, it also shows higher performance, around 12% in ACC, 7% in NMI, and 11% in F1 score. These results symbolize that MDB method is significantly profitable for learning how to discriminate similar utterances without a domain dependency. Additionally, by observing TTF model's performance improvement upon Baseline (TTF-kmeans), we can derive the same result.

Furthermore, comparing FTF and FTT, the PGT module boosts performance by bridging the gap between clustering and our model. On Banking dataset, our FTT-spectral improves FTF-spectral upon around 3.5% in ACC, 1.7% in NMI, and 3.3% in F1. And, on Finance dataset, 1.5% in ACC, 0.3% in NMI, and 1% in F1.

Comparing FTF and TTF, the general representations induced by GE module contribute to the performance. On Banking dataset, our TTF-spectral improves FTF-spectral upon around 6% in ACC, 3% in NMI, 6% in F1. And, on Finance dataset,

Table 1: Intent Detection Datasets Summary

Dataset	#Domain	#Intents	#Utters	Vocab	Length(min / max / avg)
ATIS	1	25	5,781	938	1 / 46 / 11.2
BANKING77	1	77	13,072	2,636	2 / 78 / 11.7
CLINC150	10	150	22,500	6,420	1 / 28 / 8.3
HWU64	21	64	11033	4661	1 / 25 / 6.6
MCID	1	16	1745	1415	1 / 20 / 6.7
RESTAURANT8K	1	13	4181	3949	1 / 84 / 15.1

	Banking			Finance			Summary		
Models	ACC	NMI	F1	ACC	NMI	F1	ACC	NMI	F1
Baseline (TFF-kmeans)	70.76	83.97	79.9	56.46	76.22	67.83	63.61	80.095	73.865
FTF - kmeans	74.4472	87.338	82.5436	70.177	82.717	78.1243	72.3121	85.0275	80.33395
FTF - spectral	83.7838	89.4275	86.402	68.5841	83.8913	78.7872	76.18395	86.6594	82.5946
FTT - kmeans	75.1843	85.8193	81.5178	65.2212	80.6355	74.0729	70.20275	83.2274	77.79535
FTT - spectral	87.2236	91.1721	89.7293	70.177	84.2486	79.6696	78.7003	87.71035	84.69945
TTF - kmeans (Submit)	79.36	87.71	83.66	57.52	78.44	70.38	73.62385	86.476	82.4171
TTF - spectral	89.6806	92.6607	92.3042	70.6195	**84.9659**	**80.1991**	80.15005	**88.8133**	**86.25165**
TTT - kmeans (Submit)	74.2	86.98	82.1	60.8	80.48	73.73	66.91385	82.1102	76.64015
TTT - spectral	**90.172**	**92.9917**	**92.6801**	**71.0619**	84.2045	79.7353	**80.6170**	88.6008	86.2077

Table 2: Results represent the performance of our method applied to Banking and Finance domain datasets. We notate T(True) and F(False) to signify each module's existence (GE-MDB-PGT). FTF refers to a model using MDB, FTT refers to a model using MDB and PGT, TTF refers to a model using GE and MDB, and finally TTT refers to a model using GE, MDB and PGT

2% in ACC, 1% in NMI, 1.5% in F1. GE module is prominently helpful for banking dataset. We conjecture that Banking utterances are closer to ordinary language than Finance utterances. Finally, TTF-spectral and TTT-spectral show that the combination of GE and PGT boosts ACC on Banking and Finance, around 0.5% for the two datasets.

In sum, simply changing from K-means to Spectral clustering improves the performance significantly in the model we submitted. Our TTT-spectral shows remarkable performance in two different domains (e.g., Banking, Finance) without additional training process. Mainly, the MDB method boosts performance by a large margin, and the PGT module raises the performance to a higher level. We empirically recognize that Spectral clustering shows better synergy with our models than K-means clustering. Furthermore, MDB and PGT methods work well regardless of the domain without additional fine-tuning processes.

8 Conclusion

In TOD systems, it is noteworthy to capture users' intents regardless of domain. We figure out that simply adopting PLM does not perform well in dialogue corpus. Therefore, PLM needs more training. We suggest the multi-view model with GE, MDB, and PGT modules. The MDB method with cosine softmax utilizes an existing dataset to bridge between PLM and dialogue domain. The novel PGT method, a methodology for fine-tuning based on K-means, is presented to enhance the clustering capability. As a result, the performance increases in Finance and Banking datasets. According to our clustering experiments, we found that Spectral clustering is best fitted for our model, resulting in more significant and higher performance than simple K-means methods.

Limitations

The first limitation of our approach is that the hidden representation dimension increases as more views are used. Therefore, the clustering phase may take longer than other models. Second, interactive information among these multi-views is not considered in our model. Thus, we will introduce meta-attention to harmonize them, not just a concatenation, to reflect interactive information among modules. Lastly, in order to apply MDB, an existing task-related dataset must exist. Otherwise, it is impossible to train the MDB module.

Acknowledgement

K. Jung is with ASRI, Seoul National University, Korea. This work was supported by Institute of Information & communications Technology Planning & Evaluation(IITP) grant funded by the Korea government(MSIT) [No. 2022-0-00184, Development and Study of AI Technologies to Inexpensively Conform to Evolving Policy on Ethics]. This work was partly supported by Institute of Information & communications Technology Planning & Evaluation (IITP) grant funded by the Korea government(MSIT) [NO.2021-0- 02068, Artificial Intelligence Innovation Hub (Artificial Intelligence Institute, Seoul National University) & NO.2021-0-01343, Artificial Intelligence Graduate School Program (Seoul National University)]

References

Roee Aharoni and Yoav Goldberg. 2020. Unsupervised domain clusters in pretrained language models. In *Proceedings of the 58th Annual Meeting of the Association for Computational Linguistics*, pages 7747–7763, Online. Association for Computational Linguistics.

Siqi Bao, Huang He, Fan Wang, Hua Wu, and Haifeng Wang. 2020. PLATO: Pre-trained dialogue generation model with discrete latent variable. In *Proceedings of the 58th Annual Meeting of the Association for Computational Linguistics*, pages 85–96, Online. Association for Computational Linguistics.

Markus M. Breunig, Hans-Peter Kriegel, Raymond T. Ng, and Jörg Sander. 2000. Lof: Identifying density-based local outliers. In *Proceedings of the 2000 ACM SIGMOD International Conference on Management of Data*, SIGMOD '00, page 93–104, New York, NY, USA. Association for Computing Machinery.

Tom B. Brown, Benjamin Mann, Nick Ryder, Melanie Subbiah, Jared Kaplan, Prafulla Dhariwal, Arvind Neelakantan, Pranav Shyam, Girish Sastry, Amanda Askell, Sandhini Agarwal, Ariel Herbert-Voss, Gretchen Krueger, Tom Henighan, Rewon Child, Aditya Ramesh, Daniel M. Ziegler, Jeffrey Wu, Clemens Winter, Christopher Hesse, Mark Chen, Eric Sigler, Mateusz Litwin, Scott Gray, Benjamin Chess, Jack Clark, Christopher Berner, Sam McCandlish, Alec Radford, Ilya Sutskever, and Dario Amodei. 2020. Language models are few-shot learners. *CoRR*, abs/2005.14165.

Iñigo Casanueva, Tadas Temčinas, Daniela Gerz, Matthew Henderson, and Ivan Vulić. 2020. Efficient intent detection with dual sentence encoders. In *Proceedings of the 2nd Workshop on Natural Language Processing for Conversational AI*, pages 38–45, Online. Association for Computational Linguistics.

Ajay Chatterjee and Shubhashis Sengupta. 2020. Intent mining from past conversations for conversational agent. In *Proceedings of the 28th International Conference on Computational Linguistics*, pages 4140–4152, Barcelona, Spain (Online). International Committee on Computational Linguistics.

Minhua Chen, Badrinath Jayakumar, Michael Johnston, S. Eman Mahmoodi, and Daniel Pressel. 2022. Intent discovery for enterprise virtual assistants: Applications of utterance embedding and clustering to intent mining. In *Proceedings of the 2022 Conference of the North American Chapter of the Association for Computational Linguistics: Human Language Technologies: Industry Track*, pages 197–208, Hybrid: Seattle, Washington + Online. Association for Computational Linguistics.

K. Chidananda Gowda and G. Krishna. 1978. Agglomerative clustering using the concept of mutual nearest neighbourhood. *Pattern Recognition*, 10(2):105–112.

Samuel Coope, Tyler Farghly, Daniela Gerz, Ivan Vulić, and Matthew Henderson. 2020. Span-ConveRT: Few-shot span extraction for dialog with pretrained conversational representations. In *Proceedings of the 58th Annual Meeting of the Association for Computational Linguistics*, pages 107–121, Online. Association for Computational Linguistics.

Jacob Devlin, Ming-Wei Chang, Kenton Lee, and Kristina Toutanova. 2019. BERT: Pre-training of deep bidirectional transformers for language understanding. In *Proceedings of the 2019 Conference of the North American Chapter of the Association for Computational Linguistics: Human Language Technologies, Volume 1 (Long and Short Papers)*, pages 4171–4186, Minneapolis, Minnesota. Association for Computational Linguistics.

Martin Ester, Hans-Peter Kriegel, Jörg Sander, and Xiaowei Xu. 1996. A density-based algorithm for discovering clusters in large spatial databases with noise. In *Proceedings of the Second International Conference on Knowledge Discovery and Data Mining*, KDD'96, page 226–231. AAAI Press.

Charles T. Hemphill, John J. Godfrey, and George R. Doddington. 1990. The ATIS spoken language systems pilot corpus. In *Speech and Natural Language: Proceedings of a Workshop Held at Hidden Valley, Pennsylvania, June 24-27,1990.*

Matthew Henderson, Paweł Budzianowski, Iñigo Casanueva, Sam Coope, Daniela Gerz, Girish Kumar, Nikola Mrkšić, Georgios Spithourakis, Pei-Hao Su, Ivan Vulić, and Tsung-Hsien Wen. 2019. A repository of conversational datasets. In *Proceedings of the First Workshop on NLP for Conversational AI*, pages 1–10, Florence, Italy. Association for Computational Linguistics.

Stefan Larson, Anish Mahendran, Joseph J. Peper, Christopher Clarke, Andrew Lee, Parker Hill,

Jonathan K. Kummerfeld, Kevin Leach, Michael A. Laurenzano, Lingjia Tang, and Jason Mars. 2019. An evaluation dataset for intent classification and out-of-scope prediction. In *Proceedings of the 2019 Conference on Empirical Methods in Natural Language Processing and the 9th International Joint Conference on Natural Language Processing (EMNLP-IJCNLP)*, pages 1311–1316, Hong Kong, China. Association for Computational Linguistics.

Sharon Levy and William Yang Wang. 2020. Cross-lingual transfer learning for COVID-19 outbreak alignment. In *Proceedings of the 1st Workshop on NLP for COVID-19 at ACL 2020*, Online. Association for Computational Linguistics.

Ting-En Lin and Hua Xu. 2019. Deep unknown intent detection with margin loss. In *Proceedings of the 57th Annual Meeting of the Association for Computational Linguistics*, pages 5491–5496, Florence, Italy. Association for Computational Linguistics.

Ting-En Lin, Hua Xu, and Hanlei Zhang. 2019. Discovering new intents via constrained deep adaptive clustering with cluster refinement. *CoRR*, abs/1911.08891.

Ting-En Lin, Hua Xu, and Hanlei Zhang. 2020. Discovering new intents via constrained deep adaptive clustering with cluster refinement. *Proceedings of the AAAI Conference on Artificial Intelligence*, 34(05):8360–8367.

Xingkun Liu, Arash Eshghi, Pawel Swietojanski, and Verena Rieser. 2019. Benchmarking natural language understanding services for building conversational agents. *CoRR*, abs/1903.05566.

Yinhan Liu, Myle Ott, Naman Goyal, Jingfei Du, Mandar Joshi, Danqi Chen, Omer Levy, Mike Lewis, Luke Zettlemoyer, and Veselin Stoyanov. 2020. Ro{bert}a: A robustly optimized {bert} pretraining approach.

J. MacQueen. 1967. Some methods for classification and analysis of multivariate observations.

Bodhisattwa Prasad Majumder, Shuyang Li, Jianmo Ni, and Julian McAuley. 2020. Interview: Large-scale modeling of media dialog with discourse patterns and knowledge grounding. In *Proceedings of the 2020 Conference on Empirical Methods in Natural Language Processing (EMNLP)*, pages 8129–8141, Online. Association for Computational Linguistics.

Grégoire Mesnil, Yann Dauphin, Kaisheng Yao, Yoshua Bengio, Li Deng, Dilek Hakkani-Tur, Xiaodong He, Larry Heck, Gokhan Tur, Dong Yu, and Geoffrey Zweig. 2015. Using recurrent neural networks for slot filling in spoken language understanding. *IEEE/ACM Transactions on Audio, Speech, and Language Processing*, 23(3):530–539.

Andrew Ng, Michael Jordan, and Yair Weiss. 2001. On spectral clustering: Analysis and an algorithm. In *Advances in Neural Information Processing Systems*, volume 14. MIT Press.

Hugh Perkins and Yi Yang. 2019. Dialog intent induction with deep multi-view clustering. In *Proceedings of the 2019 Conference on Empirical Methods in Natural Language Processing and the 9th International Joint Conference on Natural Language Processing (EMNLP-IJCNLP)*, pages 4016–4025, Hong Kong, China. Association for Computational Linguistics.

Nils Reimers and Iryna Gurevych. 2019. Sentence-BERT: Sentence embeddings using Siamese BERT-networks. In *Proceedings of the 2019 Conference on Empirical Methods in Natural Language Processing and the 9th International Joint Conference on Natural Language Processing (EMNLP-IJCNLP)*, pages 3982–3992, Hong Kong, China. Association for Computational Linguistics.

Xiang Shen, Yinge Sun, Yao Zhang, and Mani Najmabadi. 2021. Semi-supervised intent discovery with contrastive learning. In *Proceedings of the 3rd Workshop on Natural Language Processing for Conversational AI*, pages 120–129, Online. Association for Computational Linguistics.

Kaitao Song, Xu Tan, Tao Qin, Jianfeng Lu, and Tie-Yan Liu. 2020. Mpnet: Masked and permuted pre-training for language understanding. In *Advances in Neural Information Processing Systems*, volume 33, pages 16857–16867. Curran Associates, Inc.

Ivan Vulic, Pei hao Su, Sam Coope, Daniel Gerz, Paweł Budzianowski, Iñigo Casanueva, Nikola Mrkvsi'c, and Tsung-Hsien Wen. 2021. Convfit: Conversational fine-tuning of pretrained language models. In *EMNLP*.

Jason Wei, Maarten Bosma, Vincent Zhao, Kelvin Guu, Adams Wei Yu, Brian Lester, Nan Du, Andrew M. Dai, and Quoc V Le. 2022. Finetuned language models are zero-shot learners. In *International Conference on Learning Representations*.

Chien-Sheng Wu, Steven C.H. Hoi, Richard Socher, and Caiming Xiong. 2020. TOD-BERT: Pre-trained natural language understanding for task-oriented dialogue. In *Proceedings of the 2020 Conference on Empirical Methods in Natural Language Processing (EMNLP)*, pages 917–929, Online. Association for Computational Linguistics.

Zhilin Yang, Zihang Dai, Yiming Yang, Jaime Carbonell, Russ R Salakhutdinov, and Quoc V Le. 2019. Xlnet: Generalized autoregressive pretraining for language understanding. In *Advances in Neural Information Processing Systems*, volume 32. Curran Associates, Inc.

Hanlei Zhang, Hua Xu, Ting-En Lin, and Rui Lyu. 2021a. Discovering new intents with deep aligned clustering. *Proceedings of the AAAI Conference on Artificial Intelligence*, 35(16):14365–14373.

Haode Zhang, Yuwei Zhang, Li-Ming Zhan, Jiaxin Chen, Guangyuan Shi, Xiao-Ming Wu, and Albert Y.S. Lam. 2021b. Effectiveness of pre-training for few-shot intent classification. In *Findings of the Association for Computational Linguistics: EMNLP 2021*, pages 1114–1120, Punta Cana, Dominican Republic. Association for Computational Linguistics.

Jianguo Zhang, Trung Bui, Seunghyun Yoon, Xiang Chen, Zhiwei Liu, Congying Xia, Quan Hung Tran, Walter Chang, and Philip Yu. 2021c. Few-shot intent detection via contrastive pre-training and fine-tuning. In *Proceedings of the 2021 Conference on Empirical Methods in Natural Language Processing*, pages 1906–1912, Online and Punta Cana, Dominican Republic. Association for Computational Linguistics.

Yuwei Zhang, Haode Zhang, Li-Ming Zhan, Xiao-Ming Wu, and Albert Lam. 2022. New intent discovery with pre-training and contrastive learning. In *Proceedings of the 60th Annual Meeting of the Association for Computational Linguistics (Volume 1: Long Papers)*, pages 256–269, Dublin, Ireland. Association for Computational Linguistics.

Xueliang Zhao, Wei Wu, Can Xu, Chongyang Tao, Dongyan Zhao, and Rui Yan. 2020. Knowledge-grounded dialogue generation with pre-trained language models. In *Proceedings of the 2020 Conference on Empirical Methods in Natural Language Processing (EMNLP)*, pages 3377–3390, Online. Association for Computational Linguistics.

Yunhua Zhou, Peiju Liu, and Xipeng Qiu. 2022. KNN-contrastive learning for out-of-domain intent classification. In *Proceedings of the 60th Annual Meeting of the Association for Computational Linguistics (Volume 1: Long Papers)*, pages 5129–5141, Dublin, Ireland. Association for Computational Linguistics.

A Kmeans vs Spectral in Banking Dataset

A.1 Analysis about Banking Dataset

Table 3 shows some simple statistics for Banking Dataset. Some utterances do not belong to the gold intent sets, regarded as noises. As shown in the Tabel 4, the utterances are colloquial and usually include filler words. In some cases, samples include utterances which are different from its label. Furthermore, some samples require context to fully capture their intention, such as "I need to make a deposit like now." Additionally, some utterances could be annotated with multiple labels. For example, "Can I close my savings account and transfer the remaining balance from my savings account into my checking account?", can be labeled as not only CloseBankAccount but also, InternalFundTransfer.

We used the utterances, including noise, to make an intent schema where 2,325 instances (63%) were noise. They are daily conversations regardless of banking. Therefore, it is important to distinguish noise from other gold labels effectively.

There is a huge data imbalance with respect to the number of instances included in each gold cluster; for example, the label "CheckAccountBalance" has 243 samples, while "AskAboutCreditScore" has only three samples. The number of samples for each intent label is shown in Table 5.

A.2 Analysis about Intent Schema and Test Prediction

For noise detection, in the case of Kmeans clustering, this algorithm finds 28 intent clusters out of 30 gold clusters, whereas Spectral clustering found 34 intent clusters. Kmeans clustering detect 251 noise utterances out of 2325 noise instances and showed an F1 score of 0.189, while Spectral clustering found 838 noise instances and showed a significantly higher F1 score of 0.478. According to detected labels, the intent schema created through Kmeans clustering contained a lot of noise, resulting in an average F1 score of 0.288 without noise. In contrast, the intent schema created through Spectral clustering achieved a significantly higher average F1 score of 0.379 without noise.

Spectral clustering presented a better performance for labeled data with noise. However, Kmeans clustering tended to concentrate on certain words and did not consider the meaning of the entire sentence. This makes it difficult to distinguish noise from the other gold labels and decide the boundaries between clusters, which share similar semantic with some variations such as "UpdateEmail" and "UpdateStreetAddress." In contrast, Spectral clustering tended to consider the meaning of the entire sentence, filtering out noises consisting of daily conversations. In fact, noises are labeled sentences within additional four clusters.

Spectral clustering also showed better performance for labeled data without noise. Throughout table 6, Spectral clustering clustered sentences which have similar meanings. It also appropriately handled unrelated utterances as NaN, while Kmeans clustering failed to do so. Analyzing the results among the labels, i.e., "UpdateEmail" and "UpdateStreetAddres," Spectral clustering considered the meaning of the entire sentence more, further accurately distinguishing noise from labeled utterances. We recognize that it detects seemingly insignificant word changes such as "email" and "street," preserving overall similar semantics. However, Kmeans clustering focused on specific words rather than the entire meaning of the sen-

Table 3: Simple statistics about Banking Dataset

Dataset file name	# of Utterances	# of Intent	# of Noise
Dialogue.jsonl (InformIntent)	3696	30	2325
Test-utterance.jsonl	407	18	0

Table 4: Examples of Samples in Banking Dataset

Utterances	Intent
I need to make a deposit like now.	FindBranch
No, can you help me find one please?	FindBranch
Well I've got the mobile app. And I'll probably just go ahead and use that because I think I could get directions straight from it. Yeah, I'm new to this new place, anyways. So what about fees? What do they do with those cause I know you when I lived in Alabama we had locations you everywhere and I didn't have to worry about those new fees because I was always using you Intellibank's ATMs but so what what's like the fees like if I if I don't use an Intellibank?	AskAboutATMFees
Can I close my savings account and transfer the remaining balance from my savings account into my checking account?	CloseBankAccoun
All right. So where are you from?	N/A
All righty. So are are you in Raleigh?	N/A
gonna take very long?	N/A
I just need the balance for my checking account, please.	N/A
All right. That sounds great. Is is there a fee associated with this?	N/A
And I need some money transferred to my daughter to pay her bills.	N/A

Table 5: Number of samples included in each gold intent cluster in Banking

AskAboutATMFees	8	GetBranchHours	64
AskAboutCardArrival	10	GetBranchInfo	20
AskAboutCashDeposits	15	GetWithdrawalLimit	20
AskAboutCreditScore	3	InternalFundsTransfer	130
AskAboutTransferFees	11	OpenBankingAccount	83
AskAboutTransferTime	24	OpenCreditCard	5
CheckAccountBalance	243	OrderChecks	9
CheckAccountInterestRate	10	ReportLostStolenCard	70
CheckTransactionHistory	23	ReportNotice	17
CloseBankAccount	63	RequestNewCard	15
DisputeCharge	89	SetUpOnlineBanking	18
ExternalWireTransfer	109	UpdateEmail	34
FindATM	86	UpdatePhoneNumber	20
FindBranch	110	UpdateStreetAddress	49
GetAccountInfo	13	SUM	1371

tence, resulting in misclassifying instances to noise or wrong label even if it contains the exact same keyword with the label. Moreover, their aligned utterances share semantic information; update something. Thus, they tend to locate nearby, obscuring boundaries in terms of the distance-based method. That is, Kmeans clustering cannot distinguish the subtle changes in meaning.

We applied the test-utterance dataset to the classifier trained on the Intent schema to conduct the final evaluation. As mentioned in the Results 7, the classifier trained on the schema created using spectral clustering showed remarkably high performance. When Spectral clustering algorithm creates the schema, it groups similar utterances discerning noises. On the other hand, Kmeans focused on specific words or misclassified daily conversations irrelevant to the topic, which lowered the quality of the schema and caused the classifier to make many errors. As a result, spectral clustering showed significantly higher performance in ACC.

A.3 Alignment

In the organizer's code, predicted labels are assigned one-to-one with reference labels. The one-to-one assignment is the Hungarian mapping method relying on the number of references, so duplicate allocation to the same reference is not allowed. Therefore, when predicted clusters (23 labels) exceed the number of gold clusters (18 labels), almost similar clusters are divided into two different intents, one of which is abandoned. If we aligned the reference label to the predicted cluster allowing overlapping, both Kmeans and Spectral results show that ACC increased by about 4.5% (0.786 and 0.953, respectively). Spectral F1 score also increased by 2%, while Kmeans F1 score raised by 0.1%. It indicates that spectral clustering was well-trained in sensitivity to noise and effectively separated existing clusters.

B Kmeans vs Spectral in Finance Dataset

This section presents an empirical analysis of the results obtained from "TTT-kmeans" and "TTT-spectral" on the finance dataset. The Kmeans clustering tends to prioritize specific keywords over the overall context. For instance, in the first example provided in Table 7, taking a look at the bold phrases, it can infer "ScheduleAppointment" from "see a notary," but may provide incorrect answers if it fails to comprehend such chunks. Moreover, in cases such as "OrderCheck," where it encounters the word "check," it tends to blindly map it to "CancelCheck," and for sentences containing the word "pin," it predicts "ChangePin." Additionally, when it incorrectly predicts "UpdateEmail," it directly maps the word "update" to "UpdateEmail," and there is a tendency to link the word "liquidity" to "purchase."

On the other hand, spectral clustering tends to focus less on specific keywords than Kmeans clustering, but may still make errors in distinguishing relatively ambiguous labels in Table 8. In cases where it makes incorrect predictions, there are often instances of multi-labeling depending on how to interpret utterances. For example, in table 9, the sentence "what's the nearest branch I can visit in person?" carries an ambiguous meaning, such as where I can go and which branch is currently open. However, given the erroneous mapping of "change statement" to "UpdateEmail" and the misinterpretation of "add to business account" as "PhoneNumber" due to its focus on the word "number," and the misclassification of the entity "Gerald Smith" as a location name, there is still much room for improvement.

Table 6: Examples about classifiers' predicted labels in Banking

Utterance	Gold intent	Predicted label (Kmeans)	Predicted label (Spectral)
And and is it. Is it free? Is it free?	NaN	AskAboutATMFees	AskAboutATMFees
Oh, thanks. What about you? Are you having weather?	NaN	AskAboutCardArrival	NaN
Do you guys have an app?	NaN	SetUpOnlineBanking	NaN
OK. that's what what what about my my savings account.	NaN	InternalFundsTransfer	CheckAccountBalance
I want to put money into his account.	InternalFundsTransfer	ExternalWireTransfer	InternalFundsTransfer
no, if possible, could I update my email with you? That's an old one.	UpdateEmail	UpdateStreetAddress	UpdateEmail
OK. I appreciate that. And I wanted to also update my number.	UpdatePhoneNumber	UpdateStreetAddress	UpdatePhoneNumber
... I have money taken of my account that I didn't that I did not do.	DisputeCharge	CheckTransactionHistory	DisputeCharge

Table 7: Kmeans clustering's incorrect predictions and representative examples in Finance.

Predict	Reference	utter
AddUserToAccount	ScheduleAppointment	Good morning. I need to **see a notary** for some documents by at least 2pm today please.
CancelCheck	OrderCheck	I need to order **checks** ASAP!
CancelCheck	OrderCheck	I want to order 500 **checks** for my business.
ChangePin	CloseAccount	please close account #098716253 with **pin** #65491
ChangePin	GetCreditReport	... I need my business credit report sent to me via mail. My **pin** is 94442
UpdateEmail	UpdatePhoneNumber	I'd like to **update** my phone number is 761-451-9850
UpdateEmail	UpdateStreetAddress	I'd like to **update** my street address please, my name is Helen Smithfield
PurchaseStocks	AskLiquidityRatio	i want to check **liquidity** ratio
PurchaseStocks	AskLiquidityRatio	i am jorah mont, i want to check my **liquidity** ratio
OpenAccount	CloseAccount	Hi please close my **account**, I'm switching to a different **bank**

Table 8: Spectral clustering's top incorrect prediction-label pairs in Finance.

Predict	Reference
ApplyCreditCard	RequestNewCard
checkAccountBalance	CheckCreditCardBalance
MakeCreditCardPayment	SetAutoPayment
FindBranch	ScheduleAppointment

Table 9: Spectral clustering's incorrect predictions and representative examples in Finance.

Predict	Reference	utter
GetBranchHours	FindBranch	What's the nearest branch I can visit in person?
FindBranch	ScheduleAppointment	I need to see a person about my taxes. In person thank you.
GetBranchHours	FindBranch	Which of your branches can I visit in person?
UpdateEmail	ChangeStatementDelivery	hey I want to **change** my monthly statement delivery to **email** pls
UpdatePhoneNumber	AddUserToAccount	... I need to add Luke Walker to my business account. The **account number** is 45000222
UpdateStreetAddress	AddUserToAccount	I'm Eric Daniels. I need to add **Gerald Smith** to my business account.

Adapting Text-based Dialogue State Tracker for Spoken Dialogues

Jaeseok Yoon[1*], Seunghyun Hwang[1*], Ran Han[2], Jeonguk Bang[2], Kee-Eung Kim[1,3]
[1]Kim Jaechul Graduate School of AI, KAIST, Seoul, Republic of Korea
[2]Electronics Telecommunications Research Institute (ETRI), Daejeon, Republic of Korea
[3]School of Computing, KAIST, Daejeon, Republic of Korea
{jake.yoon, steven1971}@kaist.ac.kr, {ran.han, jubang0219}@etri.re.kr, kekim@kaist.ac.kr

Abstract

Although there have been remarkable advances in dialogue systems through the dialogue systems technology challenge (DSTC), it remains one of the key challenges to building a robust task-oriented dialogue system with a speech interface. Most of the progress has been made for text-based dialogue systems since there are abundant datasets with written corpora while those with spoken dialogues are very scarce. However, as can be seen from voice assistant systems such as Siri and Alexa, it is of practical importance to transfer the success to spoken dialogues. In this paper, we describe our engineering effort in building a highly successful model that participated in the speech-aware dialogue systems technology challenge track in DSTC11. Our model consists of three major modules: (1) automatic speech recognition error correction to bridge the gap between the spoken and the text utterances, (2) text-based dialogue system (D3ST) for estimating the slots and values using slot descriptions, and (3) post-processing for recovering the error of the estimated slot value. Our experiments show that it is important to use an explicit automatic speech recognition error correction module, post-processing, and data augmentation to adapt a text-based dialogue state tracker for spoken dialogue corpora.

1 Introduction

Task-oriented dialogue (TOD) systems aim to successfully perform various tasks, such as hotel reservations, train information retrieval, and food ordering, by interacting with users. In particular, with the popularity of voice assistant systems such as Siri and Alexa, it is important to be able to take spoken languages as inputs to TOD systems. These TOD systems with the speech interface is referred to as *spoken dialogue systems*.

However, due to the differences in many aspects between text conversation and speech conversation, the existing TOD systems for text conversation can fail to achieve good performance for speech conversation. To this end, several tasks such as ATIS (Hemphill et al., 1990) and competitions (DSTC2[1], DSTC10 knowledge-grounded task-oriented dialogue modeling on spoken conversations track[2]) were proposed. In the knowledge-grounded task-oriented dialogue modeling on spoken conversations track in DSTC10, various methods were applied to spoken dialogue systems. Khan et al. (2015) introduced a method to reduce automatic speech recognition (ASR) error by making predictions using multiple hypotheses of several ASR models together. Also, Tian et al. (2021) proposed a method to reduce the discrepancy between written conversation and spoken conversation by augmenting the dataset based on ontology and pattern or generating noisy addition of spoken conversation through a text-to-speech (TTS)->ASR pipeline.

Since only ASR hypothesis data was provided in knowledge-grounded task-oriented dialogue modeling on spoken conversations track in DSTC10, it was difficult to effectively deal with errors generated in ASR, and most of the studies were focused on data augmentation to make up for the lack of data. On the other hand, in the speech-aware dialogue system technology track in DSTC11, in addition to the ASR hypothesis data, audio, transcripts used to generate the audio and augmented data were provided, allowing a more diverse approach. For this motivation, we studied how to solve problems caused by the propagation of ASR errors to the model and how to solve errors such as incorrect proper nouns generated by spoken input and participated in the speech-aware dialogue systems technology challenge track in DSTC11.

In this paper, we propose a model, which allows good performance for spoken utterance input as

*These authors contributed equally.

[1]`https://github.com/matthen/dstc`

[2]`https://github.com/alexa/alexa-with-dstc10-track2-dataset`

Proceedings of The Eleventh Dialog System Technology Challenge, pages 81–88
September 11, 2023

<table>
<tr><th>Speaker</th><th>Utterance</th><th>Dialog state</th></tr>
<tr><td>User</td><td>I'd like to find out if there are any 4-star rated guesthouses in cambridge</td><td rowspan="9">hotel-stars=4
hotel-type=guesthouse
hotel-internet=yes
restaurant-name=bangkok city
restaurant-area=centre</td></tr>
<tr><td>System</td><td>There are quite a few. what area do you prefer?</td></tr>
<tr><td>User</td><td>I'm open to any area as long as there is free wifi.</td></tr>
<tr><td>System</td><td>Then I recommend the a and b guest house. Would you like me to book you a room?</td></tr>
<tr><td>User</td><td>Does that also have free parking available?</td></tr>
<tr><td>System</td><td>No, it doesn't. should I recommend you a place with free parking instead?</td></tr>
<tr><td>User</td><td>No, but I am looking for a particular restaurant. Its name is called bangkok city</td></tr>
<tr><td>System</td><td>Bangkok city is an expensive Thai restaurant in the centre of town. They are located at 24 green street city centre. Their postcode is cb23jx. Would you like a reservation?</td></tr>
<tr><td>User</td><td>All I needed today was the address, thank you</td></tr>
</table>

Table 1: A DST example in MultiWOZ dataset

well. Our contributions are summarized as follows: (1) We show that explicit ASR error correction can improve the performance of dialogue systems with spoken corpora as input. (2) We show that post-processing can mitigate errors in words such as proper nouns. (3) We successfully construct a dialogue system that performs well with spoken utterance input.

2 Related Work

2.1 Dialogue State Tracking

Dialogue state tracking (DST) is one of the components of a task-oriented dialogue system that maps partial dialogues to the dialogue state. It usually extracts the user's goal and intent in the form of a slot-value pair through the user and system dialogue conversation. As an example in Table 1, the DST task is to extract dialogue states such as the value of *guesthouse* in the slot of *hotel-type* and the value of *bangkok city* in the slot of *restaurant-name* from user's utterance. There are several methods have recently attracted attention in DST tasks.

Dialogue Systems with Description Input Some works have been proposed which include task descriptions as input, where the descriptions related to the dialog system slot or slot value examples are added as input data (Shah et al., 2019). Zhao et al. (2022) showed that a language description-driven system shows a better understanding of task specifications, higher performance on state tracking, improved data efficiency, and effective zero-shot transfer to unseen tasks.

Prompting Dialogue System In the NLP community, it has been shown that large language models such as GPT-3 (Brown et al., 2020) and LaMDA (Thoppilan et al., 2022) can do few-shot learning without fine-tuning. In the dialogue state tracking task, Madotto et al. (2020) applied GPT-2 by priming the model with dialogue state value pair examples. Their model works well on dialogue state tracking with few shot examples without fine-tuning.

2.2 Spoken Dialogue System

In spoken dialogue systems, the discrepancy between text and speech conversations makes it difficult for text-based dialogue systems to perform well. The differences arise from different styles of spoken and written conversations, extra noise from grammatical errors, disfluencies or barge-ins, and speech recognition errors. To solve these issues, benchmark sets using audio were proposed.

Hemphill et al. (1990) and Bennett and Rudnicky (2002) proposed the speech dialogue benchmark which consists of fairly limited corpora focusing on travel reservations. Furthermore, there is no dialogue state annotation. Recently, with spoken dialog systems becoming popular, various speech dialogues benchmark sets have emerged that overcame these limitations, such as DSTC2 (Henderson et al., 2014) and DSTC10 knowledge-grounded task-oriented dialogue modeling on spoken conversations track (Kim et al., 2021). However, these benchmark sets were still insufficient to solve the speech-aware dialogue system because they had no dialog annotations, poor ASR system results, and/or a lack of audio data.

3 Speech-aware Dialog Systems Task

Here we provide background on the Speech-aware dialogue system technology track in DSTC11, which was introduced to overcome the challenges in implementing a good speech dialogue system with the previous speech dialog system benchmarks.

3.1 Dataset

The dataset combines the Multi-domain Wizard-of-Oz (MultiWOZ) dataset (Kim et al., 2019) and audio-related features. The MultiWOZ dataset

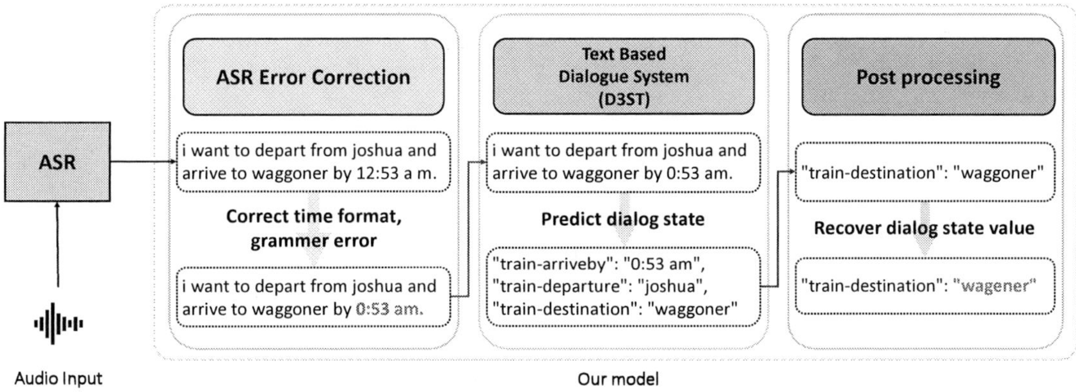

Figure 1: Our model structure

is a large-scale human-human conversational corpus spanning over seven domains, including about 10,000 multi-turn dialogues. Each dialogue is rich in annotations such as 'goal', 'meta-data', 'dialog act', and user and system utterances. Audio-related features are expressed in the following four kinds.

1. Raw audio in the standard PCM format, 2 bytes per sample, at 16KHz sampling rate. Given as two types: TTS and human.

2. Audio encoder output from the ASR system, consisting of 512-dimension vectors at a rate of 75 vectors per second.

3. Transcripts from the ASR system (ASR hypothesis).

4. Time alignment describing how the recognized words map to the encoder output sequences. For example, *w:while t:2 w:in t:5 w:cam t:8 w:bridge t:11 w:â– t:15 w:i t:15 ...*

The track tried to reduce the performance difference according to the ASR model by providing high-quality ASR results and feature vectors.

In addition, the state value of the dataset has been updated because the state value of the original MultiWOZ dataset was overlapped in the dev and test set compared to the train set, so fair evaluation could not be performed. Also, by changing the slot value in the conversation, the dataset was augmented 100 times.

Lastly, we used datasets with three kinds of audio as input to evaluate the spoken dialog system. The three types of datasets are classified according to the type of audio: *TTS-Verbatim* generated by TTS, *Human-Verbatim* by human speech, and *Human-Paraphrased* by paraphrased human speech.

3.2 Evaluation Methods

The evaluation metric is dialogue state tracking[3], one of the base evaluation metrics of the MultiWOZ dataset. Dialogue state tracking is a primary evaluation method that intuitively checks how well the dialogue model works for audio input. Joint goal accuracy(JGA) was used as the first evaluation metric, and slot error rate(SER) and F1 score were used as the second evaluation metric.

4 Methods

In this section, we describe our model that participated in the speech-aware dialogue systems technology challenge track in DSTC11. Figure 1 presents our model architecture. Our system consists of three modules: (1) ASR error correction, (2) Text Based Dialogue System, and (3) Post-processing. The overview of the process followed by our model is as follows:

1. Take the given ASR result from the audio data set to create an input.

2. Insert the input data into the **ASR error correction module** to obtain the text that corrected the ASR error.

3. Output the value of the dialog state with the **dialog system** learned based on the text

4. Run the **post processing module** to recover the dialog state value

[3]https://github.com/jasonwu0731/trade-dst

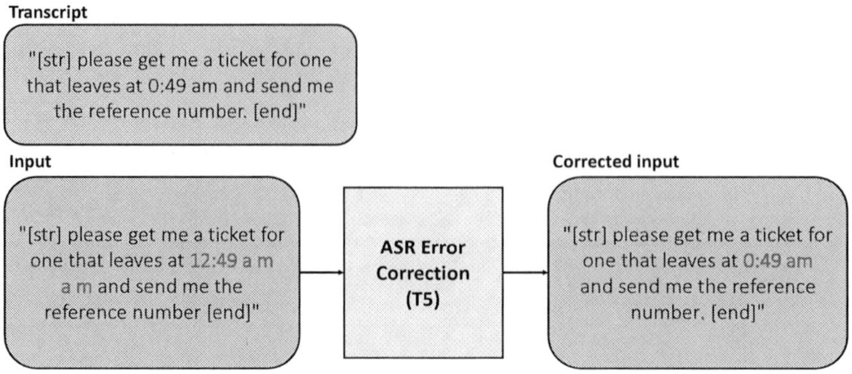

Figure 2: ASR correction example (MultiWOZ *mul0207.json*)

4.1 ASR error correction

In general, we use the ASR model to transcribe audio to text. However, errors arising from the ASR module can be propagated to the dialog system that uses them as input (Dutta et al., 2022), thus it is necessary to correct these ASR errors. Since we have the ground truth text and corresponding ASR hypothesis data, we need to calibrate the ASR hypothesis to ground truth text. As in previous studies, ASR errors can be improved by applying the n-best technique (Zhu et al., 2021), but applying the n-best technique requires audio data for training, which can be very expensive. In addition, in the case of the ASR model, text converted through ASR can be inappropriate for certain downstream tasks. Therefore, instead of the n-best technique, we utilize an ASR error correction module to convert the input to a similar text in our ground truth transcript through a seq2seq-based model.

Figure 2 shows the flow of our ASR error correction module. By comparing the ground truth text and ASR hypothesis, it can be seen that there are many differences. There are special character disappearances, errors in certain formats such as time, as well as spelling errors. To fix this, we implemented a model that was trained to generate ground truth text from the ASR hypothesis based on T5 (Raffel et al., 2020). Therefore, our model can import recovered input instead of the ASR hypothesis which has a higher error compared to the original text.

4.2 Inclusion of task description

Previously, for TOD systems, there have been two main approaches: a modular approach to solve each task by module and the end-to-end approach (Madotto et al., 2018). The end-to-end approach could not show good performance due to the propagation of ASR errors in the spoken dialog system. In addition, the dataset provided on the track was difficult to perform well compared to the conventional MultiWOZ dataset.

Therefore, we used Description-Driven DST (D3ST; Zhao et al., 2022) as a baseline to increase data efficiency by utilizing the description provided by MultiWOZ[4]. Also, we chose a T5-based generation model that showed higher efficiency in the DST Task.

Figure 3 shows an example of the input structure of our DST model. First, we transformed the input data into D3ST format and applied an index-picking mechanism, handling categorical slots. Additionally, we applied random ordering techniques to target dialogue states for each example during training to prevent dependence on the order of predicted slots. When predicting a slot using a generation-based model, this method shows that the model does not depend on the order of slots, and as a result, the slot prediction performance increases.

4.3 Post Processing

There were many proper nouns such as hotel and restaurant names, but in the case of our model, which is using the ASR result as input, it was challenging for ASR error correction to correctly fix these proper nouns. In the previous study, the slot values were recovered by applying an encoder-decoder structure in a hierarchical manner (Ren et al., 2019) or modified to a similar value using the Levenshtein distance ratio (Levenshtein et al.,

[4]https://github.com/budzianowski/multiwoz

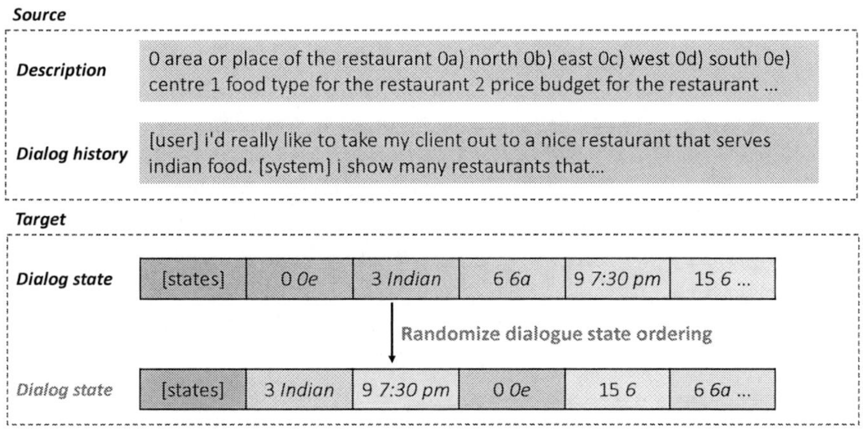

Figure 3: An example of DST model input. We applied a random ordering mechanism to D3ST-based input.

1966). To correct these proper nouns, we created a proper noun database based on Wikipedia data, and we created a module that uses word similarity to recover spelling error words.
There are various algorithms for calculating word similarity. We need to change the misrecognized word caused by ASR error to the correct word, but the spaCy library[5] could not be used because it calculates the similarity of cosine in the vector of the word. In addition, the Gestalt pattern matching (Ratcliff and Metzener, 1988) algorithm is not symmetric, so it shows different similarities depending on the input order, and the performance is slow. Therefore, we applied the Levenshtein distance ratio(Levenshtein et al., 1966) algorithm that calculates similarity by editing (add/delete/update).

5 Experiments

We trained two T5(Raffel et al., 2020) models for ASR error correction and the description dialogue system using huggingface. `T5-base`(220M) was used for ASR error correction and `T5-base`, `large`(770M) for the description dialog system. We used pre-trained weights by Wolf et al. (2020) and tokenized each sentence into sub-words using `T5Tokenizer`[6].

For fine-tuning, we used the AdamW optimizer (Loshchilov and Hutter, 2017) with $\beta_1 = 0.9$, $\beta_2 = 0.999$, weight decay = 0.01 and a learning rate of 0.0001. We used a batch size of 8, an input length of 256, the output length of 256 for ASR error correction, and batch size of 6 (3 for `T5-large`), an input length of 1024, and an output length of 512 for the description dialogue system.

5.1 ASR error correction Result

Post Processing	ASR	ASR correction
NONE	92.4%	**57.5%**
REMOVING SPECIAL CHARACTER	58.7%	**22.0%**

Table 2: Comparison of sentence error rate between the text of ASR without post-processing and of our ASR correction method. The sentence error rate is the number of incorrect sentences divided by the total number of sentences.

We compared the text enhanced by our ASR correction method to the text generated by ASR without correction. The result is summarized in Table 2. The first row shows the result without any post-processing text while the second row shows the result of removing special characters in the generated text. The sentence error rate is the number of incorrect sentences divided by the total number of sentences. We observe that our ASR correction method yields dramatic performance improvement, which is about a 35% increase in sentence error rate in both cases. This is because applying our ASR correction method makes the sentence from ASR more natural. Qualitative results are presented in Figure 2, which supports our claim.

5.2 Main Results

Table 3 shows the results of the experiment. This result is generated by training with *original transcript* and evaluating it with *tts-verbatim* of the validation set. The track organizers presented a baseline based on the `D3ST` model and showed dif-

[5] `https://spacy.io/api/token#similarity`
[6] `https://github.com/huggingface/transformers`

	Model + Feature	JGA	SER
Baseline	D3ST (T5-base)	20.0	-
	D3ST (T5-large)	21.1	-
	D3ST (T5-large) + **D**	28.4	-
	D3ST (T5-XXL) + **D**	33.7	-
Ours	UBAR (gpt-2)	19.2	-
	D3ST (T5-base)	23.3	31.7
	D3ST (T5-base) + **A**	28.7	25.9
	D3ST (T5-base) + **R**	26.2	-
	D3ST (T5-base) + **R** + **P**	34.1	23.4
	D3ST (T5-base) + **R** + **P** + **D**	40.3	19.0
	D3ST (T5-base) + **R** + **P** + **D** + **A**	**41.6**	**18.3**

Table 3: The experiment results were trained on the original transcript and evaluated on the validation set. **A**: ASR Error Correction, **R**: Random Ordering, **P**: Post Processing, **D**: Data Augmentation

ferences in performance depending on the size of the backbone model and data augmentation.

Considering that the UBAR(Yang et al., 2021) model operates in an end-to-end fashion, we implemented our backbone model based on D3ST(Zhao et al., 2022) which can effectively solve DST Tasks. On top of our backbone model, we carefully added each feature one by one to gradually increase the performance and identify its impact.

Random ordering module allows us to avoid dependence on the order of slots predicted in the inference process, and *Post Processing* module corrects prediction errors in words such as proper nouns. *ASR Error Correction* module corrected ASR errors to text similar to the original transcript. Finally, using the *Data Augmentation*, we were able to create high-performance models.

Model + Feature	Pretrain. Model (# Params.)	JGA	SER
D3ST + **R** + **P** + **D** + **A**	T5-base (220M)	41.6	**18.3**
	T5-large (770M)	**42.4**	19.0

Table 4: Comparison of performance according to model size. **A**: ASR Error Correction, **R**: Random Ordering, **P**: Post Processing, **D**: Data Augmentation

In addition, we conducted a performance comparison experiment according to the size of the T5 model. Table 4 shows the result of the experiment. The performance of our model increased as the size of the base model increased, and Zhao et al. (2022) also showed that the performance difference between the XXL model and the large model was very large for the D3ST model. It would have been nice if we had experimented with a huge model such as XXL, but due to experimental constraints, we could only experiment with the large model. Finally, we submitted our final model based on the large model.

Table 5 is the official results of the test submission by the participants. A total of 6 teams submitted, and each team could submit up to 2 systems, so a total of 11 systems were submitted. We submitted a model that recorded 42.4 in the validation set. Finally, our model achieved third place, with JGA 40.2 for *tts-verbatim* in the challenge.

In particular, our model showed a small gap between *human-verbatim* and *human-paraphrased* data because it was implemented through the *ASR Error Correction* module in a flexible form for sentence structure.

5.3 Worst-Case Analysis

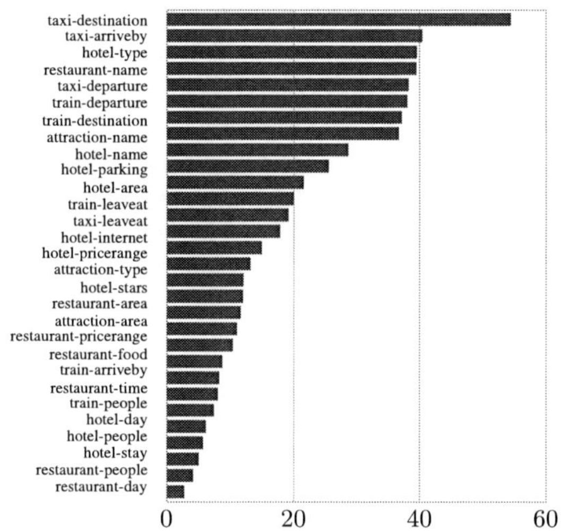

Figure 4: Slots error rate per each slot. Most slots with high slot error rates are slots with proper nouns as slot values, for example, *taxi-destination* (54.5%), *taxi-arriveby* (40.5%), and *restaurant-name* (39.5%). Red-colored slots contain proper nouns.

We hypothesize several approaches that potentially improve the performance of our model. Figure 4 shows the distribution of slot error rates for each slot. Slots containing proper nouns, such as *hotel-name* and *restaurant-name*, showed high slot error rates. Like DSTC11-Track3, in the case of a Dialogue system that uses ASR results as input, there can be many problems with proper nouns. We tried to correct these errors through post-processing, but there was still a lot of ambiguity because we have no dataset or ontology for proper nouns in the model. So we think that defining the appropriate ontology of the system

System	Joint Goal Accuracy			Slot Error Rate		
	TTS-verbatim	Human-verbatim	Human-paraphrased	TTS-verbatim	Human-verbatim	Human-paraphrased
F-p	44.0	39.5	37.9	17.1	20.0	20.4
F-s	40.4	36.1	34.3	19.2	21.9	22.4
C-p (ours)	**40.2**	**31.9**	**31.8**	**20.9**	**28.1**	**27.2**
A-s	37.7	30.1	30.7	20.3	26.9	26.2
C-s	33.1	28.6	28.1	25.0	28.7	29.5
D-s	30.3	23.5	23.2	26.6	36.5	35.1
B-p	27.3	23.9	22.6	26.2	30.0	30.6
D-p	30.3	23.5	23.2	28.0	36.7	36.0
A-p	21.9	21.2	20.0	32.8	33.5	33.8
B-s	22.4	19.2	18.3	28.7	32.2	32.6
E-p	21.3	20.0	18.2	35.1	35.5	35.3

Table 5: Official results for test submissions by DSTC11-Track3. The text in bold indicates our model. The first letter of System means **Team**, and the second letter means System, **p** is **Primary System** and **s** is **Secondary System**.

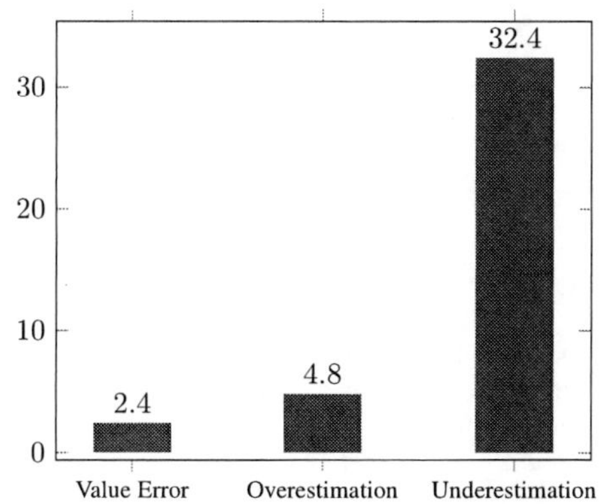

Figure 5: The cause of the error in *hotel-type* slot. Most of the reasons for the error in *hotel-type* slot were believed to have been caused by underestimation.

and post-processing will lead to even better performance.

Figure 5 shows the distribution of the error cause of the *hotel-type* slot, which showed a high slot error rate even though the slot does not include proper nouns. As a result of the analysis, most of the errors appeared to be caused by underestimation. We believe that this is caused by many cases in which hotel types are included in the hotel name, such as *guest house* and *hotel*. Therefore, we think that it would be good to solve the inference about the hotel type by separating the hotel name and the hotel type.

6 Conclusion

In this paper, we proposed an ASR dialogue pipeline model to solve the speech-aware dialogue system technology track in DSTC11. First, we reduce the gap when applying spoken data to text-based dialogue systems by modifying ASR results that differ from the original text such as time formats or special characters through the ASR error correction module. Secondly, the text-based dialogue system, a model including descriptions with several techniques, was able to get good performance even with low input data feature quality of audio data. Lastly, by recovering errors such as proper nouns that cannot be caught in ASR error correction through post-processing, a dialogue system that produces high performance even on the speech database was created. In this way, we have created a model that can overcome the limitations of speech in several parts, and in the case of T5, although the model is very sensitive to parameter size, we can confirm that it is a model with high potential for development by performing well even in a small size model.

Acknowledgments and Disclosure of Funding

This work was supported by Electronics and Telecommunications Research Institute(ETRI) grant funded by the Korean government (22ZS1100, Core Technology Research for Self-Improving Integrated Artificial Intelligence System), Institute of Information & communications Technology Planning & Evaluation(IITP) grant funded by the Korea government(MSIT) (No.2020-0-00940, Foundations of Safe Reinforcement Learning and Its Applications to Natural Language Processing; No.2019-0-00075, Artificial Intelligence Graduate School Program (KAIST)).

References

Christina Bennett and Alexander Rudnicky. 2002. The carnegie mellon communicator corpus.

Tom Brown, Benjamin Mann, Nick Ryder, Melanie Subbiah, Jared D Kaplan, Prafulla Dhariwal, Arvind Neelakantan, Pranav Shyam, Girish Sastry, Amanda Askell, et al. 2020. Language models are few-shot learners. *Advances in neural information processing systems*, 33:1877–1901.

Samrat Dutta, Shreyansh Jain, Ayush Maheshwari, Ganesh Ramakrishnan, and Preethi Jyothi. 2022. Error correction in asr using sequence-to-sequence models. *arXiv preprint arXiv:2202.01157*.

Charles T Hemphill, John J Godfrey, and George R Doddington. 1990. The atis spoken language systems pilot corpus. In *Speech and Natural Language: Proceedings of a Workshop Held at Hidden Valley, Pennsylvania, June 24-27, 1990*.

Matthew Henderson, Blaise Thomson, and Jason D Williams. 2014. The second dialog state tracking challenge. In *Proceedings of the 15th annual meeting of the special interest group on discourse and dialogue (SIGDIAL)*, pages 263–272.

Omar Zia Khan, Jean-Philippe Robichaud, Paul A Crook, and Ruhi Sarikaya. 2015. Hypotheses ranking and state tracking for a multi-domain dialog system using multiple asr alternates. In *Sixteenth Annual Conference of the International Speech Communication Association*.

Seokhwan Kim, Yang Liu, Di Jin, Alexandros Papangelis, Karthik Gopalakrishnan, Behnam Hedayatnia, and Dilek Hakkani-Tür. 2021. "how robust ru?": Evaluating task-oriented dialogue systems on spoken conversations. In *2021 IEEE Automatic Speech Recognition and Understanding Workshop (ASRU)*, pages 1147–1154. IEEE.

Sungdong Kim, Sohee Yang, Gyuwan Kim, and Sang-Woo Lee. 2019. Efficient dialogue state tracking by selectively overwriting memory. *arXiv preprint arXiv:1911.03906*.

Vladimir I Levenshtein et al. 1966. Binary codes capable of correcting deletions, insertions, and reversals. In *Soviet physics doklady*, volume 10, pages 707–710. Soviet Union.

Ilya Loshchilov and Frank Hutter. 2017. Decoupled weight decay regularization. *arXiv preprint arXiv:1711.05101*.

Andrea Madotto, Zihan Liu, Zhaojiang Lin, and Pascale Fung. 2020. Language models as few-shot learner for task-oriented dialogue systems. *arXiv preprint arXiv:2008.06239*.

Andrea Madotto, Chien-Sheng Wu, and Pascale Fung. 2018. Mem2seq: Effectively incorporating knowledge bases into end-to-end task-oriented dialog systems. *arXiv preprint arXiv:1804.08217*.

Colin Raffel, Noam Shazeer, Adam Roberts, Katherine Lee, Sharan Narang, Michael Matena, Yanqi Zhou, Wei Li, Peter J Liu, et al. 2020. Exploring the limits of transfer learning with a unified text-to-text transformer. *J. Mach. Learn. Res.*, 21(140):1–67.

John W Ratcliff and David E Metzener. 1988. Pattern-matching-the gestalt approach. *Dr Dobbs Journal*, 13(7):46.

Liliang Ren, Jianmo Ni, and Julian McAuley. 2019. Scalable and accurate dialogue state tracking via hierarchical sequence generation. *arXiv preprint arXiv:1909.00754*.

Darsh J Shah, Raghav Gupta, Amir A Fayazi, and Dilek Hakkani-Tur. 2019. Robust zero-shot cross-domain slot filling with example values. *arXiv preprint arXiv:1906.06870*.

Romal Thoppilan, Daniel De Freitas, Jamie Hall, Noam Shazeer, Apoorv Kulshreshtha, Heng-Tze Cheng, Alicia Jin, Taylor Bos, Leslie Baker, Yu Du, et al. 2022. Lamda: Language models for dialog applications. *arXiv preprint arXiv:2201.08239*.

Xin Tian, Xinxian Huang, Dongfeng He, Yingzhan Lin, Siqi Bao, Huang He, Liankai Huang, Qiang Ju, Xiyuan Zhang, Jian Xie, et al. 2021. Tod-da: Towards boosting the robustness of task-oriented dialogue modeling on spoken conversations. *arXiv preprint arXiv:2112.12441*.

Thomas Wolf, Lysandre Debut, Victor Sanh, Julien Chaumond, Clement Delangue, Anthony Moi, Pierric Cistac, Tim Rault, Rémi Louf, Morgan Funtowicz, et al. 2020. Transformers: State-of-the-art natural language processing. In *Proceedings of the 2020 conference on empirical methods in natural language processing: system demonstrations*, pages 38–45.

Yunyi Yang, Yunhao Li, and Xiaojun Quan. 2021. Ubar: Towards fully end-to-end task-oriented dialog system with gpt-2. In *Proceedings of the AAAI Conference on Artificial Intelligence*, volume 35, pages 14230–14238.

Jeffrey Zhao, Raghav Gupta, Yuan Cao, Dian Yu, Mingqiu Wang, Harrison Lee, Abhinav Rastogi, Izhak Shafran, and Yonghui Wu. 2022. Description-driven task-oriented dialog modeling. *arXiv preprint arXiv:2201.08904*.

Linchen Zhu, Wenjie Liu, Linquan Liu, and Edward Lin. 2021. Improving asr error correction using n-best hypotheses. In *2021 IEEE Automatic Speech Recognition and Understanding Workshop (ASRU)*, pages 83–89. IEEE.

CopyT5: Copy Mechanism and Post-Trained T5 for Speech-Aware Dialogue State Tracking System

Cheon-Young Park*
Korea Telecom (KT)
park.cheonyoung@kt.com

Yewon Jeong*
Korea Telecom (KT)
yewon.jeong@kt.com

Eunji Ha
Korea Telecom (KT)
eunji.ha@kt.com

Haeun Yu
Korea Telecom (KT)
haeun.yu@kt.com

Chiyoung Kim
Korea Telecom (KT)
chi-young.kim@kt.com

Joo-won Sung
Korea Telecom (KT)
jwsung@kt.com

Abstract

In a real-world environment, Dialogue State Tracking (DST) should use speech recognition results to perform tasks. However, most existing DST research has been conducted in text-based environments. This study aims to build a model that efficiently performs Automatic Speech Recognition-based DST. To operate robustly against speech noise, we proposed CopyT5, which adopts a copy mechanism, and trained the model using augmented data including speech noise. Furthermore, CopyT5 performed post-training using the masked language modeling method with the MultiWOZ dataset in T5 in order to learn the dialogue context better. The copy mechanism also mitigated named entity errors that may occur during DST generation. Experiments confirmed that data augmentation, post-training, and the copy mechanism effectively improve DST performance.

1 Introduction

Task-oriented dialogue systems are used in various fields and are intimately connected to our daily lives. They can help users perform tasks that are frequently encountered in daily life, such as restaurant reservations and train ticket reservations. However, as most of these dialogue systems are implemented using a text-based dialogue corpus, they are very weak when implemented in actual speech interface-based dialogue systems.

In actual human speech, Automatic Speech Recognition (ASR) data contains errors generated because of similar words, inaccurate pronunciation, and noise in the environment being considered, making it difficult to use it directly for learning conversation system models. Various attempts have been proposed to implement a robust speech interface-based dialogue system, such as Fazel-Zarandi et al. (2019) and Liu et al. (2021).

In Track 3 of the DSTC11 summer track, we aim to secure a dialogue system in consideration of speech recognition environments that include speech noise and paraphrasing. Accordingly, we propose a dialogue system based on voice audio and evaluate our model based on a given dataset.

We adopt simpleTOD (Hosseini-Asl et al., 2020) in an end-to-end manner, which is robust in noisy-labeled annotation among task-oriented dialogue systems. To secure a dialogue corpus of various expressions, CoCo (Li et al., 2021) and LAUG (Liu et al., 2021) toolkit were applied to augment the text corpus, and post-training (Han et al., 2022) was performed to better understand the secured text data. Furthermore, in order to improve the generation error occurring in the normal DST model, we propose a dialogue system that applies an effective copy mechanism (See et al., 2017) to out-of-vocabulary resolution and applies certain efficient post-processing techniques.

2 Related Work

2.1 SimpleTOD

A typical task-oriented dialogue system comprises three tasks: Natural Language Understanding (NLU), Dialog State Tracker (DST), and Natural Language Generation (NLG), and suggests an appropriate dialogue system for each sub-task. However, simpleTOD (Hosseini-Asl et al., 2020) proposes a casual language model that can encompass all sub-tasks. Through a simple approach to recast to a single sequence prediction problem, it achieved state-of-the-art performance in the DST task domain and confirmed that the performance impact was low even in noisy-labeled annotations. We adopted the simpleTOD model in an end-to-end manner to secure a robust dialogue system against noise errors, which is the goal of Track 3 of DSTC11 summer track.

DST aims to predict the previous dialogue con-

*Equal Contribution.

Proceedings of The Eleventh Dialog System Technology Challenge, pages 89–94 text and current dialogue states. In general, the next dialogue is predicted from the first utterance of the dialogue to the previous utterance at every dialogue turn. However, an issue arises in that it reacts sensitively to the length of dialogue in predicting the current dialogue state. As the dialogue length increases, the initial dialogue acts as noise, whereas for short dialogue lengths, there is insufficient information for prediction in the previous dialogue. Yang et al. (2021) tested the effect of context information of varying granularity on DST. Accordingly, we set the maximum value of dialogue history so that consistent and universal dialogue tracking can be conducted.

2.2 Copy Mechanism

Copy mechanism is a useful method for maintaining the context of the input sentence and solving the out-of-vocabulary problem. It improves performance by mitigating the out-of-vocabulary problem by outputting the words of the input sentences that appear less frequently in tasks from the decoder, such as machine translations (Zhang et al., 2021) and summarization (See et al., 2017). In DST, the copy mechanism is effective in inferring the dialogue state from the long-distance dialogue history (Wu et al., 2020). Based on previous research, in this study, a copy mechanism was applied to T5 to solve out-of-vocabulary problems such as entity name and to maintain the context of the input dialogue.

2.3 Data Augmentation

Data augmentation refers to generating or transforming data in order to supplement the training data. Liu et al. (2021) states that a dialogue system trained on text-based data is not robust in an audio-based data environment containing noise. CoCo (Li et al., 2021) is a method of generating a new dialogue turn by generating user utterances from system utterances and dialogues states. CoCo improved the performance of the DST model by creating a domain slot combination with a low frequency of appearance among the dialogue states of the MultiWOZ data. CopyT5 was trained LAUG and CoCo data to operate robustly on data containing speech noise and paraphrased data.

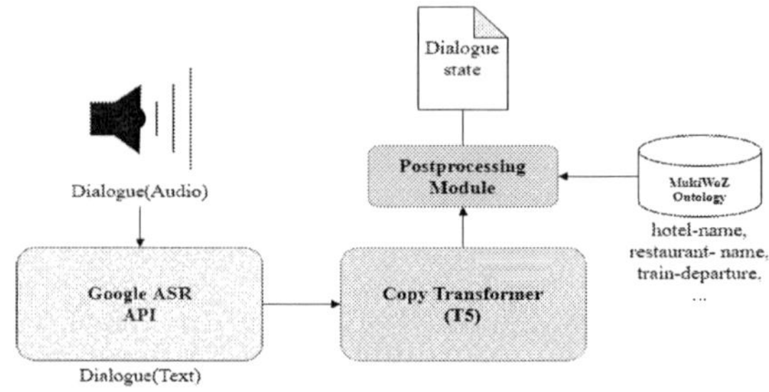

Figure 1: Overview of DST inference system.

3 Method

3.1 Overview

Figure 1 show the inference flow of our system. In the training stage, we used the training dataset provided by DSTC11 Track 3 and augmented dataset. However, in the test phase, the provided Raw Audio Data was recognized as Google ASR API[1] to reduce the noise of conversation data. Google ASR API recognizes time expression and entity name expression better, and errors in transcription are relatively low.

3.2 Post-Training

To better understand the MultiWOZ dataset, CopyT5 used post-training. Post-training means that a model is trained on dataset from the same domain before the fine-tuning stage. We train the T5 model on MultiWOZ using Masked Language Modeling (MLM) loss($\mathcal{L}_{MLM}$).

$$\mathcal{L}_{MLM} = -\sum_{j \in C} logP(y_j|x;\theta) \quad (1)$$

To learn the dialogue context better, the masked part of the dialogue history (of up to three turns) was generated. In Equation 1, j denotes the position of the masked word, C denotes the set of masked words, and y_j is the masked word. x is the input sequence, and θ is the model's parameter.

3.3 Granularity

In DST, granularity refers to the maximum number of turns to consider as current dialogue history. Dialogue has a co-reference in which the utterance of previous turns is related to the current turn. However, if all previous turns are input to the model, the input sequence becomes long and can become noise in the DST model. In contrast, if only the utterance of the current turn is used as the input

[1]https://cloud.google.com/speech-to-text

sequence to reduce the noise, the co-reference of the previous utterances cannot be identified.

Therefore, in this study, up to three turns of dialogue are considered as dialogue history, and the previous turns are replaced with the dialogue state.

3.4 Post-Processing

The generative DST model may give an error while generating dialogue states. Therefore, if the model generated a domain-slot that does not exist in the MultiWOZ dataset, it was removed, and some incorrect domain-slots were revised or deleted as per rules.

Most domain-slot information such as 'time', 'day', and 'area' slots appears in the current turn utterance. Especially in the case of 'day' and 'area' slot, the values are categorical, so we extract and reflect them in the results via a rule-based method.

ASR results may not be accurate for named entities such as restaurant names, hotel names, and station names. Consequently, we built an ontology using MultiWOZ and the named entities collected from the web. We calculated the similarity between the name-related domain-slot values inferred by the model and named entities in the ontology. If the similarity was 0.9 or higher, the value was substituted with the named entity in the ontology.

3.5 Model Architecture

In the generative DST model, an error may occur in the process of generating the named entity in the dialogue. To reduce this error, CopyT5 adopts a copy mechanism. The copy mechanism increases the generation probability of the named entity in the input, so it helps the model to output the named entity as it is in the input. Figure 2 illustrates the architecture of CopyT5.

$$h = T5Encoder(x; \theta) \quad (2)$$

$$s = T5Decoder(h, y; \theta) \quad (3)$$

$$e = v^T gelu(W_h h + W_s s) \quad (4)$$

$$a = softmax(e) \quad (5)$$

Attention a is calculated as given in Equation (5). x is the dialogue history, i.e., input sequence of the encoder, and y is the gold dialogue state, i.e., input sequence of the decoder. h is the output state of the

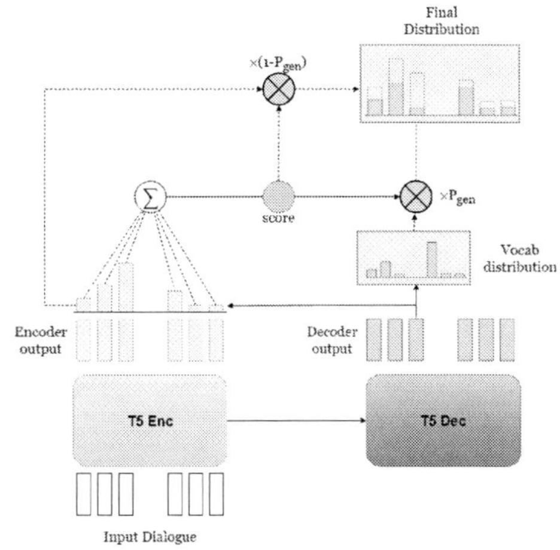

Figure 2: Overview of CopyT5.

encoder, and s is the output state of the decoder. v and W_h,W_s are learnable parameters.

$$h^* = \sum a * h \quad (6)$$

The context vector h^* is calculated by using the attention score as given in Equation (6).

$$p_{vocab} = softmax(V_s s + V_h h^*) \quad (7)$$

p_{vocab} is the probability of the entire vocabulary that the decoder can generate. p_{vocab} is calculated as in Equation (7), and V_s, V_h is the learnable parameter.

$$p_{gen} = \sigma(w_h h^* + W_s s + w_x x) \quad (8)$$

p_{gen} is a value that adjusts the probability of words in the input sequence and the words generated by the decoder. In Equation (8), x denotes the previous state of the decoder. As the transformer calculates the decoder state in parallel during the training process, x is the same as the value shifted to the right of the decoder output. w_h, w_s, w_x is the trainable parameter.

$$P(w) = p_{gen} p_{vocab}(w) + (1 - p_{gen}) a \quad (9)$$

The final output of CopyT5 is as shown in Equation (9). CopyT5 determines copy probability and generation probability according to the value of p_{gen}. $P(w)$ is probability of predicted word w.

4 Experiments and Results

4.1 Dataset

To train our models, we used several datasets including the DSTC11 training dataset. We also used

Model	Training Datasets				
	MultiWOZ 2.1			CoCo	LAUG
	Cleaned text	DSTC11 transcription	Huggingface speech2text		
CopyT5 (Base)	56,778	56,778	56,778	22,471	-
CopyT5 (Large)	56,778	56,778	56,778	22,471	36,000

Table 1: The number of turns in training datasets for each model

System	TTS Verbatim	Human Verbatim	Human Paraphrased
F-p	44.0	39.5	37.9
F-s	40.4	36.1	34.3
C-p	40.2	31.9	31.8
A-s	37.7	30.1	30.7
C-s	33.1	28.6	28.1
D-s	**30.3**	**23.5**	**23.2**
B-p	27.3	23.9	22.6
D-p	**28.6**	**21.8**	**21.4**
A-p	21.9	21.2	20.0
B-s	22.4	19.2	18.3
E-p	21.3	20.0	18.2

Table 2: Overall JGA results of DSTC11 Track 3.

System	TTS Verbatim	Human Verbatim	Human Paraphrased
F-p	17.1	20.0	20.4
F-s	19.2	21.9	22.4
A-s	20.3	26.9	26.2
C-p	20.9	28.1	27.2
C-s	25.0	28.7	29.5
B-p	26.2	30.0	30.6
B-s	28.7	32.2	32.6
A-p	32.8	33.5	33.8
D-s	**26.6**	**36.5**	**35.1**
E-p	35.1	35.5	35.3
D-p	**28.0**	**36.7**	**36.0**

Table 3: Overall SER results of DSTC11 Track 3.

our own augmented data. To make our models robust to various ASR errors and familiar with the ASR data, we augmented the training dataset with HuggingFace speech2text transcript and LAUG. We also used CoCo to augment the training data to help our models better predict proper noun values. Table 1 summarizes the number of turns of training data to train our models.

4.2 Training Details

We used two T5 models (Raffel et al., 2020) with different sizes (base, large). We also conducted post-training in the MultiWOZ domain using MLM loss. The model is trained over five epochs in the post-training stage. At the fine-tuning stage, we trained the model for up to 30 epochs and used early stopping when the performance on the dev dataset was the best. We used two GPUs with 16 batch sizes for training the base model, and four GPUs with four batch sizes for training the large model. For the other hyper-parameters, we used the default hyper-parameters setting of the HuggingFace T5 model[2].

4.3 Evaluation Metrics

We used two metrics to evaluate our models. Joint Goal Accuracy (JGA) is used as the main metric. JGA is widely used to evaluate DST models. At each turn, JGA is 1 only if all domain-slot and value pairs are predicted correctly; otherwise it is 0. This is quite strict and the model gets the worst JGA when it is wrong at the earlier turns in the dialogue. Slot Error Rate (SER) is used as a secondary metric. SER is the ratio of total number of slot errors (substitutions + deletions + insertions) and total number of slots in reference across all the dialogues.

4.4 Results

The base-sized T5 model is additionally post-trained in the MultiWOZ domain using MLM loss. However, it is not effective in the large-sized T5 model, so we used the the open-source T5 large model as it is. Tables 2 and 3 present the JGA and SER results of submissions for Track 3 of DSTC11 respectively. D-s is the base-sized CopyT5 model that conducted post-training in the MultiWOZ domain using MLM. D-p is the large-sized CopyT5 model for which post-training is ineffective, so we only conducted fine-tuning to D-p.

In terms of Slot Error Rate, our systems ranked low. However, the JGA score was ranked relatively high compare with Slot Error Rate score of our system. The CopyT5 model over-generated the 'restaurant-name', 'hotel-name', and 'attraction-

[2]https://huggingface.co/models

System	TTS Verbatim	Human Verbatim	Human Paraphrased
Base (a)	24.43	19.94	19.54
Base (b)	27.06	20.74	21.03
Base (c)	27.34	21.08	20.97
Base (d)*	30.3	23.5	23.2
Large (a)	26.33	21.50	21.32
Large (b)	23.71	18.82	18.67
Large (c)**	28.6	21.8	21.4
Large (d)	27.33	21.84	20.79

Table 4: Overall JGA results of ablation study.

System	TTS Verbatim	Human Verbatim	Human Paraphrased
Base (a)	31.83	39.72	39.29
Base (b)	28.86	38.76	36.92
Base (c)	30.97	42.47	40.76
Base (d)*	26.6	36.5	35.1
Large (a)	30.32	38.42	37.48
Large (b)	33.84	42.49	41.39
Large (c)**	28.0	36.7	36.0
Large (d)	30.59	37.94	38.24

Table 5: Overall SER results of ablation study.

name' domain-slots. We believe that the CopyT5 based DST model was trained to over-extract values for name-related named entities in dialogue history. In contrast, time-related domain-slots such as 'train-leaveat' and 'train-arriveby' were generated less often because the ASR results contained considerable noise in time-related expressions.

To prove the effectiveness of our approach, we conducted an ablation study. The list of ablation studies is as follows:

(a) simpleTOD DST model using T5 without data augmentation

(b) CopyT5 without data augmentation

(c) CopyT5 with data augmentation

(d) CopyT5 with data augmentation, post-training

Tables 4 and 5 summarize the performance of various models (* is D-s, ** is D-p). First, in the case of the base-sized model, when comparing (a) and (b), we can observe up to 2.63% increase in JGA by using the copy mechanism. Furthermore, comparing (b) and (c), JGA increased by up to 0.34% using copy mechanism and data augmentation together. The base-sized CopyT5 with data augmentation and post-processing gives the best performance. Compared to (c), (d) showed significant improvement in JGA by up to 2.96%. In contrast, in the case of the large-sized model, when the copy mechanism was used without data augmentation (comparing (a) and (b)), the performance deteriorated. If the copy mechanism is used, the number of learning parameters of the model increases. Thus, in the large-size model, we believe that the data is not enough to train the model sufficiently. Comparing (b) and (c), we can observe significant improvements in JGA up to 4.89% when we used CopyT5 with data augmentation. We also observe that post-training was not effective in the large-sized CopyT5 by comparing (c) and (d).

5 Conclusion

In this study, DST was performed using the CopyT5 model to which the copy mechanism was applied. The copy mechanism contributed to performance improvement by suitably extracting object names that appeared in the conversation. In addition, post-training helped CopyT5 improve performance in the DST fine-tuning step by pre-learning conversational domain data. However, in the large-sized CopyT5 model, the copy mechanism and post-training were not effective, but the performance improved as a result of applying data augmentation together.

Limitations

The Copy Mechanism helped improve the performance of JGA, but suffers from excessive extraction of domain-slot values. In addition, by applying the copy mechanism, the number of learning parameters increased, and the DST performance decreased despite learning the same training dataset in a large-sized model.

In the future, we will experiment with methods such as data augmentation and prompt learning to efficiently learn the increased learning parameters by applying additional mechanisms in large-scale language models.

References

Maryam Fazel-Zarandi, Longshaokan Wang, Aditya Tiwari, and Spyros Matsoukas. 2019. Investigation of error simulation techniques for learning dialog policies for conversational error recovery.

Janghoon Han, Joongbo Shin, Hosung Song, Hyunjik Jo, Gyeonghun Kim, Yireun Kim, and Stanley Jungkyu

Choi. 2022. External knowledge selection with weighted negative sampling in knowledge-grounded task-oriented dialogue systems.

Ehsan Hosseini-Asl, Bryan McCann, Chien-Sheng Wu, Semih Yavuz, and Richard Socher. 2020. A simple language model for task-oriented dialogue. In *Advances in Neural Information Processing Systems*, volume 33, pages 20179–20191. Curran Associates, Inc.

SHIYANG Li, Semih Yavuz, Kazuma Hashimoto, Jia Li, Tong Niu, Nazneen Rajani, Xifeng Yan, Yingbo Zhou, and Caiming Xiong. 2021. Coco: Controllable counterfactuals for evaluating dialogue state trackers. In *International Conference on Learning Representations*.

Jiexi Liu, Ryuichi Takanobu, Jiaxin Wen, Dazhen Wan, Hongguang Li, Weiran Nie, Cheng Li, Wei Peng, and Minlie Huang. 2021. Robustness testing of language understanding in task-oriented dialog. In *Proceedings of the 59th Annual Meeting of the Association for Computational Linguistics and the 11th International Joint Conference on Natural Language Processing (Volume 1: Long Papers)*, pages 2467–2480, Online. Association for Computational Linguistics.

Colin Raffel, Noam Shazeer, Adam Roberts, Katherine Lee, Sharan Narang, Michael Matena, Yanqi Zhou, Wei Li, and Peter J. Liu. 2020. Exploring the limits of transfer learning with a unified text-to-text transformer. *J. Mach. Learn. Res.*, 21(1).

Abigail See, Peter J. Liu, and Christopher D. Manning. 2017. Get to the point: Summarization with pointer-generator networks. In *Proceedings of the 55th Annual Meeting of the Association for Computational Linguistics (Volume 1: Long Papers)*, pages 1073–1083, Vancouver, Canada. Association for Computational Linguistics.

Peng Wu, Bowei Zou, Ridong Jiang, and AiTi Aw. 2020. GCDST: A graph-based and copy-augmented multi-domain dialogue state tracking. In *Findings of the Association for Computational Linguistics: EMNLP 2020*, pages 1063–1073, Online. Association for Computational Linguistics.

Puhai Yang, Heyan Huang, and Xian-Ling Mao. 2021. Comprehensive study: How the context information of different granularity affects dialogue state tracking? In *Proceedings of the 59th Annual Meeting of the Association for Computational Linguistics and the 11th International Joint Conference on Natural Language Processing (Volume 1: Long Papers)*, pages 2481–2491, Online. Association for Computational Linguistics.

Tong Zhang, Long Zhang, Wei Ye, Bo Li, Jinan Sun, Xiaoyu Zhu, Wen Zhao, and Shikun Zhang. 2021. Point, disambiguate and copy: Incorporating bilingual dictionaries for neural machine translation. In *Proceedings of the 59th Annual Meeting of the Association for Computational Linguistics and the 11th International Joint Conference on Natural Language Processing (Volume 1: Long Papers)*, pages 3970–3979, Online. Association for Computational Linguistics.

OLISIA: a Cascade System for Spoken Dialogue State Tracking

Léo Jacqmin[*1,2] **Lucas Druart**[*1,3] **Valentin Vielzeuf**[1]
Lina M. Rojas-Barahona[1] **Yannick Estève**[3] **Benoit Favre**[2]
[1]Orange Innovation, France
[2]LIS - Aix-Marseille Université, France
[3]LIA - Avignon Université, France
[1]{leo.jacqmin,lucas1.druart,valentin.vielzeuf,linamaria.rojasbarahona}@orange.com,
[2]{first.last}@lis-lab.fr, [3]{first.last}@univ-avignon.fr

Abstract

Though Dialogue State Tracking (DST) is a core component of spoken dialogue systems, recent work on this task mostly deals with chat corpora, disregarding the discrepancies between spoken and written language. In this paper, we propose OLISIA, a cascade system which integrates an Automatic Speech Recognition (ASR) model and a DST model. We introduce several adaptations in the ASR and DST modules to improve integration and robustness to spoken conversations. With these adaptations, our system ranked first in DSTC11 Track 3, a benchmark to evaluate spoken DST. We conduct an in-depth analysis of the results and find that normalizing the ASR outputs and adapting the DST inputs through data augmentation, along with increasing the pre-trained models size all play an important role in reducing the performance discrepancy between written and spoken conversations.[1]

1 Introduction

A majority of recent research on task-oriented dialogue (TOD) systems has focused on chat corpora such as MultiWOZ (Budzianowski et al., 2018). With voice assistants becoming more prominent in our daily lives, there has been a renewed interest in spoken dialogue systems (Faruqui and Hakkani-Tür, 2022). However, state-of-the-art systems trained on chats face robustness issues when dealing with spoken inputs (Kim et al., 2021).

In a TOD system, the role of DST is to predict at each turn and based on the dialogue history the current belief state, *i.e.* a condensed and updated representation of the user needs. DST plays a central role as the system relies on the belief state to decide which action to take next. The belief state is typically frame-based and represented as a list of <slot, value> pairs.

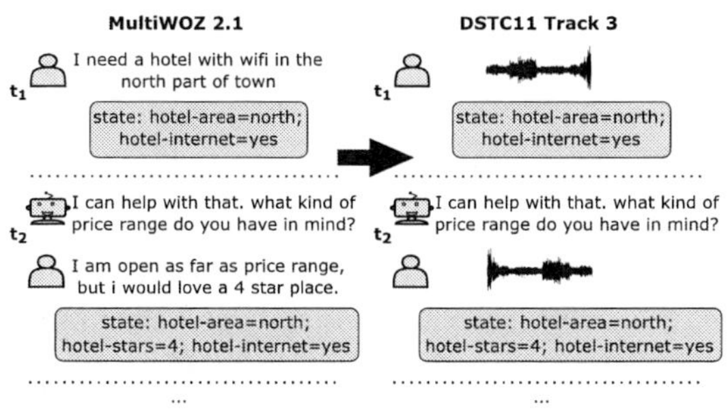

Figure 1: DSTC11 Track 3 introduced a spoken version of MultiWOZ 2.1 (Eric et al., 2019) with user utterances voiced by crowdworkers.

While both cascade and end-to-end approaches have been well studied for Spoken Language Understanding (SLU, Serdyuk et al. (2018)), there has been little recent work on spoken DST. Considering the entire dialogue context, as opposed to only the current turn, requires tricky strategies for end-to-end systems (Tomashenko et al., 2020). In order to leverage state-of-the-art models, a cascade approach with separate ASR and DST components is thus preferred. However, these two components do not benefit from joint optimization and often lack integration.

To address these shortcomings, we propose OLISIA, a cascade system composed of an ASR model and a DST model. OLISIA integrates these two components through adaptations in the ASR outputs and the DST inputs. With this design, our system ranked first in the Speech-Aware Dialog Systems Technology Challenge (DSTC11 Track 3),[2] a benchmark to evaluate spoken DST models. In this paper, we describe our cascade spoken DST system along with the proposed adaptations. Additionally, we conduct an analysis of these adaptations based on the results from various evaluation setups.

[1]Our code is made available at https://github.com/Orange-OpenSource/olisia-dstc11.
[*] Equal contribution.

[2]https://storage.googleapis.com/gresearch/dstc11/dstc11_20221102a.html

Proceedings of The Eleventh Dialog System Technology Challenge, pages 95–104
September 11, 2023 ©2023 Association for Computational Linguistics

Our contributions can be summarized as follows. In the context of the Speech-Aware Dialog Systems Technology Challenge, we show

- the need for post-processing the ASR output in a pipeline;
- the relevance of different data augmentation techniques for DST;
- the importance of scaling up the foundation model size – both for ASR and DST.

2 Related work

Much of the research in task-oriented dialogue (TOD) systems initially focused on spoken dialogue, for instance leveraging probabilistic modeling to account for the uncertainty associated with noisy utterances (Roy et al., 2000; Williams and Young, 2007; Thomson and Young, 2010). The first editions of the Dialogue State Tracking Challenge[3] (DSTC1 & DSTC2, Williams et al. (2013); Henderson et al. (2014)) introduced the first standardized benchmark for DST, releasing annotated spoken dialogue corpora.

However, the focus of research in TOD gradually shifted to chats, assuming that the upstream ASR model would be able to provide accurate transcriptions. Recently, there has been a renewed interest in spoken dialogue to address the lack of attention on the differences between spoken and textual inputs (Faruqui and Hakkani-Tür, 2022). DSTC10 Track 2 proposed a DST task on spoken conversations which stimulated work on this aspect, though only the n-best ASR hypotheses were provided without audio data.

When audio-only data is available, End-to-End Spoken Language Understanding (SLU) systems (Serdyuk et al., 2018) are often preferred because they benefit from joint optimization. Although cascade approaches suffer from error propagation because the textual Natural Language Understanding (NLU) model does not consider the uncertainty of the ASR transcriptions, they remain competitive. In fact several adaptation techniques can boost the cascade's performance.

Performing hypothesis rescoring with a language model specifically trained on the targeted domain proves to be effective when data is available in high quality and large quantity (Chung et al., 2012). We rather adopt a post-processing approach such as spelling correction which can also help aligning the transcriptions with the targeted domain (Hrinchuk et al., 2020), especially when focusing on domain-specific words.

With the recent advances in Text-to-Speech (TTS) technologies, adapting ASR models by fine-tuning them on synthetic speech of the target domain (Li et al., 2018; Rosenberg et al., 2019; Zheng et al., 2021) is now common. However, with only synthetic speech in the training set, such a fine-tuning might degrade the performances on human speech (Laptev et al., 2020). Simulating ASR hidden representations from text in order to train an end-to-end SLU model reaches higher Named-Entity Recognition (NER) performances than training it on the synthesised speech (Mdhaffar et al., 2022). Therefore, relying on the text NLU model to tolerate and correct some errors of the ASR model seems more adapted in our setting.

Recent approaches have focused on data augmentation techniques to simulate spoken data (Wang et al., 2020; Liu et al., 2021; Tian et al., 2021) in order to make the language understanding components of TOD systems more robust to spoken inputs. Other approaches have sought to leverage the multiple hypotheses provided by the upstream ASR model in the hope that these different hypotheses complement each other to help language understanding (Rojas-Barahona et al., 2016; Li et al., 2020; Ganesan et al., 2021). Similarly, others used a more compact representation of these hypotheses, such as word confusion networks (Henderson et al., 2012; Pal et al., 2020).

3 Speech-Aware Dialog Systems Technology Challenge

The lack of recent work on spoken dialogue can be attributed in part to the lack of available datasets. Track 3 of the Dialog Systems Technology Challenge 11[4] seeks to promote work on spoken dialogue by releasing a spoken version of Multi-WOZ. This Multi-domain (restaurant, hotel, attraction, taxi, train, hospital and police) Wizard-of-Oz dataset is a large-scale human-human task-oriented conversational corpus commonly used for training and evaluating dialogue state tracking (DST), policy optimization and end-to-end dialogue modeling systems. The goal of this track is to characterize the performance of DST models in the presence

[3]Rebranded as the Dialog Systems Technology Challenge since DSTC6.

[4]https://dstc11.dstc.community/

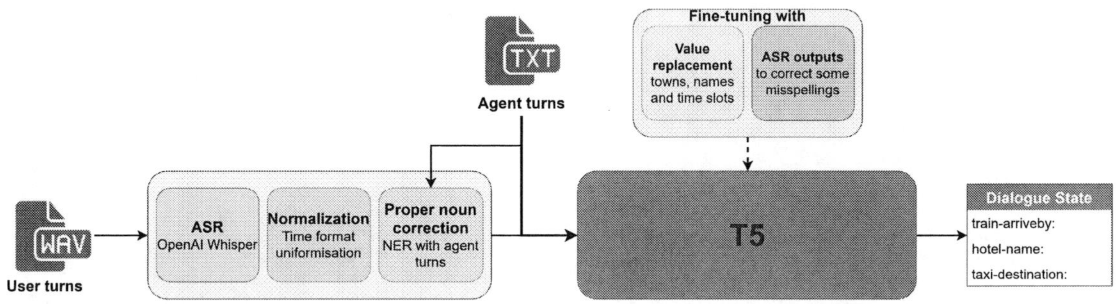

Figure 2: Illustration of OLISIA, our cascade system with adaptations of ASR and DST models to handle their respective errors.

of ASR errors and speech phenomena such as disfluencies. The organizers released a new version of MultiWOZ 2.1 (Eric et al., 2019) with user utterances voiced by crowdworkers, as illustrated in Figure 1.

Despite being widely used by the research community, MultiWOZ has been shown to exhibit an entity bias and a large overlap in the distribution of slot-values between the training and the evaluation sets which can lead to memorization in generative models (Qian et al., 2021). To encourage generalization, the organizers introduced modifications in the dev and test sets: the values for the slots `hotel-name`, `restaurant-name`, `train-departure` and `train-destination` were replaced with unseen entities, and time mentions were offset by a constant amount.

User utterances in the dev and test sets are vocalized by crowdworkers. A speech synthesized version of the training data is also provided in the aim of assessing the validity of such data to mitigate the lack of real spoken conversations.

Two verbatim versions of the dev set are provided to the participants, i.e. user utterances are vocalized as is by a TTS system (**TTS-v**) and human crowdworkers (**Human-v**). The test set includes the same setup along with a third version containing paraphrased user utterances vocalized by humans to sound more natural (**Human-p**).[5]

System submissions are evaluated using Joint Goal Accuracy (JGA) and Slot Error Rate (SER), defined as follows:

$$JGA = \frac{C}{N_t} = \frac{No.\ of\ correct\ state\ pred.}{No.\ of\ turns}$$

$$SER = \frac{S + D + I}{N_s} = \frac{No.\ of\ slot\ errors}{No.\ of\ slots\ in\ ref.}$$

where S, D and I respectively denote substitutions, deletions and insertions of <slot, value> pairs. Regarding the challenge constraints, any type of model can be used but only MultiWOZ is allowed as training data for the dialogue component.

4 Method

In this section, we present our cascade approach with an ASR component which converts the user spoken inputs into text and a DST component which predicts the current dialogue state from the transcript of the previous turns. The overall architecture of the system is shown in Figure 2

On the ASR side, given that the turns are perfectly segmented, we can easily transcribe the user's turns with Open AI Whisper (Radford et al., 2022) transformer model with a forced English decoding. On the DST side, we use a generative DST model based on a pre-trained T5 model (Raffel et al., 2020), which proved to be more robust to spoken inputs than an extractive model in preliminary experiments.

The input to the DST model consists of the entire dialogue history at a given turn, with agent and user utterances separated by delimiter tokens. At each turn, the model outputs the current dialogue state from scratch in the form of <slot-name, slot-value> pairs. Formally, let U_i and A_i respectively be user and agent utterances at turn i. The input at turn T is linearized by concatenating the utterances (U_0, A_1, ..., A_{T-1}, U_T) and prepending the delimiters `"user:"` and `"agent:"`. The output dialogue state is linearized as a semicolon-separated list of strings `"slot-name=slot-value"`.

Our contribution lies in the adaption of the transcriptions outputted from the ASR for DST and the adaptation of the DST component to handle speech specificities, which are discussed in the next two

[5] No further details were provided regarding the value replacement and paraphrasing processes.

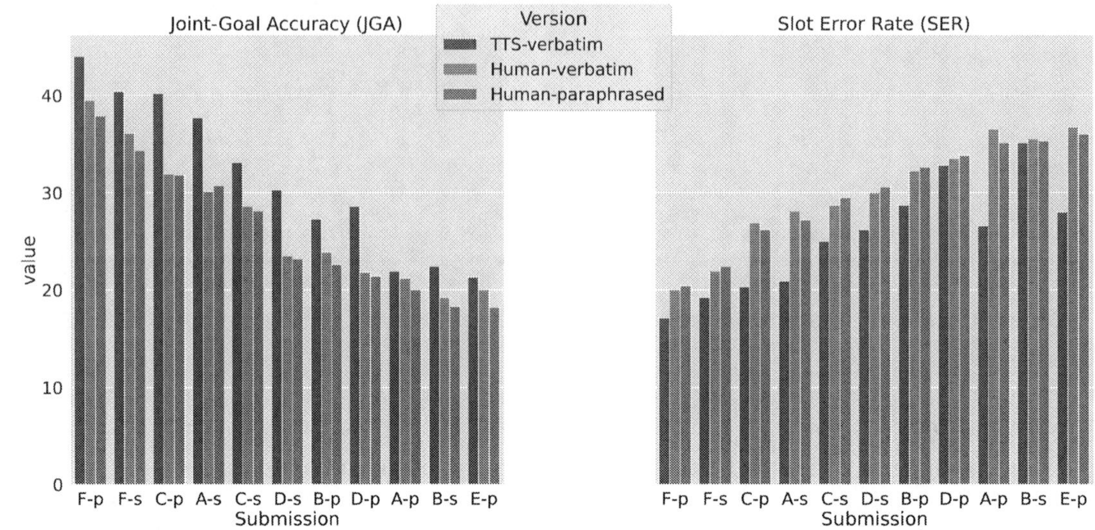

Figure 3: Overall test set results (JGA↑ / SER↓) of the challenge for all submissions. Our primary and secondary submissions respectively correspond to *F-p* and *F-s*.

sections.

4.1 ASR normalization

The first adaptation we apply to Whisper's transcriptions is time normalization. Given the data sources on which Whisper was trained, the outputted time formats vary a lot. We use several regular expressions to identify the most salient patterns (*e.g.* "5 o' 8 am", "2 to 3 pm", "midnight", "quarter past 10 am") and map them to the standard "[hour]:[minutes] [am|pm]" format found in Multi-Woz.

The second adaptation we apply is proper noun correction which impacts the values of the slots `hotel-name`, `restaurant-name`, `taxi-destination`, `train-destination`, `taxi-departure` and `train-departure`. Many proper nouns are either misspelled by the user (*e.g.* the American city Itta Bena is pronounced "I-T-T-A bena") or incorrectly recognized by Whisper (*e.g.* Itta Bena transcribed as "Itta Benna"). In both cases, we use a Named Entity Recognition (NER) model[6] from Nvidia NeMo (Kuchaiev et al., 2019) to identify lists of proper nouns from both agent and user turns. We then score each pair of user and agent identified named entities with Character Error Rate (CER) and tune a threshold in order to replace the user turns' misspelled proper nouns with their matching ones from the agent turns.

More formally, given a list of user proper nouns l_u, a list of agent proper nouns l_a and a threshold δ, we have:

$$\forall u \in l_u, a \in l_a \; u = \begin{cases} u \text{ if } \mathrm{CER}(u,a) > \delta \\ a \text{ otherwise} \end{cases}$$

Where u and a refer respectively to user and agent proper nouns.

4.2 DST data augmentation

To improve robustness and reduce the discrepancy between training and testing data, our DST model is fine-tuned on an augmented version of the provided train set. We apply value replacement, paraphrasing and speech simulation, in this order.

In a similar way to how the dev and test sets were modified by the track organizers, our value replacement concerns named entities (town, restaurant and hotel names) and time slots. To replace entity values, we create a new ontology based on data from OpenStreetMap[7]. We then sample entities with a uniform distribution over our ontology. Values with time mentions are replaced with a random time.

The value replacement process goes as follows:

1. Successively go through each dialogue state in a dialogue, sample one value from our ontology for each distinct value and replace it in the dialogue state;

[6] https://docs.nvidia.com/deeplearning/nemo/user-guide/docs/en/v1.0.0/nlp/token_classification.html

[7] https://wiki.openstreetmap.org/wiki/Overpass_API

	Dev				Test					
	TTS-v		Human-v		TTS-v		Human-v		Human-p	
	JGA↑	SER↓	JGA↑	SER↓	JGA↑	SER↓	JGA↑	SER↓	JGA↑	SER↓
Baseline	26.3	27.5	22.6	31.6	n.a.					
OLISIA$_1$	47.2	15.7	43.2	17.9	44.0	17.1	39.5	20.0	37.9	20.4
OLISIA$_2$	44.1	17.3	40.3	19.5	40.4	19.2	36.0	21.9	34.3	22.4
	JGA↑		SER↓		JGA↑			SER↓		
OLISIA$_1$ (oracle)	57.2		12.5		53.2			13.9		
OLISIA$_2$ (oracle)	55.0		13.6		51.1			15.0		

Table 1: Performance (JGA↑ / SER↓) of our submission compared with the challenge's baseline and our system with text oracle on both dev and test sets. The baseline results on the test set were not shared.

2. Track these replacements with a mapping between replaced value and new value;
3. Based on the obtained mapping, perform a string replacement in the dialogue context.

This process ensures dialogue consistency: if a value for a slot is updated during the dialogue, a new value is sampled thanks to the first step, if a value is shared between multiple slots, the same replacement value is used thanks to the second step, and finally, the string replacement in the third step is performed by decreasing lengths in order to avoid replacing sub-strings (*e.g.* city names can be present in restaurant or hotel names).

Based on this new train set with replaced values, we paraphrase the user utterances using SG-GPT (Peng et al., 2020) which allows us to condition the generation of the paraphrase on the previous turn along with the desired dialogue state for the current turn, preventing annotation inconsistencies due to hallucinations or omissions.

Lastly, we obtain the ASR transcripts for the speech simulation by synthesizing the augmented user turns with a Tacotron2-based (Shen et al., 2018) TTS system using SpeechBrain[8] and transcribing them with Whisper.

5 Results

We propose an overview of the challenge's results in section 5.1 and further analysis of the impact of each adaptation on our system's performance in the following sections.

5.1 Overview

The challenge's leaderboard is shown in Figure 3. All submissions have a gap between their TTS performance and human performance (14.32% average relative JGA decrease and 19.19% average relative SER increase). The gap between the human-verbatim and human-paraphrased is less pronounced (3.36% average relative JGA decrease and 0.08% average relative SER decrease).

Our primary submission (*F-p* in Figure 3) consists in an ensemble of 5 instances of our system described in section 4 with transcriptions provided by Whisper-Large[9] and a T5-Large model[10] fine-tuned on the variations of the training data presented in Table 2. **Replace-S** refers to one version of the train set with value replacement. With **Replace-L**, a different version of the train set is used at each epoch until convergence,[11] with newly sampled entities for value replacement along with the TTS-ASR and optional paraphrasing pipeline.

We used majority vote on each predicted slot value as ensembling strategy. Our secondary submission (*F-s* in Figure 3) consists in the best instance of the models in the ensemble (fine-tuning on T_2). For all models, we use a learning rate of $5e^{-4}$ and a batch size of 16. We compare their performance on the dev and test set with the challenge baseline and our system with text oracle[12] in Table 1. Note that we exclude the ASR-TTS data augmentation for the system evaluated on the text oracle (+5 JGA increase).

While there is still room for improvement (10 JGA points between our system and without text oracle), both our submissions achieved over 40 JGA on the TTS-verbatim test set. Our per-

[8]https://speechbrain.github.io/

[9]https://github.com/openai/whisper

[10]https://huggingface.co/t5-large

[11]Four epochs for T5-Large.

[12]Text oracle considers the ground truth user turns' transcriptions. We provide these results in order to give an upper bound of our system's performances.

formance decrease (4 JGA points) from the TTS-verbatim to the Human-verbatim version is steady across the dev and test sets. We observe a smaller decrease (2 JGA points) from the Human-verbatim to the Human-paraphrased version. Finally, the difference between the dev and test sets (4 JGA points) can be explained by overfitting, a difficulty difference, or both.

	Replace-S	Replace-L	TTS-ASR	Paraphrase
T_1	✓			
T_2	✓		✓	
T_3		✓	✓	
T_4		✓	✓	✓
T_5		✓*	✓*	

Table 2: Composition of the training sets used to fine-tune the models in the ensemble for our primary submission (**OLISIA**$_1$); * denotes the augmented data provided by the track organizers.

5.2 ASR cascade adaptations

Given that only a few words in the users' utterances are really important to the dialogue state, Word Error Rate (WER) is not a good measure for the quality of the transcriptions (Wang et al., 2003). Therefore we compute both JGA and WER at each correction step with the same T5-Large trained on the training set with value replacements. We present the results in Table 3.

	TTS-v	Human-v	Human-p
Whisper raw outputs	37.9 / 4.92	33.8 / 8.4	32.0 / _
+ Time normalization	40.0 / 4.49	35.6 / 7.89	33.5 / _
+ Noun correction	40.3 / 4.36	36.1 / 7.71	34.3 / _

Table 3: Impact of the ASR post-processing steps on the test set performances (JGA↑ / WER↓).

Unsurprisingly, the TTS-verbatim version of the test set is much cleaner than the Human-verbatim version because of the higher diversity of the crowd-workers pronunciations compared to the synthetic voices. Hence we observe over 70% relative WER increase on every correction's step outputs. This noisier version only impacts the JGA by around 10% relative JGA decrease, confirming that only a few words matter to DST.[13]

Time normalization improves equally all three versions of the test set (around 5% relative JGA increase).

Proper noun correction does not help much the clean TTS-verbatim (0.75% relative JGA increase), however, it seems to be much more valuable for the noisier Human-verbatim and Human-paraphrased versions (respectively 1.4% and 2.4% relative JGA increase) again illustrating differences between synthetic and natural speech.

5.3 Data augmentation strategies

In order to better understand how each data augmentation technique we used contributes to the overall performance, we conduct an ablation study on different versions of the training data. We incrementally add one augmentation technique at a time to the default train set and fine-tune a T5-Large model on each version. The results are shown in Table 4.

	TTS-v	Human-v	Human-p
Default train set	32.2	28.3	26.8
+ Value replacement	40.2	35.5	33.2
+ Speech simulation	40.3	36.0	34.3
+ Paraphrasing	37.3	33.9	31.5

Table 4: Contribution of the different data augmentation techniques for DST in terms of JGA on the test set.

We observe that introducing new values for the slots `hotel-name`, `restaurant-name`, `train-departure` and `train-destination` greatly alleviates the issue of memorization with MulitWOZ and enables the model to generalize more, with a 7% to 8% absolute increase in JGA. The speech simulation provides an additional slight improvement which is particularly marked on the Human-paraphrased test set (+1%). This shows that using speech synthesized training data in the absence of real spoken data can help address spoken dialogues at inference. On the other hand, paraphrasing the user utterances leads to an overall worse performance. One possible explanation for this result is the noisy nature of the process, using a generation model can lead to potential inconsistencies both in the flow of the dialogue and in the annotation.

5.4 Model size

When dealing with noisy data and robustness issues we often observe that models with more parameters perform better. However, there is a trade-off between the computation resources needed for large

[13]Note that WER values are missing for the Human-paraphrased test set as no ground truth transcripts were provided for this version.

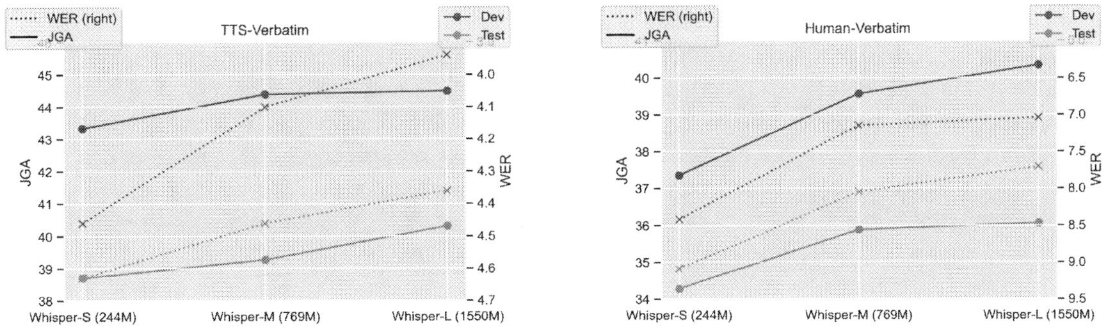

Figure 4: Impact of ASR model size (no. of parameters in parenthesis) in terms of JGA↑ in comparison with WER↓ on both dev and test sets.

models and the performance gains. In this section we attempt to explore this trade-off by exposing the performance gained by each model size increase. For the ASR part, we consider Whisper-Small (244M), Whisper-Medium (769M) and Whisper-Large (1550M). For the DST part, we consider T5-Small (60M), T5-Base (220M), T5-Large (738M) and T5-XL (3B), fine-tuning each model on our best training set (T_2). We present the impact of the size of the ASR and DST models respectively in Figure 4 and 5.

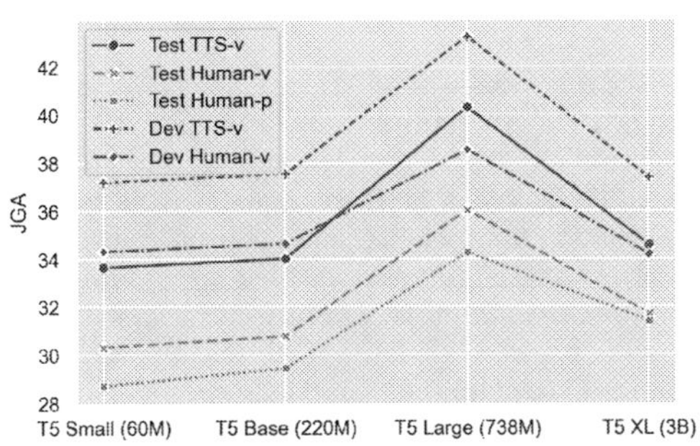

Figure 5: Impact of DST model size (no. of parameters in parenthesis) in terms of JGA on the dev and test sets.

Interestingly JGA does not increase much when moving from T5-Small to T5-Base whereas it increases by almost 6 points when using T5-Large instead of T5-Base. The performance then drops back 6 points when using T5-XL, although this larger model seems to be more robust to the paraphrased test set. This suggests that XL models tend to overfit, while Large models provide a good compromise between the number of parameters and generalization. For Whisper this trend is different: using Whisper-Medium instead of Whisper-Small increases JGA of at least 2 points on the Human-verbatim dev set while using Whisper-Large instead of Whisper-Medium only increases JGA of 1 point or less. It is noteworthy that the lower parameter ratio between the Large and Medium models might explain this lower JGA increase.

While our whisper models were not fine-tuned on any data, we can already observe that the decrease of WER obtained by using Whisper-Large instead of Whisper-Medium on the TTS-verbatim version is not found on the Human-verbatim version.

5.5 Ensemble

We compare two different ensembling strategies with a single model fine-tuned on T_2 in Table 5 (all models are based on T5-Large). Both ensembling strategies consisted of a majority vote for each slot-value. In one case, we used five models fine-tuned on the same train set with different random seeds and in the other, we fine-tuned five models on five different variations of the train set (*c.f.* Table 2).

	TTS-v	Human-v
1 model (no ensemble)	44.1	40.2
5 models - same train set	44.4	40.4
5 models - different train sets	47.8	43.5
9 models - different train sets	48.5	43.9

Table 5: Comparison of different ensembling strategies on the dev set in terms of JGA.

We find that the value of the ensemble from the same train set is limited, only providing a slight increase in JGA compared to the single model. The advantage of ensembling appears with five models fine-tuned on different train sets, providing a 3%

absolute increase in JGA. This suggests that the ensemble benefits from having contrasting views of the same instance at evaluation, and by extension that T5 models fail to learn invariant representations of proper nouns (or that our method does not enable that). It is also noteworthy that performance does not increase that much beyond 5 models, with marginally better results at 9 models,[14] likely showing a performance ceiling.

6 Limitations

Overall, the dataset released in this challenge is a good step towards bridging the gap between written and spoken dialogue systems. However, as the user utterances were read aloud by humans, this spoken data lacks in spontaneity associated with actual speech. It would be interesting to see if our findings hold on spontaneous spoken dialogue.

One limitation of our system lies in the use of Transformer-based models for both ASR and DST. While these models provide attractive performances they come with their own limitation of quadratic memory and limited input size. Dialogues in MultiWOZ are relatively short and this was not a concern in this work, but this could become problematic when dealing with longer, more realistic conversations. One alternative would be to reduce the input context to the most recent turns and include the linearized previous dialogue state in the DST input.

Another concern is the use of large pre-trained models to achieve competitive results. As pointed out before (Strubell et al., 2019), training these large models on abundant data requires a substantial electrical consumption. In light of the human impact on the environment, we should promote efficiency as the main performance factor rather than metric scores.

7 Conclusion and future work

This work introduced OLISIA, a cascade system for spoken DST that integrates an ASR and a DST model through several adaptations. We used ASR normalization and DST data augmentation to adjust each component to its counterpart. We have shown the importance of these adaptations in improving robustness to spoken inputs and our system achieved first place in the Speech-Aware Dialog Systems Technology Challenge.

[14]Post-evaluation experiments

While having user turns as speech and agent turns as text is a natural setup for a spoken dialogue system, this mix of modalities makes it more challenging to develop end-to-end systems. Recent progress on speech and text multimodal models could prove to be useful in addressing this problem (Ao et al., 2022). Another possibility would be to exploit agent turns using an audio only model, either as synthesized speech or as intermediary ASR representations (Mdhaffar et al., 2022).

This work focused on a cascade approach but a thorough comparison of end-to-end and cascade approaches could also be helpful in further research on spoken dialogue systems.

Acknowledgements

We thank Marco Dinareli for the valuable discussions and fruitful suggestions regarding end-to-end spoken DST.

This work was partially funded by the ANR CIFRE contracts N°2022/0286 and N°2022/0011 and by Orange Innovation.

This work was performed using HPC resources from GENCI-IDRIS (Grant 2022-AD011011407R2).

References

Junyi Ao, Rui Wang, Long Zhou, Chengyi Wang, Shuo Ren, Yu Wu, Shujie Liu, Tom Ko, Qing Li, Yu Zhang, Zhihua Wei, Yao Qian, Jinyu Li, and Furu Wei. 2022. SpeechT5: Unified-modal encoder-decoder pre-training for spoken language processing. In *Proceedings of the 60th Annual Meeting of the Association for Computational Linguistics (Volume 1: Long Papers)*, pages 5723–5738, Dublin, Ireland. Association for Computational Linguistics.

Pawe\l Budzianowski, Tsung-Hsien Wen, Bo-Hsiang Tseng, Iñigo Casanueva, Stefan Ultes, Osman Ramadan, and Milica Gašić. 2018. MultiWOZ - A Large-Scale Multi-Domain Wizard-of-Oz Dataset for Task-Oriented Dialogue Modelling. In *Proceedings of the 2018 Conference on Empirical Methods in Natural Language Processing*, pages 5016–5026, Brussels, Belgium. Association for Computational Linguistics.

Euisok Chung, Hyung-Bae Jeon, Jeon-Gue Park, and Yun-Keun Lee. 2012. Lattice rescoring for speech recognition using large scale distributed language models. In *Proceedings of COLING 2012: Posters*, pages 217–224, Mumbai, India. The COLING 2012 Organizing Committee.

Mihail Eric, Rahul Goel, Shachi Paul, Adarsh Kumar, Abhishek Sethi, Peter Ku, Anuj Kumar Goyal, Sanchit Agarwal, Shuyang Gao, and Dilek Hakkani-Tur. 2019. MultiWOZ 2.1: A Consolidated Multi-Domain Dialogue Dataset with State Corrections and State Tracking Baselines. *arXiv:1907.01669 [cs]*.

Manaal Faruqui and Dilek Hakkani-Tür. 2022. Revisiting the Boundary between ASR and NLU in the Age of Conversational Dialog Systems. *Computational Linguistics*, 48(1):221–232.

Karthik Ganesan, Pakhi Bamdev, Jaivarsan B, Amresh Venugopal, and Abhinav Tushar. 2021. N-Best ASR Transformer: Enhancing SLU Performance using Multiple ASR Hypotheses. In *Proceedings of the 59th Annual Meeting of the Association for Computational Linguistics and the 11th International Joint Conference on Natural Language Processing (Volume 2: Short Papers)*, pages 93–98, Online. Association for Computational Linguistics.

Matthew Henderson, Milica Gašić, Blaise Thomson, Pirros Tsiakoulis, Kai Yu, and Steve Young. 2012. Discriminative spoken language understanding using word confusion networks. In *2012 IEEE Spoken Language Technology Workshop (SLT)*, pages 176–181.

Matthew Henderson, Blaise Thomson, and Jason D. Williams. 2014. The second dialog state tracking challenge. In *Proceedings of the 15th Annual Meeting of the Special Interest Group on Discourse and Dialogue (SIGDIAL)*, pages 263–272, Philadelphia, PA, U.S.A. Association for Computational Linguistics.

Oleksii Hrinchuk, Mariya Popova, and Boris Ginsburg. 2020. Correction of automatic speech recognition with transformer sequence-to-sequence model. In *ICASSP 2020 - 2020 IEEE International Conference on Acoustics, Speech and Signal Processing (ICASSP)*, pages 7074–7078.

Seokhwan Kim, Yang Liu, Di Jin, A. Papangelis, Karthik Gopalakrishnan, Behnam Hedayatnia, and Dilek Z. Hakkani-Tür. 2021. "How Robust R U?": Evaluating Task-Oriented Dialogue Systems on Spoken Conversations. *2021 IEEE Automatic Speech Recognition and Understanding Workshop (ASRU)*.

Oleksii Kuchaiev, Jason Li, Huyen Nguyen, Oleksii Hrinchuk, Ryan Leary, Boris Ginsburg, Samuel Kriman, Stanislav Beliaev, Vitaly Lavrukhin, Jack Cook, et al. 2019. Nemo: a toolkit for building ai applications using neural modules. *arXiv preprint arXiv:1909.09577*.

Aleksandr Laptev, Roman Korostik, Aleksey Svischev, Andrei Andrusenko, Ivan Medennikov, and Sergey Rybin. 2020. You do not need more data: Improving end-to-end speech recognition by text-to-speech data augmentation. In *2020 13th International Congress on Image and Signal Processing, BioMedical Engineering and Informatics (CISP-BMEI)*, pages 439–444.

Jason Li, Ravi Teja Gadde, Boris Ginsburg, and Vitaly Lavrukhin. 2018. Training neural speech recognition systems with synthetic speech augmentation. *ArXiv*, abs/1811.00707.

Mingda Li, Weitong Ruan, Xinyue Liu, Luca Soldaini, Wael Hamza, and Chengwei Su. 2020. Improving Spoken Language Understanding By Exploiting ASR N-best Hypotheses. *arXiv:2001.05284 [cs, eess]*.

Jiexi Liu, Ryuichi Takanobu, Jiaxin Wen, Dazhen Wan, Hongguang Li, Weiran Nie, Cheng Li, Wei Peng, and Minlie Huang. 2021. Robustness Testing of Language Understanding in Task-Oriented Dialog. In *Proceedings of the 59th Annual Meeting of the Association for Computational Linguistics and the 11th International Joint Conference on Natural Language Processing (Volume 1: Long Papers)*, pages 2467–2480, Online. Association for Computational Linguistics.

Salima Mdhaffar, Jarod Duret, Titouan Parcollet, and Yannick Estève. 2022. End-to-end model for named entity recognition from speech without paired training data. In *Proc. Interspeech 2022*, pages 4068–4072.

Vaishali Pal, Fabien Guillot, Manish Shrivastava, Jean-Michel Renders, and Laurent Besacier. 2020. Modeling ASR Ambiguity for Neural Dialogue State Tracking. In *Interspeech 2020*, Shangai (Virtual Conf), China.

Baolin Peng, Chenguang Zhu, Chunyuan Li, Xiujun Li, Jinchao Li, Michael Zeng, and Jianfeng Gao. 2020. Few-shot natural language generation for task-oriented dialog. In *Findings of the Association for Computational Linguistics: EMNLP 2020*, pages 172–182, Online. Association for Computational Linguistics.

Kun Qian, Ahmad Beirami, Zhouhan Lin, Ankita De, Alborz Geramifard, Zhou Yu, and Chinnadhurai Sankar. 2021. Annotation Inconsistency and Entity Bias in MultiWOZ. In *Proceedings of the 22nd Annual Meeting of the Special Interest Group on Discourse and Dialogue*, pages 326–337, Singapore and Online. Association for Computational Linguistics.

Alec Radford, Jong Wook Kim, Tao Xu, Greg Brockman, Christine McLeavey, and Ilya Sutskever. 2022. Robust Speech Recognition via Large-Scale Weak Supervision. Technical report, OpenAI.

Colin Raffel, Noam Shazeer, Adam Roberts, Katherine Lee, Sharan Narang, Michael Matena, Yanqi Zhou, Wei Li, and Peter J. Liu. 2020. Exploring the limits of transfer learning with a unified text-to-text transformer. *Journal of Machine Learning Research*, 21(140):1–67.

Lina M. Rojas-Barahona, Milica Gasic, Nikola Mrkšić, Pei-Hao Su, Stefan Ultes, Tsung-Hsien Wen, and Steve Young. 2016. Exploiting sentence and context representations in deep neural models for spoken language understanding. *arXiv preprint arXiv:1610.04120*.

Andrew Rosenberg, Yu Zhang, Bhuvana Ramabhadran, Ye Jia, Pedro Moreno, Yonghui Wu, and Zelin Wu. 2019. Speech recognition with augmented synthesized speech. In *2019 IEEE Automatic Speech Recognition and Understanding Workshop (ASRU)*, pages 996–1002.

Nicholas Roy, Joelle Pineau, and Sebastian Thrun. 2000. Spoken dialogue management using probabilistic reasoning. In *Proceedings of the 38th Annual Meeting on Association for Computational Linguistics - ACL '00*, pages 93–100, Hong Kong. Association for Computational Linguistics.

Dmitriy Serdyuk, Yongqiang Wang, Christian Fuegen, Anuj Kumar, Baiyang Liu, and Yoshua Bengio. 2018. Towards end-to-end spoken language understanding. In *2018 IEEE International Conference on Acoustics, Speech and Signal Processing (ICASSP)*, pages 5754–5758.

Jonathan Shen, Ruoming Pang, Ron J. Weiss, Mike Schuster, Navdeep Jaitly, Zongheng Yang, Z. Chen, Yu Zhang, Yuxuan Wang, R. J. Skerry-Ryan, Rif A. Saurous, Yannis Agiomyrgiannakis, and Yonghui Wu. 2018. Natural tts synthesis by conditioning wavenet on mel spectrogram predictions. *2018 IEEE International Conference on Acoustics, Speech and Signal Processing (ICASSP)*, pages 4779–4783.

Emma Strubell, Ananya Ganesh, and Andrew McCallum. 2019. Energy and policy considerations for deep learning in NLP. In *Proceedings of the 57th Annual Meeting of the Association for Computational Linguistics*, pages 3645–3650, Florence, Italy. Association for Computational Linguistics.

Blaise Thomson and Steve Young. 2010. Bayesian update of dialogue state: A POMDP framework for spoken dialogue systems. *Computer Speech & Language*, 24(4):562–588.

Xin Tian, Xinxian Huang, Dongfeng He, Yingzhan Lin, Siqi Bao, Huang He, Liankai Huang, Qiang Ju, Xiyuan Zhang, Jian Xie, Shuqi Sun, Fan Wang, Hua Wu, and Haifeng Wang. 2021. TOD-DA: Towards Boosting the Robustness of Task-oriented Dialogue Modeling on Spoken Conversations. *arXiv:2112.12441 [cs]*.

Natalia Tomashenko, Christian Raymond, Antoine Caubrière, Renato De Mori, and Yannick Estève. 2020. Dialogue history integration into end-to-end signal-to-concept spoken language understanding systems. In *ICASSP 2020-2020 IEEE International Conference on Acoustics, Speech and Signal Processing (ICASSP)*, pages 8509–8513. IEEE.

Longshaokan Wang, Maryam Fazel-Zarandi, Aditya Tiwari, Spyros Matsoukas, and Lazaros Polymenakos. 2020. Data Augmentation for Training Dialog Models Robust to Speech Recognition Errors. In *Proceedings of the 2nd Workshop on Natural Language Processing for Conversational AI*, pages 63–70, Online. Association for Computational Linguistics.

Ye-Yi Wang, A. Acero, and C. Chelba. 2003. Is word error rate a good indicator for spoken language understanding accuracy. In *2003 IEEE Workshop on Automatic Speech Recognition and Understanding (IEEE Cat. No.03EX721)*, pages 577–582.

Jason Williams, Antoine Raux, Deepak Ramachandran, and Alan Black. 2013. The Dialog State Tracking Challenge. In *Proceedings of the SIGDIAL 2013 Conference*, pages 404–413, Metz, France. Association for Computational Linguistics.

Jason D. Williams and Steve Young. 2007. Partially observable Markov decision processes for spoken dialog systems. *Computer Speech & Language*, 21(2):393–422.

Xianrui Zheng, Yulan Liu, Deniz Gunceler, and Daniel Willett. 2021. Using synthetic audio to improve the recognition of out-of-vocabulary words in end-to-end asr systems. In *ICASSP 2021 - 2021 IEEE International Conference on Acoustics, Speech and Signal Processing (ICASSP)*, pages 5674–5678.

Speech-Aware Multi-Domain Dialogue State Generation with ASR Error Correction Modules

Ridong Jiang[†] **Shi Wei**[†] **Bin Wang**[†] **Chen Zhang**[⋆]
Yan Zhang[⋆] **Chunlei Pan**[⋆] **Jung Jae Kim**[†] **Haizhou Li**[⋆⋆,⋆,‡]
[†]Institute for Infocomm Research (I^2R), A*STAR, Singapore
[⋆]National University of Singapore [‡]Kriston AI Lab, China
[⋆⋆]The Chinese University of Hong Kong, Shenzhen, China
jjkim@i2r.a-star.edu.sg

Abstract

Prior research on dialogue state tracking (DST) is mostly based on written dialogue corpora. For spoken dialogues, the DST model trained on the written text should use the results (or hypothesis) of automatic speech recognition (ASR) as input. But ASR hypothesis often includes errors, which leads to significant performance drop for spoken dialogue state tracking. We address the issue by developing the following ASR error correction modules. First, we train a model to convert ASR hypothesis to ground truth user utterance, which can fix frequent patterns of errors. The model takes ASR hypotheses of two ASR models as input and fine-tuned in two stages. The corrected hypothesis is fed into a large scale pre-trained encoder-decoder model (T5) for DST training and inference. Second, if an output slot value from the encoder-decoder model is a name, we compare it with names in a dictionary crawled from Web sites and, if feasible, replace with the crawled name of the shortest edit distance. Third, we fix errors of temporal expressions in ASR hypothesis by using hand-crafted rules. Experiment results on the DSTC 11 speech-aware dataset, which is built on the popular MultiWOZ task (version 2.1), show that our proposed method can effectively mitigate the performance drop when moving from written text to spoken conversations.

1 Introduction

Conversational agents are evolving rapidly in the last decade and providing solutions for almost every industry including e-commerce, travel, finance, food & beverage, hospitality, gaming and healthcare. The agents that can perform certain tasks or provide transactional services such as restaurant booking and hotel booking need to understand user's intent and track the dialogue states throughout the conversation, known as DST task. The performance of the agents very much depends on the DST results for a fluent and accurate task completion. With the advancement in AI and machine learning, especially the breakthroughs in Natural Language Processing such as Attention, Sequence-to-sequence model and the Transformer Architecture, the research on DST has attracted much attention in the past few years. DST is typically formulated as the problem of estimating user's goal in the form of a list of slot-value pairs when a dialogue progresses with multiple turns. When multiple domains are involved in the conversation (e.g. MultiWOZ datasets (Budzianowski et al., 2018)), the task becomes more challenging because the developed DST model needs to deal with multiple domains and their slot values in every dialogue turn. Different DST models have been developed. The methodologies can be broadly classified into two types. One is classification based method (Wu et al., 2019; Heck et al., 2020; Hosseini-Asl et al., 2020) and another one is generation based method (Zhao et al., 2021, 2022). However, both types of methods are mostly developed for written dialogues. These models do not perform well on spoken dialogues, because the audio form of user utterances in spoken dialogues should be transcribed by an automatic speech recognition (ASR) system, and the transcription involves ASR errors.

Consider a multi-domain spoken dialogue with both ground truths and ASR hypotheses of user utterances below. The ground truth user utterances are associated with, if any, their dialogue states that are affected by ASR errors observed in the corresponding ASR hypotheses. For instance, digits in the ground truth (e.g. "7", "2") are converted into English words in the corresponding ASR hypothesis (e.g. "seven", "two"). A name (e.g. "rosepine", "naturita") is incorrectly split into two words (e.g. "rose pine") and incorrectly transcribed (e.g. "natur") in some ASR hypotheses. The word "pm" is incorrectly transcribed into two words "p m". An example is given below with both ground truth and ASR hypothesis from the user

Proceedings of The Eleventh Dialog System Technology Challenge, pages 105–112
September 11, 2023

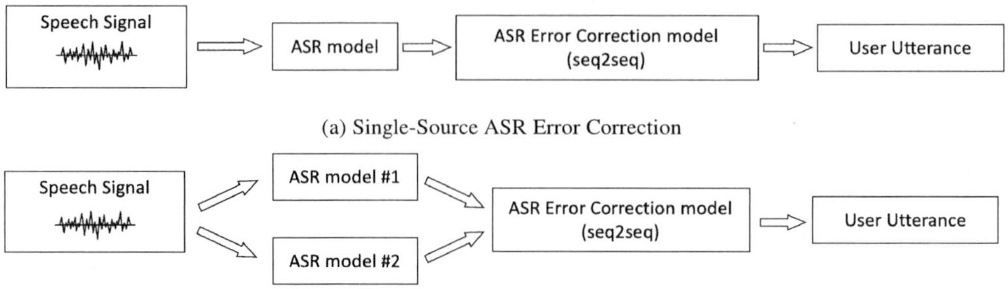

(a) Single-Source ASR Error Correction

(b) Multi-Source ASR Error Correction

Figure 1: An illustration of two types of ASR error correction methods.

side.

USER (GROUND-TRUTH) : i am looking to get some information on the resort at summerlin.

USER (ASR HYPOTHESIS) : i am looking to get some information on the resort at summerlin

SYSTEM : the resort at summerlin is in the centre of town and in the expensive price range.

USER (GROUND-TRUTH) : great can you get me a room for 7 people for 2 nights starting saturday? (hotel-people="7", hotel-stay="2")

USER (ASR HYPOTHESIS) : great can you get me a room for seven people for two nights starting saturday

SYSTEM : yes, i can! you're booked with reference number i34y32y9. is there anything else i can help you with

USER (GROUND-TRUTH) : yes, i also need to find a train going to rosepine. (train-destination="rosepine")

USER (ASR HYPOTHESIS) : yes i also need to find a train going to rose pine

SYSTEM : okay, i have quite a few. can you give me some more information?

USER (GROUND-TRUTH) : i'm departing from naturita on saturday. i want to arrive by 12:58 pm. (train-departure="naturita", train-arriveby="12:58 pm")

USER (ASR HYPOTHESIS) : i'm departing from natur on saturday i want to arrive by 12:58 p m

SYSTEM : i would recommend train id tr5049 which leaves naturita at 11:46 am and arrives in rosepine at 12:36 pm. there are earlier options as well if you wish.

USER (GROUND-TRUTH) : that would be perfect. for 7 people. (train-people="7")

USER (ASR HYPOTHESIS) : that would be perfect for seven people

In this work, we address the issue that errors in the ASR hypotheses of spoken dialogues affect dialogue states, by learning to fix them before passing the ASR hypotheses as input to a DST model and also by fixing them after the DST model generates slot values. Prior work have investigate the possibility to correct errors from ASR engines based on edit alignment (Leng et al., 2021b), non-auto-regressive generation (Leng et al., 2021a) and auto-regressive sequence-to-sequence models (Dutta et al., 2022). Here, we investigate the possibility to merge the multi-source ASR predictions using a pre-trained sequence-to-sequence model as shown in Figure 1. We experiment with DSTC 11 speech-aware dataset. Results and ablation studies show that our proposed approach can effectively mitigate the noise introduced by ASR hypothesis and performance drop when moving from written text to spoken conversations.

2 Methodology

Our model has three parts: pre-processing, encoder-decoder, and post-processing. In the stage of pre-processing, we in particular fix ASR errors in ASR hypothesis that is given as input to the encoder-decoder model, which generates dialogues states as output. In the stage of post-processing, we further try to fix remaining errors in the generated dialog states.

2.1 Pre-processing: Multi-Source ASR Error Correction

The first step of handling speech-based dialogue state tracking tasks is to use the Automatic Speech Recognition (ASR) technique to convert speech signals into textual format. As mentioned before, it introduces undesired ASR errors which largely impact the performance of existing DST models that take ASR hypothesis (or transcript) as input. It is because most existing DST models are trained and designed to handle the ground truth strings (or "clean text") of both user and agent utterances. Therefore, to bridge the gap between speech-based DST tasks and clean-text-based DST systems, we propose a multi-source ASR error correction module that learns to convert ASR-generated transcripts to clean text. We hypothesize that even though the conversion is not perfect, it still fix some of the ASR errors and thus enhance DST performance.

The input to the ASR error correction is the ASR-generated transcripts and the desired output is the original clean text. First, we use a pre-trained sequence-to-sequence model to handle this task. In experiments, we leverage the pre-trained *T5-small* model. We also experimented with other popular pre-trained models including *T5-base* and *BART-base*, but did not witness significant improvement with increased model sizes.

Second, to better recover the information from speech signals, we propose to leverage ASR transcripts from multiple (two) ASR models. This is because different ASR models may have complementary characteristics which can compensate for each other's weaknesses. As an example, the two utterances and their audio's transcripts from two ASR models (ASR 1 - Our in-house ASR model; ASR 2 - The model used to generate the track dataset) are shown below. Each of the two examples shows an error (highlighted in italic face) by one of the two ASR models, respectively.

USER (GROUND-TRUTH) : i am looking to book a train that is leaving from leaf river to carpentersville on friday.

USER (ASR 1 HYPOTHESIS) : i am looking to book a train that is leaving from **life** river to carpentersville on friday

USER (ASR 2 HYPOTHESIS) : i am looking to book a train that is leaving from leaf river to carpentersville on friday

USER (GROUND-TRUTH) : howdy, i need a train heading into floyd.

USER (ASR 1 HYPOTHESIS) : howdy i need a train heading into floyd

USER (ASR 2 HYPOTHESIS) : **howey** i need a train heading into floyd

The proposed ASR error correction model based on two ASR models is illustrated in Fig. 1. In the Experiments section, we show that the combination of multiple ASR transcripts can lead to better ASR error correction performance than using a single ASR transcript.

Third, besides the multi-source ASR transcription fusion, we also utilize a two-step fine-tuning process for better modeling of data distributions. Instead of directly fine-tuning the pre-trained encoder-decoder model on a multi-source format (Fig. 1b), we first fine-tune the model on single-source data (Fig. 1a). For the first stage of fine-tuning, we use the augmented 100x data which are auto-generated with DST slot replacements as introduced in the Experiments section. During this process, the model learns the mapping between ASR transcripts to clean text with much more amount of data. In the second stage, the model is further fine-tuned in a multi-source ASR error correction format to synergistically incorporate two ASR systems.

2.2 Dialogue state generation using encoder-decoder

Consider a task-oriented dialogue (TOD) which consists of multiple turns of conversation between a user and an agent. We denote the dialogue history at turn T:

$$C_T = \{(u_1, r_1), (u_2, r_2), ...(u_T, r_T)\} \quad (1)$$

, where $u_i, r_i,\ i \in [1, T]$ are user utterance and system response at turn T, respectively. C_T is thus the dialogue context at turn T. This context C_T is used to generate the dialogue state B_T of user utterance at turn T u_T. The dialogue state B_T is represented as slot-value pairs:

$$B_T = \{(S_1^d, V_1^{dT}), (S_2^d, V_2^{dT}), ...(S_j, V_j^{dT})\} \quad (2)$$

, where $S_i^d, V_i^{dT},\ i \in [1, j_T]$ are the i-th slot name and its value at turn T, respectively. The $d \in [1, M]$ denotes the domain, M is the total number of domains, and j_T is the number of slots with non-empty values at turn T. In DSTC11, there are total of 35 slots in 7 domains.

All the utterances and slot names S are concatenated into one sequence as input of the encoder, the decoder generates the belief state with slot values:

$$B_T = seq2seq(C_T, S) \quad (3)$$

We employ T5 pre-trained seq2seq model. The learning objective of this T5 generation model is to minimize the log-likelihood of B_T given C_T and S:

$$\mathcal{L} = -\sum \log p(B_T|C_T, S), \quad (4)$$

For all user utterances and system responses, we add "user:" and "system:" prefixes to every u_i and r_i, respectively, to differentiate the user's input from system's response.

Following is an example of input to the model:

> user: i would like a taxi from saint john's college to pizza hut fen ditton. $\langle sep \rangle$ taxi-destination: $\langle extra\_id\_0 \rangle$ $\langle sep \rangle$ taxi-departure: $\langle extra\_id\_1 \rangle$ $\langle sep \rangle$ hotel-parking: $\langle extra\_id\_2 \rangle$ $\langle sep \rangle$ ...

, and the corresponding output:

> $\langle extra\_id\_0 \rangle$ saint john's college $\langle extra\_id\_1 \rangle$ pizza hut fen ditton $\langle extra\_id\_3 \rangle$ none $\langle extra\_id\_4 \rangle$ ...

We used a special token (e.g. $\langle extra\_id\_0 \rangle$) to indicate each slot type and make connection between the slot name in input and the slot value in output. For instance, the slot value "pizza hut fen ditton" in the example output is for the slot whose name is "taxi-departure" in the example input, which are connected via $\langle extra\_id\_1 \rangle$.

2.3 Post-processing

The purpose of the proposed post-processing is to fix prediction errors from the encoder-decoder model due to the ASR errors. As shown in the Fig. 1, the ASR errors can lead to the incorrect prediction on, for instance, time, names of hotel and restaurant, and names of location (e.g. train departure and destination).

2.3.1 Name Error Correction

Name recognition is especially challenging to ASR engines. It is error prone for the recognition of names in spoken dialogue. We thus devise a method of correcting name errors with a dictionary of names that are collected from the training and development data and crawled from Web sites.

For every slot value of name, we apply fuzzy match to find the most similar name from the name dictionary of the slot type. The matching can be one of the following results:

a) Correct match: prediction is correct, matching result is correct (no change to DST accuracy).

b) Good match: prediction is incorrect, matching result is correct (Increasing the DST accuracy).

c) Bad match: prediction is correct, matching result is incorrect (Decreasing the DST accuracy).

d) Wrong match: prediction is incorrect, matching result is still incorrect (no change to DST accuracy).

Obviously, we want to have more good match (Case b) and try to reduce the bad match (Case c). We designed following matching rules to maximize the good match:

i) Get the top 10 similar matching

ii) Reject the shorter items with one word

iii) Reject too long items which are two words longer than the input value

iv) Change to top the rank of the matches which found in "system" utterance

Slot with name values	Size of dictionary
hotel	32,093
restaurant	1,102
taxi-departure	23,269
taxi-destination	23,314
train-departure	23,086
train-destination	23,089

Table 1: Dictionary size for each slot type whose values are names

Slot Type	Source URLs
hotel	wikipedia-1 wikipedia-2 wikipedia-3 wiki-accomodation
restaurant	easyleadz wikipedia opentable leading restaurants bloomberg
train	great american stations wikipedia rail advent
location	britannica-1 britannica-2 wikipedia-1 wikipedia-2 wikipedia-3

Table 2: Web sites from which we crawled potentially relevant names. 'location' can be useful for multiple slot types, including 'taxi-departure/destination' and 'train-departure/destination'.

v) Remove items whose score is lower than the preset threshold

After some experiments, we found that the matching rules are beneficial in terms of the evaluation metrics when applied to the categories of hotel, train departure, and train destination. When the slot types are restaurant, taxi-departure and taxi-destination, we keep the original model prediction. We are now using the crawled list of names as shown in Table 2. We believe the correction method can be more generalizable if more accurate candidates can be collected.

2.3.2 Time Error Correction

In this Speech-Aware Dialog Systems Technology Challenge, the ground truth of temporal expressions in dialog states is using "12-hour clock" time convention. The Latin abbreviations "a.m." and "p.m." are normalized to "am" and "pm". We noticed that the temporal expression in ASR hypothesis is different from the ground truth format in both the time convention and the Latin suffixes, as exemplified in the Introduction section. For instance, "3:08 am" in ground truth becomes "3o8 a m" in ASR hypothesis. In addition, ASR output "12o4am" needs to be normalized to "0:04 am". After analyzing ASR outputs, we designed some time normalization rules as a part of the post-processing for further improvement on the DST accuracy.

3 Experiments

3.1 Dataset and Metrics

The challenge dataset is based on MultiWOZ dataset version 2.1 with the following changes:

- Increased the domains from 5 to 7 (new domains: bus and hospital) and valid slots from 30 to 35 (new slots: bus-departure, bus-destination, bus-leaveat, bus-day and hospital-department)
- The original slot values were replaced with new values in the dev and test sets. The main purpose of the changes is to remove the slot values that overlap between the two sets and the training data.
- All time mentions were offset by a constant amount for each dialogue, and the format was standardized to "12-hour clock" with Latin abbreviations "am" or "pm".

TTS Verbatim	**Dev**		**Test**	
	JGA↑	**SER↓**	**JGA↑**	**SER↓**
D3ST-XXL	26.30	27.50	-	-
D3ST-XXL (100x)	40.80	-	-	-
TripPy (4x)	-	-	21.90	32.80
Ours (4x)	44.34	16.79	37.49	20.42
Human Verbatim	**Dev**		**Test**	
D3ST-XXL	22.60	31.60	-	-
D3ST-XXL (100x)	-	-	-	-
TripPy (4x)	-	-	21.20	33.50
Ours (4x)	-	-	29.96	26.94
Human-paraphrased	**Dev**		**Test**	
D3ST-XXL	-	-	-	-
D3ST-XXL (100x)	-	-	-	-
TripPy (4x)	-	-	20.00	33.80
Ours (4x)	-	-	30.66	26.26

Table 3: Performance of our method against baselines. The results w.r.t. D3ST-XXL are provided by the track organizers. The models are evaluated by joint goal accuracy (JGA) and slot error rate (SER). The number in the bracket indicates the amount of augmented data used for model training. For example, "(100x)" means that the amount of augmented data is 100 times of the original MultiWOZ training data. "-" indicates that result for that particular entry is not available.

- Provided 100x training data from data augmentation.

Two evaluation metrics are used to evaluate the performance of the multi-domain DST model. The Joint Goal Accuracy (JGA) and Slot Error Rate (SER) are the primary and secondary metrics, respectively. The metrics can be calculated using the standard MultiWOZ evaluation script[1] after applying the released patch from the organizer[2].

3.2 Implementation

We implement the proposed method with the above described pre-processing and post-processing based on the T5-base model. The model has 220M parameters and 12 encoder-decoder layers. Each layer has 12-headed attention with hidden size 768. We train the model with batch size 32 for 10 epochs. The learning rate is 0.0001 with early stopping patience of 3. The input and output sequence lengths are set to 512 and 128 respectively.

The computational cost is not high. For our training using MultiWOZ 2.1 dataset (4x) on a work-

[1] https://github.com/Tomiinek/MultiWOZ_Evaluation

[2] https://storage.googleapis.com/gresearch/dstc11/patch.2022-11-02.txt

Task	Correction Method	Test set	
		JGA	SER
TTS Verbatim	No correction	29.48	25.55
	ASR correction	34.07	22.28
	Name correction	32.08	23.65
	Time correction	31.97	23.40
	Name & time correction	35.20	21.50
	All corrections	**37.49**	**20.42**
Human Verbatim	No correction	25.49	30.81
	ASR correction	27.40	28.90
	Name correction	27.62	28.95
	Time correction	26.17	30.06
	Name & time correction	28.51	28.20
	All corrections	**29.96**	**26.94**
Human Paraphrased	No correction	24.47	30.63
	ASR correction	27.78	28.14
	Name correction	26.98	28.74
	Time correction	25.20	29.81
	Name & time correction	28.09	27.92
	All corrections	**30.66**	**26.26**

Table 4: Ablation Study of pre-processing and post-processing on test dataset

station with the following specifications: Intel(R) Xeon(R) Gold 6226R CPU @ 2.90GHz, 256G Memory, using one NVIDIA RTX A6000 GPU, every epoch takes about 48 minutes and 141 minutes for T5-small and T5-base respectively.

3.3 Baselines

We compare our proposed approach against two baselines, D3ST (Zhao et al., 2022) and TripPy (Heck et al., 2020).

- D3ST adopts a seq2seq backbone for dialogue state tracking, and relies on slot and intent descriptions to instruct the model. The input to D3ST is a concatenation of slot descriptions, intents, and the dialogue history. The decoder of D3ST will generate the active slot key-value pairs and the corresponding intents of the current user utterance. We report the results with respect to the best D3ST version, D3ST-XXL (11B parameters), which are released by the track organizers.

- TripPy makes use of three different copy mechanisms for DST, extracting values from the dialog context on-the-fly and combining span-based slot filling methods with memory-based methods. Different from D3ST and our proposed method, the backbone of TripPy is BERT (Devlin et al., 2019), a bidirectional encoder-only model. We hypothesize that it may not generalize as well as seq2seq model, such as T5 (Raffel et al., 2022) to out-of-distribution dialogue with unseen slot key-value pairs.

3.4 Results and Analysis

We used 4x out of the 100x augmented data as additional training data, as we did not have time to process the whole 100x data for training. Table 3 shows the performance evaluation results of our model as well as the baselines w.r.t. the development and test datasets of the challenge. From the results, we can make the following observations: (1) the JGA the D3ST-XXL (100x) is significantly better than D3ST-XXL. The original D3ST-XXL model performs poorly on the modified dev set, which contains a different set of slot key-value pairs than the training data. D3ST-XXL (100x) is less impacted by the modification. This showcases that data augmentation is useful in improving the generalization of the DST models. (2) Our approach performs better than D3ST-XXL (100x) on the development set by 3.54 JGA scores. In addition, it is more data efficient as we only use 4% of the augmented data while D3ST-XXL (100x) utilizes all the augmented data. This can be attributed to the incorporation of ASR correction module. (3) Our approach performs significantly better than TripPy across all the three settings in terms of both JGA and SER. A possible reason is that TripPy is a BERT-based classification model, which may not be robust to distribution shift (in terms of both change in slot key-value pairs and the ASR errors). In addition, the copy mechanisms of TripPy heavily rely on the ontology of the MultiWOZ dataset, which is not present in the data provided by the track organizers.

Table 4 shows the results of ablation study, estimating the impact of the pre-processing of ASR error correction and the post-processing of name error correction and time error correction. The results prove that all the proposed pre-processing and post-processing modules are impactful. In particular, the post-processing (name and time error correction) has the highest performance gain probably due to the high frequency of temporal expressions and the name recognition errors in dialog states. The ASR correction module can help on the time normalization but it is hard to correct and name recognition errors.

Index	ASR Input	2-stage FT	ROUGE-1	ROUGE-2	ROUGE-L
Error Corr. 1	ASR #1	No	96.46	93.57	96.97
Error Corr. 2	ASR #2	No	97.40	95.34	97.78
Error Corr. 3	Multi-Source	No	97.54	95.56	97.89
Error Corr. 4	Multi-Source	Yes	**97.87**	**96.26**	**98.17**

Table 5: Detailed evaluation results of ASR error correction with different hyper-parameters, including using multiple ASR models' hypotheses or not and using the 2-stage fine-tuning or not, on the development set. ASR #1 and #2 refer to our own ASR model and Google ASR model, respectively. The joint model means we use both ASR transcripts.

Error Corr. model	TTS-JGA.	TTS-Slot Acc.	Human-JGA	Human-Slot Acc.
ASR #1	22.76	94.66	17.21	93.44
ASR #2	27.67	95.72	23.69	94.88
ASR #1 + Error Corr. 1	27.71	95.65	21.27	94.44
ASR #2 + Error Corr. 2	29.59	95.86	24.99	95.03
Error Corr. 3	30.58	96.13	25.98	95.36
Error Corr. 4	**32.71**	**96.40**	**26.14**	**95.40**
Ground Truth	44.71	97.21	44.71	97.21

Table 6: Benchmarking results with different ASR error correction methods. The results on dev set are reported. ASR #1 and #2 refer to our own ASR model and Google ASR model, respectively. Error Corr. 1$\tilde{4}$ are ASR error correction models listed in Table 5. Ground Truth indicates using ground truth of user utterance instead of ASR hypothesis. "Slot Acc." indicates slot value accuracy.

3.5 Ablation Study on ASR Error Correction

We further conduct ablation study on our pre-processing module: multi-source ASR error correction. We choose the naive T5 model to test the ASR error correction module and filter the possible effect of other components. The results are shown in Table 5 and Table 6. In Table 5, the result is evaluated by ROUGE scores to determine the similarity between clean text with references. We can see that 1) the Google ASR model provides more reliable results than our own ASR model; 2) The performance can be boosted by integrating both models in a multi-source ASR error correction framework; and 3) the two-stage fine-tuning process can further boost the model performance.

Further, we did experiments of integrating the different methods of ASR error correction with the *T5-small* model for the DST task and evaluate the model performance on the development set. The results are shown in Table 6. The results show that each of the two ASR models contributes to significant improvement of the DST model performance and also have synergy when used together for ASR error correction. From the results, we can conclude that the ASR error correction model contributes to the speech-aware DST task.

4 Conclusions

We present our submissions to the Speech Aware Dialog Systems Technology Challenge of DSTC 11. Our works are based on pre-trained encoder-decoder language models. We enhance their performance by integrating ASR error correction, name correction and time correction modules. Our ASR error correction module utilizes two ASR models synergistically. We crawled names from Web sites and use them for the name correction module, instead of relying on the given training data. We manually wrote rules to fix errors of temporal expressions in ASR hypothesis.

References

Paweł Budzianowski, Tsung-Hsien Wen, Bo-Hsiang Tseng, Inigo Casanueva, Stefan Ultes, Osman Ramadan, and Milica Gašić. 2018. Multiwoz–a large-scale multi-domain wizard-of-oz dataset for task-oriented dialogue modelling. *arXiv preprint arXiv:1810.00278*.

Jacob Devlin, Ming-Wei Chang, Kenton Lee, and Kristina Toutanova. 2019. BERT: Pre-training of deep bidirectional transformers for language understanding. In *Proceedings of the 2019 Conference of the North American Chapter of the Association for Computational Linguistics: Human Language Technologies, Volume 1 (Long and Short Papers)*, pages 4171–4186, Minneapolis, Minnesota. Association for Computational Linguistics.

Samrat Dutta, Shreyansh Jain, Ayush Maheshwari, Ganesh Ramakrishnan, and Preethi Jyothi. 2022. Error correction in asr using sequence-to-sequence models. *arXiv preprint arXiv:2202.01157*.

Michael Heck, Carel van Niekerk, Nurul Lubis, Christian Geishauser, Hsien-Chin Lin, Marco Moresi, and Milica Gasic. 2020. TripPy: A triple copy strategy for value independent neural dialog state tracking. In *Proceedings of the 21th Annual Meeting of the Special Interest Group on Discourse and Dialogue*, pages 35–44, 1st virtual meeting. Association for Computational Linguistics.

Ehsan Hosseini-Asl, Bryan McCann, Chien-Sheng Wu, Semih Yavuz, and Richard Socher. 2020. A simple language model for task-oriented dialogue. *Advances in Neural Information Processing Systems*, 33:20179–20191.

Yichong Leng, Xu Tan, Rui Wang, Linchen Zhu, Jin Xu, Wenjie Liu, Linquan Liu, Tao Qin, Xiang-Yang Li, Edward Lin, et al. 2021a. Fastcorrect 2: Fast error correction on multiple candidates for automatic speech recognition. *arXiv preprint arXiv:2109.14420*.

Yichong Leng, Xu Tan, Linchen Zhu, Jin Xu, Renqian Luo, Linquan Liu, Tao Qin, Xiangyang Li, Edward Lin, and Tie-Yan Liu. 2021b. Fastcorrect: Fast error correction with edit alignment for automatic speech recognition. *Advances in Neural Information Processing Systems*, 34:21708–21719.

Colin Raffel, Noam Shazeer, Adam Roberts, Katherine Lee, Sharan Narang, Michael Matena, Yanqi Zhou, Wei Li, and Peter J. Liu. 2022. Exploring the limits of transfer learning with a unified text-to-text transformer. *J. Mach. Learn. Res.*, 21(1).

Chien-Sheng Wu, Andrea Madotto, Ehsan Hosseini-Asl, Caiming Xiong, Richard Socher, and Pascale Fung. 2019. Transferable multi-domain state generator for task-oriented dialogue systems. In *Proceedings of the 57th Annual Meeting of the Association for Computational Linguistics*, pages 808–819, Florence, Italy. Association for Computational Linguistics.

Jeffrey Zhao, Raghav Gupta, Yuan Cao, Dian Yu, Mingqiu Wang, Harrison Lee, Abhinav Rastogi, Izhak Shafran, and Yonghui Wu. 2022. Description-driven task-oriented dialog modeling. *arXiv preprint arXiv: Arxiv-2201.08904*.

Jeffrey Zhao, Mahdis Mahdieh, Ye Zhang, Yuan Cao, and Yonghui Wu. 2021. Effective sequence-to-sequence dialogue state tracking. In *Proceedings of the 2021 Conference on Empirical Methods in Natural Language Processing*, pages 7486–7493, Online and Punta Cana, Dominican Republic. Association for Computational Linguistics.

Three Ways of Using Large Language Models to Evaluate Chat

Ondřej Plátek, Vojtěch Hudeček, Patricia Schmidtová, Mateusz Lango and **Ondřej Dušek**
Charles University, Faculty of Mathematics and Physics
Institute of Formal and Applied Linguistics
Prague, Czech Republic
oplatek@ufal.mff.cuni.cz

Abstract

This paper describes the systems submitted by *team6* for ChatEval, the DSTC 11 Track 4 competition. We present three different approaches to predicting turn-level qualities of chatbot responses based on large language models (LLMs). We report improvement over the baseline using dynamic few-shot examples from a vector store for the prompts for ChatGPT. We also analyze the performance of the other two approaches and report needed improvements for future work. We developed the three systems over just two weeks, showing the potential of LLMs for this task. An ablation study conducted after the challenge deadline shows that the new Llama 2 models are closing the performance gap between ChatGPT and open-source LLMs. However, we find that the Llama 2 models do not benefit from few-shot examples in the same way as ChatGPT.

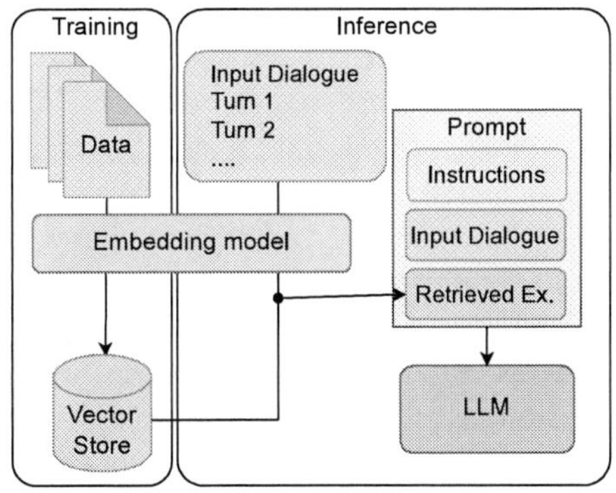

Figure 1: The architecture of the vector store approach with a LLM. During training, we construct the vector store from embedded annotated dialogues. At inference time, the input dialogue is embedded, and most similar examples from the vector store are retrieved to be included in the prompt.

1 Introduction

This paper describes the systems submitted by *team6* for ChatEval, the DSTC 11 Track 4 competition aimed at evaluating open-domain chat.[1] We participated in Task 2, which focuses on evaluating multiple criteria on the level of individual dialogue turns. The task of evaluating responses in a chat is challenging because it requires an understanding of the interlocutor's roles (pragmatics), the conversation's context, and the response's meaning (semantics). At the same time, the conversations are often ungrammatical (Rodríguez-Cantelar et al., 2023) and vary in style (Zhang et al., 2018). The commonly used metrics, such as BLEU (Papineni et al., 2002), METEOR (Banerjee and Lavie, 2005), or BERTScore (Zhang et al., 2019), are based on comparison to human references and thus correlate poorly with human judgments on the turn-level, as they penalize many correct responses for a given chat context (Zhao et al., 2017). At the same time, human evaluation is expensive and time-consuming. Previous referenceless metrics based on neural networks and language models still do not reach sufficient correlations with human judgements (Zhang et al., 2020; Lowe et al., 2017).

In our work, we followed up on the recent development of pretrained Large Language Models (LLMs) with instruction finetuning (Brown et al., 2020; Raffel et al., 2020), which have been found to be capable evaluators in machine translation, summarization as well as dialogue (Kocmi and Federmann, 2023; Liu et al., 2023). Therefore, we applied LLMs and specific prompting to elicit ratings for the multiple qualities evaluated in DSTC11 Track 4 Task 2: appropriateness, content richness, grammatical correctness, and relevance. We present three different systems used for our three submissions, all of which are based on LLMs and few-shot prompting: (1) We evaluate a straightforward approach with manually designed fixed prompts for off-the-shelf open LLMs checkpoints.

[1]Results & task description at chateval.org/dstc11. Our experimental code is available at github.com/oplatek/chateval-llm.

Proceedings of The Eleventh Dialog System Technology Challenge, pages 113–122
September 11, 2023 ©2023 Association for Computational Linguistics

(2) We train a simple feed-forward regression neural network (FNN) on top of frozen LLM embeddings to predict the turn-level metrics scores. (3) We used the ChatGPT API and few-shot examples retrieved dynamically from the development set to improve the prompting performance. As no data annotated with the target metrics were available for the challenge, we heuristically mapped existing annotations from the development set to the target metrics, and we manually annotated a small rehearsal dataset for hyperparameter search.

Based on the human annotations released after the challenge finished, our *team6* achieved second place thanks to our third method, dynamically prompted chatGPT with few-shot examples. This approach showed that LLM prompting is a viable option for prototyping chat evaluation. However, the two other methods we explored scored worse: open LLMs with fixed prompts generally showed poor performance, and the regression FFN worked well on the development set but did not generalize well to the test set.

2 Task & Data

The goal of the DSTC11 Track 4 Task 2 was to predict several turn-level metrics automatically on the test set. For each dialogue turn, considering the preceding dialogue history, the participants were to submit a system to predict the score of the target metrics, defined by the organizers as:

- *Appropriateness* – The response is appropriate given the preceding dialogue.
- *Content Richnes* – The response is informative, with long sentences including multiple entities and conceptual or emotional words.
- *Grammatical Correctness* – Responses are free of grammatical and semantic errors.
- *Relevance* – Responses are on-topic with the immediate dialogue history.

Table 1 shows chat conversations from the rehearsal dataset with the turn-level metric annotations.

The organizers provided the participants with training, development, and test sets (Rodríguez-Cantelar et al., 2023), each coming from different domains and annotated with different metrics:

- *Training set* – consists of 390k dialogues, annotated with sentiment and toxicity labels. This set was not used in our experiments at all since our goal was to fine-tune or select LLMs that are already well-performing with no finetuning.
- *Development set* – consists of 24 datasets, some annotated with dataset-specific metrics. For our experiments, we created a heuristic mapping to the target metrics on a subset of the development set (see Section 3).
- *Test set* – consists of 3,470 dialogues and 130k turns, annotated with the target metrics. The data was only published in an anonymized form and at the end of the challenge, with no annotations or metadata, so that challenge participant could produce their model outputs. The annotations were published after the challenge was finished.
- *Rehearsal set* – this is a set of 156 turns collected in the same way as the test set, released earlier than the test set. We manually annotated this set with the target metrics (see Section 3) and used the result for hyperparameter search.

The submitted systems were benchmarked for the quality of their ranking using the Spearman correlation coefficients (SCC) (Zar, 2005) computed between the predicted scores and the human judgments. As a secondary measure, the Pearson correlation coefficients (PCC) (Freedman et al., 2007) were used to evaluate the correlation. The measures were computed for each of the target metrics separately. The overall submissions' ranking was determined using the average of the four SCCs.

3 Data Preprocessing

Since no information was provided on how the individual development dataset metrics relate to the target dialogue metrics, we built a heuristic to obtain target metric scores. The heuristic uses a linear combination of one or more dataset-specific metrics to the target metrics, chosen based on individual descriptions from the literature.[2] Using the development set and the heuristic, we created a supervised dataset and split it into training and development splits. We used this *development dataset* for model selection or supervised training, and we use this dataset to develop the three systems described in Section 4.

[2]See the line 354 for the turn metric mapping for different datasets.

Dialogue Turns	Appr	Rich.	Gram.	Rel
My boss gave me a 10 raise just last month And it was a nice surprise	5	5	5	-
It's great and he might think you're doing a great job	5	5	5	5
We have always been very nice He has always been very supportive of me	4	5	5	5
That's a good thing	4	3	5	4
do you have any pets?	5	4	3	-
I am retired so I love to travel so pets would slow me down	4	4	3	4
I understand that my idea of traveling is a hot hot bubble bath	3	4	2	2
Yes I have dogs and cats I like to take them with me on trips	2	4	2	2

Table 1: Two examples of complete conversations from the rehearsal set are annotated with turn-level metrics: appropriateness, content richness, grammatical correctness, and relevance. The context for each turn are the previous turns (lines) in the conversation. The second conversation at the bottom of the table shows an inappropriate response in the last turn because the last response contradicts previous responses of the system.

During our experiments, we struggled to find representative labels and input data which could be used as a development set. Therefore, we decided to annotate the additional 156 turns from the *rehearsal set* with the target metrics described in Section 2. We used this data to find our submitted systems' optimal hyperparameters. We assumed that this data came from the same distribution as the test set, but this later proved clearly not to be the case, as seen in Figure 2.

Note that we did not use the training set at all.

4 Submitted Systems

Inspired by (Kocmi and Federmann, 2023), we used pre-trained LLMs with prompts for predicting the individual metrics. We started with the simplest approach possible and manually designed the prompts.

4.1 Method 1: Simple Prompting

We experimented with prompting GPT-NeoX-20B (Black et al., 2022), OPT-30B (Zhang et al., 2022b), and TK-Instruct-11B (Wang et al., 2022).[3] We tried several prompt templates for each model and selected the best-performing one on the development set and the manually annotated rehearsal set. The templates were slightly adapted for each model to control for the deviations in model pretraining or instruction finetuning procedures, i.e., the wording of instructions or tags denoting a user-system interaction.

We used templates evaluating a single quality of each turn (i.e., calling the LLM four times to predict all metrics). We focus on a single-metric template because most of the open-source models

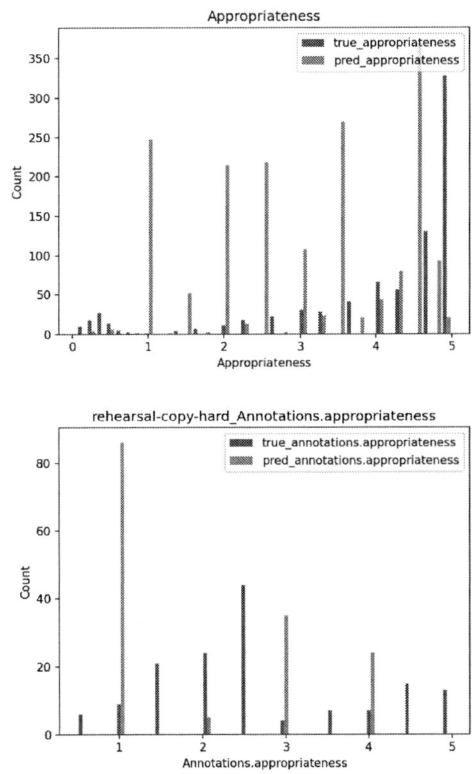

Figure 2: The histogram of predicted and human-annotated scores for *appropriateness* of a reply, on the test set (above) and on our manually annotated development set (below). Predicted scores are from ChatGPT with dynamic few-shot examples (see Section 4.3). Note that the rehearsal set is not representative of the test set – compare the blue bars representing the human-annotated scores. Interestingly, ChatGPT-predicted scores on the test set are not concentrated at the extremes, unlike on the rehearsal set.

[3]The numbers identify each exact model checkpoint by the number of parameters.

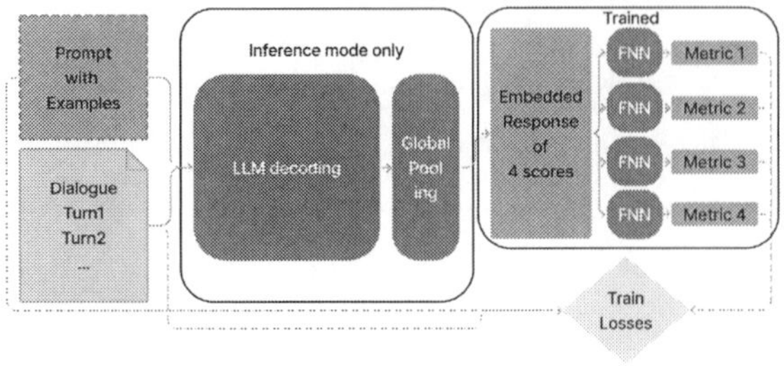

Figure 3: The architecture of the FFN trained on top of embeddings of LLM responses.

have trouble sticking to the desired output format when asked to generate a structured response with all four quality scores. Our templates included two hardcoded examples from the DailyDialog set (Li et al., 2017), one of the provided development datasets.

We developed the prompt templates iteratively. Every time we rephrased the prompt templates, we evaluated them on the DailyDialog dev set, which is part of the challenge dev set.

4.2 Method 2: Feed-Forward Regressor on Top of LLMs

Our second method attempts to solve the problem that the prompted LLMs sometimes produce malformed output. We assumed that LLMs extract relevant features even when the decoder produces a malformed one-best hypothesis. Therefore, we aimed to use LLM contextual embeddings as features for a simple regressor. However, instead of using the LLM's output directly, we implemented a simple embedding extractor on top of the LLM, and we trained a regression model to predict all four scores based on the embeddings. We use global max and average pooling over decoder layers and time steps of the decoded output to obtain the prompted response embedding.

We designed the prompts so the LLMs' replies contain information about all four metrics, so a single call to the LLMs is sufficient to obtain all four scores. At the same time, we designed the prompt so the LLM replies are as short as possible. To train the regressor, we used our heuristically mapped development data (see Section 3). We trained four simple feed-forward networks (FFNs), each modeling one of the target metrics using the same input embeddings. See Figure 3 for the architecture of the FNN.

4.3 Method 3: Dynamic Few-Shot Examples from a Vector Store

The previous two approaches used fixed few-shot examples. However, the performance of the in-context LLM learning can be improved by providing examples that are contextually similar to the instance being evaluated (Brown et al., 2020). We, therefore, implement a vector store with a dynamic few-shot example selection. First, we take dialogues from the development set relevant to a given metric (based on our mapping described in Section 3), and compute turn-level embeddings. These are then used as keys in a vector store optimized for similarity search. At runtime, we retrieve a set of examples based on their similarity to the input and include them in the LLM prompt. See Figure 1 for a detailed overview of the vector store architecture.

5 Experiments

We experimented with the three methods described in Section 4. First, we we experimented with the Simple Prompting method using the open-source LLMs (Section 4.1). Based on the results, we started two independent experiments. Section 5.2 describes the FFN training and Section 5.3 describes the development of vector storage which we used with ChatGPT API. For all three methods, we used the *rehearsal* set to select the best-performing model-template combination and hyperparameters.

5.1 Simple Prompting Submision

For our baseline submission, we selected the best-performing model-template combinations for each quality separately and then combined the results. Appropriateness and Relevance were generated by OPT-30b (Zhang et al., 2022b). Content Richness was generated by TK-Instruct (Wang et al., 2022). As the outputs for "Grammatical Correctness" were malformed in most cases, we replaced the outputs with randomly generated scores.

5.2 FFN Fine-Tuning setup

We trained the FFN using two layers with 1024 hidden units and ReLU activation with batch size 2048 and learning rate 5e-5. We used the log-cosh (Saleh and Saleh, 2022) loss function. We split the original development set into training and validation sets. We trained until early stopping based on the validation set using SCC for *appropriateness* as a stopping criterion. We extracted the embeddings from the prompted LLMs on the

```
Following is a dialogue context and the response to it.
Express how the response is appropriate given the context
with a continuous number between 1 and 5.
The higher the score, the more appropriate the sentences are.
Here are a few examples:
--------
{examples}
--------
Now complete the following with just a single float number:
Context: {dialogue_context}
Response: {response}
Appropriateness Score:
```

Figure 4: Prompt template used with the few-shot dynamic examples retrieval with ChatGPT has a placeholder for the *examples*. Each *example* contains the turn *response* together with its *dialogue context* and the ground truth *appropriateness score*. The other methods used a similar template, with only a slight rewording.

training and validation sets and cached them. We used the same LLM checkpoints as in the simple prompting method. We only used dev datasets whose annotations mapped to all four target metrics (see Section 3).; *DailyDialog* (Li et al., 2017), *Fed-Turn* (Mehri and Eskenazi, 2020a), *Persona-See* (See et al., 2019), and *Persona-Usr* (Mehri and Eskenazi, 2020b).

5.3 Vector Store Implementation

We use FAISS (Johnson et al., 2019) to implement vector storage that can perform effective similarity-based retrieval. To convert the dialogues into embeddings that are saved to the vector store, we used the MPNet (Song et al., 2020) pretrained sentence representation model (Reimers and Gurevych, 2019). We store the same development datasets in the vector store that we used for FFN training (Section 5.2), with the heuristically mapped scores for all four metrics.

We used the prompt template in Figure 4 with dynamically retrieved examples using vector store for the prompt and ChatGPT as the prompted LLM.[4]

6 Results & Discussion

We report positive findings related to Method 3 (Section 4.3), but we also report lessons learned from implementing the other two methods and, in general, using the data provided for the challenge. First, we summarize observations from our use of the data (Section 6.1). Then we report negative results from the simple prompting and FFN fine-tuning (Sections 6.2 and 6.3, respectively). We also report our best results from the vector store (Section 6.4) and discuss what our best model in the challenge is capable of evaluating. Finally, we add an ablation study in Section 6.5 performed after the challenge was complete, comparing few-shot capabilities of ChatGPT with the newly released Llama 2 model.

We are aware that LLMs are trained on large datasets, some of which (e.g., ChatGPT) are not public. However, due to the novelty of the test set (Rodríguez-Cantelar et al., 2023), we believe that the test set has not leaked to their training set.

6.1 Dataset Analysis

The test set contains dialogue samples from various datasets unseen in the development and rehearsal sets: *BlenderBot3, ChatGPT, DSTC10Persona, DSTC10Topical, ESL, GPT3, NCM*. The distribution of the test set was unknown to the participants, and most of the data comes from the unseen *BlenderBot3* and *ChatGPT* datasets. We observed that scores for individual metrics were not normalized across the datasets as the *ESL* and *NCM* datasets had a range of 0-1, while the other datasets had a range of 1-5.

This discrepancy in data distributions most likely resulted in our model selection and hyperparameter search on the rehearsal dataset being detrimental to the final performance of our systems. See the mismatch in the distribution of our own manual annotations on the rehearsal set and human annotation on the test set in Figure 2. Furthermore, we argue that we could have achieved better results if we ran our model selection not only on the appropriateness metric but optimized for all four metrics.

6.2 Simple Prompting is Fragile

In our informal experiments with simple prompting, we noticed that instruction-tuned LLM checkpoints produce results with intended formats more reliably. We also experimented with templates evaluating all four metrics using a single prompt. However, single-quality templates were generally more reliable and yielded outputs adhering to the expected formats more often. We consistently observed that adding examples to the templates improved the reliability of the outputs.

Manual development of prompts, which relies on observing a small set of examples, was impractical for a diverse development dataset. We frequently developed a promising prompt only to discover that the model produces malformed outputs when run on conversations from a different system. The typical problem was that LLMs would interpret part of

[4]We used the gpt-3.5-turbo-0301 API version.

System		Avg. Spearman
Baseline (Zhang et al., 2020)		0.3387
Winning submision (*team4*)		0.4890
Ours:	Simple Prompting	0.0807
	FFN Regressor	0.1742
	ChatGPT + Vector Store	0.4190

Table 2: The overall performance of the baseline, the challenge winning submission and our three submissions.

the input conversation as instruction. Consequently, instead of replying with the metric score, the model replied with a next turn fitting the conversation prefix. Whenever the model did not respond in the desired format, we used an uninformed response score of 3. The number of informed responses was the largest factor in the overall lower score for the simple prompting method.

6.3 FFN is Fast but Lacks Normalization

The training of the FFN is very efficient because we ran the LLMs only once in inference mode. Note that the training was faster than extracting the embeddings from the LLMs, and a single FFN layer adds negligible computational and memory costs at inference time. The FNN regression model solved the problem of LLMs producing malformed outputs. However, our submission suffered from unnormalized scores in different development dataset splits, and the model performed poorly on the test set. The results of our FFN training in Method 2 thus were influenced by incorrectly scaling the target metric values: For example, the *FedTurn* scores lie in the range $[0, 2.2]$ instead of $[1, 5]$.

6.4 Are we Comparing Systems or Turns?

Method 3 (Section 4.3) was the most successful in our experiments. We argue that we could achieve even better results if we did model selection not only on the appropriateness metric but optimized for all four metrics. We also argue that data mismatch between the rehearsal and test sets was detrimental to the performance of the systems. Despite that, we placed second as a team, improved upon a baseline, and are relatively close to the best system in terms of the overall ranking. See Table 2 for the comparison of the systems based on the average of the SCC over the four metrics. See Figure 2.

Our third method, ChatGPT with vector store examples (Section 4.3), was the most successful in our experiments. We observed that it easily contrasts between responses from different datasets but does not distinguish well among turns coming from the same dialogue system and the same dataset. The SCC scores in Table 3 shows that the score for the whole test set is better than most of the individual subsets based on different source datasets.

Dataset	Appropriateness	Relevance	Content richness
TEST-ALL	0.488	0.361	0.452
BLENDERBOT3	0.383	0.287	0.303
CHATGPT	0.122	0.060	0.181
DSTC10PERSONA	0.803	0.968	0.216
DSTC10TOPICAL	0.300	0.401	0.200
ESL	0.199	-	-
GPT3	0.091	0.007	0.242
NCM	0.061	-	-

Table 3: The performance of our best system as Spearman correlation coefficients scores on the test set split for the metrics *Appropriateness*, *content richness*, and *relevance*. The first row *TEST-ALL* reports the results on the whole dataset. For brevity, we do not report *grammatical correctness* per splits which is 0.402 for the whole test set. The test set contains conversations from different systems, including ChatGPT and GPT3.

6.5 Revisiting Few-Shot Prompts in Ablation

We present an additional ablation study, which we ran after the challenge was completed and evaluated on the *Appropriateness* quality. Using both ChatGPT and the newly released Llama 2 models (Touvron et al., 2023), we investigate the influence of the few-shot examples on the performance of the models.[5] In order to do so, we made two changes to the prompts: (1) we designed a single prompt template that can be used both with and without few-shot examples, (2) we normalized the use of newlines at the end of the prompt and in the few-shot examples, which improved performance. We also (3) further improved the prompt by iterative experiments on the DailyDialog development set.

We label the improved prompt (with changes 1+2+3) as *Pimpr*; we compare to a prompt closer to the original (with only changes 1+2 applied) as *Pnorm*. We then compared both ChatGPT and Llama 2 using both prompts *Pimpr* and *Pnorm* in three variants: (a) base without few-shot examples, (b) with two static examples (labeled *-fix-2egs*),

[5]We used the Llama2-7b-chat-hf checkpoint (`https://huggingface.co/meta-llama/Llama-2-7b-chat-hf`) and the `gpt-3.5-turbo-0613` version of the ChatGPT API. The `gpt-3.5-turbo-0301` was used for the *Porig* experiments with the original prompts from our submission.

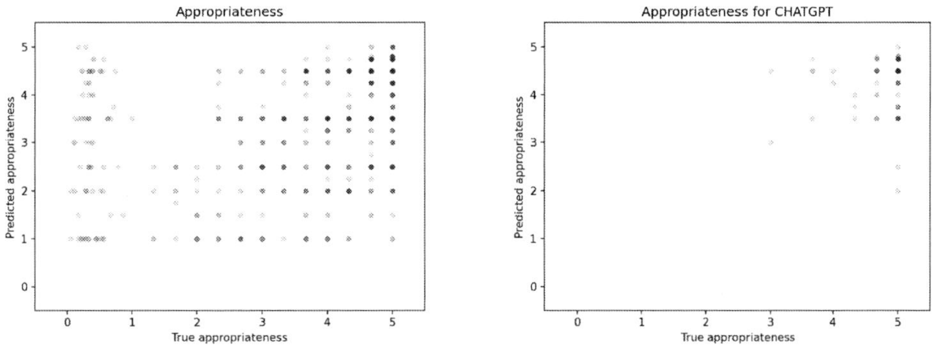

Figure 5: The two scatterplots show the correlation of ground truth turn-level scores for appropriateness and the prediction of our best system, on the whole test set (left) and for the test set turns generated by ChatGPT (right). Our system shows a relatively good correlation over the whole test set and evaluates the ChatGPT results correctly as high-quality, but it fails at distinguishing the quality of individual ChatGPT turns.

and (c) with two dynamically retrieved examples using the vector store (labeled *dyn-2egs*, cf. Section 4.3. We also include a comparison to the original ChatGPT with the prompt used in our model submitted to the challenge (labeled as *Porig*, see Section 5.3). Finally, we ran an experiment with variants of *Porig*/*Pnorm* where we prompted the model to evaluate all the four qualities in a single prompt (labeled as *-All*).

Our results in Table 4 suggest that it pays off to design the prompt carefully, and it is beneficial to use few-shot examples in the prompts. However, using dynamic examples form the vector store instead of fixed ones does not bring further improvements. We can see on ChatGPT results that our prompt improvements had an effect, and we were able to improve substantially over our challenge submission. There is a notable gap between ChatGPT and Llama 2; on the other hand, the Llama 2 results are much better than any of our previous results with open models (see Sections 6.2 and 6.3). We observe that predicting four qualities at once is not as good as predicting appropriateness only. However, it still seems an attractive alternative since such template use is roughly four times more effective when predicting four qualities individually. The percentage of failures for all reported systems is lower than 1% and thus does not play a significant role in the evaluation.

System	Prompt	Spearman Appr.	(%fail)
Llama 2 7B Chat	*Pimpr*	0.3310	(0.04%)
	Pimpr-fix-2egs	0.3756	(0.56%)
	Pimpr-dyn-2egs	0.3683	(0.36%)
ChatGPT 3.5-turbo-0613	*Pimpr*	0.4536	(0.01%)
	Pimpr-fix-2egs	0.6136	(0.00%)
	Pimpr-dyn-2egs	0.5962	(0.00%)
Llama 2 7B Chat	*Pnorm*	0.3914	(0.98%)
	Pnorm-fix-2egs	0.3551	(0.06%)
	Pnorm-dyn-2egs	0.3756	(0.65%)
	Pnorm-All	0.3710	(0.01%)
ChatGPT 3.5-turbo-0613	*Pnorm*-dyn-2egs	0.5462	
	Pnorm-fix-All	0.5334	
ChatGPT 3.5-turbo-0301	*Porig*-dyn-2egs	0.4880	
	Porig-fix-All	0.3616	

Table 4: Ablation study with the ChatGPT and Llama 2 7B Chat models for the *Appropriateness* quality (see Section 6.5 for prompt variants explanation). "%fail" indicates the percentage of LLM outputs that failed to parse due to incorrect format.

7 Related Work

Recent works in chat evaluation focus on referenceless approaches, as these do not suffer from penalizing appropriate responses based on surface dissimilarity to a single human-written reference response (Liu et al., 2017; Lowe et al., 2017). Here, Lowe et al. (2017) trained a neural network from scratch on relatively large annotated data to predict a single score, but this approach was later found to generalize poorly, even to basic data perturbations, let alone other datasets (Sai et al., 2019; Lowe, 2019).

Later works leveraged pretrained language models for better generalization abilities, such as BERT Zhang et al. (2020); Gao et al. (2020), RoBERTa (Mehri and Eskenazi, 2020c), GPT-2 (Sinha et al., 2020) or DialoGPT Mehri and Eskenazi (2020a). These metrics are trained on human-labeled sets of system outputs based on popular open-domain datasets, similar to the ChatEval development data. Some of them use additional data augmentation techniques, such as self-training Zhang et al. (2022a). While they do achieve good correlations on some datasets, generalization with respect to unseen datasets is still not guaranteed (Yeh et al., 2021).

Sai et al. (2021) stressed the importance of predicting multiple qualities, such as, fluency and appropriateness, in dialogue evaluation. At the same time, they asserted that metrics should be sensitive enough to distinguish between similar responses. Using simple text perturbations targeting the individual qualities, they show that most existing metrics are not robust enough.

Two very recent works, closely related to ours, propose the usage of instruction-tuned LLMs to evaluate generated text in various tasks like summarization and dialogue response generation (Liu et al., 2023), or machine translation (Kocmi and Federmann, 2023). Both approaches use in-context learning and multiple prompting techniques to obtain scalar metric predictions or candidate rankings. They achieved good results and correlations with human judgments. However, they used only closed models for the evaluation and did not experiment with few-shot prompting using relevant examples.

8 Conclusion

We presented three simple approaches to using LLMs for turn-level chat evaluation. We achieved promising results using ChatGPT prompting with few-shot example retrieval from a vector score, and ranked as the second-best team. Based on the results of our best system, we argue that chat turn evaluation systems based on current state-of-the-art LLMs are usable only for system-level evaluation but not for segment-level evaluation, i.e., they cannot distinguish between the quality of individual turns, especially for outputs of high-quality latest systems based on LLMs such as ChatGPT and GPT3.

We observed that LLMs are fragile to the prompts, few-shot examples and cannot be used out-of-the-box for chat evaluation. We also report implementing a simple regressor on top of embeddings obtained from the prompted LLM decoder. We attribute its poor performance to our incorrect implementation of data preparation.

We also presented an ablation study that investigated the influence of the few-shot examples on the performance of LLMs. We found that few-shot examples help the LLMs to generalize better to unseen data, especially with respect to fitting the desired output format. However, using examples dynamically obtained from the vector store instead of hand-picked fixed examples did not bring any additional improvements.

We reached a new best Spearman correlation coefficient of 0.6136 for appropriateness with ChatGPT and fixed few-shot examples in our ablation study. In addition, the Llama 2 open model used in our ablation showed significant improvements over the challenge baseline.

9 Acknowledgements

This research was supported by Charles University projects GAUK 40222 and SVV 260575 and by the European Research Council (Grant agreement No. 101039303 NG-NLG). It used resources provided by the LINDAT/CLARIAH-CZ Research Infrastructure (Czech Ministry of Education, Youth, and Sports project No. LM2018101). The authors thank the anonymous reviewers for their valuable feedback, Milan Fučík and Mateusz Krubiński for their suggestions and technical support.

References

Satanjeev Banerjee and Alon Lavie. 2005. Meteor: An automatic metric for mt evaluation with improved correlation with human judgments. In *Proceedings of the acl workshop on intrinsic and extrinsic evaluation measures for machine translation and/or summarization*, pages 65–72.

Sid Black, Stella Biderman, Eric Hallahan, Quentin Anthony, Leo Gao, Laurence Golding, Horace He, Connor Leahy, Kyle McDonell, Jason Phang, Michael Pieler, USVSN Sai Prashanth, Shivanshu Purohit, Laria Reynolds, Jonathan Tow, Ben Wang, and Samuel Weinbach. 2022. Gpt-neox-20b: An open-source autoregressive language model.

Tom B. Brown, Benjamin Mann, Nick Ryder, Melanie Subbiah, Jared Kaplan, Prafulla Dhariwal, Arvind Neelakantan, Pranav Shyam, Girish Sastry, Amanda Askell, Sandhini Agarwal, Ariel Herbert-Voss, Gretchen Krueger, Tom Henighan, Rewon Child, Aditya Ramesh, Daniel M. Ziegler, Jeffrey Wu, Clemens Winter, Christopher Hesse, Mark Chen, Eric Sigler, Mateusz Litwin, Scott Gray, Benjamin Chess, Jack Clark, Christopher Berner, Sam McCandlish, Alec Radford, Ilya Sutskever, and Dario Amodei. 2020. Language Models are Few-Shot Learners. ArXiv:2005.14165 [cs].

David Freedman, Robert Pisani, and Roger Purves. 2007. Statistics (international student edition). *Pisani, R. Purves, 4th edn. WW Norton & Company, New York*.

Xiang Gao, Yizhe Zhang, Michel Galley, Chris Brockett, and Bill Dolan. 2020. Dialogue response ranking training with large-scale human feedback data. In *Proceedings of the 2020 Conference on Empirical Methods in Natural Language Processing (EMNLP)*, pages 386–395, Online. Association for Computational Linguistics.

Jeff Johnson, Matthijs Douze, and Hervé Jégou. 2019. Billion-scale similarity search with GPUs. *IEEE Transactions on Big Data*, 7(3):535–547.

Tom Kocmi and Christian Federmann. 2023. Large Language Models Are State-of-the-Art Evaluators of Translation Quality. ArXiv:2302.14520 [cs].

Yanran Li, Hui Su, Xiaoyu Shen, Wenjie Li, Ziqiang Cao, and Shuzi Niu. 2017. DailyDialog: A Manually Labelled Multi-turn Dialogue Dataset. ArXiv:1710.03957 [cs] version: 1.

Chia-Wei Liu, Ryan Lowe, Iulian V. Serban, Michael Noseworthy, Laurent Charlin, and Joelle Pineau. 2017. How NOT To Evaluate Your Dialogue System: An Empirical Study of Unsupervised Evaluation Metrics for Dialogue Response Generation. ArXiv:1603.08023 [cs].

Yang Liu, Dan Iter, Yichong Xu, Shuohang Wang, Ruochen Xu, and Chenguang Zhu. 2023. G-Eval: NLG Evaluation using GPT-4 with Better Human Alignment. ArXiv:2303.16634 [cs].

Ryan Lowe. 2019. Introducing Retrospectives: 'Real Talk' for your Past Papers. Library Catalog: thegradient.pub.

Ryan Lowe, Michael Noseworthy, Iulian Vlad Serban, Nicolas Angelard-Gontier, Yoshua Bengio, and Joelle Pineau. 2017. Towards an Automatic Turing Test: Learning to Evaluate Dialogue Responses. In *Proceedings of the 55th Annual Meeting of the Association for Computational Linguistics (Volume 1: Long Papers)*, pages 1116–1126, Vancouver, Canada. Association for Computational Linguistics.

Shikib Mehri and Maxine Eskenazi. 2020a. Unsupervised Evaluation of Interactive Dialog with DialoGPT. In *Proceedings of the 21th Annual Meeting of the Special Interest Group on Discourse and Dialogue*, pages 225–235, 1st virtual meeting. Association for Computational Linguistics.

Shikib Mehri and Maxine Eskenazi. 2020b. USR: An Unsupervised and Reference Free Evaluation Metric for Dialog Generation. In *Proceedings of the 58th Annual Meeting of the Association for Computational Linguistics*, pages 681–707, Online. Association for Computational Linguistics.

Shikib Mehri and Maxine Eskenazi. 2020c. USR: An unsupervised and reference free evaluation metric for dialog generation. In *Proceedings of the 58th Annual Meeting of the Association for Computational Linguistics*, pages 681–707, Online. Association for Computational Linguistics.

Kishore Papineni, Salim Roukos, Todd Ward, and Wei-Jing Zhu. 2002. Bleu: a method for automatic evaluation of machine translation. In *Proceedings of the 40th Annual Meeting of the Association for Computational Linguistics*, pages 311–318, Philadelphia, Pennsylvania, USA. Association for Computational Linguistics.

Colin Raffel, Noam Shazeer, Adam Roberts, Katherine Lee, Sharan Narang, Michael Matena, Yanqi Zhou, Wei Li, and Peter J. Liu. 2020. Exploring the Limits of Transfer Learning with a Unified Text-to-Text Transformer. ArXiv:1910.10683 [cs, stat].

Nils Reimers and Iryna Gurevych. 2019. Sentence-bert: Sentence embeddings using siamese bert-networks. In *Proceedings of the 2019 Conference on Empirical Methods in Natural Language Processing*. Association for Computational Linguistics.

Mario Rodríguez-Cantelar, Chen Zhang, Chengguang Tang, Ke Shi, Sarik Ghazarian, João Sedoc, Luis Fernando D'Haro, and Alexander Rudnicky. 2023. Overview of Robust and Multilingual Automatic Evaluation Metrics for Open-Domain Dialogue Systems at DSTC 11 Track 4. ArXiv:2306.12794 [cs].

Ananya B. Sai, Tanay Dixit, Dev Yashpal Sheth, Sreyas Mohan, and Mitesh M. Khapra. 2021. Perturbation checklists for evaluating nlg evaluation metrics.

Ananya B. Sai, Mithun Das Gupta, Mitesh M. Khapra, and Mukundhan Srinivasan. 2019. Re-Evaluating ADEM: A Deeper Look at Scoring Dialogue Responses. In *Proceedings of the AAAI Conference on Artificial Intelligence*, pages 6220–6227, Honolulu, HI, USA. Number: 01.

Resve A. Saleh and A. K. Md Ehsanes Saleh. 2022. Statistical Properties of the log-cosh Loss Function Used in Machine Learning. ArXiv:2208.04564 [cs, stat].

Abigail See, Stephen Roller, Douwe Kiela, and Jason Weston. 2019. What makes a good conversation? How controllable attributes affect human judgments. In *Proceedings of the 2019 Conference of the North American Chapter of the Association for Computational Linguistics: Human Language Technologies, Volume 1 (Long and Short Papers)*, pages 1702–1723, Minneapolis, Minnesota. Association for Computational Linguistics.

Koustuv Sinha, Prasanna Parthasarathi, Jasmine Wang, Ryan Lowe, William L. Hamilton, and Joelle Pineau. 2020. Learning an unreferenced metric for online dialogue evaluation. In *Proceedings of the 58th Annual Meeting of the Association for Computational*

Linguistics, pages 2430–2441, Online. Association for Computational Linguistics.

Kaitao Song, Xu Tan, Tao Qin, Jianfeng Lu, and Tie-Yan Liu. 2020. MPNet: Masked and Permuted Pre-training for Language Understanding. ArXiv:2004.09297 [cs].

Hugo Touvron, Louis Martin, Kevin Stone, Peter Albert, Amjad Almahairi, Yasmine Babaei, Nikolay Bashlykov, Soumya Batra, Prajjwal Bhargava, Shruti Bhosale, Dan Bikel, Lukas Blecher, Cristian Canton Ferrer, Moya Chen, Guillem Cucurull, David Esiobu, Jude Fernandes, Jeremy Fu, Wenyin Fu, Brian Fuller, Cynthia Gao, Vedanuj Goswami, Naman Goyal, Anthony Hartshorn, Saghar Hosseini, Rui Hou, Hakan Inan, Marcin Kardas, Viktor Kerkez, Madian Khabsa, Isabel Kloumann, Artem Korenev, Punit Singh Koura, Marie-Anne Lachaux, Thibaut Lavril, Jenya Lee, Diana Liskovich, Yinghai Lu, Yuning Mao, Xavier Martinet, Todor Mihaylov, Pushkar Mishra, Igor Molybog, Yixin Nie, Andrew Poulton, Jeremy Reizenstein, Rashi Rungta, Kalyan Saladi, Alan Schelten, Ruan Silva, Eric Michael Smith, Ranjan Subramanian, Xiaoqing Ellen Tan, Binh Tang, Ross Taylor, Adina Williams, Jian Xiang Kuan, Puxin Xu, Zheng Yan, Iliyan Zarov, Yuchen Zhang, Angela Fan, Melanie Kambadur, Sharan Narang, Aurelien Rodriguez, Robert Stojnic, Sergey Edunov, and Thomas Scialom. 2023. Llama 2: Open Foundation and Fine-Tuned Chat Models. ArXiv:2307.09288 [cs].

Yizhong Wang, Swaroop Mishra, Pegah Alipoormolabashi, Yeganeh Kordi, Amirreza Mirzaei, A. Arunkumar, Arjun Ashok, Arut Selvan Dhanasekaran, Atharva Naik, David Stap, Eshaan Pathak, Giannis Karamanolakis, Haizhi Gary Lai, Ishan Purohit, Ishani Mondal, Jacob Anderson, Kirby Kuznia, Krima Doshi, Maitreya Patel, Kuntal Kumar Pal, M. Moradshahi, Mihir Parmar, Mirali Purohit, Neeraj Varshney, Phani Rohitha Kaza, Pulkit Verma, Ravsehaj Singh Puri, Rushang Karia, Shailaja Keyur Sampat, Savan Doshi, Siddharth Deepak Mishra, Sujan C. Reddy, Sumanta Patro, Tanay Dixit, Xu dong Shen, Chitta Baral, Yejin Choi, Hannaneh Hajishirzi, Noah A. Smith, and Daniel Khashabi. 2022. Benchmarking generalization via in-context instructions on 1,600+ language tasks.

Yi-Ting Yeh, Maxine Eskenazi, and Shikib Mehri. 2021. A comprehensive assessment of dialog evaluation metrics. In *The First Workshop on Evaluations and Assessments of Neural Conversation Systems*, pages 15–33, Online. Association for Computational Linguistics.

Jerrold H Zar. 2005. Spearman rank correlation. *Encyclopedia of Biostatistics*, 7.

Chen Zhang, Luis D'Haro, Rafael Banchs, Thomas Friedrichs, and Haizhou Li. 2020. Deep am-fm: Toolkit for automatic dialogue evaluation. *Conversational Dialogue Systems for the Next Decade*, pages 53–69.

Chen Zhang, Luis D'Haro, Thomas Friedrichs, and Haizhou Li. 2022a. Mdd-eval: Self-training on augmented data for multi-domain dialogue evaluation. *Proceedings of the AAAI Conference on Artificial Intelligence*, 36:11657–11666.

Saizheng Zhang, Emily Dinan, Jack Urbanek, Arthur Szlam, Douwe Kiela, and Jason Weston. 2018. Personalizing Dialogue Agents: I have a dog, do you have pets too? ArXiv:1801.07243 [cs].

Susan Zhang, Stephen Roller, Naman Goyal, Mikel Artetxe, Moya Chen, Shuohui Chen, Christopher Dewan, Mona Diab, Xian Li, Xi Victoria Lin, Todor Mihaylov, Myle Ott, Sam Shleifer, Kurt Shuster, Daniel Simig, Punit Singh Koura, Anjali Sridhar, Tianlu Wang, and Luke Zettlemoyer. 2022b. Opt: Open pre-trained transformer language models.

Tianyi Zhang, Varsha Kishore, Felix Wu, Kilian Q Weinberger, and Yoav Artzi. 2019. Bertscore: Evaluating text generation with bert. *arXiv preprint arXiv:1904.09675*.

Tiancheng Zhao, Ran Zhao, and Maxine Eskenazi. 2017. Learning discourse-level diversity for neural dialog models using conditional variational autoencoders. In *Proceedings of the 55th Annual Meeting of the Association for Computational Linguistics (Volume 1: Long Papers)*, pages 654–664, Vancouver, Canada. Association for Computational Linguistics.

Parallel Corpora Alignment Framework for Multilingual and Robust Automatic Dialogue Evaluation

Xinglin Wang ♠ **Jiayi Shi** ♠ **Peiwen Yuan** ♠ **Kan Li** ♡
School of Computer Science & Technology, Beijing Institute of Technology
{wangxinglin, shijiayi, yuanpw, likan}@bit.edu.cn

Abstract

Open-domain automatic dialogue evaluation plays an important role in dialogue systems. While recent efforts are being put into making learning-based evaluation metrics correlate better with human evaluation, robust metrics for parallel corpora and multiple domains remain unexplored. Parallel corpora refer to corpora that express the same idea in different ways (e.g., translation, paraphrasing and back-translation). In this paper, we propose **P**arallel **C**orpora **A**lignment **F**ramework (PCAF), which improves the consistency and robustness of model evaluation on parallel corpora. Firstly, parallel corpora are aligned in semantic space through parallel-corpora-aligned contrastive learning. Then, parallel-corpora-aligned distillation on multiple datasets is applied to further improve model's generalization ability across multiple data domains. Our approach ranks second on the final test data of DSTC11 track4 sub-task1 ("Multilingual Automatic Evaluation Metrics", turn-level) and third on the sub-task2 ("Robust Automatic Evaluation Metrics", turn-level), which proves the strong generalization ability and robustness of our proposed approach.

1 Introduction

Open-domain automatic dialogue evaluation, which aims to evaluate dialogues efficiently and accurately, plays an important role in dialogue systems. On the one hand, it provides a basis for cross-model comparison, on the other hand, it points out the direction for model improvement. While recent efforts are being put into making learning-based evaluation metrics correlate better with human evaluation, robust metrics for parallel corpora and multiple domains remain unexplored. Parallel corpora refer to corpora express the same idea in different ways (e.g., translation, paraphrasing or back-translation). In Dialogue System Technology Challenge 11 (DSTC11)[1], the track4 "Robust and Multilingual Automatic Evaluation Metrics for Open-Domain Dialogue Systems" proposes such a challenge, which consists of two sub-tasks. In sub-task1 ("Metrics for multilingual data"), all participants need to develop effective automatic open-ended and multilingual (i.e., English, Spanish and Chinese) dialogue evaluation metrics that perform similarly when evaluated over all the languages. In sub-task2 ("Robust metrics"), all participants need to develop effective automatic open-ended dialogue evaluation metrics that perform robustly when evaluated over back-translated/paraphrased sentences in English. For both tasks, the developed metrics should be correlated to human judgements well and explainable.

Current automatic dialogue evaluation metrics include word overlap-based metrics, embedding-based metrics and learning-based metrics. Word overlap-based metrics (e.g., BLEU (Papineni et al., 2002), ROUGE (Lin, 2004) and METEOR (Banerjee and Lavie, 2005)) evaluate candidate response through its overlapping words with reference response. Embedding-based metrics (e.g., Greedy Matching (Rus and Lintean, 2012) and Vector Extrema (Forgues et al., 2014)) firstly obtain sentence representation through word embedding (e.g., word vector (Mikolov et al., 2013)), then, the semantic similarity between candidate response and reference response is calculated by their representation for dialogue evaluation. However, due to the one-to-many nature of open-domain dialogue (Zhao et al., 2017), the two referenced based metrics above have been shown to be poorly correlated with human evaluation (Liu et al., 2017). Learning-based metrics aim to predict the score of certain quality of candidate response and have shown great correlation with human evaluation (Tao et al., 2018). Previous study of learning-based

♠ Equal Contribution.
♡ Corresponding Author.

[1]https://dstc11.dstc.community/home

Proceedings of The Eleventh Dialog System Technology Challenge, pages 123–132
September 11, 2023 ©2023 Association for Computational Linguistics

metrics have explored topic transition dynamics in dialogue (Huang et al., 2020), composition of fine-grained qualities (Mehri and Eskenazi, 2020b; Phy et al., 2020; Zhang et al., 2022) and quantifiable dialogue coherence evaluation (Ye et al., 2021). However, all of the current metrics are tested on a monolingual setup, and fail to consider the robustness of metrics in noisy settings.

To address the above issues, we propose **P**arallel **C**orpora **A**lignment **F**ramework (PCAF), which improves the consistency and robustness of model evaluation on parallel corpora. Parallel corpora refer to corpora that express the same idea in different manners (e.g., translation, paraphrasing or back-translation). Firstly, parallel corpora are aligned in semantic space through parallel-corpora-aligned contrastive learning. Then, parallel-corpora-aligned knowledge distillation (Hinton et al., 2015) on multiple datasets is applied to improve model's evaluation capability across multiple data domains. Our approach ranks second on the final test data of DSTC11 track4 sub-task1 ("Multilingual Automatic Evaluation Metrics", turn-level) with an average Spearman correlation score of 36.57% and third on the sub-task2 ("Robust Automatic Evaluation Metrics", turn-level) with an average Spearman correlation score of 38.30%.

Our contributions are summarized as follows:

- We propose a novel framework PCAF which improves the consistency and robustness of model evaluation on parallel corpora.
- Our approach ranks second on the final test data of DSTC11 track4 sub-task1 ("Multilingual Automatic Evaluation Metrics", turn-level) and third on the sub-task2 ("Robust Automatic Evaluation Metrics", turn-level), which proves the strong generalization ability and robustness of our proposed approach.

2 Related Work

Automatic dialogue evaluation is of great importance to dialogue systems. It can be divided into dialogue-level and turn-level, while dialogue-level pays attention to the overall evaluation of dialogue system, turn-level mainly evaluate the quality of candidate response according to the provided dialogue history. This paper mainly focus on turn-level automatic dialogue evaluation.

Word overlap-based metrics and embedding-based metrics are standard automatic evaluation metrics (Zhang et al., 2022). However, these metrics which assess dialogue based on reference response have been shown to be inaccurate for dialogue evaluation (Liu et al., 2017). Learning-based metrics was then proposed, which adopts deep learning models and aims to predict human-like scores to input responses (Lowe et al., 2017).

Learning-based metrics can be divided into supervised and self-supervised. Supervised metrics (Lowe et al., 2017) highly depend on human-annotated training data, which are not widely studied due to the lack of such data. Self-supervised metrics utilize human response as positive responses, and negative responses are obtained through negative sampling, thus, positive-negative responses pairs are constructed for model training. As human conversations are readily available (e.g., DailyDialogue (Li et al., 2017)), various self-supervised metrics have been proposed. Grade (Huang et al., 2020) applies graph reasoning to model topic transition dynamics in dialogue. Maude (Sinha et al., 2020) distinguishes the positive and negative responses using NCE loss (Gutmann and Hyvärinen, 2010). USR (Mehri and Eskenazi, 2020b) trains one language model and two dialogue retrieval models to measure five qualities respectively and regresses them to an overall score. MME-CRS (Zhang et al., 2022) trains five sub-models to evaluate five qualities respectively and weighted them to an overall judgement.

However, all of the current metrics are tested on a monolingual setup, and fail to consider metrics' robustness to changes in domain and expression. PCAF can effectively alleviate these problems and shows great generalization ability and robustness.

3 Methodology

Figure 1 illustrates the pipeline of our proposed PCAF, a two-stage training framework which aligns parallel corpora in semantic space and improves model's generalization ability. In this section, we will introduce parallel-corpora-aligned pre-training and parallel-corpora-aligned knowledge distillation for generalization in detail.

3.1 Model Architecture

The metric model consists of a encoder for feature extraction and a predictor for score prediction. Specifically, we adopt XLM-RoBERTa (Conneau et al., 2020) and RoBERTa (Liu et al., 2019) as the encoder network for sub-task1 and sub-task2 re-

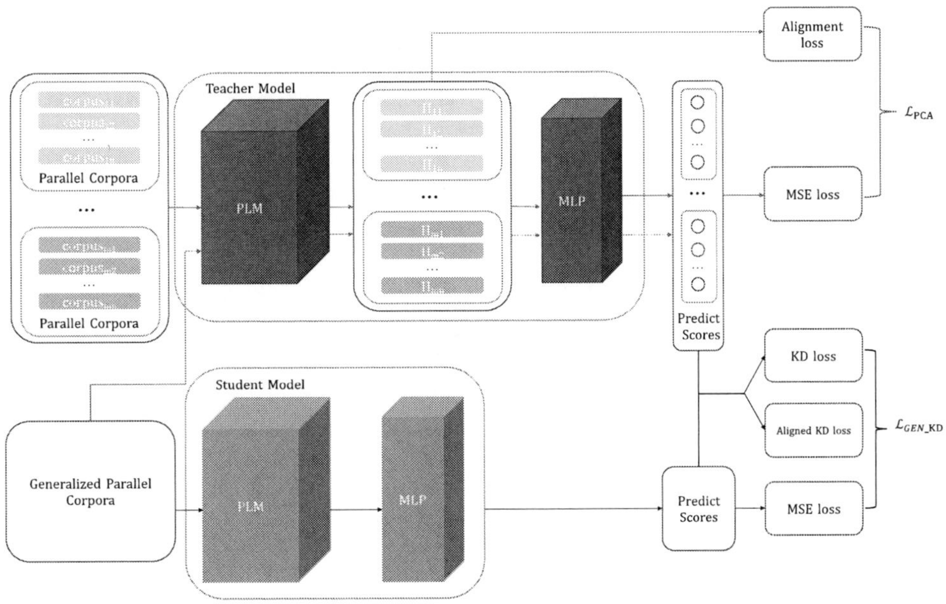

Figure 1: The overall pipeline of our PCAF, including parallel-corpora-aligned pre-training and knowledge distillation on multi-dataset. The solid blue one-way arrows show the process of parallel-corpora-aligned pre-training stage. During pre-training stage, parallel corpora are aligned in semantic space through contrastive learning, and model's prediction capability is optimized by MSE loss. The solid black one-way arrows and dotted blue one-way arrows illustrate the KD stage, where the student model is initialized with the teacher model and optimized by GEN_KD loss to improve model's generalization ability.

spectively, and a three-layer multi-layer perceptron (MLP) is used as the predictor network.

Given the context $\mathbf{c} = \{u_1, u_2, ..., u_{|\mathbf{c}|}\}$ and response $\mathbf{r} = \{u_r\}$ where u_i is utterance of context or response, the representation of response is firstly obtained by the pooled output feature of XLM-RoBERTa:

$$v_r = Pooler(Encoder(\mathbf{c}, \mathbf{r})) \tag{1}$$

Then, the quality score of response is predicted by:

$$s = MLP(v_r) \tag{2}$$

3.2 Parallel-Corpora-Aligned Pre-training

Parallel corpora refers to corpora that express the same idea in different ways. Common parallel corpora are utterances written in different languages or their paraphrased, back-translated versions. Aligning parallel corpora in semantic space can not only improve model's evaluation capability in multi-lingual settings, but also make model robust to changes in form of the utterances. Besides, training an aligned model on one language can improve model's performance on another language as well.

Parallel corpora is aligned in semantic space through contrastive learning. Formally, given a training dataset $\mathcal{D}_{pc} = \{\mathcal{P}_i\}$, $\mathcal{P}_i = \{(c_{ij}, r_{ij}, \overline{r}_{ij})\}$ where c_{ij} and r_{ij} are a ground-truth context-response pair and $\overline{r}_{ij}$ is a negative response sampled by negative sampling strategy. Each dialogue in $\mathcal{P}_i$ except the negative responses expresses the same idea but in different manners , while dialogues in $\mathcal{P}_i$ express different ideas with dialogues in $\mathcal{P}_j$ $(i \neq j)$. Let $v_{ij}, \overline{v}_{ij}$ be the representation of $r_{ij}, \overline{r}_{ij}$, the similarity between all responses is:

$$\begin{aligned} S_{all} = & \sum_{i=1}^{|\mathcal{D}_{pc}|-1} \sum_{j=1}^{|\mathcal{P}_i|} \sum_{m=i+1}^{|\mathcal{D}_{pc}|} \sum_{n=1}^{|\mathcal{P}_m|} exp(cos\_sim(v_{ij}, v_{mn})/\tau) \\ & + \sum_{i=1}^{|\mathcal{D}_{pc}|-1} \sum_{j=1}^{|\mathcal{P}_i|} \sum_{m=i+1}^{|\mathcal{D}_{pc}|} \sum_{n=1}^{|\mathcal{P}_m|} exp(cos\_sim(\overline{v}_{ij}, v_{mn})/\tau) \\ & + \sum_{i=1}^{|\mathcal{D}_{pc}|-1} \sum_{j=1}^{|\mathcal{P}_i|} \sum_{m=i+1}^{|\mathcal{D}_{pc}|} \sum_{n=1}^{|\mathcal{P}_m|} exp(cos\_sim(\overline{v}_{ij}, \overline{v}_{mn})/\tau) \end{aligned} \tag{3}$$

the similarity between responses in $\mathcal{P}_i$ is:

Dataset	Spanish Translation	Chinese Translation	Paraphrases	English Back-translation
DBDC (Higashinaka et al., 2016)	✓	-	✓	✓
CMU_DoG (Zhou et al., 2018)	✓	-	✓	✓
Cornell Movie-Dialogs (Danescu-Niculescu-Mizil and Lee, 2011)	-	✓	✓	✓
DailyDialog (Li et al., 2017)	✓	✓	✓	✓
DECODE (Nie et al., 2021)	✓	-	✓	✓
EmotionLines (Hsu et al., 2018)	✓	-	✓	✓
EmpathicDialogues (Rashkin et al., 2019)	✓	✓	✓	✓
Holl-E (Moghe et al., 2018)	✓	-	✓	✓
MEENA (Adiwardana et al., 2020)	✓	-	✓	✓
MELD (Poria et al., 2019)	✓	-	✓	✓
MetalWOz (Lee et al., 2019)	✓	-	✓	✓
Movie-DiC (Banchs, 2012)	✓	-	✓	✓
PersonaChat (Zhang et al., 2018)	✓	✓	✓	✓
SentimentLIAR (Upadhayay and Behzadan, 2020)	✓	-	✓	✓
Switchboard Coherence (Cervone and Riccardi, 2020)	-	✓	✓	✓
Topical-Chat (Gopalakrishnan et al., 2019)	✓	✓	✓	✓
Wizard of Wikipedia (Dinan et al., 2019)	✓	✓	✓	✓
WOCHAT (D'Haro et al., 2016)	✓	-	✓	✓

Table 1: Training sets provided by DSTC11 Track4 organizers. The source language of these datasets is English, and all of them are provided with English back-translation and paraphrases.

$$S_{\mathcal{P}_i} = \sum_{j=1}^{|\mathcal{P}_i|-1} \sum_{k=j+1}^{|\mathcal{P}_i|} exp(cos\_sim(v_{ij}, v_{ik})/\tau) \quad (4)$$

and the alignment loss is:

$$l_{align} = -\sum_{i=1}^{|\mathcal{D}_{pc}|} log \frac{S_{\mathcal{P}_i}}{S_{all}} \quad (5)$$

together with the MSE loss:

$$l_{mse} = \sum_{i=1}^{\mathcal{D}_{pc}} \sum_{j=1}^{\mathcal{P}_i} ((1 - s_{ij})^2 + \overline{s}_{ij}^2) \quad (6)$$

the final loss of parallel-corpora-align pre-training is:

$$\mathcal{L}_{PCA} = l_{align} + l_{mse} \quad (7)$$

3.3 Knowledge Distillation on Multiple Datasets

After parallel-corpora-aligned pre-training, the model M is further trained by parallel-corpora-aligned knowledge distillation on multiple datasets to attain a better generalization ability.

Given parallel corpora $\mathcal{P} = (c_i, r_i, \overline{r}_i)$ where r_i and $\overline{r}_i$ are positive-negative response pair, M_t is the teacher model, and M_s is the student model which is initialized with the teacher model. Let the teacher model and student model predict the score of the response pair respectively, and get $s_{ti}, \overline{s}_{ti}, s_{si}, \overline{s}_{si}$.

The student model is firstly optimized by MSE loss:

$$l_i^{kd\_mse} = (1 - s_{si})^2 + \overline{s}_{si}^2 \quad (8)$$

Then, we utilize the teacher model's predictions as soft targets. Besides, considering the parallel corpora all express the same idea, we take the average of teacher model's predictions of positive responses as the label for the entire parallel corpora's positive responses, and the KD loss is formulated as:

$$l_i^{kd} = (s_{ti} - s_{si})^2 + (\overline{s}_{ti} - \overline{s}_{si})^2 + (\frac{\sum_{k=1}^{|\mathcal{P}|} s_{ti}}{|\mathcal{P}|} - s_{si})^2 \quad (9)$$

The overall loss in KD stage is the weighted sum of $l_i^{kd\_mse}$ and l_i^{kd}:

$$\mathcal{L}_{GEN\_KD} = \frac{1}{|\mathcal{P}|} \sum_{i=1}^{|\mathcal{P}|} (\alpha * l_i^{kd\_mse} + (1 - alpha) * l_i^{kd}) \quad (10)$$

where α is the hyperparameter.

4 Experiments

4.1 Datasets

As shown in Table 1, the organizers of DSTC11 Track4 provide 18 human-human dialogue datasets as training set. Table 2 shows the result of our preliminary experiment of datasets comparison. For each dataset, we randomly sampled 3k data to train a BERT + MLP model which is further tested on the provided development sets respectively. As the model trained on DailyDialog(Li et al., 2017) shows the highest Spearman correlation among the 18 human-human dialogue datasets, we select DailyDialog as the pre-training dataset. Besides, SentimentLIAR and Switchboard Coherence are excluded as they encountered training collapse in our preliminary experiment.

Dataset	Spearman(%)	rank
DBDC	21.41	15
CMU_DoG	24.31	13
Cornell Movie-Dialogs	27.26	9
DailyDialog	31.48	1
DECODE	27.43	7
EmotionLines	30.25	2
EmpatheticDialog	28.37	6
Holl-E	24.00	14
MEENA	24.44	12
MELD	27.37	8
MetalWOz	25.28	11
Movie-DiC	28.81	5
PersonaChat	25.55	10
SentimentLIAR	-	-
Switchboard Coherence	-	-
Topical-Chat	29.98	3
Wizard of Wikipedia	29.11	4
WOCHAT	29.11	16

Table 2: Result of preliminary experiment of datasets comparison. We test the BERT + MLP model trained with 3k English data from each dataset respectively on provided development sets. The Spearman correlation is the average result of all development sets.

As for the development set, the organizers provide the following 14 turn-level datasets which have been automatically translated to Spanish and Chinese, and back-translated to English:

- CONVAI2-GRADE (CG) (Huang et al., 2020)
- DAILYDIALOG-GRADE (DH) (Huang et al., 2020)
- DAILYDIALOG-GUPTA (DG) (Gupta et al., 2019)
- DAILYDIALOG-ZHAO (DZ) (Zhao et al., 2020)
- DSTC7 (D7) (Galley et al., 2019)
- EMPATHETIC-GRADE (EG) (Huang et al., 2020)
- FED-TURN (FT) (Mehri and Eskenazi, 2020a)
- HUMOD (HM) (Merdivan et al., 2020)
- PERSONA-USR (PU) (Mehri and Eskenazi, 2020b)
- PERSONA-ZHAO (PZ) (Zhao et al., 2020)
- TOPICAL-USR (TU) (Mehri and Eskenazi, 2020b)

Team	EN	ZH	ES	Multilingual AVG
Deep AM-FM	29.40	7.53	18.26	18.40
TOP 1	48.18	39.36	58.90	48.81
TOP 2 (**ours**)	22.14	31.12	56.44	36.57
TOP 3	37.02	7.01	19.83	21.29
TOP 4	14.69	10.54	8.08	11.10

Table 3: The Spearman correlation (%) of baseline Deep AM-FM and top 4 teams on the test datasets of sub-task1 (turn-level). Only the best result of each team is shown in the table.

Team	Robust AVG
Deep AM-FM	0.3387
TOP 1	0.4890
TOP 2	0.4190
TOP 3 (**ours**)	0.3833
TOP 4	0.2697

Table 4: The Spearman correlation (%) of baseline Deep AM-FM and top 4 teams on the test datasets of sub-task2 (turn-level). Only the best result of each team is shown in the table.

- JSALT (JS) (Zhang et al., 2021)
- CHATEVAL (CS) (Sedoc et al., 2019)
- DSTC10 (D10) (Zhang et al., 2021)

Considering the multilingual setting of sub-task1, model M_1 is only trained on DailyDialog, EmpatheticDialog, PersonaChat, Topical-Chat and Wizard of Wikipia, which are translated into both Chinese and Spanish. While DailyDialog is used as the pre-training dataset, all of the 5 datasets above take part in the knowledge distillation stage of PCAF.

For sub-task2, all of the training sets except for SentimentLIAR and Switchboard Coherence are used to train model M_2. Still, DailyDialog is used as the pre-training dataset and all of these datasets above take part in the knowledge distillation stage of PCAF.

4.2 Implementation Details

In sub-task1, we adopt XLM-RoBERTa-Large as the encoder, and the parallel corpora is English-Chinese-Spanish corpora.

In sub-task2, we adopt RoBERTa-Large as the encoder, and the parallel corpora is English-Paraphrases corpora.

For both of the two tasks, we adopt Adam (Kingma and Ba, 2017) as the optimizer and set

Model	Language	Appropriateness	Content Richness	Grammatical Correctness	Relevance	Average
Deep AM-FM	EN	34.32	31.03	19.37	32.90	29.40
Deep AM-FM	ZH	12.32	14.18	3.61	0.02	7.53
Deep AM-FM	EZ	0.94	2.36	32.97	36.79	18.26
PCAF	EN	15.53	57.28	2.52	17.22	23.14
PCAF	ZH	23.18	49.56	7.43	46.35	31.63
PCAF	ES	53.48	77.86	36.87	57.57	56.44

Table 5: Fine-grained result of Deep AM-FM and our best submission on the test datasets of sub-task1 (turn-level).

Model	Coherence	Engageness	Informativeness	Overall	Average
Deep AM-FM	29.37	37.91	30.66	37.54	33.87
PCAF	39.66	42.45	28.34	42.87	38.33

Table 6: Fine-grained result of Deep AM-FM and our best submission on the test datasets of sub-task2 (turn-level).

batchsize as 32, learning rate as 5e-6, τ as 0.05, α as 0.2, and the model is trained on one single RTX 3090. Besides, epochs of the pre-training stage and KD stage are both set as 10.

4.3 Comparison Result

According to DSTC11 Track4, the turn-level metrics are evaluated by the following dimensions in both sub-task1 and sub-task2:

- **Appropriateness** - The response is appropriate given the preceding dialogue.
- **Content Richness** - The response is informative, with long sentences including multiple entities and conceptual or emotional words.
- **Grammatical Correctness** - Responses are free of grammatical and semantic errors.
- **Relevance** - Responses are on-topic with the immediate dialogue history.

For each submission, Spearman correlation at dimension-level will be calculated separately for each task. Then, the Spearman correlation scores obtained will be averaged. Finally, the Spearman correlation scores will be ranked.

We compare our approach with Deep AM-FM (Zhang et al., 2020) and the top 4 teams in sub-task1 and sub-task2 in Table 3 and Table 4 respectively, and the fine-grained results are reported in Table 5 and Table 6. PCAF ranks second and third in sub-task1 and sub-task2 in the comparison with Deep AM-FM and other teams' approaches, showing the effectiveness of our approach.

4.4 Ablation Studies

To verify the contribution of parallel-corpora-aligned pre-training and parallel-corpora-aligned

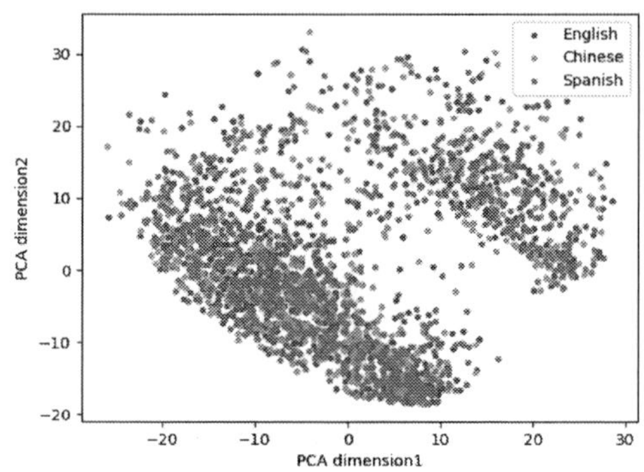

(a) aligned

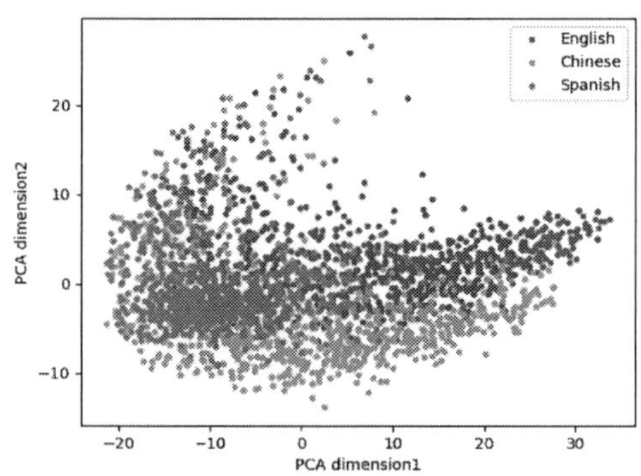

(b) unaligned

Figure 2: PCA results of metric model M trained with (top) and without (bottom) alignment loss on DailyDialog dataset

Metric	EN	ZH	ES	Multilingual AVG
PCAF	42.26 ± 0.001	40.49 ± 0.001	39.75 ± 0.002	40.83 ± 0.001
kd on DailyDialog	40.94 ± 0.001	38.76 ± 0.001	38.80 ± 0.001	39.50 ± 0.001
w/o kd	39.42 ± 0.009	37.86 ± 0.007	37.13 ± 0.007	38.13 ± 0.007
w/o kd & align	37.70 ± 0.030	37.35 ± 0.007	33.39 ± 0.054	36.15 ± 0.029

Table 7: The Spearman correlation (%) of PCAF ablation study. KD on DailyDialog means the knowledge distillation is only apply to DailyDialog training set. W/o align means the alignment loss is not involved in pre-training stage. Standard deviations are presented in gray color.

Corpora	Original	Paraphrase	English Back-translation
ori	36.67 ± 0.018	27.80 ± 0.018	32.96 ± 0.022
para	37.30 ± 0.011	31.63 ± 0.005	36.91 ± 0.006
bt	32.84 ± 0.016	27.07 ± 0.011	30.64 ± 0.014
ori + para	39.44 ± 0.001	32.34 ± 0.003	37.25 ± 0.011
ori + bt	34.62 ± 0.022	25.53 ± 0.018	26.57 ± 0.022
ori + para + bt	38.85 ± 0.007	32.55 ± 0.007	35.86 ± 0.021
ori + para + kd	42.33 ± 0.001	34.05 ± 0.001	39.47 ± 0.002

Table 8: Ablation study of different corpora combination, where ori, para, bt, kd stands for original utterances, paraphrases, back-translation and knowledge distillation respectively. Models are tested on the original, paraphrases and English back-translation corpora of development sets by Spearman correlation (%) respectively. Standard deviations are presented in gray color.

knowledge distillation on multiple datasets, we further conduct ablation studies on the provided development sets.

Table 7 shows the results of ablation study on sub-methods of PCAF. According to the results, both parallel-corpora-aligned pre-training and parallel-corpora-aligned knowledge distillation make contribution to the improvement of the model's performance. The alignment loss not only improves the evaluation ability of the model, but also improves the stability of the model training according to the standard deviation of model's validation results. We further visualize the encoded features on DailyDialog through Principal Component Analysis (PCA). As shown in Figure 2, compared to models trained without alignment loss, model trained with alignment loss has a more compact feature distribution on parallel corpora for the same sequence, showing that alignment loss effectively aligns model's representation of parallel corpora. We suppose that, as the representation of parallel corpora is pre-aligned in multilingual language model, the absence of alignment loss during pre-training may disturb model's original multilingual-aligned knowledge, which is shown in Figure 2(b). Besides, knowledge distillation is an important stage of PCAF, and the comparison between kd single DailyDialog and kd on five datasets shows that kd on multiple datasets do improves the generalization ability of model.

Training data of different parallel corpora combination of sub-task2 is also explored, Table 8 shows the result of this experiment. The combination of ori + para achieves the highest performance of the provided development sets, while the English back-translation corpora always degrades the performance of the model. The reason of such phenomena is unclear at present, and we leave it to our future work.

5 Conclusion

In this paper, we propose PCAF, a parallel-corpora-aligned training framework for training multilingual and robust turn-level automatic dialogue evaluation metrics. PCAF treats corpora express the same idea in different ways as parallel-corpora, which is aligned during both PCAF pre-training stage and PCAF knowledge distillation stage. Experiment results show that PCAF achieves a great performance, which demonstrates the effectiveness of PCAF. The effectiveness of each sub-method of PCAF is also proved through ablation study.

6 Limitations

DSTC11 Task4 requires the proposed metrics to evaluate the dialogues on multiple fine-grained qualities. However, we only train the metric model to evaluate the appropriateness of dialogues, whose results are further used as the evaluation results of other qualities. As PCAF can be integrated into the training process under any parallel-corpora setting, we can further try to train the model to evaluate other fine-grained qualities of dialogues with PCAF.

Besides, despite the DSTC11 Task4 organizers allow the participants to fine-tune their system over a subset of the development data, our submitted model is not fine-tuned with those human-annotated datasets. While we train our metric model under self-supervised learning framework, fine-tuning it on supervised datasets may improve models evaluation performance, which will be explored in our future work.

References

Daniel Adiwardana, Minh-Thang Luong, David R. So, Jamie Hall, Noah Fiedel, Romal Thoppilan, Zi Yang, Apoorv Kulshreshtha, Gaurav Nemade, Yifeng Lu, and Quoc V. Le. 2020. Towards a human-like open-domain chatbot.

Rafael E. Banchs. 2012. Movie-DiC: a movie dialogue corpus for research and development. In *Proceedings of the 50th Annual Meeting of the Association for Computational Linguistics (Volume 2: Short Papers)*, pages 203–207, Jeju Island, Korea. Association for Computational Linguistics.

Satanjeev Banerjee and Alon Lavie. 2005. METEOR: An automatic metric for MT evaluation with improved correlation with human judgments. In *Proceedings of the ACL Workshop on Intrinsic and Extrinsic Evaluation Measures for Machine Translation and/or Summarization*, pages 65–72, Ann Arbor, Michigan. Association for Computational Linguistics.

Alessandra Cervone and Giuseppe Riccardi. 2020. Is this dialogue coherent? learning from dialogue acts and entities.

Alexis Conneau, Kartikay Khandelwal, Naman Goyal, Vishrav Chaudhary, Guillaume Wenzek, Francisco Guzmán, Edouard Grave, Myle Ott, Luke Zettlemoyer, and Veselin Stoyanov. 2020. Unsupervised cross-lingual representation learning at scale. In *Proceedings of the 58th Annual Meeting of the Association for Computational Linguistics*, pages 8440–8451, Online. Association for Computational Linguistics.

Cristian Danescu-Niculescu-Mizil and Lillian Lee. 2011. Chameleons in imagined conversations: A new approach to understanding coordination of linguistic style in dialogs. In *Proceedings of the 2nd Workshop on Cognitive Modeling and Computational Linguistics*, pages 76–87, Portland, Oregon, USA. Association for Computational Linguistics.

Emily Dinan, Stephen Roller, Kurt Shuster, Angela Fan, Michael Auli, and Jason Weston. 2019. Wizard of wikipedia: Knowledge-powered conversational agents.

Luis F D'Haro, Bayan Abu Shawar, and Zhou Yu. 2016. Rewochat 2016–shared task description report. In *Proceedings of the workshop on collecting and generating resources for chatbots and conversational agents-development and evaluation (RE-WOCHAT)*, page 39.

Gabriel Forgues, Joelle Pineau, Jean-Marie Larchevêque, and Réal Tremblay. 2014. Bootstrapping dialog systems with word embeddings. In *Nips, modern machine learning and natural language processing workshop*, volume 2, page 168.

Michel Galley, Chris Brockett, Xiang Gao, Jianfeng Gao, and Bill Dolan. 2019. Grounded response generation task at dstc7. In *AAAI Dialog System Technology Challenges Workshop*.

Karthik Gopalakrishnan, Behnam Hedayatnia, Qinlang Chen, Anna Gottardi, Sanjeev Kwatra, Anushree Venkatesh, Raefer Gabriel, and Dilek Hakkani-Tür. 2019. Topical-chat: Towards knowledge-grounded open-domain conversations.

Prakhar Gupta, Shikib Mehri, Tiancheng Zhao, Amy Pavel, Maxine Eskenazi, and Jeffrey Bigham. 2019. Investigating evaluation of open-domain dialogue systems with human generated multiple references. In *Proceedings of the 20th Annual SIGdial Meeting on Discourse and Dialogue*, pages 379–391, Stockholm, Sweden. Association for Computational Linguistics.

Michael Gutmann and Aapo Hyvärinen. 2010. Noise-contrastive estimation: A new estimation principle for unnormalized statistical models. In *Proceedings of the Thirteenth International Conference on Artificial Intelligence and Statistics*, volume 9 of *Proceedings of Machine Learning Research*, pages 297–304, Chia Laguna Resort, Sardinia, Italy. PMLR.

Ryuichiro Higashinaka, Kotaro Funakoshi, Yuka Kobayashi, and Michimasa Inaba. 2016. The dialogue breakdown detection challenge: Task description, datasets, and evaluation metrics. In *Proceedings of the Tenth International Conference on Language Resources and Evaluation (LREC'16)*, pages 3146–3150, Portorož, Slovenia. European Language Resources Association (ELRA).

Geoffrey Hinton, Oriol Vinyals, and Jeff Dean. 2015. Distilling the knowledge in a neural network.

Chao-Chun Hsu, Sheng-Yeh Chen, Chuan-Chun Kuo, Ting-Hao Huang, and Lun-Wei Ku. 2018. Emotion-Lines: An emotion corpus of multi-party conversations. In *Proceedings of the Eleventh International*

Conference on Language Resources and Evaluation (LREC 2018), Miyazaki, Japan. European Language Resources Association (ELRA).

Lishan Huang, Zheng Ye, Jinghui Qin, Liang Lin, and Xiaodan Liang. 2020. GRADE: Automatic graph-enhanced coherence metric for evaluating open-domain dialogue systems. In *Proceedings of the 2020 Conference on Empirical Methods in Natural Language Processing (EMNLP)*, pages 9230–9240, Online. Association for Computational Linguistics.

Diederik P. Kingma and Jimmy Ba. 2017. Adam: A method for stochastic optimization.

S Lee, H Schulz, A Atkinson, J Gao, K Suleman, L El Asri, M Adada, M Huang, S Sharma, W Tay, et al. 2019. Multi-domain task-completion dialog challenge. *Dialog system technology challenges*, 8(9).

Yanran Li, Hui Su, Xiaoyu Shen, Wenjie Li, Ziqiang Cao, and Shuzi Niu. 2017. DailyDialog: A manually labelled multi-turn dialogue dataset. In *Proceedings of the Eighth International Joint Conference on Natural Language Processing (Volume 1: Long Papers)*, pages 986–995, Taipei, Taiwan. Asian Federation of Natural Language Processing.

Chin-Yew Lin. 2004. ROUGE: A package for automatic evaluation of summaries. In *Text Summarization Branches Out*, pages 74–81, Barcelona, Spain. Association for Computational Linguistics.

Chia-Wei Liu, Ryan Lowe, Iulian V. Serban, Michael Noseworthy, Laurent Charlin, and Joelle Pineau. 2017. How not to evaluate your dialogue system: An empirical study of unsupervised evaluation metrics for dialogue response generation.

Yinhan Liu, Myle Ott, Naman Goyal, Jingfei Du, Mandar Joshi, Danqi Chen, Omer Levy, Mike Lewis, Luke Zettlemoyer, and Veselin Stoyanov. 2019. Roberta: A robustly optimized bert pretraining approach.

Ryan Lowe, Michael Noseworthy, Iulian Vlad Serban, Nicolas Angelard-Gontier, Yoshua Bengio, and Joelle Pineau. 2017. Towards an automatic Turing test: Learning to evaluate dialogue responses. In *Proceedings of the 55th Annual Meeting of the Association for Computational Linguistics (Volume 1: Long Papers)*, pages 1116–1126, Vancouver, Canada. Association for Computational Linguistics.

Shikib Mehri and Maxine Eskenazi. 2020a. Unsupervised evaluation of interactive dialog with DialoGPT. In *Proceedings of the 21th Annual Meeting of the Special Interest Group on Discourse and Dialogue*, pages 225–235, 1st virtual meeting. Association for Computational Linguistics.

Shikib Mehri and Maxine Eskenazi. 2020b. USR: An unsupervised and reference free evaluation metric for dialog generation. In *Proceedings of the 58th Annual Meeting of the Association for Computational Linguistics*, pages 681–707, Online. Association for Computational Linguistics.

Erinc Merdivan, Deepika Singh, Sten Hanke, Johannes Kropf, Andreas Holzinger, and Matthieu Geist. 2020. Human annotated dialogues dataset for natural conversational agents. *Applied Sciences*, 10(3).

Tomas Mikolov, Ilya Sutskever, Kai Chen, Greg S Corrado, and Jeff Dean. 2013. Distributed representations of words and phrases and their compositionality. In *Advances in Neural Information Processing Systems*, volume 26. Curran Associates, Inc.

Nikita Moghe, Siddhartha Arora, Suman Banerjee, and Mitesh M. Khapra. 2018. Towards exploiting background knowledge for building conversation systems. In *Proceedings of the 2018 Conference on Empirical Methods in Natural Language Processing*, pages 2322–2332, Brussels, Belgium. Association for Computational Linguistics.

Yixin Nie, Mary Williamson, Mohit Bansal, Douwe Kiela, and Jason Weston. 2021. I like fish, especially dolphins: Addressing contradictions in dialogue modeling. In *Proceedings of the 59th Annual Meeting of the Association for Computational Linguistics and the 11th International Joint Conference on Natural Language Processing (Volume 1: Long Papers)*, pages 1699–1713, Online. Association for Computational Linguistics.

Kishore Papineni, Salim Roukos, Todd Ward, and Wei-Jing Zhu. 2002. Bleu: A method for automatic evaluation of machine translation. In *Proceedings of the 40th Annual Meeting on Association for Computational Linguistics*, ACL '02, page 311–318, USA. Association for Computational Linguistics.

Vitou Phy, Yang Zhao, and Akiko Aizawa. 2020. Deconstruct to reconstruct a configurable evaluation metric for open-domain dialogue systems. In *Proceedings of the 28th International Conference on Computational Linguistics*, pages 4164–4178, Barcelona, Spain (Online). International Committee on Computational Linguistics.

Soujanya Poria, Devamanyu Hazarika, Navonil Majumder, Gautam Naik, Erik Cambria, and Rada Mihalcea. 2019. MELD: A multimodal multi-party dataset for emotion recognition in conversations. In *Proceedings of the 57th Annual Meeting of the Association for Computational Linguistics*, pages 527–536, Florence, Italy. Association for Computational Linguistics.

Hannah Rashkin, Eric Michael Smith, Margaret Li, and Y-Lan Boureau. 2019. Towards empathetic open-domain conversation models: A new benchmark and dataset. In *Proceedings of the 57th Annual Meeting of the Association for Computational Linguistics*, pages 5370–5381, Florence, Italy. Association for Computational Linguistics.

Vasile Rus and Mihai Lintean. 2012. A comparison of greedy and optimal assessment of natural language student input using word-to-word similarity metrics. In *Proceedings of the Seventh Workshop on Building Educational Applications Using NLP*, NAACL HLT '12, page 157–162, USA. Association for Computational Linguistics.

João Sedoc, Daphne Ippolito, Arun Kirubarajan, Jai Thirani, Lyle Ungar, and Chris Callison-Burch. 2019. ChatEval: A tool for chatbot evaluation. In *Proceedings of the 2019 Conference of the North American Chapter of the Association for Computational Linguistics (Demonstrations)*, pages 60–65, Minneapolis, Minnesota. Association for Computational Linguistics.

Koustuv Sinha, Prasanna Parthasarathi, Jasmine Wang, Ryan Lowe, William L. Hamilton, and Joelle Pineau. 2020. Learning an unreferenced metric for online dialogue evaluation. In *Proceedings of the 58th Annual Meeting of the Association for Computational Linguistics*, pages 2430–2441, Online. Association for Computational Linguistics.

Chongyang Tao, Lili Mou, Dongyan Zhao, and Rui Yan. 2018. Ruber: An unsupervised method for automatic evaluation of open-domain dialog systems. *Proceedings of the AAAI Conference on Artificial Intelligence*, 32(1).

Bibek Upadhayay and Vahid Behzadan. 2020. Sentimental liar: Extended corpus and deep learning models for fake claim classification. In *2020 IEEE International Conference on Intelligence and Security Informatics (ISI)*, pages 1–6.

Zheng Ye, Liucun Lu, Lishan Huang, Liang Lin, and Xiaodan Liang. 2021. Towards quantifiable dialogue coherence evaluation. In *Proceedings of the 59th Annual Meeting of the Association for Computational Linguistics and the 11th International Joint Conference on Natural Language Processing (Volume 1: Long Papers)*, pages 2718–2729, Online. Association for Computational Linguistics.

Chen Zhang, Luis D'Haro, Rafael Banchs, Thomas Friedrichs, and Haizhou Li. 2020. *Deep AM-FM: Toolkit for Automatic Dialogue Evaluation*, pages 53–69.

Chen Zhang, João Sedoc, Luis Fernando D'Haro, Rafael Banchs, and Alexander Rudnicky. 2021. Automatic evaluation and moderation of open-domain dialogue systems.

Pengfei Zhang, Xiaohui Hu, Kaidong Yu, Jian Wang, Song Han, Cao Liu, and Chunyang Yuan. 2022. Mme-crs: Multi-metric evaluation based on correlation re-scaling for evaluating open-domain dialogue.

Saizheng Zhang, Emily Dinan, Jack Urbanek, Arthur Szlam, Douwe Kiela, and Jason Weston. 2018. Personalizing dialogue agents: I have a dog, do you have pets too? In *Proceedings of the 56th Annual Meeting of the Association for Computational Linguistics (Volume 1: Long Papers)*, pages 2204–2213, Melbourne, Australia. Association for Computational Linguistics.

Tiancheng Zhao, Ran Zhao, and Maxine Eskenazi. 2017. Learning discourse-level diversity for neural dialog models using conditional variational autoencoders.

Tianyu Zhao, Divesh Lala, and Tatsuya Kawahara. 2020. Designing precise and robust dialogue response evaluators. In *Proceedings of the 58th Annual Meeting of the Association for Computational Linguistics*, pages 26–33, Online. Association for Computational Linguistics.

Hao Zhou, Minlie Huang, Tianyang Zhang, Xiaoyan Zhu, and Bing Liu. 2018. Emotional chatting machine: Emotional conversation generation with internal and external memory. *Proceedings of the AAAI Conference on Artificial Intelligence*, 32(1).

Simple LLM Prompting is State-of-the-Art for Robust and Multilingual Dialogue Evaluation

John Mendonça[1,2,*], **Patrícia Pereira**[1,2],
Helena Moniz[1,3], **João Paulo Carvalho**[1,2], **Alon Lavie**[4,5] and **Isabel Trancoso**[1,2]
[1] INESC-ID, Lisbon
[2] Instituto Superior Técnico, University of Lisbon
[3] Faculdade de Letras, University of Lisbon
[4] Carnegie Mellon University, Pittsburgh
[5] Phrase, Pittsburgh
john.mendonca@inesc-id.pt

Abstract

Despite significant research effort in the development of automatic dialogue evaluation metrics, little thought is given to evaluating dialogues other than in English. At the same time, ensuring metrics are invariant to semantically similar responses is also an overlooked topic. In order to achieve the desired properties of robustness and multilinguality for dialogue evaluation metrics, we propose a novel framework that takes advantage of the strengths of current evaluation models with the newly-established paradigm of prompting Large Language Models (LLMs). Empirical results show our framework achieves state of the art results in terms of mean Spearman correlation scores across several benchmarks and ranks **first place on both the Robust and Multilingual tasks** of the DSTC11 Track 4 "Automatic Evaluation Metrics for Open-Domain Dialogue Systems", proving the evaluation capabilities of prompted LLMs.

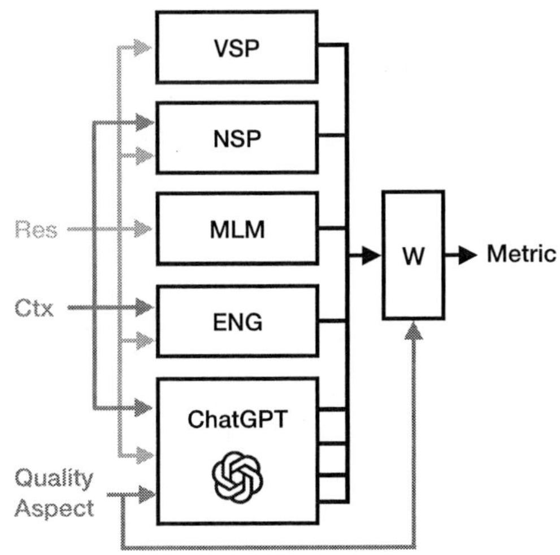

Figure 1: Proposed framework architecture. The **Response**, **Context** and **Quality Aspect** under evaluation are fed to the submetrics: **VSP** (Valid Sentence Prediction), **NSP** (Next Sentence Prediction), **MLM** (Masked Language Modelling), **ENG** (Engagement) and **ChatGPT**. Each submetric score is then weighted according to the aspect, yielding the final metric.

1 Introduction

Automatic dialogue evaluation has largely been focused on evaluating select few languages. The main reason for this constraint is the lack of linguistic diversity in dialogue corpora, which leads to a lack of chatbots that cover other languages. As a result, the need for multilingual metrics has also been limited.

A possible solution to this issue is to leverage the latest batch of Large Language Models (LLMs) to synthetically generate multilingual dialogues. Some research has already been conducted to study the capabilities of these models (Guo et al., 2023; Bubeck et al., 2023) and the consensus appears to be that these models have achieved a proxy of a *formal* linguistic competence in the most studied languages. That is, its responses follow linguistic conventions and are fluent and grammatical, but they might be inaccurate or even hallucinate (Guerreiro et al., 2023). More importantly, pertaining to dialogue, they also show signs of *functional* linguistic competence in its responses, i.e., discursive coherence, narrative structure and linguistic knowledge, even if not fully consistent (sometimes they do not consider context or situated information, and fail to adapt to users and domains).

Irrespective of these models' limitations, it is clear their emergent capabilities allow for the development of chatbots with capabilities vastly beyond what earlier models were able to achieve. Yet,

* Work conducted as a visiting scholar at CMU.

Proceedings of The Eleventh Dialog System Technology Challenge, pages 133–143
September 11, 2023

an interesting research question lingers: *If these models are able to write responses that follow formal and functional linguistics rules, are they also capable of evaluating responses/dialogues in terms of these same rules?* Prior work has confirmed the language understanding capabilities of instruction-based LLMs for dialogue evaluation (Huynh et al., 2023). However, we are the first to study the evaluation capabilities of the newest batch of LLMs in terms of multilinguality and paraphrase robustness.

This paper presents our contribution to the DSTC11 track on Robust and Multilingual Automatic Evaluation Metrics for Open-Domain Dialogue Systems (Rodríguez-Cantelar et al., 2023), where we participated in both the Multilingual and Robustness tasks. This track is an excellent venue to benchmark the capabilities of these new LLMs for dialogue evaluation, as it evaluates properties that have been observed in these models. We propose a comprehensive framework, incorporating earlier encoder-based approaches and ChatGPT, as illustrated in Figure 1. By combining multiple models and submetrics through ensembling, our approach aims to improve the performance and robustness of dialogue evaluation, ultimately contributing to the advancement of dialogue system research and development.

Overall, our contributions are the following:

- We show that ChatGPT is a *strong* evaluator of dialogues, outperforming typical encoder frameworks.
- We propose a new framework for dialogue evaluation that is multilingual and robust to paraphrases. In fact, our combined Encoder and ChatGPT framework ranks **1st place** on both the Multilingual and Robust metrics task.
- We discuss the outlook of Dialogue Evaluation in this new realm of LLMs.
- We open source the code and checkpoints of the submetrics at `github.com/johndmendonca/DialEvalML`.

2 Related work

2.1 Automatic Evaluation Metrics

Statistic-based metrics such as BLEU (Papineni et al., 2002), ROUGE (Lin, 2004), and METEOR (Banerjee and Lavie, 2005), are a popular choice to evaluate NLG (Natural Language Generation) models as they are easy to employ. These metrics assume valid responses have significant word-overlap with the ground truth. However, this is not a valid assumption for dialogue: there are many equally good responses for a single utterance. As such, the correlation with Human Evaluation (HE) annotations is very low for these metrics (Liu et al., 2016), and they cannot be used to evaluate models whenever a gold-response is not available.

Earlier learned metrics such as ADEM (Lowe et al., 2017) and RUBER (Tao et al., 2018) explicitly predict HE annotations by initialising pretrained Recurrent Neural Network response generators. Unlike ADEM, which is trained with HE-annotated data in a supervised manner, RUBER leverages negative samples. In both cases, a reference response is used to score the candidate response. As such, these metrics still suffer the same issues as word-overlap metrics.

The primary motivation for the negative sampling approach in RUBER was the need for extensive HE annotations in ADEM. Approaches similar to this are now the norm for training open-domain dialogue evaluation metrics. By using well-defined self-supervised tasks which correlate well with their corresponding aspects, the annotation limitations are mostly circumvented.

The most widely used self-supervised task is Next Sentence Prediction (NSP), as it is known to correlate well with HE that evaluate *"Context Awareness"*. The typical approach is to finetune a pretrained encoder model with this automatically generated data (Mehri and Eskenazi, 2020b; Phy et al., 2020; Mendonca et al., 2022; Zhao et al., 2020; Zhang et al., 2022). More complex approaches leverage graph representations to model dialogue interactions explicitly (Huang et al., 2020; Zhang et al., 2021a). Another typically employed self-supervised task is Valid Sentence Prediction (VSP), which uses word-level noising techniques to generate negative samples and correlates well with HE that evaluate *Fluency* (Phy et al., 2020; Mendonca et al., 2022; Zhang et al., 2022).

Parallel to this trend, other annotation-free approaches in the literature have surfaced. For instance, qualities such as *Specificity* correlate reasonably well with metrics obtained directly from the MLM (Masked Language Modelling) loss calculated using pretrained encoder models (Mehri and Eskenazi, 2020b; Phy et al., 2020; Zhang et al., 2022).

Given the multifaceted nature of dialogue, dialogue quality metrics typically employ a combination of submetrics. Mehri and Eskenazi (2020a) leverage follow-up utterance from a pretrained decoder model to calculate 18 turn and dialogue-level submetrics, which are then used as inputs to a regression model for overall quality. In fact, Linear Regression is frequently used as a feature aggregation method in the literature (Jiang et al., 2022; Mehri and Eskenazi, 2020b). Alternatively, Phy et al. (2020) propose a hierarchical composition where they incorporate the quality aspects together in a way that aspects in the lower hierarchy need to be satisfied before aspects higher up are considered. Also worth mentioning is the work of Zhang et al. (2022), which proposes the so called Correlation Re-scaling method. Here, the contribution of each aspect is calculated from the individual correlations of the submetrics, obtained from a subset of HE.

2.2 Large Language Models

The widespread use of LLMs was established, practically speaking, with the work of Devlin et al. (2019), where a transformer architecture (Vaswani et al., 2017) is pretrained with substantial amounts of unlabelled text with a Masked Language Modelling (MLM) objective. With this architecture, a new paradigm in NLP surfaced, where the adaptation to downstream tasks was conducted by finetuning the pretrained model with supervised data. Later on, GPT-3 (Brown et al., 2020), which is trained with an autoregressive objective, showed competitive results by leveraging few-shot prompting. Nevertheless, given their training objective function, it was difficult for autoregressive LLMs to successfully perform downstream NLP tasks without substantial prompt engineering.

Ouyang et al. (2022) propose finetuning GPT-3 using a 3-step approach named Reinforcement Learning through Human Feedback (RLHF). In detail, the model is (1) initially finetuned using supervised data obtained from labelling prompts (SFT); (2) a reward model is trained using ranked responses given a prompt; (3) the policy is optimised against the reward model using the Proximal Policy Optimisation reinforcement learning algorithm (Schulman et al., 2017). As a testament to the power of this approach, ChatGPT took the world by storm in late 2022 thanks to its incredible human-like generation capabilities. This was achieved by including dialogues in all steps of RLHF.

3 Problem Formulation

The main goal of this track was to develop and benchmark automatic open-ended dialogue evaluation metrics. Two tasks were proposed this year, Metrics for Multilingual Data and Robust metrics. For the Metrics for Multilingual Data task, participants were asked to construct quality metrics that perform well on a multilingual setup. For the the Robust metrics task, the goal was to develop metrics that perform robustly when evaluated over back-translated/paraphrased sentences in English.

In both tasks, the proposed metrics were evaluated at the turn and dialogue level, without access to a reference. In a *turn-level* evaluation setting, the goal is, given prior dialogue history (frequently denoted as context) c of varying amount of turns, and a response r, to learn a scoring function (also known as metric) that assigns a score $f(c, r) \rightarrow s$. Conversely, in a *dialogue-level* evaluation setting, the goal is to evaluate the performance throughout the full dialogue.

Irrespective of the level of evaluation, the proposed metrics' outputs are typically compared against HE annotations that use a Likert scale, where the lowest value means lowest quality and highest value maximum quality. For this track, the performance of these metrics was evaluated by calculating the Pearson correlation between the calculated score and HE.

4 Methodology

Our framework, which we call DIALEVALML, can be viewed as a dual layered ensemble which are done at the **model** and **submetric** level, and that employ strong multilingual pretrained encoder and decoder models which were finetuned or prompted[1]. In this section, we describe the step-by-step process of DIALEVALML, detailing the various components and methods employed.

4.1 Submetrics

Similar to other frameworks, including the best performing ones in last year's track (Zhang et al., 2022; Jiang et al., 2022) which take inspiration from the works of Phy et al. (2020); Sinha et al. (2020); Mehri and Eskenazi (2020b), we employ

[1]We tried experimenting with metrics that use graph representations, but found implementing these metrics to be Multilingual and Robust, and including them in our framework, to be impractical, not to mention detrimental to performance in some instances.

several submetrics to evaluate dialogue responses – ranging from zero-shot prediction using pretrained LLMs to trained models using self-supervised and supervised methods – and weigh them according to the aspect we wish to predict.

4.1.1 VSP: Valid Sentence Prediction

Following Sinha et al. (2020), we train a regression model that is optimised to differentiate between positive samples and synthetic negative samples. **Positive** samples are perturbed by randomly applying one of the following: (1) no perturbation, (2) punctuation removal, (3) stop-word removal. **Negative** samples are generated by randomly applying one of the following rules: (1) word reorder (shuffling the ordering of the words); (2) word-drop; and (3) word-repeat (randomly repeating words).

4.1.2 NSP: Next Sentence Prediction

With the binary **NSP** (Next Sentence Prediction) task, the goal is to distinguish a positive example from a semantically negative one, given a context. We train a discriminative regression model using the following sampling strategy: **positive** responses are drawn directly from the dialog; **negative** responses are randomly selected and a token coverage test discards semantically similar sentences. All responses are processed using the positive-sample heuristic used by **VSP**.

For both tasks, the underlying goal is that paraphrased and/or translated responses should have the same coherence score as the original response, since they (in theory) convey the same message. In order to increase the robustness of our framework to paraphrased responses we propose a Siamese Neural Network. Simply put, we train an encoder model (denoted NSP-Siamese) to jointly optimise a Cosine Embedding Loss between the hidden states of the encoder model for the original and a paraphrase, and the individual errors between the predictions and the ground truth. We hypothesise this enables the model to compare the semantic coherence of the responses w.r.t the context, instead of more spurious features such as syntax.

A similar approach could've been employed for multilingual metrics, however, scaling to more languages is computationally expensive: one would either need a new model for each language, or a training procedure requiring a forward pass for each language, for each example.

4.1.3 MLM: Masked Language Modelling

Similar to Mehri and Eskenazi (2020b); Phy et al. (2020), we use a pretrained encoder model to calculate the MLM loss of all tokens of the response. The resulting **MLM** submetric is calculated as the sum of the individual losses.

4.1.4 ENG: Engagement

An important quality aspect of dialogue that is frequently overlooked is *Engagement*. Some work attempt to equate this aspect with *Specificity* and related metrics. However, we argue this is a reductive solution, as engagement is an abstract and multi-dimensional concept, thereby making a surface level evaluation of the response in terms of diversity insufficient.

As such, and following the methodology used for **VSP** and **NSP**, we train a discriminate model using RED (Reddit-based Engagement Dataset) (Xu et al., 2022) which we then use as a submetric denoted in our framework as **ENG**. This dataset is sourced from Reddit and is curated using a novel distant-supervision framework. This framework aggregates emotional, attentional, behavioural and reply engagement onto a single score denoted ENDEX, which then has a hyperparameter threshold applied to it to cluster posts into positive and negative samples.

4.2 Exploiting Data Augmentation for Robust and Multilingual Evaluation

The main novelty of this year's track is the release of training and development dialogue data that has been augmented with MT (Machine Translation) – for the Multilingual task – and Paraphrases – for the Robust task. These augmentations are subsequently scored to determine similarity against the original data: for MT, several COMET QE (Quality Estimation) scores (Rei et al., 2020; Zerva et al., 2021; Rei et al., 2022) were provided; for Paraphrases, the organisers provided cosine similarity scores of the sentence embeddings.

A naive approach to obtain competitive metrics in both tasks would be to simply introduce the full amount of augmented data during self-supervised and supervised training. However, Mendonca et al. (2023) showed that low quality augmentation affects the performance of models trained on MT augmented data, especially for **VSP**. Following this work, we select 5 and 75 % of the best translated data (ranked using COMET QE) for training of the **VSP** and **NSP** models respectively. For **ENG**, we train different proportions of data and select the best performing ones.

4.2.1 ChatGPT

We briefly experimented with different prompts, and found the best performing prompt (irrespective of language) in a held-out internal set to be simply:

- Turn-level: *"Given the Context, evaluate from 1-5 the Response in terms of {aspect}. Provide a single score and nothing else."*
- Dialogue-level: *"Evaluate the following dialogue from 1-5 in terms of {aspect}. Provide a single score and nothing else."*

Unlike GPT-3, the API for ChatGPT does not output the log probabilities of the most likely tokens. As such, the measurement of quality is non-deterministic. We attempt to reduce output variability by reinforcing the desired output in the prompt (*"Provide a single score and nothing else."*) and by setting the temperature to 0. We report a mean absolute deviation of 0.0182 across 3 runs when querying *Appropriateness* on the provided `en/dailydialog-grade` dataset included in the development set. To facilitate ensembling in later stages, we normalise the predictions to [0,1].

The default processing step consists of searching for an integer in the response. However, there are some instances where ChatGPT fails to output the desired score: (1) When conducting dialogue level evaluation, the model sometimes outputs scores for each individual response. In these cases, we calculate the average score, similar to the dialogue-level encoder scores. (2) Less frequently, ChatGPT ignores the task and continues the conversation. Here, we prompt the model again until a score is provided.

4.3 Submetric Ensembling

Despite having a key role in NLG evaluation, HE has been performed while suffering from nontransparent and inconsistent annotation procedures. As such, annotations from different works one expects to report the same quality are frequently only nominal in nature. A good example is *Coherence*, with some definitions referring to it as (1) semantic relevance with respect to a previous sentence; (2) a theme/topic; or even (3) *Readability*, which is considered a different quality in other guidelines. Howcroft et al. (2020) provides an in-depth survey of 165 NLG papers with human evaluations where these issues are highlighted.

Taking into account these facts, it is not clear we can successfully apply an empirical surjective mapping function from our submetrics to the quality aspects. Instead, we take a data-driven approach to generate this mapping, similar to the one proposed in Zhang et al. (2022). The main difference between the original Correlation Re-Scaling method and our approach is that, instead of zeroing the weights of submetrics that have a negative correlation with the given aspect, we take a probabilistic approach where we conduct a statistic significance test, i.e., we check if the p-value is higher than a given threshold. This ensures submetrics which are strongly and negatively correlated with the aspect (for example, **MLM** and *Fluency*) are still included in the ensembling [2].

4.4 Dialogue-level Evaluation

We obtain dialogue-level quality predictions from the encoder models – **NSP**, **VSP**, **MLM** and **ENG** – by averaging the individual turn-level predictions. These are combined with the dialogue-level predictions obtained by prompting ChatGPT with the full dialogue in the prompt.

5 Experiments

5.1 Datasets

For data preprocessing we used spaCy. For the **VSP** and **NSP** models, we followed prior work and base the self-supervised data on DailyDialog (Li et al., 2017). For the language specific and multilingual models, we rank the translations using the provided WMT22 scores. Models using paraphrased responses are trained using the least similar responses (lowest score[3]).

The **ENG** model was trained using the RED dataset, more specifically on the 80k split with negative sampled data (Xu et al., 2022). Given it is an English dataset, we use `MBART50`[4] (Liu et al., 2020) to augment the original dataset with Spanish and Chinese MT. Finally, we score it using the `WMT20-COMET-QE-DA` model (Rei et al., 2020).

[2] For some annotations, none of the metrics were statistically significant. In these cases, we resort to the original proposed approach.

[3] We also trained models using the highest scoring responses and report lower performance. This is in line with our intuition that lower scoring responses are more diverse, and as such more informative for training.

[4] We chose `MBART50` as it is lightweight and open source.

For the paraphrase augmentation, we follow the organisers' approach of using Parrot Paraphraser (Damodaran, 2021) and scoring the paraphrases with Cosine Similarity.

5.2 Training and Hyperparameters

We used `XLM-RoBERTa-large` (Conneau et al., 2020) as the encoder model for the experiments. This model is the multilingual version of `RoBERTa`, pretrained on CommonCrawl data containing 100 languages. We used a single Quadro RTX 6000 24GB GPU for the encoder experiments, and accessed ChatGPT (`gpt-3.5-turbo`) in late March using the OpenAI API.

For the **VSP**, **NSP** and **ENG** metrics, a token representing the speaker was added for each turn, and a maximum history length of 3 turns was used during training. For predictions in the development and test sets we include the full conversational context whenever possible. If it surpasses input size limitations, we iteratively remove turns from the context, starting from the oldest one. We applied a regression head consisting of a 2-layer MLP with a hidden size of 1024 and a hyperbolic tangent function as activation for prediction. All parameters were trained/finetuned using Adam optimiser (Kingma and Ba, 2015). The fully finetuned models used a learning rate of 3e-6 and were trained for 3 epochs using a batch size of 16. Evaluation was conducted every 10,000 steps. The best performing model on the evaluation set was selected for testing. For the **MLM** metric, we used the existing LM head available in the Transformers library (Wolf et al., 2020).

With respect to the model-level ensembling, we conduct simple unweighted averaging of the predictions of the models. For the submetric-level ensembling, we define the mask threshold as $p > 0.05$ and square the correlations following Zhang et al. (2022). For testing, we define a mapping from the development quality aspects to the test-set aspects and obtain the final weights by averaging the weights obtained on the test set.

5.3 Model ensembling

In order to determine the best combination of models to include in our model ensemble, all encoder based models that require training were trained using different subsets of data. This includes the original (EN) English data, the corresponding augmentations in Chinese (ZH), Spanish (ES) and Paraphrases (PA) and the QE-ranked multilingual augmentation (MLXX) [5].

Submetric	Model	Language EN	ES	ZH	PA	ALL
VSP	**EN**	0.195	0.173	0.161	**0.067**	0.149
	ES	0.156	0.183	0.158	0.012	0.127
	ZH	0.179	0.111	0.102	0.086	0.119
	PA	**0.212**	**0.193**	**0.198**	0.062	**0.166**
	ML5	0.195	0.168	0.157	0.040	0.140
NSP	EN	0.279	0.256	0.286	0.267	0.272
	ES	0.266	0.257	0.282	0.251	0.264
	ZH	0.246	0.238	0.298	0.232	0.254
	PA	**0.307**	0.279	0.286	**0.279**	0.288
	ML75	0.300	**0.284**	**0.311**	0.272	**0.292**
ENG	EN	0.319	0.275	0.251	0.260	0.276
	ML5	0.310	0.268	0.214	0.275	0.267
	ML10	0.334	0.296	0.243	0.279	0.288
	ML20	**0.379**	**0.324**	**0.274**	**0.316**	**0.324**
	ML50	0.340	0.263	0.258	0.289	0.287
	PA	0.265	0.245	0.213	0.265	0.247

Table 1: Spearman Correlation scores of our trained model variants on all Language benchmarks on the full development set. The best score for each submetric and language is highlighted in **bold**. Models included in the final ensemble are in **bold**, except for NSP, which also includes NSP-Siamese.

Spearman correlation results are presented in Table 1. For the **VSP** submetric, we note that the inclusion of translations is detrimental to performance. In fact, the best performing models are PA, followed by EN. This contrasts with **NSP**, where we observe that the inclusion of more translated data improves performance. For **ENG**, the best performance is obtained with 20% of translated data. We include the 10 and 50% models in our framework to take advantage of ensembling.

5.4 Track Results

For the track we submitted 4 different systems, exploring the contribution of the different components of our framework:

- **System 1 (DIALEVALML)**: Submetric ensembling of ChatGPT + XLM-R.
- **System 2**: Submetric ensembling of XLM-R.
- **System 3**: Submetric ensembling of ChatGPT.
- **System 4**: Direct mapping of ChatGPT submetrics.

Table 2 identifies the turn-level weights calculated for testing for System 1.

[5]We only include the best performing ML models.

Aspect	VSP	NSP	MLM	ENG	cGPT-A	cGPT-R	cGPT-C	cGPT-G
Appropriateness	0.039	0.176	0.017	0.0511	0.165	**0.185**	0.181	**0.185**
Relevance	0.014	**0.214**	0.003	0.023	0.188	0.210	0.160	0.190
Content Richness	0.176	0.085	0.181	**0.238**	0.039	0.022	0.210	0.048
Grammatical Correctness	0.021	0.084	-0.06	0.061	0.238	0.242	0.155	**0.258**

Table 2: Calculated submetric weights of System 1 for test set quality aspects. Highest weight per aspect in **bold**.

	EN		ZH		ES		ML-AVG		Rank	
Team	Turn	Dial	Turn	Dial	Turn	Dial	Turn	Dial	Turn	Dial
Baseline (AM-FM)	0.2940	0.2414	0.0753	0.4648	0.1826	**0.8080**	0.1840	0.5047	4	2
Team 2	0.1469	-	0.1054	-	0.0808	-	0.1110	-	5	-
Team 4 (us)									1	1
- *S1* (DIALEVALML)	***0.4818***	***0.5342***	***0.3936***	***0.7133***	***0.5890***	***0.8080***	***0.4881***	***0.6852***		
- S2	0.2625	0.3295	0.3096	0.7030	0.5056	0.2500	0.3592	0.4275		
- S3	0.4795	0.5251	0.3656	0.6701	0.5409	0.8080	0.4620	0.6677		
- S4	0.4586	0.5039	0.3618	0.5859	0.5412	0.5915	0.4539	0.5604		
Team 5	0.3702	0.1865	0.0701	0.1356	0.1983	0.6830	0.2129	0.3350	3	3
Team 7	0.2214	-	0.3112	-	0.5644	-	0.3657	-	2	-

Table 3: Average Spearman correlation across the 4 dimensions evaluated for the baseline Deep AM-FM (Zhang et al., 2021b) and all participating teams on the Task 1 (Multilingual metrics) test set. **Bold** denotes the best result for the corresponding Language, *italic* denotes our best submission.

Task 1: Multilingual Metrics The results for each team for Task 1 are presented in Table 3, together with all of our submissions. In all languages at both the dialogue and turn level, our submissions vastly outperform others, with the exception of S2, which has comparable results with other participants. This clearly demonstrates the conversational understanding ChatGPT possesses. As expected, the best submission is S1, which conducts submetric ensembling with the XLM-R submetrics. This is followed by S3 and S4, which are exclusive ChatGPT submissions with and without ensembling, respectively.

Task 2: Robust Metrics The results for each team for Task 2 are presented in Table 4. Similar to Task 1, in Task 2, our ChatGPT submissions outperform other teams. However, at the dialogue level, the best performing model is AM-FM.

Team	Turn (rank)	Dial (rank)
Baseline (AM-FM)	0.3387 (4)	**0.4800** (1)
Team 1	0.1537 (6)	0.1111 (4)
Team 3	0.2697 (5)	0.2196 (3)
Team 4 (us)		
- *S1* (DIALEVALML)	***0.4890 (1)***	*0.3031 (2)*
- S2	0.3320	0.2335
- S3	0.4756	0.2979
- S4	0.4427	0.2492
Team 6	0.4190 (2)	-
Team 7	0.3833 (3)	-

Table 4: Average Spearman correlation and corresponding rank across the 4 dimensions evaluated for the baseline Deep AM-FM and all participating teams on the Task 2 (Robust metrics) test set. **Bold** denotes the best result for the corresponding Language, *italic* denotes our best submission.

5.5 Example predictions

Given the widely publicised emergent capabilities of current LLMs, it is worthwhile exploring where their quality predictions diverge from the annotators. To do so, we checked all instances where ChatGPT (System 4) diverges from the Human Evaluation (HE) annotations by more than 3 points. In all of the detected examples, we noted ChatGPT consistently underestimated the quality of the response when compared to HE.

We present in Table 5 two representative examples. In the first example, we see that ChatGPT erroneously underestimates quality due to the inclusion of *"weed"* in the response. We posit this is due to the RLHF finetuning, which conditions the model to avoid inappropriate or divisive topics. In the second example, we see ChatGPT has trouble understanding the conversation. Although one could argue the HE scores for *Correctness* and *Appropriateness* are too high, it seems clear the response is undeserving of a minimum score for all aspects. In fact, if one prompts the model to provide an explanation for *Content Richness*, it replies the following: *"The response attempts to provide some content related to the topic of adolescent sadness, but it is vague and lacks depth. The mention of "Qibing" without any explanation or context*

Chatbot: Tennis racquets used to be made from cloth strips stuffed with feathers haha! Then eventually evolved into today's technology
Human: oh i never knew that
Chatbot: Indeed, there was also aluminium construction improvements allowed for the introduction of oversized rackets by 1975 which was manufactured by weed

	A	C	G	R
Label:	4.7	4.7	4.3	5.0
ChatGPT:	1.0	2.0	2.0	1.0

"The mention of "weed" as the manufacturer may cause confusion or be perceived as inappropriate without further context."

	A	C	G	R
Best:	2.2	2.6	1.9	2.2

Human: Don't cry for breakfast.
Chatbot: Cry t for comfort
Human: In the end, young people are always inexplicably sad in adolescence. Which one is Qibing?

	A	C	G	R
Label:	-	5.0	5.0	3.0
ChatGPT:	1.0	1.0	1.0	1.0

"The response does not directly relate to the context or provide a meaningful answer. It seems unrelated and out of place. The mention of "Qibing" without any explanation further adds to the confusion.

	A	C	G	R
Best:	1.3	1.9	1.1	1.2

Table 5: Example turn-level predictions for *Appropriateness*, *Content Richeness*, *Grammatical Correctness* and *Relevance*. We include the ChatGPT explanation for *Appropriateness*.

leaves the reader confused. The response could benefit from more specific and informative details about the topic to increase its content richness.". However, if anything, the inclusion of the last sentence increases the richness of the response. Yet, it seems ChatGPT is conflating *Content Richness* with *Relevance*. We observe the same behaviour in all other instances we studied, and is in line with the submetric weights (Table 2).

6 Discussions

The results from our work on both tasks (Section 5.4) reveals that ChatGPT vastly outperforms typical encoder approaches that are trained to discriminate positive samples from artificially generated negative ones. It is important to note that, compared to the months worth of research dedicated to optimise our encoder models (including curation, training and selection), we were able to easily outperform all other teams and our own encoder models with a day's worth of prompt engineering. This is, in our opinion, a turning point in the paradigm of dialogue evaluation.

In any case, we do find instances where ChatGPT fails to accurately evaluate aspects of quality, as identified in Section 5.5. Future research directions may attempt to tackle the issues of score calibration by providing prompts that include examples and/or explicitly provide guidelines for scoring.

However, given the current landscape on dialogue generation, and as our submission suggests, dialogue evaluation, it is important to reflect on the value of current quality estimation frameworks. One might argue performing HE or developing metrics that evaluate responses and/or dialogues in terms of linguistic competence (e.g. *Grammatical Correctness* or *Coherence*) is no longer informative for the current and future crop of LLMs. Besides becoming ever so clear that these models no longer output responses that are incoherent or incorrect, we are reaching the point where these models are better evaluators than humans themselves (Gilardi et al., 2023). As such, developing metrics that correlate well with HE is becoming increasingly questionable.

One of the main contention points w.r.t the deployment of these models to the public pertain to their "safety" and "trustworthiness". But while "trustworthiness" can be evaluated by connecting the outputs to external and verifiable sources, the notion of "safety" is much more ambiguous. Kempt et al. (2023) suggests considering Positionality, Acceptability, and Value Alignment (PAVA) as features chatbots should have to fulfil appropriateness requirements. However, automatically evaluating if a chatbot has these features using current dialogue evaluation protocols seems implausible. Instead, the development of challenge sets for validation (such as the ones proposed in Valmeekam et al. 2023) appears to be the logical next step for evaluation of future chatbots[6].

7 Conclusion

This paper presents a novel open-domain and reference-free dialogue evaluation framework that leverages strong pretrained LLMs using finetuning and zero-shot prompting. These models, combined with effective ensembling strategies, substantially outperform the previous automatic evaluation paradigm of only training LMs with semisupervised training objectives. In fact, DIALEVALML ranks 1st on both the Robust (1st turn-level, 2nd dialogue level) and Multilingual (1st on both levels) tasks of Track 4 at DSTC11.

[6]See OpenAI Evals for recent collaborative research efforts in this direction.

Acknowledgements

This research was supported by the Portuguese Recovery and Resilience Plan through project C645008882-00000055 (Responsible.AI), and by national funds through *Fundação para a Ciência e a Tecnologia* (FCT) with references PRT/BD/152198/2021 and UIDB/50021/2020, and by the P2020 program MAIA (LISBOA-01-0247-FEDER-045909).

References

Satanjeev Banerjee and Alon Lavie. 2005. METEOR: An automatic metric for MT evaluation with improved correlation with human judgments. In *Proceedings of the ACL Workshop on Intrinsic and Extrinsic Evaluation Measures for Machine Translation and/or Summarization*, pages 65–72, Ann Arbor, Michigan. Association for Computational Linguistics.

Tom Brown, Benjamin Mann, Nick Ryder, Melanie Subbiah, Jared D Kaplan, Prafulla Dhariwal, Arvind Neelakantan, Pranav Shyam, Girish Sastry, Amanda Askell, et al. 2020. Language models are few-shot learners. *Advances in neural information processing systems*, 33:1877–1901.

Sébastien Bubeck, Varun Chandrasekaran, Ronen Eldan, Johannes Gehrke, Eric Horvitz, Ece Kamar, Peter Lee, Yin Tat Lee, Yuanzhi Li, Scott Lundberg, Harsha Nori, Hamid Palangi, Marco Tulio Ribeiro, and Yi Zhang. 2023. Sparks of Artificial General Intelligence: Early experiments with GPT-4.

Alexis Conneau, Kartikay Khandelwal, Naman Goyal, Vishrav Chaudhary, Guillaume Wenzek, Francisco Guzmán, Edouard Grave, Myle Ott, Luke Zettlemoyer, and Veselin Stoyanov. 2020. Unsupervised cross-lingual representation learning at scale. In *Proceedings of the 58th Annual Meeting of the Association for Computational Linguistics*, pages 8440–8451, Online. Association for Computational Linguistics.

Prithiviraj Damodaran. 2021. Parrot: Paraphrase generation for NLU.

Jacob Devlin, Ming-Wei Chang, Kenton Lee, and Kristina Toutanova. 2019. BERT: Pre-training of deep bidirectional transformers for language understanding. In *Proceedings of the 2019 Conference of the North American Chapter of the Association for Computational Linguistics: Human Language Technologies, Volume 1 (Long and Short Papers)*, pages 4171–4186, Minneapolis, Minnesota. Association for Computational Linguistics.

Fabrizio Gilardi, Meysam Alizadeh, and Maël Kubli. 2023. ChatGPT Outperforms Crowd-Workers for Text-Annotation Tasks.

Nuno M. Guerreiro, Duarte Alves, Jonas Waldendorf, Barry Haddow, Alexandra Birch, Pierre Colombo, and André F. T. Martins. 2023. Hallucinations in large multilingual translation models.

Biyang Guo, Xin Zhang, Ziyuan Wang, Minqi Jiang, Jinran Nie, Yuxuan Ding, Jianwei Yue, and Yupeng Wu. 2023. How Close is ChatGPT to Human Experts? Comparison Corpus, Evaluation, and Detection.

David M. Howcroft, Anya Belz, Miruna-Adriana Clinciu, Dimitra Gkatzia, Sadid A. Hasan, Saad Mahamood, Simon Mille, Emiel van Miltenburg, Sashank Santhanam, and Verena Rieser. 2020. Twenty years of confusion in human evaluation: NLG needs evaluation sheets and standardised definitions. In *Proceedings of the 13th International Conference on Natural Language Generation*, pages 169–182, Dublin, Ireland. Association for Computational Linguistics.

Lishan Huang, Zheng Ye, Jinghui Qin, Liang Lin, and Xiaodan Liang. 2020. GRADE: Automatic graph-enhanced coherence metric for evaluating open-domain dialogue systems. In *Proceedings of the 2020 Conference on Empirical Methods in Natural Language Processing (EMNLP)*, pages 9230–9240, Online. Association for Computational Linguistics.

Jessica Huynh, Cathy Jiao, Prakhar Gupta, Shikib Mehri, Payal Bajaj, Vishrav Chaudhary, and Maxine Eskenazi. 2023. Understanding the effectiveness of very large language models on dialog evaluation.

Zhihua Jiang, Guanghui Ye, Dongning Rao, Di Wang, and Xin Miao. 2022. IM^2: an interpretable and multi-category integrated metric framework for automatic dialogue evaluation. In *Proceedings of the 2022 Conference on Empirical Methods in Natural Language Processing*, pages 11091–11103, Abu Dhabi, United Arab Emirates. Association for Computational Linguistics.

Hendrik Kempt, Alon Lavie, and Saskia K. Nagel. 2023. Appropriateness is all you need!

Diederik P. Kingma and Jimmy Ba. 2015. Adam: A method for stochastic optimization. In *3rd International Conference on Learning Representations, ICLR 2015, San Diego, CA, USA, May 7-9, 2015, Conference Track Proceedings*.

Yanran Li, Hui Su, Xiaoyu Shen, Wenjie Li, Ziqiang Cao, and Shuzi Niu. 2017. DailyDialog: A manually labelled multi-turn dialogue dataset. In *Proceedings of the Eighth International Joint Conference on Natural Language Processing (Volume 1: Long Papers)*, pages 986–995, Taipei, Taiwan. Asian Federation of Natural Language Processing.

Chin-Yew Lin. 2004. Rouge: A package for automatic evaluation of summaries. In *Text summarization branches out*, pages 74–81.

Chia-Wei Liu, Ryan Lowe, Iulian Serban, Mike Noseworthy, Laurent Charlin, and Joelle Pineau. 2016. How NOT to evaluate your dialogue system: An empirical study of unsupervised evaluation metrics for dialogue response generation. In *Proceedings of the 2016 Conference on Empirical Methods in Natural Language Processing*, pages 2122–2132, Austin, Texas. Association for Computational Linguistics.

Yinhan Liu, Jiatao Gu, Naman Goyal, Xian Li, Sergey Edunov, Marjan Ghazvininejad, Mike Lewis, and Luke Zettlemoyer. 2020. Multilingual denoising pre-training for neural machine translation. *Transactions of the Association for Computational Linguistics*, 8:726–742.

Ryan Lowe, Michael Noseworthy, Iulian Vlad Serban, Nicolas Angelard-Gontier, Yoshua Bengio, and Joelle Pineau. 2017. Towards an automatic turing test: Learning to evaluate dialogue responses. In *Proceedings of the 55th Annual Meeting of the Association for Computational Linguistics (Volume 1: Long Papers)*, pages 1116–1126.

Shikib Mehri and Maxine Eskenazi. 2020a. Unsupervised evaluation of interactive dialog with DialoGPT. In *Proceedings of the 21th Annual Meeting of the Special Interest Group on Discourse and Dialogue*, pages 225–235, 1st virtual meeting. Association for Computational Linguistics.

Shikib Mehri and Maxine Eskenazi. 2020b. USR: An unsupervised and reference free evaluation metric for dialog generation. In *Proceedings of the 58th Annual Meeting of the Association for Computational Linguistics*, pages 681–707, Online. Association for Computational Linguistics.

John Mendonca, Alon Lavie, and Isabel Trancoso. 2022. QualityAdapt: an automatic dialogue quality estimation framework. In *Proceedings of the 23rd Annual Meeting of the Special Interest Group on Discourse and Dialogue*, pages 83–90, Edinburgh, UK. Association for Computational Linguistics.

John Mendonca, Alon Lavie, and Isabel Trancoso. 2023. Towards multilingual automatic open-domain dialogue evaluation. In *Proceedings of the 24th Annual Meeting of the Special Interest Group on Discourse and Dialogue*, Prague, Czechia. Association for Computational Linguistics.

Long Ouyang, Jeff Wu, Xu Jiang, Diogo Almeida, Carroll L. Wainwright, Pamela Mishkin, Chong Zhang, Sandhini Agarwal, Katarina Slama, Alex Ray, John Schulman, Jacob Hilton, Fraser Kelton, Luke Miller, Maddie Simens, Amanda Askell, Peter Welinder, Paul Christiano, Jan Leike, and Ryan Lowe. 2022. Training language models to follow instructions with human feedback.

Kishore Papineni, Salim Roukos, Todd Ward, and Wei-Jing Zhu. 2002. Bleu: a method for automatic evaluation of machine translation. In *Proceedings of the 40th Annual Meeting of the Association for Computational Linguistics*, pages 311–318, Philadelphia, Pennsylvania, USA. Association for Computational Linguistics.

Vitou Phy, Yang Zhao, and Akiko Aizawa. 2020. Deconstruct to reconstruct a configurable evaluation metric for open-domain dialogue systems. In *Proceedings of the 28th International Conference on Computational Linguistics*, pages 4164–4178, Barcelona, Spain (Online). International Committee on Computational Linguistics.

Ricardo Rei, Craig Stewart, Ana C Farinha, and Alon Lavie. 2020. Unbabel's participation in the WMT20 metrics shared task. In *Proceedings of the Fifth Conference on Machine Translation*, pages 911–920, Online. Association for Computational Linguistics.

Ricardo Rei, Marcos Treviso, Nuno M. Guerreiro, Chrysoula Zerva, Ana C Farinha, Christine Maroti, José G. C. de Souza, Taisiya Glushkova, Duarte Alves, Luisa Coheur, Alon Lavie, and André F. T. Martins. 2022. CometKiwi: IST-unbabel 2022 submission for the quality estimation shared task. In *Proceedings of the Seventh Conference on Machine Translation (WMT)*, pages 634–645, Abu Dhabi, United Arab Emirates (Hybrid). Association for Computational Linguistics.

Mario Rodríguez-Cantelar, Chen Zhang, Chengguang Tang, Ke Shi, Sarik Ghazarian, João Sedoc, Luis Fernando D'Haro, and Alexander Rudnicky. 2023. Overview of robust and multilingual automatic evaluation metrics for open-domain dialogue systems at dstc 11 track 4. In *DSTC11: The Eleventh Dialog System Technology Challenge*, 24th Meeting of the Special Interest Group on Discourse and Dialogue (SIGDIAL), Prague, Czechia.

John Schulman, Filip Wolski, Prafulla Dhariwal, Alec Radford, and Oleg Klimov. 2017. Proximal Policy Optimization Algorithms.

Koustuv Sinha, Prasanna Parthasarathi, Jasmine Wang, Ryan Lowe, William L. Hamilton, and Joelle Pineau. 2020. Learning an unreferenced metric for online dialogue evaluation. In *Proceedings of the 58th Annual Meeting of the Association for Computational Linguistics*, pages 2430–2441, Online. Association for Computational Linguistics.

Chongyang Tao, Lili Mou, Dongyan Zhao, and Rui Yan. 2018. Ruber: An unsupervised method for automatic evaluation of open-domain dialog systems. In *Proceedings of the AAAI Conference on Artificial Intelligence*, volume 32.

Karthik Valmeekam, Sarath Sreedharan, Matthew Marquez, Alberto Olmo, and Subbarao Kambhampati. 2023. On the Planning Abilities of Large Language Models (A Critical Investigation with a Proposed Benchmark).

Ashish Vaswani, Noam Shazeer, Niki Parmar, Jakob Uszkoreit, Llion Jones, Aidan N Gomez, Ł ukasz Kaiser, and Illia Polosukhin. 2017. Attention is all you need. In *Advances in Neural Information Processing Systems*, volume 30. Curran Associates, Inc.

Thomas Wolf, Lysandre Debut, Victor Sanh, Julien Chaumond, Clement Delangue, Anthony Moi, Pierric Cistac, Tim Rault, Remi Louf, Morgan Funtowicz, Joe Davison, Sam Shleifer, Patrick von Platen, Clara Ma, Yacine Jernite, Julien Plu, Canwen Xu, Teven Le Scao, Sylvain Gugger, Mariama Drame, Quentin Lhoest, and Alexander Rush. 2020. Transformers: State-of-the-art natural language processing. In *Proceedings of the 2020 Conference on Empirical Methods in Natural Language Processing: System Demonstrations*, pages 38–45, Online. Association for Computational Linguistics.

Guangxuan Xu, Ruibo Liu, Fabrice Harel-Canada, Nischal Reddy Chandra, and Nanyun Peng. 2022. EnDex: Evaluation of dialogue engagingness at scale. In *Findings of the Association for Computational Linguistics: EMNLP 2022*, pages 4884–4893, Abu Dhabi, United Arab Emirates. Association for Computational Linguistics.

Chrysoula Zerva, Daan van Stigt, Ricardo Rei, Ana C Farinha, Pedro Ramos, José G. C. de Souza, Taisiya Glushkova, Miguel Vera, Fabio Kepler, and André F. T. Martins. 2021. IST-unbabel 2021 submission for the quality estimation shared task. In *Proceedings of the Sixth Conference on Machine Translation*, pages 961–972, Online. Association for Computational Linguistics.

Chen Zhang, Yiming Chen, Luis Fernando D'Haro, Yan Zhang, Thomas Friedrichs, Grandee Lee, and Haizhou Li. 2021a. DynaEval: Unifying turn and dialogue level evaluation. In *Proceedings of the 59th Annual Meeting of the Association for Computational Linguistics and the 11th International Joint Conference on Natural Language Processing (Volume 1: Long Papers)*, pages 5676–5689, Online. Association for Computational Linguistics.

Chen Zhang, Luis Fernando D'Haro, Rafael E. Banchs, Thomas Friedrichs, and Haizhou Li. 2021b. *Deep AM-FM: Toolkit for Automatic Dialogue Evaluation*, pages 53–69. Springer Singapore, Singapore.

Pengfei Zhang, Xiaohui Hu, Kaidong Yu, Jian Wang, Song Han, Cao Liu, and Chunyang Yuan. 2022. MME-CRS: Multi-Metric Evaluation Based on Correlation Re-Scaling for Evaluating Open-Domain Dialogue. *arXiv preprint arXiv:2206.09403*.

Tianyu Zhao, Divesh Lala, and Tatsuya Kawahara. 2020. Designing precise and robust dialogue response evaluators. In *Proceedings of the 58th Annual Meeting of the Association for Computational Linguistics*, pages 26–33, Online. Association for Computational Linguistics.

Towards Optimizing Pre-trained Language Model Ensemble Learning for Task-oriented Dialogue System

Zhiyuan Zhu[1], **Yusheng Liao**[1], **Zhe Chen**[1], **Yu Wang**[1,2,*], **Yunfeng Guan**[1,*]
[1]Cooperative Medianet Innovation Center, Shanghai Jiao Tong University
[2]Shanghai AI Laboratory
{zzysjtu_iwct, liao20160907, chenzhe2018, yuwangsjtu, yfguan69}@sjtu.edu.cn

Abstract

Task-oriented dialogue systems that employ external knowledge to generate informative responses have become an important field of research. This paper outlines our contribution to Track 5 of the Eleventh Dialog System Technology Challenge (DSTC11), which focuses on constructing high-performing, subjective knowledge-enriched task-oriented dialogue systems. Specifically, we investigate the complementarity of various language models to tackle the diverse knowledge selection task that involves multiple external sources. Based on this investigation, we propose pre- and post-generation model ensemble approaches to mitigate potential biases inherent in using a single model for the knowledge selection task. Finally, we utilize the consensus decoding approach to combine fine-tuned ensemble models and improve the performance of the generation system. Our system ranked **1st** in human evaluation, even outperforming human annotation.

1 Introduction

External knowledge is critical for task-oriented dialogue (TOD) (Rastogi et al., 2020; Ghazvininejad et al., 2018) systems to reduce hallucinations when assisting users with specific tasks. Extensive effort has been investigated into knowledge-enriched TOD systems. DSTC9 Track 1 (Kim et al., 2020) is the first challenge that focuses on generating system responses using external knowledge. Previous works (He et al., 2021a; Han et al., 2022; Thulke et al., 2023) mainly utilize BERT, RoBERTa, and ELECTRA (Devlin et al., 2019; Liu et al., 2019; Clark et al., 2020) to perform knowledge selection, which achieve satisfactory result.

The DSTC10 Track2 challenge (Kim et al., 2021) focuses on improving the robustness of the dialogue system in the presence of automatic speech recognition (ASR) recognition errors (Weng et al., 2020) and speaker disfluencies (Liu et al., 2021). Existing works (Tian et al., 2021; Tam and *et al.*, 2022; Yan et al., 2022) combine data augmentation with pre-trained models like GPT2, DialoGPT, and PLATO-XL(Radford et al., 2019; Zhang et al., 2019; Bao et al., 2022) to bridge the gap between written and spoken conversation.

In contrast to the previous tasks, DSTC11 Track 5 proposed a more practical challenge (Zhao et al., 2023). In this task, dialogue systems are expected to provide not only factual information but also subjective insights from different knowledge domains. Additionally, a single dialogue may involve multiple knowledge snippets. Nevertheless, the presence of multiple external knowledge sources, each containing different subjective intents, can confuse the dialogue system and make it difficult to generate an appropriate response. The recent development of the Large Language Model (LLM) such as ChatGPT[1], LLaMA, and Alpaca (Touvron et al., 2023; Taori et al., 2023) become popular in generation tasks. However, the performance of these models on knowledge-enriched TOD systems is far from being well-studied. In this paper, we contribute to the challenge from the following perspectives:

1) We explore the retrieval performance of various discriminative models and quantitatively analyze their complementarity.

2) To mitigate potential biases inherent in using a single model in the knowledge selection, we design pre- and post-generation model ensemble methods to leverage both the capacity and diversity of the different fine-tuned models.

3) We explore the utilization of the recent popular LLaMA-7b on this task. Experiments show that our best single model outperforms LLaMA-7b finetuned on this task in two out of four metrics.

4) We utilize the consensus decoding (Mi and *et al.*, 2021) method to combine language model

* Corresponding author.

[1]https://chat.openai.com/

Proceedings of The Eleventh Dialog System Technology Challenge, pages 144–149
September 11, 2023 ©2023 Association for Computational Linguistics

ensemble with different initializations to improve the generalization of the generation. Our final system ranks **1st** place in the human evaluation, which performs even better than human annotation.

2 Methodology

We define the dialogue context of the t-th utterance turn as $W_t = \{w_{t-u+1}, \cdots, w_{t-1}, w_t\}$, where u is the window size of the truncated dialogue context. The knowledge snippets in the external knowledge base are defined as $K = \{k_1, \cdots, k_M\}$, where M is the size of the knowledge base.

2.1 Knowledge-Seeking Turn Detection

The first issue that the dialogue system needs to handle is whether external knowledge should be used in the current dialogue turn i.e. whether the generation of the system utterance w_{t+1} of current user turn w_t requires external knowledge. This turn detection task can be formulated as a binary classification problem, given the dialogue context W_t as the model input, the training objective is to minimize the binary cross-entropy loss:

$$\begin{aligned}\mathcal{L}_{\text{detect}} = & -y_t \log p_{\theta_d}\left(y_t \mid W_t\right) \\ & -\left(1-y_t\right) \log \left(1-p_{\theta_d}\left(y_t \mid W_t\right)\right),\end{aligned} \tag{1}$$

where θ_d is the model parameters, the probability p_{θ_d} is determined by the binary classification model, and y_t is the ground truth label indicating whether user utterance turn w_t requires knowledge.

2.2 Knowledge Selection

The dialogue system retrieves relevant knowledge snippets from the external knowledge base when decides to use external knowledge to generate a response, indicated by the current user turn w_t.

In this paper, for each dialogue instance that requires external knowledge, we randomly sample negative candidates from those belonging to the same entity that is queried in the dialogue context. To formalize the training process of knowledge selection, we define the set of sampled negative candidates as $K_N = \{\tilde{k}_1, \tilde{k}_2, \ldots, \tilde{k}_C\}$ and the ground truth knowledge snippets for the current dialogue instance as $K_G = \{\hat{k}_1, \hat{k}_2, \ldots, \hat{k}_D\}$, where C is the number of sampled negative candidates and D is the number of ground truth knowledge snippets used in the current dialogue instance. The training objective is to minimize the following loss:

$$\mathcal{L}_{\text{selection}} = -\sum_{j \in K_G \cup K_N} \log p_{\theta_s}\left(l_{k_i} \mid W_t\right), \tag{2}$$

where θ_s is the selection model parameters, p_{θ_s} is determined by the selection model, and l_{k_i} is the ground truth label of the knowledge candidate k_i. During inference, the selected knowledge snippets can be written as $K_S = \{k \mid p(l_k \mid W_t) > \tau, k \in K\}$, where τ is the threshold that yields the best model performance on the validation set.

2.3 Knowledge Grounded Generation

The dialogue model generates a response based on the dialogue history context and the selected knowledge snippets. Our model uses an auto-regressive architecture to generate the response, and the training loss is minimized by reducing the negative log-likelihood (NLL) loss.

$$\mathcal{L}_{\text{generation}} = -\log p_{\theta_g}\left(r_g \mid W_t, K_S\right), \tag{3}$$

where θ_g is the parameters of the dialogue generation model and r_g is the ground truth response. During training, we use ground truth knowledge snippets as input. During inference, the knowledge selection model selects relevant knowledge snippets for the following response generation.

2.4 Model Ensemble

Our final submitted system uses the model ensemble combination for both knowledge selection and dialogue generation subtasks. This enhances the robustness and diversity of the whole system.

Knowledge Selection: We propose two different model ensemble methods, named pre-generation and post-generation model ensembles, as shown in Figure 1. The pre-generation ensemble averages the selection probability output from each fine-tuned knowledge selection model to obtain the final selected results. These results are then fed into each dialogue generation model. However, this ensembling method may limit the diversity that can be provided by each selection-generation model pair. To address this problem, we also explore the post-generation ensemble approach, which involves feeding the output of each knowledge selection model into every generation model instead of initially combining multiple knowledge selection results into a single one.

Dialogue Generation: In our system, we use the consensus decoding algorithm (Mi and *et al.*, 2021) to combine the ensembles, which generate the final system response using the following equation:

$$S^* = \underset{S'}{\operatorname{argmax}} \sum_i \psi_i\left(\mathbf{S}, S'\right) w_i, \tag{4}$$

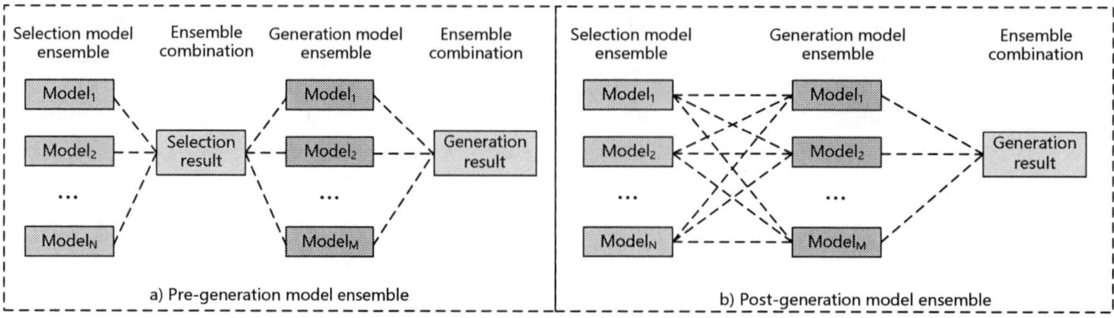

Figure 1: We employ two different model ensemble techniques in our system: a) pre-generation ensemble, in which ensemble knowledge selection results before response generation. b) post-generation ensemble, in which model ensemble is performed only once based on all the final generated responses from various generation models.

where **S** refers to the set of 1-best system responses generated from the beam search of each dialogue generation model, and S' is a system response from the response pool that consists of all N-best responses generated by each generation model. ψ_i denotes the i-th similarity function that computes the similarity scores between **S** and S', and w_i corresponds to the weight of the similarity function. The similarity function is built using nine different metrics: BLEU-1/2/3/4, METEOR, ROUGE-1/2/L, and negative normalized word error rate.

3 Experiments

3.1 Datasets

We use the DSTC11 Track 5 dataset [2] as our training data. The key difference between DSTC11 and the previous DSTC10 and DSTC9 challenges is that DSTC11 includes not only factual knowledge but also subjective knowledge in the dialogue. Therefore, the response generation model needs to be aware of the sentiment orientation embedded in the knowledge snippets when generating a system response. Furthermore, there are multiple ground truth knowledge snippets to consider, as opposed to only one in the previous challenge.

3.2 Experimental Setting

The model training setting of each subtask in Section 2 is described below, models for each subtask are trained on a single RTX 3090 GPU.

Knowledge-Seeking Turn Detection: To address the binary classification problem, we used a single large-sized DeBERTaV3 (He et al., 2021b) as our backbone model, given its outstanding performance in pre-training language models. We set the batch size to 16 and employed an AdamW optimizer with a learning rate of 3e-5 and an ϵ of 1e-8. The training epoch was set to 10. The automated metrics we used include Precision, Recall, and F1.

Knowledge Selection: To leverage the complementary capabilities of different pre-trained models in knowledge selection, we utilize 5 different large-sized pre-trained language models as our backbone model, which includes BERT (Devlin et al., 2019), DeBERTaV3 (He et al., 2021b), RoBERTa (Liu et al., 2019), ELECTRA (Clark et al., 2020), and XLNet (Yang et al., 2019). The final selection probability shown in Eq. 2 is the average value of all models' output. The training batch size for each pre-trained model is 256 and we adopt an AdamW optimizer with a learning rate of 5e-5 and an ϵ of 1e-8, the total training epoch is set to 6. The evaluation metrics include Precision, Recall, and Exact Matching Accuracy.

Knowledge-Grounded Generation: To improve the model robustness and diversity, we combine the generation responses from five fine-tuned large-sized BART (Lewis et al., 2020) ensemble models initialized with different random seeds as our final result. The training batch size for each pre-trained model is 16 and we adopted an AdamW optimizer with a learning rate of 5e-5 and an ϵ of 1e-8, the epoch is set to 16. The metrics include BLEU-1/2/3/4, METEOR, and ROUGE-1/2/L.

3.3 Evaluation Results

Details of each submitted entry of our team are described as follows:

Entry 0 uses the pre-generation ensemble and the threshold τ is chosen so that the ensembled knowledge selection probability yields the best performance on the validation set.

[2] https://github.com/alexa/dstc11-track5

ID		Task 1: Turn Detection			Task 2: Knowledge Selection				Task 3: Response Generation				
Team	Entry	Precision	Recall	F1	Precision	Recall	F1	Exact Match	BLEU	METEOR	ROUGE-1	ROUGE-2	ROUGE-L
Baseline		0.9982	0.9979	0.9980	0.7901	0.7877	0.7889	0.3906	0.1004	0.1748	0.3520	0.1430	0.2753
2	3	0.9940	0.9986	0.9963	0.8093	0.7858	0.7974	0.4156	0.0984	0.1774	**0.3658**	0.1509	0.2875
6 (ours)	0	0.9968	**0.9996**	0.9982	0.8039	0.8775	0.8391	0.5547	0.1017	**0.1894**	0.3629	0.1478	0.2804
	1	0.9968	**0.9996**	0.9982	0.7607	**0.9025**	0.8256	0.5385	0.1008	0.1889	0.3616	0.1467	0.2782
	2	0.9968	**0.9996**	0.9982	0.8125	0.8768	0.8434	0.5691	0.1005	0.1886	0.3617	0.1464	0.2794
	3	0.9968	**0.9996**	0.9982	0.7712	0.9013	0.8312	0.5538	0.1005	0.1886	0.3617	0.1464	0.2794
8	0	0.9979	0.9982	0.9980	0.8240	0.8141	0.8190	0.5130	0.1029	0.1764	0.3587	0.1479	0.2822
7	4	0.9979	0.9993	**0.9986**	0.8183	0.8506	0.8342	0.5314	0.1075	0.1744	0.3585	0.1459	0.2794
12	2	**0.9986**	0.9986	**0.9986**	0.7538	0.8227	0.7868	0.4291	0.0961	0.1715	0.3572	0.1467	0.2798
13	3	0.9964	0.9982	0.9973	**0.8590**	0.8449	**0.8519**	**0.6432**	**0.1081**	0.1819	0.3652	0.1528	0.2872
14	0	0.9979	0.9989	0.9984	0.7856	0.8035	0.7944	0.4183	0.1066	0.1748	0.3599	**0.1577**	**0.2899**

Table 1: Automatic evaluation results of the inclusion teams for human evaluation, with the highest values highlighted in bold, while underlining indicates the second highest value. Our best system ranked **1st** in Recall (detection) and METEOR (generation) in Recall (selection).

Entry 1 uses the pre-generation ensemble and the threshold τ is the average of every single model's threshold defined in Subsection 2.2.

Entry 2 uses the post-generation ensemble. Since the knowledge selection result is required for system evaluation, we use the same selection result as Entry 0 for the purpose of final evaluation.

Entry 3 uses the post-generation ensemble. For the same reason as Entry 2, we use the same selection result as Entry 1.

The automatic evaluation results of the selected team for the final human evaluation on the DSTC11 Track 5 test set are summarized in Table 1[3]. Our top-performing system demonstrates excellent results across multiple evaluation metrics, ranking 5th place in the overall system performance. Furthermore, our system achieves first place in Recall for turn detection and knowledge selection, as well as in METEOR for dialogue generation. In addition to our first-place achievement, our system ranks second place in the other four metrics.

Rank	Team	Entry	Accuracy	Appropriateness	Average
1	**6 (ours)**	0	2.9095	**3.6596**	**3.2846**
	Ground Truth		**2.9189**	3.6422	3.2806
2	8	0	2.9005	3.6535	3.2770
3	13	3	2.9100	3.6321	3.2710
4	2	3	2.8908	3.6487	3.2697
5	7	4	2.9046	3.6348	3.2697
	Baseline		2.8715	3.6348	3.2531

Table 2: Human evaluation on the DSTC11 Track 5 test set. Our system achieved **1st** place in human evaluation, which performs even better than human annotation.

The final ranking is determined by human evaluation. Crowdsourcing workers evaluate each system response based on two metrics: accuracy and appropriateness. The evaluation scores for each metric range from 1 to 5, with higher scores indicating better-generated system responses. As shown in Table 2 [3], our best system ranked **1st** place in human evaluation, outperforming even human annotators. This outstanding performance illustrates that our system can generate human-like responses using external factual and subjective knowledge.

3.4 Ablation On Knowledge Selection

We also investigate the performance of various pretrained models on the validation set of the knowledge selection subtask. To avoid the influence of the turn detection subtask, we use the ground truth result of turn detection as model input.

Model	Precision	Recall	F1	Exact Match	Total
Baseline	0.7482	**0.9371**	0.8321	0.4423	2.9597
BERT	0.8055	0.9236	0.8605	0.5566	3.1462
DeBERTaV3	0.8119	0.9348	0.8690	0.5965	3.2122
RoBERTa	0.8005	0.9285	0.8598	0.5590	3.1477
ELECTRA	0.8376	0.9277	0.8804	0.5918	3.2375
XLNet	0.7878	0.9343	0.8548	0.5773	3.1541
Ensemble	**0.8539**	0.9170	**0.8843**	**0.6087**	**3.2639**

Table 3: Different model performances on the knowledge selection. The results after the ensemble shows a significant improvement compared to the baseline.

As shown in Table 3, five different fine-tuned pre-trained models generate comparable results on the validation set. Furthermore, the results of the ensemble model achieved considerable improvement compared to other methods, which demonstrated that model ensemble can achieve higher quality and more robust results by leveraging the complementarity of various models. In this paper, we quantitively evaluate the complementarity of different fine-tuned models in knowledge selection tasks by calculating the **'cross EM'** score between

[3]https://github.com/alexa/dstc11-track5

each fine-tuned model. The **'cross EM'** score is defined as using the output of a particular model as the ground truth to score the output Exact Matching accuracy of other models. A lower score indicates greater inconsistency and stronger complementarity between the two models, while a higher score indicates weaker complementarity. Table 4 shows the cross EM between each fine-tuned model, which illustrates the complementarity between models, and the performing model ensemble is effective.

	BERT	DeBERTaV3	RoBERTa	ELECTRA	XLNet
BERT	-	0.7389	0.7379	0.7496	0.7573
DeBERTaV3	0.7389	-	0.7707	0.7634	0.7831
RoBERTa	0.7379	0.7707	-	0.7285	0.7526
ELECTRA	0.7496	0.7634	0.7285	-	0.7514
XLNet	0.7573	0.7831	0.7526	0.7514	-

Table 4: Cross EM of each fine-tuned model, which demonstrates the complementarity between models

The DSTC11 Track 5 challenge features two distinct domains, namely hotels, and restaurants, in its knowledge base. This paper also explores the difficulty of selecting knowledge across these domains on the validation set. As Table 5 illustrates, knowledge selection in the restaurant domain proves more challenging than that in the hotel domain. This may come from the domain imbalance of different domains, which highlights the significance of the model ensemble in this subtask.

	Domian: Hotel			Domian: Restaurant		
	F1	EmAcc	Total	F1	EmAcc	Total
BERT	0.9325	0.6330	1.5655	0.8155	0.4921	1.3067
DeBERTaV3	0.9350	0.6616	1.5966	0.8392	0.5628	1.4020
RoBERTa	0.9276	0.6156	1.5882	0.8238	0.5426	1.3664
ELECTRA	0.9421	0.6602	1.6023	0.8533	0.5541	1.4074
XLNet	0.9333	0.6504	1.5837	0.8090	0.5310	1.3400

Table 5: The performance of the fine-tuned model on two knowledge domains, the retrieval in the restaurant domain is more difficult than in the hotel domain.

3.5 Ablation On Dialogue Generation

To investigate the performance of different pretrained language models on the dialogue generation task, we fine-tune encoder-decoder-based and pure decoder-based models on DSTC11 Track 5 dataset, which contains comparable parameter quantities except for LLaMA-7b. We use the ground truth knowledge snippets as model input and we fine-tuned LLaMA-7b on eight RTX3090 GPUs with a learning rate of 5e-7, other training settings follow the description in Subsection 3.2.

As shown in Table 6, where the notations -B, -L, and -M represent the model sizes of Base, Large, and Medium. BART-Large performed the best in the total score. It should be noted that we obtained the results of LLaMA-7b after the end of the DSTC11 challenge, and we did not use LLaMA-7b in our final submitted system. Additionally, the encoder-decoder-based model outperformed the decoder-based model. Even with the much larger language model LLaMA, the performance of LLaMA-7b could not completely surpass the fine-tuned BART-L model. This indicates the importance of the encoder in this type of task.

Stucture	Model	BLEU	METEOR	ROUGE-2	ROUGE-L
Baseline	BART-B	10.55	17.29	15.31	29.01
Encoder	T5-B	**11.07**	18.01	15.53	29.40
-Decoder	BART-L	10.24	**20.19**	15.77	29.61
Pure-Decoder	GPT2-M	9.68	17.28	14.37	28.26
	DialogGPT-M	9.85	17.16	14.76	28.58
	LLaMA-7b	*10.60*	*18.02*	***16.22***	***30.08***

Table 6: The performance of different models on dialogue generation tasks, with the encoder-decoder-based model outperforming the decoder-based model.

Finally, we conduct an ablation experiment on the validation set to determine the best composition of similarity functions as defined in Eq. 4. where 'All' indicates that all nine functions are used for consensus decoding. As shown in Table 7, the best performance on the validation set is achieved when only the ROUGE-L-based similarity function is used. Thus, we only used a ROUGE-L-based consensus decoding for ensemble combination in our final submitted system.

Metric	BLEU	METEOR	ROUGE-1	ROUGE-2	ROUGE-L
Baseline	*10.55*	*17.29*	*36.90*	*15.31*	*29.01*
ALL	10.74	20.18	38.22	16.05	29.89
BLEU	10.73	20.14	38.18	16.05	29.86
METEOR	10.52	**20.30**	38.10	15.91	29.75
ROUGE-1	10.66	20.23	**38.37**	16.06	29.95
ROUGE-2	10.71	20.14	38.21	16.07	29.89
ROUGE-L	**10.75**	20.17	38.27	**16.10**	**30.00**

Table 7: Ablation study on similarity functions, the optimal performance on the validation set was achieved by only using the ROUGE-L similarity function.

4 Conclusions

In this paper, we present the details of our submission to the DSTC11 Track 5 challenge, where our system achieved the top ranking among 14 participating teams on human evaluation. Our system not only achieved great results in the final evaluation conducted by the organizers but also demonstrated outstanding performance in the extensive experiments that we conducted. We have also explored the potential of the recent large language model on this challenging knowledge-enriched TOD task. We believe that our findings and methods can contribute to the advancement of TOD dialogue systems and can inspire future research in this area.

Acknowledgements

This work was supported by National Key R&D Program of China (No.2022ZD0162101), Shanghai Science and Technology Committee (No.21511101100), Shanghai Key Lab of Digital Media Processing and Transmission (STCSM 22DZ2229005)

References

Siqi Bao, Huang He, Fan Wang, and *et al.* 2022. PLATO-XL: Exploring the large-scale pre-training of dialogue generation. In *Proc. Findings of ACL*, Online only.

Kevin Clark, Minh-Thang Luong, and Quoc V. Le *et al.* 2020. ELECTRA: Pre-training text encoders as discriminators rather than generators. In *ICLR*.

J. Devlin, M-W. Chang, and K. Lee *et al.* 2019. BERT: Pre-training of deep bidirectional transformers for language understanding. In *Proc. NACL*.

Marjan Ghazvininejad, Chris Brockett, Ming-Wei Chang, and *et al.* 2018. A knowledge-grounded neural conversation model. In *Proc. AAAI*.

Janghoon Han, Shin, Joongbo, and *et al.* 2022. External knowledge selection with weighted negative sampling in knowledge-grounded task-oriented dialogue systems. *arXiv preprint arXiv:2209.02251*.

Huang He, Hua Lu, and Bao, Siqi *et al.* 2021a. Learning to select external knowledge with multi-scale negative sampling. *arXiv preprint arXiv:2102.02096*.

Pengcheng He, Jianfeng Gao, and Weizhu Chen. 2021b. Debertav3: Improving deberta using electra-style pre-training with gradient-disentangled embedding sharing. *arXiv preprint arXiv:2111.09543*.

Seokhwan Kim, Mihail Eric, and Karthik Gopalakrishnan *et al.* 2020. Beyond domain apis: Task-oriented conversational modeling with unstructured knowledge access. *arXiv preprint arXiv:2006.03533*.

Seokhwan Kim, Yang Liu, and Di Jin *et al.* 2021. "how robust r u?": Evaluating task-oriented dialogue systems on spoken conversations.

Mike Lewis, Yinhan Liu, and Naman Goyal *et al.* 2020. BART: Denoising sequence-to-sequence pre-training for natural language generation, translation, and comprehension. In *In Proc. ACL*.

Jiexi Liu, Ryuichi Takanobu, Jiaxin Wen, and *et al.* 2021. Robustness testing of language understanding in task-oriented dialog. In *Proc ACL*.

Yinhan Liu, Myle Ott, and Naman Goyal *et al.* 2019. Roberta: A robustly optimized bert pretraining approach. *arXiv preprint arXiv:1907.11692*.

Haitao Mi and Qiyu Ren *et al.* 2021. Towards generalized models for beyond domain api task-oriented dialogue. In *AAAI-21 DSTC9 Workshop*.

Alec Radford, Jeffrey Wu, Rewon Child, and *et al.* 2019. Language models are unsupervised multitask learners. *OpenAI blog*.

Abhinav Rastogi, Xiaoxue Zang, Srinivas Sunkara, and *et al.* 2020. Towards scalable multi-domain conversational agents: The schema-guided dialogue dataset. In *Pro. AAAI*.

Yik-Cheung Tam and Jiacheng Xu *et al.* 2022. Robust unstructured knowledge access in conversational dialogue with asr errors. In *In Proc. ICASSP*. IEEE.

Rohan Taori, Ishaan Gulrajani, Tianyi Zhang, and *et al.* 2023. Stanford alpaca: An instruction-following llama model.

David Thulke, Nico Daheim, and *et al.* 2023. Task-oriented document-grounded dialog systems by hltpr@rwth for dstc9 and dstc10. *IEEE/ACM Transactions on Audio, Speech, and Language Processing*.

Xin Tian, Xinxian Huang, and Dongfeng He *et al.* 2021. Tod-da: towards boosting the robustness of task-oriented dialogue modeling on spoken conversations. *arXiv preprint arXiv:2112.12441*.

Hugo Touvron, Thibaut Lavril, Gautier Izacard, and *et al.* 2023. Llama: Open and efficient foundation language models. *arXiv preprint arXiv:2302.13971*.

Yue Weng, Sai Sumanth Miryala, Chandra Khatri, and *et al.* 2020. Joint contextual modeling for asr correction and language understanding. In *Proc ICASSP*.

Ruijie Yan, Shuang Peng, and Haitao Mi *et al.* 2022. Towards generalized models for task-oriented dialogue modeling on spoken conversations. *arXiv preprint arXiv:2203.04045*.

Zhilin Yang, Zihang Dai, and Yiming Yang *et al.* 2019. Xlnet: Generalized autoregressive pretraining for language understanding. In *Proc. NeurIPS*.

Yizhe Zhang, Siqi Sun, Michel Galley, and *et al.* 2019. Dialogpt: Large-scale generative pre-training for conversational response generation. *arXiv preprint arXiv:1911.00536*.

Chao Zhao, Spandana Gella, Seokhwan Kim, and *et al.* 2023. " what do others think?": Task-oriented conversational modeling with subjective knowledge. *arXiv preprint arXiv:2305.12091*.

Enhancing Task-Oriented Dialog System with Subjective Knowledge: A Large Language Model-based Data Augmentation Framework

Haein Jung* **Heuiyeen Yeen*** **Jeehyun Lee*** **Minju Kim*** **Namo Bang** **Myoung-Wan Koo**
Department of Artificial Intelligence, Sogang University, Korea
{haeindain, yeen214, jhlee22, 0307mjk, namo950815, mwkoo}@sogang.ac.kr

Abstract

As Task-Oriented Dialog (TOD) systems have advanced, structured DB systems, which aim to collect relevant knowledge for answering user's questions, have also progressed. Despite these advancements, these methods face challenges when dealing with subjective questions from users. To overcome this, DSTC11 released a subjective-knowledge-based TOD (SK-TOD) dataset and benchmark. This paper introduces a framework that effectively solves SK-TOD tasks by leveraging a Large Language Model (LLM). We demonstrate the proficient use of LLM for each sub-task, including an adapters-based method and knowledge-grounded data augmentation. Our proposed methods, which utilize LLM as an efficient tool, outperform baseline performance and approaches that directly use LLM as a one-step sub-task solver, showing superior task-specific optimization.

1 Introduction

In many Task-Oriented Dialog (TOD) systems, to ensure accurate responses to user inquiries, it is often necessary to generate system responses by extracting relevant information from a preprocessed database (Liu and Lane, 2017; Zhong et al., 2018). However, this method shows a generalization limitation, making it difficult to extend to other domains or new information. To overcome this limitation, research has been conducted to generate system responses based on factual information using Frequently Asked Questions (FAQs), a readily available source of factual information (Kim et al., 2022).

However, DSTC11 Track5[1] presents a new limitation that previous research and datasets cannot handle users' subjective requests (e.g.*"Do they have nice outdoor dining area?"*). Therefore, they have released a subjective-knowledge-based TOD

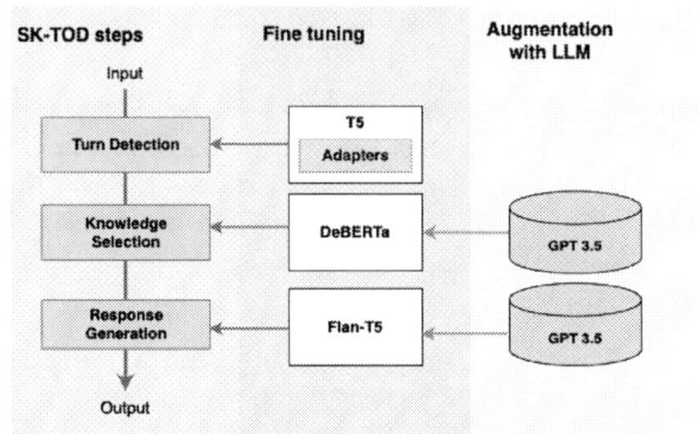

Figure 1: Diagram for each step of solving the SK-TOD task. The leftmost (blue) section represents the overall pipeline for addressing SK-TOD. The middle (orange) section shows the types of models fine-tuned specifically for each task. The rightmost (green) section indicates the augmentation process enhanced through LLM to improve the performance of the fine-tuned models.

(SK-TOD) dialog dataset, which allows for appropriate subjective knowledge (reviews) for user's subjective requests (Zhao et al., 2023).

DSTC11 Track5 defines three sub-tasks to generate appropriate system responses through the SK-TOD dataset. (1) Finding knowledge-seeking turns, (2) Selecting knowledge (reviews or FAQs) based on the dialog history of each knowledge-seeking turn, and (3) Generating system responses based on the selected knowledge and dialog history. The baseline of DSTC11 Track5 selects optimized models for each pipeline and fine-tunes them on the given dataset. However, about 50 percent of the total dataset requires knowledge selection turns, so from Task2 onwards, the dataset for the learning process decreases, which may similarly result in performance degradation.

In particular, recent research shows that Large Language Models (LLMs) demonstrate excellent generalization performance across various tasks (OpenAI, 2023), including conversation-related tasks (Zhang et al., 2023), even in few-shot or zero-shot scenarios. However, a disadvantage of LLMs

*Equal contribution, co-first authors
[1]https://github.com/alexa/dstc11-track5

Proceedings of The Eleventh Dialog System Technology Challenge, pages 150–165
September 11, 2023 ©2023 Association for Computational Linguistics

is that optimizing for specific tasks or domains is difficult.

Therefore, this paper proposes a framework that primarily fine-tunes task models suitable for each sub-task, while efficiently utilizing LLMs for performance improvement. By researching the use of LLMs ideal for the characteristics of each stage, it is shown that the mentioned limitations can be overcome by using LLMs and fine-tuning models appropriately. As a result, it has outperformed the benchmark baseline performance in all three sub-tasks of the officially released DSTC11 Track5 test set.

To summarize the contributions of this paper:

- It presents how to use LLMs suitable for the sub-tasks of the SK-TOD task: knowledge-seeking turn detection, knowledge selection, and response generation, and proposes a framework for learning by appropriately integrating LLMs and task models.
- It releases datasets augmented with LLM for each task. These datasets can be utilized for further research.

2 Task Description

The detailed formulation of the SK-TOD Task in DSTC11 Track5 follows the paper (Zhao et al., 2023). A formal dialog context $C = [U_1, S_1, U_2, S_2, ..., U_t]$ is given between the user and the system. Each user utterance U_i is followed by the system response utterance S_i, except the last user utterance U_t. The dialog is accompanied by subjective background knowledge $B = [(e_1, R_1), (e_2, R_2), ...]$, which consists of one or more entities $E = [e_1, ..., e_m]$ and their corresponding customer reviews R. Each entity e can have multiple reviews $R = [R_1, R_2, ...]$, which can be divided into segments $[K_1, K_2, ...]$ such as paragraphs, sentences, or sub-sentences.

Therefore, each sub-task can be redefined as follows:

1. **Knowledge-Seeking Turn Detection (KTD)**: Determine if the last user utterance U_t in the given dialog requires knowledge access.
2. **Knowledge Selection (KS)**: For the turns that require knowledge access, extract the entities (hotel names, restaurant names, etc.) appearing in those turns using a word-matching-based approach. Based on the extracted entities and the dialog history C, extract relevant knowledge snippets K^+.
3. **Response Generation (RG)**: Generate the final system response S_t based on the extracted knowledge.

	Train	Vaild	Test
Full Data	28,431	4,173	5,475
Knowledge-Seeking Data	14,768	2,129	2,798

Table 1: Dialog instance statistics for the SK-TOD dataset.

The statistics of the publicly available dataset for training, validation, and testing are shown in Table 1.

3 Methodology

3.1 Knowledge-Seeking Turn Detection

To determine if knowledge is required, we apply a sequence generation approach with a language modeling objective. The model predicts the next token in the dialog context and is trained with categorical cross-entropy loss to generate either "True" or "False" as the output

Adapter Tuning We leverage a pre-trained language model, which was trained on a large-scale dialog dataset, using an adapter-based approach. Adapter modules (Houlsby et al., 2019) are integrated into each transformer layer, keeping the base model's parameters frozen. These adapters consist of two feed-forward layers that project the feature size into a reduced dimension and then restore it to the original dimension. Throughout the training process, we freeze the pre-trained layers and exclusively train the adapters. One key advantage of using adapters is their ability to mitigate the catastrophic forgetting problem, enabling the model to preserve knowledge from previously learned tasks while adapting to new ones. We focus on retraining the encoder and decoder layer adapters specifically for the KTD task while preserving pre-trained knowledge.

3.2 Knowledge Selection

3.2.1 Entity Tracking

To streamline the pool of potential knowledge candidates, we implement entity matching as delineated in Zhao et al., 2023. The goal is to identify an entity that is relevant to both the dialog history

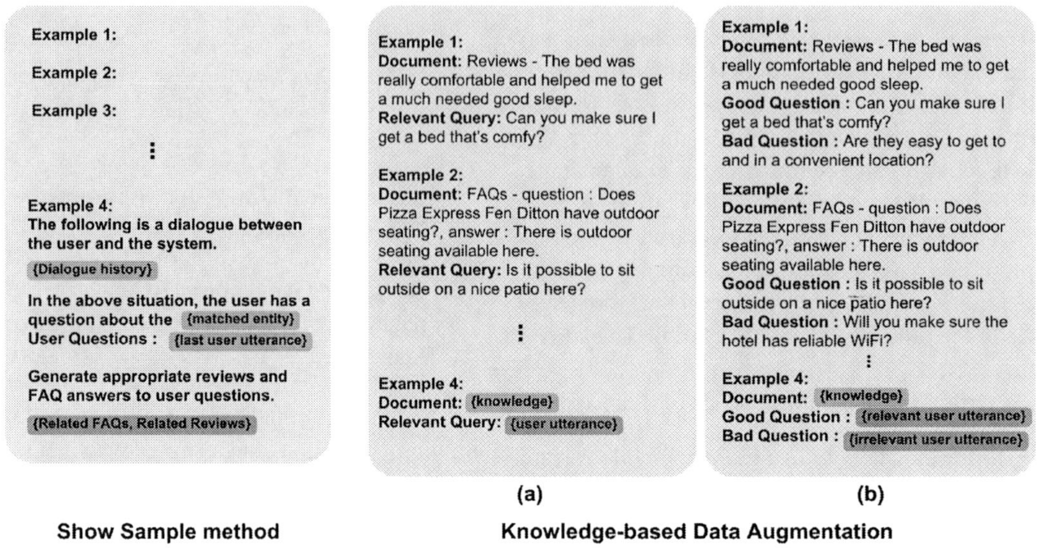

Figure 2: Example prompts for the *Show Sample Method* and *Knowledge-based Data Augmentation* methods used in the KS task. The bold text represents the default prompt format, and the input provided is highlighted in green. The blue text denotes the portion generated by the model.

and the user request among the potential candidates. Therefore, the matching process is carried out based on a word-matching-based methodology.

3.2.2 Data Augmentation for Knowledge Selection

During the training process, positive (C, K) pairs are constructed using all relevant knowledge snippets, and an equal number of negative pairs are randomly sampled. The model is trained to minimize the binary cross-entropy loss. Therefore, it is necessary to construct various positive pairs depending on the case to find appropriate K^+ for a given C. We leverage LLM to improve performance by transforming and augmenting datasets.

Show Sample Method In Wang et al., 2022, generating rationales for given questions and finetuning them through question matching with a small model enhanced performance. This approach outperforms alternatives like using prompts in existing QA tasks or direct fine-tuning. Incorporating pre-training knowledge from the LLM enables more enriched training.

We follow the approach (Wang et al., 2022) to generate FAQs and reviews, instead of rationales, which can represent the dialog history, last user utterance, and the matched entity. The prompt includes 2-shot exemplars so that it could be created in a similar way. The actual prompt is structured as shown in Figure 2. It is concatenated with the last user utterance and fed into the model for training. In actual inference, the dialog history is first input to the LLM, and representative samples are generated. The inference is then conducted by appending these generated samples to the last user utterance.

Knowledge-based Data Augmentation From a different perspective, our work draws inspiration from the paper (Bonifacio et al., 2022), which introduces a data augmentation method for training a ranker that extracts relevant knowledge. In this context, we adapt a similar approach to generate user's subject requests matching each knowledge (reviews, FAQs) attached to all entity lists.

Two prompting methods are employed in the experiments, as depicted in Figure 2. In method (a), relevant queries are generated based on the provided knowledge (K). On the other hand, method (b) generates both relevant and irrelevant queries. In both prompting methods, 3-shot exemplars are given. For method (b), only the portion corresponding to a relevant query is extracted and used after generation. The generated utterancesare labeled as single-turn dialogs requiring knowledge access and are associated with the underlying knowledge as the corresponding labels.

	BLEU	MT	R-1	R-2	R-L
Flan-T5-XL	9.61	17.15	35.72	14.67	27.98
+ pre-train (SM)	**10.19**	17.42	35.91	14.55	27.85
+ pre-train (LR)	10.16	**18.68**	**37.16**	**15.22**	**28.72**

Table 2: Comparison of pre-train methods on the RG task. SM stands for span masking, and LR stands for last response. Also, MT stands for METEOR metric, and R stands for Rouge metric.

3.2.3 Fine-tuning

For the cross-encoder approach, we encode the concatenation of C and K to obtain the contextualized representation. The actual training is conducted through binary cross-entropy loss by combining positive and negative pairs based on labels, identical to the paper (Zhao et al., 2023).

$$h = Enc(C, K) \quad (1)$$
$$P(C, K) = softmax(FFN(h)).$$

3.3 Response Generation

RG tries to answer the user's question accurately based on the reviews or FAQs, after the knowledge snippets ($K+$) retrieved from the KS stage and the dialog context. In this paper, we explore two methodologies to study how LLM can be effectively used to generate responses: a method of fine-tuning the Flan-T5-XL model (Wei et al., 2021), and in-context learning (Brown et al., 2020) using GPT-3.5-turbo model from Open AI[2].

3.3.1 Fine-tuning

Various Instruction Templates for Fine-tuning We use Flan-T5 model for fine-tuning because it was developed to understand and respond to natural language instructions, and it helps understand the context of the user's conversation and conduct knowledge-based QA. Since this model is vital in understanding instructions better, we expect to get better fine-tuning results by using specific instruction templates. We experiment with various instruction templates, and instruction of fine-tuning with span masking tokens works best. The specific prompts we experiment with can be found in appendix B.

Dialog Domain Adaptive Pre-train Since Flan-T5 is a model optimized for instruction rather than conversation, we perform further domain adaptive pre-train with dialog datasets to better understand the context of the conversation and generate answers naturally (Zhang et al., 2019; Mehri et al., 2019). We use the pre-training corpora which was used to train PPTOD (Su et al., 2021, 2022), and we perform pre-train in two ways: learning with span masking and generating only last response to the last question. For span masking, 15% of the tokens are randomly selected and masked. As described in the table 2, we find that last response generation pre-train task performs better. It seems the pre-train and fine-tuning tasks are similar in that they generate the final response based on the conversation.

Data Augmentation Methods In order to train the model on a larger amount of data, we adopt data augmentation techniques proposed by Dai et al., 2023; Wang et al., 2023. Our focus is on effectively augmenting data using LLM and achieving higher performance compared to using LLM directly as a problem solver. We propose three data augmentation approaches. The first is to augment the data by masking and changing some words, the second is to paraphrase the entire conversation, and the third is to augment the conversation based on knowledge. Appendix C gives details.

First, we adopt the inpaint method proposed in the paper like Wei and Zou, 2019. It is important to preserve the speech style and format of the dataset while augmenting dialogs, knowledge, and system responses through filling in the blanks. As part of the inpaint method, we experiment with two data augmentation techniques: synonym replacement and masked language modeling approach. Inspired by the synonym replacement method introduced in Wei and Zou, 2019, we randomly select one adjective and adverb from each utterance and replace them with synonyms. We use WordNet[3]'s synonym list. Similarly, we explore the masked language modeling approach (Gao et al., 2023) by masking candidate indices from each utterance, making predictions, and augmenting the data based on these predictions. We utilize a pre-trained XLM-Roberta-Large model (Conneau et al., 2020). By doing so, we introduce diversity and contextually relevant variations in the dataset while maintaining the underlying speech style and format.

Second, we employ the back-translation (Sennrich et al., 2016) method, which changes an existing utterance from the source language to a target language and then translates it back to the original

[2] https://platform.openai.com/docs/models/gpt-3-5

[3] https://wordnet.princeton.edu/

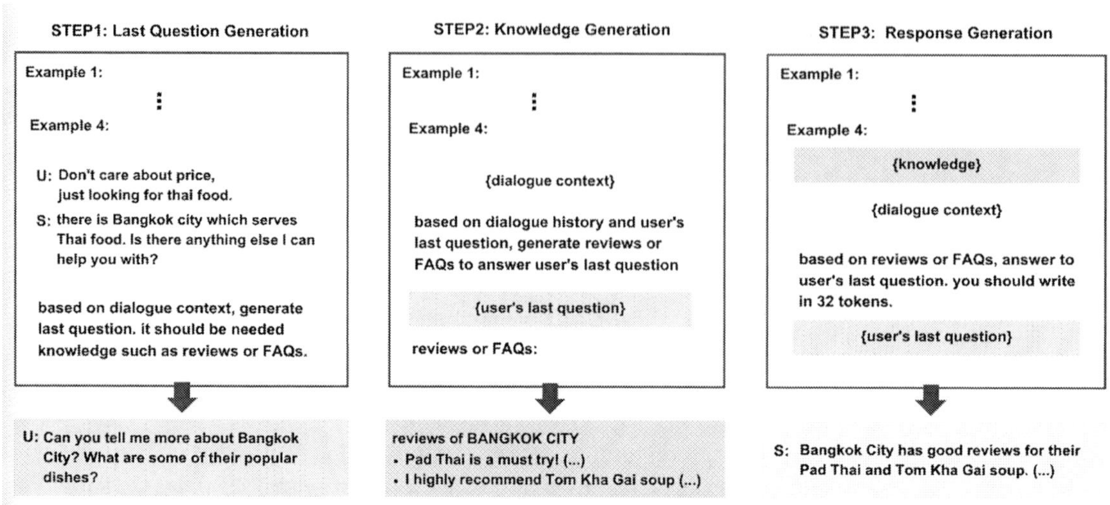

Figure 3: Knowledge-grounded data augmentation methods using GPT-3.5-turbo model.

language. We utilize the nlpaug[4] package for inference, which uses fairseq[5]'s pre-trained model to perform the translation. We also experiment with a paraphrase method using pre-trained language model (Gao et al., 2020; Niu et al., 2021; Chowdhury et al., 2022) to generate utterances that have the same meaning and context as existing sentences while ensuring fluency and grammatical correctness. We use the Parrot package (Damodaran, 2021), which provides a paraphrase-based utterance augmentation framework specialized for natural language understanding tasks, and the PEGASUS (Zhang et al., 2020) model, a self-supervised encoder-decoder-based pre-training transformer structure for large documents.

Third, we perform knowledge-grounded augmentation using the GPT-3.5-turbo model as described in figure 3. First, we input the dialog context except the user's last question to GPT, and then use knowledge to generate the user's question that needs to be answered. Next, we input the dialog context and the newly augmented user question, and generate the reviews or FAQs needed to answer it. Finally, we add the augmented knowledge, the dialog context, and the user's last question and have the system to generate a response using based on knowledge. All three stages of data augmentation are performed using 4-shot exemplars.

[4]https://github.com/makcedward/nlpaug

[5]https://github.com/facebookresearch/fairseq

3.3.2 In-context Learning

Fine-tuning methodologies achieve high performance, but they also require a lot of data and training resources. (Brown et al., 2020) Therefore, we conduct experiments for in-context learning using GPT-3.5-turbo model and try additional prompt engineering methods.

First, we conduct experiments to find the optimal prompt using the manual prompt method. Through this, we find that bundling knowledge or dialog context in the form of python's dictionary data structure generated better responses even if it takes several few-shot exemplars. It seems like GPT understands data better in code structure. In particular, it is the most effective way to present specific instructions at the end, so we put the last question and instruction at the end as described in appendix D.

Second, we use clue-based generation prompts, which is an idea to overcome GPT's strict answers and its inability to ask probing questions based on user intent. GPT generates clues from the dialog context, such as (1) what the user wants, (2) what information should be provided to the user, and (3) what can be asked of the user. GPT then generates an answer by adding the clue, knowledge, and the user's last question.

Third, we use the summary-clue generation method. Similar to the second method, GPT creates a summary-clue that describes the situation, and reinserts this summary-clue when generating a response.

	Precision	Recall	F1
BERT	99.75	99.61	99.68
RoBERTa	99.86	99.64	99.75
ALBERT	99.64	99.36	99.50
DeBERTa	**99.86**	99.57	99.71
Baseline	99.82	99.79	**99.80**
Ours	99.54	**99.93**	99.73

Table 3: Results of the KTD task.

Version	# of Data	Precision	Recall	F1	Exact Match
Baseline	28,431	79.01	78.77	78.89	39.06
Ver1	28,431	54.78	**93**	68.95	28.19
Ver2	39,313	77.66	83.12	80.3	42.54
Ver3	39,313	75.33	86.53	80.54	43.36
Ver4	50,195	**83.35**	82.17	**82.76**	**47.71**
Ver5	**71,959**	78.34	86.84	82.37	47.37

Table 4: Results of the KS task by training data version.

4 Experiments

4.1 Knowledge-Seeking Turn Detection

4.1.1 Experimental Setup

Metrics We report the Precision, Recall, and F1-score for the KTD task.

Model & Hyper-parameters As a starting point, we use the base version of the PPTOD (Su et al., 2022) checkpoint, which has been pre-trained on a large-scale multi-turn task-oriented dialog dataset. For optimization, We use Adafactor (Shazeer and Stern, 2018) with a learning rate of 0.00001. Throughout the training process, we maintain a batch size of 32. We conduct 19 epochs of training exclusively for the adapter modules. The bottleneck dimension of the adapters is set to half of the hidden dimension of the T5 model following Bang et al., 2023. We adopt the baseline provided by the DSTC11 organizer, and the remaining results are from the task introductory paper (Zhao et al., 2023).

4.1.2 Results

The results of the KTD task on the test set are presented in Table 3. Our proposed model, denoted as "Ours," achieves competitive performance with a F1-score of 99.73%. It outperforms all other models with a Recall of 99.93%. These results highlight the model's ability to detect and classify actual knowledge seeking turns in the dialog context. By leveraging the advantages of adapters, we could enhance the model's performance, effectively addressing the challenges of the KTD task.

4.2 Knowledge Selection

4.2.1 Experimental Setup

Metrics Precision, Recall, and F1-score have been computed at the knowledge snippet level. Instead of calculating the P/R/F1 for each dialog at the snippet level, the P/R/F1 is calculated for all (C, K) pairs in the entire dataset. Additionally, the exact matching score is used as an additional metric, which measures the ratio of dialogs which all knowledge snippets are exactly extracted from the total number of dialogs.

Model & Hyper-parameters The LLM used for creating and augmenting the dataset is the GPT-3.5-turbo model released by Open AI. The model used for fine-tuning the selection task is the DeBERTa (He et al., 2020). For fine-tuning, we set the AdamW optimizer (Kingma and Ba, 2014) as the optimizer, with a train batch size of 4, learning rate of 3e-5, and max sequence length of 512. The GPU used for training is a single NVIDIA RTX A5000 24G.

Dataset The datasets and versions used in the experiment are in total five, as shown in the Table 4. **1)** The version where FAQs and reviews representative of the dialog are attached to the last user utterance using the show sample method. **2)** The original dataset + knowledge-based data augmentation prompt style (a). **3)** The original dataset + knowledge-based data augmentation prompt style (b). **4)** The original dataset + version 2 + version 3. **5)** version 4 + The data where the history of single user utterances generated in versions 1 and 2 was created and appended.

4.2.2 Results

We compare the performance of the models trained on the dataset built through the LLM with the baseline released in DSTC11 Track5. In fact, version 1 achieves first place in the *Recall* metric part of the DSTC11 Track5 benchmark, and other versions mostly shows higher performance than the baseline. In particular, All scores for versions 2-5 increase significantly compared to the baseline. The overall evaluation results are shown in Table 4. The followings are the points of analysis for these results.

4.2.3 Analysis

Generating Representative Samples & Diverse Examples The first method involves creating representative reviews and FAQs for each given dialog instance, allowing us to build a dataset that can retrieve similar types of knowledge. While this approach results in many similarly structured or typed reviews and FAQs, we believe its accuracy score is lower due to the generated samples failing to encompass all the relevancy of the actual labels pertaining to knowledge.

On the other hand, referring to the dataset gathering process in the paper (Zhao et al., 2023), they initially created FAQs and user persona-based reviews for 33 hotels and 110 restaurants, then constructed a new database. Subsequently, they inserted a subjective user request that aligned with the existing conversation. This method is very similar to the knowledge-based data augmentation presented in our paper. Therefore, we believe our generation method contributes significantly to performance improvement by showing the model examples with a similar distribution to the original dataset and providing diverse cases.

Presence or Absence of History in Generated Examples For dataset version 2-4, as a single last user utterance is created that corresponds to one piece of knowledge, the dataset has been augmented with single utterance-style data that lacks history. Accordingly, version 5 is also devised to generate the history preceding these newly created utterances. The generated history is limited to start with the user and end with the system, with no more than five utterances. Detailed prompting examples are provided in Appendix A.

Looking at Table 4, adding history in this way to the dataset used in version 4 results in lower precision performance, despite having the most data. However, it does show a higher Recall score. In fact, in the RG stage following the KS, having a higher Recall performs much better when the F1 score is the same (as having more knowledge candidates leads to better generation performance), so ultimately, we use the model trained with version 5 in the RG stage.

4.3 Response Generation

4.3.1 Experimental Setup

Metric For automatic evaluation, we use BLEU, METEOR, ROUGE-1, ROUGE-2, and ROUGE-L to measure the model-generated response alignment with the gold response. In addition, human evaluation is conducted to compensate for the fact that automatic evaluation is not always reliable. (Zhao et al., 2023)

Model & Hyper-parameters Flan-T5-XL model is the backbone for fine-tuning. The dialog domain further pre-train is performed on 8 NVIDIA A100 80G, with a max length of 256, batch size of 4, learning rate of 1e-4, and AdamW optimizer. For fine-tuning with publicly available train sets and augmented data, we use the Adam optimizer with a max length of 512, a batch size of 4, and a learning rate of 1e-4. We utilize the GPT-3.5-turbo model for additional data augmentation. The baseline follows DSTC11 Track5 method.

Fine-tuning and Data Augmentation Methods					
	BLEU	MT	R-1	R-2	R-L
Baseline	10.04	17.48	35.20	14.30	27.53
Flan-T5-XL	9.61	17.15	35.72	14.67	27.98
Synonym Replacement	10.22	17.18	35.63	14.28	27.93
Filling Mask	10.01	17.28	35.77	14.33	27.83
Back-translation	10.15	17.20	35.85	14.49	28.00
Paraphrase (Parrot)	10.15	17.39	35.57	13.98	27.52
Paraphrase (PEGASUS)	10.09	17.10	35.59	14.29	27.77
ChatGPT Augmentation	**10.35**	**19.01**	**37.91**	**15.42**	**29.37**
In-context Learning Results					
	BLEU	MT	R-1	R-2	R-L
Manual Prompt	6.26	**17.74**	33.70	11.81	24.47
Clue-based Generation	6.36	17.15	33.11	11.38	24.11
Summary-Clue Generation	**6.78**	17.18	**34.14**	**12.02**	**24.87**

Table 5: Results of the RG task.

4.3.2 Results

The results for the RG task are summarized in Table 5. The table is organized into the fine-tuned part at the top, and the in-context learning part without fine-tuning at the bottom. It can be seen that the performance of the fine-tuned part is higher than the in-context learning part, which can be attributed to the better learning of the benchmark's speech style and format.

To enhance performance of fine-tuning models, we conduct dialog domain-adaptive pre-train and data augmentation. The rows below the general fine-tuning are the results of further pre-training the model on the dialog domain, followed by augmented data tuning. When comparing the data augmentation methods, we can see that the performance of the knowledge-grounded dialog augmentation method (GPT augmentation) is higher than the paraphrasing method (synonym replacement, filling mask, back-translation, paraphrase). This is due to the nature of knowledge-grounded dialogs, it is important to understand the context of the conversation, as well as to learn various knowledge forms so that relevant knowledge can be summarized and answered appropriately.

In the in-context learning results, the summary-clue generation method achieves the highest performance. Compared to clue-based generation, it seems to generate responses that reflect the characteristics of the benchmark dataset well by including many few-shot exemplars. Also, it seems to generate better responses because it directly writes down the user's intention rather than including the dialog as it is.

4.3.3 Human Evaluation Results

We gather three crowd workers to evaluate 50 randomly sampled data samples per model. We select four models that achieve good performance on the automatic metric. We evaluate three fine-tuning models trained with data augmented with back-translation, synonym replacement, and knowledge-grounded GPT augmentation, and one in-context model generated with summary-clue prompts. The evaluation criteria are accuracy, which measures how accurately the model reflects knowledge, and appropriateness, which measures how appropriate the response is as seen by a human, according to (Zhao et al., 2023). The results of the human evaluation are shown in Table 6. Unlike automatic evaluation, the preferences for in-context learning and fine-tuning are not significantly different. However, the model fine-tuned by including GPT-augmented data received the highest preference score from users. This confirms that our proposed approach, which appropriately uses LLM to learn in cooperation with a specific task model, is very effective. More details of the human evaluation can be found in appendix E.

	Accuracy	Appropriateness	Average
Back-translation	3.37	3.98	3.67
Synonym Replacement	3.42	3.78	3.60
GPT Augmentation	3.58	4.59	4.08
Summary-based Prompt	3.29	4.14	3.71

Table 6: Results of human evaluation.

Knowledge-Seeking Turn Detection					
	Precision		Recall		F1-score
GPT-3.5-turbo	49.95		100		66.62
Ours	99.54		99.93		99.73
Knowledge Selection					
	Precision		F1-score		EMAcc
Embedding search	40.90		44.43		0.82
Ours	83.35		82.76		47.71
Response Generation					
	BLEU	MT	R-1	R-2	R-L
GPT-3.5-turbo	6.78	17.18	34.14	12.02	24.87
Ours	10.35	19.01	37.91	15.42	29.37

Table 7: Comparison with LLM sub-task solver.

5 Comparison with LLM Sub-task Solver

We have shown how to effectively use LLM to solve sub-tasks efficiently. By using a fine-tuning methodology through adapters and data augmentation methodology based on LLM's knowledge, we are able to significantly increase the performance per task.

Our proposed methodology does not simply use LLM as a one-step sub-task solver, but utilizes LLM to improve the performance of the task solver model. To verify that our methodology outperforms LLM directly solving tasks, we compare the performance of our proposed methodology with that of LLM directly solving tasks. This is summarized in Table 7. In the KS task, similarity calculation is performed using embeddings from the *text-embedding-ada-002* model. As described in the table, we can see that utilizing LLM as in our proposed methodology is effective in solving SK-TOD problems.

6 Conclusion

We propose an LLM-based framework for SK-TOD. In the KTD task, we fine-tune T5 using task-specific adapters. To address the challenge of relatively reduced data classified as knowledge-seeking turns in the KS and RG tasks, we employ knowledge-based data augmentation through LLM. Our three-stage data augmentation methodology involves last question generation, knowledge generation, and response generation for the RG task, as well as generating good and bad questions for the KS task. Experimental results show that our LLM-based framework achieves significantly higher performance compared to the baselines in the KS and RG tasks. Furthermore, our proposed framework for SK-TOD outperforms using LLM directly as a task solver, indicating its promising efficiency for SK-TOD tasks. Further research may be required to explore its efficiency further and understand its potential advantages more comprehensively. We plan to make the augmented data publicly available, hoping to contribute to the advancement of SK-TOD and future research in knowledge-based data augmentation.

Limitations

We based our entire framework on the LLM. We have tried to find the optimal prompts and made them publicly available. However, it is important to note that an LLM may generate different or unexpected responses when reproducing the experiment.

Ethics Statement

The augmented data was fully examined before publication. We filtered the data to ensure that it did not contain discrimination and hatred of any particular race, gender, region, or age. If we subsequently discover data that does contain bias, we will take immediate action to remove it.

Acknowledgements

This work was supported by Institute of Information & communications Technology Planning & Evaluation (IITP) grant funded by the Korea government (MSIT) (No.2022-0-00621,Development of artificial intelligence technology that provides dialog-based multi-modal explainability)

References

Namo Bang, Jeehyun Lee, and Myoung-Wan Koo. 2023. Task-optimized adapters for an end-to-end task-oriented dialogue system. In *Findings of the Association for Computational Linguistics: ACL 2023, Toronto, Canada, July 9-14, 2023*, pages 7355–7369. Association for Computational Linguistics.

Luiz Bonifacio, Hugo Abonizio, Marzieh Fadaee, and Rodrigo Nogueira. 2022. Inpars: Data augmentation for information retrieval using large language models. *arXiv preprint arXiv:2202.05144*.

Tom Brown, Benjamin Mann, Nick Ryder, Melanie Subbiah, Jared D Kaplan, Prafulla Dhariwal, Arvind Neelakantan, Pranav Shyam, Girish Sastry, Amanda Askell, et al. 2020. Language models are few-shot learners. *Advances in neural information processing systems*, 33:1877–1901.

Jishnu Ray Chowdhury, Yong Zhuang, and Shuyi Wang. 2022. Novelty controlled paraphrase generation with retrieval augmented conditional prompt tuning. In *Thirty-Sixth AAAI Conference on Artificial Intelligence, AAAI 2022, Thirty-Fourth Conference on Innovative Applications of Artificial Intelligence, IAAI 2022, The Twelveth Symposium on Educational Advances in Artificial Intelligence, EAAI 2022 Virtual Event, February 22 - March 1, 2022*, pages 10535–10544. AAAI Press.

Alexis Conneau, Kartikay Khandelwal, Naman Goyal, Vishrav Chaudhary, Guillaume Wenzek, Francisco Guzmán, Edouard Grave, Myle Ott, Luke Zettlemoyer, and Veselin Stoyanov. 2020. Unsupervised cross-lingual representation learning at scale. In *Proceedings of the 58th Annual Meeting of the Association for Computational Linguistics, ACL 2020, Online, July 5-10, 2020*, pages 8440–8451. Association for Computational Linguistics.

Haixing Dai, Zhengliang Liu, Wenxiong Liao, Xiaoke Huang, Yihan Cao, Zihao Wu, Lin Zhao, Shaochen Xu, Wei Liu, Ninghao Liu, Sheng Li, Dajiang Zhu, Hongmin Cai, Lichao Sun, Quanzheng Li, Dinggang Shen, Tianming Liu, and Xiang Li. 2023. Auggpt: Leveraging chatgpt for text data augmentation.

Prithiviraj Damodaran. 2021. Parrot: Paraphrase generation for nlu.

Jun Gao, Changlong Yu, Wei Wang, Huan Zhao, and Ruifeng Xu. 2023. Mask-then-fill: A flexible and effective data augmentation framework for event extraction. *CoRR*, abs/2301.02427.

Silin Gao, Yichi Zhang, Zhijian Ou, and Zhou Yu. 2020. Paraphrase augmented task-oriented dialog generation. In *Proceedings of the 58th Annual Meeting of the Association for Computational Linguistics, ACL 2020, Online, July 5-10, 2020*, pages 639–649. Association for Computational Linguistics.

Pengcheng He, Xiaodong Liu, Jianfeng Gao, and Weizhu Chen. 2020. Deberta: Decoding-enhanced bert with disentangled attention. *arXiv preprint arXiv:2006.03654*.

Neil Houlsby, Andrei Giurgiu, Stanislaw Jastrzebski, Bruna Morrone, Quentin de Laroussilhe, Andrea Gesmundo, Mona Attariyan, and Sylvain Gelly. 2019. Parameter-efficient transfer learning for NLP. In *Proceedings of the 36th International Conference on Machine Learning, ICML 2019, 9-15 June 2019, Long Beach, California, USA*, volume 97 of *Proceedings of Machine Learning Research*, pages 2790–2799. PMLR.

Seokhwan Kim, Yang Liu, Di Jin, Alexandros Papangelis, Behnam Hedayatnia, Karthik Gopalakrishnan, and Dilek Hakkani-Tür. 2022. Knowledge-grounded task-oriented dialogue modeling on spoken conversations track at dstc10.

Diederik P Kingma and Jimmy Ba. 2014. Adam: A method for stochastic optimization. *arXiv preprint arXiv:1412.6980*.

Bing Liu and Ian Lane. 2017. An end-to-end trainable neural network model with belief tracking for task-oriented dialog. *arXiv preprint arXiv:1708.05956*.

Shikib Mehri, Evgeniia Razumovskaia, Tiancheng Zhao, and Maxine Eskenazi. 2019. Pretraining methods for dialog context representation learning. In *Proceedings of the 57th Annual Meeting of the Association for Computational Linguistics*, pages 3836–3845, Florence, Italy. Association for Computational Linguistics.

Tong Niu, Semih Yavuz, Yingbo Zhou, Nitish Shirish Keskar, Huan Wang, and Caiming Xiong. 2021. Unsupervised paraphrasing with pretrained language models. In *Proceedings of the 2021 Conference on Empirical Methods in Natural Language Processing, EMNLP 2021, Virtual Event / Punta Cana, Dominican Republic, 7-11 November, 2021*, pages 5136–5150. Association for Computational Linguistics.

OpenAI. 2023. GPT-4 Technical Report. *arXiv e-prints*, page arXiv:2303.08774.

Rico Sennrich, Barry Haddow, and Alexandra Birch. 2016. Improving neural machine translation models with monolingual data. In *Proceedings of the 54th Annual Meeting of the Association for Computational Linguistics, ACL 2016, August 7-12, 2016, Berlin, Germany, Volume 1: Long Papers*. The Association for Computer Linguistics.

Noam Shazeer and Mitchell Stern. 2018. Adafactor: Adaptive learning rates with sublinear memory cost. In *Proceedings of the 35th International Conference on Machine Learning*, volume 80 of *Proceedings of Machine Learning Research*, pages 4596–4604. PMLR.

Yixuan Su, Lei Shu, Elman Mansimov, Arshit Gupta, Deng Cai, Yi-An Lai, and Yi Zhang. 2021. Multi-task pre-training for plug-and-play task-oriented dialogue system. *arXiv preprint arXiv:2109.14739*.

Yixuan Su, Lei Shu, Elman Mansimov, Arshit Gupta, Deng Cai, Yi-An Lai, and Yi Zhang. 2022. Multi-task pre-training for plug-and-play task-oriented dialogue system. In *Proceedings of the 60th Annual Meeting of the Association for Computational Linguistics (Volume 1: Long Papers)*, pages 4661–4676, Dublin, Ireland. Association for Computational Linguistics.

Xin Tian, Yingzhan Lin, Mengfei Song, Siqi Bao, Fan Wang, Huang He, Shuqi Sun, and Hua Wu. 2022. Q-tod: A query-driven task-oriented dialogue system.

Peifeng Wang, Aaron Chan, Filip Ilievski, Muhao Chen, and Xiang Ren. 2022. Pinto: Faithful language reasoning using prompt-generated rationales. *arXiv preprint arXiv:2211.01562*.

Yizhong Wang, Yeganeh Kordi, Swaroop Mishra, Alisa Liu, Noah A. Smith, Daniel Khashabi, and Hannaneh Hajishirzi. 2023. Self-instruct: Aligning language models with self-generated instructions.

Jason Wei, Maarten Bosma, Vincent Y Zhao, Kelvin Guu, Adams Wei Yu, Brian Lester, Nan Du, Andrew M Dai, and Quoc V Le. 2021. Finetuned language models are zero-shot learners. *arXiv preprint arXiv:2109.01652*.

Jason Wei and Kai Zou. 2019. Eda: Easy data augmentation techniques for boosting performance on text classification tasks.

Jingqing Zhang, Yao Zhao, Mohammad Saleh, and Peter J. Liu. 2020. PEGASUS: pre-training with extracted gap-sentences for abstractive summarization. In *Proceedings of the 37th International Conference on Machine Learning, ICML 2020, 13-18 July 2020, Virtual Event*, volume 119 of *Proceedings of Machine Learning Research*, pages 11328–11339. PMLR.

Qiang Zhang, Jason Naradowsky, and Yusuke Miyao. 2023. Ask an expert: Leveraging language models to improve strategic reasoning in goal-oriented dialogue models. *arXiv preprint arXiv:2305.17878*.

Yizhe Zhang, Siqi Sun, Michel Galley, Yen-Chun Chen, Chris Brockett, Xiang Gao, Jianfeng Gao, Jingjing Liu, and Bill Dolan. 2019. Dialogpt: Large-scale generative pre-training for conversational response generation. *arXiv preprint arXiv:1911.00536*.

Chao Zhao, Spandana Gella, Seokhwan Kim, Di Jin, Devamanyu Hazarika, Alexandros Papangelis, Behnam Hedayatnia, Mahdi Namazifar, Yang Liu, and Dilek Hakkani-Tur. 2023. "what do others think?": Task-oriented conversational modeling with subjective knowledge.

Victor Zhong, Caiming Xiong, and Richard Socher. 2018. Global-locally self-attentive dialogue state tracker. *arXiv preprint arXiv:1805.09655*.

Appendices

A How to Build Version 6 data for Knowledge Selection Task

This method involves generating a history of previous system and user utterances for various single utterances generated through data augmentation techniques. Given the last user utterance, previous system and user utterances are generated sequentially. 2-shot exemplars are provided. A detailed prompt example looks like the Figure 4.

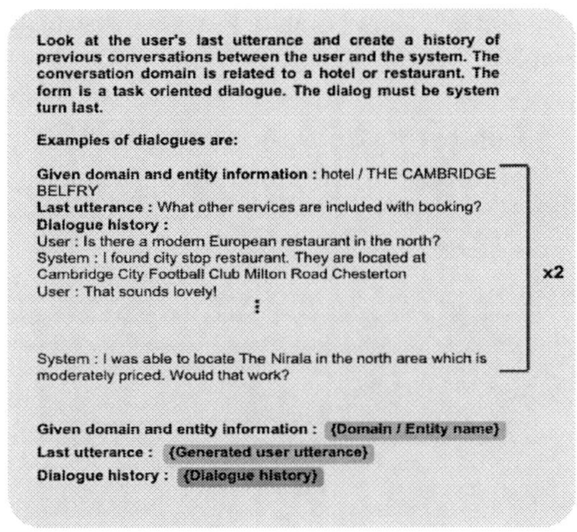

Figure 4: Example of history generation prompts for building version 6 data in the KS task. The bold text represents the default prompt format, and the input provided is highlighted in green. The blue text denotes the portion generated by the model.

B Details of Flan-T5-XL Instruction Template

As a preliminary step for Flan-T5 fine-tuning, we conducted an experiment to determine which in-

	BLEU	MT	R-1	R-2	R-L
(a) instruction	9.61	17.15	35.72	14.67	27.98
(b) instruction	9.17	16.82	34.02	13.28	25.88

Table 8: Comparison of Flan-T5-XL instruction templates.

struction format is most effective for the instructions in Flan-T5 prompts. We compared the form (a) *"system: <extra_id_0>"*, which contains special token, which is mainly used to format the input and output text of T5, and the form (b) *"generate system response based on knowledge and dialog context: "*, which describes the task to be performed by the model in natural language (Tian et al., 2022). The results of fine-tuning using each instruction and comparing the performance are summarized in table 8. As a result, the special token form (a) outperformed the natural language form (b). Since the Flan model is instruction tuned by focusing on the model's understanding of natural language instructions, we expected that the performance would be higher when using natural language instructions, but the performance was higher when using special token. Therefore, we unified the instructions in all fine-tuning experiments to (a) with special token. Also, Table 9 shows examples of each instruction template.

C Context-based Data Augmentation Methods for Response Generation Task

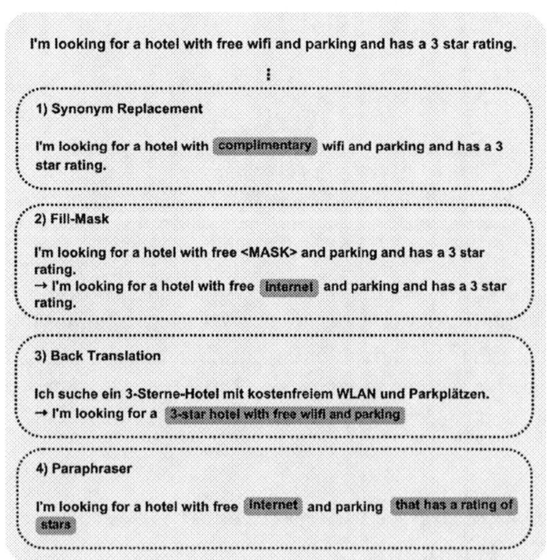

Figure 5: Examples of inpaint methods without knowledge for the RG task.

When fine-tuning the Flan-T5-XL model, we used context-based data augmentation to increase performance. The augmentation methods without using Knowledge are shown in the figure 5.

D In-context Learning Prompt Examples

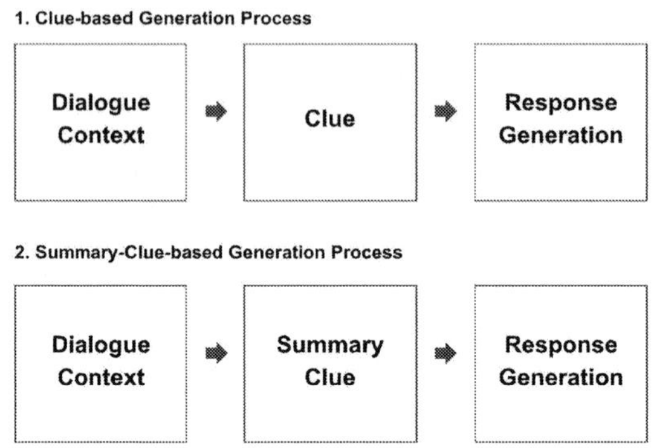

Figure 6: Clue-based Generation Prompting.

Manual prompt, contains knowledge and dialog context in the form of a python dictionary data structure. It also organizes the prompt by putting the user's question at the end and the instruction to answer it at the end. The performance presented in the paper is the result of a 2-shot prompt. Table 10 shows the examples.

Clue-based generation prompting is a way to have GPT generate the clues it needs to generate an answer, and then generate a response based on those clues. In the two-stage generation process, the GPT initially generates three clues: 1) what the user wants, 2) what information it needs to provide to the user, and 3) what it can ask the user back. An example prompt might look like this. The performance presented in the paper is based on a 4-shot prompt. Figure 6 shows the process and table 11 shows the examples.

Summary-clue generation is a two-stage generation process where GPT summarizes the context of the conversation and creates a summary-clue of what the user wants. The ability to include more few-shot exemplars improves performance by showing more example answers that can be used to generate answers that fit the automatic metric. Figure 6 shows the process and table 12 shows the examples.

E Human Evaluation

We asked crowd workers to evaluate each response generated from different models according to the

Example of (a) Instruction
From domain hotel and entity BRIDGE GUEST HOUSE, knowledge1: The room was clean and comfortable and not expensive. knowledge2: It could ruin your stay if you mind that kind of thing. knowledge3: Sadly though, I found that the bed in the room wasn't very comfortable at all. knowledge4: I do have to say, though, the bed is extremely uncomfortable. knowledge5: and the interior of the room was very good and bed was also very much comfortable. user:Can you help me find a place to stay that is moderately priced and includes free wifi? system:sure, i have 17 options for you user:Are any of them in the south? I'd like free parking too. system:Yes, two are in the south and both have free parking and internet. I recommend the Bridge Guesthouse. Would you like me to book a reservation? user:I have back issues. Does this place have comfortable beds? system: <extra_id_0>
Example of (b) Instruction
From domain hotel and entity BRIDGE GUEST HOUSE, knowledge1: The room was clean and comfortable and not expensive. knowledge2: It could ruin your stay if you mind that kind of thing. knowledge3: Sadly though, I found that the bed in the room wasn't very comfortable at all. knowledge4: I do have to say, though, the bed is extremely uncomfortable. knowledge5: and the interior of the room was very good and bed was also very much comfortable. user:Can you help me find a place to stay that is moderately priced and includes free wifi? system:sure, i have 17 options for you user:Are any of them in the south? I'd like free parking too. system:Yes, two are in the south and both have free parking and internet. I recommend the Bridge Guesthouse. Would you like me to book a reservation? user:I have back issues. Does this place have comfortable beds? generate system response based on knowledge and dialog context:

Table 9: Examples of T5 instruction templates.

following criteria:

- Appropriateness: how well the response is naturally connected to the conversation
- Accuracy: how accurate a system agent's response reflects the opinions and sentiments

This criteria is based on DSTC9 Track1 and DSTC10 Track2 human evaluation processes. Figure 7 shows the details of human evaluation instruction which was given as a guideline to crowd workers.

Manual Prompt Example

```
##
{"reviews of HOBSONS HOUSE":
["I also saw some hairs in the bathroom, which was evidently not well cleaned.",
"Upon using the bathroom facilities, we all saw that they were pristine and it looks like they had been recently cleaned.",
"The view from the room was also amazing, and the cleanliness of the bathroom was top notch."],
"dialog context": ["U: Can you help me find guesthouses in the west of town?",
"S: Of course, I have two available one is cheap and one is moderate what do you prefer?",
"U: Do either of them have a 3 star rating?",
"S: Yes, the Hobsons House has 3 stars and meets your criteria.
Would you like me to make a reservation for you?"]}

answer as a system based on reviews and FAQs
U: Are their bathrooms adequately sanitized?
S: Yes, most of the guests at Hobsons House have rated the bathrooms very high on cleanliness,
although there is at least one report of stray hairs in the bathroom.

##
{"reviews of THE CAMBRIDGE BELFRY":
["One of the best things about the hotel is the view of the mountains from the balcony.",
"The staff was polite they took out luggage to our room, and our room had a spectacular view of the forest and nature."],
"dialog context": ["U: I'm looking for information on the cambridge belfry hotel.",
"S: the cambridge belfry is cheap, located in the west, and has 4 stars. It has free internet and parking."]}

answer as a system based on reviews and FAQs
U: Do you know anything about the views from the rooms as I hope to have a nice view?
S: Yes, the rooms at the Cambridge Belfry have very nice views.
Can I answer anything else, or would you like to book it?

##
{"reviews of ASHLEY HOTEL":
["Looking out of the window was a great view, and we loved it.",
"There was a nice size refrigerator and a beautiful view out the window of the 7th floor."],
"dialog context": ["U: I'm looking to stay at a 3 star hotel in the north.",
"S: Sorry, I have no results for that query. Would you like to try a different area of town?",
"U: Are there any moderate priced hotels in the North?",
"S: Yes I have two. Would you like me to book one?",
"U: I need a hotel to include free parking; does either have that?",
"S: Yes both of them have free parking.",
"U: Which one would you recommend?",
"S: How about the Ashley hotel?",
"U: Is the Ashley hotel a 3 star hotel?",
"S: the ashley is actually a 2 star hotel."]}

answer as a system based on reviews and FAQs
U: Does this hotel have rooms with a good view of the neighborhood?
S:
```

Table 10: Examples of manual prompt.

Clue-based Generation Example
{"dialog context": ["U: I'm looking to stay at a 3 star hotel in the north.", "S: Sorry, I have no results for that query. Would you like to try a different area of town?", "U: Are there any moderate priced hotels in the North?", "S: Yes I have two. Would you like me to book one?", "U: I need a hotel to include free parking; does either have that?", "S: Yes both of them have free parking.", "U: Which one would you recommend?", "S: How about the Ashley hotel?", "U: Is the Ashley hotel a 3 star hotel?", "S: the ashley is actually a 2 star hotel.", "U: Does this hotel have rooms with a good view of the neighborhood?"]} based on dialog context, figure out 1) what the user wants 2) what information you should provide to answer user's last question 3) what can you ask user? write in one to two sentences.
role: you are a chatbot assistant system. {"reviews of ASHLEY HOTEL": ["There was a nice size refrigerator and a beautiful view out the window of the 7th floor.", "Looking out of the window was a great view, and we loved it."],} based on FAQs or reviews, answer the question "U: Does this hotel have rooms with a good view of the neighborhood?" [clues] 1) The user wants a moderate priced hotel in the north with free parking and rooms with a good view of the neighborhood. (basic) 2) To answer the user's last question, you should provide information about whether the Ashley hotel has rooms with a good view of the neighborhood. (important) 3) You can ask the user if they would like you to check the availability of rooms with a good view at the Ashley hotel or if they have any other preferences regarding the hotel. (optional) answer in 32 tokens.

Table 11: Examples of clue-based generation prompt. First row shows the input of GPT to generate clues. Second row shows the input of GPT to generate responses based on knowledge and clues.

Summary-clue Generation Example
{"dialog context": ["U: I am looking for a place to dine that has expensive romanian food.", "S: No I'm sorry. Something else perhaps?", "U: Is there one that serves Chinese instead?", "S: I'm showing 9 entries throughout the area. Do you have a preference between center, north, east, or south?", "U: I have no preference. I just need to book it for 8 at 12:45 on Thursday.", "S: I have you booked at Yu Garden. The table will be reserved for 15 minutes. Your reference number is: D6LEPNCC. Anything else I can do for you?", "U: Do you know if the restaurant has a good outdoor dining space?"]} summarize dialog context and what the user wants, with a focus on the last question. write in one to two sentences.
role: you are a chatbot assistant system. situation: The user is asking if the restaurant they have booked, Yu Garden, has a good outdoor dining space. {"FAQs of YU GARDEN": ["YU GARDEN does offer outdoor seating."], "reviews of YU GARDEN": ["When I first arrived I noticed out front there was a nice place for outdoor dining so I asked to be seated there.", "However, the view from our table was facing a wall and cramped wish they would have sat us outside."]} based on FAQs or reviews, answer the user's question: Do you know if the restaurant has a good outdoor dining space? you should answer in 32 tokens.

Table 12: Examples of summary-clue generation prompt. First row shows the input of GPT to generate clues. Second row shows the input of GPT to generate responses based on knowledge and situations.

Human Evaluation Instruction

We provide a conversation between a user and a system agent which ends with a user input, and the entire user reviews that are relevant to the user's input.

Please first read a conversation and relevant reviews(knowledges), and score the generated responses on a scale of 1 - 5 on the following criteria:

- Appropriateness: Appropriateness means how well the response is naturally connected to the conversation. A score of 1 means that the response is very inappropriate and it is not naturally connected to the conversation. A score of 5 means that the response is very appropriate and it is very naturally connected to the conversation.
- Accuracy: Accuracy means how accurate a system agent's response reflects the opinions and sentiments that you obtained from the reviews. A score of 1 means that the response is completely wrong. A score of 5 means that the response is completely accurate against the sentiment distribution of given knowledge snippets.

Figure 7: Example of human evaluation instruction.

Semantic data augmentation for meaning maintenance on Task-Oriented Conversation with Large-size Language Model

Jaehwan Lee[*] Kwanyoung Son[*] EunKyung Yoo[†] Eugene Kim[†] Hoseok Do, Daeyeon Yi
AI Lab, CTO Division, LG Electronics, South Korea
{jaehwan314.lee, kwanyoung.son, eunkyung.ryu, white.kim, hoseok.do, daeyeon.yi}@lge.com

Abstract

This paper presents our approach to building a generalized model for Track 5 in DSTC11: "Task-oriented Conversational Modeling with Subjective Knowledge" which addresses the challenge of generating responses to users' utterances based on a variety of factual and subjective knowledge. To tackle this challenge, we first augmented the training data by leveraging contextual word embedding and back translation, thereby increasing the quantity of available data. Then, we utilized a large-size language model to enhance the acceptability of the augmented data and fine-tuned the model using augmented data. Specifically, we applied the DeBERTa-v3-large model for knowledge detection and selection, and the BART-large model for response generation. Our best model achieved the seventh rank in the objective evaluation and the second rank in the final official human evaluation. These outcomes serve as solid evidence that data augmentation and using a large-size model were highly effective for developing a conversational model system that incorporates objective and subjective knowledge.

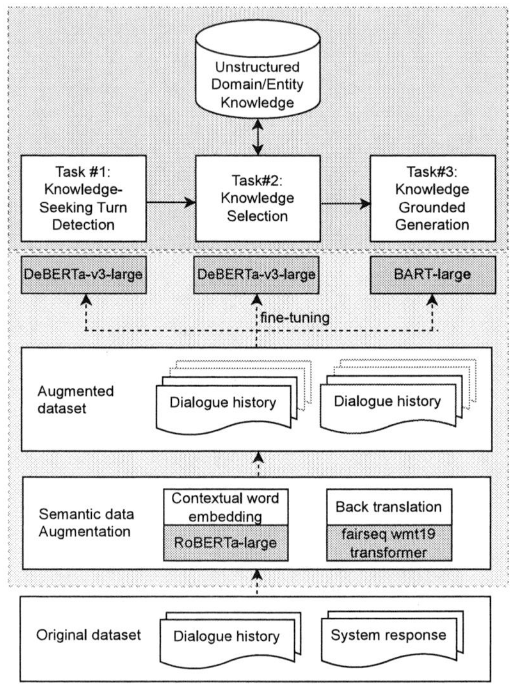

Figure 1: Overall structure of our method: The blue box is a block diagram of DSTC11 Track 5. The yellow box is an illustration of our best model. Dialog history and system response of the original dataset were augmented using contextual word embedding and back translation, and then fine-tuned to large-size models.

1 Introduction

Over the past decade, AI technology has brought about many changes and has been used in various applications and devices that permeate our lives, such as chatbots, personal assistants, and smart kiosks. Traditional studies on task-oriented dialogue systems have focused primarily on providing information and performing actions limited to specific databases or application programming interfaces (API). However, recent studies have focused on tasks beyond available APIs and databases, incorporating relevant domain knowledge. Knowledge-grounded task-oriented conversational modeling tasks are being introduced to address the demands in this research field (Kim et al., 2020; Mi et al., 2021; Kim et al., 2021).

Subjective information, such as customer reviews, rather than objective knowledge from the web, can be meaningful if used well. For these reasons, DSTC11 Track 5 proposes the challenge "Task-Oriented Conversation Modeling through Subjective Knowledge" (Zhao et al., 2023). This challenge comprises three sub-tasks: Knowledge-seeking Turn Detection, Knowledge Selection, and Knowledge-grounded Response Generation. The first sub-task determines whether knowledge access is required for a given utterance and dialog history.

[*]These authors contributed equally to this work.
[†]These authors contributed equally to this work.

Proceedings of The Eleventh Dialog System Technology Challenge, pages 166–176
September 11, 2023 ©2023 Association for Computational Linguistics

The second sub-task selects the relevant subjective knowledge. Finally, the third sub-task generates an appropriate sentence as a system response based on the selected knowledge.

Our best model adopted two major improvements: data augmentation and large-size language models. As shown in Figure 1, we applied back translation and contextual word embedding for semantic-preserving data augmentation. For the knowledge-seeking turn detection and knowledge selection, we adopted the DeBERTa-v3-large language model. Additionally, for response generation, we utilized the BART-large language model. Fine-tuning our model with augmented data, we achieved outstanding performance. Our model secured the second rank in the official human evaluation.

2 Related work

2.1 Augmentation

Data augmentation is used to increase the size of the training dataset, prevent overfitting, and increase the performance of models in low-resource tasks. Recent studies have demonstrated that data augmentation plays an important role in improving the performance of text classification and text generation tasks (Bayer et al., 2022b; Xu et al., 2021). Some studies augment the data by replacing words or phrases with synonyms (Zhang et al., 2015) and replacing similar word embedding using the k-nearest neighbor algorithm and cosine similarity (Wang and Yang, 2015). By developing this methodology, a method of replacing contextualized word embedding using the language model was also devised. Several attempts have been made, such as replacing words with top-k probability using a bi-directional language model and CNN (Kobayashi, 2018), or using BERT's masked language modeling, which masks several words, predicts them at once, and replaces them from original data (Wu et al., 2019).

In the neural machine translation task, a back translation methodology is devised which translates target language sentences into source language sentences and adds them to training data (Sennrich et al., 2016). A method for generating entirely new sentences was also studied. Anaby-Tavor et al. (2020) generated new sentences by inputting part of the beginning of the original sentence to fine-tune GPT-2.

Alternatively, some studies augmented data by randomly reproducing, inserting, swapping, and deleting words in the original text like Easy Data Augmentation (EDA) without maintaining the meaning of the original text, and demonstrating that it can help prevent overfitting and increase the robustness of the model (Wei and Zou, 2019). However, other studies have shown that EDA lowers the classification scores (Bayer et al., 2022a; Luu et al., 2020). Considering the importance of entities and the meaning of the sentence in selection and generation tasks, augmentation methods that effectively preserve these elements are prioritized over techniques like EDA.

2.2 Transformer-based Language Models

Pre-trained language models (PLMs) were created based on the "Transformer" architecture (Vaswani et al., 2017). They have been applied to Natural Language Processing (NLP) tasks while making improvements in model structure, size, and training strategy. We reviewed and applied the following models in our study.

RoBERTa (Liu et al., 2019) is an improved model of BERT (Devlin et al., 2018) trained using a larger training corpus and longer steps. RoBERTa also dynamically changes the masking pattern applied to the training data. DeBERTa (He et al., 2020) is an improved version of BERT and RoBERTa models that uses a disentangled attention mechanism and an enhanced mask decoder. DeBERTa-v3 (He et al., 2021) improves the original DeBERTa model by replacing mask language modeling with replaced token detection, a more sample-efficient pre-training task. BART (Lewis et al., 2020) is a seq2seq model with a bidirectional encoder and an autoregressive decoder. It is pre-trained by corrupting the text with an arbitrary noising function and learning a model to reconstruct the original text. T5 (Raffel et al., 2020) is also a seq2seq model. It was pre-trained on a multi-task mixture of unsupervised and supervised tasks. Multiple NLP tasks were converted into a unified "text-to-text" format and used in the pre-training.

2.3 Open-ended text generation

The aim of open-ended text generation is to produce coherent and contextually relevant sentences based on a given input or context. Many studies have concentrated on decoding methods (Bengio et al., 2000; Fan et al., 2018; Holtzman et al.,

2020; Su et al., 2022) and these utilize open-ended text generation tasks such as story generation (Fan et al., 2018), response generation in dialogue systems(Zhao et al., 2023), and contextual text completion (Radford et al., 2019). Greedy and beam search, a widely used deterministic method, selects a token with the highest probability of appearing next among candidates based on previous conversation history. However, these approaches are ineffective for tasks with subjective content requiring free-form answers (Murray and Chiang, 2018; Yang et al., 2018) and often suffer from dullness, repetition, and degeneration (Holtzman et al., 2020; Welleck et al., 2020; Shao et al., 2017; Li et al., 2016). In the stochastic methods, sampling-based decoding methods including randomness according to the conditional probability distribution have been introduced (Fan et al., 2018). Recently, contrastive search (Su et al., 2022) has been proposed to solve the lack of coherence by model degeneration on the anisotropic distribution of token representations.

3 Method

We try to improve the model in three ways based on the baseline code and dataset of DSTC11 Track 5 (Zhao et al., 2023). First, we employ augmentation techniques, such as contextual word embedding and back translation, to enrich the training data. Second, we test various large-size language models and fine-tune the model using augmented data. Finally, we implement the contrastive search method for response generation to our model and check the feasibility.

3.1 Data Augmentation

For data augmentation, we basically augmented user-system conversations, and desirable system responses. We only augmented user reviews and FAQs when we do named entity recognition-based augmentation. Back translation, contextual word embedding, and ontology-based methods can preserve the entities and meaning of the sentences as much as possible. Consequently, we applied those methods for augmenting the training data of our task. Table 1 summarizes the data augmentation results using each methodology. The first two sentences are examples of back translation results. For contextual word embeddings, we utilized two ways: inserting and substituting words considering the meaning of the sentence while ensuring they retain coherence. The experiments were performed by augmenting the data using each method to increase it by a factor of $\times 1$ and $\times 2$, respectively. Next, word concept-based methods are also used, which replace sets of synonyms for words that are contained in sentences. Finally, a named entity recognition-based method replaces entity names with external knowledge. As presented in Table 1, these models provide suitable alternative sentences through grammatical variations, word order changes, and word substitutions while preserving the overall meaning. Details of each methodology are described below.

Back Translation We used En-De, and En-Ru language pairs to obtain new round-trip translated data because they are easy to implement (Ma, 2019), many studies have been conducted on these language pairs, and there is also a huge dataset for these language pairs(Barrault et al., 2019). Furthermore, as Murthy et al. (2019) proved that translation between languages with similar word orders works better than translation between languages that do not, we used these language pairs. In order to confirm the superior performance improvement effect of back translation to a language with similar word order, a back translation experiment via Korean was also conducted. For back translation implementation, fairseq wmt19 transformer (Ng et al., 2019) En→De, De→En, En→Ru, and Ru→En models were used. To implement back translation via Korean, the OPUS-MT (Tiedemann, 2020) En→Ko, Ko→En model was used.

Contextual Word Embedding Research has proven that the semantic fidelity of augmented data using the BERT model and back translation model is the highest (Kumar et al., 2020), and because the quality of data generated by RoBERTa is better than that of BERT, the contextual word embedding method was applied using RoBERTa to augment the data.

Ontology-based augmentation Ontology-based data augmentation is a common strategy to improve performance in insufficient data environments. We used two strategies for text enrichment: word concept-based and named entity recognition-based augmentation. Word concept-based augmentation comprises two steps: pre-processing and replacing words in target sentences.

Pre-processing When dealing with large-size models, the effect of several data omissions or inaccuracies tends to be less pronounced. However, when

Augmentation Method	Sentence
Original text	Before you do that can you confirm whether Kymmoy offers good views?
Back translation(wmt19-En-De-En)	Can you confirm in advance whether Kymmoy offers good prospects?
Back translation(wmt19-En-Ru-En)	Before you do, can you confirm that Kimmoy offers good views?
Contextual word embedding(insert) $\times 1$	Before you can do all that can you also confirm whether Kymmoy offers any good views?
Contextual word embedding(insert) $\times 2$	Before you do that though can you confirm first whether Mr Kymmoy offers good political views? Before that you do that can can you confirm whether Kymmoy offers you good political views?
Contextual word embedding(substitute) $\times 1$	Before we do that should we confirm whether Kymmoy offers similar results?
Contextual word embedding(substitute) $\times 2$	Before you answer that can you confirm if this offers good value? Before you answer that can we confirm that Kymmoy offers any value?
Word concept-based	Before you do that can you check whether Kymmoy provides good views?
Named Entity Recognition-based	Before you do that can you confirm whether Madera offers good views?

Table 1: Various data augmentation methods and their examples.

Generation method	Response
Label	Acorn guest house's reviews all agree that the hotel is a place of peace and quiet, without any loud or disruptive patrons.
Contrastive Search	The Acorn Guest House gets high marks for their quietness with guests saying it was quiet and relaxing. Would you like to know more about them?
Baseline	Yes, the Acorn Guest House is quiet. Past guests have said that they were not disturbed by any loud or disruptive patrons.
Label	It is not clear if there is a big room available, but one customer said the room they got was spacious while another said the one they got was cramped.
Contrastive Search	The Avalon gets mixed reviews on room size. Some say the rooms are spacious while others say they felt cramped and small. Would you like me to find another place with larger rooms?
Baseline	According to the reviews I have on hand for that location, the opinions are mixed. Half found the rooms cramped and small, while half found them spacious and enjoyable.

Table 2: Example of contrastive search response. The parameters are set as $\alpha = 0.6, k = 4$.

dealing with small datasets, it becomes crucial to increase the precision of the modeling process. Accordingly, we propose a semi-automated approach to data cleaning and correction.

Word concept-based augmentation Next, we propose to augment the data by leveraging the concept of words and their relationships. With WordNet, you can replace a wide range of slot values without any restrictions on part-of-speech. It is an effective method to enhance the quality and consistency of data by ensuring semantic preservation and contextual considerations.

Named Entity Recognition-based augmentation

We choose hotel and restaurant names as the main entities in our oriented task. As entities are captured from the existing training logs, labels, and knowledge data, they are replaced with values from other external entity sets.

3.2 Large Language Model

We used the DeBERTa-v3 model for the detection and selection task, because it showed almost the best performance as a single LLM in NLU benchmarks such as MNLI, SQuAD, and GLUE (He et al., 2021), and was easy to implement. BART and T5 models are used for the generation task because they showed superior performance on sentence generation-related tasks (Lewis et al., 2020; Raffel et al., 2020), and they were easy to implement too. Furthermore, we used each one's large version, because recent studies have shown that the performance of PLMs can be improved by increasing the size of the model parameters (Kaplan et al., 2020). Many experimental results have proved that the large version of the language model is better than the base model too. We also apply the fine-tuning technique using augmented data for better performance.

3.3 Contrastive Search

We try the contrastive search for encoder–decoder models such as BART and T5 for the response generation sub-task. In contrastive search, there are two main parameters as given in Equation 1.

$$x_t = \arg\max_{v \in V^{(k)}} \{(1-\alpha) \times p_\theta(v|x_{<t}) \\ -\alpha \times (max\{s(h_v, h_{x_j}) : 1 \leq j \leq t-1\})\} \quad (1)$$

Name	CWE Substitute, Insert	BT	Ontology Based	Task#2	Task#3	CS	Total Data Size
M1	.	.	.	DeBERTa-v3-base	BART-base	.	×1
M2	.	.	.	DeBERTa-v3-base	T5-base	.	×1
M3	.	.	.	DeBERTa-v3-base	T5-base	O	×1
M4	.	.	.	DeBERTa-v3-large	BART-large	.	×1
M5	.	.	Wordnet	DeBERTa-v3-base	BART-base	.	×2
M6	.	En-De	.	DeBERTa-v3-base	BART-base	.	×2
M7	.	En-Ru	.	DeBERTa-v3-base	BART-base	.	×2
M8	.	En-Ko	.	DeBERTa-v3-base	BART-base	.	×2
M9	RoBERTa-large(×1)	.	.	DeBERTa-v3-base	BART-base	.	×3
M10	RoBERTa-base(×2)	.	.	DeBERTa-v3-base	BART-base	.	×5
M11	RoBERTa-large(×2)	.	.	DeBERTa-v3-base	BART-base	.	×5
M12	RoBERTa-large(×3)	.	.	DeBERTa-v3-base	BART-base	.	×7
M13	RoBERTa-large(×3)	.	.	DeBERTa-v3-large	BART-large	.	×7
M14	RoBERTa-large(×3)	En-De, En-Ru	.	DeBERTa-v3-base	BART-base	.	×9
M15	**RoBERTa-large(×3)**	**En-De, En-Ru**	.	**DeBERTa-v3-large**	**BART-large**	.	**×9**
M16	RoBERTa-large(×3)	En-De, En-Ru	.	DeBERTa-v3-large	BART-large	O	×9
M17	RoBERTa-large(×3)	En-De, En-Ru	Named Entity	DeBERTa-v3-base	BART-base	.	×10
M18	RoBERTa-large(×3)	En-De, En-Ru	Named Entity	DeBERTa-v3-large	BART-large	.	×10

Table 3: Experiments conducted by our team. CWE stands for Contextual Word Embedding. BT stands for Back Translation. LM stands for Language Model, and it is composed of DeBERTa-v3, and BART. In case of T5-base in Task#3, we used DeBERTa-v3 base-size for the detection and selection task and T5 base-size for the generation task. CS stands for Contrastive Search. ×10 means the overall training data size is ten times bigger than the original data. M1 is the baseline in DSTC11 Track 5 and our best model is M15 highlighted on the yellow background.

The top-k parameter denotes the number of $k \in N$ prediction candidates with the highest probability from the model's probability distribution. Penalty alpha $\alpha \in [0, 1]$ is a weight factor for model confidence and degeneration penalty. The closer the value is to 1, the higher is the weight given to the denaturation penalty term. We tested various cases for the penalty alpha and top-k parameters and double-checked the objective measures and subjective quality of the generated responses manually. Table 2 lists the output of the contrastive search on response generation on the BART-base model.

4 Experiments and Results

Table 3 summarizes the experiments list conducted while participating in this competition. In case of the WordNet-based data augmentation method, when used with a base-size language model, the performance was lower than the baseline, so it was not used for large-size language model experiments. T5 also had poorer performance than BART when using the base size, so large-size T5 was not used for other experiments. We cannot discover the correlation between response generation scores and others. For this reason, we check the subjective quality of generation output. We designed the experiment setting focusing on em accuracy. Table 5 lists the types of hyperparameters used in contrastive search and the performance change according to each value. Although not all cases were tested, the performance was the best when the value of penalty alpha was 0.4 and the top-k value was 4. Therefore, those values were used in subsequent tests related to the contrastive search.

4.1 Objective Evaluation

Table 4 lists the experiments submitted by our team and the performance of each. The first four results represent the performance results on the validation set, while the next four results represent the performance results on the test set. We have the following observations: 1) Using a large-size language model plays a direct role in improving performance. In all tasks, the overall performance of models with large-size models is better than models with base models. In the case of the detection task, since the performance of the base-size model itself was very high at 99.84(The performance of the published baseline was also 99.95), it was difficult to derive much performance improvement even when using the large-size model. 2) Contrastive search is not appropriate for generating responses for task-oriented conversation. There have been performance degradations in basic as well as large-size models with contrastive search. 3) Ontology-based augmentation was not that effective. Ontology-based models

	Base	Valid set				Test set			
		Base-NE (id 2)	Large (id 0)	Large-NE (id 3)	Large-CS (id 1)	Base-NE (id 2)	Large (id 0)	Large-NE (id 3)	Large-CS (id 1)
$Detect_{f1}$	99.84	99.86	99.86	**99.88**	99.86	99.75	**99.80**	99.79	**99.80**
$Select_{f1}$	84.51	84.35	**86.00**	**86.00**	**86.00**	74.92	**81.90**	81.87	**81.90**
$Select_{emacc}$	44.81	47.84	**49.88**	49.86	**49.88**	44.10	**51.30**	51.27	**51.30**
Gen_{bleu}	10.09	10.04	10.54	9.53	**10.90**	9.46	**10.29**	9.51	4.45
Gen_{meteor}	17.44	17.50	**17.99**	17.56	17.30	16.68	**17.64**	17.37	11.39
Gen_{rouge_1}	35.82	35.91	**36.77**	35.71	36.04	34.08	**35.87**	35.18	28.01
Gen_{rouge_2}	14.36	14.53	**15.06**	14.12	14.63	13.66	**14.79**	13.79	10.46
Gen_{rouge_l}	28.28	28.37	**29.20**	27.80	28.70	26.67	**28.22**	27.05	22.76

Table 4: Our final entries submitted on DSTC11 Track 5, and their performance. Our best model is entry id 0. Context word embedding augmentation using RoBERTa-large was applied, and En-De and En-Ru back translations were applied. 'Base' and 'Large' refer to the base-size language model and the large-size language model respectively. NE stands for Named entity recognition-based data augmentation and CS stands for Contrastive Search.

exhibit a slight performance decrease in generation and selection tasks. Augmented data using this method appears to have acted as noise because, among many sets of augmented data, new entities are added to only one set of augmented data. Ontology-based augmentation using synonym sets tends to work at the token level. Therefore, it is necessary to impose numerous constraints to ensure semantic maintenance as the quality of the data may contain biases. However, in this study, we have overlooked this process. Named entity recognition-based augmentation should have been applied to the entire augmented data set rather than just one set of data.

Table 6 presents the change in performance according to various back translations. Data augmentation using En-De back translation and En-Ru Back translation improved performance respectively, and using both methods together performed better than using them separately, as it showed 85.77 of F1 score and 43.92 of EM accuracy score. Furthermore, En-Ko, a language pair with dissimilar word order, was not very helpful in improving performance.

Table 7 lists various experiments using contextual word embedding data augmentation and their results. Empirically, the performance tended to improve as more data was augmented using contextual word embedding and when large-size language models were used. The experimental setting which applied CWE×3 augmentation with the large-size model showed the best performance as a 84.43 of F1 score and 49.6 of EM accuracy score.

	Case 1	Case 2	Case 3	Case 4	Case 5
$Penalty\ \alpha$	0.8	0.6	0.6	0.5	0.4
Top - k	4	5	4	4	4
Gen_{bleu}	4.45	8.45	8.53	8.91	**9.02**
Gen_{meteor}	14.81	16.57	16.62	17.08	**17.29**
Gen_{rouge_1}	27.56	33.84	34.05	35.05	**35.44**
Gen_{rouge_2}	7.27	12.67	12.71	13.58	**13.84**
Gen_{rouge_l}	19.73	26.49	26.64	27.49	**27.77**

Table 5: Performance variation according to some combinations of hyperparameters used in the contrastive search.

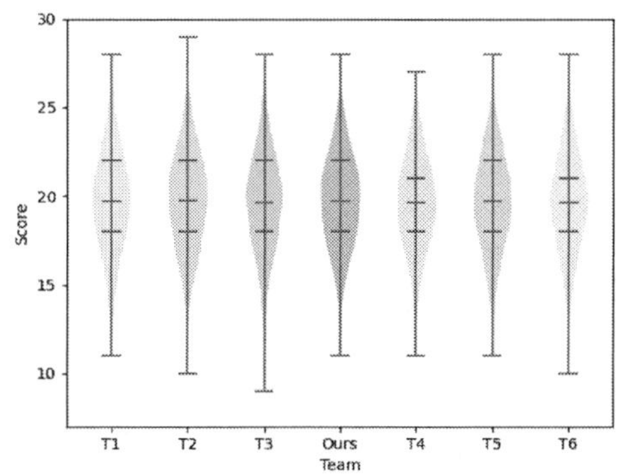

Figure 2: Comparison of human evaluation for the top-6 teams. The vertical axis is the sum of scores for each response.

4.2 Human Evaluation

Conventional reference-based metrics such as BLEU and ROUGE are well-known and widely used as automatic evaluation methods for natural language generation systems. Specifically, the automatic evaluation methods are mainly based on n-grams. BLEU is based on n-gram precision, whereas ROUGE is based on recall. An automatic evaluation method is quick, inexpensive, and language-independent (Papineni et al., 2002). However, they have been shown to have a relatively low correlation with human judgments, especially for

	baseline	En-De BT	En-Ru BT	En-De BT, En-Ru BT	En-Ko BT
$Detect_{f1}$	99.84	99.93	99.91	**99.95**	99.91
$Select_{f1}$	81.08	84.39	83.20	**85.77**	81.07
$Select_{emacc}$	37.27	41.10	41.43	**43.92**	37.02
Gen_{bleu}	9.89	10.22	10.32	**10.50**	10.15
Gen_{meteor}	**17.92**	17.86	17.85	17.72	17.57
Gen_{rouge_1}	35.99	**36.65**	36.46	36.31	35.99
Gen_{rouge_2}	14.38	14.88	**14.89**	**14.89**	14.63
Gen_{rouge_1}	28.19	**28.86**	28.75	28.80	28.49

Table 6: Experiments related to back translation and their performance.

CWE multiple **RoBERTa model size** **LM size (fine-tune)**	**Baseline**	$\times 1$ **large** **base**	$\times 2$ **large** **base**	$\times 2$ **base** **base**	$\times 3$ **large** **base**	$\times 3$ **large** **large**	**No aug.** **large**
$Detect_{f1}$	99.84	99.91	99.81	99.79	99.86	99.86	**99.93**
$Select_{f1}$	81.08	81.95	82.75	83.74	83.46	**84.43**	83.97
$Select_{emacc}$	37.27	43.29	43.62	42.40	44.08	**49.6**	41.76
Gen_{bleu}	9.89	10.30	10.34	**10.64**	10.30	9.79	10.28
Gen_{meteor}	**17.92**	17.66	17.59	17.78	17.76	17.45	17.87
Gen_{rouge_1}	35.99	36.26	36.18	**36.62**	36.44	35.89	36.30
Gen_{rouge_2}	14.38	14.84	14.83	14.99	14.90	14.29	**15.04**
Gen_{rouge_1}	28.19	28.61	28.50	**28.83**	28.72	27.94	28.71

Table 7: Performance of context word embedding augmentation as multiple increments in various settings of language model size.

Speaker	**Text**
	... *Omit previous dialog* ...
User	Also I need to find an expensive chinese restaurant book the table for 3 at 16:45 on tuesday
System	Is there a particular part of town you would like to go to?
User	I need that in the north please.
System	I have 2 chinese restaurants in the north, the hakka and the hotpot, both expensive. Phone number is 22.568988 and 22.3366552 respectively. Would you like me to book reservations for you?
User	I love to try different beers. Do they have lots of different beer options at either Hakka or Hotpot?
Speaker	**Response**
Label	Yes, they do have a lot of beer options at Hakka. One past guest mentioned a good selection of high end beer.
Ours	The Hakka has a good selection of high-end beers to choose from, while the Hotpot has a limited selection of alcoholic drinks.
Response 1	Yes, both Hakka and The Hotpot have a good selection of high-end beers. Would you like me to book a reservation for you?
Response 2	Yes, Hakka does serve alcoholic beverages. The Hotpot does not. Would you like me to book reservations for you?
Response 3	The Hakka restaurant does serve alcoholic beverages, but I am not sure what beer they serve. Would you like me to book reservations for you?
Response 4	Both Hakka and Hotpot have mixed reviews on the selection of beers. Would you like me to book a reservation for you?
Response 5	Hakka has a great selection of high-end beers to choose from. Would you like me to book reservations for you?
Response 6	The Hakka has a great selection of high-end beers to choose from. Would you like me to book a reservation for you?

Table 8: Example of conversations and responses that scored well on human evaluation. Our response contains accurate facts as well as pertinent extra details. Blue : Correct, Violet : Additional info., Orange : Unclear, Red : Wrong info.

tasks that require creativity and diversity (Yang Liu, 2023). Simply put, even if you have two sentences that differ by only one token, their meaning, and usage can be completely different. Therefore, including human evaluation to measure performance is essential. In a qualitative evaluation by humans, factors such as creativity, spontaneity, relevance, fluency, naturalness, and appropriateness will be given higher weightage than automaticity. We placed seventh in the automatic evaluation but second overall through the human evaluation. We believe that we were able to receive a good evaluation because accuracy and appropriateness are the two key factors in human evaluation in DSTC11 Track 5.

Tables 8 and 9 present examples of our responses being more appropriate than others. Since the DSTC11 organizing committee revealed the team id, entry id, entry information and contents of the top 7 teams as a result of human evaluation, the responses of other teams corresponding to

Speaker	Text
User	What can you tell me about the Lovell Lodge?
System	It is a hotel in the north part of town in the moderate price range with a 2 rating, free internet, and free parking
User	Thanks, could you give me the address and phone number?
System	No problem. The Lovell Lodge is located at 365 Milton Road and their phone number is 22.3425478. Is there anything else I can help you with?
User	**Does this place have a strong shower?**
Speaker	**Response**
Label	According to a review I found, the water pressure in the showers at Lovell Lodge is low. Would you like me to look for another option?
Ours	No, Lovell Lodge doesn't seem to have a strong shower. Past guests have said that the bathroom was not as clean as they would have liked and the water pressure was low.
Response 1	According to the reviews I have on hand for that location, the opinions are mixed. Half found the bathrooms exceptionally clean, while half thought they weren't as clean as they would have liked.
Response 2	The Lovell Lodge does have a strong shower according to one guest, but I am not sure how strong it is. Is there anything else I can help you with?
Response 3	The Lovell Lodge has exceptionally clean bathrooms according to most guests, but one guest did say that the bathroom was not as clean as they would have liked.
Response 4	The Lovell Lodge has a strong shower according to one guest. Do you want to make a reservation there?
Response 5	According to the reviews I have on hand for that location, the water pressure there is low and the bathroom wasn't as clean as they would have liked. Sorry to disappoint!
Response 6	The Lovell Lodge does have a weak shower. One reviewer said that the water pressure was low and the bathroom wasn't as clean as she would have liked. Is there anything else I can help you with?

Table 9: Another example of conversations and responses that scored well during human evaluation. Our response clearly answers 'yes/no' to the question and also provides extra information to the user.

our response sentence were extracted and written in Tables 8 and 9. In Table 8, our model gave an appropriate answer to the user's last question and provided additional useful information to the user. Other answers provided incorrect or unclear information or provided correct answers only without providing additional helpful information. In Table 9, we are the only ones who responded with a direct answer of "No", including correct information. A question that starts with the auxiliary verb "Do" means that the question must be answered using yes/no, and questions using 'either A or B' need to be answered as a comparison. In the examples in Tables 8 and 9, it can be seen that our model answered these satisfactorily.

Figure 2 depicts the score of the human evaluation from the DSTC11 Track 5 official release. The y-axis represents the sum of scores regarding the accuracy and appropriateness parts of the three raters. We received mostly higher scores than others and rarely had low scores.

5 Conclusion

In DSTC11 Track 5, we applied data augmentation methods that retain meaning and used a large-size language model. As a result, we obtained the seventh place in the objective evaluation and second place in the final human evaluation. Through various and gradual experimental innovations in the designs, it was found that data augmentation using contextual word embedding and back-translation technique play a major role in improving performance. Using the DeBERTa-v3-large and BART-large language models was also crucial. It was also found that ontology-based augmentation and contrastive search were not very helpful for this task.

6 Future Works

Our experiments have left open various questions and possibilities for future work. Owing to the limitations of the competition period, only empirical results of data augmentation and the use of language models were included in this study. Research on finding the combination of various corpus augmentation methods, finding the optimal amount of augmented data, and finding the best combination of language models needs to be conducted. It is also necessary to test other data augmentation methods that retain meaning, such as data augmentation using ChatGPT and other ontology-based methods similar to WordNet. We hope that these works will be addressed in the future.

References

Ateret Anaby-Tavor, Boaz Carmeli, Esther Goldbraich, Amir Kantor, George Kour, Segev Shlomov, N. Tepper, and Naama Zwerdling. 2020. Do not have enough data? deep learning to the rescue! In *AAAI Conference on Artificial Intelligence*.

Loïc Barrault, Ondřej Bojar, Marta R. Costa-jussà,

Christian Federmann, Mark Fishel, Yvette Graham, Barry Haddow, Matthias Huck, Philipp Koehn, Shervin Malmasi, Christof Monz, Mathias Müller, Santanu Pal, Matt Post, and Marcos Zampieri. 2019. Findings of the 2019 conference on machine translation (WMT19). In *Proceedings of the Fourth Conference on Machine Translation (Volume 2: Shared Task Papers, Day 1)*, pages 1–61, Florence, Italy. Association for Computational Linguistics.

Markus Bayer, Marc-André Kaufhold, Björn Buchhold, Marcel Keller, Jörg Dallmeyer, and Christian Reuter. 2022a. Data augmentation in natural language processing: a novel text generation approach for long and short text classifiers. *International Journal of Machine Learning and Cybernetics*, 14(1):135–150.

Markus Bayer, Marc-André Kaufhold, and Christian Reuter. 2022b. A survey on data augmentation for text classification. *ACM Computing Surveys*, 55(7):1–39.

Yoshua Bengio, Réjean Ducharme, and Pascal Vincent. 2000. A neural probabilistic language model. In *Advances in Neural Information Processing Systems*, volume 13. MIT Press.

Jacob Devlin, Ming-Wei Chang, Kenton Lee, and Kristina Toutanova. 2018. Bert: Pre-training of deep bidirectional transformers for language understanding. *arXiv preprint arXiv:1810.04805*.

Angela Fan, Mike Lewis, and Yann Dauphin. 2018. Hierarchical neural story generation. In *Proceedings of the 56th Annual Meeting of the Association for Computational Linguistics (Volume 1: Long Papers)*, pages 889–898, Melbourne, Australia. Association for Computational Linguistics.

Pengcheng He, Jianfeng Gao, and Weizhu Chen. 2021. Debertav3: Improving deberta using electra-style pretraining with gradient-disentangled embedding sharing. *arXiv preprint arXiv:2111.09543*.

Pengcheng He, Xiaodong Liu, Jianfeng Gao, and Weizhu Chen. 2020. Deberta: Decoding-enhanced bert with disentangled attention. *arXiv preprint arXiv:2006.03654*.

Ari Holtzman, Jan Buys, Li Du, Maxwell Forbes, and Yejin Choi. 2020. The curious case of neural text degeneration. In *International Conference on Learning Representations*.

Jared Kaplan, Sam McCandlish, Tom Henighan, Tom B Brown, Benjamin Chess, Rewon Child, Scott Gray, Alec Radford, Jeffrey Wu, and Dario Amodei. 2020. Scaling laws for neural language models. *arXiv preprint arXiv:2001.08361*.

Seokhwan Kim, Mihail Eric, Karthik Gopalakrishnan, Behnam Hedayatnia, Yang Liu, and Dilek Hakkani-Tur. 2020. Beyond domain APIs: Task-oriented conversational modeling with unstructured knowledge access. In *Proceedings of the 21th Annual Meeting of the Special Interest Group on Discourse and Dialogue*, pages 278–289, 1st virtual meeting. Association for Computational Linguistics.

Seokhwan Kim, Yang Liu, Di Jin, Alexandros Papangelis, Karthik Gopalakrishnan, Behnam Hedayatnia, and Dilek Hakkani-Tür. 2021. "how robust ru?": Evaluating task-oriented dialogue systems on spoken conversations. In *2021 IEEE Automatic Speech Recognition and Understanding Workshop (ASRU)*, pages 1147–1154. IEEE.

Sosuke Kobayashi. 2018. Contextual augmentation: Data augmentation by words with paradigmatic relations. In *Proceedings of the 2018 Conference of the North American Chapter of the Association for Computational Linguistics: Human Language Technologies, Volume 2 (Short Papers)*, pages 452–457, New Orleans, Louisiana. Association for Computational Linguistics.

Varun Kumar, Ashutosh Choudhary, and Eunah Cho. 2020. Data augmentation using pre-trained transformer models. In *Proceedings of the 2nd Workshop on Life-long Learning for Spoken Language Systems*, pages 18–26, Suzhou, China. Association for Computational Linguistics.

Mike Lewis, Yinhan Liu, Naman Goyal, Marjan Ghazvininejad, Abdelrahman Mohamed, Omer Levy, Veselin Stoyanov, and Luke Zettlemoyer. 2020. BART: Denoising sequence-to-sequence pre-training for natural language generation, translation, and comprehension. In *Proceedings of the 58th Annual Meeting of the Association for Computational Linguistics*, pages 7871–7880, Online. Association for Computational Linguistics.

Jiwei Li, Michel Galley, Chris Brockett, Jianfeng Gao, and Bill Dolan. 2016. A diversity-promoting objective function for neural conversation models. In *Proceedings of the 2016 Conference of the North American Chapter of the Association for Computational Linguistics: Human Language Technologies*, pages 110–119, San Diego, California. Association for Computational Linguistics.

Yinhan Liu, Myle Ott, Naman Goyal, Jingfei Du, Mandar Joshi, Danqi Chen, Omer Levy, Mike Lewis, Luke Zettlemoyer, and Veselin Stoyanov. 2019. Roberta: A robustly optimized bert pretraining approach. *arXiv preprint arXiv:1907.11692*.

Son Luu, Kiet Nguyen, and Ngan Nguyen. 2020. Empirical study of text augmentation on social media text in Vietnamese. In *Proceedings of the 34th Pacific Asia Conference on Language, Information and Computation*, pages 462–470, Hanoi, Vietnam. Association for Computational Linguistics.

Edward Ma. 2019. Nlp augmentation. https://github.com/makcedward/nlpaug.

Haitao Mi, Qiyu Ren, Yinpei Dai, Yifan He, Jian Sun, Yongbin Li, Jing Zheng, and Peng Xu. 2021. Towards generalized models for beyond domain api task-oriented dialogue. In *AAAI-21 DSTC9 Workshop*.

Kenton Murray and David Chiang. 2018. Correcting length bias in neural machine translation. In *Proceedings of the Third Conference on Machine Translation: Research Papers*, pages 212–223, Brussels, Belgium. Association for Computational Linguistics.

Rudra Murthy, Anoop Kunchukuttan, and Pushpak Bhattacharyya. 2019. Addressing word-order divergence in multilingual neural machine translation for extremely low resource languages. In *Proceedings of the 2019 Conference of the North American Chapter of the Association for Computational Linguistics: Human Language Technologies, Volume 1 (Long and Short Papers)*, pages 3868–3873, Minneapolis, Minnesota. Association for Computational Linguistics.

Nathan Ng, Kyra Yee, Alexei Baevski, Myle Ott, Michael Auli, and Sergey Edunov. 2019. Facebook fair's wmt19 news translation task submission. *arXiv preprint arXiv:1907.06616*.

Kishore Papineni, Salim Roukos, Todd Ward, and Wei-Jing Zhu. 2002. Bleu: A method for automatic evaluation of machine translation. In *Proceedings of the 40th Annual Meeting on Association for Computational Linguistics*, ACL '02, page 311–318, USA. Association for Computational Linguistics.

Alec Radford, Jeffrey Wu, Rewon Child, David Luan, Dario Amodei, Ilya Sutskever, et al. 2019. Language models are unsupervised multitask learners. *OpenAI blog*, 1(8):9.

Colin Raffel, Noam Shazeer, Adam Roberts, Katherine Lee, Sharan Narang, Michael Matena, Yanqi Zhou, Wei Li, and Peter J Liu. 2020. Exploring the limits of transfer learning with a unified text-to-text transformer. *The Journal of Machine Learning Research*, 21(1):5485–5551.

Rico Sennrich, Barry Haddow, and Alexandra Birch. 2016. Improving neural machine translation models with monolingual data. In *Proceedings of the 54th Annual Meeting of the Association for Computational Linguistics (Volume 1: Long Papers)*, pages 86–96, Berlin, Germany. Association for Computational Linguistics.

Yuanlong Shao, Stephan Gouws, Denny Britz, Anna Goldie, Brian Strope, and Ray Kurzweil. 2017. Generating high-quality and informative conversation responses with sequence-to-sequence models. In *Proceedings of the 2017 Conference on Empirical Methods in Natural Language Processing*, pages 2210–2219, Copenhagen, Denmark. Association for Computational Linguistics.

Yixuan Su, Tian Lan, Yan Wang, Dani Yogatama, Lingpeng Kong, and Nigel Collier. 2022. A contrastive framework for neural text generation. In *Advances in Neural Information Processing Systems*.

Jörg Tiedemann. 2020. The tatoeba translation challenge – realistic data sets for low resource and multilingual MT. In *Proceedings of the Fifth Conference on Machine Translation*, pages 1174–1182, Online. Association for Computational Linguistics.

Ashish Vaswani, Noam Shazeer, Niki Parmar, Jakob Uszkoreit, Llion Jones, Aidan N Gomez, Łukasz Kaiser, and Illia Polosukhin. 2017. Attention is all you need. *Advances in neural information processing systems*, 30.

William Yang Wang and Diyi Yang. 2015. That's so annoying!!!: A lexical and frame-semantic embedding based data augmentation approach to automatic categorization of annoying behaviors using #petpeeve tweets. In *Proceedings of the 2015 Conference on Empirical Methods in Natural Language Processing*, pages 2557–2563, Lisbon, Portugal. Association for Computational Linguistics.

Jason Wei and Kai Zou. 2019. EDA: Easy data augmentation techniques for boosting performance on text classification tasks. In *Proceedings of the 2019 Conference on Empirical Methods in Natural Language Processing and the 9th International Joint Conference on Natural Language Processing (EMNLP-IJCNLP)*, pages 6382–6388, Hong Kong, China. Association for Computational Linguistics.

Sean Welleck, Ilia Kulikov, Stephen Roller, Emily Dinan, Kyunghyun Cho, and Jason Weston. 2020. Neural text generation with unlikelihood training. In *International Conference on Learning Representations*.

Xing Wu, Shangwen Lv, Liangjun Zang, Jizhong Han, and Songlin Hu. 2019. Conditional bert contextual augmentation. In *Computational Science – ICCS 2019*, pages 84–95, Cham. Springer International Publishing.

Xinnuo Xu, Guoyin Wang, Young-Bum Kim, and Sungjin Lee. 2021. AugNLG: Few-shot natural language generation using self-trained data augmentation. In *Proceedings of the 59th Annual Meeting of the Association for Computational Linguistics and the 11th International Joint Conference on Natural Language Processing (Volume 1: Long Papers)*, pages 1183–1195, Online. Association for Computational Linguistics.

Yilin Yang, Liang Huang, and Mingbo Ma. 2018. Breaking the beam search curse: A study of (re-)scoring methods and stopping criteria for neural machine translation. In *Proceedings of the 2018 Conference on Empirical Methods in Natural Language Processing*, pages 3054–3059, Brussels, Belgium. Association for Computational Linguistics.

Yichong Xu Shuohang Wang Ruochen Xu Chenguang Zhu Yang Liu, Dan Iter. 2023. G-eval: Nlg evaluation using gpt-4 with better human alignment.

Xiang Zhang, Junbo Zhao, and Yann LeCun. 2015. Character-level convolutional networks for text classification. In *Advances in Neural Information Processing Systems*, volume 28. Curran Associates, Inc.

Chao Zhao, Spandana Gella, Seokhwan Kim, Di Jin, Devamanyu Hazarika, Alexandros Papangelis, Behnam Hedayatnia, Mahdi Namazifar, Yang Liu, and Dilek Hakkani-Tur. 2023. "what do others think?": Task-oriented conversational modeling with subjective knowledge.

Ensemble Method via Ranking Model for Conversational Modeling with Subjective Knowledge

Xin Huang, Kye Min Tan, Richeng Duan, Bowei Zou
Institute for Infocomm Research (I2R), A*STAR, Singapore
{huangx2,tan_kye_min,Duan_Richeng,zou_bowei}@i2r.a-star.edu.sg

Abstract

This paper describes our submission to the fifth track of the 11th Dialog System Technology Challenge (DSTC11), which focuses on "Task-oriented Conversational Modeling with Subjective Knowledge". We focus on response generation and leverage a ranking strategy to ensemble individual models of BART, Long-T5, and a fine-tuned large language model based on LLaMA. The strategy is supplemented by other techniques like low rank adaptation to maintain efficient utilization of these large models while still achieving optimal performance. The experiments show that the ensemble method outperforms individual models and the baseline method. Our model was ranked 1st place in ROUGE_1, 2nd place in ROUGE_L score and 4th place in human evaluation among a total of 14 participating teams.

1 Introduction

The task of developing effective and engaging task-oriented dialogue systems has been a subject of ongoing research and development in the field of natural language processing (NLP). Traditional approaches to task-oriented dialogue systems have focused on providing information and performing actions based on predefined rules or accessing back-end databases or APIs. However, user requests may sometimes require information outside the scope of these structured resources, requiring the system to incorporate additional domain knowledge from external unstructured sources.

Past challenges such as DSTC9 track 1 (Kim et al., 2021a) and DSTC10 track 2 (Kim et al., 2021b) have proposed the use of unstructured knowledge from FAQs to build a knowledge-grounded task-oriented dialogue system. The tasks proposed in DSTC11 track 5 build off past work by including subjective knowledge from customer reviews, which also involves addressing the complexity of differentiating multiple aspects within a single review post, conflicting opinions, and comparison requests between entities.

We primarily focus on the third sub-task of this challenge, which involves response generation. Our approach combines the utilization of large foundational language models with a ranking strategy for response prioritization. Additionally, we employ the method of low rank adaptation (LoRA) (Hu et al., 2021) to keep resource usage low while training and using such large models. To enhance generation performance, we employ an ensemble technique that combines multiple individual models, leveraging the capabilities of GPT-4 (OpenAI, 2023) in the process. Our final model achieved impressive rankings in the evaluation metrics. It secured the 1st place in ROUGE_1, the 2nd place in ROUGE_L score, and the 4th place in human evaluation. This demonstrates the effectiveness and competitiveness of our approach in the challenge.

2 Related Work

Several methods of improving knowledge-grounded task-oriented dialogue systems have been explored by participants in past DSTC challenges. Thulke et al. (2023) implemented a noisy channel model to separate the tasks of generating a response and incorporating knowledge by reranking multiple candidate responses. He et al. (2021a) and Tian et al. (2021) both use large pre-trained language models exceeding 1 billion parameters to generate the final response. The former focuses on incorporating structured knowledge from MultiWOZ 2.2 (Zang et al., 2020) and negative sampling for the knowledge selection task, while the latter explores several approaches to generating more synthetic dialogue data.

The scaling up of large language models in recent years has continued to show gains in terms of performance and abilities (Wei et al., 2022). However, the prohibitive cost of fine-tuning all the parameters in these models has led to the exploration

Proceedings of The Eleventh Dialog System Technology Challenge, pages 177–184
September 11, 2023 ©2023 Association for Computational Linguistics

of parameter efficient fine-tuning strategies, such as adapter layers (Houlsby et al., 2019), prompt tuning (Liu et al., 2021; Li and Liang, 2021; Liu et al., 2022), and LoRA (Hu et al., 2021).

3 Task Description

The aim of this challenge track is to generate a relevant response given a set of user and agent turns, and a knowledge base which may contain information relevant to the user's query. This is further divided into 3 sub-tasks:

1. Knowledge Turn Detection: Determining whether a given query is knowledge-seeking and should be handled by the following steps
2. Knowledge Selection: Selecting knowledge snippets consisting of user reviews and FAQs relevant to the query
3. Response Generation: Generating a response to the query based on knowledge snippets selected in the previous step

The training data provided for this challenge includes 28,431 dialogues, of which 14,768 are knowledge-seeking turns which will be processed by the knowledge selection and response generation steps. A knowledge base containing subjective knowledge in the form of user reviews and objective knowledge in the form of FAQs is also provided. The dialogues are augmented from MultiWoz 2.1 to include additional knowledge-seeking turns which require information from the knowledge base. All dialogues and knowledge snippets belong to either the hotel or restaurant domain. Table 1 shows the quantities of dialogue data and knowledge for these two domains. Additionally, each knowledge snippet is labeled with the name of the entity (hotel or restaurant) it refers to, the reviewer profile for user reviews (solo, couple, family, friends, colleagues), and the food and drink items mentioned in restaurant reviews. On average, each knowledge seeking turn in the train set has 3.80 relevant knowledge snippets, while the validation set has 4.07 relevant knowledge snippets.

4 Methodology

Figure 1 depicts the overall architecture of our methods.

Type	Hotel	Rest.
Dialogues (Train)	7859	6909
Dialogues (Valid)	1436	693
Entities	33	110
Reviews	330	1100
FAQs	1219	1650

Table 1: Quantity of data by domain.

4.1 Knowledge Seeking Detection (KTD)

In sub-task 1, which focuses on knowledge-seeking turn detection, we employ the baseline method which utilizes a DeBERTa (He et al., 2021b) model to encode the concatenated input of the dialogue context $C = [U_1, S_1 ... U_t, S_t]$, including user utterance U_i and system response S_i at each step of the conversation. To classify whether the current user utterance contains a knowledge-seeking request, we utilize a binary classifier, which leverages the encoded representation of the dialogue context produced by the DeBERTa model to make predictions.

$$h = DeBERTa(C)$$

$$P(C) = softmax(Dense(h))$$

4.2 Knowledge Entity Matching

The goal of knowledge entity matching process is to select entities $E = \{e_1, ..., e_m\}$ which are relevant to the user utterance given dialogue context C and a list of knowledge snippets. We follow the baseline which uses a word-matching method based on Jin et al. (2021) for entity extraction. Specifically, the method first applies a list of heuristic rules which are used to normalize entity names, then uses n-gram fuzzy matching between the normalized entity names and all dialogue turn utterances. The longest contiguous matching subsequence (LCS) algorithm is used to calculate the similarity between a entity name and a user utterance, and a threshold of 0.95 is used to determine whether an entity is considered a match. Finally, the method selects the entities from the last dialogue turn in which entities are detected.

4.3 Knowledge Selection

The knowledge selection task aims to select knowledge snippets which are relevant to the current user utterance at each turn given dialogue context C and a list of candidate knowledge snippets $K^E = \{k_1^E, ..., k_n^E\}$ where each element of the

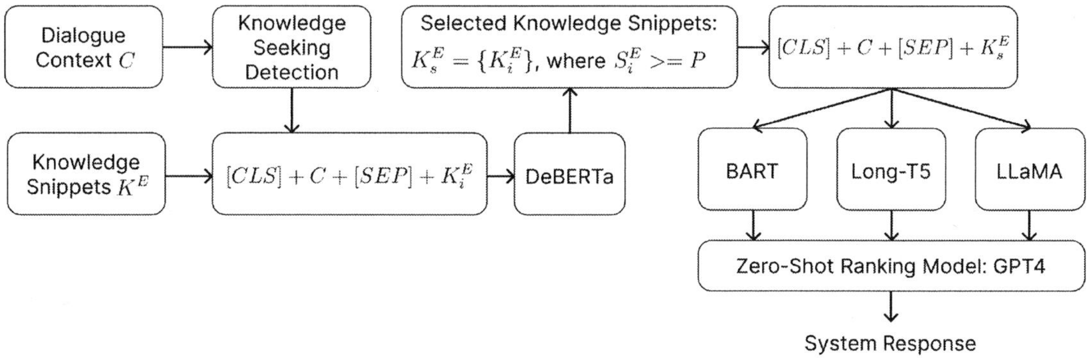

Figure 1: The overall architecture of our methods

knowledge snippets belongs to the selected entities E during the entity matching process.

We consider the knowledge selection process as a sequence classification task. Formally, for each turn, the method first concatenates the dialogue history with each candidate knowledge snippet k_i^E from the matched knowledge entities E. A DeBERTa encoder is used to encode the concatenated input to obtain hidden representation h_i and then a classification head followed by a softmax function is used to obtain the relevance probability of the candidate knowledge snippet.

$$U_i^E = [C, K_i^E]$$
$$h_i^E = Deberta(U_i^E)$$
$$S_i^E = Softmax(Dense(h_i^E))$$

During training, a sampling approach is used to reduce the number of negative candidate snippets from the large candidate space in the knowledge base. Following the baseline, we only sample negative candidates from entities which are relevant to the dialogue. A binary cross-entropy loss is used to optimize the model. As the number of knowledge snippets required for each dialogue varies, a threshold P is applied to the relevance probabilities to select candidate snippets during inference. P is estimated based on the validation set. As the optimal P for the test set may be different, we dynamically vary the threshold during inference by lowering it if no knowledge candidates meet the original threshold. We repeat this process until at least one knowledge snippet is selected.

4.4 Response Generation

The response generation task aims to generate a proper system response for user requests for knowledge given dialogue context C and selected knowledge snippets K_s^E. We first adapt the following transformer based models including encoder-decoder models and decoder-only models to generate a system response based on the concatenated input of dialogue context C and concatenated knowledge snippets K_s^E as a single string:

1. BART model (Lewis et al., 2020): the same model used in the baseline, we increase the maximum input knowledge token size from 256 to 512 to avoid knowledge cutoff for some turns.

2. Long-T5 model (Guo et al., 2022): Long-T5 model purposes local attention and transient global attention methods which show improved performance for long sentence generation tasks such as summarization. We hypothesize that a model with strong summarization capabilities will be beneficial for combining information across multiple user reviews, thus improving the quality of the response.

3. LLaMA model (Touvron et al., 2023): The LLaMA model is a foundation decoder-only model which is pre-trained on more than 1 trillion tokens. Recent research like Peng et al. (2023) also show that the LLaMA model is capable of GPT-4 like performance after instruction tuning. In this challenge, we explore directly fine-tuning the original LLaMA model.

We first train all 3 models including BART, Long-T5 and LLaMA model individually with all 3 models using the same input from the knowledge-seeking detection and knowledge selection task. For BART and T5 model, we reuse the baseline approach to train the model while only changing the tokenizer and encoder-decoder model. For LLaMA model, we use the parameter efficient tuning method LoRA for model fine-tuning which can avoid memory issues using limited GPU resources. We train the model to maximize next token probability via aligned language modeling.

4.5 Response ranking

To encourage diversity of the system response and utilize strong points from different models, we propose an ensemble method for generating the final response via ranking of the three models by a ranking model.

The goal of the ranking model is to give scores S_j for the quality of the response given the concatenated input of dialogue context C, concatenated knowledge snippets K_s^E and output of each generation model $o_j, j \in \{1, 2, 3\}$. We designed a customized prompt p_c for the independent model in order to perform zero-shot evaluation on the response generation by different models. We make use of a large language model GPT-4 and use their API for the evaluation.

$$S_j = GPT4([p_c, C, K_s^E, o_j]), j \in \{1, 2, 3\}$$

Then we ensemble the model outputs using two methods: 1) select the model output with the highest score for each turn. 2) select the model output with the highest score only if the output of the best reference model scores below or equal to a threshold S_t, otherwise we select the output of the best reference model instead. We consider the best reference model using human evaluation on the dev-set with a likert scale of 1 to 5 by sampling N utterances as our best reference model.

5 Experiments

5.1 Sub-task 1: Knowledge-Seeking Turn Detection (KTD)

For the knowledge turn detection task, we use the baseline implementation of a DeBERTa v3 model with a binary classifier.

Data: For training, we use all 28431 dialogue samples in the provided dataset. For validation, we use all 4173 dialogue samples in the dataset.

Metrics: The evaluation metrics for KTD are precision, recall, and F1.

Hyperparameters: We use the baseline hyperparameters of learning rate $\alpha = 3 * 10^{-5}$, number of epochs $E = 10$, maximum history token size of 510, and Adam optimizer with $\epsilon = 10^{-8}$ and $\beta_1 = 0.9, \beta_2 = 0.999$.

5.2 Sub-task 2: Knowledge Selection (KS)

For the knowledge selection task, we also use the DeBERTa model as a cross encoder followed by a classifier as implemented in the baseline. During inference, we begin by filtering knowledge snippets by the probability estimated by the model using the threshold P, and repeatedly lower it by 0.5 if none of the candidates meet the threshold.

Data: For training, we use 14768 dialogue samples which require knowledge access. The validation set consists of 2129 dialogue samples.

Metrics: The evaluation metrics for KS are precision, recall, and F1 on the snippet level, where the metrics are calculated across all <C, K_S> pairs.

Hyperparameters: We use the baseline hyperparameters of learning rate $\alpha = 3 * 10^{-5}$, number of epochs $E = 3$, maximum history and knowledge token size of 256 each, and Adam optimizer with $\epsilon = 10^{-8}$ and $\beta_1 = 0.9, \beta_2 = 0.999$.

5.3 Sub-task 3: Response Generation (RG)

For RG, our initial experimentation involves generating responses independently from individual models, including BART, Long-T5, and LLaMA. To further enhance the quality and effectiveness of the responses, we employ an ensemble approach. We utilize GPT-4 to score the responses generated by the individual models for each dialogue turn. The scores assigned by GPT-4 are used to determine the most suitable response from the ensemble of models, which allows us to leverage the strengths of each individual model while mitigating their weaknesses.

Data: Similar to the KS task, we use 14768 training samples and 2129 validation samples which have knowledge and system response labels.

Metrics: The automatic evaluation metrics for RG task include BLEU (Papineni et al., 2002), ROUGE (Lin, 2004), and METEOR (Banerjee and Lavie, 2005). Apart from the official human evaluation, we also internally assess the results of different models for aspect accuracy.

Hyperparameters: For the Bart and Long-T5 model, we chose the same hyperparameters of learning rate $\alpha = 5 * 10^{-5}$, number of epochs $E = 3$, maximum history and knowledge token size of 512, and we use the Adam optimizer with $\epsilon = 10^{-8}$ and $\beta_1 = 0.9, \beta_2 = 0.999$. We select transient-global attention for Long-T5 model.

For the LLaMA model we select the pretrained LLaMA model with 7 billion parameters, and we chose LoRA rank $r = 8$ which applies to W_q, W_v for this experiment. For the ensembled model, we set the reference model as LLaMA model because it scores highest based on our human evaluation on the dev-set. We chose ensembling score threshold $S_t = 3$ with a scoring likert scale of 1 to 5.

6 Results and Analysis

We present our experimental results and analyses in this section.

6.1 Sub-task 1: Knowledge-Seeking Turn Detection (KTD)

Data Split	P	R	F1
Validation	99.92	99.95	99.93
Test	99.86	99.79	99.82

Table 2: Evaluation results for Task 1 on validation and test set.

Data		Metrics		
Train	Val	P	R	F1
H	H	99.86	99.86	99.86
	R	99.33	86.00	92.19
R	H	99.91	79.46	88.52
	R	99.86	100.0	99.93
All	H	100.0	99.86	99.93
	R	99.86	99.86	99.86

Table 3: Analysis of domain masking for Task 1 on the validation set. H and R represent hotel and restaurant domains respectively

The performance of the baseline model for sub-task 1 is presented in Table 2. Although the model demonstrates near-perfect performance on both the validation and test sets, we conducted an examination of its generalization capability through domain masking in this work. Table 3 shows the performance of the model in the cross-domain evaluation setting. The results reveal a substantial decline in performance when validating on the masked domains, especially in terms of recall, suggesting that the model's effectiveness diminishes when confronted with unseen domains. This drop in performance underscores the challenge of domain adaptation in KTD, as in most NLP tasks. These findings also emphasize the need to carefully consider domain adaptation during test set construction and further explore this aspect in future research endeavors.

6.2 Sub-task 2: Knowledge Selection (KS)

Model	P	R	F1	EM
Fixed P	**77.11**	82.01	79.48	42.39
Dynamic P	77.03	**82.17**	**79.52**	**42.47**

Table 4: Evaluation results for Task 2 on test set.

Data		Metrics			
Train	Val	P	R	F1	EM
H	H	72.94	92.99	81.75	32.34
	R	33.59	83.79	47.96	18.59
R	H	72.21	80.56	76.15	28.44
	R	73.22	78.90	75.96	35.73
All	H	81.64	94.39	99.93	43.32
	R	68.59	80.70	74.15	36.46

Table 5: Analysis of domain masking for Task 2 on the validation set. H and R represent hotel and restaurant domains respectively

We analyze the effect of dynamically adjusting the threshold, P for KS. Using a fixed P obtained from tuning on the validation set, we find that no knowledge snippets are retrieved for 31 out of 2796 samples filtered by the KTD step. We observe a small uplift in recall, F1, and exact match metrics in the test set after using a dynamic P value, as shown in Table 4.

As with the KTD task, we also evaluated the KS model by domain masking, presented in Table 5. We observe that masking domains in this case also negatively impacts the performance of unmasked domains, which may be due to the limited amount of training data used. We also note that performance on the restaurant domain is comparatively weaker, which may be due to the larger number of knowledge snippets (as shown in Table 1) and the additional aspect of food types compared to the hotel domain. Hence, further improvement to the KS task may be obtained by focusing on improving the quality or availability of restaurant domain data.

6.3 Sub-task 3: Response Generation (RG)

Table 7 provides a summary of the automatic evaluation results for various models on the task 3 test set. Notably, each individual model exhibits its own strengths: Long T5 achieves the highest BLEU

U: Is there any restaurants located in the north side of town? S: There is one. It is da vinci pizzeria. Shall I book it? U: Does Da Vinci Pizzeria serve portions that are plentiful?
BART: Yes, Da Vinci Pizzeria does serve portions that are plentiful. Past guests have said that the portions are plentiful. Would you like to know more about them? **Long-T5**: The Da Vinci Pizzeria serves plentiful portions, but some customers have said that the portions are too small. **LLaMA**: Yes, Da Vinci Pizzeria does serve portion sizes that are plentiful. Would you like to know more about them? **E2.**: The Da Vinci Pizzeria serves plentiful portions, but some customers have said that the portions are too small. **GPT-4 (standalone)**: Some customers feel that Da Vinci Pizzeria serves portions that are plentiful and satisfying, while others think the portions are relatively small. It can vary depending on personal preferences and appetites. If you enjoy hearty portions, you might want to explore other options or consider ordering extra items to ensure you're fully satisfied.
Reference: Some past customers do feel that the portions are plentiful, but there are others who felt that they are too small.

Table 6: Sampled output of our different models. For GPT-4 (standalone), we directly instruct prompting the GPT-4 using input of dialogue context C and selected knowledge K_s^E for answer generation.

Model	BLEU	MT	R-1	R-2	R-L
Baseline	10.04	17.48	35.20	14.30	27.53
Long T5	**10.50**	16.91	34.72	14.66	27.93
BART	10.20	17.50	35.28	14.34	27.60
LLaMA	9.44	17.47	36.52	14.94	**28.75**
E1.	9.84	17.74	**36.58**	**15.09**	**28.75**
E2. ($S_t = 3$)	10.24	**17.76**	36.33	15.08	28.65

Table 7: Automatic evaluation results on test-set for Task 3. Evaluation metrics including BLEU-4 (BLEU), ROUGE (R-1, R-2, R-L), METEOR (MT). E1. stands for our first ensemble method, and E2. stands for the second ensemble method with threshold $S_t = 3$.

Model	Score		PCC
	Human	GPT-4	
BART	3.64	4.12	0.3626
Long T5	3.36	4.07	0.2856
LLaMA	3.88	4.28	0.2884
E1.	**3.90**	4.52	0.1785
E2. ($S_t = 3$)	3.82	**4.73**	0.3026

Table 8: Comparison between the average scores of our internal human evaluation and GPT4 evaluation for Task 3, and Pearson correlation coefficients (PCC).

score, BART excels in METEOR, and LLaMA performs best in terms of ROUGE score. Furthermore, we observe that the performance of $E1.$ closely approaches that of the reference model LLaMA, suggesting that a naive ranking method may not outperform the strongest individual model. The method $E2.$ with $S_t = 3$ yields the best overall performance and we use Table 6 to showcase sampled outputs from different models. It is evident that the results generated by BART and LLaMA lack some negative opinions, while Long T5 effectively summarizes the reviews in this case. The ensemble model successfully selects Long T5 as the final output, thereby maintaining the appropriateness of the response compared to the standalone zero-shot response generation by GPT-4.

Table 8 illustrates the results obtained from both human assessors and GPT-4 for our models on the test set for RG. For human evaluation, we enlist the expertise of four NLP experts who employ a Likert scale, ranging from 1 to 5, to rate the responses. The experts are provided with the dialogue context, oracle knowledge snippets, and predicted response for each model. To ensure consistency and reliability, we randomly sample a total of 120 instances and divide them into four groups. Among these groups, each pair has a 30% overlap, enabling us to assess the consistency of scores. The scores assigned by the experts aim to evaluate the aspect accuracy of the response. To determine the level of agreement among the experts, we calculate the average score difference. This amounts to 0.3, which indicates a mutual agreement regarding the scoring of the response, ensuring a reliable evaluation process.

From Table 8, we first see the two ensemble methods outperform individual models in terms of both human and GPT-4 ratings, suggesting that the responses generated by the ensemble approach are better. We can also observe that GPT-4's scores generally align with the scores given by the human evaluators for the different models, which indicates that GPT-4 possesses a reasonable ability to assess Task 3, though not completely consistent with human judgments. We also calculate Pearson correlation coefficients using the equation:

$$\rho_{X,Y} = \frac{\sum_{i=1}^{n}(X_i - \bar{X})(Y_i - \bar{Y})}{\sqrt{\sum_{i=1}^{n}(X_i - \bar{X})^2 \sum_{i=1}^{n}(Y_i - \bar{Y})^2}}$$

, where n is the number of samples in the test set, X is human evaluators' score and Y is GPT-

4's score, for each of the models and ensemble methods, which shows that GPT-4's and the human evaluators' judgement is weakly correlated. Further investigation of individual samples with negative correlation reveals cases where both the human raters and GPT-4 assigned scores inconsistent with judging criteria. For future evaluations, well-defined judging criteria and experimenting with different prompts may improve the accuracy and consistency of scores.

GPT-4's scoring is based on its training data and may excel in assessing certain aspects such as grammar or syntax but might struggle with understanding context-dependent nuances that human evaluators are typically adept at capturing. The alignment between the scores assigned by GPT-4, human evaluations, and the ROUGE scores obtained through automatic evaluation in Table 7 highlights an intriguing consistency. This suggests that ROUGE can offer valuable insights into the correctness of text generation. Nevertheless, for a comprehensive assessment, it is crucial to consider multiple evaluation criteria and perspectives when evaluating response generation models.

Model	Approp.	Asp-Acc	Average
Baseline	3.6348	2.8715	3.2531
Best Team	**3.6596**	**2.9095**	**3.2846**
E2. ($S_t = 3$)	3.6487	2.8908	3.2697

Table 9: Official human evaluation results for Task 3.

The official human evaluation results for this challenge are presented in Table 9, assessing the appropriateness of the response and aspect accuracy as evaluation metrics. Our submission of the ensemble method with $S_t = 3$ achieved the 4th place in the official human evaluation. However, the top-performing model only exhibited a marginal improvement of 0.0149 in terms of average score compared to our method. We attribute our performance gap relative to the best model primarily to our weaker performance in task 2, where the best model demonstrated a significant 4.2% absolute improvement over our submission in terms of F1 score for knowledge snippet selection. The incorrect selection of knowledge snippets can adversely impact the performance of both individual models and the ranking model.

7 Conclusion

In this work, we demonstrated an ensemble method that utilizes a ranking strategy to combine outputs from various large models for response generation. Our submission to the DSTC11 Track 5 challenge achieved the highest Rouge_1 score and secured the 2nd place for Rouge_L score in sub-task 3, despite relatively weaker performance in sub-task 1 and 2. Furthermore, we conducted an analysis on domain masking for sub-task 1 and 2 to assess performance in handling requests from unseen domains. Our findings highlight the need for further exploration to improve performance when the system encounters domains that significantly differ from the training data.

8 Limitations

Currently, our method uses GPT-4 for ranking individual models, but this introduces a dependency on an external service that may not always be available. In our future work, we intend to explore the utilization of an easily accessible ranking model to mitigate this dependency.

Additionally, our method requires a list of different models for result ensembling which further adds to inference cost. We plan to investigate the usage of a single open-source large language model for both answer generation and self evaluation in future work.

As with most large language models currently published, we are unable to guarantee the safety and freedom from bias of its output as it was trained on clean data, and further work in ensuring safety is recommended before the system is used as part of a large scale operation.

References

Satanjeev Banerjee and Alon Lavie. 2005. METEOR: An automatic metric for MT evaluation with improved correlation with human judgments. In *Proceedings of the ACL Workshop on Intrinsic and Extrinsic Evaluation Measures for Machine Translation and/or Summarization*, pages 65–72, Ann Arbor, Michigan. Association for Computational Linguistics.

Mandy Guo, Joshua Ainslie, David Uthus, Santiago Ontanon, Jianmo Ni, Yun-Hsuan Sung, and Yinfei Yang. 2022. LongT5: Efficient text-to-text transformer for long sequences. In *Findings of the Association for Computational Linguistics: NAACL 2022*, pages 724–736, Seattle, United States. Association for Computational Linguistics.

H. He, Hua Lu, Siqi Bao, Fan Wang, Hua Wu, Zhengyu Niu, and Haifeng Wang. 2021a. Learning to select external knowledge with multi-scale negative sampling. *ArXiv*, abs/2102.02096.

Pengcheng He, Xiaodong Liu, Jianfeng Gao, and Weizhu Chen. 2021b. Deberta: Decoding-enhanced bert with disentangled attention.

Neil Houlsby, Andrei Giurgiu, Stanislaw Jastrzebski, Bruna Morrone, Quentin de Laroussilhe, Andrea Gesmundo, Mona Attariyan, and Sylvain Gelly. 2019. Parameter-efficient transfer learning for nlp. In *International Conference on Machine Learning*.

Edward J. Hu, Yelong Shen, Phillip Wallis, Zeyuan Allen-Zhu, Yuanzhi Li, Shean Wang, Lu Wang, and Weizhu Chen. 2021. Lora: Low-rank adaptation of large language models.

Di Jin, Seokhwan Kim, and Dilek Hakkani-Tur. 2021. Can I be of further assistance? using unstructured knowledge access to improve task-oriented conversational modeling. In *Proceedings of the 1st Workshop on Document-grounded Dialogue and Conversational Question Answering (DialDoc 2021)*, pages 119–127, Online. Association for Computational Linguistics.

Seokhwan Kim, Mihail Eric, Behnam Hedayatnia, Karthik Gopalakrishnan, Yang Liu, Chao-Wei Huang, and Dilek Hakkani-Tur. 2021a. Beyond domain apis: Task-oriented conversational modeling with unstructured knowledge access track in dstc9.

Seokhwan Kim, Yang Liu, Di Jin, Alexandros Papangelis, Karthik Gopalakrishnan, Behnam Hedayatnia, and Dilek Hakkani-Tur. 2021b. "how robust r u?": Evaluating task-oriented dialogue systems on spoken conversations.

Mike Lewis, Yinhan Liu, Naman Goyal, Marjan Ghazvininejad, Abdelrahman Mohamed, Omer Levy, Veselin Stoyanov, and Luke Zettlemoyer. 2020. BART: Denoising sequence-to-sequence pre-training for natural language generation, translation, and comprehension. In *Proceedings of the 58th Annual Meeting of the Association for Computational Linguistics*, pages 7871–7880, Online. Association for Computational Linguistics.

Xiang Lisa Li and Percy Liang. 2021. Prefix-tuning: Optimizing continuous prompts for generation. In *Proceedings of the 59th Annual Meeting of the Association for Computational Linguistics and the 11th International Joint Conference on Natural Language Processing (Volume 1: Long Papers)*, pages 4582–4597, Online. Association for Computational Linguistics.

Chin-Yew Lin. 2004. ROUGE: A package for automatic evaluation of summaries. In *Text Summarization Branches Out*, pages 74–81, Barcelona, Spain. Association for Computational Linguistics.

Xiao Liu, Kaixuan Ji, Yicheng Fu, Weng Tam, Zhengxiao Du, Zhilin Yang, and Jie Tang. 2022. P-tuning: Prompt tuning can be comparable to fine-tuning across scales and tasks. In *Proceedings of the 60th Annual Meeting of the Association for Computational Linguistics (Volume 2: Short Papers)*, pages 61–68, Dublin, Ireland. Association for Computational Linguistics.

Xiao Liu, Yanan Zheng, Zhengxiao Du, Ming Ding, Yujie Qian, Zhilin Yang, and Jie Tang. 2021. Gpt understands, too.

OpenAI. 2023. Gpt-4 technical report.

Kishore Papineni, Salim Roukos, Todd Ward, and Wei-Jing Zhu. 2002. Bleu: a method for automatic evaluation of machine translation. In *Proceedings of the 40th Annual Meeting of the Association for Computational Linguistics*, pages 311–318, Philadelphia, Pennsylvania, USA. Association for Computational Linguistics.

Baolin Peng, Chunyuan Li, Pengcheng He, Michel Galley, and Jianfeng Gao. 2023. Instruction tuning with gpt-4.

David Thulke, Nico Daheim, Christian Dugast, and Hermann Ney. 2023. Task-oriented document-grounded dialog systems by hltpr@rwth for dstc9 and dstc10.

Xin Tian, Xinxian Huang, Dongfeng He, Yingzhan Lin, Siqi Bao, Huang He, Liankai Huang, Qiang Ju, Xiyuan Zhang, Jian Xie, Shuqi Sun, Fan Wang, Hua Wu, and Haifeng Wang. 2021. Tod-da: Towards boosting the robustness of task-oriented dialogue modeling on spoken conversations.

Hugo Touvron, Thibaut Lavril, Gautier Izacard, Xavier Martinet, Marie-Anne Lachaux, Timothée Lacroix, Baptiste Rozière, Naman Goyal, Eric Hambro, Faisal Azhar, Aurelien Rodriguez, Armand Joulin, Edouard Grave, and Guillaume Lample. 2023. Llama: Open and efficient foundation language models.

Jason Wei, Yi Tay, Rishi Bommasani, Colin Raffel, Barret Zoph, Sebastian Borgeaud, Dani Yogatama, Maarten Bosma, Denny Zhou, Donald Metzler, Ed H. Chi, Tatsunori Hashimoto, Oriol Vinyals, Percy Liang, Jeff Dean, and William Fedus. 2022. Emergent abilities of large language models. *Transactions on Machine Learning Research*. Survey Certification.

Xiaoxue Zang, Abhinav Rastogi, Srinivas Sunkara, Raghav Gupta, Jianguo Zhang, and Jindong Chen. 2020. MultiWOZ 2.2 : A dialogue dataset with additional annotation corrections and state tracking baselines. In *Proceedings of the 2nd Workshop on Natural Language Processing for Conversational AI*, pages 109–117, Online. Association for Computational Linguistics.

Exploring Back Translation with Typo Noise for Enhanced Inquiry Understanding in Task-Oriented Dialogue

Jihyun Lee[1*], Junseok Kim[2*], Gary Geunbae Lee[1,2]
[1]Graduate School of Artificial Intelligence, POSTECH, Republic of Korea
[2]Department of Computer Science and Engineering, POSTECH, Republic of Korea
{jihyunlee, junseokkim00, gblee}@postech.ac.kr

Abstract

This paper presents our approach to the DSTC11 Track 5 selection task, which focuses on retrieving appropriate natural language knowledge sources for task-oriented dialogue. We propose typologically diverse back-translation method with typo noise, which could generate various structured user inquries. Through our noised back translation, we augmented inquiries by combining three different typologies of language sources with five different typo noise injections. Our experiments demonstrate that typological variety and typo noise aids the model in generalizing to diverse user inquiries in dialogue. In the competition, where 14 teams participated, our approach achieved the 5th rank for exact matching metric.

1 Introduction

Task-oriented dialogue (TOD) systems have been developed to offer information and perform specific tasks such as making reservations. In general, TOD systems depend on domain-specific APIs and pre-defined databases (DB), limiting their ability to handle a wide range of scenarios. (Eric et al., 2019; Rastogi et al., 2020). In order to enhance their capabilities and offer more valuable assistance, recent studies have incorporated unstructured textual information from the web into a dialogue system (Dimitrakis et al., 2018; Kim et al., 2020; Majumder et al., 2022).

However, in order to effectively integrate unstructured information, a more advanced comprehension of the user's utterances is needed. For example, when a user mentions having a backache and asks for hotel recommendations, the model should accurately comprehend the user's core intentions (e.g., "need a *comfortable* bed") and extract relevant information from the hotel review set rather than rely only on a pre-defined DB. By precisely understanding the user's question and leveraging others' comments, the model can respond with up-to-date information and diverse perspectives. Unfortunately, precise methods for effectively utilizing these knowledge sources have not been thoroughly researched yet in TOD systems.

DSTC11-track 5 selection task (Zhao et al., 2023) was introduced to address this challenge. Unlike previous TOD approaches that rely on a pre-defined DB, this task offers an external natural language form knowledge source that contains reviews and Q&As. Participants are required to devise approaches that select the relevant information from the provided knowledge source. This track's objective is to improve the system's capacity to accurately address user inquiries by integrating external sources, going beyond the structured information.

Even if a user is asking a commonly asked question, the inquiry form can vary in their words or sentence structure, highlighting the importance of comprehending the core intent behind the user's utterance. To address this, a larger training dataset is essential to ensure robustness and generalize to a diverse form of inquiries. To tackle this challenge, we augment user inquiries by leveraging the back translation, which has been widely used for low-resource problems (Hoang et al., 2018a; Burlot and Yvon, 2019; Caswell et al., 2019; Marie et al., 2020). However, previous studies have shown that machine translations may lack diversity compared to a human-generated dataset (Gimpel et al., 2013; Ott et al., 2018; Vanmassenhove et al., 2019; Soto et al., 2020). To overcome this limitation, we conducted back translation across various typological languages, including fusional, isolating, and agglutinative languages. In total, we carefully selected 12 distinct languages for the back translation.

Another effective approach to generating diverse back-translated sentences involves introduc-

[*]These authors contributed equally to this work.

Proceedings of The Eleventh Dialog System Technology Challenge, pages 185–192
September 11, 2023 ©2023 Association for Computational Linguistics

ing noise into the translated data (Edunov et al., 2018). Moreover, applying typo errors to human-written datasets has been improve robustness across various tasks (Martins and Silva, 2004; Zhang et al., 2020; Zhuang and Zuccon, 2021). Building on these previous achievements, we propose adopting typo noises to the back-translated dataset to enhance the stability and performance when dealing with user-written inquiries.

During the experiment, we compared our performance to the baseline and achieved an exact matching score of 0.448 using our augmentation methods, which surpassed the average score for this task. Furthermore, in our analysis, we extensively examined the impact of typological diversity and typo noise in the back translation process. In the competition, our method achieved the 5th position in the exact matching score among the 14 participating teams.

2 Related Work

Back translation was initially introduced to enhance neural machine translation performance through augmented monolingual datasets (Sennrich et al., 2016) and has proven effective when language resources are limited. Subsequently, various methods have been developed to enhance the augmented dataset. For the training method, iterative back translation method leverages two translation models and continues the training of each model with an augmented dataset until no further improvement is observed in both directions (Hoang et al., 2018b; Artetxe et al., 2020). Alternatively, some researchers (Wang et al., 2019) focus on selecting among the translated datasets based on model confidence scores to ensure dataset quality. similarly, distinguishing between back-translated and original datasets by adding tags to the training set (Caswell et al., 2019; Ranathunga et al., 2023) and assigning weights based on the quality of translated sentences (Dou et al., 2020; Khatri and Bhattacharyya, 2020) also helps in using the back translation method with the original dataset.

In the context of our study, Edunov et al. (2018) is particularly relevant. They enhanced back translation by incorporating noise during decoding with beam search, improving the machine translation performance. We, too, introduce noise to our back-translated data, but in our case, we adopted a typo as the injecting noise method.

Many natural language applications such as retriever (Martins and Silva, 2004; Gao et al., 2010), optical character recognition (OCR) (Soper et al., 2021), and language model pre-training (Liu et al., 2021; Zhang et al., 2021) have dealt with typos to impart robustness to a human-generated dataset. By injecting typo noise into the user inquiries, we also aim to be more stable to some erroneous conversation inquiries.

3 DSTC11-Track5

In the DSTC11-Track5 selection task, participants are required to retrieve relevant knowledge from a provided review dataset in response to a user's utterance. The dialogue dataset consists of 32,604 dialogue data instances and 244,032 turns, which contain the system and user's utterances. The dialogue dataset is a revised version of MultiWoZ 2.1 (Eric et al., 2019), by specifically modifying several turns to be necessary subjective and factual knowledge.

The knowledge data comprises 143 entities, representing individual hotels or restaurants. In total, there are 4,299 reviews and Q&As available for these entities. It is worth noting that this knowledge data exhibits several unique characteristics compared to previous challenges. First, a single review can encompass multiple aspects. Second, there are multiple review posts from diverse individuals, which may include conflicting opinions.

During the training and testing of the selection model, participants are provided with user and system dialogue that includes the entity relevant index. Participants can use this entity index when retrieving the knowledge set. For additional guidance, participants can access the baseline and evaluation scripts on the website. [1].

4 Method

We now introduce our back translation method with typo noise. We denote the conversation dataset as D, and i-th dialgoue in D is denoted as $d_i = (u_1^i, s_1^i, u_2^i, s_3^i, ..., u_t^i)$ where u_t^i is a user utterance and s_t^i is a system utterance at turn t. Here, the last user turn u_{last}^i is the utterance that requires seeking information from external sources in order to provide a response. The knowledge source consists of n number of entities $K = \{e_1, e_2, e_3 \ldots , e_n\}$, and for the j-th entity, e_j consists of k number of reviews and Q&A data, denoted as $e_j = \{r_1, r_2, r_3, \ldots ,r_k\}$. In the training as well as test phases,

[1]https://github.com/alexa/dstc11-track5

Table 1: Typology and languages used for back translation. Language codes follow ISO 639-1.

Typology	Example
Fusional	da, de, es, hi, ine
Agglutinative	fi, hu, ko, tr
Isolating	id, zh,tl

Table 2: Examples of each typo injection method.

Method	Example
Random Delete	"typo technique" → "typo tecnique"
Swap Adjacent	"typo technique" → "typp technique"
Swap Char	"typo technique" → "typo techinque"
Rand Insert	"typo technique" → "typio technique"
Rand Substitute	"typo technique" → "type technique"

the conversation-relevant entity index j is given for each dialogue d_i, and participants should retrieve relevant reviews in the given entity e_j.

4.1 Back Translation

In order to ensure a robust system that can handle various inquiry sentences, we first employed the back translation method for data augmentation. For each dialogue d_i, we obtained the last user turn u^i_{last}, translated the utterances into targeted languages, and then translated them back into English. In translation, to enhance the diversity of augmented utterances, we leveraged various typology languages, including fusional, isolating and agglutinative. We utilized the open source translation model, available in Tiedemann and Thottingal (2020) for translation. The languages we used are in Table 1, and in total, we generated 12 different augmented datasets. We combined 12 different back-translated datasets with original dialogue dataset D, and denoted augmented dataset as $\bar{D}$, which is 13 times larger than D.

4.2 Typos

To enhance the robustness to user's inquiry, we augmented the data by injecting typos into the back-translated inquiry dataset. We employed the following types of typos at random: (1) Random Delete - randomly deleting a character, (2) Swap Adjacent - randomly swapping adjacent characters, (3) Swap Char - randomly swapping a single character with one of its neighbor, (4) Rand Insert - randomly inserting a character, and (5) Rand Substitute - randomly substituting a character. These types of typos were selected based on the errors commonly found in actual human-written sentences. We added these noises randomly to $\bar{D}$ and denoted this noised dataset as $\check{D}$. Examples of each methods are in Table 2.

4.3 Back Translation with Typo

The overall process of data augmentation is depicted in Figure 1. Initially, we perform back-translation using typologically diverse languages. Subsequently, we introduce five distinct typos randomly into the translated data. For the submission, we utilized all back-translation languages and typo methods together with the original dataset, resulting in a dataset that is 13 times larger than the originally provided dataset. Augmented examples are presented in Appendix A.1

4.4 Model Description

To retrieve plausible candidates from the subjective knowledge and return a relevant review list, we leveraged the pre-trained transformer encoder model DeBERTa (He et al., 2020). DeBERta is the enhanced version of BERT (Devlin et al., 2019), with an disentangled attention mechanism and decoding reflecting absolute position. In the given scenario, the input consists of the latest user and system utterance, denoted as s_{last-1} and u_{last}, respectively. Then, this context input is concatenated with the review from the knowledge source, using separate tokens. The model structure and input example is shown in Figure 2. If a review is required to answer the user's inquiry, the corresponding label is assigned as 1; otherwise, it is assigned as 0. Binary cross-entropy loss is calculated between the predicted probabilities and the true labels as in Equation 1,

$$L = -\frac{1}{NM}\sum_{i=0}^{N}\sum_{j=0}^{M}[y\log(P(\hat{y}|s^i_{last-1}, u^i_{last}, r_j)) + (1-y)\log(P(1-\hat{y}|s^i_{last-1}, u^i_{last}, r_j)] \quad (1)$$

Here, N is the number of dialogue numbers in $\check{D}$ and M is the number of reviews and Q&As for a given entity index.

5 Experiments

5.1 Evaluation Metrics

For evaluating our methods, we used precision, recall, F1 and exact matching (EM) as a metrics. Precision measures the proportion of retrieved data

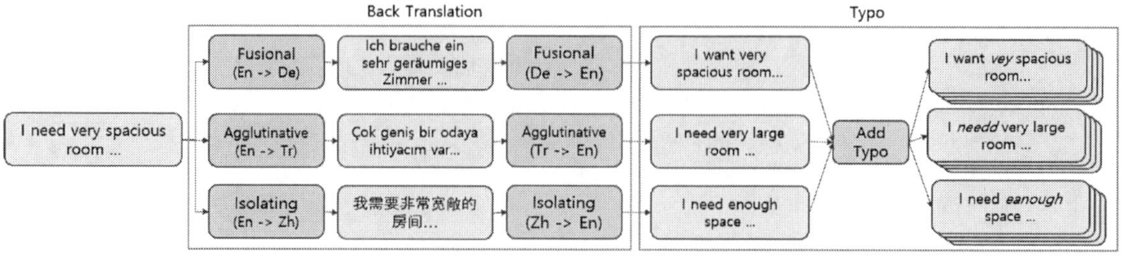

Figure 1: Overview of back translation with typo noise method.

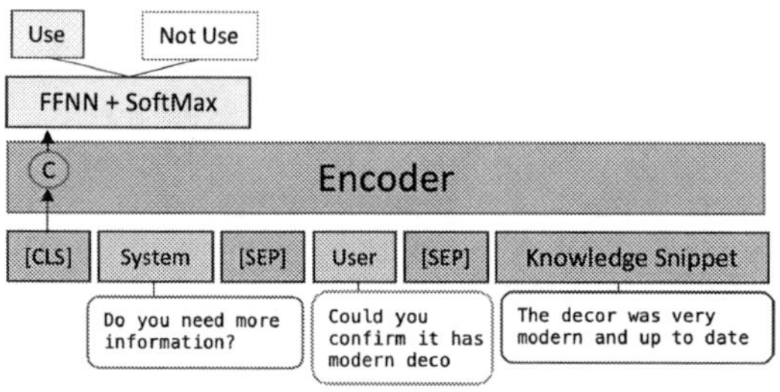

Figure 2: Overview of the model and input example.

that is relevant to the user query. Recall computes the proportion of retrieved relevant knowledge from the total amount of relevant knowledge. F1 computes the harmonic mean of precision and recall. EM computes the proportion of accurate knowledge among the total knowledge entity set.

5.2 Main Result

Table 3: Main result and ablation study of back translation and typo noise. Here, back translation is denoted as BT.

Model	Prec	Recall	F1	EM
	Dev data			
DeBERTa	0.795	0.884	0.837	0.405
+BT	**0.782**	0.906	**0.840**	0.440
+BT+Typo (Ours)	0.751	**0.912**	0.823	**0.498**
	Test data			
Average	0.794	0.800	0.784	0.449
Ours	0.774	0.856	0.813	0.468
Best (Team 13)	**0.834**	**0.871**	**0.855**	**0.657**

To show the effectiveness of our back translation and typo noise methods, we conduct an ablation study by adding them to the backbone model (Table 3). The result indicates that the back translation helps to improve the score in EM (0.440), and injecting the typo could achieve additional progress in performance (0.498). It shows that incorporating the typo noise reduces over fitting and is more robust to written-form dialogue inquiries. Eventually, through our submission we were able to achieve the fifth-highest score of EM among other participants [2]. However, when noise is added to the back-translated dataset, the Precision and F1 scores decrease. This suggests that introducing noise makes the model more likely to predict information that is not necessarily relevant or accurate.

5.3 Analysis of Typology in Back Translation

To assess the impact of utilizing different typologies in back translation, we conducted an analysis of each typology's effect on language pairs, as summarized in Table 4 [3]. The results revealed that the effect varies based on language typology. Fusional languages contribute to improving precision, agglutinative languages encourage recall, and isolating languages enhance the EM score. These findings demonstrate that various language typologies generate distinct sentence structures. We can infer that incorporating diverse typologies leads to a variety of augmented sentences, addressing the monotony problem observed in previous back-translation researches.

5.4 Effect of Typo Noise in Back Translation

In this experiment, we conducted a detailed analysis of the effects of typo noise by individually applying each method to the back-translated data (Table 5). The findings indicated that incorporating most of the noise methods resulted in improved EM scores when compared to using back translation alone. Notably, the random-deletion and character-swapping noise methods exhibited more promising performance. Furthermore, when the five noise methods were combined together, their synergistic effect further enhanced the EM score.

[2]Compared the best submission score of each participant.

[3]We chose 9 languages out of 12 that achieved a BLEU score exceeding 25 by referencing Tiedemann and Thottingal (2020).

Table 4: Result from data augmented by each language on dev data. Fus. means fusional, Agg. means agglutinative, and Iso. means isolating.

Typology	Language	Prec	Recall	F1	EM
Fus.	da	0.762	0.882	0.818	0.390
	de	0.800	0.878	0.837	0.429
	es	0.784	0.869	0.824	0.409
	Avg	**0.782**	0.876	**0.826**	0.409
Agg.	fi	0.758	0.876	0.812	0.369
	hu	0.745	0.891	0.811	0.370
	tr	0.783	0.886	0.831	0.403
	Avg	0.762	**0.884**	0.818	0.381
Iso.	id	0.819	0.870	0.844	0.429
	tl	0.758	0.887	0.817	0.408
	zh	0.767	0.864	0.813	0.404
	Avg	0.781	0.874	0.825	**0.414**

Table 5: Effect of typo noise methods with back translation on dev data.

Model	Prec	Recall	F1	EM
DeBERTa	0.795	0.884	0.837	0.405
DeBERTa +BT	0.782	0.906	0.840	0.440
+ RandDelete	**0.816**	0.892	**0.853**	0.460
+ SwapAdjacent	0.800	0.899	0.847	0.457
+ SwapChar	0.815	0.893	0.852	**0.465**
+ RandInsert	0.795	0.905	0.846	0.438
+ RandSubstitute	0.814	0.893	0.852	0.453
+ ALL	0.751	**0.912**	0.823	**0.498**

5.5 Analysis of Typo Noise

In the experiment in Table 6, we focused solely on the effects of typo noise itself, without using back translation. The results revealed that random insertion and character swapping were effective in enhancing the EM score. However, other types of typo noise either demonstrated similar results or even worse performance. This suggests that introducing noise without augmenting the dataset does not contribute to stable training.

5.6 Conclusion

In this study, we present an effective augmentation method that incorporates typo noise into back translation. In addition, to further enhance the diversity of the augmented text, we employed a range of typologically diverse languages in the back-translation process. Through our experiments, we observed that the noised back translation could improve retrieving accuracy on diverse user inquiries. In the competition, our methods for back translation with typo noise achieved a 5th ranking in terms of EM score, out of a total of 14 participants.

Table 6: Effect of typo noise methods on dev data.

Typo	Prec	Recall	F1	EM
DeBERTa	0.795	0.884	**0.837**	0.405
+ randDelete	0.768	0.887	0.823	0.360
+ swapAdjacent	**0.794**	0.874	0.832	0.392
+ swapChar	0.763	**0.889**	0.821	0.410
+ randInsert	0.791	0.888	**0.837**	**0.434**
+ randSubstitute	0.784	0.875	0.827	0.399

Acknowledgements: This work was supported by Institute of Information & communications Technology Planning & Evaluation(IITP) grant funded by the Korea government(MSIT) (No.2021-0-00575, Development of Voicepishing Prevention Technology Based on Speech and Text Deep Learning) and MSIT under the ITRC (Information Technology Research Center) support program (IITP-2023-2020-0-01789) supervised by the IITP.

References

Mikel Artetxe, Gorka Labaka, Noe Casas, and Eneko Agirre. 2020. Do all roads lead to rome? understanding the role of initialization in iterative back-translation. *Knowledge-Based Systems*, 206:106401.

Franck Burlot and François Yvon. 2019. Using monolingual data in neural machine translation: a systematic study. *arXiv preprint arXiv:1903.11437*.

Isaac Caswell, Ciprian Chelba, and David Grangier. 2019. Tagged back-translation. *arXiv preprint arXiv:1906.06442*.

Jacob Devlin, Ming-Wei Chang, Kenton Lee, and Kristina Toutanova. 2019. Bert: Pre-training of deep bidirectional transformers for language understanding.

Eleftherios Dimitrakis, Konstantinos Sgontzos, Panagiotis Papadakos, Yannis Marketakis, Alexandros Papangelis, Yannis Stylianou, and Yannis Tzitzikas. 2018. On finding the relevant user reviews for advancing conversational faceted search. In *EMSASW@ ESWC*, pages 22–31.

Zi-Yi Dou, Antonios Anastasopoulos, and Graham Neubig. 2020. Dynamic data selection and weighting for iterative back-translation. *arXiv preprint arXiv:2004.03672*.

Sergey Edunov, Myle Ott, Michael Auli, and David Grangier. 2018. Understanding back-translation at scale. *arXiv preprint arXiv:1808.09381*.

Mihail Eric, Rahul Goel, Shachi Paul, Abhishek Sethi, Sanchit Agarwal, Shuyag Gao, and Dilek Hakkani-Tur. 2019. Multiwoz 2.1: Multi-domain dialogue state corrections and state tracking baselines. *arXiv preprint arXiv:1907.01669*.

Jianfeng Gao, Chris Quirk, et al. 2010. A large scale ranker-based system for search query spelling correction. In *The 23rd International Conference on Computational Linguistics*.

Kevin Gimpel, Dhruv Batra, Chris Dyer, and Gregory Shakhnarovich. 2013. A systematic exploration of diversity in machine translation. In *Proceedings of the 2013 Conference on Empirical Methods in Natural Language Processing*, pages 1100–1111.

Pengcheng He, Xiaodong Liu, Jianfeng Gao, and Weizhu Chen. 2020. Deberta: Decoding-enhanced bert with disentangled attention. *arXiv preprint arXiv:2006.03654*.

Vu Cong Duy Hoang, Philipp Koehn, Gholamreza Haffari, and Trevor Cohn. 2018a. Iterative back-translation for neural machine translation. In *Proceedings of the 2nd Workshop on Neural Machine Translation and Generation*, pages 18–24, Melbourne, Australia. Association for Computational Linguistics.

Vu Cong Duy Hoang, Philipp Koehn, Gholamreza Haffari, and Trevor Cohn. 2018b. Iterative back-translation for neural machine translation. In *Proceedings of the 2nd workshop on neural machine translation and generation*, pages 18–24.

Jyotsana Khatri and Pushpak Bhattacharyya. 2020. Filtering back-translated data in unsupervised neural machine translation. In *Proceedings of the 28th international conference on computational linguistics*, pages 4334–4339.

Seokhwan Kim, Mihail Eric, Karthik Gopalakrishnan, Behnam Hedayatnia, Yang Liu, and Dilek Hakkani-Tur. 2020. Beyond domain apis: Task-oriented conversational modeling with unstructured knowledge access. *arXiv preprint arXiv:2006.03533*.

Shulin Liu, Tao Yang, Tianchi Yue, Feng Zhang, and Di Wang. 2021. Plome: Pre-training with misspelled knowledge for chinese spelling correction. In *Proceedings of the 59th Annual Meeting of the Association for Computational Linguistics and the 11th International Joint Conference on Natural Language Processing (Volume 1: Long Papers)*, pages 2991–3000.

Bodhisattwa Prasad Majumder, Harsh Jhamtani, Taylor Berg-Kirkpatrick, and Julian McAuley. 2022. Achieving conversational goals with unsupervised post-hoc knowledge injection. *arXiv preprint arXiv:2203.11399*.

Benjamin Marie, Raphael Rubino, and Atsushi Fujita. 2020. Tagged back-translation revisited: Why does it really work? In *Proceedings of the 58th Annual Meeting of the Association for Computational Linguistics*, pages 5990–5997.

Bruno Martins and Mário J Silva. 2004. Spelling correction for search engine queries. In *Advances in Natural Language Processing: 4th International Conference, EsTAL 2004, Alicante, Spain, October 20-22, 2004. Proceedings 4*, pages 372–383. Springer.

Myle Ott, Michael Auli, David Grangier, and Marc'Aurelio Ranzato. 2018. Analyzing uncertainty in neural machine translation. In *International Conference on Machine Learning*, pages 3956–3965. PMLR.

Surangika Ranathunga, En-Shiun Annie Lee, Marjana Prifti Skenduli, Ravi Shekhar, Mehreen Alam, and Rishemjit Kaur. 2023. Neural machine translation for low-resource languages: A survey. *ACM Computing Surveys*, 55(11):1–37.

Abhinav Rastogi, Xiaoxue Zang, Srinivas Sunkara, Raghav Gupta, and Pranav Khaitan. 2020. Towards scalable multi-domain conversational agents: The schema-guided dialogue dataset. In *Proceedings of the AAAI Conference on Artificial Intelligence*, volume 34, pages 8689–8696.

Rico Sennrich, Barry Haddow, and Alexandra Birch. 2016. Improving neural machine translation models with monolingual data.

Elizabeth Soper, Stanley Fujimoto, and Yen-Yun Yu. 2021. Bart for post-correction of ocr newspaper text. In *Proceedings of the Seventh Workshop on Noisy User-generated Text (W-NUT 2021)*, pages 284–290.

Xabier Soto, Dimitar Shterionov, Alberto Poncelas, and Andy Way. 2020. Selecting backtranslated data from multiple sources for improved neural machine translation. *arXiv preprint arXiv:2005.00308*.

Jörg Tiedemann and Santhosh Thottingal. 2020. OPUS-MT — Building open translation services for the World. In *Proceedings of the 22nd Annual Conferenec of the European Association for Machine Translation (EAMT)*, Lisbon, Portugal.

Eva Vanmassenhove, Dimitar Shterionov, and Andy Way. 2019. Lost in translation: Loss and decay of linguistic richness in machine translation. *arXiv preprint arXiv:1906.12068*.

Shuo Wang, Yang Liu, Chao Wang, Huanbo Luan, and Maosong Sun. 2019. Improving back-translation with uncertainty-based confidence estimation. *arXiv preprint arXiv:1909.00157*.

Ruiqing Zhang, Chao Pang, Chuanqiang Zhang, Shuohuan Wang, Zhongjun He, Yu Sun, Hua Wu, and Haifeng Wang. 2021. Correcting chinese spelling errors with phonetic pre-training. In *Findings of the Association for Computational Linguistics: ACL-IJCNLP 2021*, pages 2250–2261.

Shaohua Zhang, Haoran Huang, Jicong Liu, and Hang Li. 2020. Spelling error correction with soft-masked bert.

Chao Zhao, Spandana Gella, Seokhwan Kim, Di Jin, Devamanyu Hazarika, Alexandros Papangelis, Behnam Hedayatnia, Mahdi Namazifar, Yang Liu, and Dilek Hakkani-Tur. 2023. "what do others think?": Task-oriented conversational modeling with subjective knowledge.

Shengyao Zhuang and Guido Zuccon. 2021. Dealing with typos for bert-based passage retrieval and ranking. *arXiv preprint arXiv:2108.12139*.

A Appendix

A.1 Augmented Dataset Example

Table 7: Examples of augmented dataset. RI: Random insertion, RD : Random delete, RS : Random substitution, SC : Swap character, SA : swap adjacent

Method	Example
Original	A : I have back issues. Does this place have comfortable beds? B : Do they have nice outdoor dining area? C : Do you know if the Bridge Guest House has cozy beds? D : Is the staff friendly, polite, and responsive? E : Are they easy to get to and in a convenient location?
Fusional	A : I have back problems. Does this place have comfortable beds? B : Do you have a nice outdoor dining area? C : Do you know if Bridge Guest House has comfortable beds? D : Is the staff friendly, courteous and receptive? E : Are they easy to reach and in a convenient location?
Fusional + Typo	A :I have **bacJk** problems. Does this place have comfortable beds? (RI) B :Do you have a nice outdoor dining **ara**? (RD) C :Do **yBu** know if Bridge Guest House has comfortable beds? (RS) D :Is the staff **rfiendly**, courteous and receptive? (SC) E :Are they easy to reach and in a **donvenient** location? (SA)
Agglutinative	A : Are there any nice beds here? B : Do they have a nice walkroom? C : Do you know if there's any nice beds in Bridge Guest House? D : Are the staff friendly, polite and receptive? E : Are they easily accessible and comfortable?
Agglutinative + Typo	A :Are there **anAy** nice beds here? (RI) B :Do **hey** have a nice walkroom? (RD) C :Do you know if **there'H** any nice beds in Bridge Guest House? (RS) D :Are **hte** staff friendly, polite and receptive? (SC) E :**Sre** they easily accessible and comfortable? (SA)
Isolating	A : Have I ever had a comfortable bed in this area? B : Do they have a beautiful dining place outside the house? C : Do you know if there's a comfortable bed in the bridge guest room? D : Are staff friendly, polite and responsive? E : Is it easy to go and put in a convenient place?
Isolating + Typo	A :Have I ever had a comfortable bed in **Nthis** area? (RI) B :Do they have a beautiful **dinng** place outside the house? (RD) C :Do you know if **thMre's** a comfortable bed in the bridge guest room? (RS) D :Are staff friendly, **ploite** and responsive? (SC) E :Is it easy to go and put in a **conveniebt** place? (SA)

Leveraging Few-Shot Data Augmentation and Waterfall Prompting for Response Generation

Lea Krause
Vrije Universiteit Amsterdam
l.krause@vu.nl

Selene Báez Santamaría
Vrije Universiteit Amsterdam
s.baezsantamaria@vu.nl

Michiel van der Meer
Leiden University
m.t.van.der.meer@liacs.leidenuniv.nl

Urja Khurana
Vrije Universiteit Amsterdam
u.khurana@vu.nl

Abstract

This paper discusses our approaches for task-oriented conversational modelling using subjective knowledge, with a particular emphasis on response generation. Our methodology was shaped by an extensive data analysis that evaluated key factors such as response length, sentiment, and dialogue acts present in the provided dataset. We used few-shot learning to augment the data with newly generated subjective knowledge items and present three approaches for DSTC11: (1) task-specific model exploration, (2) incorporation of the most frequent question into all generated responses, and (3) a waterfall prompting technique using a combination of both GPT-3 and ChatGPT.

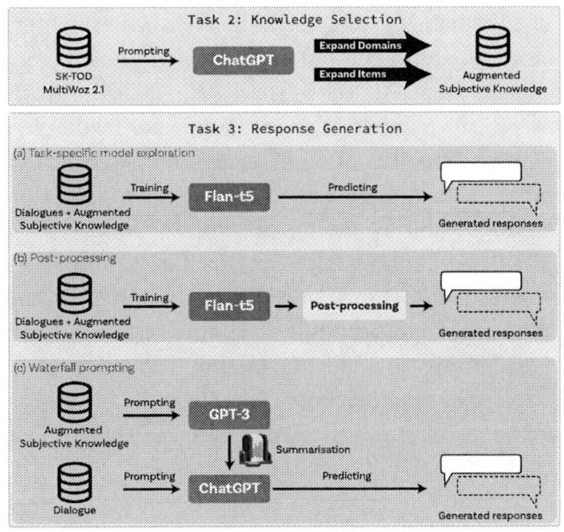

Figure 1: Overview of the approaches for *Knowledge Selection* and *Response Generation*. For approach 3a only the best-performing model is depicted.

1 Introduction

Task-Oriented Dialogue (TOD) Systems are traditionally designed to facilitate users in achieving specific objectives, such as looking up train times or booking a flight in a dialogue setting. For these tasks, the models are often given access to a database of factual information to complete the task. However, other tasks necessitate not only factual but also subjective insights, which are derived from other users' opinions. Handling subjective knowledge and using it for generating dialogue responses is the core of the *Subjective-Knowledge-based Task-Oriented Dialogue (SK-TOD)* (Zhao et al., 2023) challenge. The challenge is set up as conversations between users and artificial assistants, inquiring about and potentially booking hotels or restaurants. The organisers provided dialogue snapshots and a knowledge base with subjective reviews and FAQs related to said hotels and restaurants.

The challenge consists of three interlinked subtasks: 1) *Knowledge Seeking Turn Detection*, where it is determined whether a turn needs knowledge to create an appropriate response; 2) *Knowledge Selection*, where relevant items are selected from the knowledge base; and 3) *Knowledge-Grounded Response Generation*, where the dialogue history and the selected knowledge items must be aggregated to generate a concise response for the user.

Our primary interest was in sub-task 3, but due to the high correlation of performance with subtask 2, we simultaneously worked on improving the knowledge selection (see Figure 1). Furthermore, we experimented with splitting sub-task 3 into two smaller tasks. First, we perform few-shot data augmentation, supported by a detailed data analysis, to substantially increase the knowledge base and address generalisation to new domains. Despite its marginal impact on the final test set, given no new domains were added, it forms a robust strategy for future generalisations. Second, we undertook the exploration of task-specific models, we found that using a larger model leads to slight improvements in task performance. In addition, we augmented the generated responses by integrating the most frequently asked question, aiming to

Proceedings of The Eleventh Dialog System Technology Challenge, pages 193–205
September 11, 2023

enhance conversation coherence and engagement. Lastly, we also employed a waterfall prompting technique that integrated a combination of Large Language Models. This strategy, though it scored lower in quantitative metrics compared to the baseline, possibly due to the abstractive nature of these models, is a promising avenue for further research[1].

2 Related work

Data Augmentation In low-resource data scenarios, synthetic data augmentation has been shown to be a cost-efficient and effective way to increase dataset size (Anaby-Tavor et al., 2020). Traditional data augmentation techniques for natural language processing often include simple transformations like synonym substitution, random insertion, deletion, and swapping of words (Wei and Zou, 2019). A more complex approach is paraphrasing, where the meaning stays the same but words and syntax change, a popular example of this is back-translation in machine translation (Sennrich et al., 2016). Data augmentation was also used in successful approaches of last year's edition of DSTC (Tian et al., 2021; Thulke et al., 2022)

Recently, the emergence of large language models (LLMs) like GPT-3 (Brown et al., 2020) has opened up new avenues for data augmentation. One approach is to prompt these models to generate additional data that fits the distribution of the original dataset (Kumar et al., 2020; Xia et al., 2020; Lee et al., 2021). This leverages the capacity of LLMs to generate coherent and contextually appropriate sentences, thereby creating augmented data that closely mirrors real-world linguistic diversity.

Waterfall Prompting Combining prompts or re-running the same prompt has shown increased performance and robustness. For example, Singhal et al. (2023) coin the term *ensemble refinement* which involves using a two-step prompting approach. In the first iteration, multiple answers are generated for a prompt, and in the second iteration, these answers are incorporated into the prompt to develop a final solution that is more robust for the given task. Similar efforts have been explored such as self-consistency (Wang et al., 2023), recitation-augmentation (Sun et al., 2023), and rational-augmentation (Wang et al., 2022). Pitis et al. (2023) expand on this framework by incorporating multiple rounds of prompting, each building upon the improvements made in the previous round. However, these still focus on prompting a single model and differ from a typical ensemble where different models' output is aggregated (Wang et al., 2023). To the best of our knowledge, there is limited work on waterfall prompting or assembling the responses from different language models.

Previous DSTC editions According to system reports from the DSTC9 and DSTC10 challenges, enhancing the performance of sub-task 2 significantly affects the overall task performance (Kim et al., 2020). In the DSTC9 iteration, it was found that ensemble model approaches are effective for knowledge selection (Kim et al., 2020). In DSTC10, successful approaches used a separate entity tracking component for knowledge selection to narrow down the search space before document ranking (Kim et al., 2022).

3 Data Analysis

Before developing our approach to the DSTC tasks, we analyse the available data. We 1. inspect the correlation between features, 2. investigate the sentiment of the available data, and 3. examine the distribution of dialogue act types.

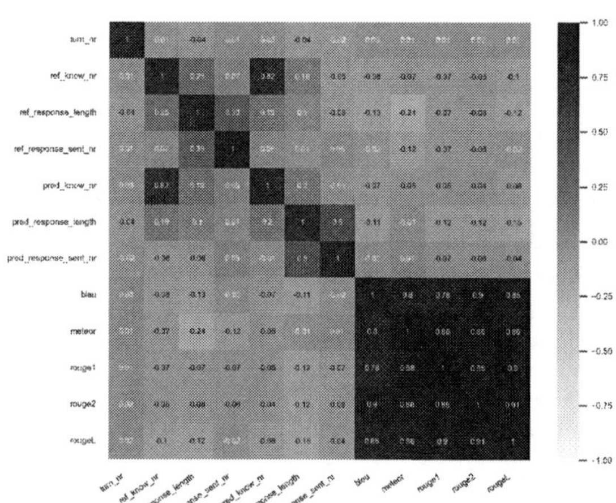

Figure 2: Correlation between reference data, baseline predictions, and automatic scores, on the validation set.

3.1 Feature correlation

To steer our approach, we investigate the potential influence of various factors on automatic metric scores. We examine correlations between the following variables: (1) the number of dialogue turns, (2) the number of selected knowledge items, and

[1]Our code is available at `https://github.com/lkra/dstc11-track5/tree/main/CLTeamL`

(3) the lengths of both the reference and prediction in terms of characters and sentences (Figure 2). After not finding strong correlations among these parameters, we decide to split the response into two sub-tasks. Namely, we process system responses by separating them into two parts:

```
summary + [optional] question
```

These two parts are defined as follows:

- Summary: This part of the response focuses on summarising the selected knowledge items.
- Question: If included, this part of the response pertains to dialogue management, where the system can offer assistance in continuing with the current task, such as making a reservation.

3.2 Summary analysis

We enrich the dataset by adding two types of sentiment scores. Firstly, we calculate a sentiment score using the spaCy library[2] across all knowledge items selected for that dialogue. Secondly, we calculate a sentiment score specifically for the summary part of the ground truth responses. Our intuition is that the sentiment of the summary should align with the sentiment of the knowledge items used to generate the response. Our belief is supported by positive correlations observed in all data splits (train=0.41, val=0.53, test=0.54) and overall (all=0.45).

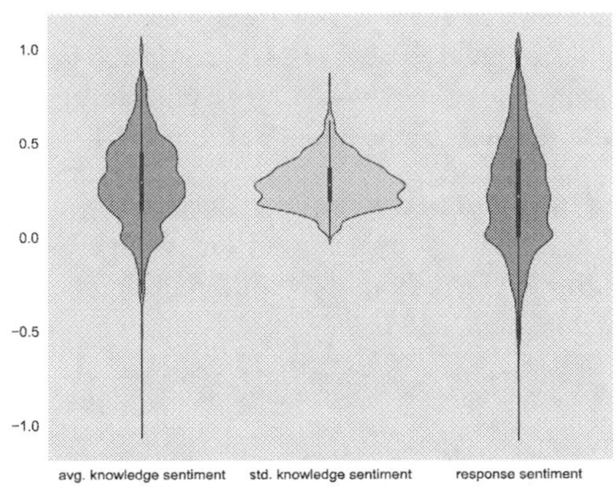

Figure 3: Sentiment distributions across dialogues for knowledge items (left) and responses (right). For knowledge items, we also show the distribution of standard deviation sentiment scores inside dialogues (centre).

Furthermore, we examined the data distributions of these new features, as depicted in Figure 3. The average sentiment of the knowledge items and the sentiment of the responses have similar distributions. They both have positive medians, positive interquartile ranges, and a long tail extending into the negative range, indicating that the sentiment of the system's responses tends to be neutral to positive. The average sentiment of the knowledge items is slightly higher than the sentiment of the responses. The standard deviation of the spread of the knowledge sentiment scores inside dialogues is around 0.25, indicating that most knowledge items are not highly polarised, and their sentiment values are relatively close to each other.

3.3 Dialogue management analysis

Dialogue acts We generate a dialogue act tag MIDAS (Yu and Yu, 2019) for each of the user's last utterances in the dialogue context and explore the baseline performance per act type (Table 1). Our findings reveal that questions are quite frequent, as users often rely on them to interact with the artificial assistant in task-oriented dialogues. It is worth noting that *yes/no questions* are the most frequent type and typically elicit short system responses, consisting of simple answers like "yes" or "no." Furthermore, we observe that some questions seek opinions, which may require subjective knowledge derived from reviews for an appropriate response, in contrast to factual questions that can potentially be answered using FAQs.

Optional questions We examined how frequently questions appear in the system's responses. Our findings indicate that 34.94% of the responses contain a question at the end.

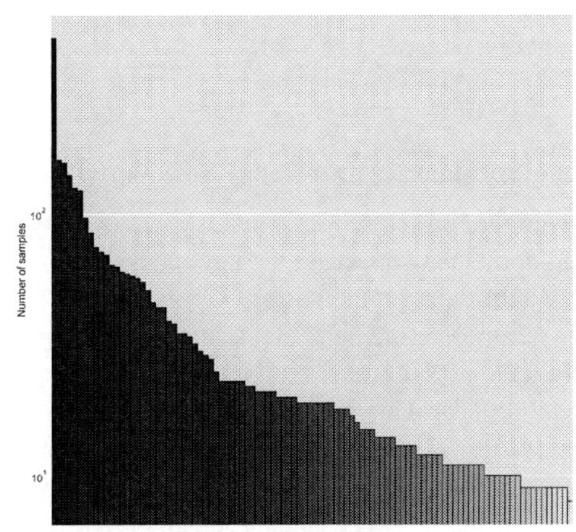

Figure 4: Question frequency distribution across all data splits. Only the first 100 elements are plotted.

[2] https://spacy.io/

Act	Freq.	Res. Len.	BLEU	METEOR	ROUGE-1	ROUGE-2	ROUGE-L
yes_no_question	1078	131.85	0.097	0.187	0.368	0.151	0.292
open_question_opinion	288	133.52	0.107	0.189	0.379	0.163	**0.301**
open_question_factual	203	134.51	0.094	0.179	0.358	0.148	0.285
statement	188	137.44	0.081	0.170	0.345	0.131	0.260
command	184	132.82	0.087	0.182	0.355	0.141	0.280
opinion	166	139.07	0.089	0.183	0.366	0.143	0.280
pos_answer	14	135.78	0.053	0.151	0.312	0.108	0.230
complaint	5	138.20	**0.110**	0.160	0.333	0.122	0.277
comment	1	181.00	0.038	0.084	0.196	0.081	0.117
neg_answer	1	**104.00**	0.069	**0.319**	**0.611**	**0.294**	0.5
nonsense	1	189.00	0.014	0.089	0.184	0.0	0.123

Table 1: Data statistics (frequency and average system response length) and baseline performance per dialogue act.

When analysing the questions, we observe that the data distribution exhibits a single peak and a long tail (Figure 4). Out of the 2,522 unique questions, 79% (n=1,994) appear only once. The most commonly occurring question is *"Would you like to know more about them?* accounting for 19% of the occurrences. Moreover, we notice that the most frequent questions are generic. The top five questions, which make up 42% of the data, include: *"Do you have any other questions?"*, *"Is there anything else I can help you with?"*, *"Would you like to make a reservation?"*, and *"Is there anything else you'd like to know about them?"*.

To evaluate the impact of optional questions, we conducted an ablation study where we remove the questions at the end of the responses (Table 2). This leads to slightly lower scores. Additionally, we experiment with adding the most frequent question (MFQ) to the responses that did not already contain a question. This improves the performance for longer responses.

4 Method

4.1 Sub-task 2: Knowledge Selection

Given the limited scope of reviews, traveller types and domains, we expand the knowledge base with few-shot data augmentation. Utilising ChatGPT, we synthesise artificial data, supplementing the MultiWoz 2.1 dataset's augmented version (Eric et al., 2020). This process involves creating new reviews for existing items within existing domains, in addition to the introduction of three new domains from the DSTC10 data set, all enriched with subjective knowledge. In total, our additional data contains 1,006 extra reviews. We combine these with the existing data for use in both the Knowledge Seeking Turn Detection and Knowledge Selection tasks. For a data example see A.

Extension of item reviews The original knowledge data had 143 entities and 1,430 reviews (8,013 sentences) in the *hotel* and *restaurant* domains. We added 715 reviews to this by adding five different traveller types and producing five sentences for each type. This led to 25 extra sentences per entity, for a total of 2,145 reviews and 11,609 sentences. We significantly expanded and diversified the present traveller types. The original data had only 6 types, we increased this to 26, though some like *"Group of friends"* and *"Friends getaway"* could be merged into the same type. For a complete overview see Table 7. The average sentence length for the original reviews is 73.73 compared to 76.93 for the added reviews. The prompt to generate these reviews can be found in Prompt 4.1

Extension to new domains Inspired by Thulke et al. (2022), we expand our knowledge base by adding reviews from three different domains: *attraction, taxi,* and *train.*

Prompt 4.1: extension of new reviews

Please provide new reviews for the **{entity_name}** but for five different traveler_type.
Continue the counting of the reviews and make sure the new reviews are in a dict format like this:
"<id>": {{"traveler_type": "<traveler_type>", "sentences": {{"<id>": "<review>", "<id>": "<review>", "<id>": "<review>", "<id>": "<review>"}}}},

These are the existing reviews: **{reviews_all}**.

Take this start and continue. Use double quotes to comply with json format.

"10": {{"traveler_type":

Approach	BLEU	METEOR	ROUGE-1	ROUGE-2	ROUGE-L
Baseline	**0.102**	0.179	**0.365**	0.149	**0.287**
Strip questions	0.083	0.165	0.359	0.148	0.284
Append MFQ	0.094	**0.181**	0.363	**0.150**	0.286

Table 2: Results of investigation regarding questions on the validation set.

We use the validation data from DSTC10[3] which contains entities and respective FAQs from these different domains. The data did not contain subjective reviews for any of the domains. Hence, we generate three reviews for each entity by prompting ChatGPT with their entity name and FAQs. Due to the limited context width of the ChatGPT API, we restrict the reviews to two sentences.

We generate the reviews with Prompt 4.2, which resulted in 291 reviews for the *attraction* domain.

Prompt 4.2: extension to new domains

Given this example:

{ **<entity_id>**: { "name": **<entity_name>**, "faqs": { **<faq_id>**: { "question": **<question>**, "answer": **<answer>** } } } },

can you generate three more reviews, not more than 2 sentences, as: traveler type: review?

Although we prepared the data for the *taxi* and *train* reviews, we excluded these two domains as there were no transportation-related domains present in the released test set.

4.2 Sub-task 3: Response Generation

4.2.1 Model exploration

The generation baseline provided by the organisers uses BART (Lewis et al., 2020), specifically bart-base[4], fine-tuned for ten epochs using Adam with a learning rate of 3e-5 and epsilon of 1e-8.

Instead of sticking to the base BART model, we opted to browse publicly available trained models on different tasks and investigate their performance after fine-tuning on the DSTC data. This approach is inspired by *model recycling* (Choshen et al., 2022), which suggests that there exist models that are generally better at being adapted to perform domain-specific tasks. We browsed the `HuggingFace Hub`[5] for models with a better fit (in the task they were trained for or in the data they used for pre-training). Ultimately, we retrained the baseline architecture, as well as Flan-T5 (Chung et al., 2022) in its small, base and large variants, and a trained BART model, trained on the SAMSum dataset (Gliwa et al., 2019). See Table 3 for the results. For training the larger architectures, including flan-t5-large, bart-large and flan-t5-base, we modified the optimisation parameters (learning rate 4e-05, a warm-up ratio of 0.2). We found that using a larger model has small benefits over the original baseline model in most evaluation metrics. We did not find that training on intermediate tasks that are related to our objective improved performance substantially.

4.2.2 Prompting

We used OpenAI's APIs[6] to generate system responses given the baseline output for sub-task 1 and 2. To ensure consistent results, we set the temperature value to 0 for all configurations.

Model comparison To compare GPT-3 and ChatGPT, we conducted experiments using simple prompts while adhering to the respective API requirements. The prompts consisted of two components: a) the dialogue history and b) the selected subjective knowledge. The subjective knowledge was formatted as a list, explicitly specifying whether each item was a **Review** or an **FAQ**.

```
{knowledge_type}: {text}
```

The initial prompt for GPT-3 is shown in Prompt 4.3

Prompt 4.3: GPT-3, initial prompt

DIALOGUE:
{dialogue_context}

KNOWLEDGE:
{knowledge}

RESPONSE:

[3]Data downloaded using the following script: https://tinyurl.com/j8pvkcnx

[4]`https://huggingface.co/facebook/bart-base`

[5]`https://huggingface.co/models`

[6]`https://platform.openai.com/docs/api-reference`

Model name	BLEU	METEOR	ROUGE-1	ROUGE-2	ROUGE-L
bart-large-cnn-samsum	0.095	**0.184**	**0.363**	0.144	0.278
bart-base	0.096	0.173	0.347	0.139	0.271
flan-t5-base	0.096	0.173	0.345	0.140	0.274
flan-t5-large	**0.104**	0.179	0.360	**0.147**	**0.281**
flan-t5-small	0.098	0.164	0.337	0.136	0.272

Table 3: Models explored, shown performance is on the test set.

Model name	BLEU	METEOR	ROUGE-1	ROUGE-2	ROUGE-L
ChatGPT	0.041	0.147	0.280	0.085	0.207
GPT-3	0.051	0.137	0.302	0.105	0.237
ChatGPT + CoT	0.050	0.155	0.305	0.099	0.228
ChatGPT + CoT + 3 examples	**0.069**	**0.161**	**0.325**	**0.117**	**0.243**
Waterfall	0.056	0.152	0.312	0.100	0.236
Waterfall + 3 examples	0.057	0.160	0.311	0.103	0.225

Table 4: Prompting settings explored, shown performance is on the validation set.

ChatGPT requires API requests to be given as a series of messages with a "role" that can have three values: *System*, *User* or *Assistant*. As they explain in their documentation, *System* messages can be used to give instructions to the model, while *User* and *Assistant* messages can be used to carry on a dialogue with the model. As such, we use the *System* messages to give the subjective knowledge to the model and then send each of the dialogue history messages as either *User* or *Assistant* messages. The initial prompt for ChatGPT is shown in Prompt 4.4.

Prompt 4.4: ChatGPT, initial prompt

{"role": "system",
"content": "You are a helpful assistant with access to the following:
{knowledge}" },
{"role": "user",
"content": "**{dialogue_context}**" },
{"role": "assistant",
"content": "**{dialogue_context}**" },
{"role": "user",
"content": "**{dialogue_context}**" }

Although ChatGPT is optimised for dialogue and we expected it to perform better, it scored lower than GPT-3 in the automatic metric evaluation, as seen in Table 4. Upon further examination of the generated responses, we observed that ChatGPT tends to produce much longer responses. In fact, 367 API requests were truncated due to their length. On the other hand, GPT-3 generates more concise responses compared to both the baseline and the ground truth (Table 5). This difference in response length has a negative impact on most natural language generation metrics, as they tend to penalise longer and wordier responses.

Approach	#Sentences		#Characters	
	Avg.	Std.	Avg.	Std.
GPT-3	1.55	0.77	120.04	70.16
Ground truth (val)	1.69	0.66	133.55	32.05
Ground truth (test)	1.70	0.66	135.55	32.12
Ground truth (train)	1.71	0.65	136.61	33.49
Baseline (val)	1.91	0.53	129.66	29.07
ChatGPT	2.09	0.79	182.62	74.61

Table 5: Length statistics on responses, ordered by ascending average length

Chain Of Thought We focus on optimising the prompts for the best performance of a single model, specifically ChatGPT. To achieve this, we adopt recommended techniques from the OpenAI Cookbook[7] for prompting ChatGPT, such as Chain of Thought (CoT) (Wei et al., 2022). For this, we divide the task into two sub-tasks: summarisation and dialogue management (See Section 3). The resulting prompt is shown in Prompt 4.5.

To accommodate CoT answers, which tend to be longer, we double the value of the "max_tokens"

[7]https://github.com/openai/openai-cookbook/blob/main/techniques_to_improve_reliability.md

parameter. This modification leads to improved performance (refer to Table 4); however, it also increases the number of truncated API responses to 1,110.

Prompt 4.5: ChatGPT, Chain Of Thought

> You are assisting a user. Create a response for the user, using the following procedure:
> *(1) First, summarise the available knowledge into a couple sentences.*
> *(2) Then, create a short follow-up question given the dialogue history.*
> *(3) Create the final response to the user as <summary><follow-up>*
>
> Knowledge:
> **{knowledge}**
>
> Dialogue history:
> **{dialogue_context}**
>
> Solution:
> *(1) summary:*

Few-shot learning In order to further enhance the prompt, we incorporate few-shot learning (Brown et al., 2020). After initial exploration, we select three examples that pose the most difficulty. To identify these examples, we analyse instances with the lowest performance and examine their data trends. We observe that ChatGPT struggles with dialogues that involve a high number of items and have a predominantly negative sentiment. Consequently, we select dialogues from the training dataset that meet the following criteria:

1. Filter by the number of knowledge items that are "higher than usual", between [mean+std, mean+2std]
2. Filter by the average sentiment that is "lower than usual", between [mean-2std, mean-std]
3. Since around one-third of responses contain a question, we sample accordingly

By applying these selection criteria, we focus on dialogues that require better summarisation due to the increased number of knowledge items with slightly negative sentiment, and a mix of dialogues with and without a question. This setting yields the best performance and reduces the number of truncated API responses to 380.

Waterfall prompting Additionally, we explore combining prompts and models by utilising the output of one prompted model as part of the input prompt for a subsequent model, in a waterfall manner. We use GPT-3 for summarisation since it behaves better at this part of the task (Bhaskar et al., 2023). We also separate the FAQs, containing factual information, from the reviews, which have opinionated information. The prompt we use for this task is shown in Prompt 4.6.

Prompt 4.6: GPT-3, Summarisation

> Summarize the following into one or two sentences max:
>
> FAQs:
> **{faqs}**
>
> Reviews:
> **{reviews}**

We then use ChatGPT to generate the system response in dialogue, using the output of GPT-3 as part of the prompt. The final prompt is shown in Prompt 4.7. Interestingly, we observed a decline in performance when using this waterfall approach compared to a single model setting.

Prompt 4.7: ChatGPT, Final prompt

> You are assisting a user. Create a response for the user, using the following procedure:
> *(1) First, summarise the available knowledge into a couple sentences.*
> *(2) Then, create a short follow-up question given the dialogue history.*
> *(3) Create a final brief response to the user as <summary><follow-up>*
>
> Knowledge:
> **{knowledge}**
>
> Dialogue history:
> **{dialogue_context}**
>
> Solution:
> *(1) summary:*
> **{GPT-3 summary}**
> *(2) follow-up:*

5 Results

Table 6 shows the submitted approaches' results for all three sub-tasks. We ranked as the 8th best team; hence we did not get official human evaluation results on our submissions. Two of our approaches perform better than the baseline on automatic evaluation metrics, and our identifier in the official results is Team 10.

In the sub-task of **Knowledge Seeking Turn Detection**, our added knowledge induced a slight decrement in performance, with precision declining from 0.998 to 0.995 and F1 score from 0.998 to 0.997, albeit recall experienced a marginal increase (refer to Table 6 for further details).

Conversely, **Knowledge Selection** saw an improvement with the augmentation, resulting in a small uplift across all metrics: precision from 0.790 to 0.796, recall from 0.788 to 0.794, F1 from 0.789 to 0.795, and Exact Match from 0.91 to 0.418.

We submitted three different approaches for the **Response Generation** task. (1) Our first submission is based on the model exploration mentioned in 4.2.1. After fine-tuning flan-t5-large this approach outperforms the baseline on all metrics, leading to a mean reciprocal rank (MRR) of 0.068 compared to 0.039 of the baseline. On BLEU this approach ranked 7th out of 49 submissions. (2) Based on our data analysis (3.3), we extended this approach in post-processing with the most frequently appearing question from the training set appended to the end of the review summaries. This approach, although underperforming relative to our first except in terms of METEOR, still surpassed the baseline on all metrics, apart from BLEU, with an MRR of 0.045. (3) Despite lower performance relative to the baseline in quantitative metrics, our waterfall prompting approach involving a combination of ChatGPT and GPT-3 gave qualitatively promising results. Presented with non-matching knowledge items it did not generate a summary, but flagged them as not relevant to the questions at hand. A full human evaluation would be an interesting step to investigate the perceived accuracy and appropriateness of such responses.

5.1 Submissions

CLTeamL-0 Baseline with augmented data for Knowledge-seeking Turn Detection and Knowledge Selection, flan-t5-large for Response Generation

CLTeamL-1 Baseline with augmented data for Knowledge-seeking Turn Detection and Knowledge Selection, flan-t5-large for Response Generation. Additionally, we do post-processing on the output, adding the most frequent question from the training set as a follow-up question to each review summary.

CLTeamL-2 Baseline for Knowledge-seeking Turn Detection and Knowledge Selection. For the Response Generation, we prompted ChatGPT with Chain Of Thought instructions, to first generate a summary of the knowledge and then append a follow-up question given the dialogue history. We provided three examples, selected from the most challenging cases in the training data according to the data trends on the validation set. Unfortunately, due to server problems, the data samples after 4500, are lacking a review summary. A full run (see Approach 2b in Table 6) after submission showed slight improvements across all metrics but still did not outperform the baseline or our other approaches.

6 Conclusion

In conclusion, our work on the Task-Oriented Conversational Modeling with Subjective Knowledge task produced three key contributions: Firstly, our detailed data analysis could serve as a basis for future dataset scoping within this domain. Secondly, we significantly expanded the knowledge dataset size utilising few-shot data augmentation. Lastly, our most successful model was a fusion of the baseline with augmented data and flan-t5-large. Our waterfall prompting approach incorporating a blend of Large Language Models demonstrated lower metrics compared to the baseline, but upon a qualitative assessment, the results were deemed satisfactory, albeit the absence of official human evaluation impedes a definitive judgement.

A preliminary qualitative analysis shows that ChatGPT can spot mistakes during knowledge selection. Thus, future work could explore incorporating an initial step where ChatGPT is employed to evaluate the relevance of the selected knowledge items. Additionally, we plan to experiment with summarising positive and negative reviews separately before creating a consolidated summary. This method may enhance performance when dealing with polarised reviews.

Limitations

The APIs provided by OpenAI come with particular length parameters which pose certain constraints in terms of flexibility and generalisability to larger datasets and longer sequences which are prevalent in knowledge-grounded dialogue.

There's also a financial aspect to consider, as the use of these APIs involves a monetary cost. We chose to proceed with ChatGPT instead of GPT-3 for parts of our research, even though preliminary explorations indicated higher performance by the latter, due to the additional cost associated with the use of GPT-3. Hence, there might be potential

Approach	sub-task 1			sub-task 2				sub-task 3						Total
	P	R	F1	P	R	F1	EM	BLEU	METEOR	ROUGE-1	ROUGE-2	ROUGE-L	MRR
Baseline	0.998	0.998	0.998	0.790	0.788	0.789	0.391	0.100	0.175	0.352	0.143	0.275	0.039
CLTeamL-0	0.995	0.999	0.997	0.796	0.794	0.795	0.418	0.104	0.179	0.360	0.147	0.281	0.068
CLTeamL-1	0.995	0.999	0.997	0.796	0.794	0.795	0.418	0.094	0.181	0.356	0.146	0.279	0.045
CLTeamL-2	0.996	0.998	0.997	0.772	0.818	0.794	0.423	0.060	0.121	0.241	0.087	0.186	0.025
CLTeamL-2b	0.996	0.998	0.997	0.772	0.818	0.794	0.423	0.068	0.157	0.311	0.112	0.232	NA

Table 6: Results over the test set. The final ranking is determined by the mean reciprocal rank (MRR) of all scores.

performance enhancements our approaches were not able to capture due to this cost-based decision.

Ethics Statement

We artificially increased the size of our knowledge data set with few-shot data augmentation to cover a broader range of traveller types and domains. The synthetic reviews were created using GPT-3 and ChatGPT. There exists a potential for the introduction of biases in this newly generated data due to inherent model biases that might have been propagated into the reviews. This is especially concerning for commercial LLMs, like the ones used, since their training data is not made public.

Acknowledgements

References

Ateret Anaby-Tavor, Boaz Carmeli, Esther Goldbraich, Amir Kantor, George Kour, Segev Shlomov, Naama Tepper, and Naama Zwerdling. 2020. Do not have enough data? deep learning to the rescue! *Proceedings of the AAAI Conference on Artificial Intelligence*, 34(05):7383–7390.

Adithya Bhaskar, Alexander R. Fabbri, and Greg Durrett. 2023. Prompted opinion summarization with gpt-3.5.

Tom Brown, Benjamin Mann, Nick Ryder, Melanie Subbiah, Jared D Kaplan, Prafulla Dhariwal, Arvind Neelakantan, Pranav Shyam, Girish Sastry, Amanda Askell, et al. 2020. Language models are few-shot learners. *Advances in neural information processing systems*, 33:1877–1901.

Leshem Choshen, Elad Venezian, Shachar Don-Yehia, Noam Slonim, and Yoav Katz. 2022. Where to start? analyzing the potential value of intermediate models. *arXiv preprint arXiv:2211.00107*.

Hyung Won Chung, Le Hou, Shayne Longpre, Barret Zoph, Yi Tay, William Fedus, Eric Li, Xuezhi Wang, Mostafa Dehghani, Siddhartha Brahma, et al. 2022. Scaling instruction-finetuned language models. *arXiv preprint arXiv:2210.11416*.

Mihail Eric, Rahul Goel, Shachi Paul, Abhishek Sethi, Sanchit Agarwal, Shuyang Gao, Adarsh Kumar, Anuj Goyal, Peter Ku, and Dilek Hakkani-Tur. 2020. MultiWOZ 2.1: A consolidated multi-domain dialogue dataset with state corrections and state tracking baselines. In *Proceedings of the Twelfth Language Resources and Evaluation Conference*, pages 422–428, Marseille, France. European Language Resources Association.

Bogdan Gliwa, Iwona Mochol, Maciej Biesek, and Aleksander Wawer. 2019. SAMSum corpus: A human-annotated dialogue dataset for abstractive summarization. In *Proceedings of the 2nd Workshop on New Frontiers in Summarization*, pages 70–79, Hong Kong, China. Association for Computational Linguistics.

Seokhwan Kim, Mihail Eric, Karthik Gopalakrishnan, Behnam Hedayatnia, Yang Liu, and Dilek Hakkani-Tur. 2020. Beyond domain APIs: Task-oriented conversational modeling with unstructured knowledge access. In *Proceedings of the 21th Annual Meeting of the Special Interest Group on Discourse and Dialogue*, pages 278–289, 1st virtual meeting. Association for Computational Linguistics.

Seokhwan Kim, Yang Liu, Di Jin, Alexandros Papangelis, Behnam Hedayatnia, Karthik Gopalakrishnan, and Dilek Hakkani-Tür. 2022. Knowledge-grounded task-oriented dialogue modeling on spoken conversations track at dstc10.

Varun Kumar, Ashutosh Choudhary, and Eunah Cho. 2020. Data augmentation using pre-trained transformer models. In *Proceedings of the 2nd Workshop on Life-long Learning for Spoken Language Systems*, pages 18–26, Suzhou, China. Association for Computational Linguistics.

Kenton Lee, Kelvin Guu, Luheng He, Tim Dozat, and Hyung Won Chung. 2021. Neural data augmentation via example extrapolation. *arXiv preprint arXiv:2102.01335*.

Mike Lewis, Yinhan Liu, Naman Goyal, Marjan Ghazvininejad, Abdelrahman Mohamed, Omer Levy, Veselin Stoyanov, and Luke Zettlemoyer. 2020. BART: Denoising sequence-to-sequence pre-training for natural language generation, translation, and comprehension. In *Proceedings of the 58th Annual Meeting of the Association for Computational Linguistics*, pages 7871–7880, Online. Association for Computational Linguistics.

Silviu Pitis, Michael R Zhang, Andrew Wang, and Jimmy Ba. 2023. Boosted prompt ensembles for large language models. *arXiv preprint arXiv:2304.05970*.

Rico Sennrich, Barry Haddow, and Alexandra Birch. 2016. Improving neural machine translation models with monolingual data. In *Proceedings of the 54th Annual Meeting of the Association for Computational Linguistics (Volume 1: Long Papers)*, pages 86–96, Berlin, Germany. Association for Computational Linguistics.

Karan Singhal, Tao Tu, Juraj Gottweis, Rory Sayres, Ellery Wulczyn, Le Hou, Kevin Clark, Stephen Pfohl, Heather Cole-Lewis, Darlene Neal, Mike Schaekermann, Amy Wang, Mohamed Amin, Sami Lachgar, Philip Mansfield, Sushant Prakash, Bradley Green, Ewa Dominowska, Blaise Aguera y Arcas, Nenad Tomasev, Yun Liu, Renee Wong, Christopher Semturs, S. Sara Mahdavi, Joelle Barral, Dale Webster, Greg S. Corrado, Yossi Matias, Shekoofeh Azizi, Alan Karthikesalingam, and Vivek Natarajan. 2023. Towards expert-level medical question answering with large language models.

Zhiqing Sun, Xuezhi Wang, Yi Tay, Yiming Yang, and Denny Zhou. 2023. Recitation-augmented language models.

David Thulke, Nico Daheim, Christian Dugast, and Hermann Ney. 2022. Adapting Document-Grounded Dialog Systems to Spoken Conversations using Data Augmentation and a Noisy Channel Model. In *Workshop on DSTC10, AAAI*.

Xin Tian, Xinxian Huang, Dongfeng He, Yingzhan Lin, Siqi Bao, Huang He, Liankai Huang, Qiang Ju, Xiyuan Zhang, Jian Xie, Shuqi Sun, Fan Wang, Hua Wu, and Haifeng Wang. 2021. Tod-da: Towards boosting the robustness of task-oriented dialogue modeling on spoken conversations. *arXiv preprint arXiv:2112.12441*.

Xuezhi Wang, Jason Wei, Dale Schuurmans, Quoc Le, Ed Chi, Sharan Narang, Aakanksha Chowdhery, and Denny Zhou. 2023. Self-consistency improves chain of thought reasoning in language models.

Xuezhi Wang, Jason Wei, Dale Schuurmans, Quoc Le, Ed Chi, and Denny Zhou. 2022. Rationale-augmented ensembles in language models. *arXiv preprint arXiv:2207.00747*.

Jason Wei, Xuezhi Wang, Dale Schuurmans, Maarten Bosma, Ed Chi, Quoc Le, and Denny Zhou. 2022. Chain of thought prompting elicits reasoning in large language models. *arXiv preprint arXiv:2201.11903*.

Jason Wei and Kai Zou. 2019. EDA: Easy data augmentation techniques for boosting performance on text classification tasks. In *Proceedings of the 2019 Conference on Empirical Methods in Natural Language Processing and the 9th International Joint Conference on Natural Language Processing (EMNLP-IJCNLP)*, pages 6382–6388, Hong Kong, China. Association for Computational Linguistics.

Congying Xia, Caiming Xiong, Philip Yu, and Richard Socher. 2020. Composed variational natural language generation for few-shot intents. In *Findings of the Association for Computational Linguistics: EMNLP 2020*, pages 3379–3388, Online. Association for Computational Linguistics.

Dian Yu and Zhou Yu. 2019. MIDAS: A dialog act annotation scheme for open domain human machine spoken conversations. *CoRR*, abs/1908.10023.

Chao Zhao, Spandana Gella, Seokhwan Kim, Di Jin, Devamanyu Hazarika, Alexandros Papangelis, Behnam Hedayatnia, Mahdi Namazifar, Yang Liu, and Dilek Hakkani-Tur. 2023. " what do others think?": Task-oriented conversational modeling with subjective knowledge. *arXiv preprint arXiv:2305.12091*.

A Appendix


```
{
  "hotel": {
    "0": {
      "name": "A AND B GUEST HOUSE",
      "reviews": {
        "0": {
          " traveler_type ": "Solo travelers ",
          "sentences": {
            "0": "I was really happy with my recent stay at A and B Guest House.",
            "1": "I stayed on my own, and I'm a smoker, so I was super happy that there was a designated area especially for smokers.",
            "2": "I also thought that my room was very spacious, and I was pleased with the breakfast options that were available ."
          }
        },
        "1": {
          " traveler_type ": "Couples",
          "sentences": {
            "0": "My husband was pleased to be able to park on site for free .",
            "1": "We thought it was a bit noisy at A and B especially because it was just us and we had looked forward to quiet ."
          }
        },
        "2": {
          " traveler_type ": "Business travelers ",
          "sentences": {
            "0": "I wasn't thrilled the with lack of conveniences at A and B Guest House on my recent business trip .",
            "1": "No luggage storage service was inconvenient, and I was surprised there was no safety deposit box in a room.",
            "2": "I do appreciate the good breakfast options and the comfort of the bed, though.",
            "3": "So overall , I would probably stay there again."
          }
        },
        "3": {
          " traveler_type ": "Solo travelers ",
          "sentences": {
            "0": "I stayed at this guesthouse by myself.",
            "1": "I was happy with the laundry facilities that were on site .",
            "2": "The free available Internet provided great speeds and a strong connection .",
            "3": "I was treated to a lovely filling breakfast in the morning.",
            "4": "However, when I went to use the bathroom I found that the bathroom was not clean .",
            "5": "Also, when I went to put away my luggage I found that there were no provided spaces in which to do so."
          }
        },
        "4": {
          " traveler_type ": "Solo travelers ",
          "sentences": {
            "0": "Not long ago, I stayed at A and B Guest House by myself.",
            "1": "The staff was really friendly when I checked in, and I was thrilled with how comfy the bed was.",
            "2": "I got a great night of sleep !",
            "3": "But I was sad that there was no elevator so I had to use the stairs , and overall I think the room was overpriced ."
          }
        },
        "5": {
          " traveler_type ": "Solo travelers ",
          "sentences": {
            "0": "I stayed here by myself, and it was nice to be able to wash my clothes at the laundry .",
            "1": "Looking out of the window was nice, as the view was unique.",
            "2": "The location makes it a delight to get around on foot, and see things .",
            "3": "If only the room was a bit cleaner , it would have been perfect ."
          }
        },
        "6": {
          " traveler_type ": "Solo travelers ",
          "sentences": {
            "0": "The A and B Guest House is a great place to stay .",
            "1": "It is a beautiful place in a good location .",
            "2": "Very quiet .",
            "3": "The staff went out of their way to make sure that our stay was outstanding .",
            "4": "The clerk even sent a hand drawn card to us when he found it was our anniversary .",
            "5": "I don't remember when I've slept in a bed more comfortable than the one here .",
            "6": "Fair warning if you travel with valuables ; there is no safety box in the room.",
            "7": "Be careful ."
          }
        },
        "7": {
          " traveler_type ": "Families",
          "sentences": {
            "0": "My family and I decided to stay here while we were in town.",
            "1": "It was kid friendly , so my kids weren't treated like garbage.",
            "2": "It was also in a good location with access to most important things , and parking was completely free .",
            "3": "The staff , on the other hand, were really unprofessional and laid back.",
            "4": "They were not professional at all ."
          }
        },
        "8": {
          " traveler_type ": "Solo travelers ",
          "sentences": {
```

```
        "0": "The room was very large and spacious .",
        "1": "Made it very easy to settle in and relax after a long trip , and even more relaxing with the excellent view out of my window!",
        "2": "The room included free Wi-Fi which was very much appreciated because its quite uncommon to get free internet service these
            days!",
        "3": "My only complaint was that there was no concierge service and I had to take care of this myself - a bit annoying but overall a
            great stay ."
      }
    },
    "9": {
      " traveler_type ": "Couples",
      " sentences ": {
        "0": "The A and B could be a problem if you need an accessible room you may need to book elsewhere .",
        "1": "The room was not very clean but it was large .",
        "2": "My boyfriend and I both thought the bed had a good firmness for our liking .",
        "3": "There is a great view especially at sunset ."
      }
    "10": {
      " traveler_type ": "Family travelers ",
      " sentences ": {
        "0": "We had a great time staying at A and B Guest House with our kids .",
        "1": "The staff was very accommodating and provided us with a baby crib and high chair upon request .",
        "2": "The breakfast options were great and the location was convenient for our family activities .",
        "3": "The only downside was that the room was a bit cramped for our family of four ."
      }
    },
    "11": {
      " traveler_type ": "Group travelers ",
      " sentences ": {
        "0": "Our group of friends stayed at A and B Guest House and we had a great time .",
        "1": "The staff was friendly and helpful , and the location was perfect for exploring the city .",
        "2": "The rooms were clean and comfortable , and the breakfast was delicious .",
        "3": "The only issue we had was that the Wi-Fi was a bit spotty in some areas of the guest house ."
      }
    },
    "12": {
      " traveler_type ": "Budget travelers ",
      " sentences ": {
        "0": "A and B Guest House was a great choice for our budget-friendly trip .",
        "1": "The room was clean and comfortable , and the breakfast options were good.",
        "2": "The location was also convenient for exploring the city on foot .",
        "3": "The only downside was that the room was a bit small and there was no elevator ."
      }
    },
    "13": {
      " traveler_type ": "Luxury travelers ",
      " sentences ": {
        "0": "As a luxury traveler , I was disappointed with my stay at A and B Guest House.",
        "1": "The room was small and lacked the amenities I expect from a luxury hotel .",
        "2": "The staff was friendly but not particularly attentive to my needs.",
        "3": "The only positive was the location , which was convenient for exploring the city ."
      }
    },
    "14": {
      " traveler_type ": "Pet owners",
      " sentences ": {
        "0": "We were happy to find a pet-friendly option in A and B Guest House.",
        "1": "The staff was accommodating and provided us with a pet bed and bowls upon request .",
        "2": "The location was also convenient for walking our dog.",
        "3": "The only downside was that there was no designated pet area for our dog to use the bathroom."
      }
    }
  }
},
"faqs": {
  "0": {
    "question": "Are children welcomed at this location ?",
    "answer": "Yes, you can stay with children at A and B Guest House."
  },
  "1": {
    "question": "Can I bring my pet to A and B Guest House?",
    "answer": "No, pets are not allowed at this property ."
  },
  "2": {
    "question": "Do you have onsite parking for your guests ?",
    "answer": "There is onsite parking at A and B Guest House but it costs extra ."
  },
  "3": {
    "question": "What time is check-in there ?",
    "answer": "Check-in time is from 3:30pm - 9:00pm."
  },
  "4": {
    "question": "Is smoking allowed on the property ?",
    "answer": "There are designated smoking areas throughout"
  },
  "5": {
    "question": "What languages are spoken?",
```

```
        "answer": "English, Italian , Lithuanian, Portuguese, and Russian are spoken here."
      },
      "6": {
        "question": "Should I make a reservation for parking?",
        "answer": "You need to make a reservation at A and B Guest House for parking."
      },
      "7": {
        "question": "Are children allowed to check in here?",
        "answer": "An individual has to be 18 and over to check in at A and B Guest House."
      },
      "8": {
        "question": "what time do I check out?",
        "answer": "Check out times range from 7:30 AM to 10:00 AM."
      },
      "9": {
        "question": "Can my small dog stay with me?",
        "answer": "Pets are not allowed at the A and B Guest House."
      }
    }
  },
```

Knowledge data example: Slightly shortened example from the knowledge.json. Reviews 0-9 are original, and reviews 10-14 are augmented.

Traveler Type	Count Original Reviews	Count Augmented Reviews
Families	320	95
Solo travelers	315	101
Couples	279	109
Colleagues	230	11
Friends	210	84
Business travelers	76	111
Budget travelers	0	49
Luxury travelers	0	39
Families with children	0	22
Foodies	0	19
Vegetarians	0	10
Pet owners	0	9
Business	0	6
Groups	0	6
Backpackers	0	5
Friends getaway	0	5
Families with teenagers	0	3
Adventure travelers	0	3
Retirees	0	3
Group of friends	0	2
Families with young children	0	2
Honeymooners	0	1
Senior travelers	0	1
Romantic couples	0	1
Romantic travelers	0	1
Students	0	1

Table 7: Comparison of traveler types between the original reviews and the added reviews. Some extremely similar types were combined into one e.g. "Family with children" and "Family with kids".

Leveraging Ensemble Techniques and Metadata for Subjective Knowledge-grounded Conversational Systems

Seongho Joo[*1] **Kang-il Lee**[*1] **Kyungmin Min**[*1] **Joongbo Shin**[2]
Janghoon Han[2] **Seungpil Won**[2] **Kyomin Jung**[1,3]
[1]Seoul National University, [2]LG AI Research, [3]SNU-LG AI Research Center
{seonghojoo, 4bkang, kyungmin97, kjung}@snu.ac.kr
{jb.shin, janghoon.han, seungpil.won}@lgresearch.ai

Abstract

The goal of DSTC11 track 5 is to build task-oriented dialogue systems that can effectively utilize external knowledge sources such as FAQs and reviews. This year's challenge differs from previous ones as it includes subjective knowledge snippets and requires multiple snippets for a single turn. We propose a pipeline system for the challenge focusing on entity tracking, knowledge selection and response generation. Specifically, we devise a novel heuristic to ensemble the outputs from the rule-based method and neural model for entity tracking and knowledge selection. We also leverage metadata information in the knowledge source to handle fine-grained user queries. Our approach achieved the first place in objective evaluation and the third place in human evaluation of DSTC11 track 5.

1 Introduction

Task-oriented dialogue (TOD) systems aim to provide users with specific services, such as making restaurant reservation or booking hotel. Typically, these systems utilize domain-specific APIs, which are limited to predefined functionalities. However, there are scenarios where a user's request go beyond the coverage of domain API. For instance, the user might ask about alcohol availability at a restaurant or the availability of free WiFi at a hotel. To handle such cases, TOD system that can refer to external knowledge base, or knowledge-grounded TODs, has drawn much attention (Wu et al., 2019; Kim et al., 2020).

Previous studies on knowledge-grounded TODs have focused on factual knowledge, such as FAQs about restaurants or hotels. In practice, users usually show interest not only in factual information but also in subjective information, involving the experiences, opinions, and preferences of other customers (Zhao et al., 2023). To address this aspect, DSTC11 track 5 specifically focuses on building a dialogue system that can effectively utilize subjective knowledge snippets. The subjective knowledge snippets consist of customer reviews concerned with hotels and restaurants, such as "If only the room was a bit cleaner, it would have been perfect" and "We loved the atmosphere from the moment we walked in." Furthermore, in some cases, multiple knowledge snippets need to be retrieved in order to adequately respond to a single user request, adding an additional layer of complexity to DSTC11 track 5.

To this end, we propose a pipeline system that addresses four subtasks of knowledge-grounded TOD: (1) knowledge-seeking turn detection, (2) entity tracking, (3) knowledge selection, and (4) response generation. For entity tracking, we propose a novel heuristic that combines the results of rule-based and neural entity matching models. In knowledge selection, we leverage given metadata to precisely retrieve relevant review snippets when the user's request is highly specific, such as asking about a particular menu of a restaurant. For response generation, we propose a data augmentation method using a Large Language Model (LLM) to fine-tune the response generation model, enabling it to handle cases with mixed opinions more effectively. Overall schema of our pipeline is illustrated in Figure 1.

Our approach demonstrates significant improvement over baseline method in terms of the accuracy of knowledge selection and the quality of response generation. Furthermore, our submission achieved the top in objective evaluation and the third place in human evaluation of DSTC11 track 5.

2 Task Description

DSTC11 Track 5 is about Task-oriented Conversational Modeling with Subjective Knowledge. The dialogue dataset used in this track is an extension of MultiWoz 2.1(Eric et al., 2020), where reviews

[*] Equal contribution.

Proceedings of The Eleventh Dialog System Technology Challenge, pages 206–215
September 11, 2023 ©2023 Association for Computational Linguistics

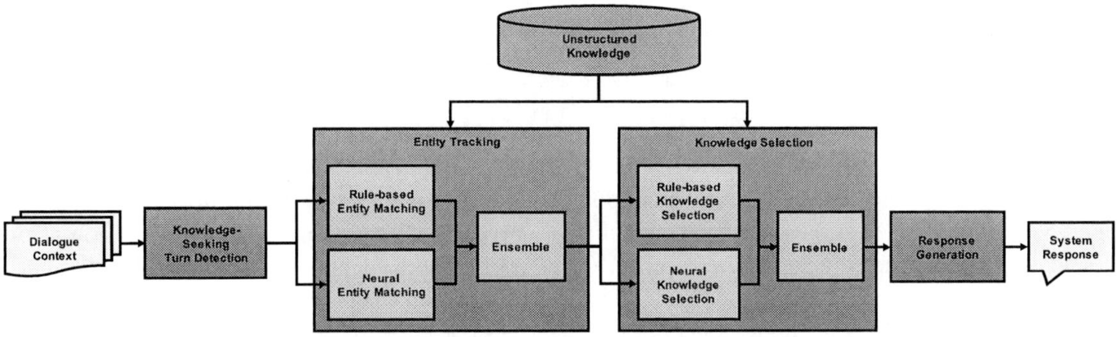

Figure 1: Overall pipeline of our conversational model.

for the exact location contain different opinions. Subjective opinions make the task more challenging than DSTC9 track 1 (Kim et al., 2020), which relied only on factual knowledge for generating responses.

The overall task can be divided into four sequential subtasks, which are as follows: knowledge-seeking turn detection, entity tracking, knowledge selection, and response generation. Knowledge-seeking turn detection determines whether subjective knowledge is required to generate the response based on the dialogue context and the user's last utterance. Entity tracking is the task of identifying the entity relevant to the user's last utterance, which helps reduce the number of candidate knowledge snippets. Knowledge selection involves finding relevant knowledge snippets to user's request from the narrowed-down knowledge pool (Reviews, FAQs) obtained by the entity tracking. Finally, response generation is the task of generating a response of the user's request grounded on the selected knowledge snippets. Given that the knowledge snippets often have conflicting opinions about entities, it is crucial to reflect both positive and negative reviews whenever possible.

The challenge dataset is structured in the following way. Firstly, it includes a dialog dataset that contains conversations between a user and a system. Secondly, there is a Knowledge dataset comprising reviews and FAQs for each domain/entity. In this context, "domain" refers to "hotel" and "restaurant", and "entity" refers to specific names such as a hotel name (e.g. CITYROOMZ) or a restaurant name (e.g. ROSA'S BED AND BREAKFAST). Each entity has its own set of review documents and FAQs. The review documents comprise sentences and also store metadata that offers additional information about each review, such as the type of traveler (e.g. couples, etc.), specific dishes (e.g. beef wellington, etc.), and beverages (e.g. beer, ale, etc.). The FAQs are stored as pairs of questions and answers.

3 Method

In this section, we explain the methods for each subtask: knowledge-seeking turn detection, entity tracking, knowledge selection, and response generation. The overall pipeline of our subtask is described in the Figure 1.

3.1 Knowledge-Seeking Turn Detection

Knowledge-seeking turn detection is a binary classification task that determines whether subjective knowledge is needed given dialogue context. We use the DeBERTa-v3-base (He et al., 2023) model as our backbone. We feed the dialogue context into the pretrained DeBERTa-v3 model and get output vectors by mean pooling. Afterward, we pass the pooled vector through a linear layer and use softmax to construct a binary classifier. This method is the same as the given baseline method in DSTC11 track 5. The model was fine-tuned by binary cross-entropy loss.

3.2 Entity Tracking

Entity tracking is a method that aims to find relevant entities based on the dialogue context and the user's request. Accurately extracting relevant entities is crucial for optimizing the performance and efficiency of a dialogue system. The more accurate the entity tracking, the fewer knowledge candidates need to be retrieved in the knowledge selection step, resulting in more precise and efficient knowledge selection process. Therefore, we perform both rule-based entity matching and neural entity matching to achieve accurate entity tracking and then ensemble those entity matching results.

3.2.1 Rule-based Entity Matching

We develop our own rule-based entity matching method based on the baseline entity matching method provided in DSTC11 track 5. In each dialogue turn in dialogue context, we perform fuzzy n-gram matching (Jin et al., 2021; Zhao et al., 2023) with all entities (143 entities). Fuzzy n-gram matching finds the longest contiguous matching sub-sequence between each dialogue turns and entities, then calculates a matching ratio. If the matching ratio exceeds a predefined threshold, we store the entity and its dialogue history turn. Based on our observation, we noticed that the more recent an entity appears, the more relevant it tends to be to the user's request. To tackle this, we track entities from the most recent dialogue history turn selected by fuzzy matching. This approach enables us to identify and prioritize the entities that are most likely to be relevant to the user's current request.

3.2.2 Neural Entity Matching

In neural entity matching, we regard the task as a sentence pair classification problem. We use the DeBERTa-v3-large model to find relevant entities. The dialogue history and entity are fed into the DeBERTa model as an input of sentence pair classification task. The training and inference are conducted in the same way as in knowledge-seeking turn detection.

Unlike knowledge-seeking turn detection, there is no negative samples provided by the dataset. Thus, we build our own set of negative samples using 4 sampling strategies with various difficulty: (1) rule-based entity matching negative, (2) similar-name negative, (3) in-domain negative, and (4) random negative. These multi-scale negatives improve the robustness of our neural entity matching model.

Rule-based entity matching negatives are sampled from aforementioned rule-based entity matching algorithm's false positives. These samples serve as hard negatives that are very informative for the neural model. Similar-name negatives are sampled from the set of entities with at least 50% token overlap with ground truth entity. In-domain negatives are sampled from the entities with the same domain and random negatives are randomly sampled from the whole entity set.

3.2.3 Ensemble

Here, we present our heuristic ensemble method that combines the outputs of rule-based entity matching and neural entity matching. We have noticed that entity annotation errors are quite common, particularly when multiple entities are involved in a single turn. These annotation errors deteriorate the neural entity matching performance in scenarios where multiple entities are present.

In contrast, the advantage of rule-based entity matching lies in its robustness against annotation errors. It has the ability to track multiple entities fairly when they appear in a single dialogue turn. However, rule-based entity matching lacks the capability to understand the dialogue context and only extracts entities from the most recent dialogue turn selected by fuzzy matching. From this perspective, neural entity matching excels as it can utilize the understanding of the dialogue context to extract entities that appear in past dialogue turns.

We have observed that when the neural model tracks only one entity in the dialogue context, it has a high level of confidence in the prediction. Consequently, if the neural model predicts only one entity, we utilize the prediction of the neural model. For dialogue contexts where the neural model extracted multiple entities, we use the entities extracted by rule-based entity matching. This heuristic of ensembling the results of two distinct models demonstrates strong performance compared to baseline entity matching.

3.3 Knowledge Selection

Knowledge selection involves identifying relevant knowledge snippets to address user inquiries effectively. Initially, the candidate knowledge snippets are narrowed down through entity tracking. The retrieval process is then conducted on these refined candidates using two distinct approaches: neural knowledge selection and rule-based knowledge selection.

3.3.1 Neural Knowledge Selection

In neural knowledge selection, context is critical when dealing with pronouns in review sentences. Without the context provided by previous sentence, it is tough to understand a review sentence containing a pronoun. Thus, we concatenate the preceding sentence in front of each candidate sentence to ascertain the relevance. In conclusion, a pair of consecutive review sentences form what we refer to as "consecutive knowledge snippets".

We use DeBERTa-v3-large as the backbone model. We construct the model input as follows: [CLS] + dialog history + [SEP] + consecutive knowledge snippets + [SEP], where [CLS] and [SEP] represent special tokens. For FAQs, consecutive knowledge snippets are constructed by concatenating the question and answer pairs. Then, binary classification is performed by mean pooling the last hidden states to determine the relevance of each knowledge snippet and the user's request.

3.3.2 Rule-based Knowledge Selection

The unstructured knowledge base provided in DSTC11 track 5 allows us to harness metadata for knowledge selection. The metadata let us know in advance which dish or drink the restaurant review document was related to. We also have found that the user's request is often associated with a specific drink or dish. In this case, utilizing metadata is a very efficient and accurate method.

To achieve this, we collect all entities related to dishes and drinks derived from the metadata, hereafter referred to as the "metadata entity set." We adopt a fuzzy n-gram matching approach to compare the user's latest utterance with the metadata entity set, facilitating the decision on whether to leverage metadata for the knowledge selection step. If the metadata is found to be relevant, an additional round of fuzzy n-gram matching is performed between all candidate knowledge snippets and the corresponding metadata to select relevant knowledge snippets.

Fuzzy n-gram matching effectively identifies specific words' presence but falls short in determining the context. To address this limitation, we employ DeBERTa-v3-large. This neural model explores the knowledge snippets and retrieves the most relevant knowledge snippet with the highest logit value among the knowledge snippets within the document containing the metadata detected by fuzzy matching. In other words, for each document containing relevant metadata, the neural model identifies the most suitable knowledge snippet. Finally, the output of rule-based knowledge selection is constructed by the union of knowledge snippets obtained through fuzzy n-gram matching and those selected by the neural model.

3.3.3 Ensemble

In the DSTC11 track 5 challenge, metadata includes information such as the names of dishes and drinks. If the user's last utterance contains metadata, we utilize the rule-based knowledge selection method. Sometimes, the metadata is mentioned in the user's last utterance but not found in any candidate knowledge snippets. In these cases, no knowledge snippet would be retrieved through fuzzy n-gram matching. In such exceptional cases, no knowledge snippets would be selected, and we rely on the results obtained from the neural knowledge selection. Also, we employ the neural knowledge selection when the user's last utterance does not contain any metadata.

3.4 Response generation

Response generation is the core task of task-oriented dialogue generation where the system response is generated based on the knowledge snippets, dialogue context, and the input utterance of the user. The main issue of response generation is properly reflecting all relevant knowledge snippets. However, we have observed that response generation models often neglect some of the knowledge snippets that are relevant to the user utterance and context history. Consequently, the model sometimes reflects only negative reviews regarding the domain or only positive reviews even if there exist both negative and positive reviews about the place.

3.4.1 Pseudo labels

To remedy the aforementioned problem, we generated pseudo labels that indicate whether given knowledge snippets have mixed opinions or not. In here, the 'mixed' means that the reviews both have positive and negative nuances about the domain. To generate the pseudo labels of knowledge snippets, the recently celebrated GPT-3 (text-davinci-003) model was used.

```
Determine whether the following
reviews contain conflicting
options related to the context:
Context: <Question 1>
Reviews: <Knolwedge Snippets1>
Opinions are conflicting: true
.
.
.
Context: <QuestionN>
Revies: <Knolwedge SnippetsN>
Opinions are conflicting: false
Context: <Question>
Reviews: <Test snippets>
Opinions are conflicting:
```

Figure 2: Example of the prompt for in-context learning

Method	Exact Match	Over Prediction	Under Prediction	Incorrect
Baseline	0.9076	0.0351	0.0129	0.0444
Rule-based	0.9316	0.0377	0.0081	0.0226
Neural	0.8987	0.0869	0.0002	0.0122
Baseline + Neural	0.9494	0.0189	0.0129	0.0189
Rule-based + Neural	**0.9545**	0.0233	0.0085	0.0137

Table 1: Results of entity tracking task on custom test set. If the predicted entity set is P and the ground-truth entity set is G, Exact Match, Over Prediction, Under Prediction, and Incorrect occurs when $P = G$, $G \subset P$, $P \subset G$, and $(P - G \neq \emptyset) \cap (G - P \neq \emptyset)$, respectively. The numbers in the table represent the proportion that each case occupies in the entire test set.

The pseudo labels are generated via in-context learning. First, pairs of knowledge snippets and user utterances are labeled manually by humans. Each sample (a knowledge snippet and a user utterance) is given a true label if the snippets have mixed opinions, and a false label otherwise. The knowledge snippets of our interest get the pseudo label by GPT-3 via in-context learning with the samples like Figure 2.

We also filter out trivial knowledge snippet cases like there is only a single ground truth knowledge snippet for the turn. After the in-context learning, pseudo labels for ground truth knowledge snippets are generated. These labels are treated as special tokens along with other tokens to generate the response.

3.4.2 Augmentation

Another speculation for why the model is vulnerable when knowledge snippets have mixed reviews is that the training set is biased towards simple cases like all reviews are positive or negative compared to mixed cases. This assumption guides us to generate mixed snippets where grounded knowledge snippets both have positive and negative reviews about the place.

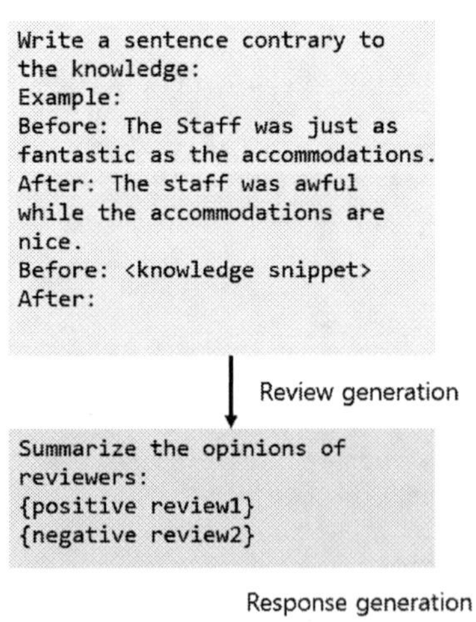

Figure 3: Example of data augmentation

We again employ the large language models to generate mixed reviews based on a positive or negative reviews. We instruct the GPT-3 (text-davinci-003) to write a review contrary to the knowledge. For example, if the input utterance is "`The staff was just as fantastic as the accommodation`", we expect that the output utterance from GPT-3 should have the opposite meaning like "`The staff was awful while the accommodations are nice`". Like the pseudo-label generation, in-context learning is used for the review generation. Finally, the response for query and snippets are generated by prompt `Summarize the opinions of reviewers`.

Although it is an effective approach for generating cases where opinions are mixed, the response might differ by a large margin from the ground truth response which leads to deteriorated BLEU score. The overall process is described in Figure 3. We observe that there is little drop in BLEU score when a small amount of augmented samples are added, but the BLEU dropped by a large margin when a large amount of augmented samples are added to the dataset.

4 Experiments

4.1 Entity Tracking

Our work focuses on two different approaches in the Entity Tracking task. The first approach aims to increase the recall score to minimize the chances of missing relevant entities. However, this approach has challenges in accurately selecting the appropriate knowledge during the selection stage. The second approach prioritizes increasing the exact match score to facilitate accurate knowledge selection. We concentrated on the latter approach and designed an ensemble method, described in section 3.2.3, to enhance the exact match ratio.

To evaluate the performance of our proposed method, we conduct experiments comparing various entity matching techniques: (1) baseline entity matching, (2) rule-based entity matching, (3) neural entity matching, (4) ensemble of baseline entity matching with neural entity matching, and (5) ensemble of rule-based entity matching with neural entity matching. To ensure the consistency of evaluation, we create a custom test set specifically for this purpose. The custom test set is designed to have no duplicate logs and contains unseen entities, accounting for 10% of the total entities.

Our findings, presented in Table 1, demonstrate that when applied to baseline method, our rule-based method improves exact match ratio from 0.91 to 0.93. This difference can be attributed to the fact that we lowered the threshold from 0.95 to 0.85. With a threshold of 0.95, even minor typos in the log's entity would result in exclusion, whereas lowering the threshold to 0.85 allowed for the inclusion of such cases. Analysis of the log data reveals a substantial occurrence of entity name typos, supporting this adjustment's effectiveness.

The neural entity matching approach alone exhibits a low exact match score, especially in multi-entity tracking. Our proposed method, which combines rule-based entity matching with neural entity matching, overcomes this weakness and the results demonstrate strong performance which make improvement in the exact match performance compared to the baseline method, with the score increasing from 0.91 to 0.95.

4.2 Knowledge Selection

In Knowledge Selection task, we use the ground truth label of the Entity tracking task as input to verify the performance of our proposed neural-based knowledge selection. We compared the performance of DeBERTa-v3-base with only one candidate knowledge snippet as the baseline method and DeBERTa-v3-base with our proposed consecutive knowledge snippets.

Table 2 shows that giving consecutive knowledge snippets is better in terms of precision, recall, F-1 score, and exact match ratio. We adopt a consecutive knowledge snippet approach and aim to analyze the impact of model size on performance. Specifically, we compare the performance of two models, DeBERTa-v3-base and DeBERTa-v3-large, to determine if increasing the model size would improve results.

Method	Precision	Recall	F-1 score	Exact match
Baseline-DeBERTa-base	0.9596	0.9416	0.9505	0.8555
Consecutive-DeBERTa-base	0.9661	0.9533	0.9597	0.8662
Consecutive-DeBERTa-large	0.9626	**0.9638**	0.9632	0.8935
Ensemble	**0.9714**	0.9553	**0.9633**	**0.9009**

Table 2: Results of Neural Knowledge Selection

The evaluation results shows that utilizing a larger model enhances the retrieval performance. Based on this finding, we select the DeBERTa-v3-large model for knowledge selection, considering its superior performance in capturing relevant information.

Moreover, we further improve our system by ensembling the DeBERTa-v3-large model through a majority voting scheme. This ensemble model is trained and validated on three separate dataset splits, allowing for diversified learning. Notably, this ensemble approach substantially enhanced the F-1 score and exact match accuracy.

Our experiments demonstrate the efficacy of employing consecutive knowledge snippets and the advantages of leveraging a larger model, DeBERTa-v3-large, for knowledge selection. Furthermore, our ensemble strategy based on multiple training partitions led to significant performance improvements, as indicated by the enhanced F-1 score and exact match accuracy.

4.3 Generation

We've used the T5-large model as the baseline in this section. First, we conducted the experiment

Model	BLEU	Mix failed
Baseline	**0.111**	52/211
1600 Aug	0.106	32/211
3200 Aug	0.104	28/211
4800 Aug	0.105	**22/211**
Baseline+Pseudo	0.103	53/211
Baseline+Pseudo+Aug	0.102	45/211
T5-3B+Pseudo	0.101	51/211
T5-3B+Pseudo+Aug	0.95	28/211

Table 3: Performance on DSTC11 validation set with the data augmentation. "Mix failed" denotes the portion of samples that fail to reflect both positive and negative samples. number+'Aug' denotes the augmentation method with n additional augmented samples. 'Pseudo' denotes the model trained with pseudo labels.

	Knowledge Selection Ensemble(Voting)	Response Generation		
		Data Augmentation	Pseudo Labeling	Composition
Entry 0	Single Model	YES	YES	NO
Entry 1	3 out of 6 votes required for Selection	YES	YES	NO
Entry 2	6 out of 6 votes required for Selection	YES	YES	NO
Entry 3	6 out of 6 votes required for Selection	NO	NO	NO
Entry 4	6 out of 6 votes required for Selection	NO	NO	YES

Table 4: Our submission entries in DSTC11 track 5. Pseudo labeling refers to incorporating a "mixed" label, identifying whether the selected knowledge snippets possess both positive and negative senses. Composition means that the model generates individual responses for each knowledge snippets and combines the responses using InstructGPT.

to verify if the augmentation approach is effective. As a first step, we first gather samples that have both positive and negative reviews from the held out DSTC11 dataset. We then compare model responses with ground truth responses from the filtered-out samples. In addition to BLEU score, we count how many samples the model succeeds to reflect both positive and negative reviews.

Table 3 shows the evaluation results of various generation methods. Overall, the augmentation approach generates lower BLEU score samples due to the style dissimilarity. However, the model with an augmentation approach shows better performance regarding mixed reviews. We have not seen a conspicuous change in BLEU score or human evaluation as we increase the number of augmentation samples. Here, 'pseudo' denotes the pseudo labels, and 'aug' denotes the data augmentation. Although T5-3B model with pseudo labels and data augmentation showed superior performance regarding reflecting both positive and negative reviews, its BLEU score drops significantly compared to the baseline.

4.4 Submission Results

The evaluation in the DSTC11 track 5 challenge involved three subtasks: knowledge-seeking turn detection (task 1), knowledge selection (including Entity tracking) (task 2), and response generation (task 3). Each participating team has the opportunity to submit a maximum of five entries. In our submissions, we employ the following method:

We use the DeBERTa-v3-base model provided in the baseline for turn detection in all five entries. All submitted entries use ensemble method for entity tracking and knowledge selection respectively. The details of the ensemble method using majority voting in the knowledge selection are described in Table 4 for each entry. In addition, the details of each entry submitted in the response generation are also reported in Table 4. Out of the 14 teams, our team is Team 13. Our submission entries ranked the highest score in precision, F-1, and exact match in knowledge selection and BLEU score in response generation. Additionally, our model secured the first place in the accuracy category of the human evaluation and obtained third place overall.

Among 5 entries, Entry ID 3 was selected as the best system and evaluated by humans. As shown in Table 5 and Table 6, our approach achieved the first place in objective evaluation and the third place in human evaluation of DSTC11 track 5.

5 Related Work

Task-oriented dialogue systems are conversational systems designed to solve specific tasks or purposes requested by users. Traditional TOD systems have solved these problems by dividing them into subtasks using a pipleline architecture (Young et al., 2013). The pipeline architecture consists of natural language understanding (NLU) (Liu and Lane, 2016; Koh et al., 2023), dialogue state tracking (DST) (Nouri and Hosseini-Asl, 2018; Lee et al., 2021), dialogue policy (Peng et al., 2017), and natural language generation (NLG) (Wen et al., 2015; Peng et al., 2020) modules. By solving these four modules sequentially, the system generates dialogues that fulfill the user's objectives. End-to-end neural models for task-oriented dialogue (TOD) systems, which build a conversational system using a single unified model, have also been continuously researched and developed (Hosseini-Asl et al., 2020; Ham et al., 2020; Lee, 2021).

Task-oriented dialogue systems have predominantly relied on pre-defined application programming interfaces (APIs) and structured databases to generate user-specific responses (Zhao et al., 2023). However, this approach has limitations as it relies on having prior knowledge of user needs and encounters challenges in storing all the necessary

Method		Task1: Turn Detection			Task2: Knowledge Selection				Task3: Response Generation				
Team ID	Entry ID	Precision	Recall	F1	Precision	Recall	F1	Exact Match	BLEU	METEOR	ROUGE-1	ROUGE-2	ROUGE-L
Baseline		0.9661	0.9979	0.9980	0.7901	0.7877	0.7889	0.3906	0.1004	0.1748	0.3520	0.1430	0.2753
6	0	0.9968	**0.9996**	0.9982	0.8039	0.8775	0.8391	0.5547	0.1017	**0.1894**	0.3629	0.1478	0.2804
	0	0.9964	0.9982	0.9973	0.8341	0.8716	0.8524	**0.6567**	0.1024	0.1826	0.3638	0.1524	0.2868
	1	0.9964	0.9982	0.9973	0.8511	0.8581	**0.8546**	0.6474	0.1017	0.1830	0.3630	0.1530	0.2870
13 (Ours)	2	0.9964	0.9982	0.9973	**0.8590**	0.8449	0.8519	0.6432	0.1017	0.1819	0.3618	0.1514	0.2865
	3	0.9964	0.9982	0.9973	**0.8590**	0.8449	0.8519	0.6432	**0.1081**	0.1819	0.3652	0.1528	0.2872
	4	0.9964	0.9982	0.9973	**0.8590**	0.8449	0.8519	0.6432	0.0931	0.1840	0.3591	0.1484	0.2808
14	0	0.9979	0.9989	0.9984	0.7856	0.8035	0.7944	0.4183	0.1066	0.1748	0.3599	0.1577	0.2899

Table 5: Objective evaluation results in DSTC11 track 5.

Rank	Team ID	Entry ID	Accuracy	Appropriateness	Average
Ground-truth			2.9189	3.6422	3.2806
1	6	0	2.9095	**3.6596**	**3.2846**
2	8	0	2.9005	3.6535	3.2770
3	**13 (Ours)**	**3**	**2.9100**	3.6321	3.2710
4	2	3	2.8908	3.6487	3.2697
5	7	4	2.9046	3.6348	3.2697
6	12	2	2.8856	3.6518	3.2687
7	14	0	2.8912	3.6427	3.2670
Baseline			2.8715	3.6348	3.2531

Table 6: Human evaluation results in DSTC11 track 5.

knowledge to generate desired responses, making it impractical in real-world scenarios. Therefore, there are lots of attempts to go beyond the limitations of APIs by utilizing knowledge from unstructured documents. DSTC9 utilized domain FAQ knowledge (Kim et al., 2020), while Chen et al. (2022) employed knowledge from Wikipedia articles, both of which served as external knowledge sources rooted in factual information. However, in DSTC11 track 5, the goal is to use user review data as subjective knowledge to meet the user's needs in a TOD system.

Knowledge-grounded dialogue generation is not only relying on the dialogue context but also leveraging external knowledge (Liu et al., 2018; Dinan et al., 2019). By leveraging external knowledge alongside the dialogue context, it is possible to generate more meaningful responses to users. To provide meaningful answers, it is crucial to obtain relevant external knowledge, making this task akin to a form of retrieval task. The key is how to determine the relevance score between a request and external knowledge, similar to the significance of assessing the relevance score between a query and a document in Question Answering task. There are two ways to measure relevance scores using dense vectors. First, there is the method of using bi-encoder models (Das et al., 2016; Chang et al., 2020; Karpukhin et al., 2020). By employing bi-encoder models, the relevance score can be calculated using inner product or cosine distance. However, the bi-encoder model lacks cross-attention between the query and document, which limits the ability to capture deeper relationships. Another method for calculating relevance scores is to utilize a cross-encoder model (He et al., 2021). This allows token-level interaction between the query and document, resulting in better retrieval performance. In this work, we used the cross-encoder approach to retrieve knowledge relevant to the user's utterance.

6 Conclusion

In this work, we proposed a pipeline system for DSTC11 track 5: Task-oriented Conversational Modeling with Subjective Knowledge, mainly focusing on entity tracking, knowledge selection and response generation. Our approach involves the following methods: (1) an heuristic ensemble method to combine the outputs from the rule-based method and neural model, (2) a knowledge selection method based on metadata information, and (3) data augmentation method to tackle mixed opinions in review snippets. As a final result, our submission ranked the top in objective evaluation and the third place in human evaluation.

Acknowledgement

K. Jung is with ASRI, Seoul National University, Korea. This work was supported in part by LG AI Research. This work was partly supported by Institute of Information & communications Technology Planning & Evaluation (IITP) grant funded by the Korea government(MSIT) [NO.2021-0- 02068, Artificial Intelligence Innovation Hub (Artificial Intelligence Institute, Seoul National University) & NO.2021-0-01343, Artificial Intelligence Graduate School Program (Seoul National University)]

References

Wei-Cheng Chang, Felix X. Yu, Yin-Wen Chang, Yiming Yang, and Sanjiv Kumar. 2020. Pre-training tasks for embedding-based large-scale retrieval. In *International Conference on Learning Representations*.

Zhiyu Chen, Bing Liu, Seungwhan Moon, Chinnadhurai Sankar, Paul Crook, and William Yang Wang. 2022. KETOD: Knowledge-enriched task-oriented dialogue. In *Findings of the Association for Computational Linguistics: NAACL 2022*, pages 2581–2593, Seattle, United States. Association for Computational Linguistics.

Arpita Das, Harish Yenala, Manoj Chinnakotla, and Manish Shrivastava. 2016. Together we stand: Siamese networks for similar question retrieval. In *Proceedings of the 54th Annual Meeting of the Association for Computational Linguistics (Volume 1: Long Papers)*, pages 378–387, Berlin, Germany. Association for Computational Linguistics.

Emily Dinan, Stephen Roller, Kurt Shuster, Angela Fan, Michael Auli, and Jason Weston. 2019. Wizard of wikipedia: Knowledge-powered conversational agents. In *International Conference on Learning Representations*.

Mihail Eric, Rahul Goel, Shachi Paul, Abhishek Sethi, Sanchit Agarwal, Shuyang Gao, Adarsh Kumar, Anuj Goyal, Peter Ku, and Dilek Hakkani-Tur. 2020. MultiWOZ 2.1: A consolidated multi-domain dialogue dataset with state corrections and state tracking baselines. In *Proceedings of the Twelfth Language Resources and Evaluation Conference*, pages 422–428, Marseille, France. European Language Resources Association.

Donghoon Ham, Jeong-Gwan Lee, Youngsoo Jang, and Kee-Eung Kim. 2020. End-to-end neural pipeline for goal-oriented dialogue systems using gpt-2. In *Proceedings of the 58th annual meeting of the association for computational linguistics*, pages 583–592.

Huang He, Hua Lu, Siqi Bao, Fan Wang, Hua Wu, Zhengyu Niu, and Haifeng Wang. 2021. Learning to select external knowledge with multi-scale negative sampling.

Pengcheng He, Jianfeng Gao, and Weizhu Chen. 2023. DeBERTav3: Improving deBERTa using ELECTRA-style pre-training with gradient-disentangled embedding sharing. In *The Eleventh International Conference on Learning Representations*.

Ehsan Hosseini-Asl, Bryan McCann, Chien-Sheng Wu, Semih Yavuz, and Richard Socher. 2020. A simple language model for task-oriented dialogue. *Advances in Neural Information Processing Systems*, 33:20179–20191.

Di Jin, Seokhwan Kim, and Dilek Hakkani-Tur. 2021. Can I be of further assistance? using unstructured knowledge access to improve task-oriented conversational modeling. In *Proceedings of the 1st Workshop on Document-grounded Dialogue and Conversational Question Answering (DialDoc 2021)*, pages 119–127, Online. Association for Computational Linguistics.

Vladimir Karpukhin, Barlas Oguz, Sewon Min, Patrick Lewis, Ledell Wu, Sergey Edunov, Danqi Chen, and Wen-tau Yih. 2020. Dense passage retrieval for open-domain question answering. In *Proceedings of the 2020 Conference on Empirical Methods in Natural Language Processing (EMNLP)*, pages 6769–6781, Online. Association for Computational Linguistics.

Seokhwan Kim, Mihail Eric, Karthik Gopalakrishnan, Behnam Hedayatnia, Yang Liu, and Dilek Hakkani-Tur. 2020. Beyond domain APIs: Task-oriented conversational modeling with unstructured knowledge access. In *Proceedings of the 21th Annual Meeting of the Special Interest Group on Discourse and Dialogue*, pages 278–289, 1st virtual meeting. Association for Computational Linguistics.

Hyukhun Koh, Haesung Pyun, Nakyeong Yang, and Kyomin Jung. 2023. Multi-view zero-shot open intent induction from dialogues: Multi domain batch and proxy gradient transfer. *arXiv preprint arXiv:2303.13099*.

Chia-Hsuan Lee, Hao Cheng, and Mari Ostendorf. 2021. Dialogue state tracking with a language model using schema-driven prompting. In *Proceedings of the 2021 Conference on Empirical Methods in Natural Language Processing*, pages 4937–4949, Online and Punta Cana, Dominican Republic. Association for Computational Linguistics.

Yohan Lee. 2021. Improving end-to-end task-oriented dialog system with a simple auxiliary task. In *Findings of the Association for Computational Linguistics: EMNLP 2021*, pages 1296–1303, Punta Cana, Dominican Republic. Association for Computational Linguistics.

Bing Liu and Ian Lane. 2016. Attention-based recurrent neural network models for joint intent detection and slot filling. *Interspeech 2016*, pages 685–689.

Shuman Liu, Hongshen Chen, Zhaochun Ren, Yang Feng, Qun Liu, and Dawei Yin. 2018. Knowledge diffusion for neural dialogue generation. In *Proceedings of the 56th Annual Meeting of the Association for Computational Linguistics (Volume 1: Long Papers)*, pages 1489–1498, Melbourne, Australia. Association for Computational Linguistics.

Elnaz Nouri and Ehsan Hosseini-Asl. 2018. Toward scalable neural dialogue state tracking. In *NeurIPS 2018, 2nd Conversational AI workshop*.

Baolin Peng, Xiujun Li, Lihong Li, Jianfeng Gao, Asli Celikyilmaz, Sungjin Lee, and Kam-Fai Wong. 2017. Composite task-completion dialogue policy learning via hierarchical deep reinforcement learning. In *Proceedings of the 2017 Conference on Empirical Methods in Natural Language Processing*, pages 2231–2240, Copenhagen, Denmark. Association for Computational Linguistics.

Baolin Peng, Chenguang Zhu, Chunyuan Li, Xiujun Li, Jinchao Li, Michael Zeng, and Jianfeng Gao. 2020. Few-shot natural language generation for task-oriented dialog. In *Findings of the Association for Computational Linguistics: EMNLP 2020*, pages 172–182, Online. Association for Computational Linguistics.

Tsung-Hsien Wen, Milica Gašić, Nikola Mrkšić, Pei-Hao Su, David Vandyke, and Steve Young. 2015. Semantically conditioned LSTM-based natural language generation for spoken dialogue systems. In *Proceedings of the 2015 Conference on Empirical Methods in Natural Language Processing*, pages 1711–1721, Lisbon, Portugal. Association for Computational Linguistics.

Chien-Sheng Wu, Richard Socher, and Caiming Xiong. 2019. Global-to-local memory pointer networks for task-oriented dialogue. In *Proceedings of the International Conference on Learning Representations (ICLR)*.

Steve Young, Milica Gašić, Blaise Thomson, and Jason D Williams. 2013. Pomdp-based statistical spoken dialog systems: A review. *Proceedings of the IEEE*, 101(5):1160–1179.

Chao Zhao, Spandana Gella, Seokhwan Kim, Di Jin, Devamanyu Hazarika, Alexandros Papangelis, Behnam Hedayatnia, Mahdi Namazifar, Yang Liu, and Dilek Hakkani-Tur. 2023. "what do others think?": Task-oriented conversational modeling with subjective knowledge.

A Difference-aware Ensemble Method for Task-oriented Dialogue with Subjective Knowledge

Changxin Ke* and **Churui Sun*** and **Longxuan Ma*** and **Weinan Zhang**† and **Ting Liu**
Research Center for Social Computing and Information Retrieval
Faculty of Computing, Harbin Institute of Technology
{cxke,crsun}@stu.hit.edu.cn {lxma,wnzhang,tliu}@ir.hit.edu.cn

Abstract

We participate in the 11th Dialog System Technology Challenges (DSTC) track-5[1] called Task-oriented Conversational Modeling with Subjective Knowledge. Introducing subjective knowledge into task-oriented dialogue (TOD) can help the DS to understand variables of subjective user needs and to suit more dialogue scenarios. Track-5 includes several sub-tasks: 1) knowledge-seeking turn detection; 2) knowledge entity tracking; 3) knowledge entry selection; and 4) use of the selected knowledge entries for response generation. Besides the challenges of each sub-tasks own, there are two challenges across different sub-tasks. The first is that there are multiple valid knowledge entries for each knowledge-seeking turn, the accuracy of the knowledge entry selection is important for the quality of response generation. The second challenge is how to address the unseen dialogue/entities/entries in the validation and the test set. In this paper, we propose a difference-aware ensemble method to address these sub-tasks and the two challenges mentioned above. Our method helps to obtain more robust results and performs well on unseen instances. Among all the submissions for the test set, our method ranks 1st on the knowledge-seeking turn detection task and achieves 3rd on the overall automatic evaluation score. Our code and data will be released on GitHub.

Subjective Knowledge (the first review):
"0": "My work colleagues and I recently visited Nandos City Centre for lunch."
"1": "We tried many Portuguese dishes such as Alheira, Caldo Verde, Francesinha, and Torricado and washed everything down with beer."
"2": "The dishes were cooked perfectly and we were able to order a lot as the prices for the dishes and the beer were very reasonable."
"3": "It did take a little longer for the food to arrive at the table. Our plates took a while to clear from the wait staff."
"4": "But overall it was a good lunch."

Subjective Knowledge (the second review):
"0": "Yesterday me and some coworkers went to Nando's City Centre."
"1": "I've never had Portuguese cuisine but my coworker insisted on it."
"2": "I was disappointed with how expensive everything was though and I hoped everything tasted good."
"3": "I was surprised with how much food there was overall, the portions were quite generous."
"4": "I'm not sure I liked the food, it didn't live up to the hype for me."

Dialogue:
User: What do you know about Nandos City Centre?
Agent: Which part do you prefer to know?
User: How is the price? Is it expensive?
Agent: The price is very reasonable because the portions were quite generous.
User: Do we need to wait a long time for the food?
Agent: Yes, some customers say it did take a little while for the food to arrive.

Table 1: SK-TOD example that the agent produces response based on the subjective knowledge (two reviews are both under the entity "Nandos City Centre").

1 Introduction

Task-oriented Dialogue Systems (TODS) aim to assist users in domain-specific tasks, such as booking a traveling ticket or a restaurant. The TODS is usually based on a domain-specific API or Database (DB) that can provide the required information for accomplishing the task, such as the price of a ticket or the location of a restaurant. However, these APIs or DBs usually do not contain information for subjective user requests (e.g., "Is this a good place for meeting colleagues?" or "Does the hotel have a good atmosphere?"). TODS trained with these APIs/DBs can only handle a limited range of scenarios. To address this issue, Zhao et al. (2023) propose a novel task called subjective-knowledge-based TOD (SK-TOD). One SK-TOD example is shown in Table 1, where the dialogue agent (DS) needs to use subjective knowledge to complete a dialogue. According to Zhao et al. (2023), a TODS should consider multiple reviews with both positive

*These three authors contributed equally.
†Corresponding author
[1]https://github.com/alexa/dstc11-track5

Proceedings of The Eleventh Dialog System Technology Challenge, pages 216–225
September 11, 2023 ©2023 Association for Computational Linguistics

and negative opinions, along with their respective proportions to make a response (as exemplified in Table 1). This two-sided response is recognized as more credible and valuable for customers, thereby fostering trust in the TODS. The SK-TOD data is used as the track-5 of the 11th Dialog System Technology Challenges (DSTC 11) workshop[2].

The track-5 (called Task-oriented Conversational Modeling with Subjective Knowledge) challenge can be divided into four sub-tasks (Zhao et al., 2023): 1) knowledge-seeking turn detection. It takes the dialogue context as input and decides whether the response to this context requires selecting external knowledge; 2) knowledge entity tracking. It selects entities from the entity pool of the subjective knowledge; 3) knowledge entry selection. It selects knowledge entries related to the selected entity from the subjective knowledge; 4) response generation uses the selected knowledge entry for generating a response. The knowledge entity tracking and entry selection sub-tasks are performed only when a response turn is detected as a knowledge-seeking turn. Each of the four sub-tasks has its own challenge. However, there are two main challenges in this competition that across different sub-tasks. The first is that there are multiple related subjective knowledge entries for each knowledge-seeking turn. This affects all knowledge entity tracking, knowledge entry selection, and response generation. The second is that there is a big portion of unseen instances in the validation and test set (see Table 3), which includes unseen dialogues/entities/entries in the train set. This affects all sub-tasks.

In this paper, we propose a difference-aware ensemble method to address the two challenges across sub-tasks. For each sub-task, we start by training a group of models that are good at specific abilities (e.g. unseen instances, noisy environment). Then we aim to combine the advantages of each model for different sub-tasks and for unseen instances. In other words, we need to assign a reasonable weight for each model based on the desired metric. To this end, we need to jointly consider three differences: 1) the different requirements of each sub-task; 2) the difference between each trained model; 3) the difference between the validation set and the test set. Our ensemble method can automatically balance these differences among tasks/models/datasets and use a unified pattern to cope with different task scenarios. Experiments show that our method largely improves performance. Among all the submissions for the DSTC 11 track-5 test set, our method ranks 1st on the knowledge-seeking turn detection task and achieves 3rd on the overall automatic evaluation score. To sum up, our contributions are:

- To address the multiple knowledge entries and the unseen instance problems, we propose a difference-aware ensemble method to leverage the advantages of different models that are good at specific abilities. Our method can automatically balance the differences between tasks/datasets/models.
- Experiments show that our method outperforms strong baselines and performs well on the DSTC 11 track-5. We give a detailed analysis of the experiments. Our code and data will be released on GitHub.

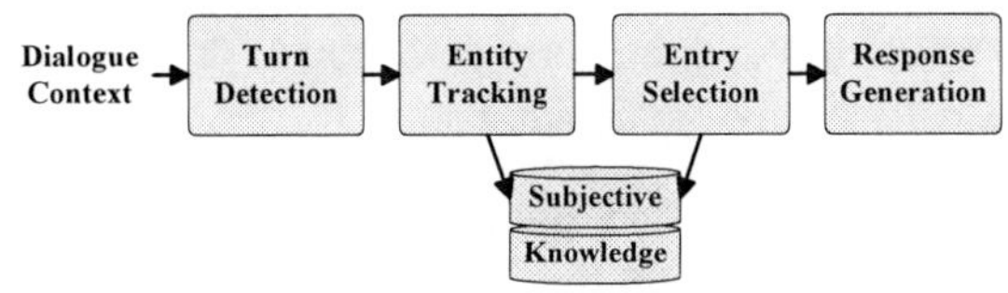

Figure 1: The pipeline we used for the SKTOD task.

2 Related Work

We introduce related work in this section, including knowledge-grounded conversation, task-oriented dialogue, large language models, and ensemble methods.

2.1 Knowledge-grounded Conversation

Knowledge-grounded conversation task first choose context-related knowledge from external sources (can be structured knowledge graph or unstructured text) and use the selected knowledge to construct a response (Zhou et al., 2018; Moghe et al., 2018; Dinan et al., 2019; Gopalakrishnan et al., 2019; Jang et al., 2022; Zhao et al., 2022). The SK-TOD task is similar to KGC with unstructured text as external knowledge, especially the knowledge selection (Kim et al., 2020a; Meng et al., 2020; Xu et al., 2022) and response generation (Zhao et al., 2020; Prabhumoye et al., 2021; Majumder et al., 2022) sub-tasks. However, the KGC task usually does not contain

[2]There are also a set of FAQs besides the subjective review knowledge. However, the dialogue is mainly grounded on subjective knowledge. Please refer to Table 3 for more details.

knowledge-seeking turn detection task and are usually open-domain dialogue.

2.2 Task-oriented dialogue and Recommendation

Task-oriented dialogues (TOD) usually rely on domain-specific APIs and databases to support the dialogue response (Levin et al., 2000; Zhao et al., 2017; Akasaki and Kaji, 2017; Yan et al., 2017). Later works ground task-oriented dialogues to web pages (Chen et al., 2022), government service documents (Feng et al., 2020), and FAQ knowledge snippets (Kim et al., 2020b). Different from these works where factual knowledge is utilized, we apply subjective knowledge to generate the response and ground in multiple knowledge snippets. There are also work in TOD (Majumder et al., 2022) and recommendation (Ni et al., 2019) that aim to generate review-based response or recommendation explanations. However, the SK-TOD requires grounding in multiple subjective knowledge and explicitly considers the diversity of opinions and the proportion of sentiments.

2.3 Ensemble Methods

The traditional ensemble iteratively minimizes the loss of the joint output (Hastie et al., 2001) and keeps the child model unchanged. Another ensemble pattern is pseudo-ensemble where the child models share parameters and structure through their parent model, which will tend to correlate the child models' behavior (Hinton et al., 2012; Bachman et al., 2014). The ensemble method is usually used in DSTC competitions (Tan et al., 2020; Chaudhary et al., 2021). Our methods belong to traditional ensemble methods that learn a robust model to input uncertainty. The difference is that our difference-aware ensemble method can jointly adjust different models/datasets/tasks.

2.4 Large Language Models

Large language models (LLMs) such as GPT-4 (OpenAI, 2023) and LLAMA (Touvron et al., 2023) show that pre-trained models with a large amount of parameters (usually more than 10 Billion) can understand complex instructions and perform well in a variety of tasks including dialogue. However, despite their success, recent studies (Bubeck et al., 2023) show that LLM still has the hallucination problem and could not perform well in domain-specific or knowledge-intense tasks even with elaborately designed instructions. In this paper, we test the response generation task with LLAMA-13B. The input is dialogue context and the selected knowledge entries. However, its performance is not as good as a smaller model such as the BART baseline.

3 Our Method

In this section, we first introduce how we train the models for each sub-tasks in DSTC 11 track-5, then introduce the difference-aware ensemble method.

3.1 Problem Statement

Formally, we have a dialogue context $\mathbf{C} = [U_1, A_1, U_2, A_2, ..., U_{|C|}]$ where each user turn U_i (i $\in$ [1,$|C|$]) is followed by a agent response turn S_i except the last user turn $U_{|C|}$. The dialogue involves one or multiple entities represented as $\mathbf{E}^C = \{E_1^C, E_2^C, ..., E_{|E^C|}^C\}$. Each entity E_i^C (i $\in$ [1,$|E^C|$]) has a group of subjective knowledge entries $\mathbf{K}^{E_i^C} = [K_1, K_2, ..., K_{|K^{E_i^C}|}]$[3]. The entity and their corresponding subjective knowledge are from a subjective knowledge source $\mathbf{B}$ = {($\mathbf{E}_1$, $\mathbf{K}^{E_1}$), ($\mathbf{E}_2$, $\mathbf{K}^{E_2}$), ..., ($\mathbf{E}_{|B|}$, $\mathbf{K}^{E_{|B|}}$) }. $|C|$, $|E^C|$, $|K^{E_i^C}|$, and $|B|$ are the number of elements in the corresponding set. The DSTC 11 track-5 needs first identify whether $U_{|C|}$ has a knowledge-seeking request and, if yes, then identifies a group of entities and their corresponding knowledge entries from the knowledge source **B**, then selects the most relevant subjective knowledge entries from the group, finally generates a response $A_{|C|}$ grounded on the selected entries. The pipeline for SK-TOD is illustrated in Figure 1. Next, we will introduce how we train models for each sub-tasks.

3.2 Knowledge-Seeking Turn Detection (KTD)

The KTD is a binary classification problem to identify whether the last user turn in context **C** requires to be addressed with subjective knowledge. The baseline is an auto-encoding pre-trained language model (DeBERTa-v3-base (He et al., 2021)). The baseline takes dialogue context **C** as input and uses the hidden state of the first token as its representation. Then it applies a classifier as follows to obtain the probability $P(\mathbf{C})$ that the current user request is a subjective knowledge-seeking turn:

[3] Each K_j can be paragraph, sentence, or segment.

$$h_C = \text{Enc}(\mathbf{C}), \quad (1)$$

$$P(\mathbf{C}) = \text{softmax}(\text{FFN}(h_C)). \quad (2)$$

The model is fine-tuned with the binary cross-entropy loss. As we introduced in Section 1, we want to obtain a group of models that are good at specific abilities (e.g. unseen instances, noisy environment) and then combine the advantages of each model for different sub-tasks. For the KTD task, we train three models.

We define the first model as an expert on seen dialogue data. It is similar to the baseline model given by the DSTC 11 track-5 organizers. We further fine-tune the model with the training set and select the checkpoint with the best performance on the validation set.

We define the second model as an expert on unseen dialogue data. To this end, we construct an unseen dialogue dataset with the given subjective knowledge and use this new unseen dataset to fine-tune a RoBERTa (Liu et al., 2019) model[4]. The unseen dialogue dataset combines original training dialogue data and the external knowledge Tan et al. (2020). This competition's training dialogue data usually starts with talking about an entity. For each entity, there are question-answering (QA) pairs in the corresponding knowledge source **B**. We first keep the starting 2 turns of a training example and randomly select the QA pairs related to this entity in **B**. We concatenate the selected QA pairs to the starting turns. Then we obtain a new unseen dialogue example that focuses on this entity. To mimic the situation of a topic shift in the real scenario, we check whether the last turn of the new example contains another entity in **B**. If so, we continue selecting QA pairs related to the second entity and add the QA pairs to the dialogue. Finally, we obtain a dialogue example that does not appear in the original training data. In practice, we use at most three entities and restrict the total length of the dialogue to 10 turns (which is similar to the average length of the training data). The length of turns under each entity is randomly decided. Training an unseen expert with this data can help the performance of unseen dialogue instances.

We define the third model as a de-noise expert. To this end, we pre-trained and fine-tuned a DeBERTa (He et al., 2021) model with an enlarged noisy training set so that the model is more aware of the noisy inputs. The pre-training is a classical word-masking training (Devlin et al., 2019; Liu et al., 2019) that randomly masks a portion (15%) of input words and asks the language model to recover them. The enlarged noisy data is obtained with a back-translation and synonym substitution process. We adopt the Google translation service[5] to translate English into other languages (such as Spanish/German/Japanese/French), then back-translated them into English[6]. Finally, we obtain 5 times dialogue and knowledge data. These data are used to pre-train the language models. We further pair the 5-times dialogue data with knowledge translated from different languages, which gives 25 times data for fine-tuning. These data are considered noise because the back-translation and synonym substitution introduces word-level and semantic-level disturbance.

After getting the seen expert, unseen expert, and de-noise expert models. We use a difference-aware ensemble method to combine their advantages, which will be introduced in Section 3.6.

3.3 Knowledge Entity Tracking (KET)

The goal of KET is to identify the entities that are relevant to the last user turn request. It can help to reduce the number of candidates in the step of knowledge selection. The baseline model given by the DSTC 11 track-5 organizers is a word-matching-based method (Jin et al., 2021) to extract relevant entities. It first normalizes entity names in the knowledge source using a set of heuristic rules. Then a fuzzy n-gram matching is performed between the normalized entity and all dialogue turns. To find the entities that are relevant to the last user request, the baseline method chooses the last dialogue turn in which the entities are detected and uses these entities as the output. We follow the baselines and have Precision=0.9516, Recall=0.9841, F1=0.9676, and accuracy=0.9398 on the validation set. It should be noted that the competition did not require to calculate results for the KET task. Meanwhile, we are limited by the schedule of the competition and fail to train well-performed experts on this sub-task. However, we believe our ensemble method is also useful for this task and we leave this training for future work.

[4]We use different PLMs because we want the difference between the seen and unseen experts to be more pronounced

[5]https://translate.google.com

[6]When the back-translation sentence is the same as the original sentence, we employ synonym substitution with Wordnet (https://wordnet.princeton.edu/) to increase diversity.

3.4 Knowledge Entry Selection (KES)

The goal of KS is to select the knowledge entries that are relevant to the user's request. The inputs are the dialogue context **C** and the knowledge candidates **K**, which is a combination of all the knowledge entries of the relevant entities in $\mathbf{E}^C$. The output $\mathbf{K}^+$ is a subset of **K** with the most relevant knowledge candidates. Note that there might be multiple knowledge snippets in $\mathbf{K}^+$. To select relevant knowledge snippets, the baseline proposed by DSTC organizers uses a bi-encoder (Mazaré et al., 2018) structure to calculate the relevance score between the dialogue context **C** and a knowledge entry $K_i \in \mathbf{K}$. The **C** and K_i are encoded separately using the same pre-trained encoder and obtain two representations, h_C and h_{K_i}. Then the concatenation of h_C, h_{K_i}, and $|h_C - h_{K_i}|$ is used as features to obtain the probability of relevance $P(\mathbf{C}, K_i)$ as follows:

$$h_C = \text{Enc}(\mathbf{C}), h_{K_i} = \text{Enc}(K_i), \tag{3}$$

$$h_{feature} = [h_C; h_{K_i}; |h_C - h_{K_i}|], \tag{4}$$

$$P(\mathbf{C}, K_i) = \text{softmax}(\text{FFN}(h_{feature})). \tag{5}$$

Similar to the KTD task, we also train three different models for KES. There are also denoted the seen expert, the unseen expert, and the de-noise expert.

3.5 Response Generation (RG)

The goal of RG is to use dialogue context **C** and the selected knowledge entries $\mathbf{K}^+$ to construct a response. The baseline for RG is a pre-trained generation model (BART (Lewis et al., 2020)) that concatenates **C** and $\mathbf{K}^+$ as the input and generates the response. The model is trained to maximize the generation probability P(A_t | **C**, $\mathbf{K}^+$). We fine-tuned BART and T5 (Raffel et al., 2020) for this task.

3.6 Ensemble Method

Algorithm 1 shows how our ensemble method balances the advantages of different models. Taking the knowledge entry selection for example, we calculate top N candidates for the k-th validation example from each model and sort them in descending order with respect to model confidence[7]. The S_k^{gt} is ground-truth results for this example with K entries, $K < N$. Each candidate is given a weight which is the reciprocal of its ranking number plus one. For instance, candidates from DeBERTa (seen expert) are S_j^D, ($j = 1, 2, ..., N$), and the corresponding weight is $W_j^D = \frac{1}{j+1}$. Similarly, S_j^R and W_j^R for RoBERTa (unseen expert), S_j^E and W_j^E for DeBERTa (de-noise expert). Then we use these candidates to form a final candidate dictionary S = $\{S_i, (i = 1, 2, ..., T)\}$, $N \leq T \leq 3N$. The ensemble weight W_i of S_i, is calculated by $W_i = p^D \cdot \tilde{W}_i^D + p^R \cdot \tilde{W}_i^R + p^E \cdot \tilde{W}_i^E$, $(i = 1, 2, ..., T)$, p is the hyper-parameter that we want to learn, $p^D + p^R + p^E = 1$. $\tilde{W}_i^D = W_j^D$ if there is a j such that $S_j^D \cong S_i$, 0 otherwise. $\cong$ means exact match here. $\tilde{W}_i^R$ and $\tilde{W}_i^E$ follows the same definition as $\tilde{W}_i^D$. Then we use a specific **Metric**, such as Recall/Precision/F1/EM (or the combination of them), to learn the optimal $\hat{p}$ with all examples in the validation set. We set a threshold for S and only reserve the candidates with W_i larger than the threshold, denoted by $S_{threshold}$. The threshold is set to $\frac{1}{6}$ according to the average entry numbers in Table 3. During testing, we use the threshold to select a set of candidates from S as our final prediction using the learned weight[8].

Next, we explain why this method can balance different tasks. According to the experiments of Zhao et al. (2023), different sub-tasks in SK-

Algorithm 1: Difference-aware ensemble method.

```
During training:
Input: S^D, S^R, S^E, S, W̃^D, W̃^R, W̃^E, S_gt.
Output: Weight for each model.
for p ∈ range(start=0, stop=1, step=0.1) do
    Score = 0
    for k ∈ {validation set} do
        Initialize W: {W_i = 0, i = 1, 2, ..., T}
        for i ∈ [1, T]; do
            W_i = p^D · W̃_i^D + p^R · W̃_i^R + p^E · W̃_i^E
        end for
        Score += Metric(S_k^threshold, S_k^gt)
    end for
    Record weight p̂ for the Best Score.
end for
During test:
for k ∈ {test set} do
    Initialize W: {W_i = 0, i = 1, 2, ..., T}
    for i ∈ [1, T]; do
        W_i = p̂^D · W̃_i^D + p̂^R · W̃_i^R + p̂^E · W̃_i^E
    end for
    S_k = S_k^threshold
end for
```

[7]In this task, the confidence is a score between 0 and 1 since we train the turn detection and entry selection with binary classification loss.

[8]For example, an entry ranks 1st in DeBERTa (seen), 3rd in RoBERTa (unseen) and 4th in DeBERTa (de-noise), p^D=0.2, p^R=0.3, p^E = 0.5 then the final weight to re-rank this entry in S is 0.2*0.5 + 0.3*0.25+0.5*0.2 = 0.275.

Models	On validation set			On final-test set		
	Precision	Recall	F1	Precision	Recall	F1
DeBERTa-v3-base (baseline)	**1.0000**	0.9990	0.9995	**0.9982**	0.9979	0.9980
DeBERTa-v3-base (seen expert)	0.9979	0.9989	0.9982	-	-	-
RoBERTa-large (unseen expert)	0.9953	0.9946	0.9949	-	-	-
DeBERTa-v3-large (de-noise expert)	0.9960	0.9983	0.9980	-	-	-
Ensemble with Precision	**1.0000**	0.9990	0.9995	-	-	-
Ensemble with Recall	0.9990	**1.0000**	0.9995	0.9979	0.9989	0.9984
Ensemble with F1	**1.0000**	**1.0000**	**1.0000**	0.9979	**0.9993**	**0.9986**

Table 2: Experimental results on the knowledge-seeking turn detection.

TOD requires different metric. For example, the knowledge-seeking turn-detection task can be seen as the simplified version the Algorithm 1. The N candidate is reduced to 1 in the turn detection task, i.e. the S_k^{gt} only has 1 ground-truth result (yes or no). We can use Exact Match between S and S_k^{gt} to learn the weight $\hat{p}$. For the KES task, both precision and recall matter since there can be multiple knowledge entries for each knowledge-seeking turn. Instead of selecting the top few results with the threshold, we can also set a threshold for the relevance score in Section 3.4.

At last, the difference-aware method is also suitable for different datasets. For example, the test set contains more portion unseen instances and multiple entity instances than the validation set. We can adjust the portion of unseen instances of the validation set so that it is similar to that of the test set. Then we can use Algorithm 1 to learn a $\hat{p}$ more suitable for the test set.

4 Experimental Settings

4.1 Data

The data set is provided by the organizers of the track[9]. The statistics are shown in Table 3. We can see that there are around 50% unseen instances in validation and test sets. The portion of the instances requiring multiple entities is also increased in the validation and test sets.

4.2 Evaluation Metrics

We use the metrics provided by the DSTC organizers [10] to show the automatic results. For the knowledge-seeking turn detection task, we report the Precision, Recall, and F1 scores. For entity tracking, we report the instance-level Accuracy score. An instance is regarded as accurate only if the predicted entities are the same as the gold entities. For knowledge entry selection, we report

	Train	Val	Test
dialogue instances	14,768	2,129	2,798
seen instances	14,768	1,057	1,349
unseen instances	0	1,072	1,449
multi-entity instances	412	199	436
Knowledge entries			
Avg.entries / instance	3.80	4.07	4.21
Avg.review / instance	3.51	3.94	3.91
Avg.FAQ / instance	0.29	0.23	0.29
Avg.tokens / entry	15.14	15.81	14.92
Dialogue			
Avg.uttrances / instance	9.29	9.44	9.36
Avg.tokens / request	8.66	8.95	9.13
Avg.tokens / response	24.27	23.69	24.05

Table 3: Data statistics of the DSTC 11 track-5.

Precision, Recall, F1, and Exact Match (EM). For response generation, we report BLEU (Papineni et al., 2002), METEOR (Lavie and Agarwal, 2007), and ROUGE-1/2/L (Lin, 2004). In the competition, the KTD task servers as the foundation of the rest sub-tasks. Specifically, when calculating the metric for each sub-task, the true positive score of sub-task 1 serves as a weight and is multiplied by other results. The overall score is calculated by the mean reciprocal rank over all the metrics.

4.3 Implementations

Our implementations of RoBERT, DeBERTa, BART, and T5 are based on the public Pytorch implementation of Transformers[11]. During pre-training, we follow the hyper-parameters setting of the original implementation. During pre-training and fine-tuning, we set the maximum input length to 512 tokens. Candidate size N in Algorithm 1 is set to 10. We use a single Tesla v100s GPU with 32 GB memory for the experiments, the pre-training time is around 48 hours and fine-tuning time is around 4 hours for each model.

5 Results and Analysis

In this competition, each team has up to five submission opportunities on the final test set. We re-

[9]https://github.com/alexa/dstc11-track5/tree/main/data
[10]https://github.com/alexa/dstc11-track5

[11]https://github.com/huggingface/transformers

Models	On validation set				On final-test set			
	Precision	Recall	F1	EM	Precision	Recall	F1	EM
DeBERTa-v3-base (baseline)	0.7951	0.8843	0.8373	0.4049	0.7901	0.7877	0.7889	0.3906
DeBERTa-v3-base (seen expert)	0.7966	0.8841	0.8379	0.4224	-	-	-	-
RoBERTa-large (unseen expert)	0.7896	0.8410	0.8252	0.4110	-	-	-	-
DeBERTa-v3-large (de-noise expert)	0.7996	0.8713	0.8358	0.4310	-	-	-	-
Ensemble with Precision	**0.8894**	0.8434	0.8658	0.4937	-	-	-	-
Ensemble with Recall	0.7278	**0.9486**	0.8236	0.4227	-	-	-	-
Ensemble with F1	0.8591	0.8889	**0.8737**	0.5148	0.8096	0.8413	0.8252	0.5210
Ensemble with EM	0.8588	0.8763	0.8675	**0.5195**	**0.8183**	**0.8506**	**0.8342**	**0.5314**

Table 4: Experimental results on the knowledge entry selection. EM is short for exact match.

port the submission results and also provide the performance on the validation set.

5.1 Sub-task 1: knowledge seeking turn detection

Table 2 shows the experimental results. We can see the baseline model already has a high performance on the validation set. However, considering there are unseen instances in the final test set, we aim to use the difference-aware method to have a better performance. We test the ensemble with Precision, Recall, and F1 and choose the last two as our final submission since a higher Recall is more useful for unseen instances. On the final test set, our method achieve better Recall and F1 than the baseline model (the results of the baselines are reported by the organizer). Specifically, we have the highest F1 and second-highest Recall among all submissions. We also have the highest sum of the Precision/Recall/F1. These results give us an advantage over the rest of the sub-tasks.

5.2 Sub-task 3: knowledge entry selection

Table 4 shows the experimental results of the knowledge entry selection task. We can see that the experts we trained all performed close to the baseline. They are only a little better on the exact match metric than the baseline. However, when using our ensemble method, the performance is largely improved. On the validation set, the highest Precision, Recall, F1, and EM results are obtained when using the corresponding metric as the ensemble indicator. These results show that 1) the different expert models are good at different aspects; 2) our ensemble method can successfully combine the advantage of the experts and achieve the desired results on specific metrics. We finally choose the last two results (ensemble with F1 and EM) for final submission according to the sum of all four metrics. On the test set, our method has consistent performance and largely outperforms the baseline. On EM, our method surpasses the baseline by 14 percent. We denote these two results as KS-F1 and KS-EM for the convenience of the next section.

5.3 Sub-task 4: response generation

Table 5 shows the experimental results on response generation. We only have five submission opportunities and all the results are shown in the Table. Notice that we did not use any ensemble in a generation. The results can reflect how the knowledge selection results affect the generation. The baseline uses the selected knowledge from the baseline in Table 4. The BART-base with KS-F1 use the fourth result of Table 4), its generation results are better than baselines on all metrics. This result shows that the KS-F1 provides higher-quality knowledge entries and again proves the effectiveness of our ensemble methods. Benefiting from more parameters, the BART-large and T5 are better than BART-base on most metrics. The BLEU of BART-large (KS-F1) ranks 2nd among all the submissions to track-5. The BART-large (KS-EM) is better on ROUGE and the T5-3B (KS-EM) is better on METEOR. However, the T5 models perform badly on BLEU on the test set and do not show an obvious advantage over BART-large. This may indicate that fine-tuning pre-trained language models with large amounts of parameters to a specific task is not always work. The DSTC 11 track-5 also performs a manual evaluation for the generation results. The organizer only chooses one of the submissions for each team based on the mean reciprocal rank over all the metrics. The BART-large (KS-F1) is chosen by the organizer since this submission has the highest overall score among our 5 submissions. We finally ranked 5th among all teams in this manual evaluation. In our own manual evaluation, the BART-large (KS-EM) is better than the BART-large (KS-F1). We also provide the results on LLAMA-13B, the results are much lower than other models.

Models	On validation set			On final-test set		
	BLEU	METEOR	ROUGE	BLEU	METEOR	ROUGE
BART-base (baseline)	0.1042	0.1810	0.3651 / 0.1506 / 0.2875	0.1004	0.1748	0.3520 / 0.1430 / 0.2753
LLAMA (fine-tuned)	0.0653	0.1012	0.2132 / 0.0975 / 0.1667	-	-	-
BART-base (KS-F1)	0.1089	0.1793	0.3689 / 0.1532 / 0.2918	0.1047	0.1764	0.3603 / 0.1463 / 0.2801
BART-large (KS-F1)	0.1087	0.1796	0.3693 / 0.1530 / 0.2925	**0.1075**	0.1744	0.3585 / 0.1459 / 0.2794
BART-large (KS-EM)	0.1103	0.1796	0.3695 / **0.1534** / **0.2929**	0.1050	0.1774	**0.3617** / **0.1474** / 0.2805
T5-3B (KS-F1)	**0.1104**	0.1773	0.3657 / 0.1524 / 0.2883	0.0897	0.1744	0.3591 / 0.1458 / **0.2840**
T5-3B (KS-EM)	0.1042	**0.1827**	**0.3743** / 0.1489 / 0.2894	0.0959	**0.1805**	0.3552 / 0.1450 / 0.2784

Table 5: Experimental results on the response generation.

6 Conclusion

We participated in track-5 of the 11th Dialog System Technology Challenges (DSTC 11), called Task-oriented Conversational Modeling with Subjective-knowledge. The task includes four sub-tasks and we propose a difference-aware ensemble method to address two main challenges in this competition. The first challenge is there are multiple reasonable knowledge entries for one context. The second challenge is that the data distribution is different in train/validation/test sets. We first train several expert models that are good at certain aspects for each sub-task. Then we use the difference-aware ensemble method to balance the abilities of expert models. Experimental results verify the effectiveness of our method and we got third on the final test set. Future work includes but is not limited to 1) testing our ensemble method on the knowledge entity tracking task; 2) designing a method to automatically learned the threshold in Algorithm 1.

Limitations

The method proposed by this work is only verified on limited data in DSTC competition and the language is only with narrow morphology (English). Whether the technique can be used for other morphology needs further verification. Another limitation is that the SK-TOD generation task needs to explicitly consider the diversity of opinions and the proportion of sentiments. This requires a specific module to assist the generation model or using a much larger language model such as GPT-4 to fully utilize the review information. We also do not perform these experiments and hope future researchers could investigate this task.

Ethics Statement

The dataset we used is from the DSTC 11 track-5. We use the back-translation and synonym substitution to construct a noise version of the data for training. The generation models trained with this noise data may learn to generate semantically incorrect or unfriendly responses.

Acknowledgements

This paper is supported by the Science and Technology Innovation 2030 Major Project of China (No. 2021ZD0113302) and National Natural Science Foundation of China (No. 62076081, No. 61772153 and No. 61936010).

References

Satoshi Akasaki and Nobuhiro Kaji. 2017. Chat detection in an intelligent assistant: Combining task-oriented and non-task-oriented spoken dialogue systems. In *ACL (1)*, pages 1308–1319. Association for Computational Linguistics.

Philip Bachman, Ouais Alsharif, and Doina Precup. 2014. Learning with pseudo-ensembles. In *Advances in Neural Information Processing Systems 27: Annual Conference on Neural Information Processing Systems 2014, December 8-13 2014, Montreal, Quebec, Canada*, pages 3365–3373.

Sébastien Bubeck, Varun Chandrasekaran, Ronen Eldan, Johannes Gehrke, Eric Horvitz, Ece Kamar, Peter Lee, Yin Tat Lee, Yuanzhi Li, Scott M. Lundberg, Harsha Nori, Hamid Palangi, Marco Túlio Ribeiro, and Yi Zhang. 2023. Sparks of artificial general intelligence: Early experiments with GPT-4. *CoRR*, abs/2303.12712.

Mudit Chaudhary, Borislav Dzodzo, Sida Huang, Chun Hei Lo, Mingzhi Lyu, Lun Yiu Nie, Jinbo Xing, Tianhua Zhang, Xiaoying Zhang, Jingyan Zhou, Hong Cheng, Wai Lam, and Helen Meng. 2021. Unstructured knowledge access in task-oriented dialog modeling using language inference, knowledge retrieval and knowledge-integrative response generation. *CoRR*, abs/2101.06066.

Zhiyu Chen, Bing Liu, Seungwhan Moon, Chinnadhurai Sankar, Paul A. Crook, and William Yang Wang. 2022. KETOD: knowledge-enriched task-oriented dialogue. In *Findings of the Association for Computational Linguistics: NAACL 2022, Seattle, WA,*

United States, July 10-15, 2022, pages 2581–2593. Association for Computational Linguistics.

Jacob Devlin, Ming-Wei Chang, Kenton Lee, and Kristina Toutanova. 2019. BERT: pre-training of deep bidirectional transformers for language understanding. In *Proceedings of the 2019 Conference of the North American Chapter of the Association for Computational Linguistics: Human Language Technologies, NAACL-HLT 2019, Minneapolis, MN, USA, June 2-7, 2019, Volume 1 (Long and Short Papers)*, pages 4171–4186. Association for Computational Linguistics.

Emily Dinan, Stephen Roller, Kurt Shuster, Angela Fan, Michael Auli, and Jason Weston. 2019. Wizard of wikipedia: Knowledge-powered conversational agents. In *7th International Conference on Learning Representations, ICLR 2019, New Orleans, LA, USA, May 6-9, 2019*. OpenReview.net.

Song Feng, Hui Wan, R. Chulaka Gunasekara, Siva Sankalp Patel, Sachindra Joshi, and Luis A. Lastras. 2020. doc2dial: A goal-oriented document-grounded dialogue dataset. In *Proceedings of the 2020 Conference on Empirical Methods in Natural Language Processing, EMNLP 2020, Online, November 16-20, 2020*, pages 8118–8128. Association for Computational Linguistics.

Karthik Gopalakrishnan, Behnam Hedayatnia, Qinglang Chen, Anna Gottardi, Sanjeev Kwatra, Anu Venkatesh, Raefer Gabriel, and Dilek Hakkani-Tür. 2019. Topical-chat: Towards knowledge-grounded open-domain conversations. pages 1891–1895. ISCA.

Trevor Hastie, Jerome H. Friedman, and Robert Tibshirani. 2001. *The Elements of Statistical Learning: Data Mining, Inference, and Prediction*. Springer Series in Statistics. Springer.

Pengcheng He, Xiaodong Liu, Jianfeng Gao, and Weizhu Chen. 2021. Deberta: decoding-enhanced bert with disentangled attention. In *9th International Conference on Learning Representations, ICLR 2021, Virtual Event, Austria, May 3-7, 2021*. OpenReview.net.

Geoffrey E. Hinton, Nitish Srivastava, Alex Krizhevsky, Ilya Sutskever, and Ruslan Salakhutdinov. 2012. Improving neural networks by preventing co-adaptation of feature detectors. *CoRR*, abs/1207.0580.

Yoonna Jang, Jungwoo Lim, Yuna Hur, Dongsuk Oh, Suhyune Son, Yeonsoo Lee, Dong-Hoon Shin, Seungryong Kim, and Heuiseok Lim. 2022. Call for customized conversation: Customized conversation grounding persona and knowledge. In *Thirty-Sixth AAAI Conference on Artificial Intelligence, AAAI 2022, Thirty-Fourth Conference on Innovative Applications of Artificial Intelligence, IAAI 2022, The Twelveth Symposium on Educational Advances in Artificial Intelligence, EAAI 2022 Virtual Event, February 22 - March 1, 2022*, pages 10803–10812. AAAI Press.

Di Jin, Seokhwan Kim, and Dilek Hakkani-Tur. 2021. Can I be of further assistance? using unstructured knowledge access to improve task-oriented conversational modeling. In *Proceedings of the 1st Workshop on Document-grounded Dialogue and Conversational Question Answering, DialDoc@ACL-IJCNLP 2021, Online, August 5, 2021*, pages 119–127. Association for Computational Linguistics.

Byeongchang Kim, Jaewoo Ahn, and Gunhee Kim. 2020a. Sequential latent knowledge selection for knowledge-grounded dialogue. In *8th International Conference on Learning Representations, ICLR 2020, Addis Ababa, Ethiopia, April 26-30, 2020*. OpenReview.net.

Seokhwan Kim, Mihail Eric, Karthik Gopalakrishnan, Behnam Hedayatnia, Yang Liu, and Dilek Hakkani-Tür. 2020b. Beyond domain apis: Task-oriented conversational modeling with unstructured knowledge access. In *Proceedings of the 21th Annual Meeting of the Special Interest Group on Discourse and Dialogue, SIGdial 2020, 1st virtual meeting, July 1-3, 2020*, pages 278–289. Association for Computational Linguistics.

Alon Lavie and Abhaya Agarwal. 2007. METEOR: an automatic metric for MT evaluation with high levels of correlation with human judgments. In *WMT@ACL*, pages 228–231. Association for Computational Linguistics.

Esther Levin, Roberto Pieraccini, and Wieland Eckert. 2000. A stochastic model of human-machine interaction for learning dialog strategies. *IEEE Trans. Speech Audio Process.*, 8(1):11–23.

Mike Lewis, Yinhan Liu, Naman Goyal, Marjan Ghazvininejad, Abdelrahman Mohamed, Omer Levy, Veselin Stoyanov, and Luke Zettlemoyer. 2020. BART: denoising sequence-to-sequence pre-training for natural language generation, translation, and comprehension. In *Proceedings of the 58th Annual Meeting of the Association for Computational Linguistics, ACL 2020, Online, July 5-10, 2020*, pages 7871–7880. Association for Computational Linguistics.

Chin-Yew Lin. 2004. Rouge: A package for automatic evaluation of summaries. In *Text summarization branches out*, pages 74–81.

Yinhan Liu, Myle Ott, Naman Goyal, Jingfei Du, Mandar Joshi, Danqi Chen, Omer Levy, Mike Lewis, Luke Zettlemoyer, and Veselin Stoyanov. 2019. Roberta: A robustly optimized BERT pretraining approach. *CoRR*, abs/1907.11692.

Bodhisattwa Prasad Majumder, Harsh Jhamtani, Taylor Berg-Kirkpatrick, and Julian J. McAuley. 2022. Achieving conversational goals with unsupervised post-hoc knowledge injection. In *Proceedings of the 60th Annual Meeting of the Association for Computational Linguistics (Volume 1: Long Papers), ACL 2022, Dublin, Ireland, May 22-27, 2022*, pages 3140–3153. Association for Computational Linguistics.

Pierre-Emmanuel Mazaré, Samuel Humeau, Martin Raison, and Antoine Bordes. 2018. Training millions of personalized dialogue agents. In *Proceedings of the 2018 Conference on Empirical Methods in Natural Language Processing, Brussels, Belgium, October 31 - November 4, 2018*, pages 2775–2779. Association for Computational Linguistics.

Chuan Meng, Pengjie Ren, Zhumin Chen, Weiwei Sun, Zhaochun Ren, Zhaopeng Tu, and Maarten de Rijke. 2020. Dukenet: A dual knowledge interaction network for knowledge-grounded conversation. In *Proceedings of the 43rd International ACM SIGIR conference on research and development in Information Retrieval, SIGIR 2020, Virtual Event, China, July 25-30, 2020*, pages 1151–1160. ACM.

Nikita Moghe, Siddhartha Arora, Suman Banerjee, and Mitesh M. Khapra. 2018. Towards exploiting background knowledge for building conversation systems. In *EMNLP*, pages 2322–2332. Association for Computational Linguistics.

Jianmo Ni, Jiacheng Li, and Julian J. McAuley. 2019. Justifying recommendations using distantly-labeled reviews and fine-grained aspects. In *Proceedings of the 2019 Conference on Empirical Methods in Natural Language Processing and the 9th International Joint Conference on Natural Language Processing, EMNLP-IJCNLP 2019, Hong Kong, China, November 3-7, 2019*, pages 188–197. Association for Computational Linguistics.

OpenAI. 2023. GPT-4 technical report. *CoRR*, abs/2303.08774.

Kishore Papineni, Salim Roukos, Todd Ward, and Wei-Jing Zhu. 2002. Bleu: a method for automatic evaluation of machine translation. In *ACL*, pages 311–318. ACL.

Shrimai Prabhumoye, Kazuma Hashimoto, Yingbo Zhou, Alan W. Black, and Ruslan Salakhutdinov. 2021. Focused attention improves document-grounded generation. In *Proceedings of the 2021 Conference of the North American Chapter of the Association for Computational Linguistics: Human Language Technologies, NAACL-HLT 2021, Online, June 6-11, 2021*, pages 4274–4287. Association for Computational Linguistics.

Colin Raffel, Noam Shazeer, Adam Roberts, Katherine Lee, Sharan Narang, Michael Matena, Yanqi Zhou, Wei Li, and Peter J. Liu. 2020. Exploring the limits of transfer learning with a unified text-to-text transformer. *J. Mach. Learn. Res.*, 21:140:1–140:67.

Chao-Hong Tan, Xiaoyu Yang, Zi'ou Zheng, Tianda Li, Yufei Feng, Jia-Chen Gu, Quan Liu, Dan Liu, Zhen-Hua Ling, and Xiaodan Zhu. 2020. Learning to retrieve entity-aware knowledge and generate responses with copy mechanism for task-oriented dialogue systems. *CoRR*, abs/2012.11937.

Hugo Touvron, Thibaut Lavril, Gautier Izacard, Xavier Martinet, Marie-Anne Lachaux, Timothée Lacroix, Baptiste Rozière, Naman Goyal, Eric Hambro, Faisal Azhar, Aurélien Rodriguez, Armand Joulin, Edouard Grave, and Guillaume Lample. 2023. Llama: Open and efficient foundation language models. *CoRR*, abs/2302.13971.

Lin Xu, Qixian Zhou, Jinlan Fu, Min-Yen Kan, and See-Kiong Ng. 2022. Corefdiffs: Co-referential and differential knowledge flow in document grounded conversations. In *Proceedings of the 29th International Conference on Computational Linguistics, COLING 2022, Gyeongju, Republic of Korea, October 12-17, 2022*, pages 471–484. International Committee on Computational Linguistics.

Zhao Yan, Nan Duan, Peng Chen, Ming Zhou, Jianshe Zhou, and Zhoujun Li. 2017. Building task-oriented dialogue systems for online shopping. In *AAAI*, pages 4618–4626. AAAI Press.

Chao Zhao, Spandana Gella, Seokhwan Kim, Di Jin, Devamanyu Hazarika, Alexandros Papangelis, Behnam Hedayatnia, Mahdi Namazifar, Yang Liu, and Dilek Hakkani-Tur. 2023. "what do others think?": Task-oriented conversational modeling with subjective knowledge. *CoRR*, abs/2305.12091.

Tiancheng Zhao, Allen Lu, Kyusong Lee, and Maxine Eskénazi. 2017. Generative encoder-decoder models for task-oriented spoken dialog systems with chatting capability. In *SIGDIAL Conference*, pages 27–36. Association for Computational Linguistics.

Xueliang Zhao, Tingchen Fu, Chongyang Tao, and Rui Yan. 2022. There is no standard answer: Knowledge-grounded dialogue generation with adversarial activated multi-reference learning. In *Proceedings of the 2022 Conference on Empirical Methods in Natural Language Processing, EMNLP 2022, Abu Dhabi, United Arab Emirates, December 7-11, 2022*, pages 1878–1891. Association for Computational Linguistics.

Xueliang Zhao, Wei Wu, Can Xu, Chongyang Tao, Dongyan Zhao, and Rui Yan. 2020. Knowledge-grounded dialogue generation with pre-trained language models. In *Proceedings of the 2020 Conference on Empirical Methods in Natural Language Processing, EMNLP 2020, Online, November 16-20, 2020*, pages 3377–3390. Association for Computational Linguistics.

Kangyan Zhou, Shrimai Prabhumoye, and Alan W. Black. 2018. A dataset for document grounded conversations. In *EMNLP*, pages 708–713. Association for Computational Linguistics.

Speech Aware Dialog System Technology Challenge (DSTC11)

Hagen Soltau, Izhak Shafran, Mingqiu Wang, Abhinav Rastogi, Jeffrey Zhao, Ye Jia
Wei Han, Yuan Cao, Aramys Miranda
Google Research
soltau,izhak,mingqiuwang,arastogi,jeffreyzhao@google.com
weihan,yuancao,aramys@google.com, jiaye@tomato.ai

Abstract

Most research on task oriented dialog modeling is based on written text input. However, users interact with practical dialog systems often using speech as input. Typically, systems convert speech into text using an Automatic Speech Recognition (ASR) system, introducing errors. Furthermore, these systems do not address the differences in written and spoken language. The research on this topic is stymied by the lack of a public corpus. Motivated by these considerations, our goal in hosting the speech-aware dialog state tracking challenge was to create a public corpus or task which can be used to investigate the performance gap between the written and spoken forms of input, develop models that could alleviate this gap, and establish whether Text-to-Speech-based (TTS) systems is a reasonable surrogate to the more-labor intensive human data collection. We created three spoken versions of the popular written-domain MultiWoz task – (a) TTS-Verbatim: written user inputs were converted into speech waveforms using a TTS system, (b) Human-Verbatim: humans spoke the user inputs verbatim, and (c) Human-paraphrased: humans paraphrased the user inputs. Additionally, we provided different forms of ASR output to encourage wider participation from teams that may not have access to state-of-the-art ASR systems. These included ASR transcripts, word time stamps, and latent representations of the audio (audio encoder outputs). In this paper, we describe the corpus, report results from participating teams, provide preliminary analyses of their results, and summarize the current state-of-the-art in this domain.

1 Introduction

In recent years, Automatic Speech Recognition (ASR) and Natural Language Processing (NLP) models have converged to utilize common components like Transformers and encoder/decoder modules. They increasingly rely on large amounts of data, large model sizes and large amounts of compute resources. This is a substantial departure from a previous era when ASR and NLP utilized different modeling architectures, chosen to inject domain-specific knowledge and constraints. This shift to a common paradigm has stimulated research in fusing audio and text modalities to substantially improve performance in tasks such as audio intent classification and speech-to-speech translation. The fusion of modalities in many cases allows the direct optimization of the end-task, overcoming the hurdles of the older cascaded approaches that often led to accumulation of errors.

Despite the general trend to develop end-to-end models for various tasks, spoken dialog systems stick out as a sore thumb. Most practical systems utilize a cascaded approach where the output of a general ASR system is fed into a dialog model trained separately on written domain. This mismatch between written and spoken inputs to the dialog models is not well-studied, largely due to the lack of a public task with spoken user inputs.

Research into combined audio-text models is limited by the lack of paired data. While the paired data requirement can be relaxed to some extent for training data via un- or self-supervised training techniques, test sets with paired data are crucial for model evaluation. In addition to an evaluation task, a training set with spoken input would also be helpful in quantifying the gains from supervised learning and recent advances in self-supervised learning.

The focus of our effort was to bring most benefit to the community with the limited resources available. While a Wizard-of-Oz style data collection in spoken domain would have been ideal to fully investigate all the phenomena of spoken domain, that would be extremely labor-intensive especially in annotating the dialog states and was beyond the scope of our effort. Instead, we chose to create a spoken version of a well-studied written-domain task, the MultiWoz task. One advantage of

Proceedings of The Eleventh Dialog System Technology Challenge, pages 226–234
September 11, 2023 ©2023 Association for Computational Linguistics

this approach was that we could directly compare the performance of the spoken version with the continuing advances in the written domain. Knowing that the current Text-to-Speech (TTS) systems have come a long way, we also chose to create a TTS-version of the MultiWoz training corpus as a surrogate for the human spoken version.

In the Speech-Aware DSTC11 challenge, participants are asked to infer the dialog states from the sequence of agent (text-input) and user (audio-input) turns. We evaluated the performance on three versions of audio inputs – TTS-Verbatim, Human-Verbatim (humans speaking the written user inputs), and Human-Paraphrased (humans paraphrasing the written user inputs). Aside from the audio-inputs, we provided transcripts from a state-of-the-art ASR system trained on 33k hours of People's Speech corpus to encourage participation from teams that did not have an easy access to ASR systems. The transcripts were accompanied with timestamps of the words and the latent representations of the acoustic encoder, which could be used by participants to train joint audio-text encoders.

In the course of developing this challenge, we developed a cascaded baseline system with data augmentation and report performances on a few variants of cascaded systems. In the process, we uncovered a bias in the MultiWoz evaluation task, the slot values in the evaluation set have a substantial overlap with those of the training set. To address this bias, we created a new version of the MultiWoz evaluation set, the dev-dsct11 and eval-dstc11. We observed that the new task surfaces many of the challenges in practical spoken dialog systems associated with mismatch in modalities, inability to recover from ASR errors, and more generally difficulty of extracting semantically relevant information from audio signals.

2 Related Work

Motivated by similar consideration as ours, Kim et al. (2022) organized a DST Challenge in 2021 where they created a task using spoken human-human dialogs on tourist information in San Francisco for three target domains: hotel, restaurant, and attraction. One of the serious limitations of the challenge was that the audio data was not released, only the ASR transcripts. The transcripts had an error rate of about 26.25% which is significantly higher than the average performance of most state-of-the-art ASR systems. The larger focus of their effort was on evaluating correctness of detecting knowledge-seeking turns, identifying the knowledge snippets and knowledge supplied in the generated responses. Prior to this effort, there have been much smaller efforts with fewer domains and dialogs in DSTC2 and DSTC3 (Henderson et al., 2014b,a). Here again the organizers only provided ASR transcripts with error rates in high 20s and low 30s, which limited the utility of the corpus as the ASR systems improved over time.

Meanwhile considerable progress has been achieved in improving the naturalness of dialog systems, for example, with chat-bots like Meena (Adiwardana et al., 2020), raising expectations of interacting with dialog systems using spoken language. Similarly, the convergence of model architectures for ASR and NLP has stimulated research in creating joint audio-text encoders that could potentially compensate for ASR errors and other spoken language phenomena (Drexler and Glass, 2019; Chen et al., 2021; Chung et al., 2020; Tang et al., 2022; Bapna et al., 2021, 2022; Chen et al., 2022), where they propose different approaches to align the speech input (frames, phones, utterances) to the corresponding text units. However, none of them have been evaluated on dialog models due to the lack of a dialog task and corpus with audio input. We hope the task and corpus released in this work will bridge this gap along with other recent speech understanding tasks such as superb and slurp (Yang et al., 2021; Bastianelli et al., 2020)

3 Data

We chose to create a spoken version of MultiWoz (2.1 version) so we could directly compare the written and spoken versions and reuse the annotations of dialog state labels, avoiding the labor-intensive process of annotating reference labels.

3.1 Redesigned DSTC11 Evaluation Sets

Before launching into the data collection and in the process of developing baseline systems, we noticed that there is a substantial overlap in slot values between the training and evaluation sets, leading to overestimation of performance of the models that memorize the slot values, as reported elsewhere (Song et al., 2020). To illustrate the issue, we probed an existing DST model with input whose slot values were replaced with other viable slot values (e.g., *cambridge* to *new york*, *ely* to *dublin*), *17:43* to *17:41* and *19:00* to *19:12*). We chose a model that achieves close to the state-of-the-art performance on the task with JGA of 55.4% (Zhao et al., 2021). The model ignores the new slot values and regurgitates the original slot values memorized from the training data, as shown in the Table 1.

Text Input	Text Output
i want to go to new york	dest=cambridge
i want to go to dublin	dest=ely
train leaving at 17:41	time=17:43
train leaving at 19:12	time=19:00

Table 1: Illustration of a model memorizing slot values: the model regurgitates memorized values and ignores the replaced slot values in the input.

This overlap in slot values between the training and evaluation sets of MultiWoz will mask the effect of misrecognition of the slot values by ASR systems in a practical spoken dialog system. For a fair evaluation of the models, we redesigned the MultiWoz evaluation sets to replace the slot values in the evaluation sets with new slot values as described below. The replacements were performed at the dialog level to maintain consistency across turns.

1. *Location Names*: The destination and departure cities for trains and buses were replaced with randomly sampled city names from 12655 cities in the United States.

2. *Hotel Names*: Hotel names were replaced with random names sampled from 1562 hotels in the United States.

3. *Restaurant Names*: Restaurant names were replaced by sampling from 214 restaurants in New York City.

4. *Time Slots*: Timestamps were offset by a random value across all the times mentioned in the dialog.

We measured the impact of the redesigned evaluation sets, henceforth referred to as dev-dstc11 and test-dstc11, using two dialog models – a seq-to-seq model (Zhao et al., 2021) and a model that utilizes the power of large language model by fine-tuning the prefix encoding with dialog-specific instructions (Zhao et al., 2022). The second model has three variants – D3ST-base, D3ST-large and D3ST-XXL – related to the size of the underlying T5x large language model. The results, shown in the Table 2, confirms our overestimation of the original MultiWoz evaluation sets. The actual performance is almost 50% worse than reported on the original evaluation sets for most models with the exception of D3ST-XXL.

Model	org. Dev	Dev-DSTC11
seq2seq	55.4	20.8
D3ST-base	54.2	22.0
D3ST-large	54.5	25.2
D3ST-xxl	57.8	43.1

Table 2: Performance of dialog models, measured in JGA, on dev-dstc11, the redesigned MultiWoz evaluation sets. The comparison with original dev set illustrates the substantial overestimation due to the overlap in training and dev slot values.

The memorization of the slot values completely distorts the effect of ASR errors on the downstream dialog models and paints an overly rosy picture. We illustrate this with a simple cascade baseline where an ASR system transcribes the input speech into written form which is fed into a seq-to-seq dialog model (Zhao et al., 2021). In the Table 3 we compare the performance degradation from switching from written to spoken input and then retraining the seq-to-seq model on the ASR transcripts. According to the performance on the original dev set, the degradation from written to ASR transcripts is 58.1% to 47.2%. Furthermore, most of the degradation is recovered by retraining on the ASR transcripts. Both these results are incorrect and misleading as will show in the Section 5.4, training on ASR output is not nearly as effective as the results in the table suggests.

Train Data	Test Data	JGA
Written	Written	58.1
Written	Spoken/ASR	47.2
Spoken/ASR	Spoken/ASR	56.0

Table 3: Results of training and evaluating a seq-to-seq model on written and ASR transcripts. The results are misleading as we will show in the Section 5.4.

3.2 Text-to-Speech Version

One of the questions we were interested in understanding was whether TTS is a good substitute for speech collected from humans. For answering this question, we generated *TTS-Verbatim*, a TTS version of the evaluation test and training sets using the system described in (Jia et al., 2021), a system that represents phonemes and graphemes to represent input text. Additionally, for training data, we generated four versions of the training data, each corresponding to a different TTS speaker. There was no overlap between the speakers in the training and evaluation sets.

3.3 Human Data Collection

We focused our data collection on the user turns since the agent turns are already available to any practical dialog system. The data collection was performed via Amazon Mechanical Turk and consisted of two versions – *Human-Verbatim* and *Human-Paraphrased*. Crow-workers were presented a full dialog in text including both user and agent turns. In the verbatim version, the workers were instructed to utter the user turns verbatim as naturally as possible, one at a time till the end of the dialog. In the paraphrased version, the workers were instructed to utter a paraphrased version of the user turn preserving the semantic meaning and the entities (e.g., names, times). After they finished the dialog, they were asked to transcribe their own paraphrased user turns.

The data was collected in several iterations. After each batch was collected, the quality of the recordings were measured and only those above certain quality were retained. There were several factors that contributed to failures: 1) missing audio, 2) incomplete dialog, 3) unintelligible speech, 4) high background noise, 5) speakers uttering verbatim when they should have paraphrased, and 6) speakers not transcribing their utterance in the paraphrased version.

We developed objective measures to perform quality control in bulk. The missing audio and incomplete dialogs were detected programmatically. To filter out utterances with unintelligible speech and high background noise, we transcribed the collected user utterances with an ASR system (for details of the system see Section 5) and measured the accuracy with respect to the corresponding transcripts. Since insertions may occur due to disfluencies, we used deletions as a stronger quality indicator and used a threshold of 25%.

Measuring the quality of paraphrased version was challenging. We iterated with objective metrics and listen to sampled utterances. After a few iterations, we converged on the following criteria: 1) paraphrased versions had at least 60% as many words as verbatim, 2) the paraphrased version differed from the verbatim version by at least 45% as indicated by the WER between recognized words and the written user prompt, and 3) less than 30% WER with respect to the crowd-worker generated transcripts. Minimum word ratio is to ensure the paraphrased speech carries enough information as in the original written user prompt. The second criterion was to ensure that the paraphrased version was sufficiently different from the written version. The last criterion was to ensure audio quality and intelligibility.

Besides the automatic quality control, we also sampled and listened to a small portion of the collected recordings. We noticed that even though the crowd-workers were asked to speak naturally, the verbatim was stilted more towards a read version. In a natural dialog, the speakers are likely to show more emotional variations and disfluencies. In comparison, the paraphrased version was more natural since they were using their own words.

In most natural conversations, speakers use 12 hour format for time (e.g., 1315 hrs vs 1:15pm). Since we wanted the crowd-workers to speak as naturally as possible, we replaced all the 24 hour time format in the original MultiWoz set with their corresponding 12 hour format.

4 Challenge Task and Evaluation

The main task in the DSTC11 Challenge is to infer the dialog states correctly from the audio inputs that were provided corresponding to the redesigned MultiWoz test set, redesigned as described in Section 3.1. For ablation studies, the participants were required to submit their results for three conditions: *TTS-Verbatim*, *Human-Verbatim* and *Human-paraphrased*, which were collected as described in Section 3.2 and 3.3. The participants were free to use their own ASR system or the outputs provided from our baseline ASR system, described in Section 5.1.

The performance in the challenge is measured using the standard Joint Goal Accuracy (JGA) as a primary metric and Slot Error Rate (SER) as a secondary metric for fine-grained comparisons. In the literature, results are often difficult to compare since research groups apply their own output normalization before scoring the results. To sidestep the resulting confusion, this challenge is evaluated using standard evaluation tool published on GitHub (Zang et al., 2020). We created a patch to support the results from this challenge and published the golden reference for our redesigned evaluation sets, which can be downloaded from the DSTC11 challenge website https://dstc11.dstc.community.

The participants were allowed to utilize any publicly available data or checkpoints, but no private data to allow fair comparisons. They were allowed to augment data and no restrictions were imposed on model sizes or computational costs.

5 Baseline

5.1 ASR and Related Outputs

As mentioned earlier, we provided the output of a baseline ASR system to reduce the barrier for participation by teams which didn't have ASR systems available to them.

The baseline ASR model is based an RNN-Transducer (Graves, 2012) which is essentially an encoder-decoder model, as illustrated in Figure 1. Unlike typical encoder-decoder models, the RNN-T uses hard attention and learns alignments via Forward-Backward algorithm similar to HMM, albeit with a different topology. These models have been extremely successful in ASR and achieves state-of-the-art performance in several benchmarks.

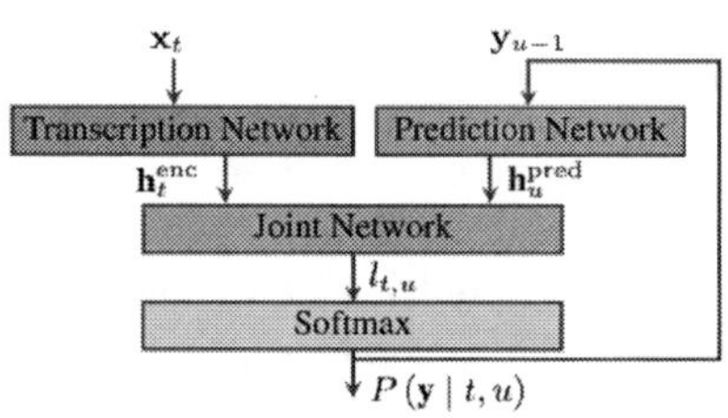

Figure 1: RNN-Transducer

Our baseline models is trained on the People-Speech corpus (Galvez et al., 2021), a supervised, publicly available data set of approx. 32,000 hours of audio data. The encoder consists of 16 Transformer layers, and the language model (decoder) is a single LSTM layer, altogether a 220m parameter model. The performance of the model on the MultiWoz evaluation sets are reported in Table 4.

We provided the following outputs as part of the DSTC11 challenge corpus.

1. *Audio Waveforms (16Khz/16-bit PCM)*: This allows researchers to investigate DST models that directly operate on audio such as end-to-end systems.

	TTS-Verbatim	Human-Verbatim
dev-dstc11	8.1(5.7/0.3/2.1)	11.9(7.7/2.7/1.5)
test-dstc11	8.2(5.7/0.3/2.1)	13.0(8.2/3.4/1.5)

Table 4: Performance of the baseline ASR model on the MultiWoz evaluation sets, reported as WER(Sub/Del/Ins)

2. *Audio Encodings (75ms frame rate, 1024-dim)*: These are the output activation from the last Transformer layer in the audio encoder. Since the input to the model are log-mel features at 25ms frame rate, and the encoder reduces the frame rate by 3x, the resulting output frame rate is 75ms, i.e. for an utterance of 15 sec, the audio encodings would be of length 200. These encodings are provided to support research in loosely-coupled ASR-DST cascaded systems.

3. *ASR Hypotheses with Time Alignment*: The ASR recognition outputs are provided to support research in different cascaded ASR-DST systems. Time alignments allow teams to pinpoint the location of recognized tokens in the audio encodings. Note, due the nature of RNN-T, multiple output tokens (words) can correspond to the same audio frame.

Typical recognition errors (ordered by frequency), illustrated in Table 5, include time formatting issues, spoken single-digit numbers, split words, and more general misspelled content words, where the last category is probably very relevant for DST purposes.

Spoken vs Written Numbers	
3 stars	three stars
031	thirty-on
Split Words	
i am	i'm
wifi	wi-fi
guesthouse	guest house
goodbye	good bye
double-checking	double checking
Misspelled content words	
hennessey	hennessy
moxee	marcy
kinbrae	kinbray

Table 5: Typical ASR Recognition Errors

Test Data	Training Data			
	Text (Ref)		ASR Hyp	
	1x	100x	1x	100x
Text	20.1	41.7	-	-
H-Paraphrased	16.5	24.1	18.3	25.6

Table 6: ASR-Vanilla Seq-to-Seq DST **base** cascaded model (JGA)

5.2 Dialog State Tracking Models

For our baseline DST experiments, we relied on two models.

1. Vanilla seq-to-seq model: This seq-to-seq model is obtained by fine-tuning a T5-base model on MultiWoz corpus (Zhao et al., 2021).

2. D3ST: This is also a seq-to-seq model trained on T5, but the input to this model contains a prompt which describes slot names in short natural language descriptions along with potential values (Zhao et al., 2022). The ordering of the slot names are randomizes to improve robustness.

5.3 Data Augmentation

Data augmentation is a common technique to improve accuracy and robustness. Since our preliminary results in Table 2 unearthed problems related to memorization, we felt the need to incorporate data augmentation into our baseline systems. We created new versions of user responses for training data by replacing slot values with randomly picked city names, time offsets and restaurant names, as described in Section 3.1. The new slot names were drawn from a different list than the ones used for generating the redesigned evaluation sets. In all, we generated about 100x training data.

5.4 Cascaded ASR-DST System

For a baseline, we created a cascades ASR-DST system where the transcripts from the ASR model in Section 5.1 were fed as input to the DST model in Section 5.2. The performance of the models of various sizes are summarized in Tables tables 6 to 9. The best baseline performance is obtained with D3ST-xxl, obtaining 33.5% JGA on the human paraphrased test set.

We point a few pertinent observations on cascaded ASR-DST models and data augmentation.

Test Data	Training Data			
	Text (Ref)		ASR Hyp	
	1x	100x	1x	100x
Text	22.0	41.6	20.9	28.6
TTS-Verbatim	19.2	27.7	19.9	27.1
H-Verbatim	17.1	23.6	17.6	22.5
H-Paraphrased	17.0	22.8	17.3	21.8

Table 7: ASR-D3ST **base** cascaded model (JGA)

Test Data	Training Data			
	Text (Ref)		ASR Hyp	
	1x	100x	1x	100x
Text	25.2	44.2	22.3	32.6
TTS-Verbatim	20.5	29.1	20.7	29.5
H-Verbatim	18.6	25.1	18.5	24.8
H-Paraphrased	18.0	23.9	17.5	23.6

Table 8: ASR-D3ST **large** cascaded model (JGA)

1. TTS (TTS-Verbatim) shows a degradation with respect to written version. However, the degradation is larger with Human-Verbatim (41.0% vs. 33.5% JGA), confirming our suspicion that we cannot rely on TTS as a surrogate for human speech.

2. Surprisingly, the drop in performance from Human-Verbatim to Human-Paraphrased is not very large. This is not because the two versions are similar since quality checks described in Section 3.3 assures us that the paraphrased version is sufficiently different from verbatim version.

3. For models of smaller sizes, the differences in model type (Vanilla seq-to-seq vs D3ST) seems less relevant. However, scaling the D3ST model from D3ST-Large (3B params) to D3ST-XXL (11B params) has substantial impact on performance (24.8% vs 33.5% JGA). This raises a question of fairness since teams may not have resources to work with larger model sizes. Nonetheless, we did find examples in results provided by participants were smaller models were able to outperform larger models, see Section 6 for details.

4. Training DST models with ASR hypotheses is simple and improves the performance substantially from 28.2% to 33.5% even when the training data is based on TTS and not human speech.

Test Data	Training Data			
	Text (Ref)		ASR Hyp	
	1x	100x	1x	100x
Text	43.1	52.8	33.9	43.0
TTS-Verbatim	27.3	32.1	26.8	38.4
H-Verbatim	23.6	27.9	23.7	31.8
H-Paraphrased	21.8	26.1	21.9	30.9

Table 9: ASR-D3ST **xxl** cascaded model (JGA)

5. Data augmentation gives consistent gains across all conditions.

6 Results

We received 11 submissions from 6 teams and the results are shown in figures 2 and 3. The full set of numbers are also available in the link under the DSTC11 Challenge website `https://dstc11.dstc.community`.

We provide a high level overview of the results, but refer to the team's system descriptions for details. While we provided data to build direct audio-to-dst and tightly coupled models, all teams chose a cascaded approach with separately trained ASR and DST models. Many teams employed an explicit ASR error correction model and re-trained their DST models on ASR hypotheses together with various forms of TTS-based data augmentation. Within this general approach teams experimented with several variations and as a result the performance across submissions vary substantially. The highest performing submission obtains a JGA of 37.9% while the lowest performance is at 18.2%.

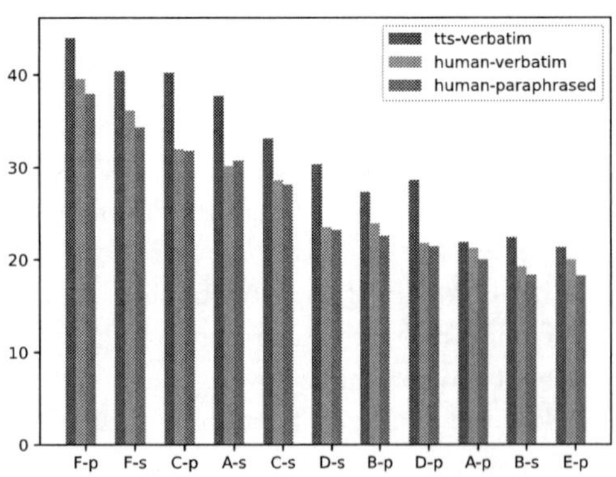

Figure 2: Joint Goal Accuracy (JGA) of team's submissions

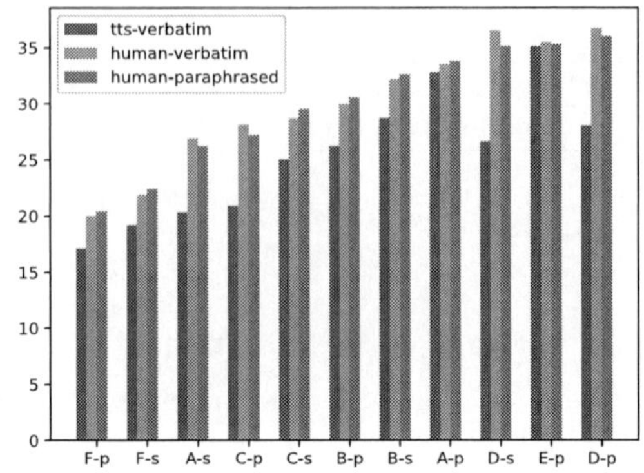

Figure 3: Slot Error Rate (SER) of team's submissions

6.1 Alternative ASR models

While we provided ASR output with our baseline ASR system, described in Section 5.1 based on *PeopleSpeech* corpus, three submissions used *Whisper* instead (Radford et al., 2022). We compared the two ASR models to tease apart the differences. As reported in Table 10, not surprisingly, we found that *Whisper* transcribes the evaluation sets more accurately than our baseline model (see Table 4) since it is trained on a magnitude order more data.

	TTS-Verbatim	Human-Verbatim
dev-dstc11	4.8(3.8/0.6/0.4)	8.5(5.8/1.4/1.4)
test-dstc11	4.6(3.7/0.6/0.3)	8.9(6.1/1.5/1.3)

Table 10: Performance of Whisper on evaluation sets, reported as WER(Sub/Del/Ins).

We evaluated *Whisper* in the cascaded ASR-DST system with two models, one trained on 100x augmented written text and one trained on *Whisper* transcripts of the TTS version of the same training data. The results shown in Table 11 clearly demonstrate that the improvements in transcription accuracy translates to improvement in DST accuracy, whereby JGA scores improve from 30.9% to 34.3% for the Human-Paraphrased test data.

7 Conclusions

In this paper, we describe a new corpus for stimulating research in modeling spoken dialogs that builds on popular written dialog corpus, MultiWoz. Having a spoken version of the same evaluation set allows researchers to study and bridge the performance gap between written and spoken dialog

Test Data	100x Training Data	
	Text (Ref)	ASR Hyp
Text	52.7	45.3
TTS-Verbatim	35.6	41.3
H-Verbatim	32.3	35.5
H-Paraphrased	30.9	34.3

Table 11: Performance in JGA of cascaded Whisper ASR-D3ST-XXL trained on text and Whisper hypotheses, evaluated on Whisper hypotheses of evaluation sets.

models. In the course of characterizing the task, we observed that there is substantial overlap between the slot values in the training and evaluation sets of the original MultiWoz corpus. We redesigned the evaluation sets (dev-dstc11 and eval-dstc11) by sampling new non-overlapping slot values and show that the new sets captures the weakness of the written dialog models better. We released three versions of the task – TTS-Verbatim, Human-Verbatim and Human-Paraphrased, where the last two were collected from crowd-workers. One caveat of this collection is that disfluencies such as speech repair are not as well represented as in natural conversations.

We have characterized this gap using a baseline cascaded ASR-DST system using ASR and DST models. While the performance improves with model size and data augmentation, even the best models (D3ST-XXL) show substantial drop in performance when switching from written version to the spoken version (53.8% to 26.1% JGA). Retraining the D3ST-XXL model on the ASR hypotheses, improves the performance to 30.9% JGA but still leaves substantial ground to be covered.

We report the results of 11 submissions from the DSTC11 Challenge. The dominant paradigm across teams was to rely on large language models for DST. Several submissions inserted ASR error correction modules of different complexities. The performance of the teams varied from a high of 37.9% to a low of 18.2% JGA.

One area of research that is not well explored is better utilization of the latent representations of the audio encoder in the ASR in the downstream DST models. Similarly, we hope the release of the audio and the audio encoders outputs will allow researchers to evaluate the power of joint audio-text encoders on dialog tasks.

References

Daniel Adiwardana, Minh-Thang Luong, David R. So, Jamie Hall, Noah Fiedel, Romal Thoppilan, Zi Yang, Apoorv Kulshreshtha, Gaurav Nemade, Yifeng Lu, and Quoc V. Le. 2020. Towards a human-like open-domain chatbot. *CoRR*, abs/2001.09977.

Ankur Bapna, Colin Cherry, Yu Zhang, Ye Jia, Melvin Johnson, Yong Cheng, Simran Khanuja, Jason Riesa, and Alexis Conneau. 2022. mslam: Massively multilingual joint pre-training for speech and text. *CoRR*, abs/2202.01374.

Ankur Bapna, Yu-An Chung, Nan Wu, Anmol Gulati, Ye Jia, Jonathan H. Clark, Melvin Johnson, Jason Riesa, Alexis Conneau, and Yu Zhang. 2021. SLAM: A unified encoder for speech and language modeling via speech-text joint pre-training. *CoRR*.

Emanuele Bastianelli, Andrea Vanzo, Pawel Swietojanski, and Verena Rieser. 2020. SLURP: A spoken language understanding resource package. *CoRR*, abs/2011.13205.

Jiawei Chen, Xu Tan, Yichong Leng, Jin Xu, Guihua Wen, Tao Qin, and Tie-Yan Liu. 2021. Speech-t: Transducer for text to speech and beyond. In *Advances in Neural Information Processing Systems*, volume 34, pages 6621–6633.

Zhehuai Chen, Yu Zhang, Andrew Rosenberg, Bhuvana Ramabhadran, Pedro J. Moreno, Ankur Bapna, and Heiga Zen. 2022. MAESTRO: matched speech text representations through modality matching. *CoRR*, abs/2204.03409.

Yu-An Chung, Chenguang Zhu, and Michael Zeng. 2020. Semi-supervised speech-language joint pre-training for spoken language understanding. *CoRR*, abs/2010.02295.

Jennifer Drexler and James R. Glass. 2019. Explicit alignment of text and speech encodings for attention-based end-to-end speech recognition. In *IEEE Automatic Speech Recognition and Understanding Workshop, ASRU 2019, Singapore, December 14-18, 2019*, pages 913–919. IEEE.

Daniel Galvez, Greg Diamos, Juan Ciro, Juan Felipe Cerón, Keith Achorn, Anjali Gopi, David Kanter, Maximilian Lam, Mark Mazumder, and Vijay Janapa Reddi. 2021. The people's speech: A large-scale diverse english speech recognition dataset for commercial usage. *CoRR*, abs/2111.09344.

Alex Graves. 2012. Sequence transduction with recurrent neural networks. *CoRR*.

Matthew Henderson, Blaise Thomson, and J. Williams. 2014a. The third dialog state tracking challenge. *2014 IEEE Spoken Language Technology Workshop (SLT)*, pages 324–329.

Matthew Henderson, Blaise Thomson, and Jason D. Williams. 2014b. The second dialog state tracking challenge. In *Proceedings of the 15th Annual Meeting of the Special Interest Group on Discourse and Dialogue (SIGDIAL)*, pages 263–272, Philadelphia, PA, U.S.A. Association for Computational Linguistics.

Ye Jia, Heiga Zen, Jonathan Shen, Yu Zhang, and Yonghui Wu. 2021. Png bert: Augmented bert on phonemes and graphemes for neural tts. In *Proc. Interspeech*. ISCA.

Seokhwan Kim, Yang Liu, Di Jin, Alexandros Papangelis, Behnam Hedayatnia, Karthik Gopalakrishnan, and Dilek Hakkani-Tur. 2022. Knowledge-grounded task-oriented dialogue modeling on spoken conversations track at dstc10. In *AAAI 2022 Workshop on Dialog System Technology Challenge*.

Alec Radford, Jong Wook Kim, Tao Xu, Greg Brockman, Christine McLeavey, and Ilya Sutskever. 2022. Robust speech recognition via large-scale weak supervision. *OpenAI Blog*.

Xiaohui Song, Liangjun Zang, Yipeng Su, Xing Wu, Jizhong Han, and Songlin Hu. 2020. Data augmentation for copy-mechanism in dialogue state tracking. *CoRR*, abs/2002.09634.

Yun Tang, Hongyu Gong, Ning Dong, Changhan Wang, Wei-Ning Hsu, Jiatao Gu, Alexei Baevski, Xian Li, Abdelrahman Mohamed, Michael Auli, and Juan Pino. 2022. Unified speech-text pre-training for speech translation and recognition. In *Proceedings of the 60th Annual Meeting of the Association for Computational Linguistics (Volume 1: Long Papers)*, pages 1488–1499, Dublin, Ireland. Association for Computational Linguistics.

Shu-Wen Yang, Po-Han Chi, Yung-Sung Chuang, Cheng-I Jeff Lai, Kushal Lakhotia, Yist Y. Lin, Andy T. Liu, Jiatong Shi, Xuankai Chang, Guan-Ting Lin, Tzu-Hsien Huang, Wei-Cheng Tseng, Ko-tik Lee, Da-Rong Liu, Zili Huang, Shuyan Dong, Shang-Wen Li, Shinji Watanabe, Abdelrahman Mohamed, and Hung-yi Lee. 2021. SUPERB: speech processing universal performance benchmark. *CoRR*, abs/2105.01051.

Xiaoxue Zang, Abhinav Rastogi, Srinivas Sunkara, Raghav Gupta, Jianguo Zhang, and Jindong Chen. 2020. MultiWOZ 2.2 : A dialogue dataset with additional annotation corrections and state tracking baselines. In *Proceedings of the 2nd Workshop on Natural Language Processing for Conversational AI*, Online. Association for Computational Linguistics.

Jeffrey Zhao, Raghav Gupta, Yuan Cao, Dian Yu, Mingqiu Wang, Harrison Lee, Abhinav Rastogi, Izhak Shafran, and Yonghui Wu. 2022. Description-driven task-oriented dialog modeling. *CoRR*, abs/2201.08904.

Jeffrey Zhao, Mahdis Mahdieh, Ye Zhang, Yuan Cao, and Yonghui Wu. 2021. Effective sequence-to-sequence dialogue state tracking. In *Proceedings of the 2021 Conference on Empirical Methods in Natural Language Processing*. Association for Computational Linguistics.

Overview of Situated and Interactive Multimodal Conversations (SIMMC) 2.1 Track at DSTC 11

Satwik Kottur[1]*, **Seungwhan Moon** [2]*, **Alborz Geramifard** [1], **Babak Damavandi** [2]
Meta Reality Labs & Meta AI
{skottur,shanemoon,alborzg,babakd}@meta.com

Abstract

With ever increasing interest in task-oriented dialog systems, the recent work on Situated and Interactive Multimodal Conversations (SIMMC 2.0) aims to develop personal assistants that interact with users, grounded in an immersive and co-observed setting of photo-realistic scenes. The dataset contains $11k$ task-oriented dialogs set in an interactive shopping scenario, spanning more than $117k$ utterances.

In order to push research towards this next generation virtual assistants, the SIMMC 2.1 challenge[1] was conducted at the Eleventh Dialog System Technology Challenge (DSTC) which had entries from across the world competing to achieve the state-of-the-art performance in the SIMMC 2.1 task. In this report, we present and compare 13 SIMMC 2.1 model entries from 5 teams across the world to understand the current progress made across the last three years (starting with SIMMC 1.0 and 2.0 challenges) for multimodal task-oriented dialog systems. We hope that our analysis throws light on components that showed promise in addition to identifying the gaps for future research towards this grand goal of an immersive multimodal conversational agent.

1 Motivation

The Situated and Interactive Multimodal Conversaitional AI (SIMMC) challenges [15, 12], held as part of DSTC9 [8] and DSTC10, pioneered the work for building the real-world assistant agents that can understand multimodal inputs (vision & conversations) and handle user requests. Throughout the two editions of the challenge, we provided two new benchmark datasets (SIMMC 1.0 and 2.0) for studying multimodal conversations with situated user context in the form of a co-observed image or virtual reality (VR) environment. Specifically, the SIMMC 2.0 dataset provided the assistant↔user task-oriented dialogs grounded on diverse photo-realistic VR renders of (synthetic) commercial stores with various referent objects, serving as a proxy for complex real-world scenarios. The earlier SIMMC challenge at DSTC10 saw a total of 16 model entries from participants around the world, establishing a new set of state-of-the-art baselines for the multimodal task-oriented dialog systems.

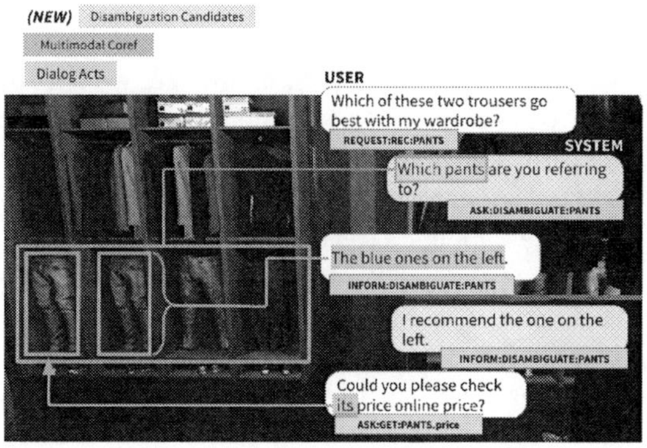

Figure 1: Illustration of a Situated Interactive Multimodal Conversation (SIMMC), which presents a task-oriented user↔assistant dialog grounded in a co-observed photorealistic multimodal context. The new version of the SIMMC dataset includes more fine-grained and precise annotations for referent disambiguation candidates, which poses new challenges for the Multimodal Coreference Resolution task (MM-Coref) and the Ambiguous Candidate Identification task.

While the new SOTA models have drastically improved the performance on the previous benchmark tasks, several challenges remain in building the production-ready agent. One such challenge is the visual disambiguation which is often encountered in real-world multimodal conversations. For instance, the user ambiguously uses *'these two trousers'* in Fig. 1, which cannot be deterministically resolved. Thus, an assistant system needs to reason about this, identify the possible ambiguous candidates, and then ask a follow-up question to disambiguate. This is important to avoid

*Joint first authors
[1]https://github.com/facebookresearch/simmc2

Proceedings of The Eleventh Dialog System Technology Challenge, pages 235–241
September 11, 2023 ©2023 Association for Computational Linguistics

a wrong resolution of such references leading to subsequent turns with false premises. Another advantage is that the assistant could insert implicit confirmation – "*Which of the two red jackets are you referring to - the one on the left or the one closer to you?*", as opposed to a generic response like: "*Which one are you referring to?*".

To this end, we conducted the third edition of the SIMMC challenge (SIMMC 2.1) for the community to tackle and continue the effort towards building a successful multimodal assistant agent. In this edition of the challenge, we specifically focused on the key challenge of fine-grained visual disambiguation, which adds an important skill to assistant agents studied in the previous SIMMC challenge. To accommodate for this challenge, we provided the improved version of the of the dataset, SIMMC 2.1, where we augment the SIMMC 2.0 dataset with additional annotations (*i.e.* identification of all possible referent candidates given ambiguous mentions) and corresponding re-paraphrases to support the study and modeling of visual disambiguation (SIMMC 2.1). This new version of the dataset poses several interesting challenges such multimodal dialog state tracking given ambiguity, coreference resolutions ("*directly behind it*", "*grey jacket to the right of the one I mentioned*"), and disambiguation strategies ("*How much is that shirt*" $\rightarrow$ "*Which shirt are you referring to?*").

2 The Third SIMMC Challenge

We now detail the new version of the multimodal conversational dataset (SIMMC 2.1) (Sec. 2.2) and the four main sub-tasks (Tab. 1, Sec. 2.3).

2.1 Problem Setup

The SIMMC challenge studies the conversational scenarios where the virtual assistant shares a co-observed scene with a user. Specifically, the dataset targets the shopping experience as the domain of study, which often induces rich multimodal interactions around browsing visually grounded items in a physical store (fashion or furniture). The assistant agent is assumed to have access to the ground-truth meta information of every object in the scene, while users observe those objects only through the visual modality to describe and compose a request, as in the real-world applications. Each dialog in the dataset includes multiple viewpoints at different time steps throughout the session, corresponding to the scenarios where users are physically navigating the scene during the conversation. Therefore, the conversational models for the SIMMC challenge need to understand both user requests using both the dialog history and the state of the environment as multimodal context.

Note that the SIMMC problem setup where user and assistant co-observe the same scene allows for more natural multimodal coreferences to be used as part of user-assistant conversations. The previous literature in multimodal dialogs [1, 10, 4, 13, 6, 5] often assumes that dialog participants take the roles of a primary and secondary observer respectively, *i.e. questioner* and *answerer* similar to the Visual Question Answering [2] tasks, which does not address the real-world consumer scenario we are targetting. The SIMMC challenge also extends many of the key dialog tasks studied in the previous literature on conventional task-oriented dialog systems [9, 18, 3, 7] (*e.g.* DST, slot carryovers) to the unique multimodal settings.

2.2 The New SIMMC 2.1 Dataset

The SIMMC 2.1 dataset extends the original SIMMC 2.0 dataset [12] with additional annotations for fine-grained referent candidates and new utterances (details below).

Collection Process: The original dataset used the two-phase pipeline to collect dialogs (multimodal dialog simulation & manual human paraphrase), which can effectively collect natrual dialogs with the minimum annotation overheads. Note that this approach extends the popular machine$\leftrightarrow$human collaborative dialog collection approaches [18, 19] to the unique multimodal settings. More details on the data collection approach can be found in [12].

Data Statistics: The dataset includes 11,244 dialogs (117,236 utterances), with the fine-grained ground-truth dialog labels (NLU/NLG/Coref) already in place. Table 2 shows the statistics of the dataset.

Additional Annotations in SIMMC 2.1. The key differences are illustrated in Fig. 1. We collect candidates in the scene for turns with ambiguous references using human annotators. Further, we also ask the annotators to paraphrase the turn in case there is not enough ambiguity. This data collection process thus allows for richer coreferences, referential expressions, and disambiguation scenarios.

Task Name	Goal	Evaluation
1. Ambiguous Candidate Identification	Given user utterances with ambiguous object mentions, resolve all referent candidate objects to their canonical ID(s) as defined by the catalog.	Object identification Precision / Recall / F1
2. Multimodal Coreference Resolution	Given user utterances with object mentions, resolve referent objects to their canonical ID(s) as defined by the catalog.	Coref Precision / Recall / F1
3. Multimodal Dialog State Tracking	Given user utterances, track user belief states across multiple turns.	Intent Accuracy, Slot Precision / Recall / F1
4. Response Generation	Given user utterances, ground-truth APIs and ground-truth object IDs, generate Assistant responses or retrieve from a candidate pool.	Generation: BLEU-4 score

Table 1: **Proposed tracks and descriptions.**

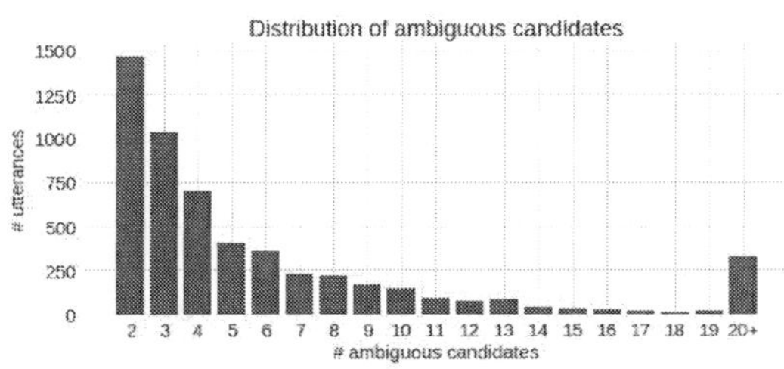

Figure 2: Distribution of ambiguous items.

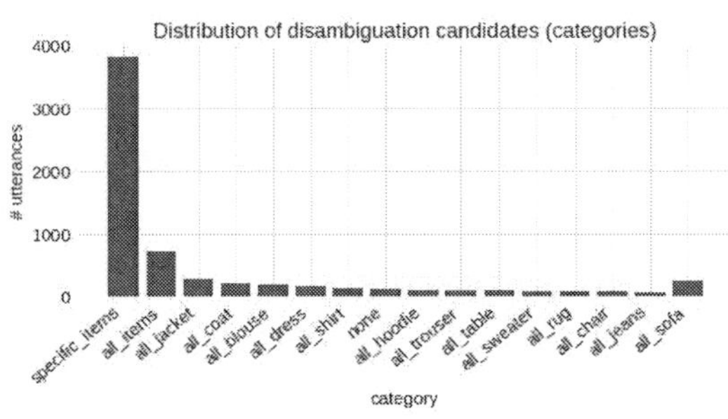

Figure 3: Distribution of ambiguous items per category.

Total # dialogs	11,244
Total # utterances	117,236
Total # scenes	3,133
Avg # words per user turns	12
Avg # words per assistant turns	13.7
Avg # utterances per dialog	10.4
Avg # objects mentioned per dialog	4.7
Avg # objects in scene per dialog	19.7
Avg # candidates per ambiguous turn	5.6

Table 2: **SIMMC 2.1 Dataset Statistics**

Annotation Analysis: We have $6.5k$ turns with ambiguous candidates, where the average number of candidates is 5.6. Fig. 2 and Fig. 3 represent the distribution of the candidates in these utterances per the number of items or per category.

Data format: The SIMMC 2.1 data has been provided in the same format as the earlier version of the datasets, making it easier for participants to use the various benchmark models publicly available [15, 12], or augment it with the previous version of the dataset for pretraining, etc. The raw pixel images of each scene as well as the pre-computed visual embeddings have been provided, allowing for easier adaptation for the NLP audience.

2.3 Challenge Tasks

We invited the DSTC community to build multimodal conversational agents for the following four benchmark tasks, addressing the key challenges in the multimodal conversational reasoning (summarized in Tab. 1). All the benchmark tasks require a strong computer vision capability as well as a multimodal conversational reasoning capability, to jointly process both the dialog and the visual contexts.

2.3.1 Ambiguous Candidates Identification

As a main focus of this edition of the challenge, this sub-task will evaluate the models' performance on identifying *all* candidate objects referred by a given user utterance, as their canonical object IDs as defined for each scene (*e.g.* U: "*How much is that blue shirt on the hanger?*" → (object IDs of all blue shirts on hangers in the scene).

The task will provide the ground-truth bounding boxes defining each object ID to make evaluation easier. The performance will mainly be measured for its F1 score.

2.3.2 Multimodal Coreference Resolution (MM-Coref)

The goal of this task is to resolve referential mentions in user utterances to their canonical object IDs as defined for each scene. The resolving contexts can come either through (1) the dialog context (*e.g.* A: "*This shirt comes in XL and is $29.*" → U: "*Please add it to cart.*", (2) the multimodal context (*e.g.* U: "*How much is that red shirt back there?*"), or (3) both (*e.g.* U: "*How much is the one next to the one you mentioned?*").

2.3.3 Multimodal Dialog State Tracking (MM-DST)

Following the earlier challenge, the goal of the MM-DST task is to predict slots and their corresponding values grounded on the co-existing multimodal context. This requires tracking the states of multimodal objects (in addition to textual tokens) as part of dialog states. Note that this task extends the traditional notion of the unimodal dialog state tracking (DST) problem widely studied by the DSTC community.

2.3.4 Assistant Response Generation

The goal of the task is to generate Assistant responses given user utterances, ground-truth APIs and object IDs. While the assistant agent has the ground-truth meta information on each object, the referent objects need to be described *as observed and understood* by the user through the co-observed scene or the dialog context, adding an interesting challenge to the traditional response generation tasks (*e.g.* `INFORM:RECOMMEND (OBJ_ID: 3)` → A: "*I recommend the blue jacket directly behind the one I mentioned*".

In addition, with the new annotations and utterances added for SIMMC 2.1, we expect that the entries that can leverage the identified ambiguous candidate list as part of the response will achieve the best performance (*e.g.* A: "*Which of the two red jackets are you referring to - the one on the left or the one closer to you?*", as opposed to a generic response like: "*Which one are you referring to?*") – which is the main focus of this edition of the challenge.

3 Baselines

There are two baselines, adopted from [12]:

(a) **MM-DST model** by [15], where we train a multi-task GPT-2 [17] based Transformer model using the joint supervision signals for the Disambiguation, MM-Coref, DST, and Response Generation tasks. Specifically, the model takes as input the dialog context and the flattened multimodal contexts (as structurally formatted strings) to predict the belief states and the responses, following the popular causal language model approach [16, 11]. We use the 12-layer GPT-2 (117M parameters) as the pre-trained language model and fine-tune for ten epochs. Note that this baseline uses the ground-truth multimodal contexts provided from the scene generator, instead of consuming raw images as input, and thus serves as a soft oracle on the proposed dataset.

(b) **Multimodal Transformer Network (MTN)** [14] for the DST and Response Generation tasks. In particular, MTN uses image features extracted from scene snapshots and attends to relevant parts as guided by the dialog. We use the same training setting and hyperparameters as [14].

Specifically for the task of ambiguous candidate identification (subtask 1), we extract the feature representation of the last token as the textual feature and compute similarity with the visual features extracted for each item in a given scene. Visual features for the items are extracted similar to the above MTN network.

4 Submitted Systems

4.1 Models

We now provide brief description of the entries submitted to the SIMMC 2.1 challenge.

Team 1 uses a large transformer-encoder based discriminative model (Longformer). To predict ambiguous candidates, coreference resolution, and belief state, they encode dialogue history and at-

Team	Model	1. ACI.	2. MM-Coref	3. MM-DST		4. Gen.
		ID F1↑	Coref F1↑	Slot F1↑	Intent F1↑	BLEU↑
Baseline	GPT-2 [15]	42.6	30.5	71.8	92.6	0.199
	MTN [14]	·	·	66.5	91.5	0.210
Team 1	Longformer	67.3	94.3	94.2	96.0	·
	FairSeq-Generative	·	·	·	·	0.409
Team 2	CoCondenser+ViT	65.2	·	·	·	·
Team 3	ALBEF	63.8	75.6	·	·	·
	BART	·	·	90.5	96.9	0.303
Team 4	Combiner	·	·	·	·	0.252
Team 5	BART-DSTCLA-Ens.	69.9	80.1	92.6	97.3	·
	BART-DSTCLA	70.5	80.3	92.7	97.3	·
	BART-Ens.	70.3	79.9	91.6	97.8	·
	BART-Sys.	·	·	·	·	0.351
	BART-Sys-Alt.	·	·	·	·	0.353
	BART-Sys-Ens.	·	·	·	·	0.365
	BART-Sys-Attr.	·	·	·	·	0.350

Table 3: Summary of the results on Test-Std split. Best results from each system are shown. **(1) Ambiguous Candidate Identification (ACI.)**, via identification F1, **(2) Multimodal Coreference Resolution (MM-Coref)**, via coref prediction F1, **(3) Dialog State Tracking (DST)**, via slot and intent F1, **(4) Response Generation (Gen.)** via BLEU. ↑: higher is better. Baseline performances: [15] (top), [14] (bottom).

tach task-specific heads to the output of encoder. Additionally, they line up the item vectors (bbox position embedding) with their respective attribute tokens in the inputted token embedding. Auxiliary heads for predicting attributes are added as additional supervision signals. For task 4, a generative multimodal model is used which takes dialogue history and non-visual attributes as textual input, and corresponding scene images as visual input. The model then generates system response autoregressively.

Team 2 proposes a model based on CoCondenser and Vision Transformer (ViT) specifically trained for Subtask 1, leveraging their powerful encoding ability. Image models were fine-tuned for the in-domain image sets (for fashion and furniture domains) to improve the visual encoding ability of the models.

Team 3 proposes separate models tuned for each subtask. For subtask 1, they train a vision language transformer model using ALBEF as backbone. Similarly, they use the same architecture for subtask 2, trained separately using only the co-reference labels as the target task. For subtask 3, they use additional pre-training on the BART model with a tailored masked language modeling task to adapt to the dialogue domain, later fine-tuned on the Dialogue State Tracking task. They use a similar model fur sub-task 4 as well, framed as a generative model. Object images are preprocessed using a ResNext model.

Team 4 did not release their implementation, thus details about their approach are not public.

Team 5 performs ablation over multiple families of models – a vanilla Encoder-Decoder architecture (BART, T5, UL-2, and BlenderBot), an Multi-Modal encoder architecture (Flava), and a Multi-Modal Encoder-Decoder, all jointly trained for a multi-task (MT) objective. With various models, they perform ablations over using the joint input of textual context, system dialog acts, tokenized objects and scene as multi-modal input.

4.2 Evaluation

The entries to the challenge set a new state-of-the-art in all four subtasks. The results are summarized in Tab. 3.

The winner of the ambiguous candidate identification subtask (subtask 1) was the multi-task BART-based model from Team 1. The winner of the multimodal coreference resolution task (subtask 2), the dialog state tracking task (subtask 3), and the response generation task (subtask 4) was from the Longformer model from Team 5.

For Subtask 1, the BART-based multi-task training from Team 1 outperforms other competing models by more than 2 point absolute gain. This result implies that the ambiguous candidate identification task can benefit from the learning signals from multiple sub-tasks.

For Subtask 2 through 4, the Longformer-based model from Team 5 shows a huge margin in performance over other models, indicating the effectiveness of the implementation in encoding the visual information (*e.g.* bbox position embeddings, understanding visual attributes of items).

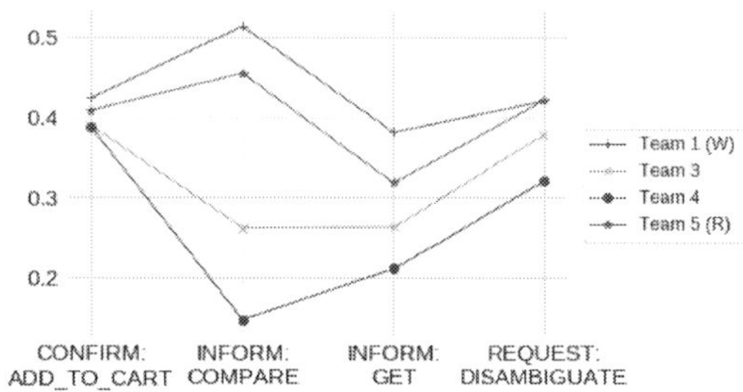

Figure 4: Distribution of BLEU score for subtask 4 over natural language generation act.

Fig. 4 shows the distribution of BLEU scores over natural language generation act, with the following key observations:

- All teams seem to perform comparable on `CONFIRM:ADD_TO_CART` intent, which is to be expected as it usually is less diverse linguistically.
- `INFORM:COMPARE` act clearly distinguishes both the winner and runner-up team from the rest, as this requires the system to understand the objects of comparison and list their attributes for the user.

5 Conclusion

The goal of the SIMMC 2.1 challenge in DSTC11 is to motivate and inspire the research community to work on the problem of creating dialog agents that can handle multiple modes of communication and handle tasks in a specific context. These agents have many practical uses and present a range of challenges related to multimodal communication.

The SIMMC 2.1 challenge specifically saw a number of submissions exploring different transformer architectures, highlighting the trade-offs in performance. We hope that the insights gained from this challenge will shed light on the challenges of multimodal dialogs and inspire further research in this area.

What next? We identify possible future directions for the SIMMC challenge to continue advancing in this area of research.

- **Incorporating additional modalities.** The current approach for the SIMMC 2.1 challenge utilizes screenshots from a shopping website as the multimodal context. While this presents its own set of challenges, it does not take into account additional forms of input such as eye gaze, head position, and gestures that would be present in a real-world setting. These additional cues are often used by human users to refer to objects, for example, "*How much is that shirt* (pointing a finger)". To include these modalities, SIMMC would need to be grounded in a virtual environment with a stream of inputs to capture users' eye gaze, head position, location in the store, *etc*.
- **Incorporating temporal reasoning.** Many of the referring expressions used in real-world scenarios are *temporally* grounded, which is not studied in the current challenge in detail. For instance, to understand a query "*I prefer the one I saw when I entered the store.*", an assistant agent would need to have a way to track the multimodal states (including human motions and movements) over time.

References

[1] H. Al Amri, V. Cartillier, R. G. Lopes, A. Das, J. Wang, I. Essa, D. Batra, D. Parikh, A. Cherian, T. K. Marks, and C. Hori. Audio visual scene-aware dialog (avsd) challenge at dstc7. 2018.

[2] Stanislaw Antol, Aishwarya Agrawal, Jiasen Lu, Margaret Mitchell, Dhruv Batra, C Lawrence Zitnick, and Devi Parikh. VQA: Visual question answering. In *ICCV*, 2015.

[3] Paweł Budzianowski, Tsung-Hsien Wen, Bo-Hsiang Tseng, Iñigo Casanueva, Stefan Ultes, Osman Ramadan, and Milica Gašić. MultiWOZ - a large-scale multi-domain wizard-of-Oz dataset for task-oriented dialogue modelling. In *Proceedings of the Conference on Empirical Methods in Natural Language Processing (EMNLP)*, 2018.

[4] Abhishek Das, Satwik Kottur, Khushi Gupta, Avi Singh, Deshraj Yadav, José MF Moura, Devi Parikh, and Dhruv Batra. Visual dialog. In *CVPR*, 2017.

[5] Harm de Vries, Kurt Shuster, Dhruv Batra, Devi Parikh, Jason Weston, and Douwe Kiela. Talk the walk: Navigating new york city through grounded dialogue. *arXiv preprint arXiv:1807.03367*, 2018.

[6] Harm de Vries, Florian Strub, Sarath Chandar, Olivier Pietquin, Hugo Larochelle, and Aaron Courville. Guesswhat?! visual object discovery through multi-modal dialogue. In *CVPR*, 2017.

[7] Mihail Eric, Rahul Goel, Shachi Paul, Adarsh Kumar, Abhishek Sethi, Peter Ku, Anuj Kumar Goyal, Sanchit Agarwal, Shuyag Gao, and Dilek Hakkani-Tur. Multiwoz 2.1: Multi-domain dialogue state corrections and state tracking baselines. *arXiv preprint arXiv:1907.01669*, 2019.

[8] Chulaka Gunasekara, Seokhwan Kim, Luis Fernando D'Haro, Abhinav Rastogi, Yun-Nung Chen, Mihail Eric, Behnam Hedayatnia, Karthik Gopalakrishnan, Yang Liu, Chao-Wei Huang, et al. Overview of the ninth dialog system technology challenge: Dstc9. *arXiv preprint arXiv:2011.06486*, 2020.

[9] Matthew Henderson, Blaise Thomson, and Jason D Williams. The second dialog state tracking challenge. In *Proceedings of the 15th annual meeting of the special interest group on discourse and dialogue (SIGDIAL)*, pages 263–272, 2014.

[10] Chiori Hori, Anoop Cherian, Tim K. Marks, and Florian Metze. Audio visual scene-aware dialog track in dstc8. *DSTC Track Proposal*, 2018.

[11] Ehsan Hosseini-Asl, Bryan McCann, Chien-Sheng Wu, Semih Yavuz, and Richard Socher. A simple language model for task-oriented dialogue. *arXiv preprint arXiv:2005.00796*, 2020.

[12] Satwik Kottur, Seungwhan Moon, Alborz Geramifard, and Babak Damavandi. SIMMC 2.0: A task-oriented dialog dataset for immersive multimodal conversations. In *Proceedings of the 2021 Conference on Empirical Methods in Natural Language Processing*, pages 4903–4912, Online and Punta Cana, Dominican Republic, November 2021. Association for Computational Linguistics.

[13] Satwik Kottur, José MF Moura, Devi Parikh, Dhruv Batra, and Marcus Rohrbach. Clevr-dialog: A diagnostic dataset for multi-round reasoning in visual dialog. *arXiv preprint arXiv:1903.03166*, 2019.

[14] Hung Le, Doyen Sahoo, Nancy Chen, and Steven Hoi. Multimodal transformer networks for end-to-end video-grounded dialogue systems. In *Proceedings of the 57th Annual Meeting of the Association for Computational Linguistics*, pages 5612–5623, 2019.

[15] Seungwhan Moon, Satwik Kottur, Paul A Crook, Ankita De, Shivani Poddar, Theodore Levin, David Whitney, Daniel Difranco, Ahmad Beirami, Eunjoon Cho, Rajen Subba, and Alborz Geramifard. Situated and interactive multimodal conversations. *arXiv preprint arXiv:2006.01460*, 2020.

[16] Baolin Peng, Chunyuan Li, Jinchao Li, Shahin Shayandeh, Lars Liden, and Jianfeng Gao. Soloist: Few-shot task-oriented dialog with a single pre-trained auto-regressive model. *arXiv preprint arXiv:2005.05298*, 2020.

[17] Alec Radford, Jeffrey Wu, Rewon Child, David Luan, Dario Amodei, and Ilya Sutskever. Language models are unsupervised multitask learners. *OpenAI blog*, 1(8):9, 2019.

[18] Abhinav Rastogi, Xiaoxue Zang, Srinivas Sunkara, Raghav Gupta, and Pranav Khaitan. Towards scalable multi-domain conversational agents: The schema-guided dialogue dataset. In *Association for the Advancement of Artificial Intelligence (AAAI)*, 2019.

[19] Pararth Shah, Dilek Hakkani-Tür, Gokhan Tür, Abhinav Rastogi, Ankur Bapna, Neha Nayak, and Larry Heck. Building a conversational agent overnight with dialogue self-play. *arXiv preprint arXiv:1801.04871*, 2018.

Intent Induction from Conversations for Task-Oriented Dialogue Track at DSTC 11

James Gung, Raphael Shu, Emily Moeng, Wesley Rose, Salvatore Romeo
Yassine Benajiba, Arshit Gupta, Saab Mansour and **Yi Zhang**
AWS AI Labs
{gungj,zhongzhu}@amazon.com

Abstract

With increasing demand for and adoption of virtual assistants, recent work has investigated ways to accelerate bot schema design through the automatic induction of intents or the induction of slots and dialogue states. However, a lack of dedicated benchmarks and standardized evaluation has made progress difficult to track and comparisons between systems difficult to make. This challenge track[1], held as part of the Eleventh Dialog Systems Technology Challenge, introduces a benchmark that aims to evaluate methods for the automatic induction of customer intents in a realistic setting of customer service interactions between human agents and customers. We propose two subtasks for progressively tackling the automatic induction of intents and corresponding evaluation methodologies. We then present three datasets suitable for evaluating the tasks and propose simple baselines. Finally, we summarize the submissions and results of the challenge track, for which we received submissions from 34 teams.

1 Introduction

Task-oriented dialogue systems used for handling high-volume customer service requests have seen growing adoption in recent years. While numerous platforms for building such dialogue systems exist, they still typically require significant time and expert knowledge to achieve good results. In particular, the process of creating non-overlapping intents and corresponding example utterances typically requires domain expertise and/or laborious analysis of a large volume of conversation transcripts. Intent induction, automatically deriving intents and corresponding utterances from conversation transcripts or customer queries, has the potential to significantly reduce the time and effort required to build a task-oriented dialogue system from the ground up.

Recent work in intent mining has often cast intent induction as a problem similar to that of short text clustering, in which unlabeled customer queries and requests are assigned labels and the effectiveness of a system is evaluated by comparing cluster assignments to labels from a ground truth intent schema (Hakkani-Tür et al., 2015; Haponchyk et al., 2018; Perkins and Yang, 2019; Chatterjee and Sengupta, 2020). Due to the lack of real world datasets capturing human-human customer support conversations, researchers have repurposed existing intent classification datasets or labeled small subsets of publicly available customer service interactions to evaluate their systems.

Despite a growing body of work, there is a lack of common evaluative settings and standardized, dedicated benchmarks for intent induction, making progress difficult to track. Existing intent classification datasets do not capture the complexity of mining intents from real customer service interactions, which typically have highly skewed distributions of intents that are embedded in noisy conversations. While dedicated, representative benchmarks have been instrumental in driving and measuring progress in natural language processing tasks (Wang et al., 2019; Ruder, 2021), there is a clear gap in this regard for intent induction.

To encourage further research and to provide a shared benchmark in the realistic setting of spoken customer service interactions, this challenge track introduces a dataset containing conversations spanning three domains: insurance, personal banking, and finance. The track explores an alternative framing of the intent induction task through the use of two related subtasks: Task 1) *intent clustering* and Task 2) *open intent induction*. For the intent clustering task, we use classic clustering metrics for evaluation. For open intent induction, which seeks to provide a more realistic and noisy setting in which

[1] https://github.com/amazon-science/dstc11-track2-intent-induction

Proceedings of The Eleventh Dialog System Technology Challenge, pages 242–259
September 11, 2023 ©2023 Association for Computational Linguistics

intents are embedded in conversations, we evaluate systems by examining the predictions of an intent classifier trained on induced intent schemas. This setting aims to bring us closer to assessing the impact of automatic induced intents on a final dialogue system.

A total of 34 teams participated in the track, with 19 teams also participating in Task 2. In this paper, we describe the tasks, evaluation methods, datasets, and baselines. We then describe the submissions from the participating teams and summarize the results and findings from the track.

2 Related Work

The majority of existing work in mining intents has focused on clustering-based methods. Perkins and Yang (2019) proposes a multi-view clustering approach for learning clustering representations by predicting cluster assignments of an alternative view of each input, such as prompts. Chatterjee and Sengupta (2020) investigates variants of DBSCAN and propose an approach that iteratively breaks down the "noise" cluster from DBSCAN to address varying densities. Others have leveraged intermediate structured prediction tasks (such as dependency parsing or abstract meaning representations) to aid in the induction of intents (Hakkani-Tür et al., 2015; Vedula et al., 2020; Zeng et al., 2021; Liu et al., 2021).

Prior work in intent mining has largely evaluated systems by re-purposing existing datasets commonly used for evaluating intent classification systems. Such datasets, including BANK77 (Casanueva et al., 2020), CLINC150 (Larson et al., 2019), SNIPS (Coucke et al., 2018), ATIS (Hemphill et al., 1990), or StackOverflow (Hamner et al., 2012; Xu et al., 2015), do not include full dialogues. Task-oriented dialogue datasets like MultiWOZ (Budzianowski et al., 2018), MultiDoGO (Peskov et al., 2019a) and SGD (Rastogi et al., 2020) span multiple domains, but individual domains contain few user intents, and conversations are not designed to be representative of real human-to-human customer service interactions. Perkins and Yang (2019) re-purpose two-turn customer support exchanges from Twitter, but only annotate a small subset of dialogues across 14 intents with broad semantics.

Hakkani-Tür et al. (2015) evaluate the classification performance of induced intents after undergoing manual mappings to reference intents. More recent work has used clustering metrics commonly used for evaluation of short text clustering in which the number of clusters is provided, such as clustering ACC, NMI, and ARI (Peskov et al., 2019a; Zhang et al., 2021c; Chatterjee and Sengupta, 2020; Kumar et al., 2022). Recent work has also investigated the intent discovery problem in which systems must discover novel intents based on a set of pre-existing intents (Lin et al., 2020; Zhang et al., 2021b,c; Shen et al., 2021; Kumar et al., 2022). In contrast to this work, this benchmark focuses on the fully unsupervised setting in which no pre-existing intents are defined and the number of reference intents are not provided in advance.

3 Tasks and Evaluation

The track consists of two subtasks providing alternative ways of framing and evaluating intent induction. This section describes the motivation for these tasks and metrics used for evaluating them.

3.1 Task 1 - Intent Clustering

Task 1 is a conversational intent clustering task. In this task, a set of conversation transcripts are provided as inputs, with each turn pre-labeled with a speaker role (i.e. *agent* or *customer*). Turns within these transcripts that contain intents are tagged for use in the task. Participants must assign each of these intentful turns to a cluster. Submissions are evaluated by comparing the resulting cluster assignment with intent labels from a reference intent schema. The number of reference intents is not provided for the task, though lower and upper limits are given (5 and 50 respectively).

3.2 Task 2 - Open Intent Induction

The clustering evaluation in Task 1 has several shortcomings. In a real world setting, the exact turns in transcripts containing intents are unknown. The goal of intent induction is to extract a set of distinctly meaningful intents, rather than assigning each turn a cluster label. The quality of a set of induced intents is likely to be judged based on the coverage and accuracy of a resulting intent classifier rather than coverage on input turns. From the perspective of chat bot development, a smaller but cleaner training set can thus be preferable to a larger but noisier and less manageable set of utterances.

To account for this, the goal of Task 2 is to instead generate a *training set* for an intent classifier

	Task 1 - Intent Clustering	Task 2 - Open Intent Induction
Goal	Assign cluster labels to a list of turns	Induce intents and training examples for an intent classifier from conversations
Input	(1) Conversation transcripts, (2) clustering turns	(1) Conversation transcripts, (2) Automatic *InformIntent* turn predictions
Output	Intent cluster labels assigned to each clustering turn	Example utterances labeled with induced intents

Table 1: Summary of the benchmark tasks proposed as part of the DSTC 11 challenge on intent induction from conversations: Intent Clustering and Open Intent Induction.

given a set of unlabeled conversations. The training set consists of utterances derived from the conversations along with corresponding intent labels[2]. Note that no explicit correspondence between utterances in the training set and the original conversations is required, so techniques such as data augmentation or paraphrasing are allowed. Unlike Task 1, to better reflect challenges of noisy data in a real world setting, we do not explicitly provide labels to tell whether a turn is intentful. However, to simplify system development for the task, automatic dialogue act classifier predictions for *InformIntent* are provided to participants.

Evaluation for the task is conducted using the predictions of an intent classifier trained with the induced intents. After training the classifier, predictions are made on a separate test set of utterances labeled with a reference intent schema. Finally, similarly to Task 1, the quality of the induced set of intents is evaluated by comparing the predicted assignment of labels with the reference intent assignment. In contrast to Hakkani-Tür et al. (2015), this evaluation approach is fully automatic and does not require manual intent mappings.

3.3 Metrics

In a realistic setting, the number of unique intents that are present in a dataset will not be known in advance. Inducing an excess of fine-grained intents may result in purer, more coherent predictions, but will then require additional manual effort and human expertise to merge intents that are duplicates of one another (semantically equivalent). On the other hand, predicting intents with too broad or coarse-grained semantics is also undesirable. We therefore select metrics that balance this trade-off and encourage approaches capable of matching the granularity of the reference intent schema in the test data.

[2]In this track, the intent labels are treated as unique IDs and are not evaluated for linguistic meaning.

Metrics for both Task 1 and Task 2 are computed by comparing the assignment of induced intents, C, with assignments to a single reference intent schema, L. For Task 1, cluster assignments are compared on turns in input conversations. For Task 2, predicted induced intents are compared on a set of test utterances collected independently from input conversations.

Clustering accuracy (ACC) is a commonly used metric for short text clustering that penalizes solutions for producing either too many or too few clusters (Huang et al., 2014). ACC is defined as

$$\text{ACC} = \frac{\sum_{i=1}^{N} \delta(map(\hat{y}_i) = y_i)}{N},$$

where $\delta(\cdot)$ is an indicator function that outputs 1 when the argument is true or 0 when false, $\hat{y}_i \in C$ and $y_i \in L$ are the predicted and ground truth labels for the ith input respectively, and N is the total number of turns/inputs. The $map(\cdot)$ function assigns the cluster label to the optimal label y_i as computed by the Hungarian algorithm (Kuhn, 1955). If too few intents are predicted, some reference intents will not receive assignments, whereas an excess of induced intents will lead to unassigned induced intents.

Clustering F_1 (Artiles et al., 2007; Haponchyk et al., 2018) also captures this trade-off by combining clustering *precision* (purity) and clustering *recall* (inverse purity, in which each reference intent is assigned to the most frequently co-occurring induced intent):

$$\text{precision (P)} = \frac{\sum_{k=1}^{|C|} \max_{j=1}^{|L|} |l_j \cap c_k|}{N},$$

$$\text{recall (R)} = \frac{\sum_{k=1}^{|L|} \max_{j=1}^{|C|} |l_k \cap c_j|}{N},$$

where $|l_k \cap c_j|$ indicates the size of the set containing inputs assigned to both reference cluster l_k and predicted cluster c_j. Clustering F_1 is then computed as the harmonic mean of the two measures.

Solutions with too few intents, or broad intents that are split between multiple different reference intents, will have lower precision/purity. Solutions with an excess of granular intents mapping to the same reference intent will have lower recall, as each reference intent can only be assigned to a single induced intent.

Finally, we also report NMI (normalized mutual information) and ARI (Adjusted Rand Index) (Rand, 1971), two commonly used measures for clustering evaluation. ACC is used as the primary metric for ranking systems for both tasks.

Intent Classifier Evaluation of Task 2 requires training an intent classifier using the induced schema. Following previous work demonstrating the effectiveness of training a simple classifier given fixed embeddings from a pre-trained sentence encoder in few-shot setting (Zhang et al., 2021d; Casanueva et al., 2020), we train a logistic regression classifier on top of off-the-shelf, static ALL-MPNET-BASE-V2 sentence embeddings from the SENTENCETRANSFORMERS library (Reimers and Gurevych, 2019; Song et al., 2020).

4 Data

Publicly available dialogue datasets have primarily focused on development and evaluation of task-oriented dialogue systems where conversations are representative of written human-to-bot (H2B) conversations adhering to restricted domains and schemas (Budzianowski et al., 2018; Rastogi et al., 2020). Such datasets are not designed to be reflective of the characteristics of human-to-human (H2H) conversations, and thus are unlikely to serve as a realistic test bed for evaluating systems designed to learn from natural conversations. However, realistic live conversations are difficult to simulate due to the training required to convincingly play the role of an expert customer support agent in non-trival domains (Chen et al., 2021) and the additional costs associated with collecting and annotating free-form synchronous conversations.

To address this gap, we introduce a benchmark dataset designed to emulate natural call center conversations between customers and customer support agents. Each conversation emulates a two-party spoken-form customer support scenario corresponding to a generated scenario based on a combination of intents, slots, and complex conversational phenomena to encourage diversity and naturalness. To naturally collect a wide variety of intents, partic-

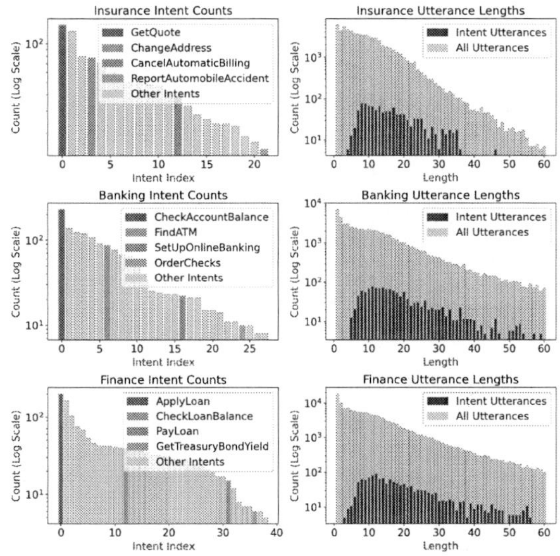

Figure 1: Intent counts and utterance length distribution across domains (logarithmic scales).

ipants were encouraged to depart from the original intents with additional requests related to each scenario. The process of annotating conversations with reference intents was decoupled from the collection of conversations in order to mimic the manual process of designing an intent schema based on conversations. Annotators shared an open intent label set that was periodically reviewed throughout the process to merge duplicate intents.

We provide three domains as part of the challenge track: *Insurance* (used as development data), *Personal Banking* and *Finance* (used as evaluation data). For evaluating Task 2, each domain also includes a H2B-style balanced test set containing utterances labeled with intents from a reference intent schema. These test sets are collected independently from the H2H-style conversations. Conversations are also labeled with automatic *InformIntent* dialogue act predictions indicating potentially relevant turns for use in Task 2, though these are non-exhaustive and include utterances that are not relevant.

We present high-level statistics for each of the domains in comparison with pre-existing dialogue datasets in Table 2. The resulting conversations include considerably more turns on average than previous task-oriented dialogue conversational datasets, suggesting a higher level of conversational complexity and diversity of flows, despite being restricted to single domains. The conversations also contain a greater variety of intents per domain,

Dataset	# conv.	# turns per conv.	# words per turn	# intents per domain
MultiDoGO (Peskov et al., 2019b)	10,829	16.7	11.4	6.7
MWOZ (Budzianowski et al., 2018)	10,437	13.7	15.4	*
SGD (Rastogi et al., 2020)	22,825	20.3	11.7	2.3
DSTC11-Insurance	948	70.5	12.3	22
DSTC11-Banking	1,000	59.2	17.4	29
DSTC11-Finance	2,000	65.1	15.7	39

Table 2: Summary statistics of DSTC 11 Track 2 datasets and comparison with previous task-oriented dialogue datasets. *User intents are not explicitly annotated in MultiWOZ, but are instead implicit to each domain.

ensuring the tasks are not trivial to distinguish between a small number of intents. Finally, as shown in Figure 1, the distribution of counts for these intents is highly skewed, similar to real intent distributions with long tails of infrequent intents and a few intents comprising a large volume of requests. Fine-grained counts of intents for conversations and test sets and further analysis of intents are provided in Sections A.1 and A.2.

5 Baselines

Task 1 Baseline The baseline system for Task 1 casts the problem as turn-level unsupervised clustering, adopting k-means (MacQueen et al., 1967) as the clustering algorithm. Utterances are encoded using a sentence embedding model from the SENTENCETRANSFORMERS library (Reimers and Gurevych, 2019), ALL-MPNET-BASE-V2, which fine-tunes MPNet (Song et al., 2020) with a contrastive objective on a dataset consisting of 1 billion sentence pairs derived from a number of datasets.

Because the number of reference intents is not provided for the task, the baseline system identifies the number of intents automatically by selecting the value for k that results in the highest intrinsic measure of clustering performance. Silhouette values (Rousseeuw, 1987; Kaufman and Rousseeuw, 2009) indicate the appropriateness of a cluster assignment for a point based on the similarity to points in its assigned cluster and dissimilarity to points in other clusters. An overall silhouette score can be computed by averaging the silhouettes for all points in a clustering. The k value that leads to the highest silhouette score is selected as the final result. To accelerate the search for optimal clustering based on Silhouette scores, we employ sequential model-based global optimization following the tree-structured Parzen estimator (TPE) approach, implemented in the HYPEROPT library (Bergstra et al., 2013).

Task 2 Baseline The baseline system for Task 2 adopts the same clustering approach as Task 1. Since clustering turns are not provided in this task, the baseline system uses the provided *InformIntent* dialogue act classifier predictions to identify turns containing intents.

6 Submissions

We received submissions from 34 teams for Task 1 and 19 teams for Task 2 encompassing a wide range of techniques. All teams that participated in Task 2 also participated in Task 1. To preserve anonymity, teams are identified with IDs T0 through T37 (several team IDs were later removed after confirming duplicate submissions from different members of the same team). This section provides a high-level summary of the submissions using self-reported descriptions and survey results of the participants. A detailed overview of submissions is provided in appendix Table 11.

Clustering Approach For both tasks, all submissions reported using clustering-based solutions. Many submissions used clustering approaches that jointly learn input representations and cluster assignments. For example, at least ten submissions (T00, T02, T05, T07, T16, T17, T24, T30, T34, and T36) reported used SCCL (Zhang et al., 2021a), a clustering approach that incorporates contrastive loss with Deep Embedded Clustering (DEC) (Xie et al., 2016). Other approaches (e.g. T06 and T37) separated representation learning from clustering, pre-training encoders with contrastive learning followed by K-Means clustering. T06 used K-Means with representations from DSSCC (Kumar et al., 2022).

Several submissions used HDBSCAN for clustering (T11, T13, T22, and T35), a density-based clustering algorithm that extends DBSCAN by allowing for clusters of varying density (Campello et al., 2013). Like DBSCAN (Ester et al., 1996), it automatically categorizes outliers in low-density regions as noise, an appealing property for a task in which many noisy, outlying input utterances are expected to be present, though only one of these teams participated in Task 2 (T13). Two teams (T13 and 35) performed dimensionality reduction on pre-trained embeddings using UMAP (McInnes et al., 2018) prior to clustering, following BERTopic (Grootendorst, 2022). Three other teams (T22, T27, and T31) also reported using some form of dimensionality reduction as part of their submissions.

Pre-trained Models Almost all submissions reported using specific pre-trained models, many of which were encoders tailored for computing utterance embeddings such as ALL-MPNET-BASE-V2 (Reimers and Gurevych, 2019), DSE-BERT-BASE, DSE-ROBERTA-LARGE (Zhou et al., 2022), and SUP-SIMCSE-ROBERTA (Gao et al., 2021). Teams T00, T15, T23 and T34 used DSE-pretrained encoders Zhou et al. (2022), which learn sentence representations tailored for dialogues using contrastive learning with consecutive utterances in dialogues. The majority of submissions also reported further fine-tuning encoders to tailor them to the task of intent induction (such as through SCCL, DEC, or supervised contrastive learning). T11 reported using two pre-trained NLI models to pre-compute a distance matrix between inputs for HDBSCAN-based clustering, further finetuning one of these models on the task development data.

Use of External Data Roughly half of submissions reported using external public data for training their models. These datasets included BANK77 (Casanueva et al., 2020), CLINC150 (Larson et al., 2019), ATIS (Hemphill et al., 1990), ACID (Acharya and Fung, 2020), HWU64 (Liu et al., 2019a), StackOverflow (Hamner et al., 2012; Xu et al., 2015), SGD (Rastogi et al., 2020) and MultiWOZ (Budzianowski et al., 2018) and SNIPS (Coucke et al., 2018). A number of teams reported using supervised pre-training (T06, T19, T23, T25, T30, T37) with labeled data, while others used semi-supervised approaches based on data augmentation to generate contrastive examples. In addition to team T23 reported using automatic English machine translations of Chinese domain-specific insurance and financial data for pre-training.

Cluster Selection Because the number of intents was not provided, submissions using parameteric clustering approaches had to devise approaches for cluster selection. Many submissions (12) explicitly reported using Silhouette scores. Two submissions (T05 and T34) used HDBSCAN (Campello et al., 2013) to determine the number of clusters prior to using SCCL. T15 reported using an iterative merging technique to determine the final number of clusters, perhaps similar to the strategy used in Chatterjee and Sengupta (2020). T00 reported using a combination of the Elbow method (Hardy, 1994) and Silhouette scores.

Use of Conversational Information Because complete conversations were provided as inputs to both tasks, participants had the option to make use of additional contextual signals for improving clustering. However, few teams reporting using conversational information beyond input turns (either given in Task 1, or predicted in Task 2) for clustering. Some teams, such as T21 and T29, reported using input dialogues for continued pre-training of their models. Team T28 identified the most relevant turn in the dialogue corresponding to each input turn using similarity scores from sentence embeddings, concatenating embeddings for the two turns as clustering inputs.

Task 2 Modifications The majority of teams that participated in Task 2 primarily used their Task 1 approaches, applying them to predicted *InformIntent* turns instead of the provided clustering turns. Although Task 2 provides *InformIntent* predictions as suggested relevant turns, several teams reported developing their own models or approaches for identifying turns in Task 2. Multiple teams (T02, T17, and T24) reported developing a custom classifier trained on public data to detect relevant turns or sentences containing intents. Team T34 used a rule-based system to identify sentences for clustering, and further augmented the input data prior to applying SCCL for clustering.

7 Results

In this section, we summarize the results for Task 1 and Task 2. To aggregate results across datasets, we use simple averages. As an alternative aggregate score, we compute the average mean reciprocal rank for ACC, F_1, and NMI, averaged over both datasets (MRR_{avg}). This approach is intended to be less sensitive to scores of the individual datasets

Team	Task 1		Task 2	
	ACC	MRR_{avg}	ACC	MRR_{avg}
T23	**69.8 (1)**	38.2 (4)	**76.3 (1)**	56.2 (2)
T07	69.6 (2)	41.0 (2)	-	-
T35	69.3 (3)	39.2 (3)	-	-
T05	69.1 (4)	**58.9 (1)**	74.5 (5)	31.7 (5)
T02	68.8 (5)	32.5 (5)	75.3 (2)	33.9 (4)
T17	67.1 (6)	12.8 (10)	73.8 (6)	**61.0 (1)**
T36	66.3 (7)	13.1 (8)	74.9 (3)	25.6 (6)
T24	66.2 (8)	19.9 (6)	74.7 (4)	36.1 (3)
T00	64.9 (9)	13.1 (9)	59.7 (17)	9.8 (12)
T34	63.7 (10)	10.7 (11)	59.3 (19)	5.9 (18)
T25	62.6 (11)	9.3 (12)	-	-
T10	62.5 (12)	6.0 (16)	-	-
T14	61.5 (13)	6.0 (17)	69.6 (7)	11.8 (8)
T30	61.1 (14)	6.7 (14)	60.9 (16)	7.0 (16)
T19	59.2 (15)	5.9 (18)	67.5 (10)	10.1 (11)
T37	58.7 (16)	5.8 (19)	-	-
T29	58.1 (17)	5.6 (21)	-	-
T26	58.0 (18)	4.8 (24)	63.6 (12)	7.4 (14)
T06	57.6 (19)	4.4 (27)	-	-
T01	57.4 (20)	7.5 (13)	-	-
T20	56.8 (21)	5.6 (20)	64.4 (11)	10.9 (9)
T28	56.6 (22)	6.5 (15)	-	-
T03	55.6 (23)	4.6 (26)	62.4 (15)	7.7 (13)
T13*	55.3 (24)	5.4 (22)	69.4 (8)	10.2 (10)
T33	54.8 (25)	14.7 (7)	-	-
T18	54.8 (26)	4.8 (23)	-	-
T21	53.8 (27)	3.9 (28)	-	-
T16	52.9 (28)	3.6 (29)	-	-
T04	50.1 (29)	4.8 (25)	63.6 (12)	7.4 (14)
T15	48.9 (30)	3.3 (32)	63.4 (14)	7.0 (17)
T27	48.9 (31)	3.5 (30)	68.7 (9)	12.6 (7)
T22	46.7 (32)	3.4 (31)	-	-
T11*	44.2 (33)	3.2 (33)	-	-
T31	35.1 (34)	3.0 (34)	59.5 (18)	5.7 (19)
Baseline	55.8 (23)	4.2 (28)	63.6 (12)	7.4 (14)

Table 3: Summary of results for both tasks. The ranking of the submission for each metric is given in parentheses. ACC (↑) is clustering accuracy and MRR_{avg} (↑) is the average mean reciprocal rank across datasets. *Did not assign labels to all inputs (see Table 4).

or biases of particular metrics. Table 3 summarizes the aggregate results and team rankings for Task 1 and Task 2. Detailed results for each dataset are provided in Section A.2

7.1 Task 1 Results

Team T23 was the overall winner for Task 1, with an honorable mention to Team T05 for having the highest MRR_{avg}.

- Team T23 had the highest overall ACC, the highest ACC on Finance, and the highest Precision (P) on Banking, and the fourth highest MRR_{avg}.
- Team T07 had the highest overall F_1 score, the 2nd highest overall ACC, and the highest F_1 on Finance.
- Team T05 had the top MRR_{avg}, the highest NMI and ARI and fourth highest overall ACC, with the highest ACC, F_1, NMI and ARI on Banking.

7.2 Task 2 Results

Team T23 was also the overall winner for Task 2, with an honorable mention for T17 for having the highest MRR_{avg}.

- Team T23 had the highest overall ACC, Recall and ARI, and the second highest MRR_{avg}, with the highest ACC, P, F1, NMI, and ARI on Banking.
- T02 had the second highest overall ACC, the second highest ACC on Banking and the 4th highest ACC on Finance.
- Team T17 had the top MRR_{avg}, the highest overall P, F1, and NMI, the highest ACC, P, F1, NMI and ARI on Finance, and the 6th highest overall ACC.

7.3 Analysis

Approaches for Top Teams SCCL (Zhang et al., 2021a), or more generally, deep embedded clustering (DEC) (Xie et al., 2016), were highly popular approaches among the top submissions for both tasks. In fact, only one of the top ten submissions, T35 (ranked third overall by both ACC and MRR_{avg}), instead used HDBSCAN for clustering. Silhouette scores were also a popular choice for cluster selection among the top-performing submissions, though T05 (top overall MRR_{avg} for Task 1) and T34 were notable exceptions that used HDBSCAN to identify the number of clusters prior to using SCCL.

Among the top-performing teams, several used DSE-ROBERTA-LARGE (Zhou et al., 2022), while many others used ALL-MPNET-BASE-V2 (Reimers and Gurevych, 2019) as the base encoder models. Many top systems also used a variety of public datasets to further adapt their models prior to clustering, either through supervised pre-training

Team	LP	ACC (Rank)	MRR_{avg} (Rank)
T11		44.2 (33)	3.2 (33)
	✓	65.8 (9)	16.9 (7)
T13		55.3 (24)	5.4 (22)
	✓	57.2 (22)	6.0 (16)

Table 4: Impact of label propagation (LP) for on submissions that used HDBSCAN, but left noise instances unassigned. For T11, the ranking changes from 33rd to 7th based on MRR_{avg}.

(multi-task with intent classification loss, or supervised contrastive learning (Gao et al., 2021)), self-supervised pre-training (e.g. via masked-language modeling (Devlin et al., 2019) or contrastive learning (Zhou et al., 2022)), or a combination of approaches. Among the top teams using DSE-ROBERTA-LARGE, compared to T00 and T34, team T23 (the overall top submission by ACC) reported further supervised and self-supervised pre-training on multiple public datasets.

Label Propagation for Noise Cluster (Task 1) We noticed that two submissions using HDBSCAN did not assign cluster labels to a number of instances in Task 1, instead leaving a large portion unassigned as automatically-detected noise (T11 and T13). Task 1 evaluation penalizes this, since clustering evaluation assumes a label should be assigned to every input. To validate this, we propagated non-noise cluster labels for these teams to the unlabeled instances by training the classifier described for Task 2 on labeled instances, and applying the resulting model to the remaining noise instances. As shown in Table 4, we observed improvements for both submissions, with a drastic improvement for team T11, with the ACC and MRR_{avg}-based rankings improving from 33rd to 9th and 7th respectively, indicating a potential shortcoming of clustering-based evaluation for comparing intent induction methods.

Sensitivity to Classifier (Task 2) Because Task 2 evaluation is dependent on the selection of a classifier, we also analyze the impact of the classifier on evaluation results. To understand this impact, we compute Task 2 evaluation results for 9 different encoders (including SimCSE, DSE, and SENTENCE-TRANSFORMERS variants, see Section A.5). Table 5 aggregates these results. When using the best-performing (highest ACC) classifier for each system, we observe the rankings for the top ten systems do not change (though ranks 11-15 fluctuate). Examining the average ACC across all classifiers, we observe that while the top system typically does not change, the standard deviation of the rankings for other systems falls between 0.3 and 1.8, indicating some degree of fluctuation. This indicates that prediction-based evaluation may introduce some noise into the process, and using high-quality classifiers or a variety of models may make evaluation results more robust.

Team	**ACC** Avg. (Rank)	**ACC** Max (Rank)	**Best Model**
T23	**74.9**$_{\pm 1.5}$ (**1.0**$_{\pm 0.0}$)	**76.6 (1)**	all-roberta-l
T02	73.7$_{\pm 1.7}$ (2.2$_{\pm 0.4}$)	75.9 (2)	multiqa-mpnet-b
T36	72.3$_{\pm 2.3}$ (4.0$_{\pm 0.9}$)	75.3 (3)	all-roberta-l
T24	72.2$_{\pm 1.8}$ (4.3$_{\pm 1.2}$)	74.7 (4)	all-mpnet-b
T05	70.9$_{\pm 2.5}$ (5.6$_{\pm 0.7}$)	74.5 (5)	all-mpnet-b
T17	72.6$_{\pm 1.4}$ (3.9$_{\pm 1.4}$)	73.9 (6)	dse-roberta-b
T14	68.7$_{\pm 1.7}$ (7.1$_{\pm 0.3}$)	71.7 (7)	all-roberta-l
T13	66.3$_{\pm 3.5}$ (9.2$_{\pm 1.8}$)	70.7 (8)	all-roberta-l
T27	66.6$_{\pm 2.7}$ (9.0$_{\pm 0.5}$)	70.5 (9)	all-roberta-l
T19	66.4$_{\pm 1.2}$ (9.0$_{\pm 1.0}$)	67.5 (10)	all-mpnet-b
T20	63.0$_{\pm 1.4}$ (12.6$_{\pm 1.3}$)	64.8 (13)	multiqa-mpnet-b
T15	58.0$_{\pm 4.4}$ (16.0$_{\pm 1.2}$)	63.4 (15)	all-mpnet-b
T03	62.6$_{\pm 0.6}$ (13.1$_{\pm 1.5}$)	63.4 (14)	all-minilml12
T30	60.1$_{\pm 1.0}$ (15.4$_{\pm 0.5}$)	61.4 (16)	all-roberta-l
T00	54.4$_{\pm 4.7}$ (18.0$_{\pm 0.7}$)	60.6 (17)	all-roberta-l
T31	53.9$_{\pm 5.1}$ (18.6$_{\pm 0.5}$)	60.2 (18)	all-roberta-l
T34	58.0$_{\pm 1.3}$ (16.9$_{\pm 1.3}$)	59.3 (19)	all-mpnet-b

Table 5: **Task 2** average and maximum ACC with corresponding rankings (in parentheses) computed for nine classifier models using different utterance encoders. Teams are ordered corresponding to their original rank based on ACC with ALL-MPNET-BASE-V2.

8 Conclusions

We presented task definitions, evaluation methods, datasets, and baselines for the DSTC 11 track on intent induction from conversations for task-oriented dialogue. The track saw a variety of submissions from 34 teams, with 19 teams submitting entries for both tasks. We summarized these track submissions and provided analysis of the trends and overall results.

The aim of the track is to provide a benchmark facilitating evaluation of methods for automatic induction of customer intents in the realistic setting of customer service interactions. We hope that the benchmark and datasets will encourage new lines of research related to the analysis of human-to-human conversations.

References

Shailesh Acharya and Glenn Fung. 2020. Using optimal embeddings to learn new intents with few examples: An application in the insurance domain. *KDD 2020 Workshop on Conversational Systems Towards Mainstream Adoption(KDD Converse 2020).*

Abhinav Arora, Akshat Shrivastava, Mrinal Mohit, Lorena Sainz-Maza Lecanda, and Ahmed Aly. 2020. Cross-lingual transfer learning for intent detection of covid-19 utterances.

Javier Artiles, Julio Gonzalo, and Satoshi Sekine. 2007. The SemEval-2007 WePS evaluation: Establishing a benchmark for the web people search task. In *Proceedings of the Fourth International Workshop on Semantic Evaluations (SemEval-2007)*, pages 64–69, Prague, Czech Republic. Association for Computational Linguistics.

James Bergstra, Daniel Yamins, and David Cox. 2013. Making a science of model search: Hyperparameter optimization in hundreds of dimensions for vision architectures. In *International conference on machine learning*, pages 115–123. PMLR.

Paweł Budzianowski, Tsung-Hsien Wen, Bo-Hsiang Tseng, Iñigo Casanueva, Stefan Ultes, Osman Ramadan, and Milica Gašić. 2018. MultiWOZ - a large-scale multi-domain Wizard-of-Oz dataset for task-oriented dialogue modelling. In *Proceedings of the 2018 Conference on Empirical Methods in Natural Language Processing*, pages 5016–5026, Brussels, Belgium. Association for Computational Linguistics.

Ricardo JGB Campello, Davoud Moulavi, and Jörg Sander. 2013. Density-based clustering based on hierarchical density estimates. In *Pacific-Asia conference on knowledge discovery and data mining*, pages 160–172. Springer.

Iñigo Casanueva, Tadas Temčinas, Daniela Gerz, Matthew Henderson, and Ivan Vulić. 2020. Efficient intent detection with dual sentence encoders. In *Proceedings of the 2nd Workshop on Natural Language Processing for Conversational AI*, pages 38–45, Online. Association for Computational Linguistics.

Inigo Casanueva, Ivan Vulić, Georgios Spithourakis, and Paweł Budzianowski. 2022. NLU++: A multi-label, slot-rich, generalisable dataset for natural language understanding in task-oriented dialogue. In *Findings of the Association for Computational Linguistics: NAACL 2022*, pages 1998–2013, Seattle, United States. Association for Computational Linguistics.

Ajay Chatterjee and Shubhashis Sengupta. 2020. Intent mining from past conversations for conversational agent. In *Proceedings of the 28th International Conference on Computational Linguistics*, pages 4140–4152, Barcelona, Spain (Online). International Committee on Computational Linguistics.

Derek Chen, Howard Chen, Yi Yang, Alexander Lin, and Zhou Yu. 2021. Action-based conversations dataset: A corpus for building more in-depth task-oriented dialogue systems. In *Proceedings of the 2021 Conference of the North American Chapter of the Association for Computational Linguistics: Human Language Technologies*, pages 3002–3017, Online. Association for Computational Linguistics.

Alice Coucke, Alaa Saade, Adrien Ball, Théodore Bluche, Alexandre Caulier, David Leroy, Clément Doumouro, Thibault Gisselbrecht, Francesco Caltagirone, Thibaut Lavril, et al. 2018. Snips voice platform: an embedded spoken language understanding system for private-by-design voice interfaces. *arXiv preprint arXiv:1805.10190.*

Jacob Devlin, Ming-Wei Chang, Kenton Lee, and Kristina Toutanova. 2019. BERT: Pre-training of deep bidirectional transformers for language understanding. In *Proceedings of the 2019 Conference of the North American Chapter of the Association for Computational Linguistics: Human Language Technologies, Volume 1 (Long and Short Papers)*, pages 4171–4186, Minneapolis, Minnesota. Association for Computational Linguistics.

Martin Ester, Hans-Peter Kriegel, Jörg Sander, Xiaowei Xu, et al. 1996. A density-based algorithm for discovering clusters in large spatial databases with noise. *kdd*, 96(34):226–231.

Tianyu Gao, Xingcheng Yao, and Danqi Chen. 2021. SimCSE: Simple contrastive learning of sentence embeddings. In *Proceedings of the 2021 Conference on Empirical Methods in Natural Language Processing*, pages 6894–6910, Online and Punta Cana, Dominican Republic. Association for Computational Linguistics.

Maarten Grootendorst. 2022. Bertopic: Neural topic modeling with a class-based tf-idf procedure. *arXiv preprint arXiv:2203.05794.*

Dilek Hakkani-Tür, Yun-Cheng Ju, Geoffrey Zweig, and Gokhan Tur. 2015. Clustering novel intents in a conversational interaction system with semantic parsing. In *Sixteenth Annual Conference of the International Speech Communication Association.*

Ben Hamner, David Fullerton, Kevin Montrose, Rebecca Chernoff, and Will Cole. 2012. Predict closed questions on stack overflow.

Iryna Haponchyk, Antonio Uva, Seunghak Yu, Olga Uryupina, and Alessandro Moschitti. 2018. Supervised clustering of questions into intents for dialog system applications. In *Proceedings of the 2018 Conference on Empirical Methods in Natural Language Processing*, pages 2310–2321, Brussels, Belgium. Association for Computational Linguistics.

André Hardy. 1994. An examination of procedures for determining the number of clusters in a data set. In *New approaches in classification and data analysis*, pages 178–185. Springer.

Charles T. Hemphill, John J. Godfrey, and George R. Doddington. 1990. The ATIS spoken language systems pilot corpus. In *Speech and Natural Language: Proceedings of a Workshop Held at Hidden Valley, Pennsylvania, June 24-27,1990.*

Peihao Huang, Yan Huang, Wei Wang, and Liang Wang. 2014. Deep embedding network for clustering. In *2014 22nd International Conference on Pattern Recognition*, pages 1532–1537.

Leonard Kaufman and Peter J Rousseeuw. 2009. *Finding groups in data: an introduction to cluster analysis.* John Wiley & Sons.

Harold W Kuhn. 1955. The hungarian method for the assignment problem. *Naval research logistics quarterly*, 2(1-2):83–97.

Rajat Kumar, Mayur Patidar, Vaibhav Varshney, Lovekesh Vig, and Gautam Shroff. 2022. Intent detection and discovery from user logs via deep semi-supervised contrastive clustering. In *Proceedings of the 2022 Conference of the North American Chapter of the Association for Computational Linguistics: Human Language Technologies*, pages 1836–1853, Seattle, United States. Association for Computational Linguistics.

Stefan Larson, Anish Mahendran, Joseph J. Peper, Christopher Clarke, Andrew Lee, Parker Hill, Jonathan K. Kummerfeld, Kevin Leach, Michael A. Laurenzano, Lingjia Tang, and Jason Mars. 2019. An evaluation dataset for intent classification and out-of-scope prediction. In *Proceedings of the 2019 Conference on Empirical Methods in Natural Language Processing and the 9th International Joint Conference on Natural Language Processing (EMNLP-IJCNLP)*, pages 1311–1316, Hong Kong, China. Association for Computational Linguistics.

Mike Lewis, Yinhan Liu, Naman Goyal, Marjan Ghazvininejad, Abdelrahman Mohamed, Omer Levy, Veselin Stoyanov, and Luke Zettlemoyer. 2020. BART: Denoising sequence-to-sequence pre-training for natural language generation, translation, and comprehension. In *Proceedings of the 58th Annual Meeting of the Association for Computational Linguistics*, pages 7871–7880, Online. Association for Computational Linguistics.

Ting-En Lin, Hua Xu, and Hanlei Zhang. 2020. Discovering new intents via constrained deep adaptive clustering with cluster refinement. *Proceedings of the AAAI Conference on Artificial Intelligence*, 34(05):8360–8367.

Pengfei Liu, Youzhang Ning, King Keung Wu, Kun Li, and Helen Meng. 2021. Open intent discovery through unsupervised semantic clustering and dependency parsing. *arXiv preprint arXiv:2104.12114*.

Xingkun Liu, Arash Eshghi, Pawel Swietojanski, and Verena Rieser. 2019a. Benchmarking natural language understanding services for building conversational agents. *arXiv preprint arXiv:1903.05566*.

Yinhan Liu, Myle Ott, Naman Goyal, Jingfei Du, Mandar Joshi, Danqi Chen, Omer Levy, Mike Lewis, Luke Zettlemoyer, and Veselin Stoyanov. 2019b. Roberta: A robustly optimized bert pretraining approach. *arXiv preprint arXiv:1907.11692*.

James MacQueen et al. 1967. Some methods for classification and analysis of multivariate observations. In *Proceedings of the fifth Berkeley symposium on mathematical statistics and probability*, 14, pages 281–297. Oakland, CA, USA.

Leland McInnes, John Healy, and James Melville. 2018. Umap: Uniform manifold approximation and projection for dimension reduction.

Hugh Perkins and Yi Yang. 2019. Dialog intent induction with deep multi-view clustering. In *Proceedings of the 2019 Conference on Empirical Methods in Natural Language Processing and the 9th International Joint Conference on Natural Language Processing (EMNLP-IJCNLP)*, pages 4016–4025, Hong Kong, China. Association for Computational Linguistics.

Denis Peskov, Nancy Clarke, Jason Krone, Brigi Fodor, Yi Zhang, Adel Youssef, and Mona Diab. 2019a. Multi-domain goal-oriented dialogues (MultiDoGO): Strategies toward curating and annotating large scale dialogue data. In *Proceedings of the 2019 Conference on Empirical Methods in Natural Language Processing and the 9th International Joint Conference on Natural Language Processing (EMNLP-IJCNLP)*, pages 4526–4536, Hong Kong, China. Association for Computational Linguistics.

Denis Peskov, Nancy Clarke, Jason Krone, Brigitta Fodor, Yi Zhang, Adel Youssef, and Mona T. Diab. 2019b. Multi-domain goal-oriented dialogues (multidogo): Strategies toward curating and annotating large scale dialogue data. In *Conference on Empirical Methods in Natural Language Processing*.

William M Rand. 1971. Objective criteria for the evaluation of clustering methods. *Journal of the American Statistical association*, 66(336):846–850.

Abhinav Rastogi, Xiaoxue Zang, Srinivas Sunkara, Raghav Gupta, and Pranav Khaitan. 2020. Towards scalable multi-domain conversational agents: The schema-guided dialogue dataset. *Proceedings of the AAAI Conference on Artificial Intelligence*, 34(05):8689–8696.

Nils Reimers and Iryna Gurevych. 2019. Sentence-BERT: Sentence embeddings using Siamese BERT-networks. In *Proceedings of the 2019 Conference on Empirical Methods in Natural Language Processing and the 9th International Joint Conference on Natural Language Processing (EMNLP-IJCNLP)*, pages 3982–3992, Hong Kong, China. Association for Computational Linguistics.

Peter J. Rousseeuw. 1987. Silhouettes: A graphical aid to the interpretation and validation of cluster analysis. *Journal of Computational and Applied Mathematics*, 20:53–65.

Sebastian Ruder. 2021. Challenges and Opportunities in NLP Benchmarking. http://ruder.io/nlp-benchmarking.

Xiang Shen, Yinge Sun, Yao Zhang, and Mani Najmabadi. 2021. Semi-supervised intent discovery with contrastive learning. In *Proceedings of the 3rd Workshop on Natural Language Processing for Conversational AI*, pages 120–129, Online. Association for Computational Linguistics.

Kaitao Song, Xu Tan, Tao Qin, Jianfeng Lu, and Tie-Yan Liu. 2020. Mpnet: Masked and permuted pre-training for language understanding. *Advances in Neural Information Processing Systems*, 33:16857–16867.

Nikhita Vedula, Nedim Lipka, Pranav Maneriker, and Srinivasan Parthasarathy. 2020. Open intent extraction from natural language interactions. In *Proceedings of The Web Conference 2020*, pages 2009–2020.

Alex Wang, Amanpreet Singh, Julian Michael, Felix Hill, Omer Levy, and Samuel R. Bowman. 2019. GLUE: A multi-task benchmark and analysis platform for natural language understanding. In *ICLR*.

Junyuan Xie, Ross Girshick, and Ali Farhadi. 2016. Unsupervised deep embedding for clustering analysis. In *Proceedings of The 33rd International Conference on Machine Learning*, volume 48 of *Proceedings of Machine Learning Research*, pages 478–487, New York, New York, USA. PMLR.

Jiaming Xu, Peng Wang, Guanhua Tian, Bo Xu, Jun Zhao, Fangyuan Wang, and Hongwei Hao. 2015. Short text clustering via convolutional neural networks. In *Proceedings of the 1st Workshop on Vector Space Modeling for Natural Language Processing*, pages 62–69, Denver, Colorado. Association for Computational Linguistics.

Zengfeng Zeng, Dan Ma, Haiqin Yang, Zhen Gou, and Jianping Shen. 2021. Automatic intent-slot induction for dialogue systems. In *Proceedings of the Web Conference 2021*, pages 2578–2589.

Dejiao Zhang, Feng Nan, Xiaokai Wei, Shang-Wen Li, Henghui Zhu, Kathleen McKeown, Ramesh Nallapati, Andrew O. Arnold, and Bing Xiang. 2021a. Supporting clustering with contrastive learning. In *Proceedings of the 2021 Conference of the North American Chapter of the Association for Computational Linguistics: Human Language Technologies*, pages 5419–5430, Online. Association for Computational Linguistics.

Hanlei Zhang, Hua Xu, and Ting-En Lin. 2021b. Deep open intent classification with adaptive decision boundary. In *AAAI*, pages 14374–14382.

Hanlei Zhang, Hua Xu, Ting-En Lin, and Rui Lyu. 2021c. Discovering new intents with deep aligned clustering. *Proceedings of the AAAI Conference on Artificial Intelligence*, 35(16):14365–14373.

Haode Zhang, Yuwei Zhang, Li-Ming Zhan, Jiaxin Chen, Guangyuan Shi, Xiao-Ming Wu, and Albert Y.S. Lam. 2021d. Effectiveness of pre-training for few-shot intent classification. In *Findings of the Association for Computational Linguistics: EMNLP 2021*, pages 1114–1120, Punta Cana, Dominican Republic. Association for Computational Linguistics.

Zhihan Zhou, Dejiao Zhang, Wei Xiao, Nicholas Dingwall, Xiaofei Ma, Andrew Arnold, and Bing Xiang. 2022. Learning dialogue representations from consecutive utterances. In *Proceedings of the 2022 Conference of the North American Chapter of the Association for Computational Linguistics: Human Language Technologies*, pages 754–768, Seattle, United States. Association for Computational Linguistics.

A Appendix

A.1 Intent Counts

To provide a benchmark that reflects a realistic setting of customer support conversations, we collected conversations from three domains (Insurance, Banking, and Finance), introduced in Section 4. The Insurance domain was used solely as development data for the challenge, while Banking and Finance were used for evaluating systems. In this section, we report further details on the characteristics of these datasets.

Tables 6, 7, and 8 show the counts of each intent appearing in conversations and Task 2 test data from Insurance, Banking, and Finance respectively. Intents with fewer than 4 corresponding annotated utterances were excluded from each dataset. Comparing intents in Banking and Finance domains, while there is overlap between the domains, it is clear that Banking focuses more on personal banking requests (such as checking account balances, transferring funds, or disputing charges. In contrast, Finance focuses more on loans and investing.

As is evident from these counts, the distribution of intents is highly skewed, while the test set counts are more evenly distributed. The decoupling of conversation annotations from test utterances provides a practical benefit for the external prediction-based evaluation of Task 2. Collecting examples from a fixed set of intents as test data is easier than annotating input conversations directly. In natural datasets, intents typically do not have balanced distributions. Identifying long tail intents may be just as important (or more so) than identifying common intents. Finally, annotating many conversations may still result in only a few examples of low-frequency intents, whereas collecting them directly ensures they are properly represented in the test data.

Intent	Count	Test Count
GetQuote	150	181
EnrollInPlan	132	32
ResetPassword	82	29
ChangeAddress	81	31
CancelPlan	74	29
ChangePlan	64	29
PayBill	63	34
ReportBillingIssue	51	32
FileClaim	51	124
AddDependent	51	33
CreateAccount	48	30
RequestProofOfInsurance	42	31
CancelAutomaticBilling	40	31
UpdatePaymentPreference	38	31
CheckAccountBalance	34	29
RemoveDependent	28	31
UpdateBillingFrequency	24	29
CheckPaymentStatus	24	31
ChangeSecurityQuestion	24	29
GetPolicyNumber	19	30
FindAgent	18	29
ReportAutomobileAccident	15	28

Table 6: Insurance domain counts for 22 intents in conversations and Task 2 test data.

Intent	Count	Test Count
CheckAccountBalance	251	30
InternalFundsTransfer	139	26
ExternalWireTransfer	124	26
FindBranch	120	21
DisputeCharge	108	32
OpenBankingAccount	92	21
FindATM	92	26
ReportLostStolenCard	77	21
GetBranchHours	73	21
CloseBankAccount	65	32
UpdateStreetAddress	60	20
UpdateEmail	35	20
CheckTransactionHistory	25	20
AskAboutTransferTime	24	21
UpdatePhoneNumber	23	20
SetUpOnlineBanking	23	20
ReportNotice	23	0
GetBranchInfo	22	0
GetWithdrawalLimit	21	20
RequestNewCard	15	0
AskAboutCashDeposits	15	10
GetAccountInfo	14	0
CheckAccountInterestRate	11	0
AskAboutTransferFees	11	0
OrderChecks	10	0
AskAboutCardArrival	10	0
OpenCreditCard	8	0
AskAboutATMFees	8	0
AskAboutCreditScore	4	0

Table 7: Banking domain counts for 29 intents in conversations and Task 2 test data.

A.2 Semantic Diversity

To be useful as an intent induction benchmark, utterances for intents should have a high degree of variation rather than rigidly follow the same structure in every conversation. To measure this, we investigate the semantic diversity of intent turns following Casanueva et al. (2022). To compute semantic diversity for a single intent, we (1) compute intent centroids as the average of embeddings for the turns labeled with the intent using the Sentence-BERT (Reimers and Gurevych, 2019) library with the pre-trained model ALL-MPNET-BASE-V2, then (2) find the average cosine distance between each individual turn and the resulting centroid. Finally, (3) overall semantic diversity scores are computed as a frequency-weighted average over intent-level scores.

The semantic diversity scores for each domain as compared to CLINC150 (Larson et al., 2019) and BANK77 (Casanueva et al., 2020), along with high level statistics are provided in Table 9. We observe that the semantic diversity for Insurance, Banking and Finance is higher than that of CLINC150 and Bank77, indicating greater potential modeling challenges. We also compare the semantic of diversity of NATCS with other datasets for specific aligned intents across datasets in Table 10.

A.3 Submission Overview

Table 11 provides a detailed overview of the track submissions. Note that because there was no open source requirement for this challenge, all details are self-reported through a survey given to participants. Thus some information may be missing or inaccurate (such as due to misinterpretations of descriptions).

A.4 Detailed Results

Table 13 provides a dataset-level detailed summary of results for Task 1 including the number of induced intents for each system. Table 14 provides a dataset-level detailed summary of results for Task 2 including the number of induced intents and average number of sample utterances for each induced intent.

A.5 Sentence Encoders used for Classifiers

In this section, we enumerate the classifiers used in Section 7 to examine sensitivity of Task 2 classifier sensitivity. We used the following 9 sentence embeddings as static (not fine-tuned) features to logistic regression classifiers:

- sentence-transformers (Reimers and Gurevych, 2019)
  - all-mpnet-base-v2
  - multi-qa-mpnet-base-cos-v1
  - all-roberta-large-v1
  - all-MiniLM-L12-v2
- DSE (Zhou et al., 2022)
  - aws-ai/dse-roberta-large
  - aws-ai/dse-roberta-base
  - aws-ai/dse-bert-base
- SimCSE (Gao et al., 2021)
  - princeton-nlp/sup-simcse-roberta-large
  - princeton-nlp/sup-simcse-roberta-base

Intent	Count	Test Count
ApplyLoan	222	106
CheckAccountBalance	183	30
GetLoanInfo	111	20
MakeTransfer	77	42
OnlineBankingInfo	73	20
GetCreditCardInfo	55	20
ScheduleAppointment	46	86
UpdatePhoneNumber	43	21
OpenAccount	43	37
GetExchangeRate	43	23
UpdateStreetAddress	41	20
ChangeStatementDelivery	41	25
CheckLoanBalance	40	22
UpdateEmail	39	26
ApplyCreditCard	39	75
ChangePin	36	20
RequestEmail	35	10
SetAutoPayment	33	62
MakeCreditCardPayment	33	28
CancelCheck	32	22
GetDebtIncomeRatio	31	22
AddUserToAccount	31	23
AskConsumerPriceIndex	29	36
CloseAccount	28	23
GetBranchHours	25	20
NetIncome	24	20
OrderCheck	23	25
AskLiquidityRatio	21	22
FindBranch	19	10
RequestNewCard	17	10
GetBankStatement	17	48
PayLoan	16	22
GetTransactions	12	0
GetPaymentDueDate	8	0
GetStockQuote	7	20
GetInvestmentReport	7	24
GetTreasuryBondYield	6	23
GetCreditReport	6	25
PurchaseStocks	5	22

Table 8: Finance domain counts for 39 intents in conversations and Task 2 test data.

Dataset	Utts./Intent	Words/Utt.	Intents/Domain	Avg. Diversity
CLINC150 (Larson et al., 2019)	157.0	8.5	15	27.4
BANK77 (Casanueva et al., 2020)	169.9	13.4	77	23.2
Insurance	52.4	20.1	22	33.3
Banking	51.8	26.9	29	30.1
Finance	40.9	31.3	39	32.4

Table 9: Comparison of intent utterances between track datasets and public intent classification datasets. Avg. Diversity corresponds to semantic diversity described in Section A.2.

Intent	DSTC11	MultiDoGO	CLINC150	BANK77	SGD
CheckBalance	**31.9**	17.9	27.8		23.1
MakeTransfer	**34.3**	24.2	29.5		25.9
ReportLostStolenCard	**29.0**	18.6	16.2	18.4	
DisputeCharge	**35.3**	23.7	26.1		
OrderChecks	**31.8**	21.5	19.0		
CloseBankAccount	**26.4**	17.6		20.1	
UpdateStreetAddress	**31.4**	17.5		28.6	
ChangePin	**27.4**		20.3	19.7	

Table 10: Comparing semantic diversity for aligned intents across MultiDoGO (Peskov et al., 2019a), CLINC150 (Larson et al., 2019), BANK77 (Casanueva et al., 2020), and SGD (Rastogi et al., 2020).

Team	Clustering	Techniques			Selection	Base Model(s)	Datasets	Rankings	
		SupPT	SSPT	Ens.				Task 1	Task 2
T23	DEC	✓	✓		sil.	dse-roberta-l	BK CC DI SO	01 / 04	01 / 02
T07	SCCL		✓		sil.	•	OD	02 / 02	•
T35	hdbscan				sil.	SBERT	•	03 / 03	•
T05	SCCL				hdb4k	all-mpnet-b	AD AS BK SO	04 / 01	05 / 05
T02	SCCL	✓	✓		•	all-mpnet-b	AS BK SO	05 / 05	02 / 04
T17	SCCL				•	all-mpnet-b	AD BK	06 / 10	06 / 01
T36	SCCL			✓	•	all-mpnet-b	AD BK CC	07 / 08	03 / 06
T24	SCCL				•	all-mpnet-b	AD BK CC	08 / 06	04 / 03
T00	SCCL				elbow sil.	dse-roberta-l	N/A	09 / 09	17 / 12
T34	DEC SCCL				hdb4k	dse-roberta-l	•	10 / 11	19 / 18
T25	k-means	✓			sil.	all-mpnet-b	BK CC SGD	11 / 12	•
T10	centroid				•	•	•	12 / 16	•
T14	centroid				sil.	roberta-b	OD N/A	13 / 17	07 / 08
T30	SCCL	✓			sil.	all-mpnet-b	BK CC HU	14 / 14	16 / 16
T19	DEC k-means	✓			sil.	all-mpnet-b	AS BK CC OD HU MD SS	15 / 18	10 / 11
T37	k-means	✓			sil.	SBERT	MW	16 / 19	•
T29	centroid	✓	✓		sil.	•	•	17 / 21	•
T26	centroid				sil.	•	N/A	18 / 24	12 / 14
T06	DSSCC k-means	✓	✓		sil.	•	BK CC DI	19 / 27	•
T01	k-means	✓	✓		•	•	•	20 / 13	•
T20	•				•	sentence-t5-l	N/A	21 / 20	11 / 09
T28	k-means				•	SBERT	•	22 / 15	•
T03	centroid				sil.	sup-simcse-roberta roberta-b	BK	23 / 26	15 / 13
Base	•				•	•	•	23 / 28	12 / 14
T13	hdbscan				•	all-minilm-l6	N/A	24 / 22	08 / 10
T33	k-means	✓	✓		•	•	•	25 / 07	•
T18	k-means	✓	✓		•	•	•	26 / 23	•
T21	centroid	✓	✓		•	all-mpnet-b	CC DI	27 / 28	•
T16	SCCL				•	•	•	28 / 29	•
T04	centroid			✓	•	multi-minilm all-mpnet-b	•	29 / 25	12 / 14
T15	centroid	✓			merge	dse-bert-b bart-b	BK CC MW	30 / 32	14 / 17
T27	DP-means hdbscan			✓	•	all-mpnet-b pp-multilingual-mpnet-b	N/A	31 / 30	09 / 07
T22	hdbscan k-means				•	•	•	32 / 31	•
T11	hdbscan	✓			•	•	•	33 / 33	•
T31	DEC UVWB				sil.	•	N/A	34 / 34	18 / 19

Table 11: Summary of submissions with corresponding rankings for Task 1 and Task 2 (ACC rank / MRR_{avg} rank). System descriptions are self-reported, as there was no open-source requirement for this challenge. See Table 12 for abbreviation definitions.

Abbreviation	Definition
N/A	No Extra Data
AD	ACID (Acharya and Fung, 2020)
AS	ATIS (Hemphill et al., 1990)
BK	BANK77 (Casanueva et al., 2020)
CC	CLINC150 (Larson et al., 2019)
DI	Development Data (Insurance)
HU	HWU64 (Liu et al., 2019a)
MD	MCID (Arora et al., 2020)
MW	MultiWOZ (Budzianowski et al., 2018)
SG	SGD (Rastogi et al., 2020)
SS	SNIPS (Coucke et al., 2018)
SO	StackOverflow (Hamner et al., 2012; Xu et al., 2015)
multi-minilm	TingChenChang/hpvqa-lcqmc-ocnli-cnsd-multi-MiniLM-v2
dse-bert-b	aws-ai/dse-bert-base (Zhou et al., 2022)
dse-roberta-l	aws-ai/dse-roberta-large (Zhou et al., 2022)
bart-b	facebook/bart-base (Lewis et al., 2020)
sup-simcse-roberta	princeton-nlp/sup-simcse-roberta (Gao et al., 2021)
roberta-b	roberta-base (Liu et al., 2019b)
all-minilm-l6	sentence-transformers/all-MiniLM-L6-v2 (Reimers and Gurevych, 2019)
all-mpnet-b	sentence-transformers/all-mpnet-base-v2 (Reimers and Gurevych, 2019)
pp-multilingual-mpnet-b	sentence-transformers/paraphrase-multilingual-mpnet-base-v2 (Reimers and Gurevych, 2019)
sentence-t5-l	sentence-transformers/sentence-t5-large (Reimers and Gurevych, 2019)
centroid	Centroid-based Clustering
hdbscan	HDBSCAN (Campello et al., 2013)
k-means	K-Means (MacQueen et al., 1967)
sil.	Silhouette Scores (Rousseeuw, 1987; Kaufman and Rousseeuw, 2009)
DEC	Deep Embedded Clustering (Xie et al., 2016)
SCCL	Supporting Clustering with Contrastive Learning (Zhang et al., 2021a)
DSSCC	Deep Semi-Supervised Contrastive Clustering (Kumar et al., 2022)
elbow	Elbow method (Hardy, 1994)
hdb4k	HDBSCAN for identifying K
merge	Iterative Merging

Table 12: Abbreviations for datasets, models, and techniques used by submissions.

Team	Banking							Finance							Avg.		
	ACC	P	R	F1	NMI	ARI	K	ACC	P	R	F1	NMI	ARI	K	ACC	F1	NMI
T23	71.5	**81.2**	75.7	78.4	77.3	62.9	29	**68.1**	70.9	76.5	73.6	72.8	55.5	32	**69.8**	76.0	75.1
T07	72.1	72.2	84.6	77.9	72.5	64.5	14	67.1	71.8	78.7	**75.1**	74.5	**55.8**	41	69.6	**76.5**	73.5
T35	73.3	79.2	76.4	77.8	73.5	63.8	53	65.4	**77.6**	70.3	73.8	**75.1**	53.5	75	69.3	75.8	74.3
T05	**75.2**	78.8	82.5	**80.6**	**78.5**	**70.7**	26	62.9	67.8	74.1	70.8	72.6	52.1	27	69.1	75.7	**75.5**
T02	75.0	78.6	82.2	80.4	78.0	70.2	26	62.6	67.5	73.9	70.6	72.3	51.6	27	68.8	75.5	75.1
T17	72.0	77.0	78.3	77.7	75.7	70.1	25	62.3	63.9	78.6	70.5	70.7	51.6	25	67.1	74.1	73.2
T36	72.5	76.6	77.9	77.3	76.1	66.7	28	60.2	67.1	71.0	69.0	71.2	49.4	28	66.3	73.1	73.6
T24	69.4	73.6	81.6	77.4	76.6	64.6	28	63.0	68.8	73.1	70.8	72.9	51.7	28	66.2	74.1	74.7
T00	66.7	74.8	75.5	75.1	71.9	51.2	17	63.2	68.1	74.1	70.9	70.3	49.5	25	64.9	73.0	71.1
T34	67.5	78.7	73.7	76.1	76.1	57.4	22	60.0	63.3	76.0	69.1	69.9	48.2	22	63.7	72.6	73.0
T25	68.2	68.2	89.7	77.5	74.1	66.3	11	56.9	57.1	83.5	67.8	70.3	54.4	18	62.6	72.7	72.2
T10	68.4	70.5	75.7	73.0	69.6	61.1	20	56.7	66.4	62.3	64.3	67.4	42.9	35	62.5	68.6	68.5
T14	67.0	69.1	77.6	73.1	72.1	66.7	21	56.0	59.7	68.0	63.6	62.6	45.0	25	61.5	68.4	67.4
T30	69.6	69.6	82.4	75.5	67.1	59.3	12	52.6	56.3	76.1	64.7	65.1	45.3	19	61.1	70.1	66.1
T19	68.7	68.7	82.3	74.9	70.6	60.6	12	49.7	49.7	81.3	61.7	64.3	46.7	14	59.2	68.3	67.4
T37	65.1	73.9	69.4	71.6	69.6	54.9	20	52.3	75.1	54.2	63.0	71.0	34.7	49	58.7	67.3	70.3
T29	60.9	74.5	67.5	70.9	71.6	52.0	23	55.4	66.8	64.4	65.6	67.5	41.3	29	58.1	68.2	69.6
T26	65.1	73.8	73.3	73.6	69.7	52.0	17	50.8	54.4	67.1	60.1	60.3	43.7	45	58.0	66.8	65.0
T06	64.4	66.4	79.1	72.2	68.7	58.3	32	50.8	54.4	67.1	60.1	60.3	43.7	45	57.6	66.1	64.5
T01	57.7	74.4	59.3	66.0	70.0	50.3	30	57.1	72.4	65.2	68.7	72.1	43.1	36	57.4	67.3	71.0
T20	62.8	62.8	**90.1**	74.0	72.0	61.6	10	50.8	72.4	52.8	61.1	68.8	33.7	50	56.8	67.6	70.4
T28	55.9	55.9	72.6	63.2	59.8	37.0	12	57.2	73.9	60.3	66.4	71.6	39.1	44	56.6	64.8	65.7
T03	57.4	57.4	88.4	69.6	67.5	55.8	9	53.9	53.9	78.3	63.8	64.1	50.3	17	55.6	66.7	65.8
T13	53.8	72.5	58.0	64.5	64.0	35.0	30	56.8	71.5	63.7	67.4	68.9	37.2	46	55.3	65.9	66.4
T33	74.5	78.5	79.7	79.1	75.2	68.2	80	35.1	38.6	84.9	53.0	47.9	15.0	88	54.8	66.1	61.6
T18	58.5	58.5	89.0	70.6	69.2	56.3	9	51.0	56.4	73.3	63.7	67.7	42.4	19	54.8	67.1	68.4
T21	59.9	62.3	70.0	65.9	60.5	46.8	14	47.7	64.9	49.9	56.4	63.4	29.2	46	53.8	61.2	62.0
T16	57.2	57.2	77.0	65.6	56.1	45.4	9	48.7	61.9	57.8	59.8	60.7	32.7	29	52.9	62.7	58.4
T04	65.7	72.9	76.4	74.6	71.9	57.4	16	34.6	35.8	**90.9**	51.4	49.1	11.6	45	50.1	63.0	60.5
T15	51.1	62.7	58.8	60.7	60.3	48.1	36	46.8	54.6	56.2	55.4	59.0	38.3	39	48.9	58.0	59.7
T27	51.0	58.4	67.5	62.6	59.8	37.9	18	46.8	50.8	73.3	60.1	61.9	37.3	19	48.9	61.3	60.8
T22	52.0	65.5	59.3	62.3	59.4	37.4	27	41.5	60.1	53.2	56.4	62.0	27.3	46	46.7	59.3	60.7
T11	42.2	50.6	58.9	54.4	49.8	7.9	37	46.1	54.3	62.2	58.0	57.1	11.9	47	44.2	56.2	53.4
T31	34.3	34.3	63.2	44.4	31.6	20.1	6	35.9	54.8	38.1	45.0	52.3	20.5	46	35.1	44.7	42.0
Base	59.7	60.7	72.0	65.9	60.3	46.1	12	51.8	69.3	54.0	60.7	65.7	33.6	46	55.8	63.3	63.0

Table 13: Per-dataset results across all metrics for **Task 1**. *Base* indicates the baseline system described in Section 5. K indicates the number of induced intents. The number of reference intents for Banking and Finance are 29 and 39 respectively. Bold denotes the best results for each dataset.

Team	Banking								Finance								Avg.		
	ACC	P	R	F1	NMI	ARI	K	U/I	ACC	P	R	F1	NMI	ARI	K	U/I	ACC	F1	NMI
T23	**88.7**	**92.1**	93.6	**92.9**	**94.2**	**84.8**	26	141.7	63.9	65.2	86.1	74.2	80.7	58.9	39	170.1	**76.3**	83.5	87.4
T02	79.4	82.6	90.2	86.2	89.1	72.3	35	47.8	71.3	73.8	86.2	79.5	85.5	65.5	36	56.7	75.3	82.9	87.3
T36	78.4	84.5	87.2	85.9	89.0	72.0	42	107.7	71.3	73.1	**88.0**	79.8	85.0	70.7	42	161.2	74.9	82.8	87.0
T24	77.9	85.0	87.7	86.3	89.4	72.6	42	103.6	71.5	74.5	87.5	80.5	85.5	68.8	42	155.5	74.7	83.4	87.5
T05	77.9	86.0	87.7	86.8	90.4	73.5	39	93.1	71.2	73.0	87.3	79.5	85.3	67.0	40	140.3	74.5	83.2	87.9
T17	75.2	87.5	84.5	86.0	89.5	71.6	40	91.5	**72.4**	**79.0**	85.2	**82.0**	**86.8**	**71.3**	43	130.8	73.8	**84.0**	**88.1**
T09	73.0	85.5	84.8	85.1	89.8	71.0	36	46.6	70.1	73.1	86.5	79.2	83.9	64.9	37	54.9	71.5	82.2	86.8
T14	75.9	77.6	89.9	83.3	87.0	70.4	30	122.8	63.2	63.7	86.0	73.2	80.3	59.8	34	195.1	69.6	78.3	83.7
T13	73.5	89.9	75.9	82.3	85.0	69.7	51	72.2	65.4	75.4	73.0	74.2	79.5	54.6	51	130.1	69.4	78.3	82.3
T27	71.7	87.2	78.4	82.6	86.1	67.4	51	72.5	65.7	73.4	76.6	75.0	81.3	60.2	51	130.9	68.7	78.8	83.7
T08	79.4	80.6	87.0	83.7	87.7	73.5	25	147.4	57.5	58.9	87.3	70.4	78.4	56.0	28	237.0	68.4	77.0	83.1
T19	74.2	74.2	91.9	82.1	87.0	69.2	19	193.9	60.8	64.0	87.0	73.7	80.5	58.1	33	201.1	67.5	77.9	83.7
T20	65.1	65.4	**96.3**	77.9	85.6	62.9	13	283.4	63.6	70.2	82.7	75.9	82.9	62.6	50	132.7	64.4	76.9	84.3
T15	66.1	76.9	77.6	77.3	82.9	61.2	36	40.8	60.6	65.0	74.8	69.5	77.5	56.2	39	45.4	63.4	73.4	80.2
T03	61.7	62.2	92.4	74.3	82.4	59.7	15	245.6	63.2	63.7	86.0	73.2	80.3	59.8	34	195.1	62.4	73.8	81.3
T30	70.3	70.3	94.3	80.5	86.0	66.2	12	122.8	51.5	52.2	82.6	64.0	72.0	44.4	19	83.4	60.9	72.3	79.0
T00	75.7	80.8	86.2	83.5	87.3	68.1	34	108.4	43.7	45.1	75.4	56.5	65.8	38.8	39	170.1	59.7	70.0	76.6
T31	69.3	78.1	70.3	74.0	79.4	61.9	41	89.9	49.7	56.6	66.3	61.1	69.8	36.7	48	138.2	59.5	67.5	74.6
T34	63.6	69.8	77.4	73.4	79.6	58.5	21	35.2	55.0	55.7	85.3	67.4	75.6	50.3	24	35.4	59.3	70.4	77.6
Base	70.8	73.7	87.2	79.9	84.0	66.1	26	141.7	56.5	64.2	71.9	67.8	76.2	48.4	50	132.7	63.6	73.9	80.1

Table 14: Per-dataset results across all metrics for **Task 2**. U/I indicates the number of utterances per intent. K indicates the number of induced intents. *Base* gives the baseline system performance (equivalent to T04 and T26). Bold denotes the best results for each dataset.

Overview of Robust and Multilingual Automatic Evaluation Metrics for Open-Domain Dialogue Systems at DSTC 11 Track 4

Mario Rodríguez-Cantelar[1], Chen Zhang[2], Chengguang Tang[3], Ke Shi[3], Sarik Ghazarian[4], João Sedoc[5], Luis Fernando D'Haro[1] and Alexander Rudnicky[6]

[1]Speech Technology and Machine Learning Group - Universidad Politécnica de Madrid, Spain
[2]National University of Singapore, Singapore
[3]Tencent AI Lab, China
[4]University of Southern California, USA
[5]Department of Technology, Operations, and Statistics, New York University, USA
[6]Carnegie Mellon University, USA

Abstract

The advent and fast development of neural networks have revolutionized the research on dialogue systems and subsequently have triggered various challenges regarding their automatic evaluation. Automatic evaluation of open-domain dialogue systems as an open challenge has been the center of the attention of many researchers. Despite the consistent efforts to improve automatic metrics' correlations with human evaluation, there have been very few attempts to assess their robustness over multiple domains and dimensions. Also, their focus is mainly on the English language. All of these challenges prompt the development of automatic evaluation metrics that are reliable in various domains, dimensions, and languages. This track in the 11th Dialogue System Technology Challenge (DSTC11) is part of the ongoing effort to promote robust and multilingual automatic evaluation metrics. This article describes the datasets and baselines provided to participants and discusses the submission and result details of the two proposed subtasks.

1 Introduction

Recent advances in large-scale neural language models (Devlin et al., 2019; Radford et al., 2019; Zhang et al., 2020) have led to significant attention in dialogue systems, especially in the open domain category. Significant research efforts are dedicated to boost the robustness of dialogue systems, that is, improving their capability to perform well across multiple domains, dimensions, and handling humans' diverse expressions of the same ideas (e.g., paraphrasing or back-translation).

Automatic evaluation is an indispensable component for speeding up the development of robust dialogue systems. Common metrics are based on word overlap, such as BLEU (Papineni et al., 2002) and ROUGE (Lin, 2004), which mainly focus on matching syntactic information with a set of golden references. Unfortunately, such metrics correlate poorly with human judgments (Liu et al., 2016) as in open-domain dialogue, there can be limitless feasible responses w.r.t. a dialogue context.

Alternatively, recently developed model-based metrics such as BERTscore (Sun et al., 2022), BLEURT (Sellam et al., 2020), FED (Mehri and Eskenazi, 2020a), and MDD-Eval (Zhang et al., 2022a), which take advantage of the strong semantic representation capability of pre-trained transformer language models, perform the evaluation at semantic and partially pragmatic levels. Some of them do not even need golden references as input. Regrettably, despite their improvement over the word-overlap metrics, these metrics are not perfect; that is, their correlation with human evaluation is still not strong. Moreover, most of them perform well only on a particular dimension (e.g., engagingness or coherence) (Zhang et al., 2022b), or specific to a single domain. In addition, their performance may be highly dependent on the datasets used for training and evaluation (Yeh et al., 2021).

Due to the lack of robust automatic evaluation metrics (Mehri and Eskenazi, 2020a), researchers have to resort to the time-consuming and cost-intensive human evaluation process to analyze the performance of their model and benchmark their proposed methods against baselines.

Furthermore, to the best of our knowledge, none of the existing metrics have been thoroughly tested in a multilingual setting. Metric generalization across different languages is highly desirable, as it

Proceedings of The Eleventh Dialog System Technology Challenge, pages 260–273
September 11, 2023

helps the transformation of state-of-the-art English-only dialogue systems into highly capable multilingual systems. Although multilingual pre-trained language models may exist and can be potentially used for training multilingual dialogue systems, human-annotations or high-quality dialogue datasets for languages other than English are very scarce or even nonexistent in the case of some low-resource languages. To address this problem, we take advantage of recent advances in neural machine translation and paraphrasing systems. Using existing high-quality services and models, it is possible to create new datasets for different languages and perform back-translation or paraphrasing to create additional data in the original language to improve and evaluate the robustness of existing metrics. To this end, we propose two subtasks in our track, and their details are listed as follows:

1.1 Track Details

This track consists of two tasks which are explained in more detail below.

Participants will develop effective open-ended and multilingual automatic dialogue evaluation metrics that perform similarly when evaluated in a new language. Participants will develop effective open-ended automatic dialogue evaluation metrics that perform robustly when evaluated over paraphrased/back-translated sentences in English. For both tasks, proposed metrics are expected to show the following two important properties, as indicated in (Deriu et al., 2021):

1. Correlated to human judgments - the metrics should produce evaluation scores that well correlate to human judgments (scores) across multiple languages or alternative responses (i.e., back-translated or paraphrased).

2. Explainable - the metrics should provide constructive and explicit feedback to the generative models in terms of the quality of their generated responses. For instance, if a generative model contradicts itself, the evaluation metrics should signal such behavior.

Participants can propose their own metrics or optionally improve the deep AM-FM (Zhang et al., 2021) baseline evaluation model provided by us. A leaderboard on the ChatEval platform[1] was provided to check the performance of their different proposed models compared to those submitted by other researchers.

For each evaluation task, Spearman's correlation was used to compare the proposed evaluation metrics against human judgments. A final average score was calculated to rank the submitted metric models. Additional instructions to participants were provided through the Github repository[2] and by email on the main DSTC distribution list.

2 Task 1: Multilingual Automatic Metrics

In this task, the goal for participants is to propose effective automatic dialogue evaluation metrics that exhibit the properties mentioned above (Section 1.1) and perform well in a multilingual setup (English, Spanish, and Chinese). In concrete, participants were asked to propose a single multilingual model that could provide high correlations with human-annotations when evaluated in multilingual dialogues (development set in Section 2.1) and perform well in the hidden multilingual test set. Participants were required to use pre-trained multilingual models and train them to predict multidimensional quality metrics using self-supervised techniques and, optionally, fine-tune their system over a subset of the development data.

Finally, participants evaluated their models on the development and test sets, expecting to show similar performance in terms of correlations with human-annotations across three languages: English, Spanish, and Chinese. Only development and test sets have human-annotations, and only the test sets were manually translated or paraphrased/back-translated to guarantee the correlations with the original human-annotations on the English data.

2.1 Datasets

Datasets summary Table 1 shows the three clusters of datasets we used or created during the competition. The table shows information about the number of data used to train, develop, and test the proposed metrics. All these datasets clusters were available in English, Spanish, or Chinese and were back-translated into English. CHANEL and CDIAL include open-domain human-human conversations, while DSTC10 includes human-annotations on human-chatbot interactions. The type of annotations or metadata and how each clus-

[1]https://chateval.org/dstc11

[2]https://github.com/Mario-RC/dstc11_track4_robust_multilingual_metrics

ter was used (training/development/test) are indicated in the last three rows.

Table 7 (Appendix A) provides a brief summary of all the statistics of the train, development, and test datasets. The datasets statistics including their number of utterances, avg. number of utterances in each conversation, avg. number of context/response words, type of annotations (turn or dialogue level), number of criteria, number of provided annotations, and type of dialogue systems used for generating responses are shown.

Train As training set, we used the data released during the CHANEL@JSALT2020[3,4] (Rudnicky et al., 2020) workshop organized by Johns Hopkins University. This cluster consisted of a total of 18 well-known human-human dialogue datasets pre-processed and distributed in a standard format. The total number of dialogues was 393k (approximately 3M turns). An additional advantage of the data in this cluster is that they have been automatically translated back and forth using the same high-quality MS Azure translation service.[5]

Development As development set, the organizers provided data from two clusters of datasets: DSTC10 and CDIAL.

The first one was collected during DSTC10 Track 5 (Zhang et al., 2022c), consisting of more than 35k turn-level human-annotations, which were automatically translated into Spanish and Chinese, and then back-translated into English using MS Azure services.

Second, we used datasets provided by THU-COAI[6] group (Conversational AI groups from Tsinghua University), naming this cluster of datasets CDIAL. It contains open-domain human-human dialogues. They are originally in Chinese and include 3,470 dialogues (approximately 130k turns). Furthermore, we provided Chinese to English translations through the SotA Tencent MT[7] system.

Furthermore, Tencent AI manually annotated $\sim$ 3k random H-H turns ($\sim$1k dialogues) of CDIAL in Chinese (at turn-and dialogue-level).

It is important to note that the development data is intended to help participants verify the multilingualism and robustness capabilities of their models in terms of correlations with human-annotations.

Test Furthermore, in order to check the generalization capabilities of the proposed metrics from the participant, the test data included new English, Chinese, and Spanish data of human-chatbot interactions (Appendix B).

A new Human-Chatbot English dataset (HCEnglish) with $\sim$2k turns ($\sim$60 dialogues) with three different SotA chatbots (ChatGPT (Radford et al., 2018), GPT-3.5 (Brown et al., 2020), and BlenderBot 3 (Shuster et al., 2022) (Giorgi et al., 2023)). This dataset was manually annotated (turn level and dialogue level) using Amazon Mechanical Turk (AMT), then translated from English to Chinese and Spanish using MS Azure.

In addition, a new Human-Chatbot Chinese dataset (HCChinese) consisting of $\sim$5k turns ($\sim$500 dialogues) was generated with three different SotA chatbots (Chinese DialoGPT, Microsoft's Xiaoice (Zhou et al., 2020b) and Baidu's Plato-XL (Bao et al., 2022)). This dataset was manually annotated (turn and dialogue level) by Tencent AI, and then translated from Chinese to English using the Tencent MT system.

Third, hidden data from the DSTC10 data was used for Spanish with a total of $\sim$1500 turns ($\sim$700 dialogues). Existing turn-level annotations were used, as well as Spanish translations and English back-translations created using MS Azure, which were subsequently manually reviewed.

Table 2 shows the number of turns and dialogues for each test dataset for each language. The DSTC10 datasets did not have annotations at dialogue-level.

Metadata Since the quality of translated sentences can play an important role in the estimation of metric scores, quality annotations between the original sentence and its respective translation were delivered for each turn of all datasets. Machine translation Quality Estimation (QE) metric scores were given to participants using the QE COMET[8] (Rei et al., 2020) system. In addition, for task 1, the cosine similarity between the original sentence and the translated sentence. Thanks to this information, participants could optionally discard dialogues or turns that potentially did not get a high translation quality estimation, therefore reducing potential noise but also allowing the creation of more robust metric systems.

[3]https://github.com/CHANEL-JSALT-2020/datasets

[4]https://www.clsp.jhu.edu/chaval-chat-dialogue-modeling-and-evaluation/

[5]https://azure.microsoft.com/en-us/products/cognitive-services/translator/

[6]https://github.com/thu-coai

[7]https://www.tencentcloud.com/products/tmt

[8]https://github.com/Unbabel/COMET

Dataset Name	CHANEL	DSTC10	CDIAL
#datasets	18	7	3
Language	English, Spanish/Chinese, and English back-translation	English, Spanish/Chinese, and English back-translation	English, Spanish/Chinese, and English back-translation
Dialogues Type	Human-Human Open-Domain	Human-Chatbot Open-Domain	Human-Human Open-Domain
#dialogues/utterances	+ 390,000 / + 3,000,000	+ 18,000 / + 55,000	+ 3,470 / +130,000
Annotations	Sentiment analysis and Toxicity	Sentiment analysis and Toxicity Turn /dialogue level human scores	Turn /dialogue level human scores
Task 1 Set	Public: Train	Public: Dev, Test Hidden: Automatic Translations	Public: Train, Dev
Task 2 Set	Public: Train	Public: Dev, Test Hidden: Manually back-translated/paraphrased	—

Table 1: Summary of train/development/test datasets.

Language	EN				ZH				ES			Global
Dataset	**HCEnglish**	**HCChinese**	**DSTC10**	**Total**	**HCEnglish**	**HCChinese**	**DSTC10**	**Total**	**HCEnglish**	**DSTC10**	**Total**	
Turns	1,700	478	114	2,292	364	1,672	123	2,159	55	333	388	4,839
Dialogues	59	40	-	99	15	160	-	175	3	-	3	277

Table 2: Summary statistics of the test dataset used for **task 1** at turn and dialogue level, and separated by language.

In addition, toxicity and sentiment analysis metadata were provided for the original turns in both the CHANEL and DSTC10 datasets for filtering and dialogue curation purposes, as well as to avoid potential biases. These metadata allowed participants to have a better reference of the dataset quality, being of great help for them to decide whether or not to use these original turn and their translations in the training of their evaluation models and, optionally, fine-tune multilingual pre-trained models allowing better performance on the proposed dialogue-oriented tasks.

Data Format All data given follow a unified data format to make the storage, handling, and retrieval easier for the participants. Detailed guidelines are available in the track repository.[9]

Dimensions For HCEnglish, Amazon Mechanical Turk (AMT) was used to collect annotations for each of the dimensions evaluated in the test data. Our annotations restricted the users to location US, >97% approval rate, >1000 HITs done, and a convenience pool of workers used for NLP evaluation tasks.[10] This pool included workers from the pipeline paper (Zhang et al., 2022d) and cloudresearch. The average compensation was ~ 15$/hr. We included text-based attention checks at the dialogue-level as well as and annotator agreement (both with an expert as well as between crowd workers [some from the DSTC10 dataset]) time-based filters on the turn-level.

For the HCChinese data, we leveraged the power of Tencent MT[11] to perform the English-to-Chinese translation of the corpus, followed by training a team of six professional Chinese annotators to annotate the dialogues. The entire annotation process spanned a month and incurred costs of approximately 6,194 US dollars, which is in line with the expenses associated with other evaluation datasets. The average cost of annotating each dialogue was 2.36 US dollars. Finally, the average correlation coefficient for Adequacy scored by six annotators is 0.79, and 0.67 for Fluency.

2.2 Dimensions Evaluated

Since open-domain dialogue systems have multifacet nature, the evaluation can be accomplished from different perspectives. Since this is the case in both development and test data of task 1 (multilingual) and task 2 (robust), we include the following dimensions at turn-level and dialogue-level annotations (Mehri et al., 2022):

- <u>**Turn-level dimensions**</u>:
  Appropriateness - The response is appropriate given the preceding dialogue.
  Content Richness - The response is informative, with long sentences including multiple entities and conceptual or emotional words.

[9] `https://github.com/Mario-RC/dstc11_track4_robust_multilingual_metrics/blob/main/dstc11/track4-datasets-format.md`

[10] Without the convenience pool our annotator agreement was near random.

[11] `https://cloud.tencent.com/product/tmt`

Grammatical Correctness - Responses are free of grammatical and semantic errors.
Relevance - Responses are on-topic with the immediate dialogue history.

- **Dialogue-level dimensions**:
Coherence - Throughout the dialogue, is the system maintaining a good conversation flow.
Engageness/Likeability - Throughout the dialogue, the system displays a likeable personality.
Informativeness - Throughout the dialogue, the system provides unique and non-generic information.
Overall - The overall quality of and satisfaction with the dialogue.

Furthermore, when choosing the test dimensions, the annotations available in the train and development data were taken into account to keep them balanced and homogeneous.

The dimensions chosen at the turn level show how much the responses are appropriate, informative including multiple entities and conceptual or emotional words, free of grammatical and semantic errors, and on-topic with the immediate dialogue history. The dimensions chosen at the dialogue level show how much the system maintains a good conversation flow, engages well with the user, provides unique and non-generic information, and the overall quality of the system.

Table 3 summarizes the dimensions for each test data set. As can be seen, the DSTC10 set only has human turn-level annotations.

Sets	Dimensions			
DSTC10				
DSTC10-turn	A	CR	GC	R
ChatEval-turn	A			
JSALT-turn	A			
HCChinese				
HCChinese-dial	C	EL	I	O
HCChinese-turn		CR	GC	R
HCEnglish				
HCEnglish-dial	C	EL	I	O
HCEnglish-turn	A	CR	GC	R
Test data				
Test-dial	C	EL	I	O
Test-turn	A	CR	GC	R

C: Coherence — EL: Engageness/Likeability
I: Informativeness — O: Overall
A: Appropriateness — CR: Content Richness
GC: Grammatical Correctness — R: Relevance

Table 3: Summary of the dimensions (human-annotations) available for each dataset used in the test data, both at the turn and dialogue level.

2.3 Baseline

We provide a multilingual variant of deep AM-FM (Zhang et al., 2021)(used previously during Track5 at DSTC10) as the baseline model. The formulation of both AM and FM remains unchanged except that we switch their original English-based pre-trained language models to multilingual models. For the adequacy metric (AM), we use XLM-R[12] (Conneau et al., 2020) to extract sentence-level embeddings of both the response and the last sentence in the corresponding dialogue context. Then, the cosine similarity of the two embeddings is the AM score assigned to the corresponding response. For the fluency metric (FM), we adopt the multilingual GPT-2[13] as the backbone language model. The conditional probability of the response w.r.t. the context given by the multilingual GPT-2 model serves as the FM score of the response. The final AM-FM score is the arithmetic mean of both metric scores. All information related to the baseline model, such as code and data, can be found in this GitHub repository.[14]

2.4 Participants

In Task 1, 4 teams participated, which provided a total of 16 submissions. Participants were asked to provide a brief description of the system for their proposals. The two system descriptions provided by the participants are shown below:

Team 4 Their approach utilizes two submetric groups, XLM-R and ChatGPT, for evaluating dialogue responses. The XLM-R group employs the XLM-Roberta-Large encoder model, consisting of NSP (Next Sentence Prediction), VSP (Valid Sentence Prediction), MLM (Masked Language Modeling), and ENG (Engagement) submetrics. The NSP submetric ensembles three models trained on English and multilingual data, while the VSP model

[12] https://huggingface.co/sentence-transformers/xlm-r-100langs-bert-base-nli-stsb-mean-tokens

[13] https://huggingface.co/ai-forever/mGPT

[14] https://github.com/karthik19967829/DSTC11-Benchmark

combines different models. The ENG submetric uses an ensemble of encoder models trained on the ENDEX engagement dataset (Xu et al., 2022). The MLM submetric utilizes the pre-trained XLM-R-large model with a Language Modeling head. The ChatGPT group prompts gpt-3.5-turbo to evaluate responses based on the dimensions of the DSTC11 test, with submetrics for dialogue and turn level. Weighted sums of the submetrics are calculated, with the weights learned from a subset of the dev dataset. For the test set, four variations were submitted, including weighted sums of XLM-R and ChatGPT, direct mapping of ChatGPT, and a weighted sum of all models.

In addition, Team 4 used the metadata provided. During their tests performed for task 1 they discovered that increasing the machine translated data affected the performance of the trained models. Therefore, they made use of the quality estimations computed with the COMET MTQE model to use only the best translated dialogues.

For task 2, they trained their models using the least similar, and separately the most similar ones, based on cosine similarity and Levenshtein distance. They found that there was a good correlation between using the paraphrase score and their model performance, with lower scores bringing higher performance and vice versa. They deduced that the lower-scored responses were more diverse and therefore more informative for training.

Team 7 Their Parallel Corpus Alignment Framework enhances model evaluation on parallel corpora, focusing on Robust and Multilingual Automatic Evaluation Metrics for Open-Domain Dialogue systems. By utilizing xlm-roberta-large and bert-base as baseline models, they leverage representations from different languages, paraphrases, and translations to align parallel corpora in the semantic space. Through contrastive learning and multi-dataset distillation, they strengthen the model's scoring robustness and evaluation capability across various data domains.

2.5 Results

Table 4 shows the results on test data for task 1 at turn and dialogue level. To calculate the scores in the table, the following procedure was followed: 1. Data are separated in each language (English, Chinese, and Spanish); 2. Then, for each language separately, Spearman's correlation coefficients are calculated for each dimension independently; 3. Next, we calculate the mean of the correlations of the dimensions in each language (columns EN, ZH, and ES); 4. Finally, we calculate the final mean (Global column) of the language columns.

		Turn-level			
Team	**EN**	**ZH**	**ES**	**Global**	**Rank**
Baseline	0.2940	0.0753	0.1826	0.1840	4
Team 2	0.1469	0.1054	0.0808	0.1110	5
Team 4	0.4818	0.3936	0.5890	**0.4881**	**1**
Team 5	0.3702	0.0701	0.1983	*0.2129*	*3*
Team 7	0.2214	0.3112	0.5644	0.3657	2
		Dialogue-level			
Team	**EN**	**ZH**	**ES**	**Global**	**Rank**
Baseline	0.2414	0.4648	0.8080	0.5047	2
Team 4	0.5342	0.7133	0.8080	**0.6852**	**1**
Team 5	0.1865	0.1356	0.6830	*0.3350*	*3*

Table 4: Spearman's correlations of the baseline and average correlations of each team's metrics on **turn-level** and **dialogue-level** test sets for **task 1**. The first position is shown in bold, the second in underline and the third in italics.

To rank each team, the best submission was used according to the calculated global score. Teams 4, 7 and 5 were the best performers at turn-level. Regarding dialogue-level, team 4 was the best performer, followed by the baseline model and then by team 3. In particular, the performance of team 4 is outstanding in all languages.

This shows that team's 4 model is very effective not only at the global multilingual level, but also in each language separately, showing a very high performance in Spanish, followed by English and then Chinese. This highlights the need of a multilingual metric capable of performing in Chinese to match the results obtained in Spanish or English.

At dialogue-level, team 4 also demonstrated a very high correlation. Having a wide margin of advantage over team 5 and the base model. It should be noted that for Spanish at the dialogue-level, the amount of data was scarse, then producing non-statistical significant results and making difficult to analyze the reason for so high correlation results.

3 Task 2: Robust Evaluation Metrics

In this task, the goal of the participants was to propose robust metrics for automatic evaluation of English dialogues that exhibit previously mentioned properties (subsection 1.1) while being robust when dealing with paraphrased/back-translated English sentences. Here, the expected performance for the proposed metrics was that they could be on par with the correlations with human-annotations obtained over the original sentences. As robustness criteria proposed, paraphrased/back-translated sentences should have the same semantic meaning as the original sentence but different wording. Task 2 was only evaluated for the English language.

Participants had the opportunity to evaluate their models with developmental data composed of paraphrased/back-translated sentences and their respective human annotations.

3.1 Datasets

Train, development, and test For task 2, the same task 1 datasets were used. However, to evaluate robustness, paraphrases and back-translated data were used. Thus, for task 2, the original datasets data was provided, in addition to the back-translations and paraphrases of the original sentences, but not the translations to other languages. Table 5 shows the number of turns and dialogues for each test data set sent to the participants. The DSTC10 datasets did not have annotations at dialogue-level.

Dataset	HCEnglish	DSTC10	Total
Turns	1,701	404	2,105
Dialogues	59	-	59

Table 5: Summary statistics of **task 2** test datasets at the turn and dialogue level.

For creating semantically similar sentences, we relied on two options: back-translations and a paraphraser model. For back-translations we used MS Azure MT services or Tencent MT system. Then for the paraphraser model, we used PARROT[15] (Damodaran, 2021). Multiple paraphrases were generated for all the original English sentences in each dataset.

For this task, paraphrases were preferable to back-translations. The reason is that current translation systems have a very high quality, so back-translations are often too similar to the original sentence, or even identical, not meeting in this case the robustness criterion proposed in task 2.

Metadata For this specific task, participants received as metadata the Levenshtein[16] distance calculated for all paraphrases generated from the original sentences, in all datasets. For task 1, QE annotations were given using the same COMET model. In this case, they were calculated between the original sentence and its respective paraphrases separately, and between the original sentence and respective back-translation.

Moreover, participants were given the Cosine Similarity calculation between the original sentence and its respective paraphrases, as well as between the original sentence and its back-translation. Finally, participants were notified of the provided metadata, as well as the toxicity and sentiment analysis annotations, for them to filter potentially biased or noised sentences.

Dimensions Human-annotations for development and test data were the same as for task 1.

3.2 Dimensions Evaluated

As the data for task 2 are the same as those in task 1, the nature of the data is common in both tasks. Therefore, the dimensions used to evaluate the models, both at the turn and dialogue level, are shared between the two tasks.

3.3 Baseline

The same baseline was used for task 2, as for task 12.3. In this case, paraphrases were used instead of multilingual sentences to evaluate robustness.

3.4 Participants

For this task, a total of 5 teams participated and sent a total of 21 submissions. Participants were asked to provide a brief description of their systems. Team 4 and 7 used the same models as for task 1, therefore they are descripted in Section 2.4. Below, we provide detailed description for teams 3 and 6.

Team 3 To address the variability of metrics in evaluating different dimensions and mitigate overfitting on scarce human-annotated data, they propose IDEL. This approach combines multiple metrics to achieve a higher correlation with human judgment across all dimensions. To avoid overfitting, they employed a list-wise learning-to-rank objective, leveraging the relative positions of examples rather than absolute coordinates. Furthermore, they utilized the LLaMa 65B dataset and the in-context-learning method for direct evaluation of examples, considering their context.

Team 6 Their approach focused on predicting turn-level qualities. They utilized pre-trained Large

[15] `https://github.com/jsedoc/Parrot_Paraphraser`

[16] The Levenshtein distance is a numerical measure indicating the similarity between two strings. A higher Levenshtein distance signifies a greater difference between the two strings.

Language Models (LLMs) with manually designed prompts and two selected dialogues as few-shot examples to adapt the LLM output. Additionally, they built a feed-forward neural network (FNN) using frozen LLM representations as features to predict the desired metrics. Another submission employed the ChatGPT API with optimized prompts and dynamically obtained dialogue examples. Hyperparameters were selected based on manual annotations of 157 testing examples. However, for grammaticality metric scores, randomly generated scores were submitted due to uninformative constant scores predicted by the LLM.

3.5 Results

Team results for turn and dialogue levels on the test data for task 2 are provided in Table 6. To calculate the scores and provide the ranking, the following procedure was followed: a. Calculate the Spearman's correlation coefficients for each dimension independently; b. Calculate the mean of the correlations of the dimensions; c. Calculate the mean (Global column) of the language columns.

Turn-level			Dialogue-level		
Team	**Global**	**Rank**	**Team**	**Global**	**Rank**
Baseline	0.3387	4	Baseline	**0.4800**	**1**
Team 1	0.1537	6	Team 1	0.1111	4
Team 3	0.2697	5	Team 3	*0.2196*	*3*
Team 4	**0.4890**	**1**	Team 4	0.3031	2
Team 6	0.4190	2			
Team 7	*0.3833*	*3*			

Table 6: Spearman's correlations of the baseline and average correlations of each team's metrics on **turn-level** and **dialogue-level** test sets for **task 2**. The first position is shown in bold, the second in underline and the third in italics.

The best presentation according to the overall score calculated was used to rank each team. Teams 4, 6 and 7 were the best performers at the turn-level. At dialogue-level, the baseline model provided the best performance, followed by team 4 and team 3.

Considering team 4 results, both in task 1 and task 2, it can be considered their model as the overall best in the competition, being good at multilingual level as well as in robustness. However, the performance of the baseline model at dialogue level is far superior to that of team 4, showing there is still room for improvement.

4 Conclusions and Future Work

This paper presents a comprehensive overview of Track 4 on "Robust and Multilingual Automatic Evaluation Metrics for Open-Domain Dialogue Systems" organized as part of the 11th Dialogue System Technology Challenge (DSTC11). The track was divided into two subtasks addressing an important problems in Dialogue Systems: the design of automatic evaluation metrics for multilingual dialogues and dialogue robustness when dealing with paraphrases or back-translations.

Each task was divided at turn and dialogue level. At the turn level, 5 teams actively participated and at the dialogue level 3 teams participated. Having some of the teams participated at both levels. Some of the teams obtained interesting results that effectively contribute to the state-of-the-art of automatic evaluation models for multilingual dialogues. However, the results at the language level show a disparate performance among the different languages, giving room for improvement in the evaluation of other languages. The overall performance of the participants was satisfactory, with some teams outperforming the baseline model both in language and globally, as well as at the turn and dialogue levels. However, we can see that the automatic evaluation is still an open problem as correlation scores are still below 0.7 in the best of the cases.

The second task was also subdivided at turn and dialogue level. At the turn level, 5 teams actively participated and at dialogue-level 3 teams, with some of the teams having participated at both levels. At the turn level, several teams outperformed the baseline model. However, no team was able to outperform the baseline model at dialogue-level, showing that there is still room for improvement.

As future work, we plan to increase the number of databases, as well as to provide better baseline models. We also want to include a larger number of dimensions so that the evaluations performed are more complete, covering more different aspects of the dialogue. For task 1, it is planned to extend the number of available languages, to create multilingual models with a wider spectrum, thus widening the scope of the competition and attracting more participants who are fluent in other languages. For task 2 we want to propose higher quality paraphrases, such as those generated with models like GPT-4 (OpenAI, 2023).

Acknowledgements

This work is supported by project BEWORD (PID2021-126061OB-C43) funded by MCIN/AEI/10.13039/501100011033 and, as appropriate, by "ERDF A way of making Europe", by the "European Union", and by the European Commission through Project ASTOUND (101071191 — HORIZON-EIC-2021-PATHFINDERCHALLENGES-01). We gratefully acknowledge valuable efforts from Tencent AI Lab who supports Chinese translation and annotation of datasets by funding and infrastructure. Thanks to THU-CoAI (Conversational AI groups from Tsinghua University) for providing their Chinese datasets as part of the challenge data. Thanks to Unbabel for providing the COMET MTQE scores annotations as part of the challenge data. This contribution was supported by national funds through Fundação para a Ciência e a Tecnologia (FCT) with references PRT/BD/152198/2021 and UIDB/50021/2020, and by the P2020 program MAIA led by Unbabel (LISBOA-01-0247-FEDER-045909). We also give thanks to MS Azure services (especially to Irving Kwong) for their sponsorship to continue processing new datasets for the research community. This research project is supported by the NYU ChatEval Team led by João Sedoc. This research project is supported in part by a grant from Amazon to Alexander Rudnicky, Carnegie Mellon University. Thanks to Karthik Ganesan, Sarik Ghazarian, James Hagerty, Zhang Chen and Alex Rudnicky for developing the baseline model as part of the challenge tasks.

References

Daniel Adiwardana, Minh-Thang Luong, David R. So, Jamie Hall, Noah Fiedel, Romal Thoppilan, Zi Yang, Apoorv Kulshreshtha, Gaurav Nemade, Yifeng Lu, and Quoc V. Le. 2020. Towards a human-like open-domain chatbot.

Rafael E. Banchs. 2012. Movie-DiC: a movie dialogue corpus for research and development. In *Proceedings of the 50th Annual Meeting of the Association for Computational Linguistics (Volume 2: Short Papers)*, pages 203–207, Jeju Island, Korea. Association for Computational Linguistics.

Siqi Bao, Huang He, Fan Wang, Hua Wu, Haifeng Wang, Wenquan Wu, Zhihua Wu, Zhen Guo, Hua Lu, Xinxian Huang, Xin Tian, Xinchao Xu, Yingzhan Lin, and Zheng-Yu Niu. 2022. PLATO-XL: Exploring the large-scale pre-training of dialogue generation. In *Findings of the Association for Computational Linguistics: AACL-IJCNLP 2022*, pages 107–118, Online only. Association for Computational Linguistics.

Tom Brown, Benjamin Mann, Nick Ryder, Melanie Subbiah, Jared D Kaplan, Prafulla Dhariwal, Arvind Neelakantan, Pranav Shyam, Girish Sastry, Amanda Askell, et al. 2020. Language models are few-shot learners. *Advances in neural information processing systems*, 33:1877–1901.

Alessandra Cervone and Giuseppe Riccardi. 2020. Is this dialogue coherent? learning from dialogue acts and entities. In *Proceedings of the 21th Annual Meeting of the Special Interest Group on Discourse and Dialogue*, pages 162–174, 1st virtual meeting. Association for Computational Linguistics.

Alexis Conneau, Kartikay Khandelwal, Naman Goyal, Vishrav Chaudhary, Guillaume Wenzek, Francisco Guzmán, Edouard Grave, Myle Ott, Luke Zettlemoyer, and Veselin Stoyanov. 2020. Unsupervised cross-lingual representation learning at scale. In *Proceedings of the 58th Annual Meeting of the Association for Computational Linguistics*, pages 8440–8451, Online. Association for Computational Linguistics.

Prithiviraj Damodaran. 2021. Parrot: Paraphrase generation for nlu.

Cristian Danescu-Niculescu-Mizil and Lillian Lee. 2011. Chameleons in imagined conversations: A new approach to understanding coordination of linguistic style in dialogs. In *Proceedings of the Workshop on Cognitive Modeling and Computational Linguistics, ACL 2011*.

Jan Deriu, Alvaro Rodrigo, Arantxa Otegi, Guillermo Echegoyen, Sophie Rosset, Eneko Agirre, and Mark Cieliebak. 2021. Survey on evaluation methods for dialogue systems. *Artificial Intelligence Review*, 54:755–810.

Jacob Devlin, Ming-Wei Chang, Kenton Lee, and Kristina Toutanova. 2019. BERT: Pre-training of deep bidirectional transformers for language understanding. In *Proceedings of the 2019 Conference of the North American Chapter of the Association for Computational Linguistics: Human Language Technologies, Volume 1 (Long and Short Papers)*, pages 4171–4186, Minneapolis, Minnesota. Association for Computational Linguistics.

Emily Dinan, Stephen Roller, Kurt Shuster, Angela Fan, Michael Auli, and Jason Weston. 2019. Wizard of wikipedia: Knowledge-powered conversational agents.

Michel Galley, Chris Brockett, Xiang Gao, Jianfeng Gao, and Bill Dolan. 2019. Grounded response generation task at dstc7. In *AAAI Dialog System Technology Challenges Workshop*.

Salvatore Giorgi, Shreya Havaldar, Farhan Ahmed, Zuhaib Akhtar, Shalaka Vaidya, Gary Pan, Lyle H. Ungar, H. Andrew Schwartz, and Joao Sedoc. 2023. Human-centered metrics for dialog system evaluation.

Karthik Gopalakrishnan, Behnam Hedayatnia, Qinlang Chen, Anna Gottardi, Sanjeev Kwatra, Anu Venkatesh, Raefer Gabriel, and Dilek Hakkani-Tür. 2019. Topical-Chat: Towards Knowledge-Grounded Open-Domain Conversations. In *Proc. Interspeech 2019*, pages 1891–1895.

Prakhar Gupta, Shikib Mehri, Tiancheng Zhao, Amy Pavel, Maxine Eskenazi, and Jeffrey P. Bigham. 2019. Investigating evaluation of open-domain dialogue systems with human generated multiple references.

Carmen Haro, Oriol A Rangel-Zúñiga, Juan F Alcalá-Díaz, Francisco Gómez-Delgado, Pablo Pérez-Martínez, Javier Delgado-Lista, Gracia M Quintana-Navarro, Blanca B Landa, Juan A Navas-Cortés, Manuel Tena-Sempere, et al. 2016. Intestinal microbiota is influenced by gender and body mass index. *PloS one*, 11(5):e0154090.

Ryuichiro Higashinaka, Kotaro Funakoshi, Yuka Kobayashi, and Michimasa Inaba. 2016. The dialogue breakdown detection challenge: Task description, datasets, and evaluation metrics. In *Proceedings of the Tenth International Conference on Language Resources and Evaluation (LREC'16)*, pages 3146–3150, Portorož, Slovenia. European Language Resources Association (ELRA).

Chao-Chun Hsu, Sheng-Yeh Chen, Chuan-Chun Kuo, Ting-Hao Huang, and Lun-Wei Ku. 2018. EmotionLines: An emotion corpus of multi-party conversations. In *Proceedings of the Eleventh International Conference on Language Resources and Evaluation (LREC 2018)*, Miyazaki, Japan. European Language Resources Association (ELRA).

Lishan Huang, Zheng Ye, Jinghui Qin, Liang Lin, and Xiaodan Liang. 2020. GRADE: Automatic graph-enhanced coherence metric for evaluating open-domain dialogue systems. In *Proceedings of the 2020 Conference on Empirical Methods in Natural Language Processing (EMNLP)*, pages 9230–9240, Online. Association for Computational Linguistics.

S Lee, H Schulz, A Atkinson, J Gao, K Suleman, L El Asri, M Adada, M Huang, S Sharma, W Tay, et al. 2019. Multi-domain task-completion dialog challenge. *Dialog system technology challenges*, 8(9).

Yanran Li, Hui Su, Xiaoyu Shen, Wenjie Li, Ziqiang Cao, and Shuzi Niu. 2017. DailyDialog: A manually labelled multi-turn dialogue dataset. In *Proceedings of the Eighth International Joint Conference on Natural Language Processing (Volume 1: Long Papers)*, pages 986–995, Taipei, Taiwan. Asian Federation of Natural Language Processing.

Chin-Yew Lin. 2004. ROUGE: A package for automatic evaluation of summaries. In *Text Summarization Branches Out*, pages 74–81, Barcelona, Spain. Association for Computational Linguistics.

Chia-Wei Liu, Ryan Lowe, Iulian Serban, Mike Noseworthy, Laurent Charlin, and Joelle Pineau. 2016. How NOT to evaluate your dialogue system: An empirical study of unsupervised evaluation metrics for dialogue response generation. In *Proceedings of the 2016 Conference on Empirical Methods in Natural Language Processing*, pages 2122–2132, Austin, Texas. Association for Computational Linguistics.

Shikib Mehri, Jinho Choi, Luis Fernando D'Haro, Jan Deriu, Maxine Eskenazi, Milica Gasic, Kallirroi Georgila, Dilek Hakkani-Tur, Zekang Li, Verena Rieser, Samira Shaikh, David Traum, Yi-Ting Yeh, Zhou Yu, Yizhe Zhang, and Chen Zhang. 2022. Report from the nsf future directions workshop on automatic evaluation of dialog: Research directions and challenges.

Shikib Mehri and Maxine Eskenazi. 2020a. Unsupervised evaluation of interactive dialog with DialoGPT. In *Proceedings of the 21th Annual Meeting of the Special Interest Group on Discourse and Dialogue*, pages 225–235, 1st virtual meeting. Association for Computational Linguistics.

Shikib Mehri and Maxine Eskenazi. 2020b. USR: An unsupervised and reference free evaluation metric for dialog generation. In *Proceedings of the 58th Annual Meeting of the Association for Computational Linguistics*, pages 681–707, Online. Association for Computational Linguistics.

Erinc Merdivan, Deepika Singh, Sten Hanke, Johannes Kropf, Andreas Holzinger, and Matthieu Geist. 2020. Human annotated dialogues dataset for natural conversational agents. *Applied Sciences*, 10(3):762.

Nikita Moghe, Siddhartha Arora, Suman Banerjee, and Mitesh M. Khapra. 2018. Towards exploiting background knowledge for building conversation systems. In *Proceedings of the 2018 Conference on Empirical Methods in Natural Language Processing*, pages 2322–2332, Brussels, Belgium. Association for Computational Linguistics.

Yixin Nie, Mary Williamson, Mohit Bansal, Douwe Kiela, and Jason Weston. 2020. I like fish, especially dolphins: Addressing contradictions in dialogue modeling. In *Proceedings of the 58th Annual Meeting of the Association for ComputationaL Linguistics, ACL 2020.*

OpenAI. 2023. Gpt-4 technical report.

Kishore Papineni, Salim Roukos, Todd Ward, and Wei-Jing Zhu. 2002. Bleu: a method for automatic evaluation of machine translation. In *Proceedings of the 40th Annual Meeting of the Association for Computational Linguistics*, pages 311–318, Philadelphia, Pennsylvania, USA. Association for Computational Linguistics.

Soujanya Poria, Devamanyu Hazarika, Navonil Majumder, Gautam Naik, Erik Cambria, and Rada Mihalcea. 2019. MELD: A multimodal multi-party dataset for emotion recognition in conversations. In *Proceedings of the 57th Annual Meeting of the Association for Computational Linguistics*, pages 527–536, Florence, Italy. Association for Computational Linguistics.

Alec Radford, Karthik Narasimhan, Tim Salimans, Ilya Sutskever, et al. 2018. Improving language understanding by generative pre-training.

Alec Radford, Jeffrey Wu, Rewon Child, David Luan, Dario Amodei, Ilya Sutskever, et al. 2019. Language models are unsupervised multitask learners. *OpenAI blog*, 1(8):9.

Hannah Rashkin, Eric Michael Smith, Margaret Li, and Y-Lan Boureau. 2019. Towards empathetic open-domain conversation models: A new benchmark and dataset. In *Proceedings of the 57th Annual Meeting of the Association for Computational Linguistics*, pages 5370–5381, Florence, Italy. Association for Computational Linguistics.

Ricardo Rei, Craig Stewart, Ana C Farinha, and Alon Lavie. 2020. COMET: A neural framework for MT evaluation. In *Proceedings of the 2020 Conference on Empirical Methods in Natural Language Processing (EMNLP)*, pages 2685–2702, Online. Association for Computational Linguistics.

Alexander Rudnicky, Rafael Banchs, Luis F. D'Haro, João Sedoc, Zhang Chen, Mario Rodríguez-Cantelar, Andrew Koh Jin Jie, et al. 2020. Chanel-metrics: Chat/dialogue modeling and evaluation report.

João Sedoc, Daphne Ippolito, Arun Kirubarajan, Jai Thirani, Lyle Ungar, and Chris Callison-Burch. 2019. ChatEval: A tool for chatbot evaluation. In *Proceedings of the 2019 Conference of the North American Chapter of the Association for Computational Linguistics (Demonstrations)*, pages 60–65, Minneapolis, Minnesota. Association for Computational Linguistics.

Abigail See, Stephen Roller, Douwe Kiela, and Jason Weston. 2019. What makes a good conversation? how controllable attributes affect human judgments. In *Proceedings of the 2019 Conference of the North American Chapter of the Association for Computational Linguistics: Human Language Technologies, Volume 1 (Long and Short Papers)*, pages 1702–1723, Minneapolis, Minnesota. Association for Computational Linguistics.

Thibault Sellam, Dipanjan Das, and Ankur Parikh. 2020. BLEURT: Learning robust metrics for text generation. In *Proceedings of the 58th Annual Meeting of the Association for Computational Linguistics*, pages 7881–7892, Online. Association for Computational Linguistics.

Lifeng Shang, Zhengdong Lu, and Hang Li. 2015. Neural responding machine for short-text conversation. In *Proceedings of the 53rd Annual Meeting of the Association for Computational Linguistics and the 7th International Joint Conference on Natural Language Processing (Volume 1: Long Papers)*, pages 1577–1586, Beijing, China. Association for Computational Linguistics.

Kurt Shuster, Jing Xu, Mojtaba Komeili, Da Ju, Eric Michael Smith, Stephen Roller, Megan Ung, Moya Chen, Kushal Arora, Joshua Lane, Morteza Behrooz, William Ngan, Spencer Poff, Naman Goyal, Arthur Szlam, Y-Lan Boureau, Melanie Kambadur, and Jason Weston. 2022. Blenderbot 3: a deployed conversational agent that continually learns to responsibly engage.

Tianxiang Sun, Junliang He, Xipeng Qiu, and Xuanjing Huang. 2022. BERTScore is unfair: On social bias in language model-based metrics for text generation. In *Proceedings of the 2022 Conference on Empirical Methods in Natural Language Processing*, pages 3726–3739, Abu Dhabi, United Arab Emirates. Association for Computational Linguistics.

Bibek Upadhayay and Vahid Behzadan. 2020. Sentimental liar: Extended corpus and deep learning models for fake claim classification. In *2020 IEEE International Conference on Intelligence and Security Informatics (ISI)*, pages 1–6. IEEE.

Yida Wang, Pei Ke, Yinhe Zheng, Kaili Huang, Yong Jiang, Xiaoyan Zhu, and Minlie Huang. 2020a. A large-scale chinese short-text conversation dataset. In *Natural Language Processing and Chinese Computing: 9th CCF International Conference, NLPCC 2020, Zhengzhou, China, October 14–18, 2020, Proceedings, Part I 9*, pages 91–103. Springer.

Yida Wang, Pei Ke, Yinhe Zheng, Kaili Huang, Yong Jiang, Xiaoyan Zhu, and Minlie Huang. 2020b. A large-scale chinese short-text conversation dataset. In *Natural Language Processing and Chinese Computing*, pages 91–103, Cham. Springer International Publishing.

Yu Wu, Wei Wu, Chen Xing, Ming Zhou, and Zhoujun Li. 2017. Sequential matching network: A new architecture for multi-turn response selection in retrieval-based chatbots. In *Proceedings of the 55th Annual Meeting of the Association for Computational Linguistics (Volume 1: Long Papers)*, pages 496–505, Vancouver, Canada. Association for Computational Linguistics.

Guangxuan Xu, Ruibo Liu, Fabrice Harel-Canada, Nischal Reddy Chandra, and Nanyun Peng. 2022. EnDex: Evaluation of dialogue engagingness at scale. In *Findings of the Association for Computational Linguistics: EMNLP 2022*, pages 4884–4893, Abu Dhabi, United Arab Emirates. Association for Computational Linguistics.

Yi-Ting Yeh, Maxine Eskenazi, and Shikib Mehri. 2021. A comprehensive assessment of dialog evaluation metrics. In *The First Workshop on Evaluations and Assessments of Neural Conversation Systems*, pages 15–33, Online. Association for Computational Linguistics.

Chen Zhang, Luis Fernando D'Haro, Thomas Friedrichs, and Haizhou Li. 2022a. MDD-Eval: Self-training on augmented data for multi-domain dialogue evaluation. In *AAAI 2022*.

Chen Zhang, Luis Fernando D'Haro, Qiquan Zhang, Thomas Friedrichs, and Haizhou Li. 2022b. FineD-eval: Fine-grained automatic dialogue-level evaluation. In *Proceedings of the 2022 Conference on Empirical Methods in Natural Language Processing*, pages 3336–3355, Abu Dhabi, United Arab Emirates. Association for Computational Linguistics.

Chen Zhang, Luis Fernando D'Haro, Rafael E Banchs, Thomas Friedrichs, and Haizhou Li. 2021. Deep am-fm: Toolkit for automatic dialogue evaluation. *Conversational Dialogue Systems for the Next Decade*, pages 53–69.

Chen Zhang, João Sedoc, Luis Fernando D'Haro, Rafael Banchs, and Alexander Rudnicky. 2022c. Automatic evaluation and moderation of open-domain dialogue systems. In *AAAI 2022*.

Lining Zhang, João Sedoc, Simon Mille, Yufang Hou, Sebastian Gehrmann, Daniel Deutsch, Elizabeth Clark, Yixin Liu, Miruna Clinciu, Saad Mahamood, and Khyathi Chandu. 2022d. Needle in a haystack: An analysis of finding qualified workers on mturk for summarization.

Saizheng Zhang, Emily Dinan, Jack Urbanek, Arthur Szlam, Douwe Kiela, and Jason Weston. 2018a. Personalizing dialogue agents: I have a dog, do you have pets too? In *Proceedings of the 56th Annual Meeting of the Association for Computational Linguistics (Volume 1: Long Papers)*, pages 2204–2213, Melbourne, Australia. Association for Computational Linguistics.

Yizhe Zhang, Siqi Sun, Michel Galley, Yen-Chun Chen, Chris Brockett, Xiang Gao, Jianfeng Gao, Jingjing Liu, and Bill Dolan. 2020. DIALOGPT : Large-scale generative pre-training for conversational response generation. In *Proceedings of the 58th Annual Meeting of the Association for Computational Linguistics: System Demonstrations*, pages 270–278, Online. Association for Computational Linguistics.

Zhuosheng Zhang, Jiangtong Li, Pengfei Zhu, Hai Zhao, and Gongshen Liu. 2018b. Modeling multi-turn conversation with deep utterance aggregation. In *Proceedings of the 27th International Conference on Computational Linguistics*, pages 3740–3752, Santa Fe, New Mexico, USA. Association for Computational Linguistics.

Tianyu Zhao, Divesh Lala, and Tatsuya Kawahara. 2020. Designing precise and robust dialogue response evaluators. In *Proceedings of the 58th Annual Meeting of the Association for Computational Linguistics*, pages 26–33. Association for Computational Linguistics.

Hao Zhou, Minlie Huang, Tianyang Zhang, Xiaoyan Zhu, and Bing Liu. 2018a. Emotional chatting machine: Emotional conversation generation with internal and external memory. In *AAAI 2018*.

Hao Zhou, Minlie Huang, Tianyang Zhang, Xiaoyan Zhu, and Bing Liu. 2018b. Emotional chatting machine: Emotional conversation generation with internal and external memory. *Proceedings of the AAAI Conference on Artificial Intelligence*, 32(1).

Hao Zhou, Chujie Zheng, Kaili Huang, Minlie Huang, and Xiaoyan Zhu. 2020a. KdConv: A Chinese multi-domain dialogue dataset towards multi-turn knowledge-driven conversation. In *Proceedings of the 58th Annual Meeting of the Association for Computational Linguistics*, pages 7098–7108, Online. Association for Computational Linguistics.

Kangyan Zhou, Shrimai Prabhumoye, and Alan W Black. 2018c. A dataset for document grounded conversations. In *Proceedings of the 2018 Conference on Empirical Methods in Natural Language Processing*, pages 708–713, Brussels, Belgium. Association for Computational Linguistics.

Li Zhou, Jianfeng Gao, Di Li, and Heung-Yeung Shum. 2020b. The design and implementation of XiaoIce, an empathetic social chatbot. *Computational Linguistics*, 46(1):53–93.

A Appendix: Datasets statistics

Table 7 shows all the data sets that make up the training, development, and test sets. In detail, it shows the number of dialogues, turns per dialogue, average number of turns per dialogue, average number of words per turn, as well as the granularity of the annotations (at turn and/or dialogue level), the original language of the dataset and into which languages it is translated.

B Appendix: Existing Benchmark Datasets

Descriptions of the datasets that constitute the DSTC10 benchmark can be found at Zhang et al. (2022c). Details of the remaining evaluation datasets are as follows:

ECM-Eval - The test instances in ECM-Eval test set are sampled from the Emotional Short-Text Conversation (ESTC) dialogue corpus (Zhou et al., 2018b), which is built on top of the Short-Text Conversation (STC) dataset (Shang et al., 2015). ESTC is designed to build Chinese empathetic dialogue systems. The dialogues are crawled from

Name	#Turns	#Dialogues	Average Turn/Dial	Average Words/Turn	Annotation Granularity	Original Language	Translation
Train							
DBDC (Higashinaka et al., 2016)	8,509	415	20.5	7.31	Turn	En	Zh/Es
CMU_DoG (Zhou et al., 2018c)	95,305	4,221	22.58	17.93	Turn	En	Zh/Es
Cornell Movie-Dialogs (Danescu-Niculescu-Mizil and Lee, 2011)	304,713	83,097	3.67	13.72	Turn	En	Zh/Es
DailyDialog (Li et al., 2017)	102,960	13,116	7.85	13.96	Turn	En	Zh/Es
DECODE (Nie et al., 2020)	296,105	35,426	8.36	15.05	Turn	En	Zh/Es
EmotionLines (Hsu et al., 2018)	14,503	1,000	14.50	10.53	Turn	En	Zh/Es
EmpathicDialogues (Rashkin et al., 2019)	107,220	24,850	4.31	15.88	Turn	En	Zh/Es
Holl-E (Moghe et al., 2018)	91,452	9,071	10.08	17.74	Turn	En	Zh/Es
MEENA (Adiwardana et al., 2020)	3,675	193	19.04	9.14	Turn	En	Zh/Es
MELD (Poria et al., 2019)	23,197	1,592	14.57	10.98	Turn	En	Zh/Es
MetalWOz (Lee et al., 2019)	432,036	37,884	11.40	8.47	Turn	En	Zh/Es
Movie-DiC (Banchs, 2012)	512,582	65,215	7.86	13.82	Turn	En	Zh/Es
PersonaChat (Zhang et al., 2018a)	162,064	10,907	14.86	11.72	Turn	En	Zh/Es
SentimentLIAR (Upadhayay and Behzadan, 2020)	12,781	12,781	1.00	20.16	Turn	En	Zh/Es
Switchboard Coherence (Cervone and Riccardi, 2020)	12,059	1,000	12.06	20.55	Turn	En	Zh/Es
Topical-Chat (Gopalakrishnan et al., 2019)	235,281	10,784	21.82	23.23	Turn	En	Zh/Es
Wizard of Wikipedia (Dinan et al., 2019)	201,999	22,311	9.05	18.83	Turn	En	Zh/Es
Wochat (Haro et al., 2016)	19,881	607	32.75	6.75	Turn	En	Zh/Es
Total	2,636,322	334,470	236.26	255.77			
Development							
ConvAI2-GRADE (Huang et al., 2020)	1,800	600	3.0	12.07	Turn	En	Zh/Es
DailyDialog-GRADE (Huang et al., 2020)	900	300	3.0	12.60	Turn	En	Zh/Es
DailyDialog-GUPTA (Gupta et al., 2019)	2,460	500	4.92	12.37	Turn	En	Zh/Es
DailyDialog-ZHAO (Zhao et al., 2020)	4,248	900	4.72	12.41	Turn	En	Zh/Es
DSTC7 (Galley et al., 2019)	34,650	9,990	3.47	15.39	Turn	En	Zh/Es
Empathetic-GRADE (Huang et al., 2020)	900	300	3.0	16.65	Turn	En	Zh/Es
FED-Dial (Mehri and Eskenazi, 2020a))	1,715	125	13.72	11.1	Dial	En	Zh/Es
FED-Turn (Mehri and Eskenazi, 2020a))	3,888	375	10.37	10.78	Turn	En	Zh/Es
HUMOD (Merdivan et al., 2020)	37,468	9,499	3.94	7.97	Turn	En	Zh/Es
Persona-SEE (See et al., 2019)	39,792	3,316	12.0	9.0	Dial	En	Zh/Es
PersonaChat-USR (Mehri and Eskenazi, 2020b)	2,790	300	9.3	12.08	Turn	En	Zh/Es
PersonaChat-ZHAO (Zhao et al., 2020)	4,614	900	5.13	12.06	Turn	En	Zh/Es
TOPICAL-USR (Mehri and Eskenazi, 2020b)	4,032	360	11.2	23.16	Turn	En	Zh/Es
ECM-Eval (Zhou et al., 2018a)	3,004	1,502	2.0	13.13	Turn	Zh	En
KdConv-Eval (Zhou et al., 2020a)	3,499	354	9.88	21.11	Turn	Zh	En
LCCC-Eval (Wang et al., 2020a)	3,009	589	5.11	11.72	Turn	Zh	En
Total	148,769	29,910	104.76	212.64			
Test							
BlenderBot3 (Giorgi et al., 2023; Shuster et al., 2022)	679	21	32.33	16.96	Turn/Dial	En	Zh/Es
ChatGPT (Giorgi et al., 2023; Radford et al., 2018)	462	21	22	91.07	Turn/Dial	En	Zh/Es
GPT-3.5 (Giorgi et al., 2023; Brown et al., 2020)	560	17	32.94	23.73	Turn/Dial	En	Zh/Es
HCChinese	2,017	187	10.79	8.08	Turn/Dial	Zh	En
ChatEval (Sedoc et al., 2019)	400	200	2	8.13	Turn	En	Zh/Es
DSTC10 (Zhang et al., 2022c)	112	28	4	14	Turn	En	Zh/Es
JSALT (Rudnicky et al., 2020)	46	13	3.54	17.26	Turn	En	Zh/Es
Total	4,276	487	107.60	179.23			

Table 7: Summary of the train, development, and test datasets. Some information comes from Yeh et al. (2021).

Weibo and post-processing, such as the removal of trivial responses and filtering out potential advertisements, has been conducted by Shang et al. (2015). The dialogues are automatically annotated by pre-trained emotion classifiers along six different emotion categories, such as angry, happy, sad, etc. The dialogues in ESTC are much shorter. Most contain only a single post-response pair.

LCCC-Eval - Data in LCCC-Eval are sampled from the Large-scale Cleaned Chinese Conversation dialogue corpus (LCCC) (Wang et al., 2020b). The LCCC corpus is designed for pretraining the Chinese dialogue model. The dialogues are mainly collected from Weibo, a Chinese microblogging website[17] and other open-source Chinese dialogue corpora, such as the Douban Conversation (Wu et al., 2017) and the E-Commerce Conversation Corpus (Zhang et al., 2018b). All the dialogues belong to the general domain and a rigorous cleaning process, which is based on a series of heuristic rules and several classifiers, is conducted to filter out dialogues with noise, such as dirty words, special characters, facial expressions, ungrammatical sentences, etc. Both ESTC and LCCC are released by the THU-COAI group for research purposes at `https://www.luge.ai/#/`

KdConv-Eval - KdConv-Eval is constructed based

[17] `https://en.wikipedia.org/wiki/Sina_Weibo`

on the KdConv corpus (Zhou et al., 2020a), a multi-domain Chinese dialogue dataset towards multi-turn knowledge-driven conversation. The corpus links the subjects of multi-turn discussions to knowledge graphs. It encompasses conversations from three categories (movies, music, and travel). These conversations involve detailed exchanges about relevant subjects and seamlessly move between a variety of topics. We sampled 354 dialogues from the original corpus to form the KdConv-Eval test dataset.

HCChinese - Dialogues in HCChinese are collected by interacting with three state-of-the-art Chinese chatbots, Baidu Plato-XL (Bao et al., 2022), Microsoft XiaoIce (Zhou et al., 2020b), and a Chinese DialoGPT model that is trained in a similar manner to DialoGPT (Zhang et al., 2020). We chat with the chatbots on a diverse set of topics, such as entertainment, relationship, arts, travel, food, etc. The discussion of sensitive topics, such as politics and race, was avoided. A manual check is performed on each dialogue, and those containing inappropriate responses were filtered out. In the end, we collected 531 human-chatbot multi-turn conversations with 207 from Plato-XL, 224 from XiaoIce, and 100 dialogues from the Chinese DialoGPT.

TBD-Q1-2023 Three Bot Dialog Evaluation Corpus (TBD-Q1-2023 OR TBD; Quarter 1 of 2023) from Giorgi et al. (2023) consists of dialogues with three chatbots: ChatGPT (Radford et al., 2018), GPT-3 (Brown et al., 2020), and BlenderBot3 (Shuster et al., 2022). Student participants were told to have a long conversation with the chatbots on a range of topics of their choosing. All conversations were collected between November 2022 and March 2023. They collected 21 dialogues with an average of 14.6 turns per dialogue. Conversations for **BlenderBot3** were directly from the website `https://blenderbot.ai/`. The **ChatGPT** conversations were taken directly from the website `https://chat.openai.com/`. Finally, **GPT3** used the text-davinci-003 model with the prompt *Hal is a chatbot that attempts to answer questions with useful responses:*. The GPT-3 model parameters were temperature of 0.5, max tokens of 289, top-p of 0.3, frequency penalty of 0.5, and presence penalty of 0.

Task-Oriented Conversational Modeling with Subjective Knowledge Track in DSTC11

Seokhwan Kim†, Spandana Gella†, Chao Zhao‡, Di Jin†, Alexandros Papangelis†, Behnam Hedayatnia†, Yang Liu†, Dilek Hakkani-Tur†

† Amazon Alexa AI ‡University of North Carolina at Chapel Hill

{seokhwk,sgella,djinamzn,papangea,behnam,yangliud,hakkanit}@amazon.com

zhaochao@cs.unc.edu

Abstract

Conventional Task-oriented Dialogue (TOD) Systems rely on domain-specific APIs/DBs or external factual knowledge to create responses. In DSTC11 track 5, we aims to provide a new challenging task to accommodate subjective user requests (e.g.,*"Is the WIFI reliable?"* or *"Does the restaurant have a good atmosphere?"*) into TOD. We release a benchmark dataset, which contains subjective knowledge-seeking dialogue contexts and manually annotated responses that are grounded in subjective knowledge sources. The challenge track received a total of 48 entries from 14 participating teams.

Figure 1: Examples of the SK-TOD task. The top part shows two hotels and their customer reviews. The bottom part shows three dialogue sessions between the system (denoted by S) and three users (denoted by U). The last user utterance is a subjective question about the WIFI quality of the hotel(s). The system needs to retrieve information from the relevant subjective knowledge, which is highlighted in the review text.

1 Introduction

Task-oriented Dialogue (TOD) Systems aim to build dialogue systems to help users to achieve specific goals (e.g., booking a hotel or a restaurant). Most solutions of TOD are either based on domain-APIs (Budzianowski et al., 2018; Rastogi et al., 2020) and structured databases (Eric et al., 2017; Wu et al., 2019), which can only handle limited scenarios. Recent works incorporate unstructured factual information (Dimitrakis et al., 2018; Kim et al., 2020, 2021b; Feng et al., 2020, 2021; Majumder et al., 2022) into dialogue modeling, which further enlarges the model's ability of task-oriented assistance.

However, in many TOD tasks, users care about not only factual information but subjective information as well, such as the experiences, opinions, and preferences of other customers. For example, when booking a hotel or a restaurant, users may ask questions like *"Is the WIFI reliable?"* or *"Does the restaurant have a good atmosphere?"*. To respond to such user requests, an agent needs to seek information from subjective knowledge sources such as online customer reviews.

In this track, we focus on enabling the TOD model to leverage subjective knowledge during task-oriented assistance. To this end, we proposed a novel task of subjective-knowledge-based task-oriented dialogue (SK-TOD) (Zhao et al., 2023). More specifically, we focus on subjective knowledge-seeking user requests and choose user reviews as external subjective knowledge sources. In Figure 1, we show three examples of such requests, where customers ask about the WiFi quality of hotels. User reviews are great resources for subjective information because even for the same aspect of the same product/service, customers may

Proceedings of The Eleventh Dialog System Technology Challenge, pages 274–281
September 11, 2023 ©2023 Association for Computational Linguistics

have different opinions and leave either positive or negative reviews.The subjectivity of reviews also indicates that a TOD system should consider multiple reviews to get a more comprehensive user opinion. Based on that, an ideal response should inform users of the diversity of opinions by including both positive and negative opinions as well as the proportions (like the response in Dialogue 3). Such a two-sided response has been observed as more credible and valuable for customers (Kamins et al., 1989; Lee et al., 2008; Baek et al., 2012), which can also protect the trust of users in the TOD system.

Building TOD upon subjective knowledge in this way brings in two unique challenges. First, instead of selecting the top few relevant knowledge snippets (as what is needed for Fact-TOD), the SK-TOD model needs to select all relevant knowledge snippets. Second, the model needs to aggregate these knowledge snippets into a concise response that can faithfully reflect the diversity and proportion of opinions. To facilitate the research of subjective-knowledge-grounded TOD, we released a large-scale dataset for this track, which contains 19,696 subjective knowledge-seeking dialogue contexts and manually annotated responses that are grounded on 143 entities and 1,430 reviews (8,013 sentences).

This paper provides an overview of the track. The rest of the paper is organized as follows. We first introduce the problem formulation (Section 2) and data statistics (Section 3). Then we introduce the baseline approach (Section 4) and the evaluation metrics (Section 5). Finally, we report the participants and results (Section 6), and we close the paper with the conclusion (Section 7).

2 Problem Formulation

Formally, we have a dialogue context $C = [U_1, S_1, U_2, S_2, \cdots, U_t]$ between a user and a system, where each user utterance U_i is followed by a system response utterance S_i except the last user utterance U_t. The dialogue involves single or multiple entities $\mathcal{E} = \{e_1, \cdots, e_m\}$. Along with the dialogue, we have a subjective knowledge source $\mathcal{B} = \{(e_1, \mathcal{R}_1), (e_2, \mathcal{R}_2), \cdots\}$ consisting of all the entities and their corresponding customer reviews. Each entity e has multiple reviews $\mathcal{R} = \{R_1, R_2, \cdots\}$. Each review can be split into multiple segments $[K_1, K_2, \cdots]$ such as paragraphs, sentences, or sub-sentential units. In this track, we regard each review sentence as a knowledge snippet.

	Train	Val	Test
# instances	14768	2129	2799
# seen instances	14768	1471	1547
# unseen instances	0	658	1252
# multi-entity instances	412	199	436
Knowledge Snippets			
Avg. # snippets per instance	3.80	4.07	4.21
Avg. # tokens per snippet	14.68	15.49	14.5
Dialogue			
Avg. # uttrances per instance	9.29	9.44	9.36
Avg. # tokens per request	8.65	8.94	9.12
Avg. # tokens per response	24.18	23.61	23.86

Table 1: Basic statistics of our dataset.

The SK-TOD task contains the following three sub-tasks.

Knowledge-Seeking Turn Detection aims to identify the user request that requires to be addressed with subjective knowledge. We regard it as a binary-classification problem, where the input is the dialogue context C and the output is a binary indicator.

Knowledge Selection is then used to select the knowledge snippets that are relevant to the user's request. The inputs are the dialogue context C and the knowledge snippets candidates $\mathcal{K}$, which is a combination of all the knowledge snippets of the relevant entities in $\mathcal{E}$. The output $\mathcal{K}^+ \subseteq \mathcal{K}$ is a subset of relevant knowledge candidates. Note that there might be multiple knowledge snippets in $\mathcal{K}^+$.

Response Generation is to create an utterance S_t that responds to the user's request based on the dialogue context C and the relevant knowledge snippets $\mathcal{K}^+$.

3 Data

We ground the data collection in MultiWOZ (Budzianowski et al., 2018; Eric et al., 2020) and select dialogues from the domains of hotels and restaurants. The data collection is conducted by a group of crowd workers through Amazon Mechanical Turk as described in (Zhao et al., 2023).

The dataset contains 19,696 instances with subjective user requests and subjective-knowledge-grounded responses in total. The average length of the subjective user request and the agent response is 8.75 and 24.07 tokens, respectively. While most of the instances contain a single entity, there are 1,047 instances where multiple entities are compared (like Dialogue 2 in Figure 1). Each instance requires on average 3.88 subjective knowledge snip-

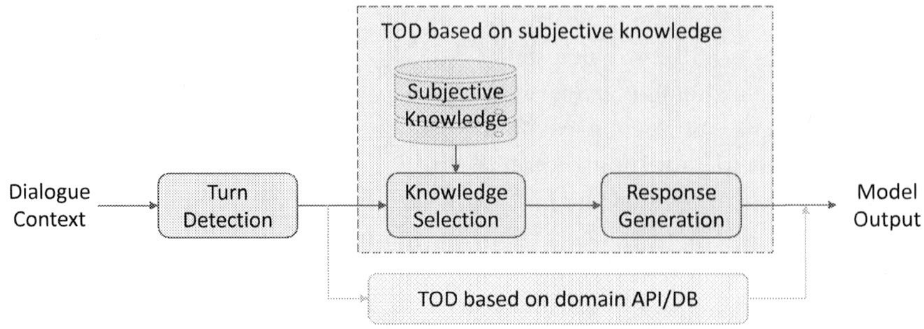

Figure 2: The pipeline architecture of SK-TOD.

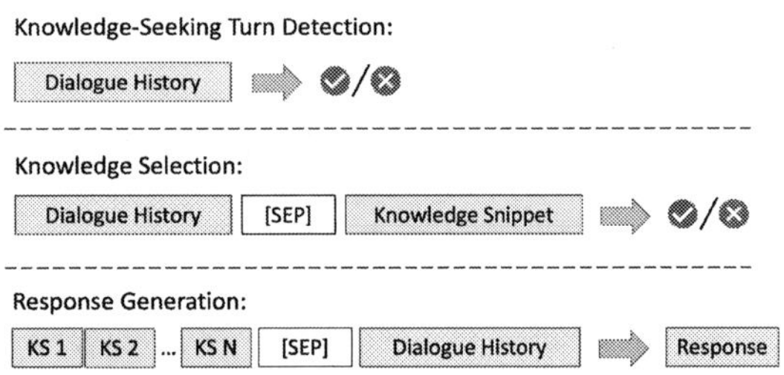

Figure 3: The Illustration of baselines for each subtask.

pets. To help identify the subjective knowledge-seeking user request, we randomly sample another 18,383 dialogues with non-subjective user requests from the original MultiWOZ dataset.

We split the dataset into training (75%), validation (10.8%), and test (14.2%) sets. Table 1 shows the detailed statistics of each subset. Our validation and test sets contain two subsets: the *seen* subset where the aspects of these instances are included in the training set, and the *unseen* subset where the aspects are not included in the training set. The unseen subset is designed to evaluate models' generalizability to arbitrary aspects.

4 Baseline

In this section, we describe the baseline method for SK-TOD. Figure 3 shows the pipeline of the baseline method which consists of three sequential sub-tasks. The details of each subtask are described as follows. They are illustrated in Figure 3.

4.1 Knowledge-Seeking Turn Detection

We employ a pre-trained language model (e.g., BERT (Devlin et al., 2019)) to encode C and adopt the hidden state of the first token as its representation. Then we apply a classifier to obtain the probability that the current user request is a subjective knowledge-seeking request. That is,

$$\begin{aligned} h &= \text{Enc}(C) \\ P(C) &= \text{softmax}\left(\text{FFN}\left(h\right)\right). \end{aligned} \tag{1}$$

The model is finetuned with the binary cross-entropy loss.

4.2 Knowledge Selection

Given a dialogue history, we first adopt a word-matching-based method used by Jin et al. (2021) to extract relevant entities. To select relevant knowledge snippets, we calculate the relevance score between the dialogue context C and a knowledge snippet $K \in \mathcal{K}$ of the corresponding entities. We regard it as a pairwise text scoring problem and consider the cross-encoder (Wolf et al., 2019) approach. We encode the concatenation of C and K to obtain the contextualized BERT representation. That is,

$$\begin{aligned} h &= \text{Enc}(C, K) \\ P(C, K) &= \text{softmax}\left(\text{FFN}\left(h\right)\right). \end{aligned} \tag{2}$$

During training, we use all relevant knowledge snippets to construct positive (C, K) pairs. Due to the large size of irrelevant knowledge snippets, we randomly sample the same number of irrelevant snippets to build negative pairs. We optimize the model using the binary cross-entropy loss. During inference, we predict the relevance probability of all knowledge snippets in the candidates. Since both precision and recall matter during KS, instead of selecting the top few results, we use a threshold to determine the relevance, which is estimated from the validation set.

4.3 Response Generation

We apply T5 (Raffel et al., 2020), a sequence-to-sequence pre-trained model as the generation model. The model receives the concatenation of dialogue context and the selected knowledge snippets as input, and has the target response as output. We train the model by maximizing $p(S_T \mid C, \mathcal{K}^+, Z)$. During the test, we generate the system response using beam-search with top-K sampling (Fan et al., 2018).

5 Evaluation Criteria

Each participating team submitted up to five system outputs each of which contains the results for all three tasks on the unlabeled test instances. We first evaluated each submission using the task-specific objective metrics by comparing to the ground-truth labels and responses. For Knowledge-Seeking Turn Detection and Knowledge Selection, we report the precision, recall, F_1 score, and accuracy score. For Response Generation, following the evaluation of other generation tasks, we employ BLEU (Papineni et al., 2002), ROUGE (Lin, 2004), and METEOR (Banerjee and Lavie, 2005) to evaluate results compared to the reference responses.

Considering the dependencies between the tasks in the pipelined architecture, the final scores for knowledge selection and knowledge-grounded response generation are computed by considering the first step knowledge-seeking turn detection recall and precision performance, as follows:

$$S_p(X) = \frac{\sum_{x_i \in X} \left(s(x_i) \cdot f_1(x_i) \cdot \tilde{f}_1(x_i) \right)}{\sum_{x_i \in X} \tilde{f}_1(x_i)},$$

$$S_r(X) = \frac{\sum_{x_i \in X} \left(s(x_i) \cdot f_1(x_i) \cdot \tilde{f}_1(x_i) \right)}{\sum_{x_i \in X} f_1(x_i)},$$

$$S_f(X) = \frac{2 \cdot S_p(X) \cdot S_r(X)}{S_p(X) + S_r(X)}, \tag{3}$$

where $f_1(x)$ and $\tilde{f}_1(x)$ are the reference and prediction for the knowledge-seeking turn detection task, respectively, and $s(x)$ is the knowledge selection or response generation score in a target metric for a single instance $x \in X$.

Then, we aggregated a set of multiple scores across different tasks and metrics into a single overall score computed by the mean reciprocal rank, as follows:

$$S_{overall}(e) = \frac{1}{|M|} \sum_{i=1}^{|M|} \frac{1}{rank_i(e)}, \tag{4}$$

where $rank_i(e)$ is the ranking of the submitted entry e in the i-th metric against all the other submissions and M is the number of metrics we considered.

Based on the overall objective score, we selected the finalists to be manually evaluated by the following two crowd sourcing tasks:

- Appropriateness: whether the response is fluent and naturally connected to the dialogue context.
- Accuracy: whether the sentiment proportion provided by the response is accordant with that of the subjective knowledge.

For Appropriateness, we only show the dialogue context and the responses. For Accuracy, we further show the oracle knowledge snippets. To increase the annotation quality, we first ask workers to annotate the sentiment label of each knowledge snippet, and then evaluate the accuracy of each response. Both measures are evaluated using the 5-Point Likert scale.

In both tasks, we assigned each instance to three crowd workers and took their average as the final human evaluation score for the instance. Those scores were then aggregated over the entire test set following Equation 3, i.e., weighted by the knowledge-seeking turn detection performance. Finally, we used the average of the Appropriateness and Accuracy scores to determine the official ranking of the systems in the challenge track.

6 Results

We received 48 entries in total submitted from 14 participating teams. To preserve anonymity, the teams were identified by numbers from 1 to 14.

6.1 Objective Evaluation Results

Table 2 shows the objective evaluation results of the best entry from each team selected based on the overall score (Equation 4). The full results including all the submitted entries are available on the track repository[1].

[1]https://github.com/alexa/dstc11-track5

Table 2: Objective evaluation results of the best entries from each team. Bold denotes the best score for each metric; and * indicates the finalists selected for the human evaluations.

	Task 1: Detection			Task 2: Selection			Task 3: Generation					
Team-Entry	P	R	F	P	R	F	EM	BLEU	METEOR	ROUGE-1	ROUGE-2	ROUGE-L
Baseline	0.9982	0.9979	0.9980	0.7901	0.7877	0.7889	0.3906	0.1004	0.1748	0.3520	0.1430	0.2753
1 - 0	0.9977	0.7702	0.8693	0.7872	0.6048	0.6841	0.3090	0.0873	0.1512	0.3061	0.1248	0.2400
2 - 3*	0.9940	0.9986	0.9963	0.8093	0.7858	0.7974	0.4156	0.0984	0.1774	**0.3658**	0.1509	0.2875
3 - 1	0.9986	0.9971	0.9979	0.7567	0.8242	0.7890	0.3966	0.0874	0.1641	0.3425	0.1372	0.2702
4 - 1	0.9982	0.9986	0.9984	0.8183	0.8442	0.8311	0.4895	0.1003	0.1731	0.3510	0.1422	0.2737
5 - 0	0.9986	0.9968	0.9977	0.7741	0.8557	0.8128	0.4675	0.0963	0.1719	0.3470	0.1379	0.2692
6 - 0*	0.9968	**0.9996**	0.9982	0.8039	**0.8775**	0.8391	0.5547	0.1017	**0.1894**	0.3629	0.1478	0.2804
7 - 4*	0.9979	0.9993	**0.9986**	0.8183	0.8506	0.8342	0.5314	0.1075	0.1744	0.3585	0.1459	0.2794
8 - 0*	0.9979	0.9982	0.9980	0.8240	0.8141	0.8190	0.5130	0.1029	0.1764	0.3587	0.1479	0.2822
9 - 1	**0.9995**	0.7691	0.8693	0.8385	0.6398	0.7258	0.3873	0.0788	0.1532	0.3141	0.1233	0.2406
10 - 0	0.9950	0.9986	0.9968	0.7955	0.7936	0.7946	0.4177	0.1035	0.1791	0.3598	0.1473	0.2812
11 - 0	0.9989	0.9982	0.9986	0.6540	0.5391	0.5910	0.3071	0.0980	0.1614	0.3368	0.1386	0.2713
12 - 2*	0.9986	0.9986	0.9986	0.7538	0.8227	0.7868	0.4291	0.0961	0.1715	0.3572	0.1467	0.2798
13 - 3*	0.9964	0.9982	0.9973	**0.8590**	0.8449	**0.8519**	**0.6432**	**0.1081**	0.1819	0.3652	0.1528	0.2872
14 - 0*	0.9979	0.9989	0.9984	0.7856	0.8035	0.7944	0.4183	0.1066	0.1748	0.3599	**0.1577**	**0.2899**

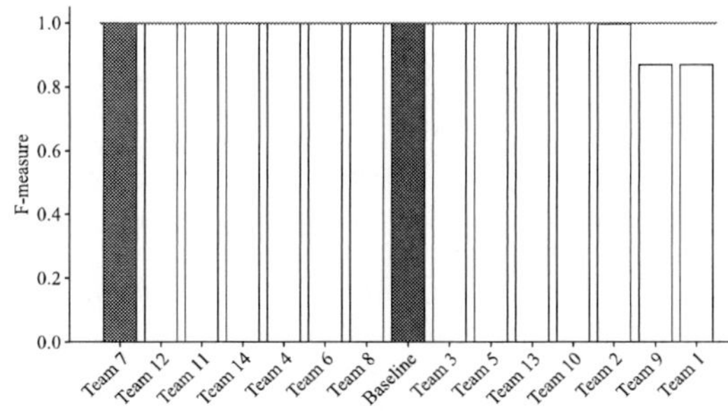

Figure 4: Knowledge-seeking turn detection performance (F-measure) from different entries. The horizontal line indicates the baseline performance.

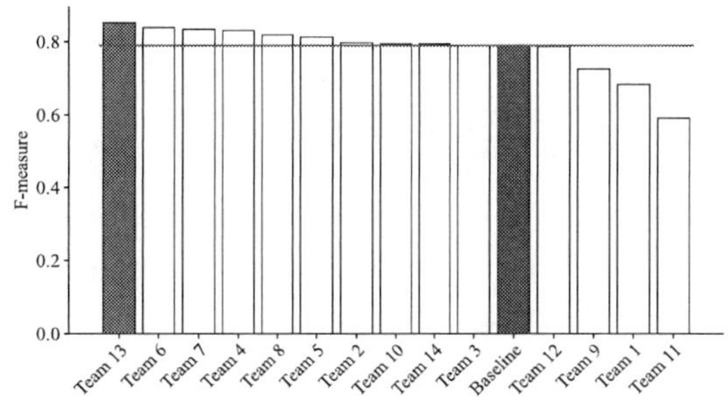

Figure 5: Knowledge selection performance (F-measure) from different entries. The horizontal line indicates the baseline performance.

Table 3: Human evaluation results. Bold indicates the best score for each metric.

Rank	Team	Entry	Accuracy	Appropriateness	Average
Ground-truth			2.9189	3.6422	3.2806
1	6	0	2.9095	**3.6596**	**3.2846**
2	8	0	2.9005	3.6535	3.2770
3	13	3	**2.9100**	3.6321	3.2710
4	2	3	2.8908	3.6487	3.2697
5	7	4	2.9046	3.6348	3.2697
6	12	2	2.8856	3.6518	3.2687
7	14	0	2.8912	3.6427	3.2670
Baseline			2.8715	3.6348	3.2531

Figure 4 shows that the majority including the baseline achieved near-perfect knowledge-seeking turn detection results with F-measure surpassing 0.99. This can be attributed to the characteristics of this data, where knowledge-seeking and non-knowledge-seeking turns are easily distinguishable from each other. For knowledge selection, the majority of the teams submitted the improved results over the baseline (Figure 5), while only half of the teams achieved higher average scores than the baseline for response generation (Figure 6). Team 13 was determined to be the best team based on the overall objective scores (Equation 4), derived from the highest F-measure and exact matching accuracy for knowledge selection, along with the averaged response generation scores.

6.2 Human Evaluation Results

We selected 7 finalists to be manually evaluated, corresponding to the best entry from each of the top half teams in the overall objective score (Equation 4). Table 3 shows the official ranking of the finalists based on the human evaluation results. Team 3 achieved the highest accuracy score, which aligns with their knowledge selection results from the objective evaluation. On the other hand, Team 6 achieved the highest appropriateness ratings, which were even higher than the scores for the reference responses. This led them to be the final winner based on the average score between accuracy and appropriateness.

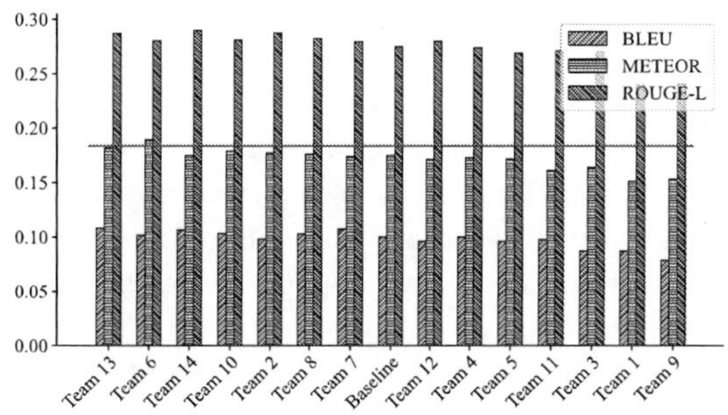

Figure 6: Knowledge-grounded generation performance from different entries. The horizontal line indicates the average of the baseline scores.

To further analyze the correlation between each automatic metric and the final human evaluation results, we calculated the Spearman's rank correlation coefficient (Spearman, 1961) of the ranked lists of all the entries in every pair of objective and human evaluation metrics, as shown in Figure 7. Consistent with the findings from our previous challenge tracks (Kim et al., 2021a, 2022), the knowledge selection metrics have the highest correlation with the accuracy ratings in the human evaluation. Among the response generation metrics, METEOR shows better alignment with the human ratings, particularly as it is the only metric with a positive correlation with appropriateness ratings. Nonetheless, none of the automatic evaluation metrics showed a strong correlation with the appropriateness ratings. This suggests a new research direction aimed at developing more reliable metrics for this task.

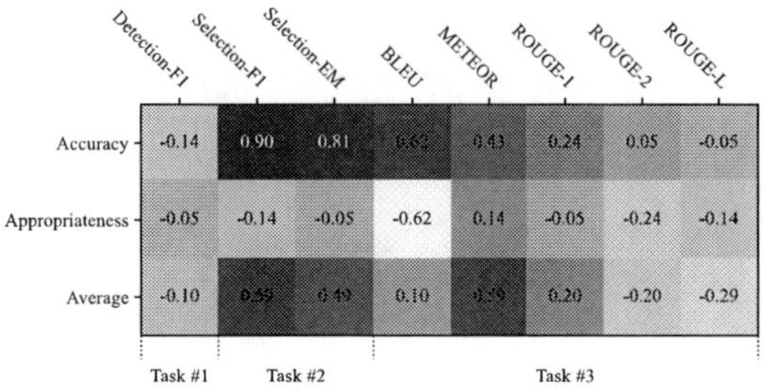

Figure 7: Correlations between the objective and human evaluation metrics in Spearman's ρ. The higher score of a pair of metrics has, the stronger correlation they have.

7 Conclusion

We presented the official evaluation results of the Task-Oriented Conversational Modeling with Subjective Knowledge Track in DSTC11 This challenge track addressed the new conversational modeling tasks to accommodate subjective user requests into task-oriented dialogue systems. A total of 14 teams participated with an overall number of 48 entries submitted. One notable thing is that some teams have used the large language models (LLMs) such as OpenAI's ChatGPT and GPT-4 for enhancing data augmentation and refining response ranking. While these methods were expected to help to improve our task performances, it was not a decisive factor to achieve elevated scores and win the benchmark in both automatic and human evaluations. This suggests a future research direction exploring more effective strategies for utilizing LLMs for the tasks.

References

Hyunmi Baek, JoongHo Ahn, and Youngseok Choi. 2012. Helpfulness of online consumer reviews: Readers' objectives and review cues. *International Journal of Electronic Commerce*, 17(2):99–126.

Satanjeev Banerjee and Alon Lavie. 2005. METEOR: an automatic metric for MT evaluation with improved correlation with human judgments. In *Proceedings of the Workshop on Intrinsic and Extrinsic Evaluation Measures for Machine Translation and/or Summarization@ACL 2005, Ann Arbor, Michigan, USA, June 29, 2005*, pages 65–72. Association for Computational Linguistics.

Paweł Budzianowski, Tsung-Hsien Wen, Bo-Hsiang Tseng, Iñigo Casanueva, Stefan Ultes, Osman Ramadan, and Milica Gašić. 2018. MultiWOZ - a large-scale multi-domain Wizard-of-Oz dataset for task-oriented dialogue modelling. In *Proceedings of the 2018 Conference on Empirical Methods in Natural Language Processing*, pages 5016–5026, Brussels, Belgium. Association for Computational Linguistics.

Jacob Devlin, Ming-Wei Chang, Kenton Lee, and Kristina Toutanova. 2019. BERT: Pre-training of deep bidirectional transformers for language understanding. In *Proceedings of the 2019 Conference of the North American Chapter of the Association for Computational Linguistics: Human Language Technologies, Volume 1 (Long and Short Papers)*, pages 4171–4186, Minneapolis, Minnesota. Association for Computational Linguistics.

Eleftherios Dimitrakis, Konstantinos Sgontzos, Panagiotis Papadakos, Yannis Marketakis, Alexandros Papangelis, Yannis Stylianou, and Yannis Tzitzikas. 2018. On finding the relevant user reviews for advancing conversational faceted search. In *EMSASW@ ESWC*, pages 22–31.

Mihail Eric, Rahul Goel, Shachi Paul, Abhishek Sethi, Sanchit Agarwal, Shuyang Gao, Adarsh Kumar, Anuj Goyal, Peter Ku, and Dilek Hakkani-Tur. 2020. MultiWOZ 2.1: A consolidated multi-domain dialogue dataset with state corrections and state tracking baselines. In *Proceedings of the 12th Language Resources and Evaluation Conference*, pages 422–428, Marseille, France. European Language Resources Association.

Mihail Eric, Lakshmi Krishnan, Francois Charette, and Christopher D. Manning. 2017. Key-value retrieval networks for task-oriented dialogue. In *Proceedings of the 18th Annual SIGdial Meeting on Discourse and Dialogue*, pages 37–49, Saarbrücken, Germany. Association for Computational Linguistics.

Angela Fan, Mike Lewis, and Yann Dauphin. 2018. Hierarchical neural story generation. In *Proceedings of the 56th Annual Meeting of the Association for Computational Linguistics (Volume 1: Long Papers)*, pages 889–898, Melbourne, Australia. Association for Computational Linguistics.

Song Feng, Siva Sankalp Patel, Hui Wan, and Sachindra Joshi. 2021. MultiDoc2Dial: Modeling dialogues grounded in multiple documents. In *Proceedings of the 2021 Conference on Empirical Methods in Natural Language Processing*, pages 6162–6176, Online and Punta Cana, Dominican Republic. Association for Computational Linguistics.

Song Feng, Hui Wan, Chulaka Gunasekara, Siva Patel, Sachindra Joshi, and Luis Lastras. 2020. doc2dial: A goal-oriented document-grounded dialogue dataset. In *Proceedings of the 2020 Conference on Empirical Methods in Natural Language Processing (EMNLP)*, pages 8118–8128, Online. Association for Computational Linguistics.

Di Jin, Seokhwan Kim, and Dilek Hakkani-Tur. 2021. Can i be of further assistance? using unstructured knowledge access to improve task-oriented conversational modeling. In *Proceedings of the 1st Workshop on Document-grounded Dialogue and Conver-

sational Question Answering (DialDoc 2021), pages 119–127.

Michael A Kamins, Meribeth J Brand, Stuart A Hoeke, and John C Moe. 1989. Two-sided versus one-sided celebrity endorsements: The impact on advertising effectiveness and credibility. *Journal of advertising*, 18(2):4–10.

Seokhwan Kim, Mihail Eric, Karthik Gopalakrishnan, Behnam Hedayatnia, Yang Liu, and Dilek Hakkani-Tur. 2020. Beyond domain APIs: Task-oriented conversational modeling with unstructured knowledge access. In *Proceedings of the 21th Annual Meeting of the Special Interest Group on Discourse and Dialogue*, pages 278–289, 1st virtual meeting. Association for Computational Linguistics.

Seokhwan Kim, Mihail Eric, Behnam Hedayatnia, Karthik Gopalakrishnan, Yang Liu, Chao-Wei Huang, and Dilek Hakkani-Tur. 2021a. Beyond domain apis: Task-oriented conversational modeling with unstructured knowledge access track in dstc9.

Seokhwan Kim, Yang Liu, Di Jin, Alexandros Papangelis, Karthik Gopalakrishnan, Behnam Hedayatnia, and Dilek Hakkani-Tür. 2021b. "how robust ru?": Evaluating task-oriented dialogue systems on spoken conversations. In *2021 IEEE Automatic Speech Recognition and Understanding Workshop (ASRU)*, pages 1147–1154. IEEE.

Seokhwan Kim, Yang Liu, Di Jin, Alexandros Papangelis, Behnam Hedayatnia, Karthik Gopalakrishnan, and Dilek Hakkani-Tür. 2022. Knowledge-grounded task-oriented dialogue modeling on spoken conversations track at dstc10. In *Proceedings of the AAAI-22 Workshop on Dialog System Technology Challenges (DSTC10)*.

Jumin Lee, Do-Hyung Park, and Ingoo Han. 2008. The effect of negative online consumer reviews on product attitude: An information processing view. *Electronic commerce research and applications*, 7(3):341–352.

Chin-Yew Lin. 2004. ROUGE: A package for automatic evaluation of summaries. In *Text Summarization Branches Out*, pages 74–81, Barcelona, Spain. Association for Computational Linguistics.

Bodhisattwa Prasad Majumder, Harsh Jhamtani, Taylor Berg-Kirkpatrick, and Julian McAuley. 2022. Achieving conversational goals with unsupervised post-hoc knowledge injection. In *Proceedings of the 60th Annual Meeting of the Association for Computational Linguistics (Volume 1: Long Papers)*, pages 3140–3153, Dublin, Ireland. Association for Computational Linguistics.

Kishore Papineni, Salim Roukos, Todd Ward, and Wei-Jing Zhu. 2002. Bleu: a method for automatic evaluation of machine translation. In *Proceedings of the 40th Annual Meeting of the Association for Computational Linguistics, July 6-12, 2002, Philadelphia, PA, USA*, pages 311–318. ACL.

Colin Raffel, Noam Shazeer, Adam Roberts, Katherine Lee, Sharan Narang, Michael Matena, Yanqi Zhou, Wei Li, Peter J Liu, et al. 2020. Exploring the limits of transfer learning with a unified text-to-text transformer. *J. Mach. Learn. Res.*, 21(140):1–67.

Abhinav Rastogi, Xiaoxue Zang, Srinivas Sunkara, Raghav Gupta, and Pranav Khaitan. 2020. Towards scalable multi-domain conversational agents: The schema-guided dialogue dataset. In *Proceedings of the AAAI Conference on Artificial Intelligence*, volume 34, pages 8689–8696.

Charles Spearman. 1961. The proof and measurement of association between two things.

Thomas Wolf, Victor Sanh, Julien Chaumond, and Clement Delangue. 2019. Transfertransfo: A transfer learning approach for neural network based conversational agents. *arXiv preprint arXiv:1901.08149*.

Chien-Sheng Wu, Richard Socher, and Caiming Xiong. 2019. Global-to-local memory pointer networks for task-oriented dialogue. In *International Conference on Learning Representations*.

Chao Zhao, Spandana Gella, Seokhwan Kim, Di Jin, Devamanyu Hazarika, Alexandros Papangelis, Behnam Hedayatnia, Mahdi Namazifar, Yang Liu, and Dilek Hakkani-Tur. 2023. "what do others think?": Task-oriented conversational modeling with subjective knowledge.

AUTHOR INDEX

Bang, Jeong-Uk ... 81
Bang, Namo ... 150
Benajiba, Yassine ... 242
Cao, Yuan ... 226
Carvalho, Joao Paulo ... 133
Cha, Hyunmook ... 25
Chang, Youngjae ... 25
Chen, Yirong ... 1
Chen, Zhe ... 144
Choi, Hyewon ... 9
Chu, Caiyuan ... 31
D'Haro, Luis Fernando ... 260
Druart, Lucas ... 95
Du, Bingzhu ... 48
Duan, Richeng ... 177
Dusek, Ondrej ... 113
Estève, Yannick ... 95
Favre, Benoît ... 95
Ge, Yongxin ... 31
Gella, Spandana ... 274
Ghazarian, Sarik ... 260
Gu, Jia-Chen ... 31
Guan, Yunfeng ... 144
Gung, James ... 242
Gupta, Arshit ... 242
Ha, Eunji ... 89
Hakkani-Tur, Dilek Z ... 274
Han, Janghoon ... 206
Han, Wei ... 226
Hedayatnia, Behnam ... 274
Hu, Guoping ... 1, 31
Huang, Fei ... 15
Huang, Xin ... 177
Hudecek, Vojtech ... 113
Hui, Binyuan ... 15
Hwang, Seunghyun ... 81
Jacqmin, Léo ... 95
Jang, Daesik ... 9
Jang, Yoonna ... 57
Jeong, Yewon ... 89
Jiang, Ridong ... 105
Jin, Di ... 274
Joo, Seongho ... 206
Jung, Haein ... 150
Jung, Kyomin ... 67, 206
Ke, Changxin ... 216
Khurana, Urja ... 193
Kim, Chi-Young ... 89
Kim, Doo Young ... 25
Kim, Eugene ... 166
Kim, Jinyoung ... 25
Kim, Jung Jae ... 105
Kim, Junseok ... 185
Kim, Kee-Eung ... 81
Kim, Keunha ... 25
Kim, Minju ... 150
Kim, Seokhwan ... 274
Kim, Yunsu ... 40
Ko, Youngjoong ... 25
Koh, Hyukhun ... 67
Koo, Myoung-Wan ... 150
Kottur, Satwik ... 235
Krause, Lea ... 193
Lango, Mateusz ... 113
Lavie, Alon ... 133
Lee, Chanhee ... 57
Lee, Gary Geunbae ... 40, 185
Lee, Jaehwan ... 166
Lee, Jeehyun ... 150
Lee, Jihyun ... 40, 185
Lee, Kang-Il ... 206
Lee, Kye-Hwan ... 25
Li, Haizhou ... 105
Li, Kan ... 123
Li, Ya ... 1, 31
Li, Yongbin ... 15
Liao, Yusheng ... 144
Lim, Heuiseok ... 57
Liu, Cong ... 1
Liu, Quan ... 1, 31
Liu, Ting ... 216
Liu, Yang ... 274
Liu, Yifan ... 31
Long, Yuxing ... 15
Ma, Longxuan ... 216
Mansour, Saab ... 242
Meer, Michiel van der ... 193
Mendonça, John ... 133
Min, Kyungmin ... 206
Min, Suyoung ... 25
Moeng, Emily ... 242
Moniz, Helena ... 133
Moon, Seungwhan ... 235
Pan, Chunlei ... 105
Papangelis, Alexandros ... 274
Park, Cheonyoung ... 89

Park, Jeiyoon 57
Park, Joonwoo 25
Pereira, Patrícia 133
Plátek, Ondřej 113
Pyun, Haesung 67
Ran, Han 81
Rastogi, Abhinav 226
Rodríguez-Cantelar, Mario 260
Rojas, Lina M 95
Romeo, Salvatore 242
Rose, Wesley 242
Rudnicky, Alexander I. 260
Santamaría, Selene Báez 193
Schmidtova, Patricia 113
Sedoc, João 260
Seo, Seungyeon 40
Shafran, Izhak 226
Shi, Jiayi 123
Shi, Ke 260
Shi, Wei 105
Shin, Joongbo 206
Shu, Raphael 242
Soltau, Hagen 226
Son, Kwanyoung 166
Su, Nan 48
Sun, Churui 216
Sung, Joo-Won 89
Tan, Kye Min 177
Tang, Chengguang 260
Trancoso, Isabel 133
Vielzeuf, Valentin 95
Wang, Bin 105
Wang, Mingqiu 226
Wang, Tao 1
Wang, Xiaojie 15
Wang, Xinglin 123
Wang, Yongliang 48
Wang, Yu 144
Won, Seungpil 206
Xing, Xiaofen 1
Xu, Xiangmin 1
Yang, Nakyeong 67
Yang, Zhenglu 15
Yeen, Heuiyeen 150
Yoon, Jaeseok 81
Yu, Haeun 89
Yuan, Caixia 15
Yuan, Peiwen 123
Zhang, Chen 105, 260
Zhang, Huibin 15
Zhang, Wei-Nan 216
Zhang, Yan 105
Zhang, Yi 242
Zhang, Yuchi 48
Zhao, Chao 274
Zhu, Zhiyuan 144
Zou, Bowei 177

Association for Computational Linguistics
209 N. Eighth Street
Stroudsburg, Pennsylvania 18360

CURRAN ASSOCIATES INC.
proceedings.com

ISBN 978-1-7138-9030-0

9 781713 890300